THE LAWBOOK EXCHANGE, LTD.

Foundations of the American Law of Lawyering

GENERAL EDITOR: Michael H. Hoeflich

SOURCES OF THE HISTORY OF THE AMERICAN LAW OF LAWYERING

Foundations of the American Law of Lawyering

The Foundations of the American Law of Lawyering Series presents reprints of works published in the nineteenth and early twentieth century that illuminate the ethical origins of the heritage of the legal profession in the United States.

Foundations of the American Law of Lawyering

SOURCES OF THE HISTORY OF THE AMERICAN LAW OF LAWYERING

MICHAEL H. HOEFLICH, EDITOR

THE LAWBOOK EXCHANGE, LTD.
Clark, New Jersey
2007

ISBN-13: 978-1-58477-759-5 (cloth)
ISBN-10: 1-58477-759-1 (cloth)
ISBN-13: 978-1-58477-861-5 (paperback)
ISBN-10: 1-58477-861-X (paperback)

The Lawbook Exchange, Ltd.
33 Terminal Avenue
Clark, New Jersey 07066-1321

Please see our website for a selection of our other publications and fine facsimile reprints of classic works of legal history:
www.lawbookexchange.com

Library of Congress Cataloging-in-Publication Data

Sources of the history of the American law of lawyering / Michael H. Hoeflich, editor.
p. cm. -- (Foundations of the American law of lawyering)
Includes bibliographical references.
ISBN-13: 978-1-58477-759-5 (cloth : alk. paper)
ISBN-10: 1-58477-759-1 (cloth : alk. paper)
ISBN-13: 978-1-58477-861-5 (pbk. : alk. paper)
ISBN-10: 1-58477-861-X (pbk. : alk. paper)
1. Legal ethics--United States--History. 2. Practice of law--Moral and ethical aspects--United States--History. 3. Practice of law--United States--History. 4. Lawyers--United States. I.
Hoeflich, Michael H.
KF306.S68 2008
174'.30973--dc22

2007040224

Printed in the United States of America on acid-free paper

Dedication

To My Lunch Buddies
Glee, Jim, and Laurence

Contents

PREFACE

Some Little Known Sources for the History of Legal Ethics in the Nineteenth Century

Given the strongly historical nature of the law and the proud heritage of the American legal profession it is somewhat surprising that most studies of legal ethics published in the United States have tended to believe that there were no significant writings on legal ethics from Lord Brougham's speech in his defense of Queen Caroline at the beginning of the nineteenth century until the end of the century and the beginning of the twentieth century and the beginnings of the lawyer codes published by the states and the American Bar Association.[1] The reason for this may well be a suspicion among the general run of lawyers and legal scholars that the ethics of the nineteenth century were less than satisfactory to modern sensibilities. In recent years, however, a small group of ethics scholars have turned their attention to this neglected period. Tom Shaffer, Russell Pearce, and Stephen Kalish have brought David Hoffman and Judge George Sharswood to the attention of the modern Bar.

David Hoffman, of course, was the first professional law teacher in Baltimore whose short-lived law school was one of the first in the United States. He was also the author of the *Course of Legal Studies*, one of the most influential handbooks on legal education of the antebellum period. The first edition of the work, published in 1817, contained a short chapter on "legal deportment." The second, expanded edition of 1836 added to this an appendix of *Fifty Rules on Professional Deportment,* a text which was to be widely circulated in later decades and which influenced the work of both Judge George Sharswood and the drafters of the early ethics code at the end of the century.[2]

---

1. See, esp., C.R. ANDREWS, P.M. PRUITT, JR., DAVID I. DURHAM, GILDED AGE LEGAL ETHICS: ESSAYS ON THOMAS GOODE JONES' CODE AND THE REGULATION OF THE PROFESSION (2003).

2. See, on Hoffman and Sharswood, esp., Thomas L. Shaffer, David Hoffman's Law School Lectures, 1822-1833, 32 J. LEGAL EDUC. 127 (1982); Russell G. Pierce, Rediscovering the Republican Origins of the Legal Ethics Codes, 6 GEO. J. LEGAL ETHICS 241 (1992);

Judge George Sharswood was a distinguished Pennsylvania lawyer, judge, and law professor who published his lectures on legal ethics at Philadelphia in 1854.[3] This text was a far more complete treatment of the problems of legal ethics with which the average practitioner would have to deal and went through several editions over the next half century and stayed in print for a remarkably long period.

Two other nineteenth century lawyers who wrote on legal ethics have also come to the attention of modern lawyers of late. George Paul Brown, reckoned by contemporaries to be the best criminal lawyer of the antebellum Philadelphia Bar published two volumes of memoirs several years after the first edition of Judge Sharswood's *Legal Ethics* appeared.[4] Several chapters in this work are, in fact, not autobiographical at all. Rather they are Brown's attempt to set forth his views on how lawyers must behave. These chapters are quite detailed and provide another source by which one can begin to understand the predominant views of legal ethics during this period. Particularly interesting is also the fact that much of Brown's chapters on ethics are, in fact, near verbatim plagiarism of Sharswood's earlier works. Nevertheless, Brown's volumes, published under the title *The Forum*, appear to have been well distributed during his life and thereafter.

Finally, scholars have also turned their attention to the writing of David Dudley Field, who in spite of great success as a lawyer and legal scholar came under stinging attack from such notables as Henry Adams and Charles Francis Adams as a result of his representation of a number of shady railroad financiers, and who felt it necessary to defend himself in several quite thoughtful disquisitions on legal ethics.[5]

Stephen E. Kalish, David Hoffman's Essay on Professional Deportment and the Current Legal Ethics Debate, 61 NEB. L. REV. 54 (1982); Maxwell W. Bloomfield, David Hoffman and the Rise of a Republican Legal Culture, 38 MD. L. REV. 673 (1979); M.H. Hoeflich, Legal Ethics in the Nineteenth Century: The Other Tradition, 47 KANS. L. REV. 793 (1999) [reprinted below].

3. George Sharswood, A COMPENDIUM OF LECTURES ON THE AIMS AND DUTIES OF THE PROFESSION OF LAW (1854).

4. DAVID PAUL BROWN, THE FORUM; OR FORTY YEARS FULL PRACTICE AT THE PHILADELPHIA BAR (1856).

5. See, Michael Schudson, Public, Private, and Professional Lives: The Correspondence of David Dudley Field and Samuel Bowles, 21 AM. J. LEG. HIST 191 (1977).

These writings are, without doubt, extremely important, for they provide major insights into the opinions of some of the leading lawyers and jurists of the period. Hoffman, though his law school failed to be a success, was known and admired by many of the leading jurists of the age, including Justice Story. His *Fifty Rules on Professional Deportment* clearly had an impact on the work of Judge Sharswood and David Paul Brown. The 1836 volume to which they were appended enjoyed a wide circulation throughout the United States and remained available for sale for decades.6 Indeed, the Rules were so well respected that they were even included in the prefatory material of a popular lawyer's diary during the latter part of the century.[7] Sharswood and Brown were members of the Philadelphia legal elite and trained many of the leading lawyers of the day through lectures and by example. Field, in spite of his questionable activities in the Erie Railroad affairs was one of the leading lights of the New York Bar, a champion of codification, and the brother of an Associate Justice of the United States Supreme Court. Thus, the work of all four men cannot be taken as representative of the Bar as a whole. These men were members of the elite urban Bar from major legal centers. Their writings on ethics must be put into their social and intellectual milieu, which has been well described by Maxwell Bloomfield.[8] All four men represent in their writing the highest aspirations of the nineteenth century Bar and the rules by which they suggest lawyers ought to live are rules that represent those rules which wealthy, established practitioners have the luxury to espouse and even follow. In their writings these men not only attempted to set forth rules for lawyers but also, in so doing, portray their profession, a profession already under popular attack, as having the highest ideals and ethical standards. Thus, if we are to understand not simply the views of the of the nineteenth century legal elite, it is necessary to find other sources with which to compare these elite sources.

Several years ago I attempted to seek other nineteenth century sources to divine commonly accepted ethical standards of the nineteenth century Bar.[9]

---

6. DAVID HOFFMAN, A COURSE OF LEGAL STUDY (2d. Ed., 1836).

7. See, MOSER'S LAWYER'S DIARY FOR 1883 (1883) [the Hoffman extract is on pp.v-xvii].

8. See, above, n. 2.

9. Reprinted below.

In that article I attempted to examine the perceived scope and limits of the lawyer client relationship not only in the work of established legal figures like Hoffman, Sharswood, Brown, and Field, but also in a less explored source: funeral orations. In this volume of collected sources I have included a number of the sources cited therein and others which I believe that lawyers and ethics scholars will find useful. The criteria for inclusion of material in this volume are simple. I have excluded book-length texts, some of which will be separately reprinted at a later time. Shorter materials which are representative of the genre and which are either of overwhelming importance, like Hoffman's Fifty Rules or are little-known today, like O'Brien's essay, are included. The reader should recognize, however, that what is included is only a fraction of the materials of the period with relevance to the study of legal ethics today and yesterday.

Michael H. Hoeflich
October 2007

Part One

Chapter I

Legal Ethics in the Nineteenth Century

The "Other Tradition"

M.H. Hoeflich

Hoeflich, M.H. Legal Ethics in the Nineteenth Century: The "Other Tradition." University of Kansas Law Review, v. 47, no. 4 (May, 1999)

ESSAYS

Legal Ethics in the Nineteenth Century: The "Other Tradition"

M.H. Hoeflich[*]

Zealous advocacy. Hired gun. Adversarial process. These phrases and others are commonly used to describe the role of a lawyer in our system. At the heart of all of these is a very specific notion of the lawyer-client relationship. This relationship is central to our modern ideology of the legal profession and the lawyer's role in it. The idea is simple: a lawyer owes the highest loyalty to his client and, within established ethical bounds, must do his all for his client. The late Irving Kaufmann used to tell students at his bar review lectures that a lawyer "was not a bus, but a concert piano." He was not a bus because he did not have to take on all comers who had the fare; but he was like a concert piano because once he began to play, he had to respond totally to the pianist.

As central as the lawyer-client relationship is to the modern conception of a lawyer's role, it is just as controversial. Most nonlawyers simply cannot understand why a lawyer will behave so aggressively for his client, particularly when that client is unattractive or unpopular or accused of a heinous crime. As the American public watched the Menendez case, the Buattofuco case, and the O.J. Simpson case on television, the confusion and outrage over lawyer zealotry and the trial tactics which derived therefrom became even greater. But it is not just the general public that is so troubled by the extremes of lawyer advocacy on behalf of clients. Many members of the profession believe that the current centrality of the lawyer-client relationship and the value placed upon loyalty to the client does a disservice to the profession and to our system of justice. Just as the adversarial system and the concept of overwhelming loyalty to, and advocacy for, a client in that system has its proponents, so, too, does it have its detractors.

Perhaps foremost amongst those who have attacked the extreme vision of lawyer advocacy on behalf of clients is Professor Thomas Shaffer of the Notre Dame Law School. In a series of articles and books, he has

* Dean and John H. & John M. Kane Distinguished Professor of Law, University of Kansas School of Law. B.A., M.A. Haverford College; M.A. Cambridge University; J.D. Yale.

argued for the reinsertion of the lawyer's personal morality into the lawyer-client relationship as a mitigating force to the notion of zealous advocacy.[1] He has grounded his arguments in a combination of religion and popular morality. He has also argued that the modern notion of the lawyer-client relationship is precisely that—a modern notion—and has argued that historically the normative view of a lawyer's obligation to his client has been far less extreme in its approach to zealotry than it is at the present day.[2] In constructing this historical view, Professor Shaffer has focused primarily on two sources, the works of David Hoffman and George Sharswood.[3] But while these two nineteenth century jurists were quite influential in shaping the boundaries of the then prevalent view of the lawyer's obligation to his client, many lawyers and nonlawyers wrote on the subject during this period. Their writings provide a fuller and richer perspective on this history. In the end, when one examines many of these little known nineteenth century sources, one discovers that Professor Shaffer is quite right and that the nineteenth century view of legal ethics differed greatly from our own.

It is rare that one can trace the exact source of a particular doctrine in the law. But the idea of zealous advocacy as the highest form of the lawyer-client relationship can be exactly dated and attributed. It first appears in the legal forum in a speech made before the House of Lords by Lord Henry Brougham.[4] Lord Brougham was born in 1778 and practiced first at the Scottish Bar and moved to London to become a barrister in 1808.[5] He became a member of Parliament soon thereafter and acquired a reputation as a first-rate trial lawyer. It was because of this that he was retained as defense counsel in one of the most celebrated

---

1. *See generally* THOMAS L. SHAFFER & R.F. COCHRAN, JR., LAWYERS, CLIENTS, AND MORAL RESPONSIBILITY (1994); THOMAS L. SHAFFER, ON BEING A CHRISTIAN AND A LAWYER (1981); Thomas L. Shaffer, *The Practice of Law as Moral Discourse*, 55 NOTRE DAME L. REV. 231 (1979); Thomas L. Shaffer, *The Gentleman in Professional Ethics*, 10 QUEEN'S L.J. 1 (1984); Thomas L. Shaffer, *The Unique, Novel, and Unsound Adversary Ethic*, 41 VAND. L. REV. 697 (1988) [hereinafter Shaffer, *Adversary Ethic*]. William Simon has also propounded this new interpretation of legal ethics. *See* William H. Simon, *Ethical Discretion in Lawyering*, 101 HARV. L. REV. 1083 (1988); *see also* THOMAS L. SHAFFER, AMERICAN LEGAL ETHICS (1985) [hereinafter SHAFFER, LEGAL ETHICS].

2. *See generally* SHAFFER & COCHRAN, *supra* note 1.

3. *See id.* at 32-35.

4. The first edition of the speech is Henry Brougham, *The First Part of Mr. Brougham's Speech in the Defense of Her Majesty Queen (Oct. 3-4, 1820)*, *in* SPEECHES OF MR. BROUGHAM, MR. DENMAN AND DR. LUSHINGTON; CONTAINING THE DEFENSE OF HER MAJESTY THE QUEEN 3-58 (London, Thomas Masters 1820) [hereinafter SPEECHES]. It is noteworthy that the first appearance in part of this speech was in the form of a broadside, intended for popular consumption. *See id.*; *see also* SHAFFER, LEGAL ETHICS, *supra* note 1, at 204-06.

5. Brougham was a prolific author and statesman who went on to become Lord Chancellor of England and one of the most forceful proponents of legal reform.

trials of his era. Queen Caroline was accused of adultery against the King of England.[6] The case was tried before the House of Lords. Brougham, as Caroline's counsel, came under severe attack on the grounds that defending against the King was an act tantamount to treason and one which no patriot nor self-respecting British subject would undertake. In his opening statement to the House of Lords, Brougham established the basis for his defense of Caroline as well as for himself:

> [A]n advocate, in the discharge of his duty, knows but one person in all the world, and that person is his client. To save that client by all means and expedients, and at all hazards and costs to other persons, and, among them, to himself, is his first and only duty; and in performing this duty he must not regard the alarm, the torments, the destruction which he may bring upon others. Separating the duty of a patriot from that of an advocate, he must go on reckless of consequences, though it should be his unhappy fate to involve his country in confusion.[7]

Lord Brougham's statement of a lawyer's duty to his client was the most extreme view to that point ever expounded. It was contradictory to the medieval tradition of legal ethics and inconsistent with the view propounded by Blackstone in his *Commentaries*. It was also successful; the prosecution against Caroline was abandoned.

Brougham's statements quickly became well-known, but they were not quickly approved. In fact, Brougham's vision of zealous advocacy—one which might well have been expressed by the Simpson defense team—was rejected by many of his contemporaries. Indeed, in the United States, Brougham's statements were attacked and viewed by contemporaries and successors as being utterly inappropriate.

The first published American treatment of legal ethics is found as an appendix to David Hoffman's 1817 treatise on legal education, *A Course of Legal Study*, which was reissued in an expanded version in 1836.[8] Hoffman was a Baltimore lawyer with an all-consuming interest in legal

6. Queen Caroline had long been estranged from her husband King George IV. She had been a long-time resident of Italy where, it was alleged, she had committed adultery. The best edition of the trial transcript is contained in MEMOIRS OF HER LATE MAJESTY QUEEN CAROLINE (J. Nightingale ed.., London, J. Robins & Co. Albion Press 1820-22); a modern popular account of the trial is ROGER FULFORD, THE TRIAL OF QUEEN CAROLINE (1967).

7. SPEECHES, *supra* note 4, at 4. The most accessible source for this excerpt is MONROE H. FREEDMAN, UNDERSTANDING LEGAL ETHICS 65-66 (1990), which quotes from *Trial of Queen Caroline* 8 (1821). Professor William Hodes has analyzed this speech and put it into the fascinating context of the O.J. Simpson case. *See* W. William Hodes, *Lord Brougham, the Dream Team, and Jury Nullification of the Third Kind*, 67 U. COLO. L. REV. 1075, 1104-08 (1996).

8. *See generally* DAVID HOFFMAN, A COURSE OF LEGAL STUDY (2d ed. Philadelphia, Thomas, Cowperthwait & Co. 1836); *see also* SHAFFER, LEGAL ETHICS, *supra* note 1, at 59-160; Maxwell Bloomfield, *David Hoffman and the Shaping of a Republican Legal Culture*, 38 MD. L. REV. 673 (1979); Thomas L. Shaffer, *David Hoffman's Law School Lectures, 1822-1833*, 32 J. LEGAL EDUC. 127 (1982).

education, professionalism, and ethics. For several years, he operated a law school in Baltimore that eventually failed for lack of students. His most important contribution to legal ethics, however, is his *Resolutions in Regard to Professional Deportment* published in the expanded 1836 version of *A Course of Legal Study*.[9] Several of these treat the lawyer-client relationship and its limitations.[10] Far from embracing Lord Brougham's expansive view of the lawyer's obligation to his client, Hoffman takes a more restrictive view. In Resolution X, he declares that a lawyer ought not put forth "frivolous or vexatious defenses" even though his client desires him to do so.[11] Resolution XI counsels the young lawyer to advise a client to abandon a client's case or claim which "*ought not, to be sustained.*"[12] He specifically rejects pushing such a claim in hopes of reaching a better settlement.[13] In Resolutions XII and XIII, Hoffman counsels against a lawyer pleading the Statute of Limitations or the incapacity because of minority of a client, if a client can otherwise pay a valid debt.[14] He refers to the use of such defenses as "knavery."[15]

Resolutions XIV and XV are, perhaps, the most significant. Resolution XIV deals with civil cases, and Resolution XV deals with criminal cases.[16] In regard to the first, Hoffman states that a lawyer's conscience must remain a "distinct entity" from his client's.[17] He goes on to say: "[I]f I am satisfied from the evidence that the fact is against my client, he must excuse me if I do not see as he does, and do not press it . . . ."[18] In criminal cases, he states that when the evidence against clients leaves "no just doubt of their guilt," then the lawyer ought not "impede the course of justice" through the use of ingenuity or "artifices of eloquence" nor through the use of any influence the lawyer might have.[19] He argues that the lawyer's duty is only to assure "a fair and dispassionate investigation of the facts of their cause and the due application of the law."[20]

In all of these Resolutions, there is implicit the notion that the lawyer must, in fact, exercise his own personal moral judgment in determining

9. *Resolutions in Regard to Professional Deportment*, *in* HOFFMAN, *supra* note 8, at 752-75.
10. *See e.g.*, *id.*, *in* HOFFMAN, *supra* note 8, at 755, 758 (Resolutions XIV and XVIII).
11. *Id.*, *in* HOFFMAN, *supra* note 8, at 754.
12. *Id.*, *in* HOFFMAN, *supra* note 8, at 754 (emphasis added).
13. *See id.*, *in* HOFFMAN, *supra* note 8, at 754.
14. *See id.*, *in* HOFFMAN, *supra* note 8, at 754-55.
15. *Id.*, *in* HOFFMAN, *supra* note 8, at 754 (Resolution XII).
16. *See id.*, *in* HOFFMAN, *supra* note 8, at 755-56.
17. *Id.*, *in* HOFFMAN, *supra* note 8, at 755 (Resolution XIV).
18. *Id.*, *in* HOFFMAN, *supra* note 8, at 754.
19. *Id.*, *in* HOFFMAN, *supra* note 8, at 755-56.
20. *Id.*, *in* HOFFMAN, *supra* note 8, at 756.

the extent to which he will go in representing a client. In so doing the lawyer becomes a sort of judge in each client's case, a notion from which Hoffman does not shrink as many modern ethicists would. And, of course, Hoffman's views quite clearly include an implicit rejection of Brougham's standard of advocacy as stated in his defense of Queen Caroline. Brougham's view of advocacy and the attorney's role in the lawyer-client relationship is amoral at best. Hoffman's view is imbued with morality from start to finish. Indeed, Professor Shaffer has characterized Hoffman's views as representing a "gentlemanly" approach to ethics.[21]

In 1834, Simon Greenleaf, a prominent Maine attorney, was appointed to the Royall professorship at Harvard Law School.[22] He delivered his inaugural address on August 26, 1834. He took as his topic the importance of law and the legal profession to the new republic. Greenleaf views the role of lawyers in the national life as of paramount importance for it was lawyers who could both "obtain reparation for wrongs done" as well as "devise the means to prevent them."[23] As part of this discussion, Greenleaf also considers the importance of the lawyer's character and his obligations to his clients.

> [T]he character of an upright lawyer shines with mild but genial lustre. He concerns himself with the beginnings of controversies, not to inflame but to extinguish them. He is not content with the doubtful morality of suffering clients, whose passions are aroused, to rush blindly into legal conflict. His conscience can find no balm in the reflection, that he has but obeyed the orders of an angry man. He feels that his first duties are to the community in which he lives . . . . I look with pity on the man, who regards himself as a mere machine of the law;—whose conceptions of moral and social duty are all absorbed in the sense of supposed obligation to his client, and this of so low a nature as to render him a very tool and slave, to serve the worst passions of men . . . .[24]

Greenleaf's advice to his listeners—the students at Harvard Law School—could not be clearer. They are men of conscience and must

---

21. SHAFFER & COCHRAN, *supra* note 1, at 35-39; *see also* David Luban, *Paternalism and the Legal Profession*, 1981 WIS. L. REV. 454 (discussing attorney-client interaction).

22. For Greenleaf's biography, see 1 CHARLES WARREN, HISTORY OF THE HARVARD LAW SCHOOL 450 (1970). Professor Al Konefsky of the Buffalo Law School has, for some years, been at work on a full biography of Greenleaf.

23. Simon Greenleaf, *A Discourse Pronounced at the Inauguration of the Author as Royall Professor of Law in Harvard University* (Cambridge, James Munroe 1854), *reprinted in* THE GLADSOME LIGHT OF JURISPRUDENCE 134 (M.H. Hoeflich ed., 1988).

24. *Id.*, *reprinted in* THE GLADSOME LIGHT OF JURISPRUDENCE 140 (M.H. Hoeflich ed., 1988) (emphasis added). This should be compared with Abraham Lincoln's advice later that the lawyer should "[d]iscourage litigation" and fulfill the role of "peace-maker." Abraham Lincoln, *Fragment: Notes for a Law Lecture (1850)*, *in* THE COLLECTED WORKS OF ABRAHAM LINCOLN: SUPPLEMENT 1832-1865, at 18, 19 (Roy P. Basler ed., 1974).

exercise their own moral judgment in carrying out their tasks as lawyers. They must not elevate their obligation to their client over their own independent moral judgment. Greenleaf, like Hoffman, sees the lawyer as the judge of his client's cause—and as his client's advisor in this cause:

> [O]ur clients are not always the best judges of their own interests,—and that having confided these interests to our hands, it is for us to advise to that course, which will best conduce to their permanent benefit, not merely as solitary individuals, but as men connected with society by enduring ties.[25]

Greenleaf ties the extent of the lawyer's obligation to his client to the lawyer's own morality and, above all, to the oath that the lawyer swears upon becoming an attorney:

> He is to deal faithfully with the merits and facts of the cause confided to his care; yet not pressing them beyond their intrinsic value, or the boundaries of justice. He has not sold himself to obtain, by right or wrong, a victory for his employer; but is engaged to see, that the cause is clearly and truly developed .... He is to perpetrate no falsehood;—he is to practise no chicanery;—he is to take no advantage of the mistakes of his brethren .... He is not to forget, that while maintaining individual rights, he is also addressing the public ....[26]

The essence of Greenleaf's statements lies in this last quotation. Greenleaf speaks less of the details of practice and more of general ethical aspirations than does Hoffman. Nevertheless, Greenleaf and Hoffman both agreed on the basic issue that a lawyer must condition his acts on his own moral judgment and not based on his fidelity to his client.

Greenleaf also introduced a very significant element into the debate on lawyer ethics: the import of the lawyer's oath. Oaths were taken quite seriously in the eighteenth and early nineteenth century.[27] They bound the taker before God and man. The lawyer's oath elevated the lawyer from being a private citizen to being a public official and, as such, gave the lawyer a whole new set of obligations. Professor Shaffer has suggested that the heightened ethics of Hoffman and his contemporaries derived both from their notion that lawyers were gentlemen and also from the ideals prevalent in the early republic.[28] Greenleaf, in stressing the role of the lawyer's oath in shaping lawyer ethics, makes this latter point clear. As an office holder, a lawyer must be concerned with the public

---

25. Greenleaf, *supra* note 23, *reprinted in* THE GLADSOME LIGHT OF JURISPRUDENCE 141 (M.H. Hoeflich ed., 1988).

26. *Id.*, *reprinted in* THE GLADSOME LIGHT OF JURISPRUDENCE 141 (M.H. Hoeflich ed., 1988).

27. There is a large literature on oaths. *See generally* J.E. TYLER, OATHS, THEIR ORIGINS, NATURE, AND HISTORY (London, Parker 1835); L. ENOCH, OBSERVATIONS ON LEGAL AND JUDICIAL OATHS (Philadelphia, J. Rakestraw 1846).

28. *See* SHAFFER & COCHRAN, *supra* note 1, at 32, 35.

welfare. Thus, a lawyer owed two loyalties—to his client and to the public. It would have been inconceivable to men of Greenleaf's generation, steeped in republican ideals, that individual welfare, even that of a client, might overcome public welfare. Thus, Greenleaf had no problem ideologically holding lawyers—as officeholders—to the moral dictates of their conscience and the needs of the public.

The Law Academy of Philadelphia was founded in 1783 with the mission to educate and maintain a high standard of learning and ethics of the bar.[29] It had as its officers many of the leading legal luminaries of the city and state. Amongst its many activities, it sponsored periodic lectures on law. In 1839, Job Tyson, a Philadelphia lawyer and Vice-Provost of the Law Academy delivered a lecture on "The Integrity of the Legal Character" before the Academy.[30] In the course of this lecture, Tyson, too, discussed the parameters of the lawyer-client relationship. Tyson believed that lawyers were of the highest importance to society. According to Tyson, a lawyer

> stands, not only as a sentinel against the inroads of a political despot, and the scourge of public abuses, but he is the shield of private injuries and the assertor of legal retribution. He is interposed between the corrupt, incompetent and erring judge, and the wronged and trembling suitor. The avenger of the innocent, he visits upon the wrong-doer the penalties of the law, and protects the weak and defenseless from the overbearing hand of oppression and power.[31]

But Tyson, like Greenleaf, also recognized that lawyers, by virtue of their oath and office, also must recognize limits to their behavior:

> [W]hile many practice the law as become the votaries of an elevated science, others degrade it into a pernicious and *driving trade*. It is indifferent to these men what may be the merits of a controversy, or which side they espouse; they ignobly pervert their oath of office, which enjoins fidelity to the interests of the client, into a pretext for sheltering him from the condign punishment of justice and law.[32]

Here, again, are echoes of Hoffman and Greenleaf and a firm rejection of the Brougham ethic. Lawyers, according to Tyson, must, as office

29. *See* William MacLean, Jr., *The Law Academy and Early Legal Education in Philadelphia*, *in* 4 PHILADELPHIA HISTORY 27, 27-36 (1935); *see also* CHARTER, CONSTITUTION AND BY-LAWS OF THE LAW ACADEMY OF PHILADELPHIA 1 (Philadelphia, Law Academy 1848) ("Preamble. The primary object of this institution is to afford the students of law and young members of the Bar, the means of improving themselves in legal and forensic accomplishments."). For a typical speech before the Law Academy, see JOHN K. KANE, A DISCOURSE PRONOUNCED BEFORE THE LAW ACADEMY AT PHILADELPHIA, 26 OCTOBER 1831 (Philadelphia, Law Academy 1831), which deals with the theory of legislation and precedent's value.

30. *See* JOB R. TYSON, DISCOURSE ON THE INTEGRITY OF THE LEGAL CHARACTER (Philadelphia, Law Academy 1839).

31. *Id.* at 8-9.

32. *Id.* at 10.

holders and oath takers, uphold a high standard of morality and cannot permit this to be weakened by their obligations to their clients. At the same time, Tyson admits that many lawyers do not live up to this ideal, but he chastises them for this failure.

Across the Atlantic, another lawyer published one of the more unusual treatments of legal ethics to appear during the century. This was Edward O'Brien's *The Lawyer, His Character and Rule of Holy Life: After the Manner of George Herbert's Country Parson*.[33] O'Brien was an Irishman trained in the law in England. He was also university-educated at Trinity College, Cambridge.[34] Most importantly, he was a devout Christian determined to interject religious and moral values into professional ethical guidelines. This volume was reprinted in Philadelphia in 1843.[35] This rather odd-sounding pamphlet of just under one hundred pages is actually a somewhat learned disquisition on legal ethics. It goes into quite a bit more detail than Hoffman's or Greenleaf's work. The basic thrust of the book is that Brougham's argument as to the ethical obligations of a lawyer, and that the lawyer's duty not to make a moral judgment as to a client's cause, are simply unacceptable.

O'Brien comments in the *apologia*, printed as a preface to the work, as follows:

> "The lawyer," it is said, "is part of the machine of justice:"—Be it so:—He is still a *man*; and as a man is endowed with a sense of what is *right* and *wrong*, of what is *true* and *false*, of what is *just* and *unjust*; and being so endowed is bound to the utmost of his power to advance what is right, true, and just, and to oppose what is contrary to these.[36]

These sentiments are carried on throughout the short work. O'Brien refers to the legal profession as a "calling," a word pregnant with theological overtones.[37] He follows the medieval tradition and considers that the lawyer's knowledge and skills are a gift of God and a sign of grace; to prostitute these divine gifts by turning them to the defense of evil and unjust causes is a sin against God.[38] Interestingly, O'Brien is one of the first modern theorists to endorse pro bono activity, for he

33. EDWARD O'BRIEN, THE LAWYER, HIS CHARACTER AND RULE OF HOLY LIFE: AFTER THE MANNER OF GEORGE HERBERT'S COUNTRY PARSON (Philadelphia, Carey & Hart 1843).

34. *See id.* at 5-8.

35. *See id.*

36. *Id.* at 11.

37. *Id.* at 23.

38. *See id.* ("A lawyer is the servant of his fellow-men for the attainment of justice: in which definition is expressed both the lowliness and the dignity of his *calling* . . . ."(emphasis added)); *see also id.* at 24-25.

argues that a lawyer's "doors are ever open to the poor as well as the rich."[39]

O'Brien is at his most interesting—and most eloquent—when he turns to the chapter in which he discusses a lawyer's duties. Here, he outlines a list of such duties as follows:

> 1. And *first* he makes it known that he will undertake the conduct of none but *just* causes; and here he esteems those causes alone to be just which under natural law, or positive laws, not contradicted by natural laws, do make such.
> . . .
>
> . . . .
>
> 2. *Secondly*, the lawyer makes it known that he will not even in a just cause make use of unjust arts: he may not do evil that good may come, for real good he is assured may never grow out of evil, to him who works it: much less will he use unjust arts in an unjust cause.[40]

In fact, O'Brien's pamphlet goes into quite detailed directions for particular situations. He has, for instance, a section on the ethical responsibilities of a lawyer when drawing pleadings, when advising on evidence, when consulting with clients.[41] In all of these sections, the basic message remains the same: the lawyer is not simply a mechanical extension of his client. Rather the lawyer is an independent creature who must exercise moral judgment at each stage in his service to his client and must always refuse to do that which is unjust or which might lead to injustice.

Back in the United States, William Porter delivered an oration before the Law Academy of Philadelphia on September 19, 1849.[42] In this oration, he addressed several crucial questions that he believed lay before the Academy and the profession as a whole. Porter addressed a related, but somewhat different, ethical question. Porter's concern was that lawyers were relying upon the technicalities and the subtleties of the law in order to avoid confronting the question of whether or not they were acting justly.[43] His answer to this was that the truly ethical lawyer would not do so, that the ethical lawyer must, at times, engage in subtlety or appeal to a technicality but only because that was a part of the law and, as such, must be followed.[44] But he did not accept the argument that such behavior must inevitably lead to injustice. Indeed, he enunciated the question in a rather bold and simple manner: "Can a lawyer, in every

39. *Id.* at 25.

40. *Id.* at 28-29.

41. *See id.* at 31.

42. *See* WILLIAM A. PORTER, THE INTRODUCTORY ADDRESS DELIVERED BEFORE THE LAW ACADEMY OF PHILADELPHIA, THE OPENING SESSION OF 1849-50 (Philadelphia, Barrington & Haswell 1849).

43. *See id.* at 10-11.

44. *See id.* at 11-12.

case, act honestly and conscientiously?"[45] His answer was a ringing affirmation.[46] It would seem, therefore, that he did not accept Brougham's idea that a lawyer should use every artifice in the cause of his client, though he also was clearly not willing to go so far as O'Brien or Hoffman and explicitly make it a duty of each lawyer to make a moral judgment about his client's case.

In this same year of 1849, one of the leaders of the Philadelphia Bar, Charles Chauncey, died. His death was the occasion for the delivery of an oration by the Reverend Henry Boardman at the Tenth Presbyterian Church in Philadelphia on the subject of "The Importance of Religion to the Legal Profession."[47] Boardman began his oration with the proposition—echoing de Tocqueville—that in the American republic no group of individuals enjoyed as high a status nor as influential a position as lawyers.[48] He extrapolates from this observation that lawyers, therefore, bear a public trust that they must discharge properly.[49] To do so, he believed, required that lawyers be pious and moral individuals and that they carry their personal morality into their professional lives, particularly in how they related to clients.[50] He asks a series of questions as to how a lawyer should react when a client, inflamed and passionate about his cause, comes to the lawyer for help:

> Are you to inflame still further their excited feelings by expatiating on their alleged injuries? . . . Are you with eager haste to assure them that the case admits of no compromise—that the law will award them with full redress, and they should be satisfied with nothing less? Are you to bring the cause into court, and employ all the arts of chicanery, such as brow-beating the witnesses, misquoting authorities, perverting the testimony, and appealing to the baser passions or the political prejudices of the jury—to conceal the merits of the question and secure a favorable verdict? *This surely is not the treatment your clients have a right to expect from you.*[51]

Boardman insists that a lawyer must always exercise his conscience in representing a client. Here again, however, Boardman is not so strict as O'Brien, nor so strict as to destroy the adversarial nature of the legal process. Instead, he shows a remarkable knowledge of, and sensitivity to, the problems lawyers face, but without accepting the radical and, in his mind, amoral views of Brougham:

45. *Id.* at 19.

46. *See id.*

47. HENRY A. BOARDMAN, THE IMPORTANCE OF RELIGION TO THE LEGAL PROFESSION: WITH SOME REMARKS ON THE CHARACTER OF THE LATE CHARLES CHAUNCEY, ESQ. (Philadelphia, Wm. S. Martien 1849).

48. *See id.* at 7-8.

49. *See id.* at 8-9.

50. *See id.* at 15-17.

51. *Id.* at 16-17 (emphasis added).

> It is not meant by this that a lawyer is to assume the functions of a judge, and take both parties under his protection. He stands before the court as a representative of one of the parties, and he is bound to omit no legitimate means which may promise to benefit his client. He may suggest arguments which are not conclusive to his own mind: the court will allow them their due weight. He may seize upon technical informalities in the proceedings of the other side. He may avail himself of all advantages which the law will allow him for vindicating his client and baffling his opponent. But he may not bring into the conduct of his cause a malicious or vindictive spirit. He may not needlessly blacken the character of the opposing party. He must not impugn the veracity of witnesses, whose only fault has been their modesty or timidity. He must not seek to carry his cause by misrepresenting the facts, or by poisoning the minds of the court and jury against the antagonist client on personal or party grounds, aside from the merits of the issue on trial.[52]

In short, Boardman's position is quite simple: you may be an adversary, but there are limits to what an adversary may do and these limits are prescribed by common morality and a perception of the distinction between right and wrong.

In 1854, another American voice entered the fray on the ethics of the lawyer-client relationship. The original title of the work was *A Compendium of Lectures on the Aims and Duties of the Profession of the Law.*[53] Its author was George Sharswood. Sharswood was a lawyer, judge, and professor of law at the University of Pennsylvania. His 1854 volume, which had originated as a series of lectures at the University of Pennsylvania, was intended to provide a basic guide to practice for young lawyers. It became immensely popular and, under several variations on the title *Legal Ethics*, went through numerous editions.[54] A substantial portion of the book consists of a discussion of what Sharswood refers to as the lawyer's duty of "fidelity to the client."[55] In this section of the book, Sharswood asks directly what the limits of the lawyer's obligation to his client are when the "legal demands or interests of his client conflict with his [the lawyer's] own sense of what is just and right."[56]

Sharswood begins his examination of this question by noting that a lawyer is not simply a client's agent but also an officer of the court.[57] He

52. *Id.* at 18.

53. GEORGE SHARSWOOD, A COMPENDIUM OF LECTURES ON THE AIMS AND DUTIES OF THE PROFESSION OF LAW (n.p., 1854); *see generally* SHAFFER, LEGAL ETHICS, *supra* note 1, at 176.

54. In this Essay, I have used the 1884 edition. *See* GEORGE SHARSWOOD, AN ESSAY ON PROFESSIONAL ETHICS (5th ed., Philadelphia, T. & J.W. Johnson 1884). I have chosen to use this edition because it contains a "memorial" biography of Sharswood as the introduction. *See id.*; *see also* G. BIDDLE, A SKETCH OF THE PROFESSIONAL AND JUDICIAL CHARACTER OF THE LATE GEORGE SHARSWOOD, CHIEF JUSTICE OF THE SUPREME COURT OF PENNSYLVANIA (Philadelphia, Law Association 1883); 17 DICTIONARY OF AMERICAN BIOGRAPHY 28-29 (1946).

55. SHARSWOOD, *supra* note 57, at 81.

56. *Id.*

57. *See id.* at 83.

also notes that certain acts which would be repugnant *in foro conscientiae* (in the forum of the conscience) will be acceptable in a court of law.[58] The example he adduces for this distinction is that of the Statute of Limitations.[59] According to Sharswood, while it may be immoral to plead the Statute to avoid paying an otherwise valid debt, it would not be illegal.[60] This distinction, absent from Hoffman's Resolutions, marks an important turning point in the ethics of legal representation. Obviously, Sharswood is willing to accept that a lawyer may, in the interests of his client, act against morals so long as he does not violate the law.[61]

Indeed, Sharswood goes on to point out that every "party has a right to have his case decided upon the law and the evidence, and to have every view presented to the minds of the judges, which can legitimately bear upon the question."[62] The presentation of these views Sharswood calls the "office of the advocate."[63] Indeed, Sharswood expressly excuses the lawyer from any moral responsibility for his client's case.[64] To do otherwise, Sharswood maintains, would be to make the lawyer his client's judge.[65]

At this point in his argument, Sharswood would appear to be much closer to Brougham's views than to those of Hoffman. Hoffman quite clearly was unwilling to separate questions of law and morality and believed that a lawyer was responsible morally if he were to act in his client's interest against morality. Indeed, Hoffman seems to have favored an approach that required the lawyer to judge the merits of his client's case and to act according to that judgment. Sharswood, on the other hand, was willing to recognize the difference between law and morals and was, in general, unwilling to have the lawyer test a client's case by his moral standards. The justification for Sharswood's position has a very modern sound to it. To do other than he stated, Sharswood feared, would undermine the entire system of justice, usurp the judge and jury's functions to the lawyer, and, in extreme cases, deny an individual the ability to have adequate representation.[66]

Sharswood, in fact, expands upon this general view of the lawyer's role. He was troubled by the notion that his position could provide an ethical justification for lawyers taking on all clients, regardless of the

58. *See id.*
59. *See id.*
60. *See id.*
61. *See id.* at 82-83.
62. *Id.* at 83.
63. *Id.*
64. *See id.*
65. *See id.* at 83-84.
66. *See id.* at 84.

merit of their cases, and taking them on, as he said, "with a view to one single end, *success*."[67] Sharswood feared that such a reaction would lead to unrestrained advocacy and public outcry.[68] He specifically rejects Brougham's view of a lawyer's duty to be unrestrained and holds Brougham's position to be against "cool reflection and sober reason."[69] He also points out that a lawyer may not always make the proper judgment of the merits of a client's case and, therefore, implicitly rejects Hoffman's position.[70] Sharswood sets out a middle ground and in so doing sets out four distinct cases: (1) when a lawyer acts as a criminal prosecutor; (2) when he acts as defense counsel; (3) when he is asked to represent a client in an "unjust claim"; and (4) when he is asked to represent a client in defending against what appears to be a just cause.[71]

In the first case, that of criminal prosecution, he has an easy answer.[72] Because there is never a professional obligation to voluntarily join in a criminal prosecution, if a lawyer believes such a prosecution to be unjust, he should stay away from it and leave it to the public prosecutor.[73] As to criminal defense cases, Sharswood argues that a defendant in such an action should have the full benefit of the law and that his attorney ought to provide this, but not more.[74] Indeed, in cases of appointed counsel, Sharswood argues that it is ethical for a lawyer to represent a client even though he believes him to be guilty.[75] In the third case, defense of a civil action, Sharswood again believes that the need of clients for representation makes it necessary for lawyers to take on such cases, even though they may not agree with their client's cause.[76] Once again, the reasoning behind this rule stems from Sharswood's belief that without lawyers, litigants would often be at a disadvantage because of wealth or knowledge and that by having lawyers both sides are equalized and a case may then be decided on the merits.

It is in regard to the fourth case, prosecution of a civil code, that Sharswood most closely approaches Hoffman and distances himself from Brougham.[77] Sharswood argues that in cases where a client seeks a lawyer to prosecute a civil claim the lawyer is duty bound "to refuse to be concerned for a plaintiff in the legal pursuit of a demand, which

---

67. *Id.*
68. *See id.*
69. *Id.* at 87.
70. *See id.* at 89.
71. *Id.* at 90.
72. *See id.* at 93.
73. *See id.*
74. *See id.* at 90-91.
75. *See id.* at 92.
76. *See id.* at 95-96.
77. *See id.* at 96.

offends his sense of what is just and right."[78] Sharswood urges the lawyer not to refuse lightly, but remains steadfast in his belief that in cases where the case is repugnant to the lawyer's personal morality then the lawyer should refuse it.[79] In support of this proposition, he cites a statement of Chief Justice Gibson that lawyers are not solely in the position of owing fidelity to a client but also are officers of the court bound by an "official oath."[80] Under this schema, a lawyer who was to prosecute an unjust claim for a client would be knowingly violating his obligation to the court.

Sharswood then goes on to discuss the celebrated *Courvoisier* case, a capital case, in which the defense counsel knew that his client was guilty.[81] Sharswood had already stated that every defendant deserved counsel. He uses this case as a means of refining this rule. Sharswood explains that while the client is entitled to legal representation, the lawyer should make only those arguments he knows to be true and fair and should neither use sharp practices, nor attempt to use his own reputation to help his client.[82] In short, the client, according to Sharswood, is entitled to be defended using all of the arguments presented by the evidence, but no others.

Sharswood's analysis of the duties owed by an attorney to his client have a modern ring to them. He chose a middle path between the extremes stated by Brougham and Hoffman. While he rejected the notion that a lawyer was, in effect, a "hired gun" owing loyalty only to his client, he also was unwilling to accept the extreme moralist view proposed by Hoffman. We may, perhaps, explain this based upon experience and context. Brougham's statement was made in court in a defense of national import and for which the popular voice was against both client and lawyer. To some degree, Brougham was faced with a potential lynch mob. Hoffman, on the other hand, was an academic speaking to law students. We may well see in his extreme moralist views the beginnings of that isolation from and misunderstanding of practice that has so long marked the relationship between legal academics and legal practitioners. Sharswood, was speaking neither in the heat of battle nor solely as an academic (although his book began life as an academic lecture). Sharswood was an experienced and successful lawyer and jurist. He was quite interested in law reform as well. He clearly understood the pressures the justice system in its adversarial form placed upon lawyers. At the same time, his own sense of professionalism and morality, as well

78. *Id.*
79. *See id.*
80. *Id.* at 96-97.
81. *See id.* at 103.
82. *See id.* at 104-05.

as his knowledge of the traditions of the bar, would not allow him to adopt either extreme view. Thus, he chose the middle road. And, as we shall see, this middle road was exactly in keeping with the general view of the lawyer-client relationship abroad in the profession of his day.

Two years after Judge Sharswood published his first edition, another Philadelphia lawyer published a two-volume work entitled *The Forum; or Forty Years Full Practice at the Philadelphia Bar*.[83] The author, David Paul Brown, was a senior member of the Philadelphia Bar, knew Judge Sharswood and his writings, and wanted to provide the bar with a history as well as commentary on practice. *The Forum*, therefore, is a combination of bar memoir and practice handbook. In the second volume is contained a chapter entitled *Forensic Ethics and Etiquette*.[84]

It is quite interesting, in the light of Sharswood's dependence upon the notion that a lawyer is an officer of the court that Brown begins his discussion of legal ethics with a discussion of the oath required of all lawyers in Pennsylvania.[85] That oath required the lawyer to fulfill his office as lawyer with all fidelity to both the court and to his client.[86] The obligation was shared. Brown then goes on to reject Brougham's view in words strongly reminiscent of those of Sharswood; in fact, Brown also quotes Chief Justice Gibson.[87] But Brown and Sharswood are not in total agreement. Brown states in several places in his volume that should a lawyer be retained in a case which he discovers to be "dishonest" or "unsound," he "is bound to abandon the cause at once."[88] This is a step that Sharswood was not willing to take. These remarks, however, would seem to be limited to civil cases. In criminal cases, Brown agrees with Sharswood that a defendant is entitled to be defended within the limits of the law and evidence.[89] Brown goes further and makes what is now a familiar argument, that a criminal lawyer can rarely be certain that his client is guilty and that the finder of fact is the jury and of law, the

83. *See* DAVID PAUL BROWN, THE FORUM; OR FORTY YEARS FULL PRACTICE AT THE PHILADELPHIA BAR (2d ed., Philadelphia, Robert Small 1856). Interestingly, these volumes were published initially by subscription (*i.e.*, a number of lawyers agreed to purchase the volumes before they were printed). Among the subscribers were leading lawyers from Pennsylvania, New York, Tennessee, New Jersey, and even Mississippi. For the purpose of this Article, the most important section of the work is in volume 2, titled *Forensic Ethics and Etiquette*.

84. *See* 2 BROWN, *supra* note 83, at 25.

85. *See id.* at 26.

86. *See id.*

87. *See id.* at 29-30. Brown quotes Brougham and then states: "[I]f carried out to the extent suggested, [Brougham's words] make the advocate worse than a highwayman, and render him, under cover of the law, a virtual outlaw." *Id.* at 28.

88. *Id.* at 36; *see also id.* at 30 ("[A] lawyer is bound to refuse a case that he believes to be dishonest, or to retire from it, the moment he discovers it to be so.").

89. *See id.* at 30-36.

judge.[90] Thus, the criminal defense lawyer can ethically defend a client even though he *believes* the client to be guilty.[91]

In a later section of this same chapter, Brown has a most interesting, and rather equivocal treatment of the problem of defending against enforcement of a date through pleading the Statute of Limitations.[92] He begins his argument sounding rather like Sharswood. He states that the Statute is a valid law.[93] But he then looks to the purpose of the Statute to determine the ethics of its use.[94] He says that the Statute is legitimated by reason because it is designed to protect parties against death, destruction, or the loss of documents, all of which may occur over the passage of time.[95] But he then goes on to ask as to how a lawyer should plead when he knows that none of these has occurred and that the debt is valid and unpaid, but his client simply wishes to avoid his moral duty by recourse to the Statute.[96] In such a case, Brown departs from Sharswood and states that "he had better not undertake the case."[97]

Although Brown and Sharswood differ in small details, their general approach to legal ethics was quite similar and fell between the two poles established by Hoffman and Brougham. The evidence of these two practitioners at the middle of the nineteenth century provides strong indications of the prevailing view about legal ethics, at least among the elite urban bars. In fact, there is another source, less conscious and direct than these volumes, which suggests that these views were widely held throughout the American legal profession.

One of the least looked to and understood sources for the history of legal ethics in the United States are eulogies and memorial addresses given upon the death of a lawyer or judge. It was the habit in the United States from the eighteenth to the twentieth centuries that when a prominent person died, his funeral would feature a series of speakers who would not only reflect upon the deceased's personal characteristics but

90. *See id.*

91. *See id.* at 41. However, he also states:

> Even in a criminal case, which is the severest test to which counsel can be subjected—though counsel may contend that the case for the prosecution is not made out by the evidence—they have no right to contend that presumptions may be built upon the evidence, which, although the evidence may possibly warrant them, the counsel know to be contrary to fact and truth.

Id. at 39.

92. *See id.* at 71.

93. *See id.* at 71-72.

94. *See id.*

95. *See id.*

96. *See id.*

97. *Id.* at 72.

also upon his professional life and standing.[98] It was also common that such speeches and memorial addresses be printed in pamphlet form, often with an engraving of the deceased as a frontispiece. These printed versions were distributed to family and friends and professional colleagues. In the case of lawyers, we often find printed versions not only of speeches actually given at the funeral, but also at memorial sessions held by bar associations and even courts.[99] These addresses provide a rich source for determining normative ethical values for lawyers, for they often paint the deceased in ideal terms. Indeed, when one studies a large number of these speeches, one quickly sees that an "ideal type" of the lawyer emerges. Not surprisingly, this lawyer typology includes a substantial treatment of the lawyer-client relationship. Thus, by studying these speeches and memorial addresses it is possible to compare the ideal lawyer-client relationship as it is portrayed there with the lawyer-client relationship as it is discussed by Brougham, Hoffman, Sharswood, and Brown.

We may properly begin with one of the most famous printed eulogies of the nineteenth century, that of Supreme Court Justice Joseph Story on Chief Justice John Marshall.[100] In telling of Marshall's approach to the law when he was a lawyer, Story notes that Marshall did not accept the idea of fidelity solely to a client.[101] Instead, according to Story, Marshall felt a "deep responsibility, not to his client alone, but to the court and to the cause of public justice."[102] Inherent in this concept is not only a rejection of Brougham's approach, but also the idea found in Sharswood and Brown that a lawyer is an officer of the court and owes equal loyalty to the justice system as to any individual client. Story stresses another aspect of Marshall's practice philosophy that is quite important in this context. Story tells his readers that Marshall eschewed any arguments except those that were "*for* the law, and *with* the law, and *from* the law."[103] Here, again, is a statement in which is inherent the idea put forward by both Sharswood and Brown, that a lawyer ought not to make arguments based upon his own reputation or designed to incite the passions of the judge and jury. Instead, Sharswood and Brown both

98. So common were such speeches that manuals with simple addresses were published during this period. *See, e.g.*, E.J. WHEELER, PULPIT AND GRAVE. A VOLUME OF FUNERAL SERMONS AND ADDRESSES (N.Y., Funk & Wagnall 1880).

99. On this genre of literature, see M.H. Hoeflich, *Legal Ephemera: A Window on Society and the Law*, 99 A.B. BOOKMANS WKLY. 785 (1997).

100. *See* JOSEPH STORY, A DISCOURSE UPON THE LIFE, CHARACTER, AND SERVICES OF THE HONORABLE JOHN MARSHALL, LL.D., CHIEF JUSTICE OF THE UNITED STATES OF AMERICA 5 (Boston, J. Munroe 1835).

101. *See id.* at 62-63.

102. *Id.*

103. *Id.* at 63.

argued for—and Marshall lived by—the notion that a lawyer was bound to argue law soberly and in a dispassionate way so as to assure justice.

This latter point is quite significant given the predilection of the day for oratory. Trial advocacy during this period was often seen as being predominantly oratory. Lawyers from Webster to Lincoln depended less upon the law and the facts dispassionately stated than upon excellent oratorical skills to sway a jury.[104] Men like Story and Sharswood and Brown feared such displays, for they believed that arguments of this sort, though they might well win a case, would inevitably lead to injustice being done. Thus, the ideal lawyer was one who did not need to depend upon oratorical tricks, nor, indeed, to stoop to such measures. Instead, the ideal lawyer maintained a sober demeanor and argued the law and the law alone, as Story stressed that Marshall did.

This theme of sober argument based upon the law alone is further elaborated in another memorial, William Hinckling Prescott's *Memoir of the Honorable John Pickering, LL.D.*, published at Cambridge, Massachusetts, in 1848.[105] Prescott was one of the greatest of America's historians in the nineteenth century.[106] His subject, John Pickering, was a Harvard graduate known for his profound learning in the law.[107] Prescott, in his memoir of Pickering, echoes and elaborates upon Story's ideal lawyer:

> As a professional man, he had studied the law profoundly as a science, penetrating to those departments of it which are, for the most part, little consulted by the profession. . . .
>
> . . . .
>
> As a lawyer, he stood high in the consideration of the community, and deservedly, for no man in the profession did more to elevate its character. At the bar, as everywhere else, his demeanor was courteous. His manner of addressing the jury was plain and impressive. He was well instructed in his case, and expounded with logical precision the legal principles that applied to

104. The role of oratory in the antebellum American legal profession needs to be studied. It is interesting to note that one of the period's greatest orators, Rufus Choate, seems to have been one of Brougham's *strongest* American supporters and according to his biographer "accepted and acted the doctrine [of Lord Brougham] with no qualification whatsoever." EDWARD G. PARKER, REMINISCENCES OF RUFUS CHOATE, THE GREAT AMERICAN ADVOCATE 133 (N.Y., Mason Bros. 1860). It is interesting to speculate whether Choate may well have represented the Broughamian tradition in America, a tradition embraced by those who favored a more populist and less "scientific" approach to law and legal ethics.

105. *See* WILLIAM H. PRESCOTT, MEMOIR OF HON. JOHN PICKERING, LL.D. 3 (Cambridge, Metcalf & Co. 1848).

106. Prescott is best known for his *History of the Conquest of Mexico*, first published in 1843. *See generally* DONALD G. DARNELL, WILLIAM HINCKLING PRESCOTT (1975).

107. Pickering, interestingly, was, perhaps, better known as a scholar to his contemporaries than as a lawyer. *See* CHARLES SUMNER, THE SCHOLAR, THE JURIST, THE ARTIST, THE PHILANTHROPIST. AN ADDRESS BEFORE THE PHI BETA KAPPA SOCIETY OF HARVARD UNIVERSITY 7 (Boston, Wm. T. Clamor 1846). In this study, the scholar was Pickering, and the jurist was Joseph Story.

> it. . . . He addressed the understanding, rather than the passions of his audience. . . . He could not be brought to regard the law as a cunning weapon.[108]

In these discourses about Marshall and Pickering is contained the crucial idea that a good lawyer is not a demagogue nor willing to utilize "tricks" to win his case. The lawyer owes a duty to his client to plead the law, and no more. Certainly, he does not owe his client oratory designed to inflame the passions or tricks and wiles that made the law no more than a "cunning weapon."[109] Again, this view is quite different from the one put forward by Brougham, although it does not require as much of the lawyer as did Hoffman.

A perspective on the lawyer-client relationship that more closely approaches that of David Hoffman than Sharswood and Brown is to be found in an anonymous memorial to James Louis Petigru.[110] Petigru was one of the leaders of the Charleston, South Carolina bar during the antebellum period.[111] He was well known for his learning and he trained many of the South's finest lawyers in his law offices. His anonymous eulogist stressed his ethical standards:

> He never was a mere lawyer to his clients. He was a friend, and a sincere friend; and, when called on for his counsel, he never stopped at expounding the law, but placed before his clients the duties their positions required. With him, *honor* was worth more than property; and he frankly and freely counseled the course that high morals required his clients to pursue, irrespective of law . . .
>
> [H]e was ever assiduous to clear himself of any complicity with moral crime which the profession of law sometimes produces.[112]

This analysis of Petigru's ethical standards for law practice is far closer to Hoffman's than Sharswood's or Brown's. Like Sharswood, Petigru recognized the difference between law and morals, but he chose,

---

108. PRESCOTT, *supra* note 105, at 23.

109. Here, again, we may advert to what appears to have been a rather strong split in the antebellum profession between those who favored oratory and those who took a more "scientific" and restrained view of legal practice. As noted, Rufus Choate was best known as an orator and supported Brougham's views. Webster, another great orator-lawyer of the period may also have fallen into this group. *See* JOEL PARKER, AN ADDRESS TO THE STUDENTS IN THE LAW SCHOOL OF THE UNIVERSITY OF CAMBRIDGE 35-40 (Cambridge, J. Bartlett 1853) ("[A lawyer] may be required, at times, to insist that the rules of the law applicable to the case before the court furnish for human tribunals the equity and justice which must govern that case, and that all beyond must be left to the personal conscience of the parties . . . ."). Is it possible that these orator-lawyers who favored the Broughamist doctrine represent an early "proto-populist" faction and that the more "scientific" lawyers represent an early "elitist" faction?

110. *See* MEMORIAL OF THE LATE JAMES L. PETIGRU (N.Y., Richardson & Co. 1826).

111. For further discussion of Petigru, see JAMES LOUIS PETIGRU: SOUTHERN CONSERVATIVE, SOUTHERN DISSENTER (1995).

112. MEMORIAL, *supra* note 115, at 20-22. The image of the lawyer as a "friend" of his clients is one examined by Professor Shaffer in his book *Lawyers, Clients, and Moral Responsibility*. *See* SHAFFER & COCHRAN, *supra* note 1, at 40-54.

apparently, like Hoffman, always to act according to morals rather than law (or, at least, his eulogist would have us believe). The similarity between Hoffman's views and Petigru's may be more than mere coincidence. During the first half of the nineteenth century, the South possessed a legal culture somewhat different from the North.[113] Lawyers in Charleston and Baltimore viewed themselves in a different light than did lawyers in Philadelphia or Boston. The southern legal profession was more literary and was more conscious of the role of the lawyer as gentleman. This may well have been a holdover of the southern cavalier tradition. Certainly, this difference affected the ethics of practice. Gentlemanliness and gentlemanly morality were more important to the southern lawyer. For instance, Hugh Swinton Legaré, another Charleston lawyer and acquaintance of Petigru, once remarked that he followed the ancient Roman, Cicero, as a role model in practice, even to the point of being unwilling to take any legal actions to collect a fee due him.[114] Thus, what we may see in the more extreme ethics of Hoffman and Petigru is a southern "aristocratic" influence which required these lawyers to always follow morality even when it meant acting against or withdrawing from the lawyer-client relationship. This is not to say that this was a solely southern view; rather, it was a view that was, perhaps, more predominant in the South.

Certainly, the evidence suggests that a full range of views from Hoffman to Sharswood existed among the bar, but that all of the Americans who wrote on the subject rejected Brougham's views. Again, this is not to say that the Americans did not understand that the limits of the lawyer-client relationship and the lawyer's obligations within it were far from clear. S.L. Southard in his *Discourse on the Professional Character and Virtues of the Late William Wirt* stated the problem in clear terms:

> There is . . . a and almost imperceptible narrow line, which is to be trodden by the practitioner. It lies between the vigilant attention and ardent prosecution of the client's rights on the one side; and proper respect for, and submission to the

---

113. Southern legal culture was, in many respects, more literary and broad-based than northern legal culture, although the North has had many literary lawyers. For instance, of Petigru, one memorialist stated: "He was a classical scholar; a man of literary habitudes; a writer of taste and elegance . . . ." MEMORIAL, *supra* note 115, at 17. On other members of the southern antebellum bar who fit into this category, see M.H. HOEFLICH, ROMAN AND CIVIL LAW AND THE DEVELOPMENT OF ANGLO-AMERICAN JURISPRUDENCE IN THE NINETEENTH CENTURY 50-73 (1997). On northern literary lawyers, see generally ROBERT A. FERGUSON, LAW AND LETTERS IN AMERICAN CULTURE (1984).

114. *See* HOEFLICH, *supra* note 113, at 67. Blackstone also adopted the Ciceronian view to a degree, holding that it was unethical for a lawyer to *sue* his client for his fee, a rule held applicable to English barristers until just recently.

> court, and regard for the feelings of the opponent, on the other. It is a point, in our practice, less successfully reached than any other.[115]

In the end, the question of the lawyer's obligation to his client versus his obligation as an officer of the court became one of individual judgment and integrity. Some lawyers took the path laid out by Hoffman, even though it might cost them success. One such lawyer, apparently, was Charles Williams of Vermont. In an obituary notice published in 1854, Isaac Redfield noted of Williams the following:

> In one essential, cardinal excellence, his reputation, as a member of the bar, is perhaps worthy of special commendation to the members of the profession every where and at all times, since the temptations there to moral delinquencies, are so constant, and so specious often as to be difficult of detection, and not easily resisted when discovered. He was never suspected of carrying his case by mere management and chicanery. He chose to lose cases which he could not gain fairly.[116]

If most lawyers did not live by Hoffman's Resolutions or by Williams's model, they also did not accept Lord Brougham's notion that a lawyer should do anything he could do legally for his client. John P. Jones, another nineteenth century lawyer-author put it quite succinctly: "Industrious cunning, and the miserable arts of mean chicane, pandering to crime and prostituting justice, may give one practice, they can never give one honour."[117] Of course, there is in this quote also the recognition that all lawyers did not live up to the standards proposed by Sharswood and Brown, let alone Hoffman or Williams. But the aspirations were there, and they were aspirations that put a far greater moral burden upon the individual lawyer than did Brougham's view of ethics. Indeed, these aspirations put a far greater moral burden on lawyers and saw them as far more dedicated to the office of lawyer and the system of justice than do our own ethical rules. In the moral universe of these lawyers, there was simply no room for the "hired gun."[118]

During the nineteenth century, as today, the question of legal ethics and particularly the lengths to which a lawyer would go in representing his client were of interest to a broader public than just the profession. One of the most interesting lay expositions of legal ethics published in

---

115. S.L. SOUTHARD, DISCOURSE ON THE PROFESSIONAL CHARACTER AND VIRTUES OF THE LATE WILLIAM WIRT 49 (Washington, Gales & Seaton 1834).

116. ISAAC F. REDFIELD, OBITUARY NOTICES AND OTHER TESTIMONIALS OF RESPECT ON THE OCCASION OF THE DEATH OF THE HON. CHAS. K. WILLIAMS, LL.D.: FORMERLY CHIEF JUSTICE OF THE SUPREME COURT, AND AFTERWARDS GOVERNOR OF THE STATE OF VERMONT (Rutland, Vt., G. Tuttle 1854).

117. JOHN PRINGLE JONES, AN EULOGIUM UPON ANTONY LAUSSAT, ESQUIRE: LATE ONE OF THE VICE-PROVOSTS OF THE LAW ACADEMY OF PHILADELPHIA 15 (Philadelphia, Joseph & William Kite 1834).

118. *See id.*

the nineteenth century is a small pamphlet written by John Brookes and published at Cincinnati in 1849 under the title *The Legal Profession: Its Moral Nature and Practical Connection with Civil Society.*[119] Brookes was a local clergymen and the occasion of his writing this piece was an invitation to speak before the Philomathesian Society at Kenyon College. The purpose of his speech was to explore the question of whether a man could practice law and remain morally upright or whether the practice of law necessarily forced a lawyer into immoral acts through his role of advocate.[120] Brookes decided that lawyers could lead moral lives, though it might not be easy:

> Is it not a main part of the business of lawyers to pervert truth? Is not willful falsehood one of the essential features of their profession? If the charge insinuated in these questions were true, it would be condemnation absolute, and we could not, of course, utter a syllable in vindication of the Bar. But, while we must acknowledge that there is much in the public duties of the profession to tempt untruthful representation, or false coloring, we can perceive nothing which necessitates it. We certainly believe it to be possible for a lawyer to pass through his professional career with a veracity as little tainted as that of the mass of good men in other pursuits . . . .[121]

This range of views of the lawyer-client relationship and the moral responsibility of lawyers within that relationship seems to have been maintained throughout the first three-quarters of the nineteenth century. The change came—the change that initiated the more modern view of the lawyer-client relationship—in the 1870s. This change brought with it a reinvigoration of Lord Brougham's perspective on the relationship and the lawyer's duties within it. Once again, it is possible to identify both the context within which this change occurred and the lawyer who most clearly and earliest enunciated it. The context was the rise of a new type of law in the United States, what we now call corporate law, and the lawyer most responsible for popularizing the view was David Dudley Field.[122]

The last quarter of the nineteenth century was a period in American history marked by the rise of the first great corporate amalgamations in railroads, in oil, and in steel. It was also the period in which the securities markets became a principal vehicle for financing new industrial enterprises. And it was the period of the first great "robber barons" who, through their force of will, ingenuity, and lack of morals, were able to build vast corporate conglomerates through the manipulation of markets

119. JOHN BROOKES, THE LEGAL PROFESSION: ITS MORAL NATURE AND PRACTICAL CONNECTION WITH CIVIL SOCIETY (Cincinnati 1849).

120. *See id.* at 9-10.

121. *Id.* at 10.

122. *See infra* notes 123-28 and accompanying text.

and the laws pertaining to them. These robber barons, men like Jay Gould, Jim Fisk, and Jim Brady, were prepared to go to any lengths—including murder—to reach their corporate ends. They amassed vast fortunes in so doing. They also needed lawyers skilled enough to be able to manipulate the law, the courts, and the justice system as a whole so that they could carry on without impediment. Not surprisingly, given the large amounts of money at stake, these robber barons were easily able to find legal talent to serve their purposes. What is significant, however, is that many of the lawyers who served men like Gould and Fisk were not the dregs of the profession, or the back-room pettifoggers despised by men like Sharswood or Hoffman. Instead, they were often individuals of the highest professional standing. Chief among them was David Dudley Field.

Field's work for Gould and Fisk and other robber barons of the late nineteenth century was immortalized in the work of Charles Francis Adams and Henry Adams titled *Chapters of Erie*.[123] The portrait of Field contained therein is far from laudable. Indeed, Field was also attacked in some of the leading newspapers and magazines of the day for his work on behalf of the railroad moguls. These attacks touched a nerve. In a series of letters to Samuel Bowles, publisher of the *Springfield Republican* (Massachusetts), Field responded to his critics and set forth a reinvigorated version of Brougham's vision of the lawyer-client relationship and of the lawyer's overwhelming and singular obligation of fidelity to his client.[124] Field's dissertations on the lawyer-client relationship and the ethical obligations of lawyers within it is, to a large extent, the harbinger of the modern idea of zealous advocacy. Of course, Field's view hearkens back to Lord Brougham and thus has the patina of antiquity, but, clearly, it draws its primary strength from the demands and rewards of the then newly emerging practice of corporate law.

In one of the letters to Field, Bowles pointed out that the issue of lawyer-client relations was not, in 1870, a thoroughly settled matter: "The province of professional duty to causes and clients, is, I believe, an open question among lawyers themselves. Even the principles of it have never been stated to general acceptance; but it is much easier to agree upon a principle than to decide upon practice under it."[125] In answer to

123. *See generally* CHARLES FRANCIS ADAMS & HENRY ADAMS, CHAPTERS OF ERIE AND OTHER ESSAYS (N.Y., H. Holt 1886).

124. *See* Michael Schudson, *Public, Private, and Professional Lives: The Correspondence of David Dudley Field and Samuel Bowles*, 21 AM. J. LEGAL HIST. 191, 197-99 (1977); *see also* Shaffer, *Adversary Ethic*, *supra* note 1.

125. *Correspondence of Messrs. David Dudley and Dudley Field, of the New York Bar, with Mr. Samuel Bowles, of the Springfield Republican* (1871), *in* ANDREW L. KAUFMAN, PROBLEMS IN PROFESSIONAL RESPONSIBILITY 418 (3d ed. 1989).

this criticism, Field replied with a suggested general rule of ethics for lawyers: "[T]he lawyer, being intrusted by the government with the exclusive function of representing litigants before the courts, is bound to represent any person who has any rights to be asserted or defended."[126] Field reiterated in his letters that he had not lied or misled a court in the course of his representation of Fisk and Gould, in spite of the popular belief that he had done so.[127] What was important to Field was that, in his opinion, he was bound to represent his clients regardless of their actions or character and, furthermore, that he was bound to use all means possible—within the law—to further his clients' cause as part of his representation.[128]

There can be little doubt in anyone's mind that David Dudley Field's position was one that was to gain support during the succeeding decades. The idea of the lawyer as moral arbiter of his client's case and the notion that a lawyer should act within severely defined limits in his representation of clients gave way to the demands of corporate and individual clients who wanted zealous advocacy not moral criticism from their attorneys. Professor Shaffer and other advocates for a more moralistic approach to the lawyer-client relationship bemoan this change and would see us move back to Hoffman's or, perhaps, Sharswood's views.[129] They attribute the movement away from this more moralistic perspective to a decline in public morality generally and a move away from the more stringent professional ideas of the nineteenth century.[130] They see the rise of corporate law practice as having a deleterious effect upon legal ethics and rightly point out that the state of things today was not always the way it was.[131]

Certainly, knowing the history of views on the lawyer-client relationship and the obligations of representation can help us in assessing our current situation. Most lawyers and legal academics are unhappy at the excesses of zealotry they see in court today.[132] One constantly hears discussion of a decline in lawyer morality. It is common to see lawyers boast of their tenacity and willingness to fight "to the death" for their clients. Such comments are far more common than claims by lawyers

126. *Id.*, *in* KAUFMAN, *supra* note 125, at 419.

127. *See id.*, *in* KAUFMAN, *supra* note 125, at 419-21.

128. *See id.*, *in* KAUFMAN, *supra* note 125, at 419-21.

129. *See generally* Shaffer, *Adversary Ethic*, *supra* note 1.

130. *See id.* at 713-15.

131. *See id.* at 705-07.

132. *See, e.g.*, Deborah L. Rhode, *Ethical Perspectives on Legal Practice*, 37 STAN. L. REV. 589, 628 (1985) ("Reported cases and surveys reveal a striking incidence of overly zealous representation ranging from garden variety discovery abuse to suppression of evidence and complicity in fraud or perjury.").

that they will judge the merits of their clients' cases and act according to that judgment.

If, in fact, many of us do desire to return to the nineteenth century ideals of legal practice as set out by Sharswood and Brown and in the various eulogies and memorial speeches discussed above, then we must also realize that one of the principle reasons for the move away from such a view of legal ethics was lawyers' response to client demands. David Dudley Field, in defending his actions in regard to the Erie Railroad never was willing to admit that he was not required to represent Fisk and Gould. They had numerous other lawyers on retainer. He accepted them as clients because it meant business. In essence, much of the move away from lawyers as judges of clients' cases toward lawyers as unstinting zealous advocates for clients' cases derives from market pressures. For every lawyer who will exercise such moral judgment, there will be another who will not. This was as true in the nineteenth century as it is today. As John Jones noted, the basic choice was one between "honor" and "practice."[133] The normative rule in the nineteenth century was that a lawyer should choose honor over financial success. Those who sought financial gain as a first priority were labeled pettifoggers or worse and were subjected to the scorn and contempt of their fellow lawyers and the general public. Peer pressure helped to maintain the ethical standards. Today, if we are to move back toward the nineteenth century model of legal ethics and of the lawyer-client relationship, we shall be able to do so only, I would suggest, if we can restore to the profession such a notion of honor and restore, as well, the peer pressure necessary to back it up. Without such a cultural change in the profession, I doubt we shall ever return to the views of Sharswood or Brown—let alone Hoffman—but instead shall live in the world of Brougham and Field where the market determines morality.

---

133. *See generally* JONES, *supra* note 117.

Chapter II

OBSERVATIONS

ON

THE PERNICIOUS PRACTICE

OF THE

LAW.

AS PUBLISHED OCCASIONALLY IN THE INDEPENDENT CHRONICLE, IN THE YEAR 1786, AND REPUBLISHED AT THE REQUEST OF A NUMBER OF RESPECTABLE CITIZENS.

WITH AN

ADDRESS NEVER BEFORE PUBLISHED.

CORRECTED AND AMENDED.

BY HONESTUS.

"Cicero insisted on the moral rectitude of a Lawyer, and asserted that every thing depended on his probity and adherence to the principles of justice."

WITH REMARKS ON THE

RIGHTS OF JURY AS JUDGES OF LAW AND EVIDENCE.

BOSTON:

PRINTED BY TRUE & WESTON.

1819.

Honestus. *Observations on the Pernicious Practice of the Law. As Published in the Independent Chronicle, in the year 1786, and Republished at the Request of a Number of Respectable Citizens. With an Address Never Before Published. Corrected and Amended. With Remarks on the Rights of Jury as Judges of Law and Evidence.* Boston: True & Weston, 1819.

A

PREFATORY ADDRESS

TO CANDID READERS.

What solid Joy is it, for a virtuous man, in the practice of the law, to think he has received a talent from God which makes him the sanctuary of the unfortunate, the protector of justice, and enables him to defend the lives, fortunes, and honour of his countrymen.—Rollin.

The republication of the following numbers "On the Pernicious Practice of the Law," is not intended to excite either a political, or personal controversy. They are now offered to the candid consideration of the public, merely to gratify the curiosity of many respectable citizens, who are desirous to peruse writings which, for so many years, have retained a peculiar celebrity. The circumstances under which they at first appeared, are different from what they are at present. The author flatters himself, that the practice within the bar has become more congenial to the happiness of society; and under this impression, acknowledges the utility of the profession, when conducted upon those honorary principles which give lustre to science. He is only desirous to place the "order" in that rank of society, which the most respectable and learned men, of all ages have been zealous to consider them. The study of the law is highly honorable. It is a science, on which the permanent interest of the community essentially depends. Without an accurate knowledge of our legitimate rights, we are destitute of those barriers, which protect the virtuous from the rapacity of the vicious. In the impartial distribution of justice, the poor and rich stand on an equality; and, in a republican government, the rights of the citizens are founded on one uniform system of jurisprudence. No local partialities are admitted within the system. But while we advocate such liberal sentiments it is necessary, that the most salutary objects should not be converted to the most injurious purposes. At the period when the following numbers appeared in the public papers, certain practices were prevalent, which called for some caustic animadversions, to check their progress. The author was then led to extend his remarks to many instances of mal-practice. The illiberal replies to his observations, naturally produced a severity on his part to stop their insolence.—Being attacked with a phalanx of veteran assailants, he was urged in self-defence to exercise the full energy of his vindication. If therefore, in the following numbers, some retorts should appear pungent, yet an apology is readily offered from the peculiar circumstances, under which the author was obliged to rebut his antagonists. From these remarks, however, he does not consider himself as making a relinquishment of his original sentiments. He still maintains the ground he then occupied, and is free to declare, that *if the same impositions, within the bar, are now continued, as were practised by some at the period when the following numbers were written, that the same mode of legislative procedure ought to be adopted as was then recommended.* But he candidly hopes, that the gentlemen of the profession have become more liberal in their practice. That the client is not *now* exposed to unreasonable delays, and illegal charges.—That the citizens of *all classes* can appeal to the laws with a full assurance, that law and justice are synonymous. That every member of the community *now* finds a remedy for his grievance, without suffering more from the man whom he styles his "*Counsel*," than from the person against whom he complains.

Upon the above acknowledgment, the author is desirous to declare, that though an abolition of the "order" is sometimes mentioned in the following numbers, yet it was not the object contemplated even at the time they were published. He would, therefore, request in perusing the present edition, that the word *regulation* should be substituted in the place of "ABOLITION." It may be proper to observe, that the following remarks apply more immediately to the *practice of the day in which they were written.*

5

The author means to say in general, that he estimates the honorable practitioner, but cannot feel a cordiality for the crafty pettifogger. The beautiful portrait drawn by Quintilian of the character of a Lawyer comes fully within his idea of the dignity attached to the profession.—He lays it down as a fundamental principle, "that eloquence should not be separated from *integrity;* without this, *eloquence,* which is the most beautiful gift, that nature can bestow on man, and by which she has distinguished him in a particular manner from other living creatures, would prove a fatal present to him.—If it is used to oppress innocence, and pervert truth, it is a weapon of the most destructive nature.—Justice and truth only have a right to the assistance of his voice, guilt has no title to it."

It has been observed, that the author has been opposed to the Judiciary.—On the contrary, he venerates the *Bench of Judges,* and there cannot be produced one sentence in the following pages which speaks disrespectfully of them. Not but Judges in their *individual capacity* may sometimes maintain improper principles, and are subject to a *critical examination* of the *opinions* they advance, and the CHARGES they give—but as a *constitutional branch* of the government, they are entitled to every honourable mark of respect and veneration. The author had no other object in the following numbers, than to distinguish, *between the pernicious practice of certain individuals within the Bar, and the purity which ought to constitute a Court of Justice.* He has strictly followed the sacred Doctrines of Quintilian and Cicero, on the duties of a Lawyer, and he defies any man to show a sentiment in the following numbers, which does not correspond with the rules laid down by those learned and philanthropic Civilians.

He is still further honored by the full approbation of Washington, in the system which he proposes, and while he can plead such *authorities,* how futile must be the attempt to depreciate the reputation of the author, or invalidate the rectitude of his principles. For if Honestus is wrong, Quintilian, Cicero and Washington are equally erroneous.

In considering the subject of reform in our judiciary proceedings, the many impositions through the medium of *trading Justices of the peace,* are not among the least of the evils we experience. This species of practice falls heavy on the middling and poorer classes of society. Some of our County Jails have almost become Bastiles, where distressed individuals are suffering for the most trifling breaches of law, the utmost rigor of professional severity. The County is burdened with an excessive tax, while trading Justices, and trading Constables are sharing the profits of this pretended legal traffic. If the town of Boston embraced the whole County, it would be in our power to rectify many errors in the conduct of such Justices, as we should have right to investigate our County concerns, in the same manner we do our Town's. Also the rigid confinement of evidences, whereby they are nearly as much punished as the culprits, require some reform from the national government.

As the foregoing remarks may be considered as extracts from the former publication of HONESTUS, the style and manner of the original have in some measure lost their energy, as the same pungency is not required now, as at the time they were written. It is now offered for a candid perusul, rather as an attempt to a reform, than as a discipline of censure.

Relying on the liberality of all classes of readers, he is willing to submit his sentiments to their candid perusal.

OBSERVATIONS, &c.

No. I.

" When will Benevolence the country warm ?
Or when plain Honesty the courtier charm ?
How flames my blood, indignant at the thought,
Should laws be barter'd ; traffick'd passions bought !
If men no more the soft sensation feel,
And gold, curs'd gold, the bosom turns to steel."

THE following observations are meant, in general, to apply to the practitioners of the law in their mal practice, and not intended to reflect on them in their particular character, as many individuals among them are gentlemen of high esteem and confidence. But as it has lately been asserted, by a person under the signature of a " Free Republican," in our public papers, that they are a " necessary order in a republic," it is presumed the subject is open to inquiry, and consequently there can be no objection in applying the general practice to support a contrary hypothesis.

Among the multiplicity of evils which we at present suffer, there are none more justly complained of, than those we labor under by the many pernicious practices in the profession of the law. It has therefore, become a subject of serious inquiry, whether this body of men, in a young republic, ought not to be controuled in their pleas.

Laws are necessary for the safety and good order of society, and consequently the execution of them is of great importance to be attended to. When therefore, *finesse* and gross impositions are practised, and under sanction of the law, every principle of equity and justice is destroyed, the persons concerned in such pernicious measures ought to be brought forward, and their conduct arraigned before the impartial tribunal of the people.

The study and practice of the law are doubtless an honourable employment; and when a man acts becoming the dignity of the profession, he ought to be esteemed by every member in the community. But when any number of men under sanction of this character are endeavouring to perplex and embarrass every judicial proceed-

8

ing; who are rendering intricate even the most simple principles of law; who are involving individuals, applying for advice, in the most distressing difficulties; who are practising the greatest art in order to delay every process; who are taking the advantage of every accidental circumstance which an unprincipled person might have, by the lenity and indulgence of an honest creditor; who stand ready to strike up a bargain, (after rendering the property in a precarious state) to throw an honest man out of three quarters of his property. When such men pretend to cloak themselves under the sacredness of law, it is full time the people should inquire, "by what authority they do these things."

Within a few years past, numerous impositions have been practised by some of this "order." Has it not become a matter of general complaint? If so, why should the community be hampered with such evils without endeavouring in some manner to remedy them? As practitioners of the law, are they to be indulged with the privilege of exposing every individual to ruin who appeals to the laws of his country? It is the peculiar right of a freeman to be secure in his property and person; but by the present frequent mode of conduct, are we not deprived the security of both? To what purpose are laws without a due execution? Or why should we boast of our liberties, if we are deprived the power of freeing ourselves from injuries?

The distresses of the people are now great, but if we examine particularly, we shall find them owing, in a great measure, to the conduct of some practitioners of the law. Seven-eighths of the causes which are now in their hands might have been settled by impartial *referees*. Why cannot the disputes of the merchant, &c. be adjusted by reference, rather than by a long tedious Court process? Or why should we engage lawyers who are wholly unacquainted with all mercantile concerns? Is it to swell the cost and then by a rule of Court have them finally determined by referees, which is generally the case? Have not the greatest distresses taken place by this "order" of men being employed as agents in litigious controvercies, &c. and if we look through the different counties throughout the Commonwealth, we shall find that the troubles of the people arise principally from debts enormously swelled by tedious law-suits.

The many pernicious modes of judiciary process which have taken place within a few years, are too notorious to mention; scarcety a petty office but has become a little distinct tribunal. What flagrant impositions are daily practised under sanction of law ! The distressed individual is often reduced to the humiliating state of submitting to the extortion of official fees without any remedy. Is it not a disgrace to a free republic that the citizens should dread appealing to the laws of their country ? To what purpose have we laws ? Or with what propriety can we call ourselves freemen, while we suffer individuals to embarrass every mode of legal proceeding ?

It has, therefore, become necessary for the welfare and security of the Commonwealth, that some mode be adopted in order to render the laws a blessing, instead of an evil. For this purpose, it is requested that some acts should be passed, declaring that in all cases left to reference in future, the decision of the referees should be binding on the parties. In all judiciary processes, the Jury, to receive the evidence from the parties, and the Judges to give their opinion on any controverted points of law. The Jury in this manner would be possessed of all that was necessary to determine on the cause, viz. Law and Evidence, without the false glosses and subterfuges too often practised by lawyers.

If such regulations were made in our Courts, the Judges could determine with more precision ; the Jury by taking the evidence, and points of law from the Judges, could, with more clearness, determine the cause ; as in many instances, a Jury becomes puzzled in their judgment by the variety of sentiments advanced by lawyers. By this method the laws would be more justly executed, as the judges are under no influence from either party, their salaries being independent. But by our present mode, the lawyers become parties by their fees, and are too apt to delay the busines while there is any prospect of further profit.

I would ask, whether there are many cases, that absolutely require the assistance of this " order ?" Or if they were not admitted, whether any great inconvenience could arise ? The law and evidence are all the essentials required, and are not the Judges with the *Jury* competent for these purposes ? Why then this intervening "order ?" The important study of law, should be followed solely with a view of doing justice; and gentlemen of talents, who meant to serve their country as Judges, should make the public good their chief object. They would not take up the profession as a set of needy persons, who meant by chicanery and finesse, to get a living by their practice ; but they would make it a point of duty, so to understand the laws, as to distribute equal justice to the rich and poor; each individual would receive the benefit of the laws, and by a speedy and impartial determination, every man would have his cause decided without the imposition of enormous Court charges, and lawyers' fees. There would be no great danger of the Judges converting their authority to any destructive purposes, "as the municipal institutions are so fixed and determined, in this Commonwealth, that it must be difficult for the Judicial Authority to trample upon them with impunity." The perplexity of our laws, therefore, are chiefly owing to the embarrassments thrown in the way by many in the profession.

It is presumed the sentiments offered will be attended to by the Legislature; and as it is a matter of universal concern, it is earnestly wished that the people throughout the State would instruct their representatives on this interesting subject.

I would again observe, that the foregoing observations do not arise from pique or resentment to the gentlemen of the profession, as individuals; but from a sincere regard to the interest and well being of the Commonwealth; and as nothing but facts are mentioned, they will be maintained with confidence.

March 9, 1786.

No. II.

Some Observations on the Pernicious Practice of the Law.

ADDRESSED TO THE PEOPLE.

IN my last, some observations were offered for the consideration of the Legislature, on the practice "of the law," as of late introduced amongst us by some attornies. It being a matter of serious concern, I hope it will not be thought unnecessary to draw the attention of my countrymen to this interesting subject. The observations in the former piece were not intended merely for speculation, and I hope they will not be considered of such trifling moment as to be treated with indifference; the people of this Commonwealth are too much interested in the decision, to rest satisfied with barely hearing of the evils they suffer, without some determinate resolutions to remedy them.

The questions are, whether we will have this "order" so far established in this Commonwealth, as to rule over us; or, whether the people of this State do think themselves free from danger, while many of them are permitted to continue in their present career? These surely are questions worthy of our attention, and ought not to be passed over without mature consideration.

If the most pernicious consequences have taken place by the conduct of many, practitioners, why should we not make some spirited exertions, to free ourselves from them? Are the people of this Commonwealth become so pleased with the parade of tedious pleadings at the bar, as to wish the continuance of it? Or are we at length become so terrified by their assuming consequence, as willingly to crouch to their controul? Shall we be content with the humble boon of making laws, but resign the prerogative of their execution into the hands of this "order?" Shall we who have fought to establish a government upon the basis of "peace, liberty, and safety," relinquish every privilege of freedom, and subject ourselves to continual animosities, impositions and distresses? If we are willing to bend under the imposition of any of this "order," all the boasted acquisitions of our independence are "sounds and nothing else." For I do maintain, when a people cannot appeal with safety to the laws of their country, they are absolute slaves.

I am not led by an heated enthusiasm, as my appeal is not only to the feelings, but the judgment of the people. That we have hitherto suffered much, not a man throughout the Commonwealth, but can attest to the melancholy truth. How many debtors now languish in prison, whose misfortunes are increased by Court charges? The merchant can witness the embarrassment of his appeal to the laws of his country. The landholder, tradesman, and mechanic, can relate the distresses of their families, and in many instances ruin of their estates, in consequence of perplexing law suits. It is time then for the people to begin seriously to think of the evil now existing, and to avoid those with which they are threatened; a few years more may put it out of our power to relieve ourselves! The disease may be too deeply rooted, to be easily eradicated.— This "order" is continually becoming more and more powerful.— Look into every public department, and who do we find? Are not individuals of this "order" exercising their influence within every important circle? Can we suppose the Republic to be free from danger, while individuals are admitted so abundantly as members of our Legislature? Is it not contrary to every principle of propriety to admit men to make laws, who are living upon the practice of them? They surely will ever find it for their interest to make them so indefinite in their construction, as to allow of many plausible objections against them in their future practice. The constitution has forbid the Judges, State's Attorney, and others in the Judiciary department, from being members of the Legislature; why then should this profession be so numerous? As it must ever be for their benefit so to frame laws as will answer every purpose and subterfuge, in their professional line. Do we not often hear this "order" make a distinction between their opinion as members of society, and as practitioners of the law; one being their real, the other their occasional sentiments? Upon these principles, therefore, I doubt not my countrymen will in future conclude, that only a proportionate number ought ever to be admitted into our Legislature.

In the former piece some regulations were mentioned as necessary to be adopted.

1st. "That all decisions by referees should be binding on the parties." On which I beg leave to observe, that no person whatever can object to this measure. What mode can be more eligible, than for the parties to have their disputes settled by the determination of three judicious men? Who can have no sinister views, and who meet solely for an amicable settlement of the contest. If any question can be adjusted with equity, this certainly must be the most likely method: Why are lawyers needed in this case? If this mode therefore is so perfectly equitable, why should we object against having a law passed to make such decisions binding on the parties? Possibly it may be said, that at court we can appeal from one term to another; so also in the method proposed; if the parties find any new evidence arise after their first hearing, they should have a right to a second appeal on the subject, before the same referees, and the last decision to be binding. A law of this kind to be passed, could not but be approved of by the people, as the most beneficial plan, calculated to prevent great trouble and expense. Provided this mode had formerly been adopted, how many disputed accounts, which are now in our courts, could have been settled by three merchants who are acquainted with mercantile concerns;

whereas we have become so inconsiderate as to place such causes in the hands of lawyers, who in general are unacquainted with the customs of merchants, &c. and after the parties have danced through every labyrinth of the law, are at last obliged to leave their cause to a rule of court, and to have it settled by the very men who should have determined it in the first instance. Thus by our own folly we subject ourselves to the costs of court, lawyers' fees, &c. which are continually augmenting throughout every period of the controversy. I have thought proper to instance in the case of the merchant, but is it not equally as inconsistent in a dispute between any other class in the Commonwealth? Cannot the tradesman, the husbandman, &c. have most of their disputes settled in this manner? If therefore a law was enacted, to make the decisions by reference binding on the parties, the greater part of our disputes might be determined by referees.

The second observation is, That the explanation of the law should be delivered to the Jury by the Judges;—Nothing more can be essential than the law and evidence; I will appeal to the gentlemen of the "Bar," whether by this method, the Jury could not be possessed with every necessary information. The Judges are supposed competent to give their opinion on any points of law; do we suppose the Judges can receive any insight from lawyers, who cannot even from their own practice, or acquired knowledge, be more acquainted with the law than the judges themselves? Two lawyers disputing cannot alter the established principles of law, though they may bewilder a Judge. They may perplex the mind, but they cannot inform the judgment. As modesty and diffidence are often attendants on real merit, some Judges, though fully possessed of the principles of law, may be confounded by the sophistry of the pleas. I need no greater proof of the danger of the improper influence of lawyers over the Judges, than what frequently takes place at our Court of Sessions. How often are a Jury hindered from coming to a speedy decision of a cause, by the laboured pleadings of the council? Though the case at first might be evident to every one of the Jury, yet after the loquacity of a lawyer, and the shifts and turns which "he has acquired by long practice," the subject has almost become lost in the tediousness of the controversy. The plainer the cause, the more ingenuity is required to confound the business, and oftentimes if they cannot succeed in any other manner, they rack their invention to find some plea to have it referred. After mentioning these particulars, does not our own judgment rise up to condemn this pernicious mode, and fully convince us of the fatal effects of such practice.

But upon the plan proposed, all these difficulties would be remedied; in the first place, most of our disputes might be decided by referees, consequently the Judges would have but a small proportion of their present trials. In those cases that require a judiciary determination, each individual could appeal to the laws as the barrier of his rights and liberties! they could lay their causes before the Judges as fathers of the people; their evidence could be delivered in the most plain manner, either in writing or otherwise; the Judges would consider of the case with the utmost impartiality, as they could have no sinister motives to induce them to act contrary, depending on neither party for their salary. The evidence could forthwith be stated to the Jury, with the opinion of the Judges as to any point of law; and the Jury, after receiving the whole warm from the bosoms of the Judges, (without being enveloped in the mist of absurd sophistry) they would be able to decide with the greatest deliberation and equity. The charges of the Court could be regulated by a fee table, (which is now too much disregarded) and the people of this Commonwealth would be secured in their property, and receive the benefit of the laws without the delays and charges they are now subject to.

Is it not trying to the feelings of "Free Republicans," to be exposed to the scoffs of some of the Bar while they are delivering their evidence in any cause, where the property and liberties of their fellow citizens are engaged? Have not our respectable citizens sometimes been treated, in the course of their examination, with indignity? and have they not often times been obliged to submit to the satirical retorts of a professionalist? Pray is such conduct "necessary."

Another pernicious practice is, making bargains upon the event of the cause. How ruinous is it to a people to have an "order" of men among them, who are rendering the laws a mere business of traffic? How disgraceful is such a mode of conduct! Are the "people" of this Commonwealth reduced to so dreadful a state, as to give one quarter part of their property to secure the remainder, when they appeal to the laws of their country? Shall we nourish individuals in the community merely to take the advantage of our distresses, and under pretence of doing us justice, demand any proportion of our property they may think fit? In a few years we may expect their influence to be so great, that no man will be able to apply to the laws without mortgaging a certain part of his estate to a lawyer. Our lands, farms, and every other property, will ere long be held under the tenure of this "order;" even wills and other conveyances by which we hold our estates, may be disputed by them for a proportion of whatever they may acquire.

"The custom of making agreements with clients, and taxing them in proportion to the nature of the cause, and the risk they run, is," says Quintillian, "an abominable kind of traffic, fitter for pirates than for lawyers, and which even those who have but a slender love for virtue will avoid." Nothing surely can be so detestable, as for a man to set up his principles for sale. "Far from the dignity of profession be those men, who make a trade of eloquence, and think of nothing but sordid gain."

One reason of the pernicious practice of the law, and what gives great influence to the "order" is, that we have introduced the whole body of English laws into our Courts; why should these States be governed by British laws? Can we suppose them applicable to the circumstances of this country? Can the monarchical and aristocratical institutions of England, be consistent with the republican principles of our constitution? Why should a young Republic be ruled by laws framed for the particular purpose of a monarchical government, or can laws which are applicable to Kings, Lords, and Commons of England, be any way consonant to the Republican establishment of this Commonwealth? We may as well adopt the laws of the Medes and Persians. A great error, therefore, lies in our want of a proper system of laws, adapted to our particular state and circumstances: the numerous precedents brought from "Old English Authorities," serve to embarrass all our judiciary causes, and answer no other purpose, than to increase the influence of lawyers; as from such authorities they can cull and select precedents to answer every purpose: the omnipotence of their laws can reconcile all contradictions; how absurd therefore to introduce into our young republic, the whole body of English laws!

Is it not melancholy to see such numerous volumes, brought into our Courts, arranged in formidable order, as the grand artillery to batter down every plain, rational principle of law? As we have framed our own constitution, and mean to support our Independence as a nation, why should the people of this Commonwealth, be subject to these English codes? Would it not be more for the honour and happiness of this State, to establish a system of laws of our own, dictated by the genuine principles of Republicanism, and made easy to be understood by every individual in the community? By this means, we should destroy the wonderful misery of law craft, and the whole science would be adapted to the most simple understanding.

The observations offered are solely intended for the public good; I have endeavoured to deliver my sentiments as familiar as possible; any inaccuracies therefore, I hope will be pardoned. Each individual will judge on the subject; if my principles are approved, let them be adopted with resolution, by giving instructions to our Representatives; but if we are willing to be governed principally by English authorities, as an individual, I must acquiesce in the determination of my countrymen.

I am far from depreciating any principles wherein real learning can any way be promoted. The professions of the law are too often studied wi h a view to pervert them by false glosses and plausible cavils. In short, they are too often read with a design to warp them to private emolument. Provided the system was simplified, I do conceive the real principles of law would be more universally practised, as they would not be so exposed to be perverted, by the whims and fancies of a numerous body of professionalists. Men of leisure, and of real abilities, would apply themselves to the study, and would make themselves such proficients (especially if British codes were exploded) as to qualify themselves for the important station of Judges. The bench might ever be filled (as it is at present) with men who are an honour to the state for their wisdom and integrity.

March 23, 1786.

No. III.

On the pernicious practice of the Law.

THE gentleman under the signature of a "Merchant" seems exceeding anxious to inform the public, that he is "no Lawyer."

17

How far this declaration may be considered as a compliment, is left to the "order" themselves to determine. A person would suppose that the gentlemen of this profession were in a very bad repute, if it is necessary to be so very explicit, in order to give force to the sentiments offered in their vindication. However, it is presumed that the public are governed so much by candour, as not to be influenced in their judgment, by unwarrantable prejudice; arguments which are conclusive, will have their due weight, whether they are delivered by a lawyer or a merchant. The enquiry is not who is the author? but what are the arguments?

For my own part, I appeal to the impartial determinations of the public, and shall willingly resign every pretension to their indulgence the moment my sentiments are condemned by them. As the Merchant has not offered any reasons to convince Honestus of his "error;" he still persists in his sentiments, (however "bold" the declaration) that the pleas of lawyers ought to be controuled.

The Merchant asks, "if there is a profession on earth that has not bad men in it, who disgrace and abuse it?" and instances in the clergy. I am equally as sensible as the gentleman, "that it would be illiberal to lisp a syllable against the clergy, because of the misconduct of some;" but if it could be proved that this "order," instead of promoting Godliness, were the cause of many immoralities practised, in this case, I should be for censuring them, however pious and devout a few individuals amongst them might be. But this manner of reasoning is entirely foreign to the point, and is artfully introduced to lead the public from the important consideration of the pernicious practice of the law. This finesse, however, it is hoped, will not avail. It is below contempt to observe the variety of methods used to throw aside the principles advanced; also the pitiful art practised by blending very unpopular sentiments under the same signature, with a view to mislead the public into a belief, that the same person is author of all the extravagant pieces under the signature of Honestus. This, however, may be considered as low cunning, and much like a rogue, who, when he is pursued, will cry out *thief* in order to escape himself amidst the general bustle.

The clergy in general are an ornament to society; no charges can be brought against them as an "order;" therefore to introduce this respectable body to justify the continuance of mal-practice in the judiciary, is an instance of law craft too gross to effect the purpose of the authors.

18

Suppose we allow "that good and bad men are in all orders, will it follow, that all "orders" are necessary? An order of clergy exists in this Commonwealth; must therefore an order of monks and friars be admitted? An order of doctors is established, but this is no argument that we should allow of an order of quacks and mountebanks, though possibly they may sometimes administer a favourable nostrum: An order of Judges is considered "necessary" in our republic, to administer justice, &c. but does it follow, that it is unnecessary to regulate the proceedings of Lawyers, especially if they frequently embarrass the citizens in their appeal to the laws of their country? The gentleman therefore by saying, that "good and bad men are in all professions," does not prove, that the evils mentioned do not exist--which is the matter of contest. His premises being admitted, his consequences do not follow; if his arguments prove any thing, they prove too much, which in general is reckoned as inconclusive, as though they proved nothing.

The Merchant declines engaging in the controversy, but has offered a few judicious observations, as the "ground work" on which he should consider the subject. Though they are principles which no one would controvert, yet I do not think that they all apply to the point in question. Every person will join with him, "that the great aim of government should be to make such laws as produce the fewest evils, and are practicable." The plan proposed, in the former papers, I am willing should stand on this test: "The fewest evils," must arise from a decision by referees; also, by the "law and evidence being submitted to the Jury by the Judges; and the "fewest evils" must arise, by forbidding any unreasonable delays in our courts by the order of lawyers. The practicability of this plan is certainly very easy, and requires but very little exertion to accomplish it.

The Merchant seems to dispute the right of the Legislature to regulate the order, by saying, "That every profession is by natural right, as well as by the principles of the constitution, entitled to equal freedom and toleration." I do not suppose the Legislature has a right to controul any man in his profession, while this profession is no ways injurious to the public: But they have a right to examine the principles upon which individuals act, and if they find that their practice is productive of great mischief, and that the community are injured by their conduct, in these cases they have a right to controul them by positive laws. It being an incontrovertible principle, " That a nation or state has a right to every thing that can secure it from threatening danger, and to keep at a distance whatever is capable of causing its ruin!

The Merchant desires me to announce to the public, " the names of the bad men of this order." This is a very disagreeable task; and as the gentleman has complimented me as being " unwilling to wound the feelings of a fellow citizen," he must excuse my declining this unwelcome declaration: but as the Merchant is so great an advocate for the profession, it would be very agreeable if he would favour the public with the names of the good men of this order; as the list would be very acceptable, he cannot deny so small a request.

I would not be thought to depreciate the characters of those gentlemen of the " order" of lawyers, who have acted worthily amongst us—we have had, and we continue to have, some who are entitled to every respect from this country: But I would not carry my praise so far as to insinuate, " that America depends upon this 'order to produce the great characters our country boasts of." We have had, and still continue to have characters equally as great, who are not of this " order"—however, when we name an Adams,* I must beg leave to be excused from " wounding the feelings of any one" by making a comparison to their injury: As a patriot and statesman, he stands conspicuous; superior to every little art which is now too generally practised.

These are serious truths, and I doubt not the people of this state will attend to them; the plan offered it is hoped will be supported by general instructions given to the members of the next General Court, as our dependence must be on the legislature. For this purpose it is necessary that the Senate and House should not consist of such a large proportion of this profession. In the mean time, the small squibs of party resentment will pass unnoticed, as too contemptible to draw the attention of the author, from the objects conemplated.

The sentiments advanced in former pieces have not been controverted; the writer under the signature of the " Free Republican" has not thought proper to make any reply, and as he was so very elaborate in his ten numbers, it is supposed from his silence, that he is fully convinced of the " error" of his assertion.

March 30, 1786.

* The American Ambassador.

20

No. IV.

" Oh that this care might universal be,
That all our species liv'd in harmony;
That the wide world, out-stretch'd in moral aid,
The cradling arm to shelter and to shade!
That tender transport melted every soul,
And one warm wish presided o'er the whole!
That all the opposing elements of life,
The gales of rage and hurricanes of strife,
Might cease; and waft our barks on silken sail,
And on life's ocean one vast calm prevail!
That mutual passions, mutual charms might lend,
And each to each be Neighbour, Father, Friend."

I AM not opposed to the body of lawyers, but to their mal-practice as individuals, and when a regulation is urged, it is not intended as a reflection upon every individual, but as a remedy to prevent the pernicious tendency of that practice which has too generally prevailed throughout this Commonwealth.

I have in former papers endeavoured to establish this principle, that the "order" of Lawyers is dangerous in our republic, if they are permitted to pursue their mal-practice by causing delays, and augmenting unreasonable charges. If any arguments had been offered to prove my position erroneous, no person in the Commonwealth would more readily have acknowledged his error. I write not from resentment, and while I can appeal to my conscience for the rectitude of my intentions, the mere puffs of individuals will ever be treated with contempt. When a hive is disturbed we must expect a great buzzing.

In Courts of Justice, all persons employed who have any influence in the cause, ought to be as unbiassed as possible; judges, jury, witnesses, &c. The parties, therefore, should not be permitted to offer any thing further, than what can be produced simply from the evidence. A Court acting upon such principles, must be considered as the most equitable and judicious. In this impartial arrangement, with what propriety can we introduce a person to embarrass the question? Can a man be unbiassed, who has received a large reward, to involve the case (if necessary) in as much perplexity as possible? It may be said, that the lawyer stands in the place of his client, and may say any thing in his defence; but is there not a material difference, between allowing a man to relate his own story, and employing a person who in consideration of his fee, may be influenced to pervert the general principles of law ? No man ought to be employed to speak to a cause, who is under a bias to misconstrue the laws ; and herein is the difference, between admitting a person to plead his own case, and employing a lawyer for this purpose; as the former must relate only plain matters of fact, but the latter (provided the cause is bad) may be led to warp the laws to answer his own particular purposes. Can the poor man (who cannot pay any of this "order") receive equal advantage with the rich, while such a body of men stand ready to speak on any subject, and like mercenary troops, can be hired to support any cause for the consideration of a large reward ? Will not the rich opponet overpower the poor man, by the greatness of his gifts to his lawyers ? The regulation proposed may remedy this evil.

I will illustrate this remark by a simple case ; suppose two persons have a dispute ; each of them repairs to his lawyer ; they accordingly take up the cause on the part of the person who applies to them —It is quite accidental on which side either of the lawyers are engaged; they might have been on the part of their antagonist; however the *fee* rivets both to become strenuous advocates for their clients ; though without doubt in some cases, they may think their employers are wholly in the wrong.—When the cause is brought into Court, one lawyer tries to intimidate, and often times abuses the evidence of the other ; instead of a fair, equitable enquiry into the subject, every little advantage is taken of each other. The parties are harrassed by constant attendance : the trial is put off under some pretence to another term ; and by the finesse practised, the Judges themselves are obliged to consent to the delay.—Finally, after sauntering at the heels of a lawyer from term to term, and burthened with expenses, the cause is either submitted to a Rule of Court, or the richest party by bearing down the estate of the other, obtains judgment in his favor.

In free governments all appeals to the laws should be on the plainest principles possible :—By this method, the poor man stands on an equality with his wealthy neighbour; and every individual would receive equal benefit from the laws, without any tedious delays. If this simple mode was adopted, the dishonest would not dare to take the advantage of the honest, as they could not have any person within the Court to plead in their favor. The quibbles of law would not be so often urged. The paltry litigious causes amongst neighbours would not exist : harmony and benevolence would more generally prevail, and agreeable to my motto,

> " Mutual passions, mutual charms might lend,
> And each to each be neighbour, father, friend."

Our courts would become places of justice, as we should have no individuals to prevent the execution of it, and every citizen would apply to the Judges with confidence becoming freemen.

Some persons have a wonderful opinion of this " order," as being necessary to explain the mysteries of the law. In the first place, the greatest part of those mysteries are owing to the introduction of British authorities. The variety of sophistry introduced by their pleadings is the principal cause of the intricacy of our laws; any man of common abilities can easily distinguish between right and wrong (a trial by Jury is on this principle) more especially when the parties are admitted to give a plain story, without any puzzle from lawyers? I dare appeal to any man who has been on a Jury, whether the greatest difficulty did not arise from the tedious loquacity of the lawyers? The most simple case can be made intricate by a person who is rewarded for this purpose. Is it not as common to employ a lawyer for his art and cunning, as for his knowledge in the law? and do we not as often find him succeed by the former as by the latter? For this reason the lawyers are crying up the intricacy of the law; and by hard words, in all their judiciary proceedings, they amuse the people, (like Romish priests in matters of religion) by vehemently asserting, that without abstruse special pleadings, the laws could not be executed. This however is a mere dogma of law craft; from which good Lord deliver us.

The manner of employing these persons must show the impropriety and fatal tendency of the general practice; sometimes half a dozen are employed or retained on one side; and a wealthy man may silence a whole bar. Does not such pecuniary influence, deprive a poor man of every necessary mean to obtain his plea?

The candor of the " Merchant" in his last performance seems wholly to have left him. He says, " Honestus has refuted himself, because he allows my principles to be incontrovertible." It is true they were so, but then the application of them to the point in question, is what I object to. If the " Merchant" had said, It was light when the sun shined, I should not have controverted this principle, but might have objected to its application respecting the subject in controversy.

The Merchant is greatly afraid, that we shall not have Judges learned in the law, if we should check or controul this "order." Quibbles of law, (which only arise from perverse practice) are not necessary to a Judge; the fundamental principles are only required, and provided our codes were simplified, gentlemen of leisure and abilities would qualify themselves fully for this important station.

As to his "2700 references and as many suppers," they are too contemptible to be noticed. "The 900 actions entered on one docket" are not doubted, and are melancholy proofs of the danger arising to the Commonwealth, without some controul over men whose existence depends on this public distress.

Great stress is laid by the "order," on the constitution, which provides, "That every person shall be heard by himself, or by his council;" and from this they infer, that the Legislature has not power to check them. The right of council does not interfere with the prerogative of the Legislature to regulate their conduct: if a person does not choose to give his evidence personally, or in writing to the Court, but will employ council, the Legislature has a right to determine whether a person ought not to be restricted, who has received a bribe from his employer; as in a Court of Justice, all monies paid by the parties to those who can influence the cause, must be considered as a bribe, given with a view to obtain that which the law will not grant. Every man is entitled to a trial by jury; but then we all know, that in many cases a Juryman is not qualified, and cannot be eligible if he has received a reward from the parties. The privilege of council, and the present practice of lawyers are very different in their establishment and consequences.

It is curious to observe the plea, often urged, "that the weak and simple would be over-matched and out-witted by the artful and cunning man," if lawyers were not allowed the utmost latitude in their pleas. But I maintain, that these advantages take place principally by admitting this indulgence. "An artful and cunning man," aided by "an artful and cunning" lawyer, would ever get the advantage of the "weak and simple." It will be answered, such persons must get a lawyer equally as "cunning" as his antagonist. In consequence of this, every action that comes into a Court of Justice, instead of resting on the fair principles of law, must depend for its

24

success on the art and cunning of parties. Judge and Jury must set for hours to hear two artful, cunning men dispute. Excellent situation for a young republic! Is this the manner in which our laws are executed? shall the success of our appeals to the laws of our country (which ought to be pure as possible) depend on law "cunning?" Shall the inhabitants of this Commonwealth obtain justice, by setting one "artful cunning" attorney to oppose the chicanery of another? Besides, a wealthy man may employ, or retain all the "cunning" men of the "order," and then what is to become of the "weak and simple" (if poor) when his antagonist is assisted by such a formidable combination? In this case, the "weak, simple" and poor must become a sacrifice, even while appealing to the justice of their country. This argument, therefore, like all others I have yet heard, is quite trifling, and upon this principle, which they think is incontrovertible in their favour, I am willing to support my position, that no individual should be employed in a court of Justice, whereby the "artful and cunning" should be assisted by others as bad as themselves, but that every man should be on a par by relating his own story, either personally or in writing. The Judges would candidly distinguish the false colouring of the culprit, and pay due attention to the diffidence of the honest man. In short, if there is any chance for the "weak and simple" man, it must be in a Court, where the "artful and cunning" can have no assistance from any quarter.

I hope my countrymen will not be led away from the essential point, of checking the pernicious practice of the law, by some *specific* legislative regulation. It is a matter of universal concern, and as we regard the happiness and welfare of our country, it is hoped the next General Court will be fully authorized to consider of this important subject.

Let us immediately attend to the weighty concern, and so arrange our laws, that freemen shall no longer consider an appeal to them as a grievance.

April 12, 1786.

25

No. V.

"Oh! When will justice ope her slumb'ring eyes,
And privilege on daring pinions rise?
The sacred rights of property secure,
And render every tenure safe and sure!

AS some judiciary mode seems necessary to be adopted, to remedy the evils we now suffer, I must request the attention of the public to the mode proposed in former papers. The author has no other motive, than to urge those who are more acquainted with the general principles of jurisprudence to offer their sentiments on the subject. It is not doubted the plan will be treated with candour, as the writer has no sinister views to answer; having as little to fear from the continuance of the evils, or to hope from their removal, as any individual in the state.

The mode is as follows—

1st. That whenever parties agree to leave their disputes to reference, the decision of the referees (if unanimous) to become binding on them; and in case any new evidence arises, the parties to be entitled to a second hearing before the same referees.

2d. That instead of the numerous codes of British laws, which are now introduced into our Courts, we should adopt a concise system, calculated upon the plainest principles, and agreeable to our Republican government. This would render useless hundreds of volumes, which only serve to make the practice mysterious.

3d. That in all civil cases brought into Court, the parties should offer their pleas personally, or in writing if they think proper. The evidence to be delivered to the Jury, and the Judges to recite the whole to the Jury, with every explanation necessary to regulate their decision both as to law and evidence.

4th. As by the Constitution, every man has the privilege of being heard by his council, in conformity to which, those persons who do not choose to make their plea in person or writing, should be heard by any friend they may choose to employ; should rather encourage every person (who has no particular hindrance) to make his plea in person or writing; this establishment would be very different from the present practice.

26

5th. As we have an Attorney-General who acts in behalf of the State, it is proposed that the Legislature appoint another person (with a fixed salary) as Advocate-General for all persons arraigned on criminal prosecutions; whose business should be to appear in behalf of all persons indicted by the State's Attorney.

Provided the foregoing mode was adopted I would ask, whether the inhabitants of this Commonwealth, would not receive greater benefits from the laws, than they now do, according to the general mode of practice, without the impositions, embarrassments, and expenses, which attend our most simple trials? By this plan our causes would be more expeditiously determined, as there would be no persons whose interest it was to perplex and delay: each man's plea would be impartially considered by the Judges, and delivered pure without any subtilty to the Jury. I dare appeal to any man, whether he had not rather trust his cause upon the determination of a Court established upon those principles, than to the long, tedious process we are now subject to? So far from disorder and anarchy taking place from this mode, all our appeals to the laws would be decided with the utmost impartiality, order and rectitude; no law-craft would be exercised, as it would be no advantage for any in Court, to embarrass or perplex the cause; candour and decision must of consequence ensue.

We have too long supposed that *Laws* depend on the loquacity of *Lawyers*; and some are apt to think, if we check the latter, the former must of consequence be annihilated; but as a friend to their due executions, I wish that the laws may be executed upon the strictest principles of equity; that the rich and the poor may ever be on an equality, while they are appealing to the justice of their country.

Some persons may think that I pay too little regard to the study of the law; so far from this, no person has a greater idea of the importance of this branch of science. The fundamental principles of our laws, I hold "necessary" to be known in our republic; but I conceive the mode (as now practised in our Courts) is no way essential to this knowledge. Our Judges come fully within my idea to answer this purpose, and a little attention will prove my remarks to be just; a lawyer takes up a cause solely for the profit; consequently he must have recourse in many cases to sophistry and "cunning." The Judges have their fixed salaries, consequently they have no inducement to be led from the fair principles of law: could

27

a Juryman hesitate a moment to determine, as to the justness of these persons' sentiments?

It is worthy of notice, that the Judges in delivering the evidence to the jury, are seldom heard to mention any observation or point of law, delivered by the lawyers of either side; and the jury when they retire, as seldom have any reference to the pleadings of the lawyers: the Law as delivered by the judges is principally attended to, and all previous debates of lawyers are considered as time spent to little purpose. The law and evidence are accurately decided by the Jury, as they have the whole subject submitted to them by their oaths.

I am sensible this reply will be made, "If we check the lawyers, from whence are to come the Judges?" I answer, the fundamental principles of our laws may be known without encouraging men to become hacknied in every quibble to puzzle and perplex; we may as well say that we can have no merchants, without first introducing an "order" of stock-jobbers; the fair principles of commerce are known, without all the finesse, "cunning," and craft of the exchange-alley.

My principles are, to make the study of the law respectable and beneficial. For this purpose we should introduce the study at our University; a Professor of Law should be established, and the youth should be early taught the fundamental principles of our laws; and from this knowledge (with small attention) they would become qualified to take the important station of Judges.

It is said, "that the Judges stand in need of the advice of the lawyers, as from the multiplicity of causes within their cognizance, they could not attend particularly to them, unless assisted by this "order." To which I answer, that if the decisions by references were binding, we should not have so great a number of cases before the Judges, as this mode would keep out of our Courts the greatest part of our actions. The Judges, therefore, would be better able to attend the business, than they are at present, as the vast variety of cases, now before them, must be attended with delay and indecision. I dare appeal to those who are conversant in Courts, whether nineteen cases in twenty could not be decided as equitably by referees, as by a tedious court process?

As the number of lawyers is so great throughout this State, there is danger of their becoming formidable as a combined body. There is no body of men among us, that can so easily render themselves

28

powerful by professional influence; being so connected with each other in their practice, they may readily unite to establish any mode of judiciary process they may think proper, and under sanction of law, the greatest impositions may be practised.

Suppose, for instance, (and I will not affirm that it has not already taken place) that the lawyers should meet every quarter, and correspond with their brethren throughout the State: that they should determine the business of every court by previous consultation, whether to close a cause at the next term, or defer it to another: that the determinations at their conventions should be minutely entered in their Bar-Book, and the whole business dealt out in Court agreeably to their pre-determined resolutions. Suppose a Grand Secretary should be chosen, to keep a particular account of all proceedings, and each one should be sacredly bound to adhere to what ever was transacted at this meeting. Also, a Committee should be appointed to examine all candidates, who should adhere strictly to the rules of this convention. In a word, suppose this "order" should establish a perfect Star-Chamber jurisdiction, as to all Court proceedings.

Provided there is danger of such a combination, is it not time that the People should be guarded against it, by checking the practice. If the inhabitants of this Commonwealth should become subject to such impositions, (as previous agreements before their causes are brought to trial.) have we not the greatest reason to apprehend the most pernicious perversion of every judiciary process? If individuals should become allied by mutual correspondence through the State, might they not subvert every principle of law by their combination, and establish a perfect aristocratical influence through the Commonwealth? In short, what security have the people in the laws, while an "order" of men exist, who have it in their power to manage them, so as to answer their own particular purposes and emolument?

Further, if such a large proportion of this "order" are admitted into our Legislature to make laws, and at the same time can become so formidable by their professional attachments, is there not the greatest danger, that in a few years they will render themselves (as a combined body) absolute, both in the Legislative and Judicial branches? What safety has the "majority of persons" as to their rights, liberties and property, when in the first instance the framers of our laws, are under the management of BAR meeting regulations?

Conclave may, in time, exercise as unlimited authority as the Spanish inquisition.

As this " order" has taken a plea from the Constitution for their mode of practice, I shall take one from the Bill of rights for their restriction. An article in our Bill of rights stands thus, " Every subject of the Commonwealth ought to find a certain remedy, by having recourse to the laws, for all injuries or wrongs, which he may receive in his person, property or character; he ought to obtain right and justice freely, and without being obliged to purchase it; completely and without denial; promptly and without delay; conformably to the laws." But, my countrymen, are our appeals to the laws conformable to this article? According to the present system, are not the people deprived of this right? instead of obtaining justice free- " ly," " completely," and " promptly," are we not often subject to the grossest impositions, by extravagant demands? our causes are carried through every tedious labyrinth; and even, if an individual obtains his case, he must in many instances, give a great part of what he recovers, to a lawyer. It is true a Fee-table is established, but how is it treated? Let the individuals of this State declare! Look into our country towns, and we shall find thousands who can express, with every sentiment of indignation, the distresses they suffer by the impositions of some practitioners. I will venture to affirm, there is no country in Europe (if the least pretensions to equity govern their conduct) where the expenses attending a lawsuit, are greater than in this State: The people cannot get the most trifling advice, without paying the most extravagant fees. The instances which I could mention are too numerous (at present) to recount: But the modes of receiving a certain proportion of what is recovered, is a practice which no free government ought to suffer: For if the inhabitants of this Commonwealth are to purchase the security of their property, upon such terms, in a few years they will have but very little property to secure. A few lawsuits would convert the greatest part into the lawyers' possession.

We are told, " that every man may now go and plead his own cause;" but according to the present mode of practice, this is an affront to our understanding. Has not this " order" established such rules among themselves, that if any man attempts to speak to his cause he would be perplexed in every particular; it is true, every man has a right to speak to his own case, but this " order" has in effect, destroyed this privilege, by certain modes of practice. To say therefore, we have a right to plead our own causes, is insulting; as we can never expect to exercise this right, without first regulating the mode of practice. When this is done, our line of conduct will be plain and easy.

The importance assumed by this "order" is another matter worthy notice. How does the poor dependent client, follow the professionalist, (often times hat in hand,) while the gentleman of the "order" stalks on with a solemn importance, and scarcely deigns to answer his client as to the state of his cause!

I am sensible the gentlemen of the Bar, are displeased with my sentiments, but their approbation I never expected to obtain. Every thing but fair argument has been attempted to throw my remarks into contempt; scurrility, abuse and forgery, have been adopted; but this low cunning I despise.

If the "order" or their friends have nothing better to offer, silence is their only weapon. As to the contemptible remarks, under the signature of *A Mechanic*, I shall not affront the public by noticing them. If such are the advocates of the "order," they may exclaim, "Miserable comforters are ye all."

As the time approaches when this state, in their Legislative capacity, can take into consideration the important business urged in these papers, it is hoped that the principal towns will give a lead to the undertaking, by inserting in their warrants, the design of instructing their Representatives on the subject. If any good takes place from my feeble attempts, my wishes and intentions will be answered. I have no favours to ask of the public; my sentiments I mean should stand or fall, agreeably to the determinations of my countrymen. But if the people of this Commonwealth are content in their present situation, and are willing, after all their struggles for freedom, to become slaves to individuals, the fatal consequences of their pusillanimity will only be lamented by

HONESTUS.

April 20, 1786.

No. VI.

AFTER my numerous opponents have gone through with their observations, I shall pursue my remarks with freedom; and being

31

willing to disarm them of one capital argument, viz. Electioneering, I shall desist till this business is fully over.

I shall endeavour to scrape from the "dirt" which surrounds the performance of "Zenas," such sentiments as are worthy notice. This writer is undoubtedly sincere in one assertion, "That he never assumed the quill with more reluctance than in the present instance."

The "twig of the branch," being tender, must be treated with delicacy. The "lawyer" writes coolly, but he is apt sometimes to take a "certainty for an uncertainty;" when this is the case, there is but little dependence on his judgment. The "Merchant" is gone away in a passion, but previously informs me there is room enough in the world for us both; hope, therefore, never to jostle against him. The Mechanic, he is——

These writers may ransack the tombs of history; they may raise a numerous host of venerable sages; but, alas! when we apply these models to the practice of the present day, how vast the disparagement! Might not the ghosts of these stern patriots address many of those who thus disturb their ashes, and profane their names, in the words of Hamlet, "Whence and what art thou?"

I doubt not in the course of my observations to prove, that the practice of many has become dangerous in our republic, and that unless they are checked, will finally establish an absolute aristocratical jurisdiction. We wish to be under a "government of laws," and not a "government of men."

The laboured writings of the "Free Republican" in former papers, (who I am jealous is one of this "order") seem calculated to pave the way for this aristocratical system. This writer earnestly recommends the mode adopted by the Romans of the "Comitia Centuriata." He says, "The richest class should have every thing at their disposal." "That we should seldom have occasion to go so low as the fourth class for a majority of votes;" and that "the people should be rarely called together, unless for matters of small moment." Are these sentiments calculated for a republican government? Rather have not the "people" the greatest reason to be alarmed, when such principles are publicly declared with impunity? Provided this mode was adopted, what security have the "weak and poor" (which Zenas pretends to be so wonderfully concerned for,) against the impositions of the "wealthy," and influential?

The unbounded scurrility of many of my opponents is unman-

32

nerly and ungenerous; some of them have acquired an importance from their profession, after hammering at other occupations; in consequence thereof, they now assume an arrogance. As for myself, I am willing to stand the test of their strictest scrutiny, being convinced, that my actions have ever been on such principles as to defy the shafts of my most malignant enemies. Their insinuations can never injure my character, I shall therefore treat them with the contempt they merit. They must excuse my not replying in kind, being from education and acquaintance wholly ignorant of the language of billingsgate. The greatest reflection I should conceive on myself or family would be, to have it insinuated that my conduct, in any instance, run parallel with some who are very liberal in their abuse.

The subject is not taken up from " resentment," or from " electioneering" views, as many would insinuate. As was said in a former piece, I have no favour to ask of the public, having no other intentions than the real good of the community. I plead not for a a dissolution of law, but for the restriction of those who are perverting every principle to their own emolument. I appeal to the experience and " feelings" of my countrymen for the justness of my sentiments, and while their approbation is secured, my opponents have full liberty to pursue their malice; for they may rest assured their spite is little regarded by

HONESTUS.

May 4, 1786.

No. VII.

" Facts are Stubborn Things."

THE multiplicity of opponents that surround me, make it difficult to select an antagonist; and to answer them separately, would be too tedious both for myself and the public. I shall, therefore, introduce the whole upon the stage, and exhibit them in one portrait.

The " Twig of the Branch" is pleasing in his manner, though not very forcible in his arguments; and I doubt not, with proper culvation, he will flourish ere long in the garden of science, un-

33

less he is injured in his growth, by the briars and thorns which so abundantly spring from the soil in which he is planted.

The "Lawyer," in the Centinel, writes with plausibility. The sentiments of the other writers, after divesting them of their supernumerary appendages, are chiefly comprised in his performances.

"Zenas" deals largely in history, and from thence endeavours to prove the necessity of indulging the Bar in all their vagaries. From his "steu boy" language, without doubt he has made the Belles Lettres his particular study. He introduces the respectable characters of "Demosthenes and Cicero," but the sound of names will not avail him in this controversy. I would ask, whether those sages lived upon the delay and embarrassments of the causes committed to their care ? Did Cataline, as a conspirator, find a friend in Cicero ? Did those orators become advocates for the enemies of their country ? Did the "liberties of Rome" depend on a set of men, in any manner analagous in the practice to those described ? If "Zenas" cannot draw these inferences from his premises, his introducing those worthies upon the present occasion, is an affront to their memories.

The character given of Demosthenes is, "That in his pleading he thought of nothing but his country ;" and of Cicero, "That he had the integrity both of witness and Judge. The principles laid down by Cicero and Quintilian, for the conduct of a lawyer, are worthy the attention of every honourable member of the Bar.

The ostentatious display of *technical formalities* in a court of Law, are ludicriously described by Cicero in his plea for L. Murena before Roman Judges.—As this is an authority drawn from the most exalted character in the profession of the Law, it is unnecessary to make any apology for alluding to his comments on their absurdity. I forbear publishing them in detail as they may be thought too pointed, but ask the indulgence, of referring to his oration on the occasion mentioned in justification of the principles advocated in these publications. If *Cicero was wrong*, I must only modestly plead, that his sentiments and my own are analagous.

I was sensible when I first introduced the idea of checking the practice, that my sentiments would be opposed by this general observation, "That we ought not to condemn a whole profession for the misconduct of a few." But this argument would hold equally good with regard to any institution or mode of government what-

34

ever. For instance it may be urged, "Will the people abolish a monarchy for a few bad princes?" But in a republic we should with one voice declare, that this form of government was in itself pernicious, and that we ought to curtail it.

Every writer who has appeared on the subject, acknowledges, that those who have been guilty of mal-conduct have brought a disgrace on the "order." The "Lawyer" also allows the "general practice" to be pernicious; if therefore, these writers admit, that so far as bad practice takes place, so far the public censure is justifiable; if it can be proved that perverse practice is frequently adopted, it will justify my sentiments of a radical reform. It being evident, that the inhabitants of this Commonwealth are deprived, in many cases of the advantages of the laws. The bills of cost which I could here exhibit, would prove this truth of the observation; but I forbear, as it might be thought by some to be pleading too forcibly to the "feelings" of the people.

I am aware of the answer that is made by many discreet persons, let us retain the "order," but destroy the evil. I find the gentlemen of the bar are willing to join in this sentiment. But from experience we are certain, that unless a thorough check takes place, the evils we now complain of will unavoidably continue. The present laws of this State are intended to restrain illegal charges; but have they effected these essential purposes? The fee-table is treated like an old almanac. They have so established certain rules amongst themselves, as a combined body, that the State may go on to regulate; but *Bar-meetings* will ever find means to augment Court charges. For while our judicial causes are subject to the controul of a body, whose interest is repugnant to that of the people, we cannot adopt any measures to effect a radical cure. Possibly, for a few months, some trifling attention may be paid to our complaints; but a few years will introduce every mischief we apprehend.

A necessary "order" implies an impossibility of doing without them. Let us then examine this hypothesis in such cases as are within every man's cognizance.

In the first place, the amount of most prosecutions that arise amongst neighbours in the country towns, are from 6*s* to 10*l*. In the heat of the dispute, the persons apply for "council." Even if the parties agree to leave their cases to reference, a lawyer is introduced to tell each man's story. In this case, surely they are not necessary. But let us suppose this dispute is carried into Court.

35

The lawyer sets out with his client to the shire town. To enable the "counsel" to pursue his journey with decency he must have more money advanced him, as a fee, than would pay his employer's annual tax. The client also must have some ready cash to bear his expenses, which is the earnings of many months' labour. The lawyer when he arrives at Court, has so many other matters to arrange, that his client must "dance attendance" for many days before his case is brought forward. In the interim, the poor man has nothing else to do but to loiter away his time with a herd of people, in the same unhappy predicament with himself, and possibly from idleness becomes subject to a thousand vicious practices, which, if he had kept at home, he would never have been exposed to. However, after waiting till his patience is wearied out, his case is at length brought forward for trial. One lawyer presents his charge, and the other prepares his vindication; while the poor plaintiff and defendant stand gaping at their honours. After going through the necessary preparations of reading, looking over papers, and calling over witnesses, the "counsel," with a very solemn phiz, agree between themselves to defer this important decision to another term. The lawyers knowing that their clients must finally pay for every day's attendance, are pertectly easy what expense accrues; and after they have wearied those unfortunate men through as many Courts as their purses will bear, both lawyers will whisper to their clients, "Make up the matter upon the best terms you can." Here ends the farce, and here they are at issue. Pray, is the "order" necessary in this case? Was it impossible for three honest neighbours to settle the dispute, without all this expense, fatigue, and trouble?

I have in the plainest terms, given a narration of those facts which commonly take place in our country towns; and if we candidly examine, we shall find these observations will apply in many cases, where we employ a lawyer. To say that this body of men are absolutely necessary for the decision of all law questions, when they often perplex the most simple case, is absurd and inconsistent.

Is this "order" so frequently necessary in our mercantile concerns? A body of merchants are ever considered the most eligible to settle commercial disputes. Since the peace, have the mercantile body experienced the necessity of this body? Have they wanted them to throw the most simple demands into confusion? Or do we conceive this "order" "necessary to regulate the customs of foreign nations

36

and merchants?" I would ask those persons who maintain that they are absolutely necessary, to point out the particular instances wherein they are so indispensable.

I cannot apprehend, from a reform of Judicial practice, that we should be in a state of anarchy, or that we should make our situation worse than it is at present. Legal impositions are the worst species of tyranny.

But, however, this "anarchy," which is predicted is all a bugbear; our laws might become so simplified, notwithstanding what has been said by the "Lawyer," that Judges might be found equal to the task of dispensing them, upon the most equitable principles, of justice and propriety. By the mode proposed, we should find every individual would receive a greater benefit from the promptitude of the laws, than from the delays of the lawyers.

But it is said by the "lawyer," "How dangerous and powerful an union might these Judges form?" This argument is somewhat similar to that which is urged against giving powers to Congress! "What an unlimited influence would they acquire?" cries Jonathan of the valley. But this argument has no more force in one case, than in the other; as the Judges are chosen during good behaviour. When, therefore, they are found to pervert the laws, the people have a remedy by impeachment. As one writer observes, "The judiciary power is as secure as the nature of government will admit."

As this "undue influence of the Judges" is a great argument used by the advocates, and particularly by the "Lawyer," let us examine from which institution the most danger is apt to arise. In the first place, the Judges may have an undue influence; they may pervert the laws; they may receive bribes. We will admit these evils to take place; but the remedy is in the people! Remove them from their office, and the evils subside. But on the other side, suppose the lawyers should be guilty of these practices, wherein is our remedy? It will be said, controul them by certain regulations; make them take a most solemn oath, that they "will not do any falsehood, or consent to any to be done, &c.;" restrain them by a strict fee-table. But it is answered, these things are already done; notwithstanding which, every man "feels" the effects of mal-practice. These laws and checks of government have but little tendency to relieve us; they are disregarded by them. Their numbers have become so great, that the evils steal through the State, and the people become entangled before they are aware. But the practice of the Judges is at one view, and when they are guilty of a breach of duty, the number being small, it is immediately felt, and we know the person on whom to lay our charge. Besides, being supported by "fixed and determinate salaries," they have not that inducement to pervert the laws, as men who are obliged to act for their clients, let their cause be good or bad. Notwithstanding the long continuance of the order of Judges, how seldom does our history furnish us with any impeachments for mal-conduct? So far from any complaint, against the present Bench, every individual is satisfied with their conduct. But is this the case with the frequent practice of lawyers? Certainly not.

Further, the permanency of this "order," establishes a perpetual power vastly superior to the Judges, who are during good behaviour, over which the people have no controul. There being no rotation or choice of members, they will become an "order," continually increasing in influence, and by "long practice" will have their clients equally as dependent upon them as vassals under the feudal system, and in time they may become so involved in the very vitals of government, that it will be out of the power of the people to regulate them. This "order" may, in a few years, establish such an ascendency within the Commonwealth, that like the Plebeians of Rome, the people will be obliged to choose a "patron" from among them.

I am sensible, "that men professing the knowledge of the laws are necessary to every free government." But I am as fully convinced that the practice of the law ought not to be within the hands of such men, who may pervert them by their mal-practice. The knowledge of the law, and the pernicious practice, are two very different points.

When a community, therefore, find any individuals, becoming so powerful that the citizens cannot appeal to the laws without being subject to their imposition, it is the duty of the community to view their conduct with jealousy. The characters of Otis, Thacher, &c. are very respectable; but the practice then and since is so opposite in many instances, as to render the establishment very different in its nature and operations, and from a "useful" has become a suspicious institution.

The "order of Judges will answer every purpose, "as men professing the knowledge of the law;" and to allow generous salaries to gentlemen in this office, would ever be an inducement for many to turn their study to this profession. The difficulty held forth respecting the impossibility of getting good Judges without this "order" is only deception. For if none but this "order" are acquainted with the general principles of jurisprudence, it must follow that they only are competent to make laws. But on the contrary I argue, that if a body of men can frame laws, who do not make this profession their whole study, it follows that wise and honest men may judge on them, notwithstanding they are not backnied in all the finesse, cunning and art too often practiced. The fundamental principles of right and wrong are level with the common understanding of mankind. For if these principles are not known, without making them the whole study of a man's life, the trial by jury, which consists of twelve men taken indiscriminately from the people, is the greatest absurdity in nature; for how can men determine upon any business with equity, if we allow in the first instance, that the subject is above their comprehension.

It appears rather a difficulty to the "Twig of the Branch" to know how we shall obtain "the different forms of conveyance requisite to secure the peaceable possession of property, provided this order were abolished." To which I answer, that the excessive intricacy of these conveyances arises principally from a multiplicity of needless and almost unintelligible words introduced into these forms; every necessary security might be had, provided a more concise mode was adopted, so as to prevent "every contention, dispute and outrage incident to verbal contracts."

Even now, amidst the multiplicity of mystical phrases, all necessary forms can be had independent of a lawyer.

I hope my countrymen will consider with candour the sentiments delivered. I mean to pursue the subject, but whether any good effects shall take place from my remarks, depend on your determinations.

May 11, 1786.

No. VIII.

"*Great is the praise, and greatly acceptable to mankind, when men labor in a profession, by which their fellow citizens are profited.*"
Cicero.

I HAVE hitherto endeavoured to treat my opponents with as much respect as decency would permit me; I have overlooked many of their insinuations and personal abuses, knowing their intentions were to draw me aside from pursuing my subject; but "Zenas" appears to be bred wholly in the school of vulgarism; and though he may assume the title of a gentleman, I dare venture to affirm, if he would reveal his name, we should find him of a most despicable original. He says in his last, that "Honestus is a designing and dishonest man." In this assertion I look upon myself as interested. If this writer had proved his charge from my writing, or had convinced the public of the justness of his accusation, I should not have blamed him for his declaration; but the contemptible wretch in the first place only deals in cant and declamation; and though he forces himself upon the public by taking up four columns of a paper, he is so far from refuting my arguments, that he is entirely ignorant of the subject he pretends to vindicate. The trial by Jury, nor the privilege of Council, on which he is so very elaborate, have never been disputed in any one paragraph I have offered to the public; neither have I urged "compulsory references." As to the gentleman whom he styles "the stern, false-hearted, and ungrateful politician,"* I should be happy could I boast of his assistance; his character as a patriot stands too exalted to be injured by "Zenas;" if any thing can sully his fame, it must be to vindicate his conduct from the aspersions of this paltry scribbler.

Having dismissed forever this ignorant "Zenas," I shall go on with my remarks, after asking pardon of the public for noticing so gross and illiberal a writer.

As many persons have received a wrong impression (notwithstanding my repeated declarations to the contrary) that my views are not only to regulate the "order" of lawyers, but to destroy the efficacy of the laws,—this being so contrary to my idea, that my whole aim has been to establish the laws upon such a foundation, that every man should receive the full benefit of them; or in other words, agreeable to our Bill of Rights, "freely without being obliged to purchase it; completely and without denial; promptly and without delay; conformably to the laws." I wish therefore that this declaration may be remembered, that my opposition is not to the laws, but to the too frequent mal-practice of many in our courts of law; my plan, I presume, can be practised without weakening the laws, or setting property afloat.

I go on as was proposed to consider the question, "whether Judges

* Samuel Adams.

40

well versed in the laws, could be procured after regulating the practice as recommended?" I have observed in a former paper, that the fundamental principles of our laws might be known, without the mode of practice introduced by the "order" of lawyers; for if it be a fact, as one of my opponents asserts, "that the municipal institutions of this Commonwealth are so fixed and determinate, that it must be difficult for the judicial authority to trample on them with impunity;" if this be the case, even now, notwithstanding the vast and "venerable pile of British codes" introduced into our Courts, provided the laws were simplified, how much more "fixed and determinate" would they become? Thus systematised, could not persons of abilities, with proper attention, make themselves acquainted with every information essential to a Judge?

It is observed by the same writer, that "the want of uniformity and system, put it in the power of the Judge, in the republic of Athens, Sparta and Rome, of bending the laws to their pleasure:" but if the institutions of this State, (as asserted by the writer) are "fixed and determinate," this "uniformity and system" are not wanting, as in "Athens," &c.—consequently the judges of this State have not the "power of bending the laws to their pleasure." The conclusion therefore is, that the laws becoming "fixed and determinate," the fundamental principles might easily be acquired, so as to enable them to take the important stations of Judges; and that certain professionalists who are puzzling and perplexing those institutions which are in their nature "fixed and determinate," are not absolutely necessary in our Republic.

The "Lawyer" (in the Centinel) seems averse to adopting a concise code of laws, but thinks it necessary to admit the body of British laws into our Courts. He says, "they are framed upon the principles of Magna Charta; and those which relate to the prince and nobility are never adopted." By his own acknowledgment, the laws by which we practice are involved amidst a multiplicity of others we have nothing to do with." Would it not be a more eligible method to frame a code of laws upon the principles of our own Bill of Rights, and adapted to the particular circumstances of the State?—That we may no longer be obliged to wade through folios from the "first Henry, and travel over numberless pages relating to the prince and nobility," and "which are repugnant to our constitution, and as little regarded as the edicts of France." If therefore those introduced into our practice are involved in a thick cloud of useless Brit-

41

ish statutes, it is a full proof that those which are applicable to our constitution, should be selected and brought to one point of view. I would ask, why this state cannot have laws framed upon the principles of their Bill of Rights, equally as well as England upon their Magna Charta? But it is said, Magna Charta is agreeable to our republican government; therefore British laws are consonant to our constitution. But according to this mode of reasoning, we might have adopted Magna Charta in the gross, and not have been at the trouble to form a Bill of Rights of our own. But I argue thus, as we have adopted a Bill of Rights, though consonant to the spirit of Magna Charta, so also we ought to frame a code of laws, though they may be agreeable to the republican laws practised in the Courts of England. Thus reduced as to bulk, if not in spirit, our laws would be adapted to every man's information, and most persons could spare some leisure moments to become acquainted with their general principles. But as our laws, at present, are so involved with the whole body of British statutes, scarcely any person, even if he has an inclination to make the laws his study, can select from the chaos those which are necessary for his attention.

I thank the "lawyer" for his friendly intention to inform me, "that the kingdoms of Media and Persia were under the government of absolute monarchs; but knowing this wonderful piece of history before, I only introduced those kingdoms to show the impropriety of our adopting British laws, as if we thought they were as "unalterable" as those of the Medes and Persians; or that we conceived ourselves bound strictly to adhere to them, notwithstanding they were blended with thousands "repugnant to our republican constitution."

But it is said by one writer, "our laws cannot be simplified, as a variety of laws are necessary in a free State, from the variety of views in which property is considered, for the payment of debts, raising a revenue, and the numberless rules necessary to the transferring property." On which I observe, that this "variety of views" is the slough of the law; and the greatest part of those "views" arise merely from the sophistry introduced by lawyers; for the more divisions, subdivisions, distinctions, and vague indefinite ideas that are introduced into any controversy, the better for them. In short, the whole bundle of perplexities originate from the metaphysical pleadings of this "order," they being studious to show a cause in as many shades as fancy can picture it; and very often the most simple cases are thrown into such a "variety of views," as to become a

42

jumble of intricacies. But the principal part of this parade is mere pageantry of profession, calculated to perplex the Jury, and deceive the wondering crowd.

If there is such a mystery in right and wrong, we ought to have a body of lawyers for Jurymen, as they are the final deciders on this heap of wonders. Can any man seriously say, that five Judges cannot give every point of "view" in which property is considered? Have they not "abilities to discern the near approaching shades of guilt verging from excusable homicide to manslaughter, and thence to murder?" Or could they not know "the natural distinction observed in the definition of any crime or offence?" Could they not know "what a writ of habeas corpus was, how enjoyed, or in what circumstances demanded?" I hope this writer does not mean to "banter" the Judges, as if they wanted information on these points. Could not a Jury take the right point of "view" from men who are under no bias to consider it but in one point, which is that of equity? But the Jury now become embarrassed in their ideas from lawyers who have an interest to make their own particular side appear the only right point of "view." I would ask, whether the Jury could not determine the truth with greater certainty from the explanation of the Judges, than from the sophistry of a dozen lawyers, who are only delivering their sentiments to persuade them to take a "view" through their optic glasses.

Further, if we were to examine all the cases since the declaration of Independence, I do not suppose we should find more than one in a hundred that required any material law question to be agitated; and even this one, it is more than probable, could have been decided without the assistance of the bar. Many causes now in our Courts, and those which have occasioned so much distress among the people, are no way connected with any law question. The common cases which are deferred from term to term, and which cost so much money in the prosecution, are in no respect intricacies of law. Our difficulties do not arise from such causes, but from the embarrassments of lawyers. The trifling litigious cases which in general are brought into our Courts, require no questions of law, but are nourished by those, who make money for themselves, from the purses of their clients. Some of the Bar too frequently play upon the feelings of their townsmen, and so far from endeavouring to reconcile any differences, are willing to urge the resentment of one neighbour, to pursue with rigour another, by which means not only their property becomes a sacrifice, but private bickerings and animosities pervade the whole town.

The "Lawyer" observes, "that the decisions by references have been decisive, time immemorial, both in this country and England." But we know the decisions by references are not always binding.—Even if an obligation is given upon such an occasion, it is sometimes set aside as invalid.

The "Lawyer" says, "every man has now a right to plead his own cause;" but every man knows, that by the mode of practice, the people are deprived of this right. The "Lawyer" says, "if a man conducted his suit with learning and propriety," he would be treated by the Bar with the greatest respect. The gentlemen of the Bar therefore are the judges of "learning and propriety:" and if a man who is interrogated with the utmost arrogance by the Lawyer, shews the least diffidence, it is considered as an "awkwardness," and "a foolish attempt to undertake a business he is totally unfit for." This is truly a novel sentiment, that a man who is telling his own story, and who must in the nature of things know more about it than any other person, should be "totally unfit" for the business. If he is not fit for the business, who can be? can a Lawyer be more fit to tell the story, than the man himself? pray how did the Lawyer receive his account, unless from the person? But it will be said, "he cannot tell his story in open court." I readily acknowledge he cannot now, while we have many within the Bar, to laugh him out of countenance; but if we adopt the mode proposed, we should find that every man would tell his story with equal ease, as he now does to a lawyer, under the gloomy shades of his office.

The "Lawyer" says, "mirthful scenes naturally excite a mirthful countenance." For my own part I know not any "mirthful scenes" in our courts! a man in distress exhibits no laughable scene! possibly a man who is living on his distress, may call it a "mirthful scene," when a poor unhappy client shows a little agitation in expressing himself, this may appear truly laughable to him. A few may take pleasure in the throbbing bosom of an unfortunate man, entangled in the web of the law; but however "mirthful" this may appear to them, yet consider ye bold, unfeeling beings, that the object of your merriment, has his property, and possibly his life, depending on the issue; and though you can shroud yourselves in your formality, and can smile on his misfortunes, yet remember, this dis-

44

tressed man and his family are suffering the most poignant miseries, owing principally to the person against whom he is engaged.

The "Lawyer" finds fault with my plan, "that any man should speak for himself or by his friend." He reprobates this idea, and says, "we could not attend to this business ourselves, and as to a friend, no one would devote himself to serve another." A decision by rule of Court, is contrary to this sentiment. Thank heaven, we often experience the indulgence of our friends, to devote themselves to a settlement of a cause, after it has travelled for years, through every round of the law. These friends we do not call "pettifoggers," but real friends, in distress. They are not pleaders who are taking an advantage of our misfortunes. They are not men who are pilfering our little remaining all. They are not growing rich by the delay of our cause. They are not taxing us with a heavy bill of costs. In a word, they are friends to "the widow and fatherless," the weak and poor; and instead of adding to their misfortunes, they endeavour to smooth the rugged paths of misery." Does the "Lawyer" call such persons pettifoggers, or does he give our Judges such opprobrious epithets? I rather suppose a troublesome, cunning Attorney, comes more justly within this idea; one, who by long, unnecessary delays, will swell a bill of costs, and who pursues this business solely for his own private emolument.

My plan solely rests here, that a man who does not choose to give his plea in person, or writing, may employ a friend for this purpose, and that the Judges should take this account in its simple state, and deliver it to the jury, with any points of law necessary for the decision. This mode I call equity; and the determination of the jury would be more just, than a thousand attornies employed to embarrass, delay and swell charges.

As to a man attending on his own business himself, this objection is quite trifling; as he is now obliged to attend every court, notwithstanding he employs a lawyer, and his expenses become augmented by supporting himself and his Counsel, through a whole term.

Another sentiment is, "that lawyers must be considered as sentinels over the enemies of the law." This idea could be well applied to the Judges, but the simile is rather unfortunate as to the general practice. Would a prudent General place a man as a sentinel, against whom the army were almost unanimously clamorous? Would a body of guards be placed on the out-posts, who by their conduct had weakened the army? who were taking the advantage of every soldier?

45

who were suspected of holding an improper correspondence? who by their art and cunning were promoting a dissention among the troops, and were fomenting every little dispute? and who by this means had amassed to themselves the greatest part of the rations, clothing and pay of the soldiery? I ask, whether a General would show his prudence to place such a body as sentinels, in a time of danger? Rather on the contrary, would it not prove his wisdom to arraign such individuals at a Court-Martial, and would it not be just to sentence them immediately to quit the camp?

Another sentiment advanced by the "Lawyer," is, "we deprive men of enterprise, from engaging in the study of the laws." I have ever conceived the principles of justice were necessary for a Judge, but the spirit of "enterprise" is quite a novel idea. It is true, the practice of some may come within this idea, but it appears perfectly absurd, that a Court of Justice should be governed by men of "enterprise;" the fair principles of law cannot be considered "enterprise"; "champarty" possibly may be considered such! It may be called "enterprise" to take up a cause, and depend on its success, by endeavouring to puzzle and perplex it in every particular: but such conduct though it may be a pleasing speculation to the professionalists, is ruinous to the community. These speculating attornies may increase their fortunes, and may by some successful causes live above their fellows, but if this enterprising conduct is pursued, Justice must ere long become most horribly perverted; and our courts become scenes of Exchange Alley traffic.

One writer arrogantly asks me, "whether I can lift up my eyes to the supreme bench of justice." That elevated seat I revere equal with him; and so great is my respect, that I should hold the man in contempt, (if any was within my knowledge,) who would quit it, to to take a stand at their Honours' footstool.

The variety of objections offered by the advocates, must apologize for the length of my observations. I shall therefore conclude this paper in the words of Æschines, in one of his orations; "In such a situation of affairs of which you yourselves, my countrymen, are sensible, the only method of saving the wrecks of government, is if I mistake not, to allow full liberty to accuse those who have invaded our laws. But if you shut them up, or suffer others to do this, I prophesy that you will fall insensibly, and that very soon, under a tyrannical power."

May 18, 1786.

F

46

No. IX.

A citizen naturally virtuous, possesses these two qualities; a steady and unshaken courage to support the Commonwealth; and a zeal that that has been proof against every thing, in every conjuncture, and particular action.

THE parade in the Exchange Advertiser, and other papers, respecting the conduct of the town of Boston, on the business of instructing their representatives, and the insinuations thrown out, as if the inhabitants in general were opposed to the sentiments contained in these papers, prevent me (for the present) from pursuing the subject mentioned in my last, that I may take notice of those pompous recitals.

It seems a worthy citizen made a motion for a reconsideration of the vote passed at a previous meeting, viz. "not to instruct their Representatives;" and mentioned particularly the consideration of the pernicious conduct of some in the practice of the law. This motion was seconded, and after a very trifling debate it was put to vote, and there appeared but a very small number of hands in favour of a reconsideration. The narrator then concludes by saying, that "Honestus may console himself that he has a few "ignorant, ridiculous, absurd beings," to join him in sentiments.

I would not pretend to reflect on the inhabitants of the town of Boston for their proceedings; but from previous conduct I have the greatest reason to suppose that my sentiments were not so generally disapproved as this writer would represent. With respect to introducing so great a number of lawyers into our legislature, which was one main object held forth, there never was a time when the sentiments of the people could be more fully known on this point, than at the last election: as gentlemen of the most respectable characters met at several parts of the town previous to the choice, and though amongst the number of candidates, seven or eight persons of the profession were nominated, yet a disapprobation was shewn by an almost unanimous negative.

I do not mention this to boast or to "banter" the gentlemen who were candidates, but to inform my countrymen of the minds of the people of this metropolis; and to convince them, that the reason of their "not" instructing their Representatives, was not owing to a disapprobation of the sentiments delivered in these papers.

47

I hope the narrator does not publish his vaunting paragraphs merely to insinuate to the public that the perverters of the law have so far established their influence in this metropolis, as to set the respectable inhabitants at defiance; or does he think the town will thank him, for treating a motion (regularly made by a worthy citizen) with so much insult and ridicule? As freemen, they all feel the privileges of a citizen; and when an individual is marked out as an object of ridicule, or as being "ignorant, ridiculous and absurd," merely for making a motion, it touches too keenly the "feelings" of his brethren, to suffer so great an insult to pass unnoticed.

The reason why this motion was not passed, I shall not pretend to say, as every individual, without doubt, has a witness within himself, which fully convinces him of the real cause of his silence.

The inhabitants of the town of Boston have ever been opposed to all illegal measures. I need only revert to that period when the arbitrary edicts of Britain roused them to assemble! when our patriots, impressed with the dangers which threatened their country, harangued their listening townsmen! When each bosom beat high in opposition to tyranny; at this crisis did not their hearts glow within them? Was not every coward sentiment that could depress the soul quickly stifled? And did not every man (a few despicable wretches excepted) readily determine with one inflamed heart, to become his country's friend?

At this period, my countrymen, would it have soothed your virtuous resentment, or have hushed your just complaints, to have been told, that a newspaper account of danger was not to be regarded?—That we ought to know the name, family, and connexion of a public writer, in order to determine whether his sentiments were worth attending to; that we should place such implicit confidence in the abilities of our Representatives, as to render it needless to instruct them? Would such arguments then, have lulled you into a supineness, to acquiesce in the wishes of your enemies?

I shall offer my sentiments with coolness, as I am convinced some "few" persons will blame me for my remarks; but as I conceive the subject to be of the utmost importance, must beg the indulgence of the public, while I consider the arguments which were urged in opposition to the motion. I would not be thought to reflect on the gentlemen who spoke on the subject, as I believe them to be sincere friends to their country. If they were wrong, it must be considered

48

only as an error in judgment, as they could have no sinister views to mislead them.

The first observation is, "A newspaper writer was not to be heeded;" or in other words, that the sentiments delivered in our papers were so little regarded, as scarcely to be worthy of notice. I am sensible we have some "few" amongst us, who heartily wish that newspaper accounts were much less regarded; but when the people of this Commonwealth pay no attention to *cautionary advice,* we may soon expect they will give but little heed to any propositions whatever. In this case, an universal lethargy would soon take place.

Pray from whence arose our opposition to Britain? Were not the sentiments delivered in our newspapers, the principal cause? At that time an "order" of tories would willingly have hushed every whisper of a public speculation. From what source did the people get their political knowledge, but from this vehicle of information? I am sensible it has, of late, become "monstrous" fashionable among a certain class, to speak contemptibly of public writings; and to boast, with a haughty indifference, that they pay no attention to what appears in a newspaper; and if by chance they hear of a writer, who is urging an attention to first principles, they will exclaim with a heavy sigh, "Peace, be still." And if they find their pitiful moanings will not answer their purposes, they will endeavour to undervalue whatever sentiments are delivered, by branding them with the cant phrases of popularity, electioneering, ungrammatical, inconsistency, absurd, and many other epithets of as little import. But if they should deign to write in reply, their flimsy arguments are to be considered as carrying indubitable conviction. Their composition, the standard of diction. And though every line of their writings should be evidently wanting in both, yet such is their arrogance, they will censure every one that differs from their prejudiced opinions. But however such persons may be affected, I hope the people will ever remember, that when this barrier of their liberties, the public prints, shall sink into disrepute, their freedom will speedily crumble from its basis.

The second objection is, "That we ought to know the name, family, and connexions of a public writer." With respect to myself, I am willing to stand the strictest scrutiny; but, however, this principle is perfectly aristocratical. Do "names, families, and connexion" alone, give force to sentiments? Must our opinions become valid, merely from high sounding dignities? Must the poor man be forever debarred from delivering his mind, lest the inquiry should be concerning his origin. Are there no observations worthy our attention, unless they are authorized by family alliances? Cannot the poor man have sentiments, that may be beneficial to his country? Must not the people listen to the voice of danger, unless it is proclaimed through the gilded trumpet of fame? Shall the grand inquiry be, who is the man, rather than what are the principles? Sorry I am that such doctrines should be attended to in republican assembly.

The third remark is, " That we should place such confidence in the abilities of our Representatives, as to render it needless to instruct them." I greatly esteem the worthy gentlemen who are chosen by the town of Boston, for their wisdom, firmness and patriotism; but I reprobate the idea of relying so fully upon their abilities, as not to instruct them. This is a most pernicious sentiment. It is the grand prerogative of the people to instruct their Representatives; but if we introduce the idea, that we ought to place implicit confidence in their integrity and abilities, it is in effect destroying the right of instructing them. If we act upon this principle, we can never exercise this right, for if we confide entirely on them this year, why not the next, and so on forever? If we would instruct them in future, it will become a matter of so much delicacy from long disuse, as to be considered an affront for their constituents to instruct them in any case whatever. For they may quere with the utmost propriety, why do you distrust our abilities, more than our predecessors? Upon these principles, therefore, I am for tenaciously adhering to this right, and surely it cannot be any reflection upon the wisdom of our Representatives, to let them know, how we would have them act upon any particular subject; for if they do not know the minds of their constituents, it is quite a chance whether they please them or not.

These observations may appear groundless! They may be considered as the mere effusions of fancy; but however singular they may be thought by some; I dare hazard my conjectures, that (unless checked by the people) a few years will introduce so perfect an aristocratical influence, as will finally sap the foundation of our republic.

Some individuals make a laugh at our attempts to regulate the practice; but we doubt not the business will be treated seriously, when it comes before that august body, from whence the people have a right to expect a redress of their grievances. For any persons,

50

therefore, to assert that we cannot obtain relief from the Legislature is not only alarming, but perfectly paradoxical; as the power which frames the laws must in its nature be competent to regulate all orders in the execution or practice of them. The happiness of the people is the sole object of all laws in a free government, consequently if their prosecution is injurious to the community by the mal-practice of any individuals, it behoves the Legislature to remedy the evils, and immediately to devise some measures whereby the laws may be executed with equity and decision.

May 25, 1786.

No. X.

By heavens, I had rather coin my heart,
And dr p my blood for drachms, than to wring
From the hard hands of the Peasants, their small trash,
When I've no right to.—SHAKESPEARE.

THE number of papers which have appeared under one signature, and upon one subject, I hope will not be considered by my countrymen as tedious or unimportant. If any consideration is worthy our attention, surely that must be whereon depends the happiness and welfare of our young republic. The laws are the barriers of freedom, and when they are perverted, the liberties of the people are in danger of falling a sacrifice to the innovation. These observations being premised, I shall pursue my remarks with confidence, not doubting they will be perused with candor by every member of the Commonwealth.

I beg leave to introduce to the public the oath taken by an Attorney, previous to his being admitted into the practice of the law, viz.

"You shall do no falsehood, nor consent to any to be done in Court; and if you know of any to be done, you shall give knowledge thereof to the Justices of the Court, or some of them, that it may be reformed. You shall not wittingly or willingly prosecute, sue or procure to be sued, any false or unlawful suit, nor give aid or consent to the same. You shall delay no man for lucre or malice; but shall use yourself in the office of an Attorney,

51

within the Court, according to the best of your knowledge and discretion, and with all good fidelity, as well to the Court as to your clients. So help you God."

The bare recital of this oath, without any comment, is sufficient to convince every one of the propriety of the foregoing remarks. The writers on the side of the "order" have repeatedly called upon me to point out the particular persons who have been guilty of malpractice; at the same time they have all candidly acknowledged, that some individuals within their knowledge have been justly censured. The "Lawyer," in particular, admits, the "general practice" to be unjustifiable. If this is fact, I now demand of them whether they have, conformably to their oaths, "given knowledge to the Justices of the Court," or have impeached any of their brethren notwithstanding they are acquainted with their pernicious practice? If any think themselves injured by my observations, let them now convince the public that they mean to adhere to their oaths, by bringing those culprits to punishment. This palpable neglect therefore proves, that however innocent the persons themselves may be, yet they are blameable for not adhering more sacredly to their obligations.

An act of this State provides, "That the parties shall employ two Attornies only, to the intent that the other should have the advantage of one at least." How does the practice of employing or retaining a great majority of the bar, by hush-money, correspond with this act? It is true "two Attornies only" are admitted to speak to any cause; yet this retaining fee may deprive the other party of every benefit from "Counsel." By this practice a rich man will ever have the advantage of a poor antagonist; as the former may bribe two lawyers for pleading, so also he can fee half a dozen more to say nothing—but "laugh." These are among the scenes of "merriment" hinted at by the "Lawyer."

Another act of this State authorizes "the Supreme Judicial Court with respect to the admission of attornies, and the creating barristers at law, and establishing rules and regulations." But the "order" have now in a great measure got this power within their own hands; at their bar-meetings no candidate is admitted without passing their examination, and sometimes the person is exposed to their malice, pique, and resentment. These censors have a wonderful effect towards establishing the importance of the bar. It is surprising to hear a man defy me to produce an instance "when the fee-table has not been the rule of conduct with an attorney." Pray

52

what is the aggregate amount of a bill of cost? Possibly this confident boaster has not the presumption to charge in open defiance of the fee-table; but let him hand to the public the sum-total of his accounts, and I dare warrant, unless he is callous to every feeling, he would blush at the enormity of his account. This Jesuitical manner of reasoning, therefore, will not answer.

How extensive must be the influence, and how great the danger of those who are practising in our Judicial Courts as a combined body? The charges alledged against them of their bar-meetings, and their correspondence, are too notorious to be controverted; and provided they would favour the public with their whole proceedings (those in particular which are not entered into the bar-book) we might then judge whether the continuance of such measures were dangerous or not. What security have the people either of their liberties or property, when all their appeals to the laws are first canvassed (unknown to the parties) by the very body of men whom they employ as counsel in their causes, and who oft times agree beforehand as to their issue when brought into Court? By such conduct, does not justice become a mere deception, and intended only as a cloak for many and great impositions? Are not our laws rendered by such practice a mere ignis fatuus to delude the people? If individuals can combine to delay and embarrass any causes they think proper, is it not in effect as fatal to the welfare of the community, as if we were without any laws whatever? How can we boast of our liberties, or be safe in our property, when they hang on such a precarious tenure?

Suppose A. commences an action against B.—when the parties apply separately to their lawyers, it is with a view to have the business settled upon the best terms possible; but if these two attornies instead of minding the interest of their employers, meet to settle the business to their own private emolument, by delaying the decision from term to term, can the parties by such conduct, be said to obtain the law agreeable to the Bill of Rights, "freely, completely, and promptly?"

May not the most dangerous consequences take place, not only to every individual, but to the state in general, by such a combination? Is there not danger that such persons will in time become so powerful in our judiciary proceedings, as to rise superior to the controul of the people? And though the "majority of persons" throughout the Commonwealth may be sensible of their impositions, yet from the influence they may acquire from their practice, they will be afraid to oppose them. Does not this dread already prevail throughout many of our considerable towns?

The "order" have often made this boast, "that the Legislature have not power to controul them." Is it not alarming to hear those whose practice is universally complained of, declaring publicly, "that they are not afraid of a restriction, and that it is out of the power of all men to do it." If this is our real state, melancholy indeed is our situation! What! are we threatened with a total abolition of our liberties, without even the possibility of a remedy? A free government thus hampered is truly a political solecism.

Another evil is, their charging all their clients for a whole term 1*s.* 6*d.* per day, although their actions are deferrred to another Court? What an amazing income must arise to the "order" by this practice, even if they had no other fees?

The questions now to be determined are simply these, whether the people of this Commonwealth shall be exposed to the imposition of any individuals, who are practising every art in their profession to enrich themselves, and are embarrassing the causes committed to their care? Or, whether some measures shall be adopted, that the people may have every privilege which they are entitled to by the eleventh article of their Bill of Rights?

Before I conclude, I would observe on two arguments, which are offered by many, first, That the delay of causes is an advantage to the debtor! This is plausible reasoning at first view, but how reverse the reality? Suppose a cause is delayed for a number of years, do not the charges become enormous when judgment takes place? The poor debtor pays most extravagantly for this respite; as the debt is daily increasing as it travels through the Courts, and finally the unhappy man falls a prey to a heavy bill of cost. The lawyers on both sides, during the whole term of delay, are swelling the charges of plaintiff and defendant. The lenient "counsel" on the part of the creditor knows that he is putting the original debt to an extravagant interest, (more possibly than a hoary usurer) and after ascertaining how far the property of the debtor can hold out, these sympathizing gentlemen have only to determine between themselves, to continue the cause just so far as will about balance the accounts of both debtor and creditor. This is the effect of law lenity! In this case, "are not their tender mercies cruelties?"

54

The second argument is, "That by the constitution we cannot controul the "order." The idea of controul is supposed by some to be nothing short of an insurrection of the people, as if we were to rouse in a mob, and turn every lawyer from his residence! we have a "few" amongst us, who would thus represent the reform recommended; these are bugbears thrown out by our aristocratical gentry; but this anarchy is foreign from my idea of reform. Order and government are objects which I have ever attended to throughout all my observations. The only measure I conceive necessary for the purpose of rectifying the present practice, is to adopt such regulations, and introduce such modes as will render the "order" beneficial to the community, rather than injurious; at least so far useful, as will comport with the happiness of the people; or in other words, that "they use themselves in all good fidelity in their practice," agreeably to the oath administered them.

If this method did not abolish the "order," it would effectually abolish the mal-practice, which is tantamount.

I shall now dismiss the subject, leaving the consideration of my observations, to our political fathers. If any good consequences take place from my remarks, I shall think my time has been usefully spent. I have no sinister views to promote, but have studied solely the welfare of my country. The malice of my enemies I disregard; they have full liberty to convince the public of the wretchedness of their cause, by adopting ribaldry and low cunning, instead of reason and fair argument. The personal abuse they have offered, does no way affect me, otherwise than it adds to the contempt I have ever entertained of them. I have always declared that I esteem many gentlemen of the profession, but the influence of the bad now overbalances the wishes of the good. Provided I receive the approbation of the honest, virtuous and patriotic, I shall never concern myself about persons of an opposite character.

"To virtue only, and its friends, a Friend,
The world beside may murmur or commend;
Know all the distant din this world can keep,
Rolls o'er my grotto, and but soothes my sleep."

HONESTUS.

June 1, 1786.

No. XI.

The Examiner, in answer to a writer in the Yankee, on trial by Jury.

THE definition of a right of trial by jury, as published in the Yankee, being written by a well disposed, (though mistaken) young Republican Lawyer, we are willing to consider the subject with that propriety of argument, which the importance of the question demands.

In the first place, all juries, (by the writer,) are to consider themselves unqualified to judge of law, and though they are sworn "well and truly," to try the case before them, according to law and evidence, yet they are to divest themselves of all the legal principles, upon which they are to predicate their verdict. They are passively to admit, that one part of their oath (as relates to law) is a mere nullity. They are to be blindfolded in this essential privilege, by a restrictive bandage, which the court alone has a right to place over their intellectual optics. They are to hear on one side of the question, as it respects evidence, but are prevented from seeing on the other, as it relates to law. They are to give a verdict between the parties, not embracing either their criminality, or justification, but as solely confined to evidence, on which the court is to decide the guilt or innocence of the individuals. Suppose for example, that a man commits homicide, and the indictment should be for murder, or manslaughter; in this case the jury being obliged to take the opinion of the court, (through the supreme judge) as the only rule for procedure, the verdict must correspond with the principles laid down by them. Suppose further, the court declared that "holding up a finger in an insulting manner, and when the insult however small, is inflicted, even by TOUCHING a person, in an unlawful manner, it amounted to a battery, which includes an assault," and therefore, killing the assailant, did not amount either to murder, or manslaughter, but defensive homicide. The jury in this case, having nothing to direct them but the law laid down by the court, must acquit the offender. They must argue thus; we are of opinion that the person is guilty of murder by using deadly weapons to defend himself against the finger touch of the assailant, yet as the judge declares, that if a finger is held up in a threatening manner, it is a battery, and amounts to an assault, we must therefore acquit the man

56

at the bar, upon the law promulgated from the bench. Will any man of common sense allow this to be correct reasoning, or admit that the lives of the citizens are to be exposed upon such vague principles? Would not all the security of life be frustrated, and would not every assassin be urged to commit murder by first provoking the object of his resentment to raise a finger against him, or touching him in anger, in order to execute the premeditated deed of laying his antagonist a lifeless corpse at his feet? As the protection of life is more essential than that of property or liberty, if the doctrine of unlimited controul over juries on points of law is correct, must it not operate in trials of murder? If so, will not murderers be released, not from a conviction of their innocence, but from the necessity of being obliged to follow the dictates of the court, whose partialities, or political intolerance may lead them to pervert the laws of God and man in the punishment of death?

We put a question in this strong point of view as it relates to homicide, as it serves to prove the fallacy of judges having the sole controul over the verdicts of jury—and to show that juries have a right to judge of law and evidence, as connected with the verdicts returned by them. It is further declared by the writer, that though jury trials are recognized by the constitution, as the "permanency of liberty," yet the citizens in general possess so little information on the subject, that a lawyer is obliged to find not "only argument' but understanding," to make them comprehend the limited extent of this privilege. He narrows this great barrier to the most contracted point, and then exultingly exclaims, that ignorance is the sole cause why the generality of the people do not submissively bow down to his profound explanation. Is it possible, at this enlightened period, the citizens should not be qualified to discharge a duty which has been practised for centuries, and which is contemplated in the constitution as "sacred," and essential to the preservation of their liberties? This doctrine would answer for Jeffries, when Sidney was arraigned before him.—It would answer in the days of tyranny, when juries were made the instruments to shed the blood of martyrs and patriots. But in 1819, where is the man that will avow himself as the advocate of a doctrine, that ignorance is a bar which ought to prevent jurymen from exercising the right of deciding controversies both upon law and evidence? Law and evidence are one and indivisible. They cannot be separated, and while we adhere to jury trials, they cannot be two distinct properties. The evidence must accompany the law, and the law must be connected with the evidence. If the jury have not the whole subject submitted to them, the evidence may be wrested by a construction of law, to destroy the whole intention of the verdict. A man may be considered a criminal by the judges, when the jury intended to consider him innocent. Would any usurping tyrant on the bench, require a more powerful weapon, to effect his purposes? This is a doctrine under which all patriots have fallen a sacrifice.

By this writer, the grand barrier of our liberties (trials by juries) is reduced to a weak mound, scarcely sufficient to afford security against the smallest rivulet, much less against the boisterous billows of despotism. He clothes the judge with the mantle of infallibility as presented to the jury. Being ignorant themselves, they are to be directed in the most "abstruse science of human wisdom, the law." They are to hear evidence, but are forbid to judge of it, as it applies to any law, consequently they say guilty or not guilty, without knowing whether the person is so or not; as the judge applies the guilt or innocence, agreeably to a law of which the jury is entirely ignorant. At length the jury are dismissed, and all this profound process is arrested by a gentleman at the bar, who doubts the correctness of the judge, charges him with a misstatement of the law, dispels all those terrific, and repulsive qualities which appeared to fetter the minds of the jury, and carries the case, together with the judge up to another tribunal, to obtain some positive law, which must controul the jury in a further process. In this case where is the jury, or even where is the judge? The lawyer appears paramount to both. We respect the court too highly to admit the position.

To prove the fallacy of this writer's reasoning, it is a doctrine in judiciary processes on libels, that the truth is not to be admitted in evidence.* Here then we arrive at the grand ultimatum of jury restrictions. Though the Jury, (as by this writer) is confined to evidence, yet in this case they are deprived even of evidence.—Having neither evidence or law, on which to found their verdict, the person arraigned is completely left to the disposal of the court—admit the doctrine of this writer, and we should soon be deprived both of evidence and law; for if evidence is denied in one case, and law in every case, what an easy transition would there be,

* See the late trial of Mary Ann Tucker.

58

to deprive a jury of every essential privilege contemplated by this "sacred" barrier of our liberties? It is too abhorrent to consider the question with seriousness.

There is such an inconsistency in the writer, that it is difficult to trace him in a direct line: while he objects to the rights of jury, he declares that the "humblest citizen has a right to contend against the opinion of the court." That a single lawyer has a right to arrest the judgment of the court, and to tell a judge that he is not satisfied with his opinion—why is he so fierce for individual rights, and so mild as to jury rights? If the humblest citizen, as he says, practises it every day, why are juries to be deprived of it? Are juries to be the only body excluded from the right of judging on law, and to be more tramelled than the humblest citizen? And while a judge submits with complacency to a censure from an individual in the bar, he is represented as frowning with just indignation at a jury, who presume to judge of the law in making up their verdict. It is supposed that this writer, when he talks in such high strains of individual rights as to doubt of the infallibility of the judges in the opinion of the law, that this is to be exclusively exercised by the counsel at the bar. He would shudder at the idea, that a jury should do this; but armed with the weapon of "bar rules," he assumes a dictatorial attitude, and frequently convinces the judge of his error. Strange that all this sanctity of judges opinion, should so soon be exploded, when applied to the counsel, but should be so sacredly adhered to when applied to the jury. They must not doubt of the law, but conform to every minutia as promulgated from the bench. The verdict must correspond with the opinion of the judges on the law, but when brought within the focus of the inspection of the counsel, then this little hero begins to display the prerogative of a citizen—Tells the judge that he has misstated the law, that he shall carry the case before another tribunal, and that he must be prepared to answer before his peers for his incorrect statement of the law to the jury. He branches out still further in the plenitude of his vaunting enquiries, "what terrific or repulsive qualities (says he) surround the judiciary tribunal, that the correctness of a judge's opinion should not be called in question?" He however checks his boasting, by qualifying the mode of appeal. He says he will apply to five judges to correct the errors of one. But what terrific or repulsive qualities surround the five, more than the one, if the whole should be erroneous in their opinion? Must the jury take their decision as infallible, and admit that though the whole have frequently been erroneous in their individual capacity, yet collectively, they are infallible? If one judge is incorrect, when all the evidence, and all the minute circumstances of the case are before him, is it certain that five will be perfect when called to decide on the same case, without such evidence and circumstances before them? If a judge is possessed of common law knowledge, he must be more competent to give the law in conformity to the case when possessed of all the particulars, than those who are deprived of such information. If one judge is incorrect under such favourable circumstances, may not the whole five be equally so, when destitute of the same means of forming a right judgment? As in the case of murder, if a supreme Judge gives in charge, that if a man " holds up his finger in a threatening manner, it shall not be murder if his antagonist kills" him, may not all the judges accede to the principle, and thus render homicide a minor transgression in the criminal code? Has not a case taken place, which we have reason to suppose was decided on this vague declaration from the bench?

What inconsistency of reason is displayed by the writer, in giving an individual a right to doubt the opinion of a judge, and yet denies the same privilege to twelve jurymen who are bound by oath to judge both of law and evidence?

We conclude by saying, that by the constitution, and from long practice previous to its adoption, the jury have a right to judge both law and evidence, in all cases submitted to them, and that whenever new trials are granted, it must be made manifest to the court, that further evidence can be produced essential to the merits of the case, or that some flagrant violation of the rights of the parties has been committed. But we deny that a partial plea of a pretended mistatement of the law by the judge, ought to arrest the verdict of a jury, or expose the victorious party to further expences, by an appeal to another tribunal; and further, that juries have a right to give a verdict without being restrained by the judges, according to their opinion of law, agreeably to the evidence furnished them. The law comprehends the guilt or innocence of the parties, but if the juries have no cognizance of this fundamental principle, the judge instead of the jury becomes the sole umpire of the decision. The citizens instead of being tried by their peers consisting of

60

twelve impartial men within the precinct, are tried by those who bring evidence to conform to their construction of law. Patriots and martyrs were never hung, burnt, or beheaded by the jury of England, but by the arbitrary provision of the law by the judges. Such we trust will never be the case in the United States, as we confide in the integrity of the present judges, and the people have a permanent security of their rights, when violated, by an IMPEACHMENT.

Chapter III

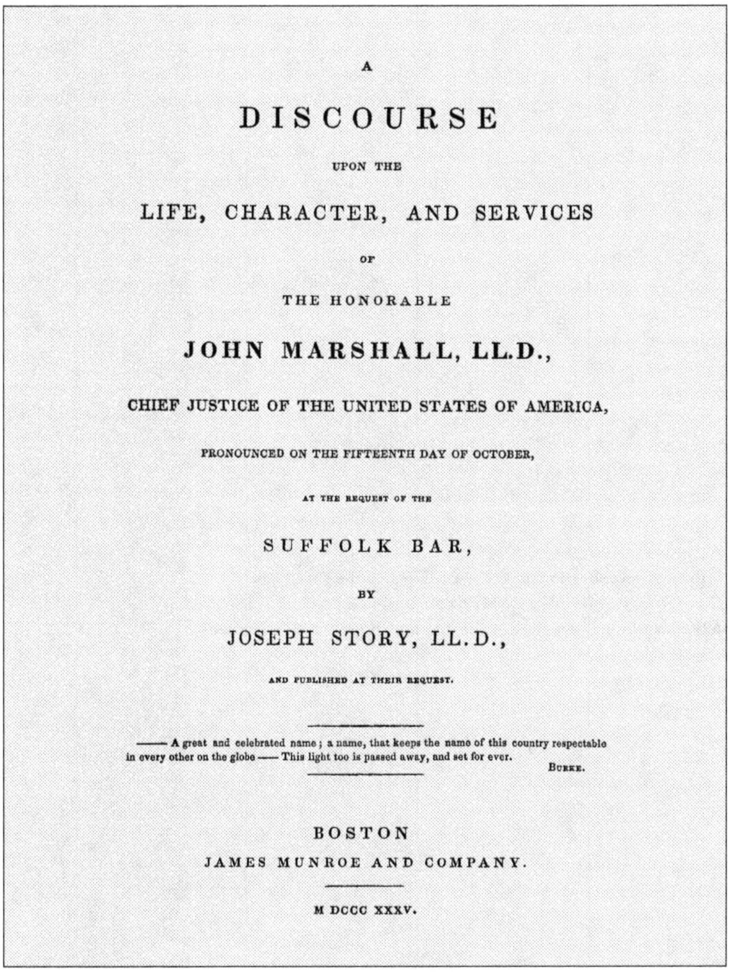

A

DISCOURSE

UPON THE

LIFE, CHARACTER, AND SERVICES

OF

THE HONORABLE

JOHN MARSHALL, LL.D.,

CHIEF JUSTICE OF THE UNITED STATES OF AMERICA,

PRONOUNCED ON THE FIFTEENTH DAY OF OCTOBER,

AT THE REQUEST OF THE

SUFFOLK BAR,

BY

JOSEPH STORY, LL.D.,

AND PUBLISHED AT THEIR REQUEST.

——A great and celebrated name; a name, that keeps the name of this country respectable in every other on the globe —— This light too is passed away, and set for ever.

BURKE.

BOSTON

JAMES MUNROE AND COMPANY.

M DCCC XXXV.

Story, Joseph. *A Discourse upon the Life, Character, and Services of the Honorable John Marshall, LL.D., Chief Justice of the United States of America, Pronounced on the Fifteenth Day of October, at the Request of the Suffolk Bar*. Boston: James Monroe and Company, 1835.

CAMBRIDGE PRESS:
METCALF, TORRY, AND BALLOU.

ADVERTISEMENT.

THE narrative of facts and some of the reflections in this Discourse are taken from a biographical sketch, written by me some years ago for the North American Review. As those parts were derived from the most authentic sources, and as the reflections connected with them naturally grew out of the subject, I have not hesitated to adopt them, whenever they were appropriate to my present purpose. It would have been mere affectation to have attempted to avoid the same train of narrative or remark. This explanation is necessary to be made, lest I should be supposed to have appropriated without acknowledgment the labors of another person.

Cambridge, Oct. 16, 1835.

DISCOURSE.

THE funeral obsequies have been performed; the long procession has passed by; and the earth has closed over the mortal remains of Chief Justice Marshall. Time has assuaged the first agonies of grief of the immediate relatives, who were called to mourn over so afflictive a loss; and others, who, looking to the claims of private friendship or to the public interests, were astounded at a blow, which, though not unexpected, came at last with a startling force, have had leisure to recover from their perturbation, and may now contemplate the event with a calm though profound melancholy.

It is under these circumstances, that we are now assembled together, to devote a brief space of time to the consideration of his life, character, and services; and then to return again to the affairs of the world, edified, as I may hope, by what he was, and warmed and elevated by a nearer approach to excellencies, which, if we may not reach, we may yet gaze on with devout respect and reverence. I am not insensible of the difficulties of the task of worthily discharging the duties of the present occasion. I am but too conscious, how much more successfully it would have been accomplished in other hands; and how little is my own ability to do justice, even to my own feelings, in attempting a sketch of such a man. I have not, however, felt at liberty to decline the part, which has been assigned to me in the commemorations of this day, lest I should be thought wanting in readiness to do homage to one, who was the highest boast and ornament of the profession. There is this consolation, nevertheless, in undertaking the task, that it requires no labored vindication of motives or actions. His life speaks its own best eulogy. It had such a simplicity, purity, consistency, and harmony, that the narrative of the events, in their natural order, invests it with an attraction, which art need not seek to heighten, and friendship may well be content to leave with its original coloring.

Of the great men, who have appeared in the world, many have been distinguished by the splendor of their birth or station; many by the boldness or variety of their achievements; and many by peculiarities of genius or conduct, which, from the extraordinary contrasts presented by them, have awakened the curiosity, or gratified the love of novelty, of the giddy multitude. I know not, how it has happened, but so, I fear, the fact will be found to be, that high moral qualities are rarely the passport to extensive popular favor or renown. Nay; a calm and steady virtue, which acts temperately and wisely, and never plunges into indiscretion or extravagance, is but too often confounded with dullness or frigidity of temperament. It seems as if it were deemed the prerogative, if not the attribute, of genius, to indulge itself in eccentricities, and to pass from one extreme to another, leaving behind it the dark impressions of its vices or its follies. The deeper movements of the soul, in the inmost workings of its thoughts, are supposed to display themselves, like volcanoes in the natural world, by occasional explosions, which awe, but at the same time excite, the crowd of eager spectators. They are struck with admiration of what they do not comprehend ; and mistake their own emotions for the presence of superior power. They are bewildered by the shifting exhibition, alternately of brilliant deeds, and debasing passions, of intellectual efforts of transcendent energy, and paradoxes of overwrought ingenuity ; and being unable to fathom the motives or sources of anomalies, they confound extravagance with enterprise, and the dreams of wild ambition with lofty and well considered designs.

And yet, if there is any thing taught us, either by the precepts of Christianity, or the history of our race, it is, that true greatness is inseparable from sound morals ; that the highest wisdom is but another name for the highest talents ; that the genius, which burns with a pure and regulated flame, throws far and wide its beneficent light, to guide and cheer us ; while occasional corruscations serve only to perplex and betray us, or (to borrow the language of poetry) serve but to make the surrounding darkness more visible. The calm and patient researches of Newton and Locke have conferred far more lasting benefits on mankind, than all the achievements of all the mere heroes and conquerors of ancient or modern times. One patriot, like Epaminondas, Scipio, or Washington, outweighs a host of Alexanders, Cæsars, and Napoleons. The fame of Justinian, as a fortunate possessor of the imperial purple, would have long since faded into an almost evanescent point in history, if his memorable Codes of Jurisprudence had not secured him an enviable immortality, by the instruction, which they have imparted to the legislation of all succeeding times. He, who has been enabled by the force of his talents, and the example of his virtues, to identify his own character with the solid interests and happiness of his country ; he, who has lived long enough to stamp the impressions of his own mind upon the age, and has left on record lessons of wisdom for the study and improvement of all posterity ; he, I say, has attained all, that a truly good man aims at, and all, that a truly great man should aspire to. He has erected a monument to his memory in the hearts of men. Their gratitude will perpetually, though it may be silently, breathe forth his praises ; and the voluntary homage paid to his name will speak a language, more intelligible and more universal than any epitaph inscribed on Parian marble, or any image wrought out by the cunning hands of sculpture.

Reflections, like these, naturally crowd upon the mind upon the death of every great man ; but especially of every one, who may be justly deemed a benefactor and ornament of his race. In the present case, there is little occasion to point out the manner or the measure of their application.

JOHN MARSHALL was born on the 24th day of September, 1755, (a little more than eighty years ago,) in the county of Fauquier, in the State of Virginia. His father was Thomas Marshall, a native of the same State, and at the time of his birth, a planter of narrow fortune and retired habits. Of this gentleman, who afterwards served with great distinction during the revolutionary war, having been appointed to the command of one of the Continental Regiments of Infantry, it is proper to say a few words in this place. He was a man of uncommon capacity and vigor of intellect; and though his original education was very imperfect, he overcame this disadvantage by the diligence and perseverance, with which he cultivated his natural endowments; so that he soon acquired, and maintained throughout the course of his life, among associates of no mean character, the reputation of masculine sense, and extraordinary judgment and ability. No better proof, indeed, need be adduced to justify this opinion than the fact, that he possessed the unbounded confidence, respect, and admiration of all his children at that mature period of their lives, when they were fully able to appreciate his worth, and to compare and measure him with other men of known eminence. I have myself often heard the Chief Justice speak of him in terms of the deepest affection and reverence. I do not here refer to his public remarks; but to his private and familiar conversations with me, when there was no other listener. Indeed, he never named his father on these occasions, without dwelling on his character with a fond and winning enthusiasm. It was a theme, on which he broke out with a spontaneous eloquence; and, in the spirit of the most persuasive confidence, he would delight to expatiate upon his virtues and talents.—"My father," (would he say with kindled feelings and emphasis,) "my father was a far abler man than any of his sons. To him I owe the solid foundation of all my own success in life." Such praise from such lips is inexpressibly precious. I know not, whether it be most honorable to the parent, or to the child. It warms, while it elevates our admiration of both. What, indeed, can be more affecting than such a tribute of filial gratitude to the memory of a parent, long after death has set its seal upon his character, and at such a distance of time, as leaves no temptation to pious sorrow to exaggerate what he was, or to excite the imagination to paint what he might have been.

Colonel Marshall had fifteen children, several of whom are still living. Some of them, besides the one of whom I am mainly to speak, have attained high distinction as scholars and statesmen ; and one, whom I do not feel privileged to name, enjoys the reputation of a thorough acquaintance with that most difficult of all studies, the Philosophy of History.

John was the eldest son, and of course was the earliest to engage the solicitude of his father. The means of obtaining any suitable education at the family residence were at that period scanty and inadequate. Fauquier was then a frontier county of the State ; and whoever will carry back his thoughts to the dangers and difficulties of such a local position, far in advance of the ordinary reach of compact population, will readily comprehend the embarrassments and sacrifices, with which it was attended. Colonel Marshall was thus compelled exclusively to superintend the education of all his children ; and perceiving the rapid development of the talents of his eldest son, he gave him a decided taste for the study of English literature, and especially for poetry and history. At the age of twelve, the latter had transcribed the whole of Pope's Essay on Man, and some of his moral essays ; and had committed to memory many of the most interesting passages of that distinguished poet.

The love of poetry, thus awakened in his warm and vigorous mind, soon exerted a commanding influence over it. He became enamoured of the classical writers of the old English school, of Milton, and Shakspeare, and Dryden, and Pope; and was instructed by their solid sense and beautiful imagery. In the enthusiasm of youth, he often indulged himself in poetical compositions, and freely gave up his leisure hours to those delicious dreamings with the muses, which (say, what we may) constitute with many the purest source of pleasure in the gayer scenes of life, and the sweetest consolation in the hours of adversity. It has, indeed, been said by Sir James Mackintosh, that all men of genius delight to take refuge in poetry, from the vulgarity and irritation of business. Without yielding to so general and sweeping a conclusion, it may be truly said, that it is not uncongenial with the highest attributes of genius, and is often found an accompaniment of its nicer sympathies.

One of the best recommendations, indeed, of the early cultivation of a taste for poetry, and the kindred branches of literature, is, that it does not expire with youth. It affords to maturer years a refreshing relaxation from the severe cares of business, and to old age a quiet and welcome employment, always within reach, and always bringing with it, if not the charm of novelty, at least the soothing reminiscences of other days. The votary of the muses may not always tread upon enchanted ground ; but the gentle influences of fiction and song will steal over his thoughts, and breathe, as it were, into his soul the fragrance of a second spring of life.

Throughout the whole of his life, and down to its very close, Mr. Marshall continued to cultivate a taste for general literature, and especially for those departments of it, which had been the favorite studies of his youth. He was familiar with all its light, as well as its more recondite, productions. He read with intense interest, as his leisure would allow, all the higher literature of modern times ; and, especially, the works of the great masters of the art were his constant delight. While the common publications of the day fell from his hands with a cold indifference, he kindled with enthusiasm at the names of the great novelists and poets of the age, and discussed their relative powers and merits, with a nice and discriminating skill, as if he were but yesterday fresh from the perusal of them.

To many persons it may seem strange, that such a love of letters, and especially of works of imagination, should ever be found combined with the severe logic and closeness of thought, which belonged to his character, and gave such a grave cast to all his juridical labors. But the truth is, that the union is far less uncommon in the highest class of minds, than slight observers are apt to suppose. There is not only no incompatibility in pursuits of such opposite tendencies ; but men of genius, more than any other persons, from their lively sensibility to excellence, are prone to have their curiosity awakened by any exhibition of it, in whatever department of knowledge or art it may be displayed. They feel the presence of superior power ; they are touched by the sublime reaches of kindred spirits ; they gaze on the wonders of that workmanship, whose exquisite proportions they understand, and whose difficulties of execution they appreciate. They see the glory of that eminence, which is so proudly won, and so bravely maintained. But they can also measure, what few other persons can, what vast resources and uncounted labors have been exhausted in the attainment. Thus, their sympathies are excited by every triumph of the human intellect ; and the very contrast of their own favorite studies and pursuits with those of others opens upon them new sources of pleasure, in surveying the variety, as well as the magnificence, of human genius. But to return to my narrative.

There being no grammar school in the neighbourhood, young Marshall, at the age of fourteen, was sent for his education about a hundred miles from his home, and was placed under the tuition of Mr. Campbell, a clergyman of great respectability. He remained with him a year, and then returned home, and was placed under the care of a Scotch gentleman, who was just then inducted as pastor of the parish, and resided in his father's family. He pursued his classical studies under the care of this reverend pastor, as long as he resided in the family, which was about a year ; and he had at that time commenced the reading of Livy and Horace. After this period, he was left to his own unassisted diligence ; and his subsequent mastery of the Classics was accomplished without any other aids than his Grammar and Dictionary. He never had the benefit of any instruction in any college, or other public institution ; and his attainments in learning, such as they were, were nourished by the solitary vigils of his own genius. In English literature, he continued to receive the fostering care and assistance of his father, who directed his studies, and contributed, in an eminent degree, to cherish his love of knowledge ; to give a solid cast to his acquirements ; and to store his mind with the most valuable materials. It is to this circumstance, that we are mainly to attribute that decided attachment to the writers of the golden age of English literature, which at all times he avowed, and vindicated with a glowing confidence in its importance, and its superior excellence. His father, too, at this period, was not only a watchful parent, but a most useful and affectionate friend; and he became the constant, as he was also almost the only intelligent, companion of his son. The time, which was not thus passed in the society of his father, he employed in hardy, athletic exercises in the open air. He engaged in field sports; he wandered in the deep woods; he indulged his solitary meditations amidst the wilder scenery of nature; he delighted to brush away the earliest dews of the morning, and to watch the varied magnificence of sunset, until its last beams ceased to play on the dark tops of the noiseless forest. It was to these early habits in a mountainous region, that he probably owed that robust and vigorous constitution, which carried him almost to the close of his life with the freshness and firmness of manhood.

It was about the time, when young Marshall entered on the eighteenth year of his age, that the controversy between Great Britain and her American Colonies, which ended in the establishment of the independence of the latter, began to assume a portentous aspect. It could not fail to engage the attention of all the Colonists, whether they were young, or old, in the retirement of private life, or in the exercise of public political functions. It was a stirring theme of conversation, involving interests of such vast magnitude, and consequences of such enduring influence, that every patriot felt himself called upon by a sense of duty to rouse himself for the approaching exigency. Young Marshall could not be indifferent to it. He entered into the controversy with all the zeal and enthusiasm of a youth, full of the love of his country, and deeply sensible of its rights and its wrongs. Partaking of the spirit and energy of his father, he immediately devoted his time, with a prophetic foresight, to the acquisition of the rudiments of military manœuvres in an independent company of volunteers, composed of gentlemen of the same county, to the training of a company of the militia of the neighbourhood, and to the diligent reading of the political essays of the day. For these animating pursuits he was quite content to relinquish all his literary studies; and the pages of Blackstone's Commentaries, to which he had already begun to direct his ambition, were forgotten amidst the din of arms, and the preparations for open hostilities.

In the summer of 1775 he was appointed the first lieutenant of a company of minute men, who were enrolled for active service, and assembled in battalion at the beginning of the ensuing September. In a few days they were ordered to march into the lower country, for the purpose of defending it against a small predatory force of Regulars commanded by Lord Dunmore, and also of assisting in the relief of Norfolk, with some other provincial troops. Hearing of their approach, Lord Dunmore took an advantageous position on the north side of Elizabeth, near the great bridge, and at a small distance from Norfolk. A battle soon afterwards took place between the opposing bodies, in which the British were repulsed with great gallantry. On this occasion Lieutenant Marshall took an active part, and had a full share of the honors of the day. The Provincials, immediately after the retreat of the British, made their way to Norfolk; and Lieutenant Marshall was present, when that city was set on fire by a detachment from the British ships, then lying in the river.

In July, 1776, he received the appointment of first lieutenant in the eleventh regiment on the Continental establishment; and in the succeeding winter he

16

marched with his regiment to the Middle States, then the scene of an harassing warfare; and in May, 1777, he was promoted to the rank of captain. From this period he remained constantly in service until the close of the year 1779. He was present at the skirmish with the British light infantry at Iron Hill; and he fought in the memorable battles of Brandywine, Germantown, and Monmouth. During this period of his military life, he was often employed to act as Deputy Judge Advocate, a situation, which brought him to a large acquaintance with the officers of the army, by whom he was greatly beloved, and among whom he deservedly acquired an extensive influence. I myself have often heard him spoken of by some of these veterans in terms of the warmest praise. In an especial manner the Revolutionary officers of the Virginia Line (now "few and faint, but fearless still") appeared almost to idolize him, as an old friend and companion in arms, enjoying their unqualified confidence.

It was during his performance of the duties of Judge Advocate, that he for the first time (I believe) became personally acquainted with General Washington, and (I am sure) with Colonel (afterwards General) Hamilton; for both of whom, it needs scarcely to be said, he always entertained the deepest respect, and whose unreserved friendship, at a subsequent period of his life, he familiarly enjoyed. His opinion of Washington is sufficiently manifested in his biography of that great man. Of Hamilton he always spoke in the most unreserved manner, as a soldier and statesman of consummate ability; and in point of comprehensiveness of mind, purity of patriotism, and soundness of principles, as among the first, that had ever graced the councils of any nation. His services to the American Republic he deemed to have been of inestimable value, and such as had eminently conduced to its stability, its prosperity, and its true glory.

There being in the winter of 1779, a great surplus of officers belonging to the Virginia Line, beyond the immediate exigencies of the service, the supernumeraries, among whom was Captain Marshall, were directed to return home, in order to take charge of such men, as the State Legislature might raise for their command. It was in this interval of military inactivity, that he availed himself of the opportunity of attending at William and Mary's College the course of law lectures of Mr. (afterwards Chancellor) Wythe, and the lectures upon natural philosophy of the then president of the college, Mr. (afterwards Bishop) Madison. He left that institution in the summer vacation of 1780; and soon afterwards received the usual license to practice law. In October of the same year he returned to the army, and continued in active service until after the termination of Arnold's invasion of Virginia. Finding, that the same redundancy of officers in the Virginia Line still continued, he then resigned his commission, and addicted himself to the study of his future profession. The Courts of law were suspended in Virginia until after the capture of Lord Cornwallis and his army at the memorable siege at Yorktown. As soon as they were reopened, Mr. Marshall commenced the practice of the law, and soon rose into high distinction at the bar.

In the spring of 1782, he was elected a member of the State Legislature; and, in the autumn of the same year, a member of the State Executive Council. In January, 1783, he married Miss Ambler, the daughter of the then Treasurer of the State, to whom he had become attached, before he quitted the army. With this

18

lady he lived in a state of the most devoted conjugal affection for nearly fifty years ; and her death, not quite three years ago, cast a gloom over his thoughts, from which I do not think he ever fully recovered. About the time of his marriage, he took up his permanent residence in the city of Richmond. In the spring of 1784, he resigned his seat at the council board, in order to devote himself more exclusively to the duties of the bar. He was immediately afterwards elected a member of the Legislature by the County of Fauquier, a tribute of respect from the spot of his nativity the more marked, because he had already ceased to have any thing but a nominal residence there. In 1787, he was elected a member of the Legislature by the County of Henrico ; and he soon embarked in all the perplexing political questions, which then agitated the state.

It is to this period, — between the close of the war of the Revolution, and the adoption of the present constitution of the United States, — that we are to refer the gradual development, and final establishment of those political opinions and principles, which constituted the basis of all the public actions of his subsequent life. He had entered the army with all the enthusiasm of a young man, ardent in the cause of liberty, devoted to his country, glowing with confidence in the wisdom and virtue of the people, and unsuspicious, that they could ever be seduced or betrayed into any conduct, not warranted by the purest public principles. He knew the disinterestedness of his own heart ; and he could not believe, nay he could not even imagine, that it was possible, that a Republic, founded for the common good, should not, at all times and under all circumstances, be exclusively administered for this single purpose. The very suggestion of any doubt upon the subject led him to distrust, not his own judgment, but the intelligence or integrity of those, who ventured to breathe that doubt, even in the softest whispers. He had never heard of the profound remark of a great statesman, that a young man, who was not an enthusiast in matters of government, must possess low and grovelling principles of action ; but that an old man, who was an enthusiast, must have lived to little purpose. He could have learned nothing worth remembering ; or remembered only what was fit to be forgotten. Like the Shepherd in Virgil, in the simplicity of his heart he thought, that all things were at Rome, as they were at Mantua ; — Sic parvis componere magna solebat. Amidst the din of arms, he found no leisure to study the science of government. He deemed it useless to consider, how Liberty was to be enjoyed and protected, until it was won. The contest for national existence was then instant and pressing. The only lights, which were on the paths of the patriot, to guide or instruct him, were those, which glanced from the point of his sword. The midnight hours were to be passed, not in the soft serenities of meditation, but in mounting guard on the outposts ; in stealthy patroles along the lines of the enemy ; or in repelling the deadly attack in the midst of the flashes and the roar of well directed musketry and cannon.

"When I recollect" (said he, in a letter written long afterwards to a friend,) "the wild and enthusiastic notions, with which my political opinions of that day were tinctured, I am disposed to ascribe my devotion to the Union, and to a government competent to its preservation, at least as much to casual circumstances, as to judgment. I had grown up at a time, when the love of the Union, and the resistance to the claims of

Great Britain, were the inseparable inmates of the same bosom; when patriotism and a strong fellow feeling with our suffering fellow citizens of Boston were identical; when the maxim, 'United we stand; divided we fall,' was the maxim of every orthodox American. And I had imbibed these sentiments so thoroughly, that they constituted a part of my being. I carried them with me into the army, where I found myself associated with brave men from different States, who were risking life and every thing valuable, in a common cause, believed by all to be most precious; and where I was confirmed in the habit of considering America as my country, and Congress as my government."

But the times were now arrived, in which the dreams of his early manhood were to be rigidly compared with the sober realities about him. The revolution, with its strong excitements, and its agitations of alternate hopes and fears, had passed away. The national Independence had been achieved; and the feverish and restless activity of the past had given place to a state of languor and exhaustion, which made the advent of peace itself a period of renewed anxieties, and heavier cares. What had been gained by the sword was now to be secured by civil wisdom; by the establishment of wholesome laws, sound institutions, and well regulated government. And deeply and painfully did every lover of his country then feel the truth of the remark of Milton, — "Peace hath her victories, no less renowned than War."

Whoever is well read in our domestic history, cannot have forgotten the dangers and difficulties of those days. The close of the war of the Revolution found the whole country impoverished and exhausted by the necessary expenditures of the contest. Some of the States had made enormous sacrifices to provide their own just contributions for the public service ; and most of them had been compelled to resort to the ruinous expedient of a paper currency, to supply their own immediate wants. The national finances were at the lowest ebb of depression. The Continental Congress had issued more than three hundred millions of paper money, purporting on its face to contain a solemn pledge of the faith of the Union for its due redemption, which pledge had been as notoriously violated. And, indeed, this paper money had sunk to the value of one dollar only for one hundred ; and at last had ceased in fact to circulate at all as currency. The national debt was not only not discharged ; but was without any means of being discharged, even as to the interest due upon it. The army had been disbanded with long arrearages of pay outstanding ; and the discontents of those noble bands, which had saved the country, were listened to, only to be disregarded. The very magnitude of the public evils almost discouraged every effort to redress them. The usual consequences of such a state of things had been fully realized. Private, as well as public, credit was destroyed. Agriculture and commerce were crippled ; manufactures could not, in any strict sense, be said to have an existence. They were in a state of profound lethargy. The little money, which yet remained in specie in the country, was subject to a perpetual drain, to purchase the ordinary supplies from foreign countries. The whole industry of the country was at a stand. Our artisans were starving in the streets, without the means, or the habits of regular employment ; and the disbanded officers of the army found themselves, not only without resources, but without occupation. Under such circumstances, the popular murmurs were not only loud, but deep; and the general distress became so appalling, that it threatened a shipwreck of all our free institutions. In short, we seemed to have escaped from the dominion of the parent country, only to sink into a more galling domestic bondage. Our very safety was felt to be mainly dependent upon the jealousy, or forbearance of foreign governments.

What aggravated all these evils was the utter hopelessness of any effectual remedy under the existing form of the national government; if, indeed, that might be said to deserve the name, which was but the shadow of a government. The union of the States at the commencement of the revolutionary contest was forced upon us by circumstances; and from its nature and objects seemed limited to that precise exigency. The Confederation, which was subsequently framed, was conceived in a spirit of extreme jealousy of national sovereignty, and withal was so feeble and loose in its texture, that reflecting minds foresaw, that it could scarcely survive the revolutionary contest. Yet feeble and loose as was its texture, it encountered the most obstinate opposition at every step of its progress; and it was not finally adopted, until the war was about to close, in 1781. The powers of Congress, under the Confederation, were, for the most part, merely recommendatory, and to be carried into effect only through the instrumentality of the States. It conferred no power to raise revenue, or levy taxes, or enforce obedience to laws, or regulate commerce, or even to command means to pay our public ministers at foreign courts. Congress could make contracts; but could not provide means to discharge them. They could pledge the public faith; but they could not redeem it. They could make public treaties; but every State in the Union might disregard them with impunity. They could enter into alliances; but they could not command men or money to give them vigor. They could declare war; but they could not raise troops; and their only resort was to requisitions on the States. In short, all the powers given by the Confederation, which did not execute themselves without any external aid, were at the mere mercy of the States, and might be trampled upon at pleasure. Even that miserable fragment of sovereignty, the power to levy a tax of five per cent. on imports, in order to pay the public debt, and until it was paid, was solemnly rejected by the States, though asked by Congress in terms of humble intreaty, and the most affecting appeals to public justice.

The result was obvious. Without the power to lay taxes, Congress were palsied in all their operations. Without the power to regulate commerce, we were left to the capricious legislation of every State. Nay more; our trade was regulated, taxed, monopolized, and crippled at the pleasure of the maritime powers of Europe. Every State managed its own concerns in its own way; and systems of retaliation for real or imaginary grievances were perpetually devised and enforced against neighbouring States. So that, instead of being a band of brothers, united in common cause, and guided by a common interest, the States were every where secret or open enemies of each other; and we were on the verge of a border warfare of interminable irritation, and of as interminable mischiefs.

24

Such was the state of things in the times, of which I have been speaking; and, strong as the coloring may seem to those, whose birth is of a later date, it falls far short of a full picture of the actual extent of the evils, which the details of the facts would justify.

It was under these circumstances, that the State Legislatures were constantly called upon by public clamor, and private sufferings, to interpose summary remedies to ward off the hardships of the times. The people, loaded with debts, and goaded on almost to madness by the thickening calamities, demanded measures of relief of the most extravagant nature. The relations of debtor and creditor, always delicate, became every day more embarrassed and more embarrassing. Laws suspending the collection of debts; insolvent laws; instalment laws; tender laws; and other expedients of a like nature, which, every reflecting man knew would only aggravate the evils, were familiarly adopted, or openly and boldly vindicated. Popular leaders, as well as men of desperate fortunes, availed themselves (as is usual on such occasions) of this agitating state of things to inflame the public mind, and to bring into public odium those wiser statesmen, who labored to support the public faith, and to preserve the inviolability of private contracts.

The whole country soon became divided into two great parties, one of which endeavoured to put an end to the public evils by the establishment of an efficient national government; the other adhered to the State sovereignties, and was determined, at all hazards, to resist the increase of the national power. Virginia bore her full share in these political controversies. They were constantly debated in the halls of her

Legislature ; and, whatever might be the fate of any particular debate, the contest was perpetually renewed ; for every victory was but a temporary and questionable triumph ; and every defeat left still enough of hope to excite the vanquished to new exertions. At this distance of time it is scarcely possible to conceive the zeal, and even the animosity, with which the opposing opinions were maintained. The question, whether the Union ought to be continued, or dissolved by a total separation of the States, was freely discussed ; and either side of it was maintained, not only without reproach, but with an uncompromising fearlessness of consequences. Those, who clung to the supremacy of the States, looked without dismay upon a dissolution of the Union ; and felt no compunctions in surrendering it. Those, on the other hand, who deemed the Union the ark of our political safety, without which independence was but a name, shrunk with horror from the thought of its dissolution ; and maintained the struggle with a desperate valor, as the death grapple for constitutional liberty.

It was in such times and under such circumstances, that Mr. Marshall, while yet under thirty years of age, was called upon to take an active part in the legislative deliberations, as well as in the popular meetings, in his native State. "My immediate entrance," said he, in the letter already alluded to, "into the State Legislature opened to my view the causes, which had been chiefly instrumental in augmenting those sufferings [meaning of the army] ; and the general tendency of State politics convinced me, that no safe and permanent remedy could be found, but in a more efficient and better organized general government." Mr. Madison was at that time, and had for some years before been, a member of the State Legislature; and stood forth on all occasions an inflexible and enlightened advocate for the Union; and General Washington was the acknowledged head and supporter of the same principles. Mr. Marshall at once arrayed himself on the side of these great leaders; and while Mr. Madison remained in the Legislature, he gave him a bold and steady support in all the prominent debates. The friendship, which was thus formed between them, was never extinguished. The recollection of their coöperation at that period served, when other measures had widely separated them from each other, still to keep up a lively sense of each other's merits. Nothing, indeed, could be more touching to an ingenuous mind, than to hear from their lips, in their latter years, expressions of mutual respect and confidence; or to witness their earnest testimony to the talents, the virtues, and the services of each other.

It was by this course of action in State Legislation at this appalling period, that Mr. Marshall was disciplined to the thorough mastery of the true principles of free government. It was here, that he learned and practised those profound doctrines of rational, limited, constitutional liberty, from which he never shrunk, and to which he resolutely adhered to the end of his life. It was here, that he became enamoured, not of a wild and visionary Republic, found only in the imaginations of mere enthusiasts as to human perfection, or tricked out in false colors by the selfish, to flatter the prejudices, or cheat the vanity of the people; but of that well balanced Republic, adapted to human wants and human infirmities, in which power is to be held in check by countervailing power; and life, liberty, and property are to be secured by a real and substantial independence, as well as division of the Legislative, Executive, and Judicial departments. It was here, that he learned to love the Union with a supreme, unconquerable love ; — a love, which was never cooled by neglect, or alienated by disappointment ; a love, which survived the trials of adversity, and the still more dangerous trials of prosperity ; — a love, which clung more closely to its object, as it seemed less dear, or less valuable in the eyes of others ; — a love, which faltered not, fainted not, wearied not, on this side the grave. Yes ; his thoughts ever dwelt on the Union, as the first and best of all our earthly hopes. The last expressions, which lingered on his dying lips, breathed forth a prayer for his country.

> " Such in that moment, as in all the past,
> ' O, save my Country, Heaven,' was then his last."

While these exciting discussions were absorbing the whole attention of the State Legislatures, the Confederation was obviously approaching its final dissolution. It had passed the crisis of its fate ; and its doom was fixed. As a scheme of government it had utterly failed ; and the moment was now anxiously expected, when, from mere debility, it would cease to have even a nominal existence, as it had long ceased to have any substantial authority. The friends of the Union determined to make one more and final effort. A Convention was called, which framed the Constitution of the United States ; and it was presented to the people for their ratification or rejection. This measure at once gave rise to new and more violent political controversies ; and the whole current of popular opinion was impetuously hurried into new channels. Parties, for and against the adoption of the Constitution, were immediately organized in every State ; and the lines of political division were for the most part the same, which marked the former parties. Virginia, as a leading State, became the scene of the most active exertions ; and, as many of her gifted and eloquent men were arrayed against the Constitution, so its friends rallied for the approaching struggle with a proportionate zeal and ability.

Mr. Marshall was chosen a member of the Convention of Virginia, which was called to deliberate upon the ratification of the Constitution, under circumstances peculiarly gratifying. — A majority of the voters of the County, in which he resided, were opposed to the adoption of it ; and he was assured, that, if he would pledge himself to vote against it, all opposition to his election should be withdrawn ; otherwise he would be strenuously resisted. — He did not hesitate for a moment to avow his determination to vote for the Constitution. To use his own language — "The questions, which were perpetually recurring in the State Legislatures ; and which brought annually into doubt principles, which I thought most sacred ; which proved, that every thing was afloat, and that we had no safe anchorage ground ; gave a high value in my estimation to that article in the Constitution, which imposes restrictions on the States. — I was consequently a determined advocate for its adoption ; and became a candidate for the Convention." — The opposition to him rallied with great force ; but such was his personal popularity, and the sense of his integrity, or (as in his modesty he chose to express it) "parties had not yet become so bitter, as to extinguish the private affections," that he was chosen by a triumphant majority.

Few assemblies have ever been convened under circumstances of a more solemn and imposing responsibility. It was understood, that the vote of Virginia would have a principal and perhaps decisive influence upon several other States; and for some weeks the question of the adoption of the Constitution hung suspended upon the deliberations of that body. On one side were enlisted the powerful influence of Grayson, the strong and searching sense of George Mason, and the passionate and captivating eloquence of Patrick Henry. On the other side were the persuasive talents of George Nicholas, the animated flow of Governor Randolph, the grave and sententious sagacity of Pendleton, the masculine logic of Marshall, and the consummate skill and various knowledge of Madison. Day after day, during the period of twenty-five days, the debate was continued with unabated ardor and obstinate perseverance. And it was not until it was known, that the Constitution had already been adopted by nine States, (which settled its fate,) that Virginia by the small majority of *ten* votes, reluctantly gave her own voice in its favor.

During the whole of this most arduous and interesting contest the leading debates were principally conducted on opposite sides by Henry and Madison. Mr. Marshall contented himself with a constant support of his leader. But on three great occasions, the debate on the power of taxation, that on the power over the militia, and that on the powers of the Judiciary, he gave free scope to his genius, and argued in their favor with commanding ability. The printed sketches of all these debates are confessedly loose, and imperfect, and do little justice to the eloquence or ability of the respective speakers. Yet with all their imperfections the most careless observer cannot fail to perceive, in what is attributed to Mr. Marshall on these occasions, the

30

closeness of logic, the clearness of statement, and the comprehensiveness of principles, which characterized his labors in the maturer periods of his life. I regret, that the brief space of time, allowed for the present notices, does not justify me in the citation of some passages to illustrate these remarks.

It is difficult, perhaps it is impossible, for us of the present generation to conceive the magnitude of the dangers, which then gathered over our country. Notwithstanding all the sufferings of the people, the acknowledged imbecility, nay the absolute nothingness of the Confederation, and the desperate state of our public affairs, there were men of high character, and patriots too, who clung to the Confederation with an almost insane attachment. They had been so long accustomed to have all their affections concentrated upon the State Governments, as their protection against foreign oppression, that a National Government seemed to them but another name for an overwhelming despotism. We have lived to see all their fears and prophecies of evil scattered to the winds. We have witnessed the solid growth and prosperity of the whole country, under the auspices of the National Government, to an extent never even imagined by its warmest friends. We have seen our agriculture pour forth its various products, created by a generous, I had almost said, a profuse industry. The miserable exports, scarcely amounting in the times, of which I have been speaking, in the aggregate, to the sum of one or two hundred thousand dollars, now almost reach to forty millions a year in a single staple. We have seen our commerce, which scarcely crept along our noiseless docks, and stood motionless and withering, while the breezes of the ocean moaned through the crevices of our ruined wharves and deserted warehouses, spread its white canvass in every clime ; and, laden with its rich returns, spring buoyant on the waves of the home ports ; and cloud the very shores with forests of masts, over which the stars and the stripes are gallantly streaming. We have seen our manufactures, awakening from a deathlike lethargy, crowd every street of our towns and cities with their busy workmen, and their busier machinery ; and startling the silence of our wide streams, and deep dells, and sequestered valleys. We have seen our wild waterfalls, subdued by the power of man, become the mere instruments of his will, and, under the guidance of mechanical genius, now driving with unerring certainty the flying shuttle, now weaving the mysterious threads of the most delicate fabrics, and now pressing the reluctant metals into form, as if they were but playthings in the hands of giants. We have seen our rivers bear upon their bright waters the swelling sails of our coasters, and the sleepless wheels of our steamboats in endless progress. Nay, the very tides of the ocean, in their regular ebb and flow in our ports, seem now but heralds to announce the arrival and departure of our uncounted navigation. We have seen all these things ; and we can scarcely believe, that there were days and nights, nay, months and years, in which our wisest patriots and statesmen sat down in anxious meditations to devise the measures, which should save the country from impending ruin. The task was, indeed, most arduous ; in which success was far more desired than expected. Obstinate prejudices were to be overcome ; and popular influences were to be resisted. They could scarcely hope for their just rewards, except from a distant posterity. But they were governed by a supreme love of their country, and the

32

consciousness of the inestimable value of the objects, if achieved. Events, indeed, have far outstripped their most sanguine imaginings. By the blessing of Providence we have risen, under the auspices of the Federal Constitution, from a feeble republic to a wide spreading empire. Many of these patriots and statesmen went down to their graves without the consolation of having witnessed the glorious results of their labors. We owe them a debt of gratitude, which can never be repaid. They laid the broad foundations of our government upon public justice, public virtue, and public liberty. They reared the superstructure with consummate skill, and of the most solid materials. It is for us to say, whether it shall remain through all ages an enduring monument of political wisdom ; or, toppling from its height, shall bury under its ruins the glory of the past and the hopes of the future. It can be preserved only by untiring watchfulness. It may be destroyed by popular violence, or the madness of party, or the deeper sappings of corruption. It may, like the fragments of other great empires, (may Heaven avert the evil !) it may

> "Leave a name, at which the world grew pale,
> To point a moral, or adorn a tale."

But these are topics, which, though not inappropriate upon the present occasion, are of themselves of too absorbing an interest to be discussed, as mere incidents in the life of any individual. They may be glanced at in order to do justice to eminent patriotism ; but they essentially belong to that philosophy, which reads in the history of the past lessons of admonition and instruction for the ascertainment of the future. Tacitus in other days arrived at the melancholy conclusion,

Reipublicæ Forma laudari facilius, quam evenire ; vel si evenit, haud diuturna esse potest.*

As soon as the adoption of the Constitution had been secured, Mr. Marshall immediately determined to relinquish public life, and to confine his labors to his profession. To this resolution, which was urged upon him by the claims of a growing family and a narrow fortune, he was not enabled to adhere with the steadfastness, which he wished. The hostility, already evinced against the establishment of the National Government, was soon transferred in Virginia to an opposition to all its leading measures. Under such circumstances, it was natural for the friends of the Constitution to seek to give it a strong support in the State Legislature. Mr. Marshall was accordingly compelled to yield to their wishes, and served as a member from 1788 to 1792. From the time of the organization of the government under President Washington, almost every important measure of his administration was discussed in the Virginia Legislature with great freedom, and no small degree of warmth and acrimony. On these occasions, it fell to the lot of Mr. Marshall to defend these measures, and to maintain the rights, duties, and powers of the National Government against every attack ; and he performed the service with great zeal, independence, and ability. In 1792, he again retired from the State Legislature, and returned to his professional labors with increased activity ; and soon found himself engaged in all the leading causes in the state and national tribunals. The excellent Reports of this period by my lamented friend, Mr. Justice Washington, exhibit ample proofs of his success in argument.†

* Tacitus, Annal. B. 4, n. 15. † See also Mr. Call's Reports.

34

But, although Mr. Marshall was thus for some years withdrawn from public life, yet he was still compelled to take an active part in political discussions. The French Revolution, which at its early dawn had been hailed with universal enthusiasm throughout America, had now burst out into extravagancies and butcheries, which disgraced the cause of liberty, and gave an unbounded license to ferocious mobs and demagogues. The monarchs of Europe, alarmed for their own safety, were soon leagued in a mighty confederacy to crush a revolution, dangerous to the claims of legitimacy, and the stability of thrones. It was easy to foresee, that if their enterprises against France were successful, we, ourselves, should soon have but a questionable security for our own independence. It would be natural after their European triumphs were complete, that they should cast their eyes across the Atlantic, and trace back the origin of the evil to the living example of constitutional liberty in this Western Hemisphere. Under such circumstances, notwithstanding all the excesses of the French Revolution, the mass of the American people continued to take the liveliest interest in it, and to cherish the warmest wishes for its success. These feelings were heightened by the grateful recollection of the services rendered to us by France in our own Revolution ; and the consideration, that she was struggling to relieve herself from oppressions, under which she had been groaning for centuries. In this posture of affairs, there was infinite danger, that we should be driven from the moorings of our neutrality, and should embark in the contest, not only as an ally, but as a party, foremost in the fight, and in the responsibility. We were just recovering from the exhaustion, and poverty, and suffering, consequent upon our own struggle; and the renewal of war would be fraught with immeasurable injuries, not only to our present interests, but to our future national advancement. France saw and felt the nature of our position; and partly by blandishments, and partly by threats, endeavoured to enlist our fortunes, as she had already succeeded in enlisting our feelings, in her favor. The other powers of Europe were not less eager in their gaze, or less determined in their future course. England, herself, had already adopted precautionary measures to compel us to support our neutrality in an open and uncompromising manner, or to assume the state of positive hostilities.

It was under these circumstances, that President Washington, having determined to preserve our own peace, and to vindicate our rights against all the belligerents with an even handed justice, issued his celebrated Proclamation of Neutrality. The whole country was immediately thrown into a flame; and the two great parties, into which we were then divided, engaged, the one in denouncing it, and the other in supporting it, with intense zeal. On this occasion Mr. Marshall found himself, much to his regret, arranged on a different side from Mr. Madison. He resolutely maintained the constitutionality, the policy, nay, the duty of issuing the Proclamation, by oral harangues, and by elaborate writings. For these opinions he was attacked with great asperity in the newspapers and pamphlets of the day, and designated by way of significant reproach, as the friend and coadjutor of Hamilton, a reproach, which at all times he would have counted an honor; but, when coupled (as it was) with the name of Washington, he deemed the highest praise. He defended himself against these attacks with an invincible firmness, and ability, proportioned to the occasion. He drew up a series of resolutions, approving the conduct of the Executive, and carried them by a decided majority at a public meeting of the citizens of Richmond.

The result of this controversy is well known. The administration was sustained in its course by the sober sense of the majority of the nation ; and the doctrine, then so strenuously contested and boldly denounced, has ever since that time been laid up as among the most undisputable of executive rights and duties. Probably, at the present day, not a single statesman can be found, of any influence in any party, who does not deem the measure to have been as well founded in constitutional law, as it was in sound policy.

In the spring of 1795, Mr. Marshall was again returned as a member of the State Legislature, not only without his approbation, but against his known wishes. It was truly an honorable tribute to his merits ; but it was demanded by the critical posture of our public affairs. The treaty with Great Britain, negotiated by that eminent patriot, Mr. Jay, was then the subject of universal discussion. As soon as the ratification of it was known to have been advised by the Senate, the opposition to it broke out with almost unexampled violence. Public meetings were called in all our principal cities for the purpose of inducing the President to withhold his ratification ; and if this step should fail, then to induce Congress to withhold the appropriations necessary to carry the treaty into effect. Such a course, if successful, (it was obvious) would at once involve us in a war with England, and an alliance with France. The denunciations of the treaty were every where loud and vehement. The topics of animadversion were not confined to the policy, or expediency of the principal articles of the treaty. They took a broader range ; and the extraordinary doctrine was advanced and vigorously maintained, that the negotiation of a commercial treaty by the Executive was an infringement of the Constitution, and a violation of the power given to Congress to regulate commerce.

Mr. Marshall took an active part in all the discussions upon this subject. Believing the treaty indispensable to the preservation of peace, and its main provisions beneficial to the United States, and consistent with its true dignity, he addressed himself with the most diligent attention to an examination of all the articles, and of the objections urged against them. It was truly a critical period, not merely for the country, but also in an especial manner for the administration. Many of its sincere friends, from the boldness and suddenness of the attacks upon it, from the inflamed state of the public mind, and from a natural distrust of their own judgment upon topics full of embarassment and novelty, remained in a state of suspense, or timidly yielded themselves to the prejudices of the times. It has been well observed in the biography of Washington, that it is difficult now to review the various resolutions and addresses, to which this occasion gave birth, without feeling some degree of astonishment, mingled with humiliation, on perceiving such proofs of the deplorable fallibility of human reason.

In no State in the Union was a more intense hostility exhibited against the treaty than in Virginia ; and in none were the objections against it urged with more unsparing or impassioned earnestness. The task, therefore, of meeting and overturning them was of no ordinary magnitude, and required the resources of a

38

well instructed mind. In some resolutions passed at a meeting of the citizens of Richmond, at which Mr. Chancellor Wythe presided, the treaty was denounced "as insulting to the dignity, injurious to the interest, dangerous to the security, and repugnant to the Constitution of the United States." At a meeting of the same citizens, subsequently held, Mr. Marshall introduced certain resolutions in favor of the conduct of the Executive, and supported them in a masterly speech; the best comment upon which is, that the resolutions were approved by a flattering majority.

But a more difficult and important duty remained to be performed, It was easily foreseen, that the controversy would soon find its way into the State Legislature, and would there be renewed with all the bitter animosity of party spirit. So odious was the treaty in Virginia, that Mr. Marshall's friends were exceedingly solicitous, that he should not engage in any legislative debates on the subject, as it would certainly impair his well earned popularity, and might even subject him to some rude personal attacks. His answer to all such suggestions uniformly was, that he would not bring forward any measure to excite a debate on the subject; but if it were brought forward by others, he would at all hazards vindicate the administration, and assert his own opinions. The subject was soon introduced by the opposition; and, among other things, the constitutional objections were urged with triumphant confidence. Especially was that objection pressed, which denied the constitutional right of the Executive to conclude a commercial treaty, as a favorite and unanswerable position. The speech of Mr. Marshall on this occasion has always been represented as one of the noblest efforts of his genius. His vast powers of reasoning were displayed with the most gratifying success. He demonstrated, not only from the words of the Constitution and the universal practice of nations, that a commercial treaty was within the scope of the constitutional powers of the Executive ; but that this opinion had been maintained and sanctioned by Mr. Jefferson, by the Virginia delegation in Congress, and by the leading members of the Convention on both sides. The argument was decisive. The constitutional ground was abandoned ; and the resolutions of the assembly were confined to a simple disapprobation of the treaty in point of expediency.

The constitutional objections were again urged in Congress, in the celebrated debate on the Treaty in the spring of 1796 ; and there finally assumed the mitigated shape of a right claimed by Congress, to grant or withhold appropriations to carry treaties into effect. The higher ground, that commercial treaties were not, when ratified by the Senate, the supreme law of the land, was abandoned ; and the subsequent practice of the government has, without serious question, been under every administration, in conformity to the construction vindicated by Mr. Marshall. The fame of this admirable argument spread through the Union. Even with his political enemies, it enhanced the estimate of his character ; and it brought him at once to the notice of some of the most eminent statesmen, who then graced the councils of the nation.

In the winter of 1796, Mr. Marshall visited Philadelphia, to argue before the Supreme Court the great case of Ware *v.* Hylton, which involved the question of the right of recovery of British debts, which had been confiscated during the revolutionary war. It is well known, that the question was decided against

40

the side, on which Mr. Marshall was employed. On this occasion he was opposed by three of the ablest lawyers, then belonging to the Pennsylvania bar. This was, of itself, under such circumstances, no small distinction. But the sketch of the argument delivered by him, as we find it in the printed Reports, affords conclusive evidence of his juridical learning, and the great skill, with which he arranged his materials, and sustained the interests of his client.

It was during this visit, that he became personally acquainted with the distinguished men, who were then in Congress, as Representatives from the Northern States. "I then became acquainted," says he, in a letter to a friend, "with Mr. Cabot, Mr. Ames, Mr. Dexter, and Mr. Sedgwick of Massachusetts, Mr. Wadsworth of Connecticut, and Mr. King of New York. I was delighted with these gentlemen. The particular subject (the British Treaty) which introduced me to their notice, was at that time so interesting, and a Virginian, who supported, with any sort of reputation, the measures of the government, was such a *rara avis*, that I was received by them all with a degree of kindness, which I had not anticipated. I was particularly intimate with Mr. Ames, and could scarcely gain credit with him, when I assured him, that the appropriations would be seriously opposed in Congress." The event proved, that he was right. The high opinion, which he then formed of these gentlemen, continued to be cherished by him through all his future life.

About this period President Washington offered him the office of Attorney General of the United States; but he declined it on the ground of its interference with his far more lucrative practice in Virginia.

He continued, however, in the State Legislature ; but he rarely engaged in the debates, except when the measures of the National Government were discussed, and required vindication. Nor were the occasions few, in which this task was required to be performed with a steady confidence. One of them shall be mentioned in his own words. "It was, I think," said he, "in the session of 1796, that I was engaged in a debate, which called forth all the strength and violence of party. Some Federalist moved a resolution, expressing the high confidence of the House in the virtue, patriotism, and wisdom of the President of the United States. A motion was made to strike out the word *wisdom*. In the debate the whole course of the Administration was reviewed, and the whole talent of each party was brought into action. Will it be believed, that the word was retained by a very small majority ? A very small majority in the Legislature of Virginia acknowledged the wisdom of General Washington ! "

Upon the recall of Mr. Monroe, as Minister to France, President Washington solicited Mr. Marshall to accept the appointment, as his successor ; but he respectfully declined it for the same reasons as he had the office of Attorney General ; and General Pinckney, of South Carolina, was appointed in his stead. "I then thought," said he, "my determination to remain at the bar unalterable. My situation at the bar appeared to me to be more independent, and not less honorable, than any other ; and my preference for it was decided."

But he was not long permitted to act upon his own judgment and choice. The French Government refused to receive General Pinckney ; and Mr. Adams, (who had then succeeded to the Presidency,) from an

42

anxious desire to exhaust every measure of conciliation, not incompatible with the national dignity, in June, 1797, appointed Mr. Marshall, General Pinckney, and Mr. (afterwards Vice-President) Gerry, Envoys Extraordinary to the Court of France. After no inconsiderable struggles in his own mind, (which are fully developed in a paper now in my possession,) Mr. Marshall accepted the appointment; and proceeded to Paris, and there, with his colleagues, entered upon the duties of the mission. It is well known, that the mission was unsuccessful; the French Government having refused to enter into any negotiations. The preparation of the official despatches addressed to that Government upon this occasion was confided to Mr. Marshall; and these despatches have been universally admired. They are models of skilful reasoning, clear illustration, accurate detail, and urbane and dignified moderation. They contain a most elaborate review of all the principles of national law, applicable to the points in controversy between the two Nations. As State Papers, there are not in the annals of our diplomacy any, upon which an American can look back with more pride, or from which he can draw more various instruction.

On his return home Mr. Marshall resumed his professional business, and had the best reasons to believe, that it would be increased rather than diminished by his temporary absence. He was determined to pursue it with renewed ardor. But from this determination he was again diverted by a personal appeal made to him by General Washington, who earnestly insisted, that he should become a candidate for Congress. After a conversation between them of the deepest interest and animation, and breathing on each side a spirit of the purest patriotism, Mr. Marshall reluctantly yielded to the wishes of General Washington, and became a candidate; and was elected after a most ardent political contest; and took his seat in Congress in December, 1799. While he was yet a candidate, President Adams offered him the seat on the Bench of the Supreme Court, then vacant by the death of Mr. Justice Iredell. He immediately declined it; and it was conferred on that excellent magistrate, Mr. Justice Washington.

The Session of Congress in the winter of 1799 and 1800 will be for ever memorable in our political annals. It was the moment of the final struggle for power between the two great political parties, which then divided the country, and ended, as is well known, in the overthrow of the federal administration. Men of the highest talents and influence were there assembled, and arrayed in hostility to each other; and were excited by all the strongest motives, which can rouse the human mind, the pride of power, the hope of victory, the sense of responsibility, the devotion to principles deemed vital, and the bonds of long political attachment and action. Under such circumstances, (as might naturally be expected,) every important measure of the administration was assailed with a bold and vehement criticism; and was defended with untiring zeal and firmness. Mr. Marshall took his full share in the debates; and was received with a distinction proportioned to his merits. Such a distinction, in such a body, is a rare occurrence; for years of public service and experience are usually found indispensable to acquire and justify the confidence of the House of Representatives.

It is not my intention to enter into a minute detail of the debates, in which Mr. Marshall took a part, or to vindicate his votes or opinions. That duty is more

44

appropriate for a different labor. On one occasion, however, he took a leading part in a most important debate, which acquired for him a wide public fame, and therefore requires notice in this place. I allude to the debate on the case of Thomas Nash, otherwise called Jonathan Robbins, who had been surrendered to the British Government for trial for a supposed murder, committed by him on board of a British ship of war. Certain Resolutions were brought forward, censuring the conduct of the Executive for this act, in terms of decided disapprobation, as unconstitutional and improper. Mr. Marshall in the course of the debate delivered a speech in vindication of the right and duty of the Executive to make the surrender, which placed him at once in the first rank of constitutional statesmen. The substance of it is now in print. It is one of the most consummate juridical arguments, which was ever pronounced in the Halls of Legislation ; and equally remarkable for the lucid order of its topics, the profoundness of its logic, the extent of its research, and the force of its illustrations. It may be said of that Speech, as was said of Lord Mansfield's celebrated Answer to the Prussian Memorial, it was *Reponse sans replique*, an answer so irresistible, that it admitted of no reply. It silenced opposition, and settled then, and for ever, the points of national law, upon which the controversy hinged. The Resolutions did not, indeed, fall lifeless from the Speaker's table, though they were negatived by a large majority. But a more unequivocal demonstration of public opinion followed. The denunciations of the Executive, which had hitherto been harsh and clamorous every where throughout the land, sunk away at once into cold and cautious whispers only of disapprobation. Whoever reads that Speech even at this distance of time, when the topics have lost much of their interest, will be struck with the prodigious powers of analysis and reasoning, which it displays ; and which are enhanced by the consideration, that the whole subject was then confessedly new in many of its aspects.

In May, 1800, President Adams, without any personal communication with Mr. Marshall, appointed him Secretary of War. Before, however, he was called to enter upon the duties of that office, the known rupture took place between the President and Col. Pickering ; and Mr. Marshall was appointed Secretary of State in the stead of the latter. The appointment was every way honorable to his merits ; and no one doubted, that he was eminently qualified for the discharge of its arduous and important duties.

And, here, I cannot but take great pleasure in recording a circumstance equally honorable to all the parties concerned. Without intending in the slightest degree to enter upon the discussion of the controversy between the President and Col. Pickering, I may be permitted to say, that the circumstances, necessarily attending the dismissal of the latter from office, were calculated to awaken a strong sense of injustice in the mind of an officer of unquestionable integrity and patriotism. The rupture grew out of a serious difference of opinion upon very grave political measures ; and Mr. Marshall entertained a serious attachment to the views of the President. Under such circumstances, it would have been not unnatural, that the late Secretary should have felt some prejudices against his successor ; and that there should have been some withdrawal of mutual confidence and perhaps respect between them. No such event occurred. On the contrary, each to the day of his death spoke of the other in terms of enviable

46

commendation ; and their mutual frank and familiar friendship was never in the slightest manner interrupted. I have often listened to the spontaneous praise bestowed on Mr. Marshall by Col. Pickering, (a man to whom might justly be applied the character — Incorrupta fides, nudaque veritas, et mens conscia recti) in his own peculiar circle of friends with unmixed delight. It was full, glowing, and affecting. It was a tribute from one of such sincerity of thought and purpose, that praise, even when best deserved, came from his lips with a studied caution of language. His conversation, always instructive, on these occasions rose into eloquence, beautiful, nay, touched with a moral sublimity. When all the circumstances are considered, I think, that I do not over estimate the value of this example of mutual confidence and friendship, when I pronounce it as gratifying, as it is rare. It prostrates in the dust all petty rivalry for public distinction. It shows, that great minds, (and perhaps great minds only,) fully understand that exquisite moral truth, that no man stands in another man's way in the road to honor ; and that the world is wide enough for the fullest display of the virtues and talents of all, without intercepting a single ray of light reflected by any.

On the 31st of January, 1801, Mr. Marshall received the appointment of Chief Justice of the United States. It is due to his memory to state, that it was conferred on him, not only without his own solicitation, (for he had in fact recommended another person for the office,) but by the prompt and spontaneous choice of President Adams upon his own unassisted judgment. The nomination was unanimously confirmed by the Senate ; and the Chief Justice accordingly took his seat on the

Bench at the ensuing term of the Supreme Court. I trust, that I am not violating any private confidence, when I quote from a letter of the distinguished Son of this distinguished Patriot a passage on this subject, to which the whole country will respond without hesitation. It enclosed a judicial commission to a gentleman, now justly enjoying the highest professional reputation ; and says with equal felicity and truth — "One of the last acts of my father's administration was the transmission of a commission to John Marshall, as Chief Justice of the United States. One of the last acts of my administration is the transmission of the enclosed commission to you. If neither of us had ever done any thing else to deserve the approbation of our country, and of posterity, I would proudly claim it of both for these acts, as due to my father and myself." The claim is, indeed, a proud claim to distinction. It has received, as it deserved, the approbation of the whole country. The gratitude of posterity will also do just homage to the sagacity, foresight, disinterestedness, and public spirit of the choice. It was in moral dignity the fit close of a political life of extraordinary brilliancy. In public importance it scarcely yielded to any act of that life, except the motion for the Declaration of Independence. Such honor from such hands was felt to be doubly dear. It was the highest praise from one, whose title to confer it had been earned by long services in the cause of liberty. The names of Adams and Marshall became thus indissolubly connected in the juridical and constitutional history of the country.

From this time until his death the Chief Justice continued in the discharge of the duties of his exalted office with unsullied dignity, and constantly increasing

48

reputation. Notwithstanding his advancing years, no sensible inroad had been made upon his general health, until the last term of the Court, when it was obvious, that his physical strength had passed the utmost stretch of its vigor, and was in a state of rapid decline. His intellectual powers still, however, retained their wonted energy; and, though he was suffering under great bodily pain, he not only bore it with an uncomplaining spirit, but continued to take his full share of the business of the Court. No better proof need be required of his intellectual ability than his opinions, which stand recorded in the last volume of Reports.

At the close of the term he returned to his residence in Virginia; and he was afterwards induced, by the solicitations of his friends, to visit Philadelphia, in the expectation of receiving some aid from the distinguished medical skill of that city. His constitution, however, had become so shattered, that little more remained to be done, during the last weeks of his life, than to smooth the downward path towards the grave. He died on the sixth day of July last past, about six o'clock in the evening, in the arms of his children, without a struggle; and to use the expressive language of one, who was present, his last breath was the softest whisper of a zephyr. Fortunately, by the considerate kindness of his friends, he was spared the knowledge of the death of his eldest son, who lost his life a few days before by a most calamitous accident; an event, which, from the high character of the son, and his strong affection for him, would have filled his last hours with inexpressible anguish.

He was fully aware of his approaching end, and prepared to meet it with a calmness built upon the fixed principles, by which he had regulated his life. Two days only before his death he wrote an Inscription to be placed on his tomb, in the following simple and modest terms : "John Marshall, son of Thomas and Mary Marshall, was born on the 24th of September, 1755, intermarried with Mary Willis Ambler the 3d of January, 1783, departed this life the —— day of —— 18—."

What can be more affecting than these few facts, the only ones, which he deemed in his last moments worth recording ! His birth ; his parentage ; his marriage ; his death ; — His parents, to whose memory he was attached with a filial piety, full of reverence ; — his marriage to the being, whom he had loved with a singleness and devotedness of affection never surpassed ; — his own birth, which seemed principally memorable to him, as it connected him with beings like these ; — his own death, which was but an event to re-unite him with those, who had gone before, in a world, where there should be no more suffering or sorrow ; but kindred souls should dwell together, even as the Angels in Heaven.

I have now finished the narrative of the life of Chief Justice Marshall, a life, which, though unadorned by brilliant passages of individual adventure, or striking events, carries with it, (unless I am greatly mistaken,) that, which is the truest title to renown, a fame founded on public and private virtue. It has happened to him, as to many other distinguished men, that his life had few incidents; and those, which belonged to it, were not far removed from the ordinary course of human events. That life was filled up in the conscientious discharge of duty. It was throughout marked by a wise and considerate propriety. His virtues expanded with the gradual development of his character. They

50

were the natural growth of deep rooted principles, working their way through the gentlest affections, and the purest ambition. No man ever had a loftier desire of excellence; but it was tempered by a kindness, which subdued envy, and a diffidence, which extinguished jealousy. Search his whole life, and you cannot lay your finger on a single extravagance of design or act? There were no infirmities, leaving a permanent stain behind them. There were no eccentricities to be concealed; no follies to be apologized for; no vices to be blushed at; no rash outbreakings of passionate resentment to be regretted; no dark deeds, disturbing the peace of families, or leaving them wretched by its desolations. If here and there the severest scrutiny might be thought capable of detecting any slight admixture of human frailty, it was so shaded off in its coloring, that it melted into some kindred virtue. It might with truth be said, that the very failing leaned to the side of the charities of life; and carried with it the soothing reflection — Non multum abludit imago. It might excite a smile; it could never awaken a sigh.

Indeed, there was in him a rare combination of virtues, such only as belongs to a character of consummate wisdom; a wisdom which looks through this world, but which also looks far beyond it for motives and objects. I know not, whether such wisdom ought to be considered as the cause, or the accompaniment, of such virtues; or whether they do not in truth alternately act upon, and perfect each other.

I have said, that there was in him a rare combination of virtues. If I might venture, upon so solemn an occasion, to express my own deliberate judgment, in the very terms most significant to express it, I should say, that the combination was so rare, that I have never known any man, whom I should pronounce more perfect. He had a deep sense of moral and religious obligation, and a love of truth, constant, enduring, unflinching. It naturally gave rise to a sincerity of thought, purpose, expression, and conduct, which, though never severe, was always open, manly, and straight forward. Yet it was combined with such a gentle and bland demeanour, that it never gave offence; but it was, on the contrary, most persuasive in its appeals to the understanding.

Among Christian sects, he personally attached himself to the Episcopal Church. It was the religion of his early education; and became afterwards that of his choice. But he was without the slightest touch of bigotry or intolerance His benevolence was as wide, as Christianity itself. It embraced the human race. He was not only liberal in his feelings, and principles, but in his charities. His hands were open upon all occasions to succour distress, to encourage enterprise, and to support good institutions.

He was a man of the most unaffected modesty. Although I am persuaded, that no one ever possessed a more entire sense of his own extraordinary talents and acquirements, than he; yet it was a quiet, secret sense, without pride and without ostentation. May I be permitted to say, that, during a most intimate friendship of many, many years, I never upon any occasion was able to detect the slightest tincture of personal vanity. He had no desire for display; and no ambition for admiration. He made no effort to win attention in conversation or argument, beyond what the occasion absolutely required. He sought no fine turns of expression, no vividness of diction, no ornate elegancies

52

of thought, no pointed sentences, to attract observation. What he said was always well said, because it came from a full mind, accustomed to deep reflection; and he was rarely languid, or indifferent to topics, which interested others. He dismissed them without regret; though he discussed them with spirit. He never obtruded his own opinions upon others; but brought them out only, as they were sought, and then with clearness and calmness. Upon a first introduction, he would be thought to be somewhat cold and reserved; but he was neither the one, nor the other. It was simply a habit of easy taciturnity, waiting, as it were, his own turn to follow the line of conversation, and not to presume to lead it. Even this habit melted away in the presence of the young; for he always looked upon them with a sort of parental fondness, and enjoyed their playful wit, and fresh and confident enthusiasm. Meet him in a stage coach, as a stranger, and travel with him a whole day; and you would only be struck with his readiness to administer to the accommodations of others, and his anxiety to appropriate the least to himself. Be with him, the unknown guest at an Inn, and he seemed adjusted to the very scene, partaking of the warm welcome of its comforts, whenever found; and if not found, resigning himself without complaint to its meanest arrangements. You would never suspect, in either case, that he was a great man; far less, that he was the Chief Justice of the United States. But, if perchance, invited by the occasion, you drew him into familiar conversation, you would never forget, that you had seen and heard that "old man eloquent."

He had great simplicity of character, manners, dress, and deportment; and yet with a natural dignity, that suppressed impertinence, and silenced rudeness. His simplicity was never accompanied with that want of perception of what is right, and fit for the occasion; of that grace, which wins respect; or that propriety, which constitutes the essence of refined courtesy. And yet it had an exquisite *naivete*, which charmed every one, and gave a sweetness to his familiar conversations, approaching to fascination. The first impression of a stranger, upon his introduction to him, was generally that of disappointment. It seemed hardly credible, that such simplicity should be the accompaniment of such acknowledged greatness. The consciousness of power was not there; the air of office was not there; there was no play of the lights or shades of rank; no study of effect in tone or bearing. You saw at once, that he never thought of himself; and that he was far more anxious to know others, than to be known by them. You quitted him with increased reverence for human greatness; for in him it seemed inseparable from goodness. If vanity stood abashed in his presence, it was not, that he rebuked it; but that his example showed its utter nothingness.

He was a man of deep sensibility and tenderness; nay, he was an enthusiast in regard to the domestic virutes. He was endowed by nature with a temper of great susceptibility, easily excited, and warm, when roused. But it had been so schooled by discipline, or rather so moulded and chastened by his affections, that it seemed in gentleness, like the distilling dews of evening. It had been so long accustomed to flow in channels, where its sole delight was to give or secure happiness to others, that no one would have believed, that it could ever have been precipitate or sudden in its movements. In truth, there was, to the

54

very close of his life, a romantic chivalry in his feelings, which, though rarely displayed, except in the circle of his most intimate friends, would there pour out itself with the most touching tenderness. In this confidential intercourse, when his soul sought solace from the sympathy of other minds, he would dissolve in tears at the recollection of some buried hope, or lost happiness. He would break out into strains of almost divine eloquence, while he pointed out the scenes of former joys, or recalled the memory of other days, as he brought up their images from the dimness and distance of forgotten years, and showed you at once the depth, with which he could feel, and the lower depths, in which he could bury his own closest, dearest, noblest emotions. After all, whatever may be his fame in the eyes of the world, that, which, in a just sense, was his highest glory, was the purity, affectionateness, liberality, and devotedness of his domestic life. Home, home, was the scene of his real triumphs. There, he indulged himself in what he most loved, the duties and the blessings of the family circle. There, his heart had its full play; and his social qualities, warmed, and elevated, and refined by the habitual elegancies of taste, shed around their beautiful and blended lights. There, the sunshine of his soul diffused its softened radiance, and cheered, and soothed, and tranquillized the passing hours.

May I be permitted also in this presence to allude to another trait in his character, which lets us at once into the inmost recesses of his feelings with an unerring certainty. I allude to the high value, in which he held the female sex, as the friends, the companions, and the equals of man. I do not here mean to refer to the courtesy and delicate kindness, with which he was accustomed to treat the sex; but rather to the unaffected respect, with which he spoke of their accomplishments, their talents, their virtues, and their excellencies. The scoffs and jeers of the morose, the bitter taunts of the satirist, and the lighter ridicule of the witty, so profusely, and often so ungenerously, poured out upon transient follies or fashions, found no sympathy in his bosom. He was still farther above the common place flatteries, by which frivolity seeks to administer aliment to personal vanity, or vice to make its approaches for baser purposes. He spoke to the sex, when present, as he spoke of them, when absent, in language of just appeal to their understandings, their tastes, and their duties. He paid a voluntary homage to their genius, and to the beautiful productions of it, which now adorn almost every branch of literature and learning. He read those productions with a glowing gratitude. He proudly proclaimed their merits, and vindicated on all occasions their claims to the highest distinction. And he did not hesitate to assign to the great female authors of our day a rank, not inferior to that of the most gifted and polished of the other sex. But, above all, he delighted to dwell on the admirable adaptation of their minds, and sensibilities, and affections to the exalted duties assigned to them by Providence. Their superior purity, their singleness of heart, their exquisite perception of moral and religious sentiment, their maternal devotedness, their uncomplaining sacrifices, their fearlessness in duty, their buoyancy in hope, their courage in despair, their love, which triumphs most, when most pressed by dangers and difficulties; which watches the couch of sickness, and smooths the bed of death, and smiles even in the agonies of its own sufferings ; — These, these were the favorite topics of his confidential conversation ; and on these he expatiated with an enthusiasm, which showed them to be present in his daily meditations.

I have hitherto spoken of traits of character, belonging in a great measure to his private life. Upon his public life we may look with equal satisfaction. It was without stain or blemish. It requires no concealment or apology ; and may defy the most critical and searching scrutiny. He was never seduced by the allurements of office to a desertion of his principles. He was never deterred from an open vindication of them by popular clamor, or party cabal ; by thefrowns of power, or the fury of mobs. His ambition took a loftier range. He aspired to that fame, which is enduring, and may justly be conferred by future ages ; not to that fame, which swells with the triumphs of the day, and dies away, long before it can reach the rising generation. To him might be applied the language of another great magistrate* — He wished for popularity ; that popularity, which follows, not that, which is run after ; that popularity, which, sooner or later, never fails to do justice to the pursuit of noble ends by noble means. He would not do, what his conscience told him was wrong, to gain the huzzas of thousands, or the daily praise of all the papers, which came from the press. He would not avoid to do, what he thought was right, though it should draw on him the whole artillery of libels ; all that falsehood or malice could invent, or the credulity of a deluded populace could swallow.

There was throughout his political life a steadfast-

* Lord Mansfield, 4 Burr. R. 2562.

ness and consistency of principle as striking, as they were elevating. During more than half a century of public service, he maintained with inflexible integrity the same political principles, with which he begun. He was content to live *by*, *with*, and *for* his principles. Amidst the extravagancies of parties at different times, he kept on the even tenor of his way with a calm and undeviating firmness, never bending under the pressure of adversity, or bounding with the elasticity of success. His counsels were always the counsels of moderation, fortified and tried by the results of an enlightened experience. They never betrayed either timidity or rashness. He was, in the original, genuine sense of the word, a Federalist — a Federalist of the good old school, of which Washington was the acknowledged head, and in which he lived and died. In the maintenance of the principles of that school he was ready at all times to stand forth a determined advocate and supporter. On this subject he scorned all disguise ; he affected no change of opinion ; he sought no shelter from reproach. He boldly, frankly, and honestly avowed himself, through evil report and good report, the disciple, the friend, and the admirer of Washington and his political principles. He had lived in times, when these principles seemed destined to secure to the party, to which he belonged, an enduring triumph. He had lived to see all these prospects blasted ; and other statesmen succeed with a power and influence of such vast extent, that it extinguished all hopes of any future return to office. Yet he remained unshaken, unseduced, unterrified. He had lived to see many of his old friends pass on the other side ; and the gallant band, with which he had borne the strife, drop away by death, one after another, until it seemed reduced to a handful. Yet he uttered neither a sigh, nor a complaint. When, under extraordinary excitements in critical times, others, with whom he had acted, despaired of the Republic, and were willing to yield it up to a stern necessity, he resisted the impulse, and clung to the Union, and nailed its colors to the mast of the Constitution.

It is no part of my duty or design upon the present occasion to expound, or vindicate his political opinions. That would of itself furnish ample materials for a discourse of a different character. But it is due to truth to declare, that no man was ever more sincerely attached to the principles of free government ; no man ever cherished republican institutions with more singleness of heart and purpose ; no man ever adhered to his country with a stronger filial affection ; no man in his habits, manners, feelings, pursuits, and actions, ever exemplified more perfectly that idol of chivalry, a patriot without fear and without reproach. But, on the other hand, no man was ever more sensible of the dangers incident to free institutions, and especially of those, which threaten our national existence. He saw and felt, where the weaknesses of the Republic lay. He wished, earnestly wished, perpetuity to the Constitution, as the only solid foundation of our national glory and independence. But he foresaw what our course would be ; and he never hesitated to express, what his fears were, and whence the ruin of the Constitution must come, if it shall come at all. In his view, the Republic is not destined to perish, if it shall perish, by the overwhelming power of the National Government ; but by the resisting and counteracting power of the State sovereignties. He thought with another kindred mind, whose vivid language still rings in my ears after many years, as a voice from the dead, that in our Government the centrifugal force is far greater than the centripetal ; that the danger is not, that we shall fall into the sun ; but that we may fly off in eccentric orbits, and never return to our perihelion. Whether his prophetic fears were ill or well founded, Time alone can decide ; — Time, which sweeps away the schemes of man's invention; but leaves immovable on their foundations the eternal truths of nature.

Hitherto, I have spoken of the attributes belonging to his moral character, and the principles, which governed his life and conduct. On these, I confess, that I dwell with a fond and reverential enthusiasm. There was a daily beauty in these, which captivated the more, the nearer they were approached, and the more they were gazed on. Like the softened plays of moonlight, they served to illuminate all objects, at the same time, that they mellowed and harmonized them. But, I am admonished, that the duties of the present occasion require me to dwell rather on his intellectual, than his moral qualities. He stands before us rather as the head of a learned profession, than as a private citizen, or as a statesman.

He was a great man. I do not mean by this, that among his contemporaries he was justly entitled to a high rank for his intellectual endowments, an equal among the master spirits of the day, if not *facile princeps*. I go farther; and insist, that he would have been deemed a great man in any age, and of all ages. He was one of those, to whom centuries alone give birth ; standing out, like beacon lights on the loftiest eminences, to guide, admonish, and instruct future generations, as well as the present. It did not happen to him, as it has happened to many men of celebrity,

60

that he appeared greatest at a distance ; that his superiority vanished on a close survey ; and that familiarity brought it down to the standard of common minds. On the contrary, it required some degree of intimacy fully to appreciate his powers ; and those, who knew him best, and saw him most, had daily reason to wonder at the vast extent and variety of his intellectual resources.

His genius was rather contemplative, than imaginative. It seemed not so much to give direction to his other intellectual powers, as to receive its lead from them. He devoted himself principally to serious and profound studies ; and employed his invention rather to assist philosophical analysis, than to gather materials for ornament, for persuasion, or for picturesque effect. In strength, and depth, and comprehensiveness of mind, it would be difficult to name his superior. He sought for truths far beyond the boundaries, to which inquisitive and even ambitious minds are accustomed to push their inquiries. He traced them out from their first dim lights and paly glimmers, until they stood embodied before him with a clear and steady brightness. His sagacity was as untiring, as it was acute ; and he saw the conclusion of his premises at such vast distances, and through such vast reaches of intermediate results, that it burst upon other minds as a sort of instant, and miraculous induction. It was said by a distinguished political opponent, who had often felt the power of his reasoning, that he made it a rule in argument, never to admit any proposition asserted by the Chief Justice, however plain and unquestionable it might seem to be ; for, if the premises were once admitted, the conclusion, however apparently remote, flowed on with an irresistible certainty. His powers of analysis were, indeed, marvellous. He separated the accidental from the essential circumstances with a subtilty and exactness, which surprised those most, who were accustomed to its exercise. No error in reasoning escaped his detection. He followed it through all its doublings, until it became palpable, and stripped of all its disguises. But, what seemed peculiarly his own, was the power, with which he seized upon a principle or argument, apparently presented in the most elementary form, and showed it to be a mere corollary of some more general truth, which lay at immeasurable distances beyond it. If his mind had been less practical, he would have been the most consummate of metaphysicians, and the most skilful of sophists. But his love of dialectics was constantly controlled by his superior love of truth. He had no vain ambition to darken counsel, or encourage doubt. His aim was conscientiously to unfold truth, as it was, in its simple majesty; to strengthen the foundation of moral, religious, social, political, and legal obligations; and to employ the gifts, with which Providence had entrusted him, to augment human happiness, support human justice, and bind together in an indissoluble union the great interests of human society. In short, if I were called upon to say, in what he intellectually excelled most men, I should say it was in wisdom, in the sense already alluded to; — a wisdom drawn from large, extensive, sound principles and various researches; — a wisdom, which constantly accumulated new materials for thought and action, and as constantly sifted and refined the old. He was not ambitious of literary distinction. But his great work on the life of Washington shows his capacity for historical composition in the most favorable light. It will for ever remain a monument of his skill, sound judgment, and strict impartiality; and must in the future, as in the past, be a standard authority for all other historians.

In contemplating his professional career it cannot for a moment be doubted, that he must have occupied the foremost rank among Advocates. Such accordingly has been his reputation transmitted to us by his contemporaries at the bar. From what has been already said, his powers of argument must have ensured him entire success. In his manner he was earnest, impressive, deliberative; but at the same time far more intent on his matter, than his manner. Never having known him, while he was at the bar, I should have silently drawn the conclusion, that his forensic arguments were more distinguished for masculine sense, solid reasoning, and forcible illustration, than for impassioned appeals, or touching pathos, even when the latter might fairly enlist the judgment of an advocate. But there have been times in private conversations and conferences, in which he has been roused by the interest of the subject to such a glowing strain of animated reasoning, that I am convinced, that he was no stranger to appeals to the heart; and that, when he chose, he could call up from the very depths of the soul its most powerful feelings.

In regard to Eloquence, if by that be merely meant, an ornamented diction, splendor of style, impassioned delivery, and fine flourishes of rhetoric, it could scarcely be said to belong to his forensic addresses. In the view of such a mind as his, there were graver duties to be performed, and more important interests to be secured. He loved the law, as a science, and not as a trade; and felt the full dignity of being a minister at its altars. He deemed himself under deep responsibility, not to his client alone, but to the court, and to the cause of public justice. He studied to know, what the precepts of the law were, that he might apply them to his cause, and not to pervert them to aid the triumph of injustice, or to swell the trophies of cunning, or avarice, or profligacy. His notions of professional morals and obligations were far different from such mean and debasing palterings with conscience. He argued *for* the law, and *with* the law, and *from* the law. He disdained to mislead the court or jury, if he could; and he gave to both on all occasions the support and the instruction of his ample studies.

But if by Eloquence be meant the power to address other men's minds in language expressive and luminous; to present the proper topics of argument in their just order and fullness; to convince the understanding by earnest and sententious appeals; and by the force of reasoning, to disarm prejudices, to subdue passions, and to dissipate popular delusions; — if these be the attributes of eloquence, then, indeed, few men might more justly aspire to such a distinction. I would not claim for him, that he possessed the power to seduce men's understandings by persuasive insinuations, or honied accents; but I affirm, that he withdrew their understandings from the potency of such artifices, so that they fell lifeless at his feet; — telumque imbelle sine ictu. To him may unhesitatingly be applied the language of Cicero, pronounced upon one of the greatest lawyers of Rome, that he possessed a mastery of the highest art of oratory; the art of analyzing, defining, and illustrating a subject; separating the true from the false; and deducing from each the appropriate consequences; — artem, quæ doceret rem universam tribuere in partes, latentem explicare definiendo, obscuram explanare interpretando; ambigua primum videre, deinde distinguere; postremo, habere regulam, quâ vera et falsa judicarentur; et quæ, quibus positis, essent, quæque non essent, consequentia. Hic enim attulit hanc artem, omnium artium maximam, quasi lucem, ad ea, quæ confuse ab aliis aut respondebantur, aut agebantur.*

But it is principally upon his character as a Magistrate, presiding over the highest tribunal of the Nation, that the solid fabric of his fame must rest. And there let it rest; for the foundations are deep, and the superstructure fitted for immortality. Time, which is perpetually hurrying into a common oblivion the flatterers of kings, and the flatterers of the people, the selfish demagogues, and the wary courtiers, serves but to make true greatness better known, by dissolving the mists of prejudice and passion, which for a while conceal its true glory. The life of the Chief Justice extended over a space rare in the annals of jurisprudence; and still more rare is such a life, with the accompaniment of increasing reputation. There was nothing accidental or adventitious in his judicial character. It grew by its own native strength, unaided by the sunshine of power, and unchecked by cold neglect, or unsparing indifference. The life of Lord Mansfield was one of the longest and most splendid in the juridical history of England. That of the Chief Justice was longer, and may fairly rival it in the variety of its labors, in the glory of its achievements, and in its rapid advancement of the science of jurisprudence.

The Chief Justiceship of the United States is a station full of perplexing duties, and delicate responsibili-

* Cicero De Clar. Orator. Cap. 41.

ties, and requiring qualities so various, as well as so high, that no man, conscious of human infirmity, can fail to approach it with extreme diffidence and distrust of his own competency. It is the very post, where weakness, and ignorance, and timidity must instantly betray themselves, and sink to their natural level. It is difficult even for the profession at large fully to appreciate the extent of the labors, the various attainments, the consummate learning, and the exquisite combination of moral qualities, which are demanded to fill it worthily. It has hitherto been occupied only by the highest class of minds, which had been trained and disciplined by a long course of public and professional service for its functions. Jay, Ellsworth, and Marshall, have been the incumbents for the whole period since the adoption of the Constitution ; and their extraordinary endowments have in a great measure concealed from the public gaze the dangers and the difficulties of this dazzling vocation.

There is nothing in the jurisprudence of the States, which affords any parallel or measure of the labors of the National Courts. The jurisprudence of each State is homogeneous in its materials. It deals with institutions of a uniform character. It discusses questions of a nature familiar to the thoughts and employments of the whole profession. The learned advocate, who finds himself transferred, by public favor or superior ability, from the state bar to the state bench, finds the duties neither new, nor embarrassing in their elements or details. He passes over ground, where the pathways are known and measured ; and he finds pleasure in retracing their windings and their passages. He may exclaim with the poet, Juvat iterare labores; and he indulges a safe and generous confidence in his own juridical attainments.

How different is the case in the National Courts! With whatever affluence of learning a Judge may come there, he finds himself at once in a scene full of distressing novelties and varieties of thought. Instead of the jurisprudence of a single State, in which he has been educated and trained, he is at once plunged into the jurisprudence of twenty-four States, essentially differing in habits, laws, institutions, and principles of decision. He is compelled to become a student of doctrines, to which he has hitherto been an entire stranger; and the very language, in which those doctrines are sometimes expressed, is in the truest sense to him an unknown tongue. The words seem to belong to the dialect of his native language; but other meanings are attached to them, either so new, or so qualified, that he is embarrassed at every step of his progress. Nay; he is required in some measure to forget in one cause, what he has learned in another, from its inapplicability or local impropriety; and new statutes, perpetually accumulating on every side, seem to snatch from his grasp the principles of local law, at the moment, when he is beginning to congratulate himself upon the possession of them. Independent of this complicated intermixture of State Jurisprudence, he is compelled to master the whole extent of Admiralty and Prize Law; the public and private Law of Nations; and the varieties of English and American Equity Jurisprudence. To these confessedly Herculean labors he must now add some reasonable knowledge of the Civil Law, and of the Jurisprudence of France and Spain, as they break upon him from the sunny regions of the farthest South. Nor is this all; (though much of what has been already stated must be new to his thoughts) he must gather up the positive regulations of the statutes and treaties of the National Government, and the silent and implied results of its sovereignty and action. He must finally expand his studies to that most important branch of National Jurisprudence, the exposition of constitutional law, demanding, as it does, a comprehensiveness of thought, a calmness of judgment, and a diligence of research, (not to speak of other qualities,) which cannot be contemplated without the most anxious apprehensions of failure. When these various duties are considered, it is scarcely too much to say, that they present the same discouraging aspect of the National Jurisprudence, which Sir Henry Spelman has so feelingly proclaimed of the municipal jurisprudence of England, in his day ; — Molem, non ingentem solum, sed perpetuis humeris sustinendam.

These, however, are but a part of the qualifications required of the man, who holds the office of Chief Justice. He must also possess other rare accomplishments, which are required of one, who, as the Head of the Court, is to preside over its public deliberations, and its private confidential conferences. Patience, moderation, candor, urbanity, quickness of perception, dignity of deportment, gentleness of manners, genius, which commands respect, and learning, which justifies confidence ; — These seem indispensable qualifications to fill up the outlines of the character. While I was yet shadowing them out in my own mind, my eyes insensibly turned (as it were) to the Judicial Hall at Washington, and to the very Chair appropriated to the office. The venerable form of Marshall seemed still seated there ! — It was but a momentary dream ;

68

—I awoke; and found, that I had but sketched the first lines of his portrait.

Yes, this great and good man was all, that we could ask, or even desire for the station. He seemed the very personation of Justice itself, as he ministered at its altars—in the presence of the nation—within the very walls, which had often echoed back the unsurpassed eloquence of the dead, of Dexter, and Pinkney, and Emmett, and Wirt, and of the living also, nameless here, but whose names will swell on the voices of a thousand generations. Enter but that hall, and you saw him listening with a quiet, easy dignity to the discussions at the bar; silent, serious, searching; with a keenness of thought, which sophistry could not mislead, or error confuse, or ingenuity delude; with a benignity of aspect, which invited the modest to move on with confidence; with a conscious firmness of purpose, which repressed arrogance, and overawed declamation. You heard him pronounce the opinion of the Court in a low but modulated voice, unfolding in luminous order every topic of argument, trying its strength, and measuring its value, until you felt yourself in the presence of the very oracle of the law. You heard, (if I may adopt the language applied to another great magistrate on a like occasion) you "heard principles stated, reasoned upon, enlarged, and explained, until you were lost in admiration at the strength and stretch of the human understanding."* Follow him into the conference room, a scene of not less difficult or delicate duties, and you would observe the same presiding genius, the same kindness, attentiveness, and deference; and, yet, when the occasion required, the same

* Mr. Justice Buller, speaking of Lord Mansfield, in Lickbarrow *v.* Mason, 2 Term Rep. 73.

power of illustration, the same minuteness of research, the same severity of logic, and the same untiring accuracy in facts and principles.

It may be truly said of him, as it was of Lord Mansfield, that he excelled in the statement of a case; so much so, that it was almost of itself an argument. If it did not at once lead the hearer to the proper conclusion, it prepared him to assent to it, as soon as it was announced. Nay more; it persuaded him, that it must be right, however repugnant it might be to his preconceived notions. Perhaps no Judge ever excelled him in the capacity to hold a legal proposition before the eyes of others in such various forms and colors. It seemed a pleasure to him to cast the darkest shades of objection over it, that he might show, how they could be dissipated by a single glance of light. He would by the most subtile analysis resolve every argument into its ultimate principles, and then with a marvellous facility apply them to the decision of the cause.

That he possessed an uncommon share of juridical learning, would naturally be presumed, from his large experience and inexhaustible diligence. Yet it is due to truth, as well as to his memory to declare, that his juridical learning was not equal to that of many of the great masters in the profession, living or dead, at home or abroad. He yielded at once to their superiority of knowledge, as well in the modern as in the ancient law. He adopted the notion of Lord Bacon, that "studies serve for delight, for ornament, and for ability,"—"in the judgment and disposition of business." The latter was his favorite object. Hence he "read not to contradict and confute; nor to believe and take for granted; nor to find talk and discourse; but to

70

weigh and consider." And he followed another suggestion of that great man, that "Judges ought to be more learned, than witty; more reverend, than plausible; and more advised, than confident." The original bias, as well as choice, of his mind was to general principles, and comprehensive views, rather than to technical, or recondite learning. He loved to expatiate upon the theory of equity; to gather up the expansive doctrines of commercial jurisprudence; and to give a rational cast even to the most subtile dogmas of the common law. He was solicitous to hear arguments; and not to decide causes without them. And no Judge ever profited more by them. No matter, whether the subject was new or old; familiar to his thoughts, or remote from them; buried under a mass of obsolete learning, or developed for the first time yesterday; whatever was its nature, he courted argument, nay, he demanded it. It was matter of surprise to see, how easily he grasped the leading principles of a case, and cleared it of all its accidental incumbrances; how readily he evolved the true points of the controversy, even when it was manifest, that he never before had caught even a glimpse of the learning, upon which it depended. He seized, as it were by intuition, the very spirit of juridical doctrines, though cased up in the armor of centuries; and he discussed authorities, as if the very minds of the Judges themselves stood disembodied before him.

But his peculiar triumph was in the exposition of constitutional law. It was here, that he stood confessedly without a rival, whether we regard his thorough knowledge of our civil and political history, his admirable powers of illustration and generalization, his scrupulous integrity and exactness in interpretation, or his consummate skill in moulding his own genius into its elements, as if they had constituted the exclusive study of his life. His proudest epitaph may be written in a single line — Here lies the Expounder of the Constitution of the United States.

I am aware of the force of this language; and have no desire to qualify it. The task, which he had to perform, was far different from that, which belongs to the debates in other places, where topics may be chosen, and pressed, or avoided, as the occasion may require. In the forum there is no choice of topics to be urged; there are no passions to be addressed; there are no interests to be courted. Critical inquiries, nice discriminations, severe inductions, and progressive demonstrations are demanded upon the very points, on which the controversy hinges. Every objection must be met, and sifted, and answered, not by single flashes of thought, but by the closest logic, reasoning out every successive position with a copious and convincing accuracy.

Let it be remembered, that, when Chief Justice Marshall first took his seat on the Bench, scarcely more than two or three questions of constitutional law had ever engaged the attention of the Supreme Court. As a science, constitutional law was then confessedly new; and that portion of it, in an especial manner, which may be subjected to judicial scrutiny, had been explored by few minds, even in the most general forms of inquiry. Let it be remembered, that in the course of his judicial life, numerous questions of a practical nature, and involving interests of vast magnitude, have been constantly before the Court, where there was neither guide, nor authority; but all was to be wrought out by general principles. Let it be

72

remembered, that texts, which scarcely cover the breadth of a finger, have been since interpreted, explained, limited, and adjusted by judicial commentaries, which are now expanded into volumes. Let it be remembered, that the highest learning, genius, and eloquence of the bar, have been employed to raise doubts, and fortify objections ; that State sovereignties have stood impeached in their legislation ; and rights of the most momentous nature have been suspended upon the issue ; that, under such circumstances, the infirmities of false reasoning, the glosses of popular appeal, the scattered fire of irregular and inconclusive assertion, and the want of comprehensive powers of analysis, had no chance to escape the instant detection of the profession ; — Let these things (I say) be remembered ; and who does not at once perceive, that the task of expounding the Constitution, under such circumstances, required almost superhuman abilities ? It demanded a mind, in which vast reaches of thought should be combined with patience of investigation, sobriety of judgment, fearlessness of consequences, and mastery of the principles of interpretation, to an extent rarely belonging to the most gifted of our race.

How this gigantic task of expounding the Constitution was met and executed by Chief Justice Marshall, let the Profession, let the Public, decide. Situated as I am, I may not speak for others upon such an occasion. But having sat by his side during twenty-four years ; having witnessed his various constitutional labors ; having heard many of those exquisite judgments, the fruits of his own unassisted meditations, from which the Court has derived so much honor ; — et nos aliquod nomenque decusque gessimus ; — I confess myself unable to find language sufficiently expressive of my admiration and reverence of his transcendent genius. While I have followed his footsteps, not as I could have wished, but as I have been able, at humble distances, in his splendid judicial career, I have constantly felt the liveliest gratitude to that beneficent Providence, which created him for the age, that his talents might illustrate the law, his virtues adorn the bench, and his judgments establish the perpetuity of the Constitution of the country. Such is my humble tribute to his memory. His saltem accumulem donis, et fungar inani munere. The praise is sincere, though it may be perishable. Not so his fame. It will flow on to the most distant ages. Even if the Constitution of his country should perish, his glorious judgments will still remain to instruct mankind, until liberty shall cease to be a blessing, and the science of jurisprudence shall vanish from the catalogue of human pursuits.

And this great Magistrate is now gone — gone, as we trust, to the high rewards of such eminent services. It is impossible to reflect, that the places, which once knew him, shall know him no more, without a sense of inexpressible melancholy. When shall we look upon his like again? When may we again hope to see so much moderation with so much firmness; so much sagacity with so much modesty; so much learning with so much purity; so much wisdom with so much gentleness; so much splendor of talent with so much benevolence; so much of every thing to love and admire, with nothing, absolutely nothing, to regret?

And yet there are some consolations even in so great a loss. Cicero, in mourning over the death of his friend, the great Roman lawyer, Hortensius, did not hesitate to pronounce his death fortunate ; for he died at a moment happy for himself, though most unfortunate for his country. Quoniam perpetuâ quâdam felicitate usus ille, cessit e vitâ, suo, magis quam suorum civium, tempore. Vixit tam diu quam licuit in civitate bene beateque vivere.* We may well apply the like remark to Chief Justice Marshall. He was not cut off in middle life, in the early maturity of his faculties, while he was yet meditating new plans of usefulness or glory. He lived to the very verge of that green old age, after which the physical strength sensibly declines, and the intellectual powers no longer reach their accustomed limits. He retained, to the very last hour of his life, the possession of all these powers in full perfection, without change — nay, without the shadow of change. Such had been his hope, earnestly and frequently expressed to his confidential friends, with deep solicitude ; for no man more than he dreaded to add another to the melancholy lessons :

> " In life's last scenes, what prodigies surprise,
> Tears of the brave, and follies of the wise."

We may well rejoice, therefore, that a life, so long and so useful, should have come to its close without any exhibition of human infirmity. The past is now secure. It is beyond the reach of accident. The future cannot be disturbed by error, or darkened by imbecility. His setting sun loomed out in cloudless splendor, as it sunk below the horizon. The last lights shot up with a soft and balmy transparency, as if the beams, while yet reflected back on this world, were but ushering in the morn of his own immortality.

* Cicero De Clar. Orator. Cap. 1.

ERRATUM.

Page 45, line 27, *for* serious, *read* decided.

Chapter IV

A

COURSE

OF

LEGAL STUDY,

ADDRESSED TO

STUDENTS AND THE PROFESSION GENERALLY;

BY

DAVID HOFFMAN,

JUR. UTR. DOCT. GÖTTINGEN.

Second Edition,

RE-WRITTEN AND MUCH ENLARGED.

IN TWO VOLUMES.

VOL. II.

BALTIMORE:

PUBLISHED BY JOSEPH NEAL.

1836.

Hoffman, David. [*Fifty Rules on*] *Professional Deportment.* From Hoffman, David. *A Course of Legal Study, addressed to Students and the Profession Generally.* Baltimore: Joseph Neal, 1836.

DIVISION IX.

'I do not here confine the name and character of HEROES to warriors and great conquerors; I extend the appellation to all persons who are in a high degree eminent, be they of the Cabinet, or of the Bar, and be they conversant in human or divine literature.'—*Balthsasar Gratian.*

'*L'on ne vaut dans ce monde que ce que l'on veut valoir.*'—LA BRUYERE.

PROFESSIONAL DEPORTMENT.

EVERY one echoes the sentiment of lord Bacon, that 'knowledge is power;' if to this we add the beautiful and correspondent sentiment of a moralist of our own time, that 'virtue is power,' we have the two great principles which, combined, form the only true and solid basis of the 'art of rising in life.' This was, no doubt the idea of the great English philosopher, though the apophthegm, usually quoted from him, speaks of knowledge only; but in this case, the mention of the one was by no means designed as an exclusion of the other. The art of 'self-advancement,' from the days of Solomon to our own, has required the joint co-operation of virtue and of knowledge; and this must ever continue the case, and will become daily more manifest, as the world becomes daily more virtuous and enlightened.

Under the preceding divisions of our work, we have attempted to arrange for the student a choice, yet extensive course of professional reading. Amongst the numerous volumes, &c. we have recommended in the *regular Course*, (few indeed in comparison with the multifarious tomes of the law library, and few even in comparison with those adverted to in our Notes,) we make no doubt of having neglected some in both of these divisions of our work, with whose merit our reading may not have made us acquainted; while of others we have perhaps, spoken in the manner rather suggested by accidental prepossessions, than due to their intrinsic worth. Both of these it has been our anxious desire to avoid; but during the entire progress of our work, having aimed to bring our student gradually on from the smallest beginnings, to the most elevated attainments, we cannot hope to have uniformly preserved the right path. We trust, however, that we may reasonably assume the merit of delineating an outline, which, though it may be partially altered by different tastes, must certainly prove better than the vague, imperfect, and injudicious course which is generally pursued.

It was the wish of correcting this unprofitable plan of legal education, and of redeeming for the student many hours of vain and desultory labour, in a study sufficiently arduous with all the aid of method and selection, that engaged us in the present undertaking—an undertaking which must be performed very ill indeed, not to be productive of decided benefit. It is sufficiently apparent from the tenor of the observations scattered through the foregoing pages, as well as from the nature of the work itself, that while we desire to suggest every encouragement to students, we would offer no hopes to the indolent and the superficial. The most extensive legal acquirements, moreover, gained by the most methodical course of reading, will not make an accomplished and efficient lawyer. The knowledge of and strict adherence to professional deportment, are altogether essential to his honourable and permanent success. Regarding law as a science equally venerable from its objects, and noble from the ingenuity and mental expansion employed and excited in its acquisition and practice, we eagerly desire to see its shrine unprofaned by knavery and ignorance, and its retainers not more eminent from the importance of their functions, than from the *honesty and skill with which they discharge them.* It is true we do not expect that this can ever happen; it is incident to the best things to be the most perverted; and while we may admire and emulate the portraiture which the votaries of law have been found to appropriate to its professors, we must be content to see its dignity often debased by the ignorant, and its liberality by the mercenary. At the same time there are many, we flatter ourselves, who, prompted by an honest passion for distinction, not less than by the hope of emolument, will enter on the study of our favourite science with the spirit and the views we have attempted to inspire; who conceiving of it far differently than as of a confused and arbitrary mass of *dictums* and decisions, regulated by no principles, and reducible to no order—as a means of subsistence degenerating into drudgery from the unscientific and mechanical manner in which it is often pursued, and for the most part more disreputable, indeed, than a mechanical pursuit—will desire to consider its philosophy and reason, and will receive with pleasure every attempt to facilitate their progress by the classification and selection of their reading. He, indeed, who has bestowed on law this kind of consideration—who has contemplated it originating in the first principles of nature and society; ever modified by circumstance, yet ever constant to those principles; ever changing its particular direction, yet never swerving from its general and inevitable objects, the good order and felicity of mankind; he too, who has exercised his genius in discerning the numerous modifications, combinations, and distinctions of its principles, the infinite number of cases seemingly alike, yet widely dissimilar, and all the subtile niceties which seem peculiarly incident to these studies, has not only been employed in the most noble and useful of human sciences, but has pursued the best discipline for invigorating his intellect, and enlarging his capacity for all other profound and useful learning. We do not wonder, therefore, at the partiality of those who remembering, in addition to the elevation of its objects, at once the learning and the skill, the patient research, and the subtile genius, the drudgery and the enterprise, the laborious lucubrations and the ready adroitness, which seem requisite to form the accomplished lawyer, are disposed to exalt it above every other art and science.

It is not our purpose, under the present title, to enter very largely on the *manner* and *conduct* which should distinguish the guardians of the laws of the land, and the champions of the rights of their fellow citizens. We have occasionally, in the course of this work, undertaken to point out what the law *is*, but our chief province has been to designate where the law may *be found*. Under the present Division, therefore, of our subject, we would not be understood as having engaged in the responsible task of defining with minuteness, the conduct of a lawyer in all his various professional relations, best adapted to advance his interests, and to maintain the dignity of his profession: this would, of itself, require a volume; but as the subject is, we may say, almost wholly new, and quite too important to be pretermitted, we shall indulge, in the course of the present title, in some hints, observations and rules, which we hope may prove useful, and be esteemed by none as a departure from the legitimate object of our work, or as savouring of arrogance or of vanity.

We believe that, in most cases, *enlarged knowledge and noble studies* exercise so happy an influence on those who have addicted themselves to them, that treatises and precepts on mere *manner* and *conduct* become comparatively unnecessary to such minds; while to others they are either unintelligible or useless. The very acquisition of liberal knowledge supposes the acquisition of liberal ideas; so that, in most cases, the possession of intellectual power begets correctness in its application to the purposes of life, and the scientific mind is always supposed to derive, from the complexion of its pursuits, more correct, more enlarged, and more *honourable* views, than one of more circumscribed knowledge. Under the influence of these sentiments, we feel less solicitude for the works which we shall have it in our power to select on this topic; especially as the student will ever bear in mind, that notwithstanding the word law is of comprehensive signification, lawyer is still more so; embracing the RICHNESS AND SOLIDITY OF LEARNING, THE PROFUNDITY OF WISDOM, THE PURITY OF MORALS, THE SOUNDNESS OF INTEGRITY, THE ORNAMENTS OF LITERATURE, THE AMIABLENESS OF URBANITY, THE GRACES OF MODESTY, AND, GENERALLY, THE DECORATIONS AND AMENITIES OF LIFE. We have, therefore, under the present division of our Course, designated a few works calculated to augment the student's acquaintance with his own mind and heart, and furnish him with rules for the regulation of his conduct, either as it respects that decorum of manners which maintains 'with an even balance the dignity betwixt ourselves and others;' prudence in every vicissitude and relation of life; or the judicious use of the means best adapted to advance his private fortune, or particular vocation. On these topics, denominated by lord Bacon, *Conversation*, the *Doctrine of various occasions*, and the *Art of rising in life*, the pen of genius and of virtue have been industriously and efficiently employed; but on the peculiar duties and conduct of the lawyer, little that is very valuable, has been written.*

☞ *On the subject of this title, we recommend to the student the following, as the best selection we have been able to make after a very careful examination; and we trust the propriety of the selection will be manifested by our Notes, read previous to the student's perusal of the works themselves.*

SYLLABUS.

1. The Proverbs of Solomon.
2. The Book of Ecclesiastes.
3. The Book of Ecclesiasticus.
4. The Book of Wisdom.

} (*Note* 1.)

*For further remarks on this subject, vide post Note 18. 'Observations on Professional Deportment, with some rules for a Lawyer's conduct through life.' Also, ante Note 13, p. 345. Note 16, p. 358. Note 17, p. 367, &c.

5. **Burgh's Dignity of Human Nature.** [*Book i. part i. the five sections. Part ii. sections* 2, 3, 4, 5, 16. *Book ii. sec.* 8. *Book iii. Introduction and sections*, 7, 8, 9.] (*Note* 2.)

6. **Watts on the Improvement of the Mind.** (*Note* 3.)

e. 7. **Rochefoucault's Maxims or Sentences.** (*Note* 4.)

E. 8. **Laconics; or the Best Words of the Best Authors.** (*Note* 5.)

9. **Bacon De Augmentis Scientiarum.** [*Sections xxiii. xxiv. xxv. Shaw's translation, or the London edition*, 1825, *page* 306 *to* 353—*or the admirable edition of Basil Montague, Esq. London*, 1833.] (*Note* 6.)

E. e. 10. **The 'Hero' of Balthazar Gracian.** (*Note* 7.)

11. **Fielding's Select Proverbs of all Nations.** *London*, 1824. (*Note* 8.)

12. **The Life of a Lawyer; written by himself.** *London*, 1830. (*Note* 9.)

e. 13. **Gisborne's Inquiry into the Duties of Men.** *Chapter ix. 'On the Duties of the Legal Profession, page* 331 *to* 416. (*Note* 10.)

14. **Edgeworth's Essays on Professional Education.** *Chap. vi. page* 318 *to* 410. *London*, 1812. (*Note* 11.)

15. **Quinctilian's Institutes of the Orator.** *Book xii.* (*Note* 12.)

e. 16. **The Barrister.** *Edition of* 1818. (*Note* 13.)

e. 17. **Letters on the Study and Practice of the Law.** *Letter* 35. *'Study of Philosophy.' Letter* 36. *'Of Integrity.' Letter* 37. *'Of*

Urbanity.' Letter 38. *'Of Modesty.' Letter* 39. *'Philosophy useful, &c.'* (*Note* 14.)

18. **Of the Examination of Witnesses.** *Vide Evans' translation of Pothier on Obligations. Vol. ii. sec. ix. page* 223.

19. **Considerations on the viva voce Examination of Witnesses at the English Bar.** (*Note* 15.)

e. 20. **Miller on the Civil Law of England.** *Section ii. 'Of Judges and Practitioners by whom justice is administered,' page* 437 *to* 476. (*Note* 16.)

21. **Bacon's Essays.** (*Note* 17.)

[☞ *Vide* (*Note* 18,) *near the close of this Title, for the author's views on the subject of* PROFESSIONAL DEPORTMENT; *and for a series of* RESOLUTIONS, *recommended to lawyers.*]

NOTES ON THE NINTH DIVISION.

(*Note* 1.) PROVERBS OF SOLOMON, &c.—The wise and sententious proverbs of Solomon, seem to form a proper, and very natural commencement of a course of reading on that moral wisdom which teaches, not only the science, but the true art of being happy, and of promoting our earthly advancement. His learning and wisdom, never equalled, were, no doubt, in part, the result of an experience pre-eminent over that of all who had lived, or perhaps ever will live. A familiar acquaintance with these terse sentences, so pregnant with living truths, seems to be expected, no less in the mere man of the world, than in the moralist and christian. Professor Jahn remarks that the Hebrew word, rendered *proverbs*, and its equivalent in the Arabic, 'do not mean proverbs in the strict sense of the term, but sententious declarations, such as the book really contains, relative to virtue and vice, to the conduct of domestic and public matters, to the education of offspring, to the government of a state, to the duties of children, parents, subjects, judges, magistrates and kings, to good and evil, and to happiness and misery. They are in some respects similar to the Golden Verses of Pythagoras, and to the Proverbs of Lockman and Meidan.'*

For further remarks on the 'Proverbs,' we refer the student to our Note on the Bible at its close; and especially to Holden's beautiful Eulogium on the excellence and utility of these proverbs. We may here remark that Holden is the author of an Attempt towards an Improved Translation of the Proverbs of Solomon, with a Preliminary Dissertation. *London*, 1819. The Book of Proverbs contains thirty-one chapters.

THE BOOK OF ECCLESIASTES, which, for like reasons we have recommended, is also called the 'Book of the Preacher,' the word *Ecclesiastes* being thus rendered and applied to Solomon, one of whose three names was 'Preacher,' which word Holden thinks does not express the full import of the original, but that our language has not a more appropriate word.† This Book, and that of the Proverbs belong to what is called the *First Canon*, concerning the authenticity of which no doubts whatever are entertained, though it is questioned by competent judges who fully admit it to be canonical, whether Solomon be really the author of the Book of Ecclesiastes. Professor Jahn contends for the negative, and Mr. Holden maintains the affirmative. The controversy is of little importance to those who are really in search of the lessons of wisdom. Its twelve chapters are replete with salutary precepts to be as faithfully studied and practised by lawyers and judges, as by divines.

THE BOOK OF ECCLESIASTICUS, also called the 'Book of the Wisdom of Jesus the son of Sirach,' is apocryphal, or

* Vide Jahn's Intro. 452.

† The word 'Solomon,' that illustrious individual's principal name, signifies a *peacemaker*. His second name, 'Idida,' is said to import *beloved of God*, and his third name, 'Ecclesiastes,' a *teacher of wisdom*.

belongs to what is called the *Second Canon.* It is in many respects very similar to the Book of Proverbs; is full of wisdom, apparently the result of much worldly experience, and is evidently the offspring of the purest morality and piety. It is supposed to have been written only about two hundred and eighty-five years before Christ. It contains fifty-one chapters.

THE BOOK OF THE WISDOM OF SOLOMON.—This contains nineteen chapters, and must not be confounded with the other Book of Wisdom, just mentioned. This is also apocryphal. It is very generally admitted to be a production long after the age of Solomon, who is merely introduced, in a manner similar to Socrates, who appears to give the recitations in Plato's treatise De Republicâ.

We have been thus minute in our information respecting these four books of the sacred volume, from two considerations; first, because we are apprehensive that many young men are really under very mistaken impressions as to their value, considered merely as sources of useful worldly knowledge; and secondly, because the more familiar our acquaintance with them has become, the more we are satisfied that for beauty of expression, sublimity of morals, as the results of actual experience, and for an intimate knowledge of man's nature, they are pre-eminent; and that it would be a reproach to any scholar (in law hardly less than in divinity) to attain even the age of twenty-five, without a familiar knowledge, not only of their contents, but of all the learning which appertains to them.*

(*Note* 2.) BURGH'S DIGNITY OF HUMAN NATURE.—We have designated only such parts of this valuable work, as more especially appertain to the present title. The volume, however, is full of instruction and sound sense. The one hundred and twenty miscellaneous directions on the art of conversation, and the two hundred similar directions on propriety of con-

* For further remarks on the general subject of *aphorisms, adages, precepts, apothegms, maxims, laconisms,* vide Notes 4 and 5 on the present Title.

duct, contained in the sixteenth section, page 108, may be regarded as the distillation of nearly the entire work. The rules are laconic and well expressed, full of moral wisdom, and of worldly prudence; and if treasured in the heart and mind, cannot fail to regulate our deportment by a standard, pure, elevated, and practical; whilst they supply an ample and varied fund to embellish discourse, or to serve as themes for more extended reflections on the various duties of life. Dr. Burgh is the author of two other well known works, 'The Art of Speaking,' and 'Political Disquisitions.' He was born in 1714, and died in 1775. His work on the 'Dignity of Human Nature,' has always been a popular production. The third English edition was published in 1812, in one volume, 8vo.

(*Note* 3.) WATTS ON THE IMPROVEMENT OF THE MIND. Among the numerous excellent works of Dr. Watts, none has been read with more pleasure and improvement than the present. It was his singular merit to raise out of chaos, an orderly and beautiful system of logic, freed from the subtleties and learned jargon of the schoolmen; and in his treatise on the *Improvement of the Mind*, he has displayed the same dislike of pedantry and useless refinement. In this work the student will find the soundest rules for the easy acquisition of knowledge. These rules are deduced from an intimate and philosophical acquaintance with man: and form a methodical and admirable system, which, if strictly pursued, cannot fail to infuse a spirit of inquiry and observation, and to regulate and strengthen the faculties which they require. Dr. Johnson, in his life of Dr. Watts, speaks of this book with marked respect. 'Few books have been perused by me with greater pleasure than his *Improvement of the Mind;* of which the radical principles may indeed be found in Locke's *Conduct of the Understanding;* but they are so expanded and ramified by Watts, as to confer on him the merit of a work in the highest degree useful and pleasing. Whoever has the care of instructing others, may be charged with deficiency in his duty, if this book is not recommended.' We may add that the work is valuable, not merely as a guide to the improvement of the mind, but of the heart also; and, as such will be found a useful monitor in regard to deportment in every relation of life. Dr. Watts was born at Southampton, in 1674, and died in 1748. He was the author of the well known treatise on Logic, and of many other works, which have been collected into six volumes, 4to.

(*Note* 4.) ROCHEFOUCAULT'S MAXIMS.—The short and terse maxims of such works as this and others contained in our syllabus, or mentioned in our notes on the present title, often force their practical philosophy on the mind more powerfully than bulky treatises of ethics. It was a no less true than felicitous saying of Swift, that 'abstracts, abridgments, summaries, maxims, &c. have the same use with burning glasses; they collect the diffused rays of wit and learning in authors, and make them point with warmth and quickness upon the reader's imagination.' Seneca thinks that 'he who lays down maxims for the government of our lives, and the control of our passions, obliges human nature, not only in the present, but in all succeeding generations.' Voltaire, whose religion was always bad, but whose morals were often good, remarks in substance, that these sentences of Rochefoucault have contributed, more than any other similar performance, to form the taste of the French people; and further, that his memoirs of the Regency of Anne of Austria are *read*, but that his Maxims or Sentences are *committed to memory*. Lord Chesterfield, whose far famed letters to his son we cannot entirely approve, remarks that 'Rochefoucault's little book of maxims which I would advise you to look into for some moments at least every day of your life, is, I fear, too like and too exact a picture of human nature. I own, it seems to degrade it, but yet my experience does not convince me, that it degrades it unjustly.' To Rochefoucault it has been often objected, that his views of human nature are harsh, and his principles ungenerous. It is true, indeed, that the young mind does not easily admit his unfavourable representations of mankind: yet he is a happy man, who reaches old age, and does not esteem this celebrated writer much more a painter than a caricaturist. He was born in 1613, and died 1680.

(*Note* 5.) LACONICS, &c.—The student must have observed that we have in our language a number of words which import *generically* nearly the same meaning, but which specifically vary their signification, although the precise limits sometimes cannot be well defined: such are the words *aphorism*, *apophthegm*, *proverb*, *rule*, *maxim*, *sentence*, *principle*, *motto*, *adage*, *device*, *precept*, *axiom*, *laconism*, *&c.* They have all, however, a common object,—the condensation of much thought in few and apt words: they convey some lesson, in pointed and impressive language; they are intended to be easily remembered, form much of the riches of popular wisdom,—and, like coins and medals, often serve as historical evidences of manners, customs, opinions, morals, &c. of individuals, classes, and even of nations. They are found in all ages, and among all people; but have been chiefly used, and so continue to be, among people whose information is but little conveyed through the medium of books and of writings. To this remark, however, there have been some signal exceptions; for fashion has sometimes revived and caused them to be much used and sought after by the *elite* of society. In the time of 'good Queen Bess' (if she ever were good) and in those of James and Charles, they were not only appealed to and greatly used in conversation, by men and women of high fashion, but the orators, and statesmen, and philosophers collected them with assiduity from all languages, and made earnest and free use of them, often bringing matters of import to a speedy conclusion by well applied proverbs and aphorisms. We have remarked that they belong to all countries, and to all ages. The seven sages of Greece had each applied to him the merit of first uttering some of these '*wise sayings;*' and Plutarch thinks that 'under the veil of these curious sentences are hid those germs of morals which the masters of philosophy have afterwards developed into so many volumes.' So famous were the Lacedæmonians for this species of tersely expressed philosophy, that their short and pregnant expressions gave rise to one of the words belonging to the *genus* under consideration,—*laconics* and *laconism* being nearly synonymous with aphorisms, proverbs. To the entire genus, however it may be specifically divided, should still belong, as Howel has well expressed it, '*shortness, and salt*,' for when amplified, they necessarily lose much of their strength, and are no longer capable of that popular tradition, and of that daily application which render them so valuable. During the luxurious age of Louis the Fourteenth, so fashionable did proverbs become, that even comedies and ballets were so contrived as to illustrate and enforce them! The best known and most useful of the proverbs were literally *acted*, and by being made, as it were, *visible*, they could not fail to leave an enduring impression.

There are two great classes of proverbs, (using this as the generical word) viz. *local* and *universal.* The first take their rise from the laws, institutions, habits, virtues, vices, employments, and peculiarities of nations,—all of which they may, in a degree, illustrate; and may be aptly cited in confirmation or rejection of the testimony of history. They manifest the peculiar modes of thinking and of acting in communities; showing us the poetical character of one people, the phlegm of another; the nomadic habits of this nation, the retired and fixed habits of that; the wary policy of one, the open and unsuspecting character of another. The truth of this observation is strikingly manifest on reading Burkhardt's Arabic Proverbs, recently published, Kelly's Scottish Proverbs, Sailer's explanation of German Proverbs, the Spanish Proverbs by Oudin, and by Nuñes; and the Italian by Florio, and by Torriano. In these, and indeed in all other collections, the national peculiarities appear in high relief, and are as true to the life and to their originals respectively, as express treatises would be on their history, habits, institutions and morals.

The second class of proverbs, which we have denominated *Universal* are based on the common nature of man and of nations: they go to the heart and to the understanding of all; and though variously expressed according to the idioms of different languages, will be found to be essentially the same in all ages and in all nations. It is a delightful and useful employment, to assure ourselves of the identity of our species by studying these universal proverbs; they show not only that man in all times and in all nations entertained on numerous subjects very similar opinions; but that in similar situations, they resorted to similar modes of enforcing virtue, and of correcting the vices and follies of those around them: and that in so doing, they used expressions of the same import, with no other variation than what is referable to idiom, or to the idiocratic character of the particular people among whom they are found. Were the proverbs of all nations collected, and philosophically classed and explained, it would be a volume rich in thoughts, 'full of the genius, wit, and spirit of nations,' as Bacon well observed,—a volume replete with the elements of moral knowledge, reflecting light on the nature of our species, and a text book to which historians, metaphysicians, moralists, legislators, publicists, and even poets might resort, with the certainty of finding themes, which as Plutarch remarked, they could develope into so many volumes.

Should our student, in after life, be disposed to pursue the subject, beyond the narrow list contained in our syllabus, which might be read in a few days, we now furnish him with the means of so doing, by the following selection of the principal collectors and explainers of proverbs, &c. in various languages and nations, many of which have been translated into English. We would advise, however, that as far as may be practicable, they should be read, if read at all, in the originals, as it is manifest that this species of writing must lose considerably in the translation: but where the language is unknown, readers will still find the translation to answer a very useful and pleasing end. It is proper to add that some of the enumerated works are extremely rare; and are now given as much for the purpose of showing the sense of all nations, as to the value of this source of moral and intellectual instruction, as with any expectation that they will be of much practical use even to the learned and studious lawyer. Most of them, however, are easily attainable, and will be found rich in thought, and varied in entertainment.

LIST OF WORKS ON MAXIMS, APOPHTHEGMS, &c. IN VARIOUS NATIONS.

1. ORIENTAL.—'Apophthegma Ebræorum ac Arabi ex variis auctoribus collecta,' 1591. 'Remarkable Sayings and Maxims of Eastern Nations,' viz. Arabic, Persian, and Turkish, 1695. 'Sentences of Ali, son-in-law to Mahomet,' 1726. 'Anthologia Sententiarum Arabicarum,' 1776. 'Selecta quædam Arabum Adagia,' 1616. 'Proverbiorum Arabicorum Centuriæ, ii. Arabicè et Latine, cum scholiis Josephi Scalegeri, et Thomæ Erpenii.' *Leyd.* 1614, *4to.* 'Burckhardt's Arabic Proverbs; or, the Manners and Customs of the Modern Egyptians.' *London,* 1830. 'Proverbia seu Sententiæ Morales Hebraicæ, et Latine, cum Commentariis Pauli Fagii,' 1542, 1660. 'Les Paroles Remarquable, les Bon Mots, et les Maximes des Orientaux,' par M. Galland, 1694.

2. GREEK.—'Sententiæ vii Sapientium Græciæ, cum Scholiis,' 1528. 'The Sayings of the Seven Wise Men of Greece,' 1547. 'Many Curious Sayings ascribed to Plato,' 1753. 'Adagia Græcorum,' 1615. 'Apostolius' Collection of Proverbs'—original work entitled 'Paræmiæ seu Proverbia.' *Basle,* 1538, *8vo.* and by Paulinus, *Leyden,* 1653. 'The Meditations of the Emperor Marcus Aurelius Antonius;' translated from the Greek. 2 *vols.* 12*mo.* *Glasgow,* 1764. *Bath,* 1792, 1 *vol.* 8*vo.* with learned and judicious notes, by R. Graves. This charming little work was early translated into French, under the title of '*Livre Dore.*' *Paris,* 1531, 4*to.* This work is too little known in our county.

3. ITALIAN.—'A Collection of Italian Proverbs.' *London,* 1598. 'Proverbi Italiani, da Orlando Pescitti.' *Ven.* 1618, 12*mo.* 'Common-Place of Italian Proverbs, and Proverbial Phrases, digested into alphabetical order; illustrated with Notes.' *London,* 1649, 1666, by Gio. Torriano. 'Il Giardino di Recreatione.' 'Six Thousand Proverbs,' by Florio. *London,* 1591. 'Scuola del Vulgo,' da Julio Varini, 1642.

4. SPANISH.—'Refranes o Proverbios Castellanos,' par Cæsar Odin, 1624. 'Proverbes Espagnols traduits en François,' par C. Oudin. *Paris,* 1605. 'A Collection of

Italian and Spanish Proverbs, by Arnoult, under the assumed name of Antoine Dumont.' *Besancon*, 1761. 'Refranes, o Proverbios en Romance.' *Salamanca*, 1555. *Madrid*, 1619.

5. GERMAN.—Bebele's Collection of German Proverbs in the 'Opuscula Bebeliana.' *Strasburg*, 1512, *4to*. 'Blum's Dictionary of German Proverbs.' *Leipsic*, 1782. 'Agricola's Explanation of Four Hundred German Proverbs,' 1530. 'Sailer's Wisdom of the Streets; or, the Meaning and Use of German Proverbs.' *Augsburg*, 1810, (in German.)

6. SWEDISH.—'Maxims and Reflections, translated from the Swedish Language.' *London*, 1791.

7. DUTCH.—'Agron's Handwoordenbock,'—French and Dutch. *Amsterdam*, 1821. 'English and Dutch Dictionary of Words and of Select Proverbs,' 1700.

8. DANISH.—'Danish Proverbs, with a French Translation.' *Copenhagen*, 1761.

9. FRENCH.—'Hecatongraphie, c'est ã dire les Descriptions de cent Figures et Histoires, contenants plusieurs apophthegmes, proverbes, sentences et dictez, tant des anciens que des modernes, par M. Carrozet.' *Paris*, 1538, *8vo*. 'Curiositẽs Françoises,' par Ant. Oudin. *Paris*, 1640, *8vo*. 'Explication de Proverbes François,' par Henry de Bellingen.

10. SCOTTISH.—'Collection of Scottish Proverbs,' by David Ferguson, 1598, 1785. 'A Collection of English and Scottish Proverbs,' by John Ray, 1670, 1721. 'A Complete Collection of Scottish Proverbs,' by James Kelly. *London*, 1721, *8vo*.—1818, *12mo*.

11. ENGLISH.—'John Heywood's Dialogue, conteyninge, the number in effect of, all the Proverbes in the English Tunge,' 1561, 1598, *4to*. 'Bank's Proverbes or Adagies.' *London*, 1539, *8vo*. 'Trusler's Proverbs Exemplified,' 1811, 1813. 'Ray's English Proverbes.' *London*, 1670,—1813, *8vo*. 'Helps for Short Memories, consisting of Maxims, Rules, Proverbial Sayings,' &c. *London*, 1803. 'Moral Maxims, by a Lady.' *London*, 1812. 'Moral Reflections upon Select English Proverbs,' by Oswald Dykes. *London*, 1708. 'Crossing of Proverbs,' &c. 1616. 'Outlandish Proverbs, Sentences,' &c. by Geo. Herbert. *London*, 1651. 'Old English Sayings Newly Expounded,' by J. Taylor. *London*, 1827. 'The Book of Aphorisms, by a Modern Pythagorean. *Glasgow*, 1834.*

12. AMERICAN.—'Franklin's Moral Works.'—*passim*. 'The Prompter; A Commentary on Common Sayings,' &c. *New York*, 1803. 'Moral Encyclopædia,' by Varlẽ. *New York*, 1831. 'The Fragments of the Choice Sayings of Publius Syrus,' vide a work entitled 'The Phœnix.' *New York*, 1835.

* The author is Dr. Robert Macnish, to whom we are indebted for the 'Philosophy of Sleep,' and the 'Anatomy of Drunkenness.'

13. MISCELLANEOUS.—'Two Thousand Maxims, Principles,' &c. 1758. 'Proverbiorum Libellus,' of Polydore Virgil. *Venice*, 1500, *4to*.—[The first of its kind in modern times.] 'Adagia,' by the same. 'Proverbes or Adagies, with newe addicions, gathered out of the Chiliads of Erasmus,' by R. Taverner. *London*, 1547, *8vo*. [a large part being a translation from Publius Syrus, who lived in the time of Augustus] 'Garden of Wysdome, conteyninge the Sayeyngs of Princes, Philosophers,' &c. *London*, 1539. 'Fuller's Adigies, Proverbes, Wise Sentiments, &c. of ancient and Modern times.' *London*, 1732. 'Mavor's Proverbs; or, the Wisdom of all Nations.' *London*, 1804. 'Proverbs chiefly taken from the Adagia of Erasmus, illustrated by examples from the Spanish, Italian and French languages; 1814, 2 *vols*, *8vo*. 'Mapletoft's Proverbs of all Nations,' 1707.

[☞ We again remind the student that the foregoing list is not designed for him; the few works of the kind which we have recommended to him in the Syllabus will be sufficient. But should he in after life have leisure to indulge a fondness for the moral sciences, this more ample list may then serve him a useful purpose.]

(*Note* 6.) LORD BACON'S ADVANCEMENT OF LEARNING.—In his treatise De Dignitate et Augmentis Scientiarum, this great philosopher proposes that, what he calls *self-policy*, or the *art of rising in life*, should be treated scientifically; and, according to his manner, he illustrates his general views by some rules of practical wisdom that might serve as hints to be enlarged into a methodical treatise by any future moral Machiavelian. Speaking of this 'architecture of fortune,' he says, 'we do not report it as a part of knowledge that is absolutely deficient; not but that it is *practised* too much, but it hath not been *reduced to writing*. And therefore, lest it should seem to any not to be comprehensible by axioms, it is requisite that we should set down some heads or passages of it.' He further remarks, 'it may appear, at the first, a new and unwonted argument to teach men how to raise and make their fortune; a doctrine wherein every man perchance will be ready to yield himself a disciple, till he seeth difficulty.'* The golden opinions of Lord Bacon on any subject have been found too

* Adv. of Learn. 323. Vide also Note 17, on this Division.

valuable not to arrest the attention of all subsequent writers. As to the topic under consideration, it is remarkable that there is not a precept, nor an intimation contained in the brief outline of the noble author, which has not been used by the numerous writers who have treated the subject,—none, indeed, with an adoption of the name, or with an express recognition that they have desired to execute the *desideratum* mentioned by Lord Bacon; but, in some cases with an evident eye on the task imposed by this illustrious pioneer, and philosophical prophet.

(*Note* 7.) THE HERO OF BALTHAZAR GRACIAN.—This work seems to have enjoyed, in its day, a very extended reputation. Its editor, Don Lastanosa, speaks of it as having undergone many impressions; been translated into many languages; applauded by the learned and polite of all nations; largely transferred into the works of numerous authors; and, to its greatest glory, placed by Philip IV. of Spain, among his choicest and most valuable books, in the royal museum! There is certainly much wisdom, close thought, accurate observation of man, sound morals, high honour, and practical sense in this volume, and its notes, as presented to the English reader by an Oxford scholar in 1726. It being among the earliest productions of Balthazar Gracian, it fortunately escaped, in a great degree, the extremely vitiated style of his other, once very popular, works, and which strongly marked the prose, as well as poetic productions of Spain, towards the close of the seventeenth century. Gracian, a jesuit in religion and politics, was a man of genius and distinguished learning. For reasons, not entirely known, be published 'El Hero,' in 1637, and subsequently, many other works, under the name of Laurence Gracian. His other works are replete with the *concetti*, and, what has been called, the *Gongorism* of the age,—especially 'El Criticon,' an allegorical picture of human life from the cradle to the grave, in the form of a romance; which, though graced with many uncommon thoughts, and bold displays of genius, is full of every strange affectation and fanciful conceit. His most popular work, and one similar in object with that of the Hero, is the 'Oraculo Manual,' a book of maxims, in which, however, the learned jesuit has been less cautious in manifesting the peculiar tenets of his dangerous school. The Hero and the Oraculo should not be passed over by the scholar in search of moral wisdom, and the art of advancing in life, both of which are so necessary to distinguished eminence in the legal profession. Legal knowledge, of itself, is not sufficient: and though the native virtues of the heart, and the lights of a good understanding may do much, both are strengthened and regulated by the lessons and experience of others, who, to a life of thought and of observation, have availed themselves of much that is valuable in these respects in the morals of Homer, Aristotle, Seneca, Cicero, Plutarch, Tacitus, Esop, Zoroaster, Confucius, Publius, Syrus, and numerous others.

(*Note* 8.) FIELDING'S SELECT PROVERBS OF ALL NATIONS. In this work, among the most modern on the subject, we have an opportunity of comparing many of the most approved proverbs of all nations,—which will be found to illustrate the views we have taken in the preceding Note 5, and to strengthen the claim of these laconics to be regarded as the distillations of practical wisdom. We repeat that judiciously selected proverbs are apt to contain the moral, political, and domestic philosophy of the thinking portion of our species; they originate in close thought and accurate observation, and are transmitted and applied only by minds capable of the like thought and observation.

(*Note* 9.) THE LIFE OF A LAWYER; WRITTEN BY HIMSELF. Those who have read with pleasure and advantage the delightful fiction, in a recent work, entitled 'Diary of a Physician,' will be pleased and edified with the 'Life of a Lawyer,' which no doubt, was conceived by the author, in consequence of the great popularity of the 'Diary.' To the young lawyer this work, though also a fiction, may prove serviceable, as it paints to the life, the eventful occurrences encountered by a young man of talents and worth, who having to contend, in a large capital, with numerous difficulties in his professional career, finally triumphs over them all, and attains the highest and most enduring honours. The hero is Baron Malverne, Lord High Chancellor of England, who once a subordinate in a country attorney's office; by the force of a due share of talent, by great industry, pure morals, and the most uncompromising honour, surmounts poverty, reaps an ample share of the emoluments of his profession, and eventually becomes judge, member of parliament, and lastly, as we have stated, Lord Chancellor. It is a pleasing tale, the moral of which is to show to the young aspirant in the law, that professional eminence, and even the highest distinctions of state are open to all who prove themselves meritorious of them, and that virtue and honour, and industry are the only effectual means of surmounting the difficulties of life, and of reaping the benefits of wealth and of distinction. If this be the case, as it certainly is in a great degree in England, it is still more so in our country, where every man's success is almost strictly in the ratio of his industry, talents and moral worth.

(*Note* 10.) GISBORNE'S INQUIRY.—There is much useful and highly interesting information in this chapter, on many of the important duties of the lawyer and judge. The author commences with a vindication of the legal profession from numerous dishonourable imputations; and shews them to be founded in prejudice and error. Like Quinctilian, he inquires into the kind of causes in which a lawyer may justifiably engage, and treats of the knowledge, habits, dispositions, and morals generally, which should claim his particular regard. His duties prior to, and at the trial of causes, are pointed out, and reasons given why he should not early engage in public employments, particularly as a legislator. The peculiar temptations and duties of the parliamentary and crown lawyer are next treated of, and many sensible observations are made on the highly responsible office of a judge. The whole is comprised in a chapter.

(*Note* 11.) EDGEWORTH'S ESSAYS, &c.—In the chapter in this work, 'Of the Profession of the Law,' there are many excellent thoughts on the discipline and education of law students. We are happy to find the sentiments which we have expressed on these points, in different parts of this Course, corroborated by so judicious a writer as Mr. Edgeworth. He insists on the lawyer's induction to general literature; on the necessity of method; the usefulness of logic; and the propriety of a knowledge of common characters and affairs. In his remarks, also, on the examination of witnesses, and on the uselessness of the usual long apprenticeships in law offices; in his observations on legal memory, and his admiration of Mr. Bentham, we entirely agree with him. This, and the chapter in Gisborne's Inquiry, mentioned in the preceding note, would occupy the student but a few hours, and should by no means be neglected, as they will amply compensate him.

(*Note* 12.) THE TWELFTH BOOK OF QUINCTILIAN'S INSTITUTES OF THE ORATOR.—In our second Division of Auxiliary Subjects, 'Forensic Eloquence and Oratory,' this justly celebrated work was recommended to the student, and we presume has been attentively read, with no less interest than improvement. We desire, however, at this time to attract his particular attention to this twelfth book. Quinctilian, after educating his Orator in all the *learning* of his art, proceeds in this concluding book to enforce the necessity of *good morals*, and prescribes various rules essential to his certain and enduring success. He ingeniously maintains, that there can be no efficient eloquence, unless the speaker be an *honest* man; points out the species of knowledge best adapted to improve the heart, and consequently to advance the orator's skill in the art of speaking; designates the particular dispositions of the mind which should be especially cultivated; speaks of the period in which his orator should commence his career; examines the difficult questions which arise as to the causes which an orator is justified in advocating, and his conduct in their management; dwells on the matters most worthy of regard in *studying* his causes, and particularly those things which he should well observe in *pleading* them; and then concludes with some remarks on the various kinds of eloquence, and the adaptation of each species to the particular cause. It is scarce necessary to state that what is thus addressed to the ancient orator, in respect to morals, conduct, and policy, is equally applicable to lawyers of the present day.

(*Note* 13.) The Barrister.—This is a charming and instructive little volume, manifestly the production of a man of law and of literature, and the offspring of an accomplished and reflecting mind. It is impossible to read this work without catching a portion of that honourable spirit which guides the pen of its author. The philosopher, the orator, and the gentleman should be intimately blended with the lawyer, to constitute that character which it is the desire of the Barrister, and the humble attempt of this Course, to form.

This work was originally published in the 'World;' and is from the pen of Thomas Ruggles, Esq. who republished it in 1792, with considerable additions, and an introduction, in two volumes, 12mo. A second edition, with corrections, appeared in 1818.

(*Note* 14.) Letters on the Study and Practice, &c.—We have not recommended the whole of this volume, though it has been much, and favourably, spoken of. This we believe has been owing, in part, to the opinion entertained by many, that it is from the pen of Sir James Mackintosh. It is sometimes written with eloquence and spirit, but abounds, we think, in verbiage throughout. We are reluctant to believe, that a book so generally wordy, tedious, and declamatory, is the production of that accomplished statesman and scholar. The chapters recommended come properly under the head of professional deportment, and merit an attentive perusal.

(*Note* 15.) CONSIDERATIONS ON THE VIVA VOCE EXAMINATIONS, &c.—This sensible essay, on a highly useful topic, is appended to a work called Deinology, by Hortensius. Scarce any part of a lawyer's professional duty requires more skill and delicacy of management, than the *viva voce* examination of witnesses. Great knowledge of the human character, the art of adapting his manner to its varieties, penetration, equanimity, amiableness, clearness of expression, &c. are requisite in extracting the precise truth from witnesses; and it is one of those arts on which a lawyer's success or discomfiture frequently depends, independently of the intrinsic merits of his cause. It is an art, in which there may be a considerable display of genius; and often more strongly commands the admiration of intelligent observers, than elaborate and eloquent speaking. The ninth section of the second volume of Evan's Pothier is recommended by us in this place, chiefly on account of some useful observations on this topic, addressed to young practitioners; and also on account of some valuable remarks on the subject of scientific evidence. We also here refer the student to Note 18, of the present Division, and particularly to the thirty-fifth, and forty-second Resolutions, for additional observations on matters connected with the present topic.

(*Note* 16.) MILLER'S INQUIRY INTO THE CIVIL LAW OF ENGLAND.—That part of the work which relates to the 'Judges and practitioners by whom justice is administered,' applies to our present subject; but may be recommended rather to statesmen, judges, legislators, and experienced lawyers, than to students or those about to commence their professional career. We have ventured, however, to hope that our work may not be wholly passed over, even by the former.

Mr. Miller's volume is one of that numerous class of valuable publications addressed to the people of England, with the view of pointing out the abuses of the law, and its defects, with suggestions for their amendment. Some of the evils complained of arise from the mistaken and unprofessional deportment, whether of judges, lawyers, officers, &c. The author inquires into the actual state of the Civil Law of England; treats of the constitution of the courts of law and of equity; their defects in organization and in practice; of various errors in the systems of personal and real law, which defects it is his object to remedy; of the means by which his improvements may be most effectually promoted; and, among other things he treats in the section now recommended, of the qualities which should characterize efficient and competent judges; and of the great importance of integrity, elevated honour, and adequate learning in them, as well as in barristers, solicitors, and all other ministers of the laws. The work at large comes more properly under the Fifth Division of Auxiliary Subjects of our Course, as it treats of what is called Codefication. It may not be out of place at this time to state only for those, however, who have taken up our 'Course' at the present point, that many of the nations of Europe, and some of our own states, have been much agitated on the subject of the imperfections and abuses of their systems of jurisprudence, both civil and criminal. In England, as well as on the continent there may be said to be three sects or schools. Some contend that the entire scheme of law is so totally defective or vicious, as well in theory as in practice, that the whole system needs to be remodeled, and reduced to a code, simple, methodical, and wholly freed from the errours of past times. Others admit the existence of partial defects and abuses, and the necessity of amendatory laws—whilst a few, tenacious of all that has been so long consecrated, are unwilling to sanction any changes; any, at least, which are suggested by what is called the Reform Party.*

(*Note* 17.) LORD BACON'S ESSAYS.—These essays are too well known to require a very special notice of them. They were written by their gifted author at various times, and seems

* For further information on this subject we refer the student to the Fifth Division of the Auxiliary Subjects of this Course, ante p. 672.

to have been highly prized by him. In an address to his brother Mr. Anthony Bacon, in 1597, he alludes to their being in the hands of many persons *in manuscriptis;* and to the propriety of publishing them to prevent 'untrue copies;' and justly remarks, that, after examination he finds nothing of them 'contrary or infectious to the state of religion or manners, but rather medicinable.' Subsequently, in his Dedication to the Duke of Buckingham, he remarks, that 'they, of all my other works, have become most current; for that, as it seems, they come home to men's business and bosoms.' The topics, fifty-nine in number, are selected with great judgment, and form a little code of morals, of prudence, and of self-policy, which may be regarded as a valuable chapter of a work on the 'architecture of fortune,' which, in his treatise De Augmentis Scientiarum, he considers as a desideratum, and which, since his time, has never been fully and ably completed in any one treatise devoted to the subject. Remote approaches to it are, perhaps, to be found in 'Burgh's Dignity of Human Nature,' the 'Hero,' of Balthazar Gracian, 'Watts on the Mind,' and 'Rochefoucault's Maxims.'*

(*Note* 18.) OBSERVATIONS ON PROFESSIONAL DEPORTMENT, WITH SOME RULES FOR A LAWYER'S CONDUCT THROUGH LIFE.

We have frequently adverted to the salutary influence which the cultivation of the moral sciences exercises over the mind and heart. The seeds of vice are seldom generated, and are never fully matured in the morning of a life engaged in such studies. Honest resolutions, the offspring of innocence, and exemption from temptation, are generally nourished by those fresh from their books, and who have had but little intercourse with the outer world. It is, however, an undeniable truth, that culpable ambition, false pride, the love of lucre, and even

* Vide Notes 2, 3, 4, and 7, of the present Division.

dishonesty, sometimes make silent, insidious, and almost imperceptible, inroads on the morals, and the virtuous resolutions of young practitioners, especially of those who have neglected to strengthen and establish their native virtues, by a careful study of the reasons and grounds on which they rest, and by which alone they can be preserved. Whilst, therefore, our *science* (which embraces morals) expands the understanding and furnishes the heart with the purest principles of action, it will often be found that the *practice* of our profession is peculiarly calculated to suppress their influence. The solution of this alarming fact lies in the very nature of man, and perhaps in the very nature also of the legal vocation. Its office is, indeed, to adjust the disputes and to preserve the harmony of individuals, and of society; to vindicate the laws of God and of man; and to lessen, or remove all the evils which arise from ignorance and vice. But such an office brings its ministers into a too intimate and dangerous acquaintance with man's depravity; it places them in the midst of temptations; and whilst engaged in rescuing others, they sometimes fall the only lamented victims. The disputes and controversies with which even eminent lawyers are often engaged, are frequently founded on bad, if not the worst of passions. On the one side, or the other, dishonesty sometimes actuates the client; and the indomitable pride of opinion, exacerbated by opposition, may mislead the counsel, and render him blind to the real merits of the controversy. The success of the client is always that of the counsel: the interests and feelings of the latter become in a measure identified with those of the former, and be they meritorious or the reverse, the tie is often of such a nature as to generate the seeds of moral evil. Perhaps in a majority of legal disputes some dereliction of sound morals lies on one side or the other; not that cases do not arise in which the question is honestly and justly disputed by both of the litigant parties. But believing, as we do, that in most cases one of the disputants is *knowingly* in the wrong, the lawyer's vocation must of necessity expose him to some portion of those feelings, and agitating passions which either generate these causes, or protract them to a long and vexatious period. In point of *interest*, also, as well as of feeling, the lawyer is occasionally too intimately connected with his client not to feel the force of those passions which lessen the ardour of virtue. He is made familiar with the artful devices of cunning; the ingenious contrivances of fraud and oppression; the well guarded schemes of the shrewd, artfully made by them to amble on the very confines of dishonesty, yet speciously to avoid an overt breach of morals; and finally, he is compelled to learn the most dangerous of all lessons, viz: the vast power, conferred by intellectual superiority, over the rights and possessions of the ignorant, or the necessitous. And though the lawyer's obligation to be faithful in the discharge of the numerous trusts reposed in him, be of the most solemn and honourable kind, yet the temptations to some indirection are so insidious, so various, and so powerful, that he needs the constant presence of the best guarded, and most confirmed moral principles, to counteract their almost insensible operation.

All this may be regarded by many as an overcharged, and too dark a portrait of the evil enticements which environ and beset the paths of the practising lawyer. But the student must not apply the eulogiums on the moral influences of the science, to those influences which arise in the actual occupations of a busy professional life: and whilst we would repel, with indignation, the opprobrium cast by vulgar prejudice, and traditional error, on the members of our profession; we are sensible that the youthful ministers at the altars of justice have great need, not only for the wisdom of man, but for that which is from above, if they would preserve through life that purity, and perfect exemption from moral contamination, with which they commence their interesting career.

Whilst, therefore, we desire to guard the young practitioner against the dangers to which we have just alluded, we are fully sensible how great is the preservative principle of a highly cultivated mind, and of a legal education based on a careful study of the moral sciences. But added to all this, the very conviction that his vocation is one of peculiarly high trust, and of honourable obligation is, of itself, a strong preventive, and a powerful antidote against temptation; and if religion and morals be not of themselves quite sufficient, the scale will sometimes be turned to the side of virtue, by those principles emphatically denominated *honourable*. We cannot perceive that it is in any degree the dictate of prejudice, when we say, that no other science is so well calculated as the Law, to excite and foster in the mind, the principles of an elevated honour. If the lawyer be subjected to temptations to do wrong, he is also powerfully excited to act fairly and honourably, and to do right. His situation, of all others, is the furthest removed from a negative one. In his intercourse with his professional brethren, and, indeed, with the world generally, he seems peculiarly bound to the observance of the most honourable and refined moral deportment: any known departure from this excites more than ordinary distrust; because, among other reasons, much is expected from his intelligence; and all are, in a degree, interested in his trustworthiness, since his vocation confers on him the capacity of being any one's trustee; or the power of promoting, or of retarding any one's interests. Character, therefore, and the best of manners are to the lawyer invaluable; the former essential, the latter worthy of all cultivation.

In no career is the great importance of courteous, correct, and honourable deportment more strikingly manifest. If the lawyer would *gain* clients, he must be popular with the world around him; if he would *preserve* them he must also be respected by the bench and the bar. Eminent success at the latter depends not solely on learning, eloquence, and sound morals; manners are also of the highest necessity. One who is beloved by his professional brethren, and by the judicial and ministerial officers of the court, soon finds a numerous list of clients, equally adhesive in their attachment, and anxious to promote his welfare and elevation. And if the practitioner should be cautious in his deportment towards clients and the members of the bar, he should be still more so in his intercourse with the court. If loyal to their clients, it is not always easy for counsel, even of the most courteous manners, to prevent collisions with the bench. The unavoidable dependence of the former, on the power of the latter, is apt to generate, in some minds, servility; in others a morbid impatience of control. These extremes should be equally avoided; for, whilst nothing is more ruinous to professional success than ill favour with the court (for clients perceiving it, are apt to magnify its effects) yet a too tame submission to the occasional arrogance, and oppression of judicial sway, is no less so. On this subject we desire not to be misunderstood. Judges are but men, and as such, are sometimes liable to the influences of passion and of prejudice. The most honest and honourable judicial minds can be cast from their pivot by circumstances. The animation of debate, so strong with counsel, is not equally felt by the court. The former is apt to misconceive the latter, and in his zeal becomes, perhaps, unintentionally offensive; the latter, in turn, feels the pride, both of opinion and of office,—an altercation ensues, which generally terminates in the discomfiture of the counsel. If, on the other hand, the court be manifestly in the wrong, and the *amende* be made, the counsel may be the victor, but it is possible he may have purchased success at too great a cost. Such collisions, therefore, ought to be avoided, if possible; but if not, a manly and respectful maintenance of the counsel's rights, becomes essential; and it should be done in such a manner that, whilst it leaves no sting, he may convince the court that as its officer, and his client's patron, he has rights which *must* be protected. It is said of lord Erskine, that whilst always deferential, he was still remarkable for the fearlessness with which he opposed the bench, when in his judgment, the occasion really demanded it. In an instance which occurred with lord Kenyon, *after firmly declining to submit to the court*, the learned counsel, in a decorous manner, explained to his lordship the rule of his conduct at the bar. 'It was the first command and counsel of my youth,' said he, 'always to do what my conscience told me to be my duty, and to leave the consequences to God. I shall carry with me the memory, and I trust, the practice of this paternal lesson to the grave. I have hitherto followed it, and have had no reason to complain, that my obedience to it has been even a temporary sacrifice. I have found it, on the contrary, the road to prosperity and wealth, and I shall point it out as such to my children.' This course, being called for by the occasion, became irresistible: but the practitioner, who is not always an Erskine, (nor the judge a Kenyon) should feel the inward and quiet consciousness that he is in the right, and that the matter is of sufficient moment to take such a stand,—otherwise it may degenerate into captiousness, or assume the appearance of mock heroism. But pass we now to other matters.

Our young lawyer may rest assured that he has every motive for the utmost assiduity in the acquisition of knowledge, and for the most inflexible honour in the practice of his profession. He has proffered to him respect and influence in society, professional reputation, high stations of honour and of profit, and all the goods of intellectual and worldly wealth, in a growing and enlightened republic. If true to himself, most, if not all of these, are within his reach; but his practical motto must be 'Id facere laus est quod decet, non quod licet.' The character of a lawyer who does justice to his profession, may not easily be drawn: but we hold him to be one, whom early education has imbued with the lessons of probity, and habituated to labour and research in all that enlarges and refines the mind, and chastens the heart. He desires to impart lustre to the utility of his learning, by fostering every honourable and amiable affection. He has tasted of the fountains of liberal science, and of polite letters, before entering on his more technical studies, and has thus protected himself from pedantry and narrow views. To this he has subsequently added the sciences most necessary to the purposes of his profession, and obtains over society a large and legitimate control, which he exercises only that he may become in it a more useful member. He is the assertor of right, the accuser of wrong, the protector of innocence, and the terror of crime. He labours not for those alone who can afford the *honorarium*, but for the widow, the fatherless and the oppressed. No prospect of gain will induce him to advise the pursuit of law against right or sober judgment; nor will any man's greatness be a shield against the justice due to his client. If he assist in the enaction of laws, which he may be afterwards called on to vindicate, it is done with an eye solely to his country's good; and whilst he respects its legislature and judiciary, he learns to reverence the constitution more than either. History presents to him the riches of her experience, and he notes, with care, the rudiments, and growth, and revolutions of his science. Rhetoric and logic are weapons by which he imparts to his oratory warmth and grace, force and clearness. From his knowledge of man, he ascertains the real nature of truth; and he loves and cultivates rectitude, for the more useful exercise of his powers. Destitute of these, he is either unprofitable, or mischievous to society,—but endued with them, he is one of its chiefest ornaments, and firmest safeguards.

Admitting, however, our student, (now about to commence the practice) to be a young man of the soundest morals, and of the most urbane, and honourable deportment; it may still be well that he should be fortified with a few rules for his future government. We have been to him (we hope as we intended) a faithful guide through a long course of preparation, and cannot even now feel as if we had fully discharged our duty, unless we leave him a momento of our regard for his welfare, long after he has bid adieu to these volumes, and when he has become fully engaged in all the perils, and honours, and emoluments of an arduous profession. We therefore submit to him the following *Resolutions*, to be adopted by him as guides, never to be departed from, and to which he will ever be faithful. We have preferred to frame them in the manner of resolutions, rather than of *didactic rules*, hoping they may thereby prove more impressive, and be the more likely to be remembered.

RESOLUTIONS

IN REGARD TO

PROFESSIONAL DEPORTMENT.

I. I WILL never permit professional zeal to carry me beyond the limits of sobriety and decorum, but bear in mind, with Sir Edward Coke, that 'if a river swell beyond its banks, it loseth its own channel.'

II. I will espouse no man's cause out of envy, hatred or malice, towards his antagonist.

III. To all judges, when in court, I will ever be respectful: they are the Law's vicegerents; and whatever may be their character and deportment, the individual should be lost in the majesty of the office.

IV. Should judges, while on the bench, forget that, as an officer of their court, I have rights, and treat me even with disrespect, I shall value myself too highly to deal with them in like manner. A firm and temperate remonstrance is all that I will ever allow myself.

V. In all intercourse with my professional brethren, I will be always courteous. No man's passions shall intimidate me from asserting fully my own, or my client's rights; and no man's ignorance or folly shall induce me to take any advantage of him; I shall deal with them all as honourable men, ministering at our common altar. But an act of unequivocal meanness or dishonesty, though it shall wholly sever any personal relation that may subsist between us, shall produce no change in my deportment when brought in *professional* connection with them; my client's rights, and not my own feelings, are then alone to be consulted.

VI. To the various officers of the court I will be studiously respectful, and specially regardful of their rights and privileges.

VII. As a general rule, I will not allow myself to be engaged in a cause to the exclusion of, or even in participation with the counsel previously engaged, unless at his own special instance, in union with his client's wishes: and it must, indeed, be a strong case of gross neglect or of fatal inability in the counsel, that shall induce me to take the cause to myself.

VIII. If I have ever had any connection with a cause, I will never permit myself (when that connection is from any reason severed) to be engaged on the side of my former antagonist. Nor shall any change in the *formal aspect* of the cause, induce me to regard it as a ground of exception. It is a poor apology for being found on the opposite side, that the present is but the *ghost* of the former cause.

IX. Any promise or pledge made by me to the adverse counsel, shall be strictly adhered to by me: nor shall the subsequent instructions of my client induce me to depart from it, unless I am well satisfied it was made in errour; or that the rights of my client would be materially impaired by its performance.

x. Should my client be disposed to insist on captious requisitions, or frivolous and vexatious defences, they shall be neither enforced nor countenanced by me. And if still adhered to by him from a hope of pressing the other party into an unjust compromise, or with any other motive, he shall have the option to select other counsel.

xi. If, after duly examining a case, I am persuaded that my client's claim or defence (as the case may be,) cannot, or rather ought not, to be sustained, I will promptly advise him to abandon it. To press it further in such a case, with the hope of gleaning some advantage by an extorted compromise, would be lending myself to a dishonourable use of legal means, in order to gain a *portion* of that, the *whole* of which I have reason to believe would be denied to him both by law and justice.

xii. I will never plead the Statute of Limitations, when based on the *mere efflux of time;* for if my client is conscious he owes the debt; and has no other defence than the *legal bar*, he shall never make me a partner in his knavery.

xiii. I will never plead, or otherwise avail of the bar of *Infancy*, against an honest demand. If my client possesses the ability to pay, and has no other legal or moral defence than that it was contracted by him when under the age of twenty-one years, he must seek for other counsel to sustain him in such a defence. And although in this, as well as in that of limitation, the *law* has given the defence, and contemplates in the one case, to induce claimants to a timely prosecution of their rights, and in the other, designs to protect a class of persons, who by reason of tender age are peculiarly liable to be imposed on,—yet, in both cases *I shall claim to be the sole judge* (the pleas not being compulsory) of the occasions proper for their use.

XIV. My client's conscience, and my own, are distinct entities: and though my vocation may sometimes justify my maintaining as facts, or principles, in doubtful cases, what may be neither one nor the other, I shall ever claim the privilege of solely judging to what extent to go. In *civil* cases, if I am satisfied from the evidence that the *fact* is against my client, he must excuse me if I do not see as he does, and do not press it: and should the *principle* also be wholly at variance with sound law, it would be dishonourable folly in me to endeavour to incorporate it into the jurisprudence of the country, when, if successful, it would be a gangrene that might bring death to my cause of the succeeding day.

XV. When employed to defend those charged with crimes of the deepest dye, and the evidence against them, whether legal, or moral, be such as to leave no just doubt of their guilt, I shall not hold myself privileged, much less obliged, to use my endeavours to arrest, or to impede the course of justice, by special resorts to ingenuity—to the artifices of eloquence—to appeals to the morbid and fleeting sympathies of weak juries, or of temporizing courts—to my own personal weight of character—nor finally, to any of the over-weening influences I may possess, from popular manners, eminent talents, exalted learning, &c. Persons of atrocious character, who have violated the laws of God and man, are entitled to no such special exertions from any member of our pure and honourable profession; and indeed, to no intervention beyond securing to them a fair and dispassionate investigation of the *facts* of their cause, and the due application of the law: all that goes beyond this, either in manner or substance, is unprofessional, and proceeds, either from a mistaken view of the relation of client and counsel, or from some unworthy and selfish motive, which sets a higher value on professional display and success, than on truth and justice, and the substantial interests of the community. Such an inordinate ambition, I shall ever regard as a most dangerous perversion of talents, and a shameful abuse of an exalted station. The parricide, the gratuitous murderer, or other perpetrator of like revolting crimes, has surely no such claim on the commanding talents of a profession, whose object and pride should be the suppression of all vice, by the vindication and enforcement of the laws. Those, therefore, who wrest their proud knowledge from its legitimate purposes, to pollute the streams of justice, and to screen such foul offenders from merited penalties, should be regarded by all, (and certainly shall be by me,) as ministers at a holy altar, full of high pretension, and apparent sanctity, but inwardly base, unworthy, and hypocritical—dangerous in the precise ratio of their commanding talents, and exalted learning.

XVI. Whatever personal influence I may be so fortunate as to possess, shall be used by me only as the most valuable of my possessions, and not be cheapened, or rendered questionable by a too frequent appeal to its influence. There is nothing more fatal to *weight of character* than its common use; and especially that unworthy one, often indulged in by eminent counsel, of solemn assurances to eke out a sickly and doubtful cause. If the case be a good one, it needs no such appliance; and if bad, the artifice ought to be too shallow to mislead any one. Whether one or the other, such *personal pledges* should be *very sparingly* used, and only on occasions which obviously demand them; for if more liberally resorted to, they beget doubts where none may have existed, or strengthen those which before were only feebly felt.

XVII. Should I attain that eminent standing at the bar, which gives *authority* to my opinions, I shall endeavour, in my intercourse with my junior brethren, to avoid the least display of it to their prejudice. I will strive never to forget the days of my youth, when I too was feeble in the law, and without standing. I will remember my then ambitious aspirations, (though timid and modest,) nearly blighted by the inconsiderate, or rude and arrogant deportment of some of my seniors; and I will further remember that the vital spark of my early ambition might have been wholly extinguished, and my hopes been forever ruined had not my own resolutions, and a few generous acts of some others of my seniors, raised me from my depression. To my juniors, therefore, I shall ever be kind and encouraging; and never too proud to recognize distinctly that, on many occasions it is quite probable their knowledge may be more accurate than my own, and that they with their limited reading and experience have seen the matter more soundly than I with my much reading and long experience.

XVIII. To my clients I will be faithful; and in their causes, zealous and industrious. Those who can afford to compensate me, *must do so;* but I shall never close my ear or heart, because my client's means are low. Those who have none, and who have just causes, are, of all others, the best entitled to sue, or be defended; and they shall receive a due portion of my services, cheerfully given.

XIX. Should my client be disposed to compromise, or to settle his claim, or defence; and especially if he be content with a verdict, or judgment, that has been rendered; or, having no opinion of his own, relies with confidence on mine, I will in all such cases greatly respect his wishes and real interests. The further prosecution, therefore, of the claim, or defence, (as the case may be) will be recommended by me only when, after mature deliberation, I am satisfied that the chances are decidedly in his favour; and I will never forget that the pride of professional opinion on my part, or the spirit of submission, or of controversy (as the case may be) on that of my client, may easily mislead the judgment of both, and cannot justify me in sanctioning, and certainly not in recommending, the further prosecution of what *ought* to be regarded as a hopeless cause. *To keep up the ball* (as the phrase goes,) at my client's expense, and to my own profit, must be dishonourable; and however willing my client may be to pursue a phantom, and to rely implicitly on my opinion, I will terminate the controversy as conscientiously for him, as I would were the cause my own.

XX. Should I not understand my client's cause, after due means to comprehend it, I will retain it no longer, but honestly confess it, and advise him to consult others, whose knowledge of the particular case, may probably be better than my own.

XXI. The wealthy, and the powerful shall have no privilege against my client, that does not equally appertain to others. None shall be so great as to rise, even for a moment, above the just requisitions of the law.

XXII. When my client's *reputation* is involved in the controversy, it shall be, if possible, judicially passed on. Such cases do not admit of compromise; and no man's elevated standing shall induce me to consent to such a mode of settling the matter: the *amende* from the great and wealthy, to the ignoble and poor, should be free, full, and open.

XXIII. In all small cases in which I may be engaged, I will as conscientiously discharge my duty, as in those of magnitude; always recollecting that 'small' and 'large' are to clients, relative terms, the former being to a poor man, what the latter is to a rich one,—and, as a young practitioner, not forgetting that large ones, which we have not, will never come, if small ones, which we have, are neglected.

XXIV. I will never be tempted, by any pecuniary advantage, however great, nor be persuaded by any appeal to my feelings, however strong, to purchase, in whole, or in part, my client's cause. Should his wants be pressing, it will be an act of humanity to relieve them myself, if I am able; and if not, then to induce others to do so. But in no case will I permit either my benevolence, or avarice,—his wants or his ignorance, to seduce me into any participation of his *pending* claim or defence. Cases may arise in which it would be mutually advantageous thus to bargain; but the experiment is too dangerous, and my rule too sacred to admit of any exception, persuaded as I am that the relation of client and counsel, to be preserved in absolute purity, must admit of no such privilege, however guarded it may be by circumstances. And should the special case, alluded to arise, better would it be that my client should suffer, and I lose a great and honest advantage, than that any discretion should exist in a matter so extremely liable to abuse, and so dangerous in precedent.

And though I have thus strongly worded my resolution, I do not thereby mean to repudiate, as wholly inadmissible, the taking of *contingent fees*,—on the contrary, they are sometimes perfectly proper, and are called for by public policy, no less than by humanity. The distinction is very clear. A claim or defence may be perfectly good in law, and in justice, and yet the expenses of litigation would be much beyond the means of the claimant or defendant—and equally so as to counsel, who if not thus contingently compensated, in the ratio of the risk, might not be compensated at all. A contingent fee looks to professional compensation only on the final result of the matter in favour of the client. None other is offered, or is attainable. The claim or defence never can be made without such an arrangement; it is voluntarily tendered, and necessarily accepted or rejected *before* the institution of any proceedings.

It flows not from the influence of counsel over client, both parties have the option to be off; no expenses have been incurred; no moneys have been paid by the counsel to the client; the relation of borrower and lender, of vendor and vendee, does not subsist between them,—but it is an independent contract for the services of counsel, to be rendered for the contingent avails of the matter to be litigated. Were this denied to the poor man, he could neither prosecute, nor be defended. All of this differs essentially from the object of my resolution, which is against *purchasing*, in whole or in part, my client's rights, after the relation of client and counsel, in respect to it, has been fully established—after the strength of his case has become known to me—after his total pecuniary inability is equally known—after expenses have been incurred which he is unable to meet—after he stands to me in the relation of debtor,—and after he desires *money from me* in exchange for his pending rights. With this explanation, I renew my resolution, never *so to purchase* my *client's* cause, in whole, or in part,—but still reserve to myself, on proper occasions, and with proper guards, the professional privilege, (denied by no law among us,) of agreeing to receive a contingent compensation, *freely offered*, for services *wholly to be* rendered, and when it is *the only* means by which the matter can either be prosecuted, or defended. Under all other circumstances I shall regard contingent fees as obnoxious to the present resolution.

XXV. I will retain no client's funds beyond the period in which I can with safety and ease, put him in possession of them.

XXVI. I will on no occasion blend with my own, my client's money: if kept *distinctly as his*, it will be less liable to be considered *as my own*.

XXVII. I will charge for my services what my judgment and conscience inform me is my due, and nothing more. If that be withheld, it will be no fit matter for *arbitration;* for no one but myself can adequately judge of such services, and after they are successfully rendered, they are apt to be ungratefully forgotten. I will then receive what the client offers, or the laws of the country may award,—but in either case, he must never hope to be again my client.

XXVIII. As a general rule, I will carefully avoid what is called the '*taking of half fees.*' And though no one can be so competent as myself to judge what may be a just compensation for my services,—yet, when the *quiddam honorarium* has been established by usage or law, I shall regard as eminently dishonourable all *underbidding* of my professional brethren. On such a subject, however, no inflexible rule can be given to myself, except to be invariably guided by a lively recollection that I belong to an honourable profession.

XXIX. Having received a retainer for contemplated services, which circumstances have prevented me from rendering, I shall hold myself bound to refund the same, as having been paid to me on a consideration which has failed; and, as such, subject to repetition, on every principle of law, and of good morals,—and this shall be repaid not merely at the instance of my client, but *ex mero motu.*

XXX. After a cause is finally disposed of, and all relation of client and counsel seems to be for ever closed, I will not forget that it once existed; and will not be inattentive to his just request that all of his papers may be carefully arranged by me, and handed over to him. The execution of such demands, though sometimes troublesome, and inopportunely, or too urgently made, still remains a part of my professional duty, for which I shall consider myself already compensated.

XXXI. All opinions for clients, verbal, or written, shall be *my opinions*, deliberately and sincerely given, and never *venal and flattering offerings to their wishes, or their vanity*. And though clients sometimes have the folly to be better pleased with having their views confirmed by an erroneous opinion, than their wishes or hopes thwarted by a sound one, yet such assentation is dishonest and unprofessional. Counsel, in giving opinions, whether they perceive this weakness in their clients or not, should act as *judges*, responsible to God and to man, as also especially to their employers, to advise them soberly, discreetly, and honestly, to the best of their ability—though the certain consequence be the loss of large prospective gains.

XXXII. If my client consents to endeavours for a compromise of his claim, or defence, and for that purpose I am to commune with the opposing counsel, or others, I will never permit myself to enter upon a system of tactics, to ascertain who shall overreach the other, by the most nicely balanced artifices of disingenuousness, by mystery, silence, obscurity, suspicion, vigilance to the letter, and all of the other machinery used by this class of tacticians, to the vulgar surprise of clients, and the admiration of a few ill judging lawyers. On the contrary,—my resolution in such a case is, to examine with great care, previously to the interview, the matter of compromise; to form a judgment as to what I will offer, or accept; and promptly, frankly, and firmly to communicate my views to the adverse counsel. In so doing, no lights shall be withheld that may terminate the matter as speedily, and as nearly in accordance with the rights of my client as possible; although a more dilatory, exacting, and wary policy, might finally extract something more than my own, or even my client's hopes. Reputation gained for this species of skill is sure to be followed by more than an equivalent loss of character: shrewdness is too often allied to unfairness,—caution to severity,—silence to disingenuousness—wariness to exaction, to make me covet a reputation based on such qualities.

XXXIII. What is wrong, is not the less so from being common. And though few *dare to be singular*, even in a right cause, I am resolved to make my own, and not the conscience of others, my sole guide. What is morally wrong, cannot be professionally right, however it may be sanctioned by time or custom. It is better to be right with a few, or even none, than wrong, though with a multitude. If, therefore, there be among my brethren, any traditional moral errors of practice, they shall be studiously avoided by me, though in so doing, I unhappily come in collision with what is (erroneously I think) too often denominated the policy of the profession. Such cases, fortunately, occur but seldom,—but when they do, I shall trust to that moral firmness of purpose which shrinks from no consequences, and which can be intimidated by no authority however ancient or respectable.

XXXIV. Law is a deep science: its boundaries, like space, seem to recede, as we advance: and though there be as much of certainty in it, as in any other science, it is fit we should be modest in our opinions, and ever willing to be further instructed. Its acquisition is more than the labour of a life; and, after all, can be with none the subject of unshaken confidence. In the language, then, of a late beautiful writer, I am resolved to 'consider my own acquired knowledge but as a torch flung into an abyss, making the darkness visible, and showing me the extent of my own ignorance.'*

XXXV. I will never be voluntarily called as a witness, in any cause in which I am counsel. Should my testimony, however, be so material that without it my client's cause may be greatly prejudiced, he must at once use his option to cancel the tie between us in the cause, and dispense with my further services, or with my evidence. Such a dilemma would be anxiously avoided by every delicate mind,—the union of counsel and witness being usually resorted to only as a forlorn hope, in the agonies of a cause,—and becomes particularly offensive, when its object be to prove an *admission* made to such counsel by the opposite litigant. Nor will I ever recognize any distinction in this respect between my knowledge of facts acquired before, and since the institution of the suit; for, in no case will I consent to sustain by my testimony any of the matters which my interest and professional duty render me

* Mrs. Jameson.

anxious to support. This resolution, however, has no application whatever, to facts contemporaneous with, and relating merely to the prosecution or defence of the cause itself; such as, evidence relating to the contents of a paper unfortunately lost by myself or by others—and such like matters, which do not respect the original merits of the controversy, and which, in truth, adds nothing to the once existing testimony; but relates merely to matters respecting the conduct of the suit, or to the recovery of lost evidence: nor does it apply to the case of gratuitous counsel,—that is, to those who have expressly given their services voluntarily.

XXXVI. Every letter or note that is addressed to me, shall receive a suitable response, and in proper time. Nor shall it matter from whom it comes, what it seeks, or what may be the terms in which it is penned. Silence can be justified in no case: and though the information sought cannot, or ought not to be given, still decorum would require from me a courteous recognition of the request, though accompanied with a firm withholding of what has been asked. There can be no surer indication of vulgar education than neglect of letters and notes; it manifests a total want of that tact and amenity, which intercourse with good society never fails to confer. But that *dogged silence* (worse than a rude reply) in which some of our profession indulge, on receiving letters offensive to their dignity, or when dictated by ignorant importunity, I am resolved never to imitate,—but will answer every letter and note with as much civility as may be due; and in as good time as may be practicable.

XXXVII. Should a professional brother by his industry, learning, and zeal, or even by some happy chance, become eminently successful in causes which give him large pecuniary emoluments, I will neither envy him the fruits of his toils or good fortune,—nor endeavour, by any indirection, to lessen them; but rather strive to emulate his worth, than enviously to brood over his meritorious success, and my own more tardy career.

XXXVIII. Should it be my happy lot to rank with, or take precedence of my seniors, who formerly endeavoured to impede my onward course, I am firmly resolved to give them no cause to suppose that I remember the one, or am conscious of the other. When age and infirmities have overtaken them, my kindness will teach them the loveliness of forgiveness. Those again, who aided me when young in the profession, shall find my gratitude increase in proportion as I become the better able to sustain myself.

XXXIX. A forensic contest is often no very sure test of the comparative strength of the combattants,—nor should defeat be regarded as a just cause of boast in the victor, or of mortification in the vanquished. When the controversy has been judicially settled against me, in all courts, I will not 'fight the battle o'er again,' *coram non judice;* nor endeavour to persuade others (as is too often done) that the courts were prejudiced,—or the jury desperately ignorant,—or the witnesses perjured,—or that the victorious counsel were unprofessional and disingenuous. In such cases, Credat Judæus Apella!

XL. Ardour in debate is often the soul of eloquence, and the greatest charm of oratory. When spontaneous and suited to the occasion, it becomes powerful. A sure test of this is when it so alarms a cold, calculating, and disingenuous opponent, as to induce him to resort to numerous vexatious means of neutralizing its force,—when ridicule and sarcasm take place of argument,—when the poor device is resorted to of endeavouring to cast the speaker from his well guarded pivot, by repeated interruptions, or by impressing on the court and jury that his just and well tempered zeal is but passion, and his earnestness but the exacerbation of constitutional infirmity,—when the opponent assumes a patronizing air, and imparts lessons of wisdom and of instruction! Such opponents I am resolved to disappoint, and on no account will I ever imitate their example. The warm current of my feelings shall be permitted to flow on; the influences of my nature shall receive no check; the ardour and fullness of my words shall not be abated,—for this would be to gratify the unjust wishes of my adversary, and would lessen my usefulness to my client's cause.

XLI. In reading to the court or to the jury authorities, records, documents, or other papers, I shall always consider myself as executing a *trust*, and, as such, bound to execute it faithfully and honourably. I am resolved, therefore, carefully to abstain from all false, or deceptious readings; and from all uncandid omissions of any qualifications of the doctrines maintained by me, which may be contained in the text, or in the notes. And I shall ever hold that the obligation extends, not only to words, syllables and letters, but also to the *modus legendi:* all intentional false emphasis, and even intonations, in any degree calculated to mislead, are petty impositions on the confidence reposed; and, whilst avoided by myself, shall ever be regarded by me in others, as feeble devices of an impoverished mind; or as pregnant evidences of a disregard for truth, which justly subjects them to be closely watched in more important matters.

XLII. In the examination of witnesses, I shall not forget that perhaps circumstances, and not choice, have placed them somewhat in my power. Whether so, or not, I shall never esteem it my privilege to disregard their feelings; or to extort from their evidence what, in moments free from embarrassment, they would not testify. Nor will I conclude that they have no regard for truth, and even the sanctity of an oath, because they use the privilege, accorded to others, of changing their language, and of explaining their previous declarations. Such captious dealing with the *words* and *syllables* of a witness, ought to produce in the mind of an intelligent jury, only a reverse effect, from that designed by those who practise such poor devices.

XLIII. I will never enter into any conversation with my opponent's client, relative to his claim or defence, except with the consent, *and* in the presence of his counsel.

XLIV. Should the party, just mentioned, have no counsel, and my client's interests demand that I should still commune with him, it shall be done in writing only,—and no verbal response will be received. And if such person be unable to commune in writing, I will either delay the matter until he employs counsel,—or, take down in writing his reply, in the presence of others; so that, if occasion should make it essential to avail myself of his answer, it may be done through the testimony of others, and not by mine. Even such cases should be regarded as the result of unavoidable necessity, and are to be resorted to only to guard against great risk, the artifices of fraud, or with the hope of obviating litigation.

XLV. Success in any profession will be much promoted by good address. Even the most cautious and discriminating minds are not exempt from its influence; the wisest judges, the most dispassionate juries, and the most wary opponents being made thereby, at least, more willing auditors,—and this, of itself, is a valuable end. But whilst address is deservedly prized, and merits the highest cultivation, I fully concur in sentiment with a high authority, that we should be 'respectful without meanness, easy without too much familiarity, genteel without affectation, and insinuating without any art or design.'

XLVI. Nothing is more unfriendly to the art of pleasing than *morbid timidity*, (*bashfulness,—mauvaise honte.*) All life teems with examples of its prejudicial influence, showing that the art of rising in life has no greater enemy than this nervous and senseless defect of education. Self-possession—calmness—steady assurance—intrepidity—are all perfectly consistent with the most *amiable modesty;* and none but vulgar and illiterate minds are prone to attribute to *presumptuous assurance*, the apparently cool and unconcerned exertions of young men at the bar. A great connoisseur in such matters, says, that 'what is done under concern and embarrassment, is sure to be ill done:' and the Judge (I have known some) who can scowl on the early endeavours of the youthful Advocate who has fortified himself with resolution, must be a man poor in the knowledge of human character, and perhaps still more so in good feelings. Whilst, therefore, I shall ever cherish these opinions, I hold myself bound to distinguish the arrogant, noisy, shallow and dictatorial impudence of some, from the gentle, though firm and manly confidence of others—they who bear the white banner of modesty, fringed with resolution.

XLVII. All reasoning should be regarded as a philosophical process—its object being conviction, by certain known and legitimate means. No one ought to be expected to be convinced by loud words—dogmatic assertions,—assumption of superior knowledge—sarcasm—invective;—but by gentleness, sound ideas, cautiously expressed—by sincerity—by ardour without extravasation. The minds and hearts of those we address are apt to be closed, when the lungs are appealed to instead of logic; when assertion is relied on, more than proof; and when sarcasm and invective supply the place of deliberate reasoning. My resolution, therefore, is to respect courts, juries, and counsel as assailable only through the medium of logical and just reasoning; and by such appeals to the sympathies of our common nature, as are worthy, legitimate, well timed, and in good taste.

XLVIII. The ill success of many at the bar is owing to the fact that their *business is not their pleasure.* Nothing can be more unfortunate than this state of mind. The world is too full of penetration not to perceive it, and much of our discourteous manner to clients, to courts, to juries, and counsel, has its source in this defect. I am, therefore, resolved to cultivate a *passion* for my profession; or, after a reasonable exertion therein, without success, to abandon it. But I will previously bear in mind, that he who abandons any profession will scarcely find another to suit him; the defect is in himself; he has not performed his duty, and has failed in resolutions, perhaps often made, to retrieve lost time, the want of which firmness can give no promise of success in any other vocation.

XLIX. Avarice is one of the most dangerous and disgusting of vices. Fortunately its presence is oftener found in age, than in youth; for if it be seen as an early feature in our character, it is sure, in the course of a long life, to work a great mass of oppression, and to end in both intellectual and moral desolation. Avarice gradually originates every species of indirection. Its offspring is meanness; and it contaminates every pure and honourable principle. It can consist with honesty scarce for a moment, without gaining the victory. Should the young practitioner, therefore, on the receipt of the first fruits of his exertions, perceive the slightest manifestation of this vice, let him view it as his most insidious and deadly enemy. Unless he can then heartily, and thoroughly eradicate it, he will find himself, perhaps slowly, but surely, capable of unprofessional—mean—and finally, dishonest acts;—which, as they cannot be long concealed, will render him conscious of the loss of character; make him callous to all the nicer feelings; and ultimately so degrade him, that he consents to live upon arts, from which his talents, acquirements, and original integrity would certainly have rescued him, had he at the very commencement fortified himself with the resolution to reject all gains, save those acquired by the most strictly honourable and professional means. I am therefore, firmly resolved, never to receive from any one, a compensation, not justly and honourably my due; and if fairly received, to place on it no undue value; to entertain no affection for money, further than as a means of obtaining the goods of life,—the art of *using money* being quite as important for the avoidance of avarice, and the preservation of a pure character, as that of *acquiring it*.

☞ With the aid of the foregoing Resolutions, and the faithful adherence to the following and last one, I hope to attain eminence in my profession, and to leave this world with the merited reputation of having lived an honest lawyer.

L. LAST RESOLUTION. I will read the foregoing forty-nine resolutions, twice every year, during my professional life.

Chapter V

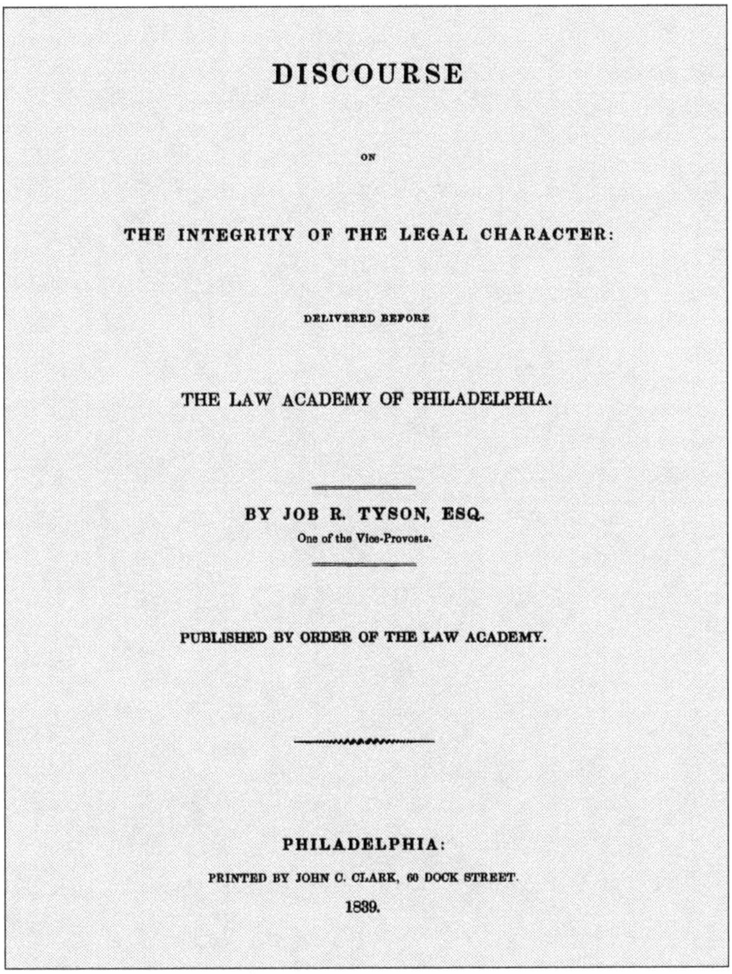

DISCOURSE

ON

THE INTEGRITY OF THE LEGAL CHARACTER:

DELIVERED BEFORE

THE LAW ACADEMY OF PHILADELPHIA.

BY JOB R. TYSON, ESQ.

One of the Vice-Provosts.

PUBLISHED BY ORDER OF THE LAW ACADEMY.

PHILADELPHIA:

PRINTED BY JOHN C. CLARK, 60 DOCK STREET.

1839.

Tyson, Job R. *Discourse on the Integrity of the Legal Character: Delivered before the Law Academy of Philadelphia*. Philadelphia: John C. Clark, 1839.

PHILADELPHIA, Oct. 24th, 1839.

DEAR SIR,—We have great pleasure in communicating to you the subjoined resolution, unanimously adopted by the Law Academy of this City, at a meeting held on Wednesday, the 23d inst.

"*Resolved*, That the thanks of the Academy be presented to JOB R. TYSON, Esq. for the appropriate and able Discourse delivered by him last evening; and that a copy be requested for publication."

Indulging the hope that the wishes of the Academy may be gratified,

We remain, with great respect,
Your friends and obedient serv'ts,

JOHN PHILIPS MONTGOMERY,
THOMAS B. DRINKER,
EDWARD HOPPER,
Committee.

JOB R. TYSON, ESQ.

GENTLEMEN,—Your kind note is received, communicating the unanimous wish of the Law Academy to have a copy of my Discourse for publication. In reply to so flattering a request, I cannot hesitate to place the MS. at their disposal.

With sentiments of personal regard,
I am, gentlemen, your friend, &c.

J. R. TYSON,
S. W. Corner Prune and Fourth Sts.
24th Oct. '39.

JOHN PHILIPS MONTGOMERY,
THOMAS B. DRINKER, and
EDWARD HOPPER, Esquires,
Committee.

DISCOURSE.

Gentlemen of the Law Academy:—

It is natural to feel a deep solicitude in the repute of a profession, which we have chosen as the business of our lives. The subject is interesting, because it powerfully appeals to us as a common sentiment, that it is our duty, as far as we are able, to extend its usefulness and enhance its estimation.—While the study of the law is highly esteemed as an elevated science, there are, perhaps, few objects against which popular prejudice has been so unsparingly directed, as the legal profession. All admit the exalting and ennobling influences of historical and legal disquisitions—of researches into the existence and effects of law upon communities and states—and yet, the class of men whose peculiar province it is to explore and trace the rise and fall of institutions and nations, seem to be regarded, by common consent, as a standing theme of alternate jest and reproach.

With some well-meaning and intelligent persons an honest lawyer is a paradox. He is accused of a cold and avaricious selfishness, and supposed to be intent upon stirring up the passions of the multitude, to their degradation and ruin, from the sordid motive of pecuniary gain. Many impute to him an absorbing ambition for the honours, as well as the emoluments of life. He is represented, in fine, as a great spider surrounded by the meshes of the web he has

6

woven, and inveigling all objects into its entangling fibres. Among this class, every instance of deviation from right and honour, is treasured up as a substantive charge against the whole fraternity.

It cannot be doubted, that some cause exists for a feeling, which, if it does not pervade all classes of society, has at least a very diffusive prevalence. As every rank in life, from the highest to perhaps the meanest, has contributed recruits to the Bar, and the light and shade of each may be seen reflected from its surface, so no one department is answerable for its errors. In other pursuits, the temptations to indirection may be equally potent and insidious; but the lawyer, from the publicity of his path, is more frequently subjected to suspicion, and his lapses are sooner and more generally known. Let a physician resort to the little arts of empiricism, let a merchant falsify or embezzle, let a tradesman keep false books and aid his scheme of deception by duplicity and falsehood;—in neither case, are mankind so unjust as to charge his crime upon the members of his body, or attribute to his peculiar vocation, an influence unfavourable to moral virtue. The character of the offender is lost in the consideration of the offence, and justice is satisfied with punishing the delinquent without reference to his class.

But censorious and unjust as may be a part of the public in this wholesale condemnation, it cannot be questioned that the severity is not wholly destitute of reason. Many bad men, wearing the panoply of the profession, have been enabled to perpetrate their deeds under its sanction. The studies of the lawyer imply an intimate acquaintance with the principles of justice; and the world will hold him to a strict account for undermining the corner stone of his temple; for sinning against the lights of that knowledge which he especially ought to hold in regard and veneration. The

7

high trusts and sacred confidences which he violates, in departing from the plain path of integrity, is an ingredient in his error which distinguishes it from the mass of moral delinquency. Men are prone to regard the abuses of trust and the betrayal of confidence, with sentiments of peculiar disgust and aversion. Nor should it be forgotten, that the secrecy with which cheats may be conducted, forms a powerful reason why the detected culprit should be visited by a signal punishment.

This tendency to censure in the popular mind, may prove a wholesome corrective with bad men, who, if they are not influenced by higher motives, may reflect that they involve their fellow members in their disgrace. It should bind together "the good men and true" of the profession, like the Hundredors in the olden times of England, who, being held responsible for the conduct of each other, made hue and cry after a delinquent, with the view of screening themselves from suspicion, and the Hundred from punishment. The dishonoured lawyer must entertain a strange idea of the responsibilities of professional life, and interpret still more strangely the declaration of Coke, that every man owes a debt to his profession. Sir William Jones thought that if he did nothing more than introduce to the notice of the English lawyer, the great work of Pothier, he would go far towards discharging this obligation. Amid the absorbing cares and worrying vexations of professional duty, it must happen, in the majority of cases, that there is little time and less inclination or ability, for the composition of a treatise which would not be a positive incumbrance to the lawyer's library. But all have it in their power to leave to their fellow members and successors, the valuable inheritance of an honoured and unspotted name.

This reflection will receive additional force, when we take into view the delicate functions and high responsibilities of the legal profession. Waiving, for the present, the consideration of those manifold and peculiar private duties, each big with importance, that every counsel may be called upon to discharge, the political and social influences of the body are great, diffusive and permanent. In all countries the firmest impediment to the encroachments of arbitrary power, is to be found in an enlightened, virtuous and independent Bar. They are the sentinels who sound the alarm at the approach of an enemy to constitutional liberty; for it is not amid the tyranny of despotic rule or in the strife and tumult of anarchy, that the expounder of the laws can find a birth-place or a home. The noble conduct of Sir Edward Coke, in resisting the disgraceful servility of a powerful court and the tyranny of a capricious monarch, is a memorable illustration of the value of the lawyer in perilous times, and a striking example of moral intrepidity and personal firmness.* In the reign of Louis XIV., and the regency of Orleans, that great lawyer, D'Aguesseau, rescued unhappy France, by his patriotism and courage, from the intrigues of ambitious favourites, the corruptions of the tribunals, and the stupendous and dazzling projects of the infamous John Law. The annals of juridical biography, over the world, teem with similar examples.

The lawyer exists, and can exist only, in the genial atmosphere of freedom. It is from him especially, that traditional errors and practical abuses must find a corrective. Reform and improvement, under his auspices, hope for stability and progress. But he stands, not only as a sentinel against the inroads of a political despot, and the scourge of public abuses, but he is the shield of private injuries and the assertor of legal retribution. He is interposed between the corrupt, incompetent and erring judge, and the wronged and

* Vide Note 1.

9

trembling suitor. The avenger of the innocent, he visits upon the wrong-doer the penalties of the law, and protects the weak and defenceless from the overbearing hand of oppression and power.

It is not necessary to remind such an assembly as this, of the position assumed by the legal profession at the darkest period of our political history, when tyranny wore the guise of a necessary tax for the public good. Who but lawyers could have roused the country to the vindication of rights merely speculative and theoretical—rights affecting abstract principle, and wholly unfelt in curtailing the happiness and enjoyments of the people? The voice of Constitutional liberty, the inheritance of Britons on both sides of the Atlantic, was heard from every bar of the Colonies; and an union, the most wonderful and instantaneous, was the result. The bickerings of private jealousy, the rancour of party spirit, the rival prejudices of distant colonies, were at once extinguished or disappeared; or united their angry forces to answer those eloquent appeals which were made to the spirit of national independence. Let it not be forgotten in the tale of our country's history, that those same lawyers who preached free principles to the people—the Dickensons, Adamses and Lees of those days,—when the flame of war converted the council chamber into a camp, they valiantly asserted the sincerity of their patriotism by offering to seal their doctrines with their blood.

But that science which may thus confer blessings on society, and ennoble its professors, is capable of the grossest perversion. Bolingbroke does only justice to the legal profession, when he pourtrays it as being, "in its nature, the noblest and most beneficial to mankind; in its abuse and debasement, the most sordid and pernicious." It was in this state of depression on the decline of Roman jurisprudence, during the latter and darker period of the empire. That noble art, which had been vindicated for so long a period by the exalted wisdom and pure integrity of its members, sustained the most pitiable declension which could befall an honourable pursuit. "It had fallen," says Gibbon, in his Decline and Fall, "into the hands of freedmen and plebeians, who, with cunning, rather than skill, exercised a sordid and pernicious trade. Some of them procured admittance into families for the purpose of fomenting differences, of encouraging suits, and of preparing a harvest of gain for themselves and their brethren. Others, recluse in their chambers, maintained the dignity of legal professors, by furnishing a rich client with subtleties to confound the plainest truths, and with arguments to colour the most unjustifiable pretensions. The splendid and popular class was composed of the advocates, who filled the forum with the sound of their turgid and loquacious rhetoric. Careless of favour and of justice, they are described, for the most part, as ignorant and rapacious guides, who conducted their clients through a maze of expense, of delay, and of disappointment."

It cannot be denied, in our own day, that while many practice the law as become the votaries of an elevated science, others degrade it into a pernicious and *driving trade*. It is indifferent to these men what may be the merits of a controversy, or which side they espouse; they ignobly pervert their oath of office, which enjoins fidelity to the interests of the client, into a pretext for sheltering him from the condign punishment of justice and law. Like Major Dalgetty, they are ever willing to fight on the *eligible* side; and exclaim in the base spirit of that mercenary soldier,

> "With pleas of right let statesmen vex their head,
> "Battle 's my business, and my guerdon bread;
> "And with the sordid Switzer, I can say
> "The best of causes is the best of pay."

11

The little arts of chicanery and falsehood, exciting differences, magnifying trivial offences, blurring the reputations of upright men;—in short, gaining an ignominious livelihood by preying upon the ignorant and poor, and plundering the weak and the rich—are malversations which have, in some instances, disgraced the exercise of our profession.

How are we to guard against the continuance of a system so fraught with public and private mischief, so full of infamy to the country, of perpetual and ineffaceable disgrace to ourselves? An obvious reply to this question, demands a higher aim in the qualifications to membership—a longer period of study,—and a loftier standard of mental and moral attainment. These requisites would certainly produce a beneficial influence, since candidates are admitted to practice whose moral training and want of intellectual fitness, instead of conferring honour upon the Bar, have only added to its odium and contempt. The acquisition of a mechanical trade, requires an apprenticeship, omitting the item of literary preparation, during as long a period as the study of the laws of the land. If the means to improve and exalt the character of the Bar be *confined* to augmented strictness in the admission to membership, it is feared that it will advance but slowly and partially the work of reform. It might insure to the public and the profession, more cultivated talents and sounder learning; but the example of England proves that a severer system of exclusion, forms no security against the inroads of bad men, and the arts of dishonest practitioners. But let it not be forgotten, that the most corrupt and infamous judge that has ever disgraced Westminster Hall,—the detestable and blood thirsty Jefferies,—assumed the gown of the barrister, if indeed he was ever regularly admitted to practice, at the early age of eighteen years, and after an unusually brief period of probation.

It might be well to consider how much could be done to purify the Bar, by an uncompromising sincerity of deport-

12

ment in those to whom the profession look for guidance and example. I speak not of that moral propriety of personal conduct which scorns meanness and dishonour, but that magnanimity of sentiment and demeanour which would refuse all countenance to the trickster and pettifogger. They should cultivate that true *esprit de corps* which would guard our reputation from the effects of private, much less any public manifestation of regard, where regard is misplaced, because it is unmerited. Affability, when undistinguishing, ceases to be a virtue. The world is influenced by appearances, and when these prove false and hollow, it is either shocked, or falls a victim to the deception. In the one case it loses its respect, and in the other, it receives an injury. The man whose moral sentiments and professional deportment are free from reproach, may learn, by the contacts of the Bar, to connive at serious delinquencies in a fellow member, from the force of pleasing manners or the fascinating influence of agreeable social qualities. The clear moral perceptions of the community, and the conduct of the Bar, may thus come into collision. While the public are ready to consign an unworthy member to the infamy he deserves, his legal brethren may extend to him the hand of cordiality and fellowship, and try to sustain him by every mark of public and private confidence. I would not be understood as recommending the abandonment of a fellow lawyer to an unreasonable outbreak of popular indignation or suspicion; the *esprit de corps* should protect him, at whatever hazard, in the fearless and independent discharge of his functions. I speak not of idle rumour with its thousand lying tongues, its appetite whetted for mischief, and greedy for its victim.

"Fama ———————————————
"Parva metu primò, mox sese attollit in auras,
"Ingrediturque solo, et caput inter nubila condit."*

* Æneid. lib. 4, v. 175.

13

Many occasions occur in the course of an extensive practice at the Bar, when, from the blindness of popular prejudice or the easiness of public credulity, a counsel finds himself in situations which may expose him to ruin, without the sympathy and support of his brethren. In the memorable case of the libel against Paine, for that part of his *Rights of Man*, which attacked the English government, Erskine stood forward his intrepid and eloquent defender. All the arts of intimidation were employed to drive him from his purpose. A conspiracy was formed to deprive Paine of the benefit of counsel; but despising promises, and regardless of threats, Erskine was true to that independence of action and integrity of purpose, which should ever characterize a member of the Bar. For this act of disobedience, he was put under the ban and deprived of office. Now that time has mellowed the passions of the moment, we look in vain for their excuse or justification. He was the defender, not of language tending to sedition; not of an inflammatory attempt to excite opposition to law, tumult, disorder or misrule; not of calumnies against the living magistrate; but of a sober effort to bring about the redress of acknowledged grievances, by addressing the universal reason of the nation. He remained under a temporary cloud, but true to himself, and fortunate in the adherence of his brethren, he emerged from the vapour which obscured him, into the brightest sunshine of popular and royal favour.*

The call for withdrawal on the part of the Bar, from the countenance and protection of a colleague, is reserved for cases, not of suspicion founded only on rumour, nor of acts performed under a delusive but honest sense of duty, but of unquestioned and indubitable dishonour. In such cases, it may be gravely contended, without the imputation of harsh-

* Vide Note 2.

14

ness, that it is not only the *right* of each member, as *amicus curiæ*, to institute a proceeding, but the *stern duty* of the body to promote and sustain it.

It is an error of an opposite nature, and one that argues not only a want of self-respect, but of *fidelity to one's profession*, to detract from, or grudgingly yield the palm of merit to a deserving compeer. Want of equal success sometimes unconsciously sours into asperity our feelings towards a man, whom we might otherwise regard with the warmest sentiments of friendship and admiration. It is a quicker and an easier task to demolish the fabric which it required years to construct, than to build up another by its side; and, however repugnant to propriety and honour may be the fact, and humiliating to our pride may be the admission, it cannot be doubted, that there are men who prefer depending for their advancement more upon the adroitness with which a competitor can be humbled, than raising themselves to the height of fair and open competition. It was one of the maxims of honourable chivalry, that knighthood was disgraced by an attempt to undervalue the honest fame of an enemy or a rival. The world is censorious enough to dwell with complacency upon ill-natured recitals of professional miscarriage, and surely he proves recreant to his order, who will minister to tastes so unwholesome and depraved. Instead of looking with spleen or envy, upon a prosperity which, unable to equal, he would insidiously destroy, it would be well to raise his eyes to the level of the character he dislikes, and attuning his mind for the effort, mount up, like the blaze of the emulous lamp, to the object above him.

An opinion prevails, that the reading of the lawyer cannot stray, with safety, from the beaten track of his profession. A sentiment of this kind is so inimical, in its spirit, to the genius of the age, and so injurious in its practical tendency, to the public and the profession, that so opportune an occasion as this, should not be omitted to present and expose its fallacy.—The law is not only a learned, but a *liberal* profession; and the lawyer, of all men, should elevate and fortify his principles by various and enlarged studies, against the insidious temptations to which he is on every side exposed.—"The sparks of every science," says Finch, "are taken up in the ashes of the law." How dark and bewildered we should grope our way, without a more certain and satisfactory guide, than these sparks can furnish?* "Your mere lawyer," says Mr. Warren, in his Law Studies, "is a pettifogger." He seldom distinguishes between principle and *technicality;*—the latter of these, according to Lord Kaimes, invariably leading to corruption and depravity. He who thus observes the *outside,* instead of advancing into the penetralia of the temple, is as partial in his scope of observation, as the underworkman, so felicitously described by Dean Swift,—and confining himself to the outworks, is a stranger to the grander conceptions which would be inspired by the amazing extent and beautiful proportions of the interior and principal structure.

Liberal studies are necessary to counteract the circumscribing and benumbing influences of a professional addiction to law. The man who devotes himself exclusively to its details, becomes as pitiable in his helplessness as the blind or hood-winked mill-horse, unsuited for every purpose but the round he is accustomed to travel, and only fitted for that, by the appliances which confine him to his circle. Too strict an adherence to legal forms cramps the energies and contracts the mental vision, rendering it acute in the perception of immediate objects, but, by disqualifying it for a wider range, lessens the sphere of its observa-

* Vide Note 3.

tion. Lawyers in this, as in all free countries, are called upon to guide the helm of state; and surely he is a worse pilot than the heavy-eyed Palinurus, who, accustomed only to view the nicely adjusted machinery of a clock through a microscope, cannot, in the distance, descry the thickening tempest in the speck which floats on the horizon.

We sometimes hear the lawyer derided, who steps aside from his profession to mingle with the world, in the attractive departments of literature and benevolence. Believe that though the law is a jealous mistress, no lawyer is less qualified to be her humane and enlightened votary, by mixing in scenes which allow play to the imagination, and give impulse to the best emotions of the heart. It is important that he should be made acquainted with other men and things, than law and lawyers; it is his duty, to cultivate an expansive philanthropy, and extend a helping hand to all the moral institutions of the age. It was to such men, that the jurisprudence and philanthropy of England are indebted for their regenerated spirit and upward movement. Bentham, whose *originality* as a legal reformer, is greater perhaps than Justinian, Alfred or Napoleon, was a man of diversified and general knowledge. Without bloodshed, temporary misrule, or the anarchy attendant on important changes, he has brought about the greatest revolution, the most extensive and valuable reforms, which have ever been witnessed in the annals of mankind. Dumont, Mackintosh, Brougham, Romilly, Wells and others, his distinguished coadjutors, were spirits whose intellects were not more enlarged by various research, than their hearts were adorned, and affections purified by the truths of religion and philosophy.

Though Bentham may justly be deemed the greatest benefactor of legal science, of this or perhaps of any age, let it not be understood that I commend the adoption of all

17

his doctrines. His Rationale of Evidence is a wonderful specimen of research, and for the most part, of just, comprehensive and luminous reasoning. But in the troubled whirlpool of agitated opinion in England, he could not escape from the leaven which was fermenting the mass. His arguments are often carried beyond the bounds of truth and logic. In the language of Brougham, he is apt "to push his discussions to the uttermost, and to strain his principles till they crack." The American lawyer, while he marks and imitates his spirit, will avoid his mistakes; he will seek the true shrine of practical improvement, and not yield himself blindly to the genius of innovation, that giddy and delusive phantom, whose aims are as unsubstantial as her behests are visionary. He will not swell the headlong and turbulent stream, which, boiling from the very bottom, pours over its banks; and instead of diffusing fertility and beauty, exhibits a scene of sad and wasteful desolation. He will learn the practice of other codes than his own, he will study those principles of eternal justice upon which enlightened law must be founded;—for ignorant of these, he is without the light of comparison, and lives and dies the inflexible and determined enemy of change.

A man when entering his profession, should reflect upon the enlarged sphere of obligations which his position has contracted, that there are duties which he owes to the Bar as well as to himself.—Professional integrity requires, in the first place, that he should possess all the learning of his art, that his legal knowledge should be profound and exact, in order to direct his client wisely.* He will be distinguished, not only for the assiduity necessary for this, but for honour, sincerity and truth, in all his relations with the client, the court, the Bar and the community. If sincerity

* Vide Note 4.

18

be loved in the common intercourse of life, how desirable to find it in a counsel into whose ear has been poured perhaps the confidential breathings which have been withheld from every other mortal! In the rude ages of chivalry, veracity was esteemed a cardinal and indispensable virtue, and without it, the dignity of knighthood attracted to its possessor only the contempt and infamy of his order. Of all the detestable properties, for which a man of liberal aspirations may be known, is falsehood, a vice equally impolitic and base. But on the other hand, how noble a consciousness does he enjoy, how proud a niche does he occupy in the hearts of his fellow men, whose lips have never been polluted with untruth, and whose promise, without the sign manual to attest its nature, has always been scrupulously, and to the letter, redeemed!

Next in importance to these, perhaps upon the community and himself, is promptitude in the discharge of professional business. *Neglect* on the part of the barrister, is an imputation as often made, and a grievance as extensively felt, as "the law's delay" and the uncertainty of its ultimate decisions. Voltaire said, "he had been twice ruined; once when he lost a law suit, and once when he gained one." The excellent motto of Sir Matthew Hale, "*festina lente*," was inscribed upon the head of his staff, and his judicial industry, and admirable resolves, attest its value as a guide. "Slow, but sure," was the favourite maxim of Lord Eldon, whose balancing mind and habitual caution, held suitors in suspense, till sometimes, from "the hope deferred which maketh the heart sick," they are said to have died of grief and vexation. Millions of pounds sterling were locked up in chancery awaiting his tardy deliberations, to the ruin of estates, and the distress and impoverishment of families. If his distinguished successor on the woolsack, had emulated Eldon in the soundness of his law, as he excelled him in the despatch of equity business, Brougham's reputation, as a jurist, would stand upon a lofty eminence. But no man is a safe counsellor who speaks when he ought to meditate, and a swift judge is a public calamity. The whisperings of sloth, on the other hand, should be silenced by the voice of honour and the dictates of integrity, whose primary lesson enjoins an *instant* obedience to its call.

The lawyer, in full practice, who faithfully and conscientiously performs his duty, passes a life of thoughtful toil, which it is not easy for an uninitiated public to appreciate. His gains are sometimes believed to be more than an equivalent for his labour. But the ordinary fees of the counsel are incomparably less in amount, than in many departments of life, in which, though less labour is bestowed, and to which inferior qualifications are sufficient, the remuneration is by no means thought to be disproportioned to the skill and responsibility. In a majority of cases, every one must not only be the best, but the *exclusive* judge of the value of his own services; but still there are certain received rules to which all honourable men will adhere.—A compensation, dependant upon the event of a controversy, has been condemned as liable to many objections. These contracts may certainly lead to deception and abuse; but on the other hand, they may be mutually convenient and beneficial to the client and counsel. The suitor may be either unable or unwilling to repay the exertions of a counsel in any other mode, and is the latter therefore to reject what, in the line of his profession, may confer a benefit? But an honourable man will not avail himself of that superior knowledge which he must possess over his client, in fixing the principle of compensation. The contracting parties seldom stand upon equal ground. The counsel, perhaps aware of the comparative ease with which the rights of the suitor can be enforced, may dictate unreasonable terms, which the ignorance or necessity of the latter only could induce him to accept. It is related of Topping, an English lawyer of celebrity, that a larger sum being tendered to him as a retainer, in an important cause, than was customary, he indignantly refused it, upon the ground, that the surplus either implied an unwillingness to do what was right, without a perquisite, or that he was expected to perform more than his duty—an alternative which he treated with scorn.

There is one faculty of the mind, to which I beg leave to call your attention as nearly connected with integrity of character, and upon the cultivation of which the happiness and usefulness of a lawyer materially depend. It is the cultivation of the temper. In the ordinary routine of professional business, in the official intercourse of the Bar, in the duties of the forum, all experience will tell how necessary it is to preserve the temper calm and unruffled, amidst a thousand circumstances, which are perpetually occurring to try it. Clients may be exacting, opponents unreasonable, the demeanour of the judge may be disagreeable, or his decision unsatisfactory, the jury may have decided hastily or from misconception—these are among the numerous causes of vexation, which a lawyer may meet with, in his daily walks, and which, without the exercise of that philosophy which "ruleth the spirit," may cloud and embitter his whole journey. The impetuosity of Coke, the irritability of Tenterden, and the occasional dogmatic violence of Ellenborough, scarcely more alienated their cotemporaries, and diminished the lustre of their judicial renown, on the bench, than it has affected the deliberate estimate of their characters with posterity.* With what upbraiding remorse must a passionate man look out upon the world whose green

* Vide Note 5.

21

spots of friendship, love and esteem he has transformed into a desert! He is forced to exclaim,

> "The thorns which I have reaped, are of the tree I planted:
> They have torn me, and I bleed!"

The Academy will not, I am sure, charge me with a desire to become its moral Mentor, when, as an old member, I take the liberty of presenting considerations which I cannot but view as important in the formation of the legal character. There are one or two reflections, gentlemen, which, I must still, however, press upon your notice. One is, that let the intellectual character be what it may, no matter how elevated and superior, if it want integrity, these endowments will be regarded as nothing, except to heap accumulated odium upon their possessor. The other is, that in the season of ingenuous youth, when all the impulses of the heart are usually generous and noble, and little has occurred to disturb or chill their genial flow, if the moral sensibilities be so blunt as to permit a departure from the principles of integrity, manhood, which brings with it greater coldness and stronger temptations, must be crowned with misery and dishonour. The effects of idleness may be retrieved; assiduity, inspired by the enthusiasm of an ambition which circumstances had checked or concealed, may repair the breaches of indolence. But let the cold steel of insincerity, falsehood, dishonour, enter, at that period of life, into the soul, and the vitality of a better principle is irrevocable; the virtuous spark, it may be feared, is dead forever.

In glancing over the pages of juridical biography, we are struck with the justice of the world in overlooking the greatest talents, when they are not joined to a virtuous life. Witness the case of Sir Francis, afterwards Lord Bacon, described by Pope, as the

> "Greatest, wisest, meanest of mankind."

D

22

who, though so eminently endowed, and excelling so much in varied accomplishments, his illustrious rival, is nevertheless seldom mentioned but in terms of reproach and disparagement. Bacon once, perhaps only once in his life, uttered the real sentiments of his heart. He has revealed, in these few words, the secret of his policy, the instrument of his promotion. "Not *too much,*" says he, "of the *honest,* is a property conducive to *fortune.*" The Lord Jefferies is only remembered as the supple and sanguinary tool of a bad king, and as the execrable judge who could insult and triumph over Baxter, and browbeat, convict and execute such men as Russell and Sidney. The means which these two men employed to attain seats of eminence and power, are expressively sketched in a single line;

> "Meanness which soars, and pride that licks the dust,—"

the one successful by ductility and sycophancy, and the other rising by his rottenness from the bottom of the stream of life.

Turn from such examples as these, to the inflexible honesty of Coke, the self-denying independence of Mansfield, the unsullied and unambitious virtue of Wilmot, the honest pride and benevolent sensibilities of Blackstone, the pure religion and energetic philanthropy of Romilly, and a multitude of others of only inferior celebrity. The virtues of these men can never be forgotten; and so genial is their effect upon the memory of their greatness, that so far from being eclipsed, it must continue to live by an union with a principle, alike co-existent and conservative.

Of Coke, it is enough to say, that with all his defects, he stands out in such high relief, as a man of integrity, that now, having outlived the petty arts by which Bacon assailed him, the majesty of his intellect shines forth with unclouded lustre in his works, which promise to endure until the great foundations of British law are broken down and destroyed.*

The character of Murray, afterwards Mansfield, presents to the lawyer, a proud subject of study and imitation. Though he has raised one branch of the law at least, which he found in elemental chaos, into the dignity of consistent science; though he has impressed upon the principles of general jurisprudence, much of his own wise and penetrating spirit; though he graced Parliament with an oratory, as effective and popular as the eloquence of Pitt;—with all these to embalm him in the perpetual remembrance of the lawyer and statesman, yet his public and private virtues, his signal integrity, and noble independence, will be the means of securing for him a deeper love, a prouder immortality. His contempt of "the huzzas of the crowd," of that popularity "which is run after," and the manly sensibility with which he looked forward to the applause of after times, to the page of impartial history, when truth should triumph over delusion, must challenge the sympathy of the enlightened and generous part of mankind. Menaced with the violence of an indignant mob, he nobly performed his duty, *ruat cœlum*, as he said, regardless of the frowns of power and the turbulence of popular commotion. It may be truly said, he had

> "A soul
> That spurned the crowd's malign control,
> A firm contempt of wrong."

With all the objections which captious men have raised against Lord Mansfield, in common with other eminent jurists, for attempting to give to the court, and not to the jury, the question of "libel or no libel," and maugre some

* Vide Note 6.

24

alloys from which humanity can scarcely be exempt, he stands a monument of genius and virtue, an assertor of human freedom, and a benefactor of legal science.

One of those remarkable men, of whom, perhaps, the present age is not very prolific, is Sir Eardley Wilmot. This eminent personage united, in an extraordinary degree, the talents and learning, the sincere piety and scupulous honour, which fitted him for the highest judicial station, with the modesty which made him shun all eclat and distinction. Averse to place or preferment, his cotemporaries frequently thrust upon him situations of dignity and emolument, without his consent, and in opposition to his wishes. He was made a puisne Judge of the King's Bench, in despite of a sincere and earnest remonstrance against it, and thence was promoted to the Chief Justiceship of the Common Pleas, in the face of as vehement a protest as his gentle nature and the silencing voices of his friends would permit. Twice offered the Great Seal, he steadily and firmly declined it, preferring the blessings of retirement and the calm virtues of private life, to the allurements which its acceptance held out to ambition. "Bread and water," said he, "are nectar and ambrosia, contrasted with the supremacy of a Court of Justice."—When he accepted the Chief Justiceship of the Common Pleas, that humble dependence upon God for aid which was the ruling principle of all his actions, appears in a letter to his son. "Now, my son," says he, "I will tell you a secret worth knowing and remembering: the elevation I have met with in life, particularly this last instance of it, has not been owing to any superior merit or abilities, but to my humility, to my not having set up myself above others, and to an uniform endeavour to pass through life void of offence towards God and man." Again he writes, "I do not in the least doubt but you will second my endeavours to cultivate your mind,

25

and principally to impregnate it with those principles of honour and truth, which constitute a gentleman; and however fortune may exalt or depress you in the world, the consciousness of having always acted upon those principles, will give you the only perfect happiness that is to be found in this world. Whether my heart be full of joy or grief, it will always beat uniformly with unremitting wishes, that all my children may be more distinguished for their *goodness*, than their *greatness*." Filial piety has bequeathed to mankind a faithful and affectionate tribute to the memory of this great and good man,—a memory which must ever be cherished by his descendants and all posterity with sentiments of lively and grateful love.

The literary attractions of the Commentaries on the Laws of England, dispose mankind, according to the influences which operate on the human heart, either to believe any thing that is favourable or the reverse, in the character of the distinguished author. It is a matter of regret, that his professional and social career, has not been more minutely delineated, as it would be gratifying to all, interested in legal biography, to follow so illustrious a penman from the retired haunts of his study into the exciting scenes of debate, in the forum. It appears an ill elocution retarded his early advances, but his intrinsic worth and elevated bearing, are shown in a single incident, which has been fortunately preserved. Being recommended by Mr. Murray, afterwards Lord Mansfield, to the Duke of New Castle, to fill the vacant chair in the University of Oxford, the Duke willing to try how far he could depend upon the flexibility of his nature, or the easiness of his principles, observed to him, that "in case of any agitation in the college, he presumed he might rely upon Mr. Blackstone's exertions in behalf of government." "Your Grace may be assured," said Blackstone, "that *I will discharge my duty in giving*

26

law lectures, to the best of my poor ability." "And your duty in the other branch too?" added the Duke. A silent flexion of the body was the only rejoinder. A few days after, Dr. Jenner was promoted to the vacant chair. But the disappointment of Blackstone, was nobly revenged by his subsequent election to the Vinerian professorship,—a station, which the elegant genius displayed in his lectures, has adorned and immortalized.

Sir William Blackstone, if he had not written the Commentaries, has vindicated a claim to high renown for his efforts, in conjunction with Howard and Eden, to reform the prisons of England. The memorable statute 19 Geo. 3, is attributed to his pen, the doctrines of which he asserted through the press, and enforced by means of charges to Grand Juries. If he had performed nothing more than writing the Commentaries, he would be entitled to our gratitude for enlarging and beautifying the literary realms of law; but, having added to our debt by his labours in the uninviting field of penal philanthropy, he must live in our hearts, with enduring freshness.

Of all the lawyers of whom past times or the present age can boast, no one can be placed in competition with Sir Samuel Romilly, as a beautiful instance of the abandonment of individual ambition to the promotion of the public good. Learned and able, far beyond the ordinary standard of learning and ability, he looked at office and station as only augmenting his responsibility, and placing in his power the means of more extensive usefulness. Though diffident to a degree, which, for years, threatened to drive him in discredit from the Bar, he overcame the barrier of physical weakness, by the force of his fine intellect and moral susceptibilities, attained a most commanding eminence in the forum, and has inscribed his name, in imperishable characters, high in the blazing scroll of philanthrophy. To him

27

more than to any man who ever lived, amid reproach and ridicule, and surrounded by every form of opposition and discouragement, are the most benign features of the penal code, and many of the best institutions of England, indebted for their existence. Sorrowing, but not disheartened, bowed down for a time, but not dismayed by keen sarcasm, unfounded misrepresentation and unexpected defeat, he reproduced his plans of improvement, year after year, and calmly waited the approach of that hour when public sentiment, having imbibed his enlightened views, and animated by his generous ardour, should be prepared for their adoption. At such a time, he was capable of making the following declaration, in Parliament, a declaration remarkable for the forbearance and elevated spirit which it breathes. "Since the last session of Parliament, I have repeatedly reconsidered the subject: I am more and more convinced of the strength of the foundation on which I stand. * * * I knew that my motives must be occasionally misunderstood by many, and might possibly be misrepresented by others. I was not blind to the road where prudence pointed to preferment; but I am not to be misled from comforts which no external honours can bestow." Again he said, "From the spirit which I have seen, I shall not be surprised, and certainly I will not be deterred, by any vote of this night. * * * It was my lot to hear in Parliament, a negative upon that bill, which was intended to deliver this enlightened nation from the reproach of the cruel and disgusting punishment of burning women alive. It was my lot, again and again, to witness in this house, the defeat of those wise and humane exertions which were intended to rescue Englishmen from the disgrace of abetting slavery. But the punishment of burning is no more, and Africa is free. No resistance, no vote of this night, shall prevent my appealing to the good sense and good feeling of the legislature and of the country. If I live another year, I will renew this bill, with the bill for repealing the punishment of death for stealing a few shillings; and whatever may be *my* fate, the seed which is scattered has not fallen upon stony ground."

Romilly is represented, by his biographer, as uniting the greatest modesty to the highest merit; as being laborious, but social; as devoted to his profession, but most disinterested in his services to the poor and unfortunate; and in all his conduct, both professional and parliamentary, distinguished for high-minded rectitude and punctilious honour.

Such was Samuel Romilly: a man whose faith, under the guidance of our holy religion, led him to elevated studies and noble acts, and anxious only to assuage the ills of humanity, and to purify it from the taint of meanness and error, he has enrolled himself in that band of great and superior spirits, who have been called, "The salt of the earth,"

"The virtuous few
Who season human kind."

If we go from the illustrious of another land, to the celebrated men of our own, we shall find that the garland of fame is more likely to retain its perfume and verdure from the virtues, than the abilities of its possessor. The purity of character which marked the judicial and social careers of Chief Justice Marshall, of the Supreme Court of the United States,—that great man who may be called *primus absque secundo;* of Judge Washington, of the United States Court for this circuit;—and of Chief Justice Tilghman of the Supreme Court of Pennsylvania; will preserve and brighten, if it does not survive the recollection of their eminent talents and profound learning. Of the lamented William Rawle, late of this Bar, we may emphatically use the fine language applied by Warburton to Bayle,—that "he had a soul superior to the attacks of fortune, and a heart practised to the best philosophy." In the noble course of this lawyer, we see much to shield our profession from the injustice of general censure and the stigma of indiscriminate reproach.

To a list, which might be extended by so many additions from the ranks of "the mighty dead," let me point you to the seats of the living. At the risk of inflicting pain, I must marshal one or two names gathered from the roll of our own records. These gentlemen, having, for the most part, retired from the active struggles of the Bar, no reason exists why we should be silent, when silence is injustice as well to them, as to ourselves. They belong to us and our community. The Philadelphia Bar, who witnessed and participated in their triumphs, may claim to assert the honours of their membership, and the benefits of their living example. It is to the high and unblemished integrity of a Du Ponceau and a Binney, of a Sergeant and a Chauncey, that we are indebted for the acknowledged pre-eminence of the Philadelphia Bar over the Union. In the homely phrase of an ancient legal writer, these gentlemen knew of "what stuff a right worthy lawyer was to be made." They well knew, that though legal learning and general knowledge were alike necessary for chamber practice and forensic display, yet that without an elevated honour, their reputation, like the Prophet's gourd, would wither in a night. They knew they would be like a ship at sea, without ballast or a compass, fearlessly exposing herself to the elements, which seemed to waft her to her port, but which were only conspiring their forces for her ruin. They knew, by the unaided exertions of their eminent talents, that "they could rise like the rocket," but without the sustaining arm of a superior power, "they must fall like the stick." It is at once a proof of the existence and effect of the principle

30

which I have feebly attempted to illustrate, that these eminent men, though engaged for a long series of years, in nearly all the important causes which were tried in this city, and though frequently on opposite sides, all the collisions of the forum have not impaired their respect for each other, nor disturbed the intimacy of their early friendship. This certainly is a spectacle worthy of all admiration.—And I am unable to express a higher wish for the personal and professional success of the members of this Academy, than that, like them, they may win a deserved renown for goodness as well as greatness; that in the evening of their days they may find warm hearts in the bosoms of their early friends and co-labourers of this institution; and that honoured themselves, and conferring honour on others, they may descend to the rich blessings of a well spent life.

NOTES.

Note 1, *Page* 6.—I refer, in the text, to the prohibitions used by Coke upon the proceedings of the High Commission Court, (Vide 12 Rep. 50,) and the manly resistance which he made to the numerous proclamations of James 1st. This monarch, in the first year of his reign, issued thirty-seven of these edicts, most of them illegal, and many of them entrenching upon the authority of Parliament. Wilson, the historian, says, "the people took them for good payment a great while, till the multitude of them lessened their valuation." (Kennet, Vol. II. p. 667.) As soon as James arrived in England, he issued a proclamation for the apprehension of William and Patrick Ruthven, two of the Gowrie conspirators. This was soon followed by edicts against monopolies; one relating to the making of starch, and another forbidding the erection of buildings in London; commanding the magistrates to pull down those which were erected contrary to the order, to sell the materials, and imprison the workmen. Some of these proclamations aimed at absolute power; such, for example, as tended to alter the law of the land, of which kind there were many. Some denounced penalties for the commission of acts to which no punishment was affixed by law; some related to matters directly rejected by Parliament, just before prorogued; some appointed punishments to be inflicted before lawful trial and conviction; and others contained penalties in the form of penal statutes. Hume, in his history of this reign, has erroneously stated that these royal proclamations had the force of law, asserting that they "were established by uniform and undisputed practice, and *even acknowledged by lawyers*, who made, however, this difference between laws and proclamations, that the authority of the former was perpetual, while that of the latter expired with the sovereign who emitted them." This declaration seems to be without foundation, except, perhaps that Bacon and the court may have suggested this ingenious gloss to so dangerous a prerogative. The judges, with Sir Edward Coke at their head, delivered the following resolution at the Michaelmas term of 1612, touching the validity of these regal ordinances: "It was resolved, that the king, by his proclamation, cannot create any offence which was not an offence before, for then he may alter the law of the land by his proclamation in a high point; for if he may create an offence where none is, upon that ensues fine and imprisonment. Also, the law of England is divided into three parts: common law, statute law, and custom: but the king's proclamation is none of them. Also, *malum aut est malum in se, aut prohibitum*, that which is

32

against common law, is *malum in se; malum prohibitum* is such an offence as is prohibited by act of parliament. Also, it was resolved, that the king hath no prerogative but that which the law of the land allows him. But the king, for prevention of offences, may admonish his subjects by proclamation that they keep the laws, and do not offend them, upon punishment to be inflicted by the law; and lastly, if the offence be not punishable in the Star Chamber, the prohibition of it by proclamation cannot make it punishable there." (12 Rep. 74.)

James himself, in one of his proclamations, disproves the assertion of Hume, by admitting the correctness of the opinion expressed by the judges in the above resolutions: "So, although we know that by the constitution of the frame and policie of this kingdom, royal proclamations and ordinances are *not of equal force*, nor in the like degrees with our laws," &c. (Vide Book of Proclamations, p. 235.)

Note 2, *Page* 13.—It is but just to mention that Erskine, though the advocate of Paine in a prosecution founded upon "The Rights of Man," displayed his detestation of the infidel opinions of this writer, as expressed in his "Age of Reason." He was employed to conduct the prosecution in the case of Williams, for the publication of this notorious book. In the course of his speech, on that occasion, he made the following eloquent profession of his religious faith: "For my own part," says he, "I have been ever devoted to the truths of Christianity; and my firm belief in the Holy Gospel, is by no means owing to the prejudices of education, (though I was religiously educated by the best of parents,) but has arisen from the fullest and most continued reflections of my riper years and understanding. It forms, at this moment, the great consolation of a life which, as a shadow, passes away; and without it, I should consider my long course of health and prosperity, (too long, perhaps, and too uninterrupted to be good for any man,) as the dust which the wind scatters, and rather as a snare than a blessing."

I extract the following narrative of some touching particulars of this case, from Roscoe's Lives, &c. It exhibits Erskine in a most amiable point of view, and disposes us to draw a veil over the infirmities which marked a subsequent period of his life. "The prosecution in this case," says Mr. Roscoe, "had been instituted by the 'Proclamation Society,' an association for the suppression of blasphemous and seditious publications, and Mr. Erskine appeared to support it by virtue of the general retainer which he held for the society. Williams was convicted, and on the motion of Mr. Erskine, was brought up for judgment. Between the time of that motion and the judgment of the court being passed upon him, some circumstances occurred which induced Mr. Erskine to suggest to

33

those who employed him, the propriety of instructing him to state that they were satisfied with the punishment already inflicted on the defendant by his commitment to Newgate. The answer from the society was, that though they did not wish to press for a severe judgment, they did not feel themselves justified in expressing a wish for lenity. This resolution being communicated by the secretary to Mr. Erskine, he declined being further concerned for the society, and returned their retainer. A statement of the circumstances, which induced Mr. Erskine to adopt this unusual step, was many years afterwards communicated by him to Mr. Howell, the editor of the State Trials, at the request of that gentleman. The narrative is a very interesting one. "Having convicted Williams, as will appear by your report of his trial, and before he had notice to attend the court to receive judgment, I happened to pass one day through the Old Turnstile, from Holborn, in my way to Lincoln's Inn Fields, when, in the narrowest part of it, I felt something pulling me by the coat: when, on turning round, I saw a woman at my feet bathed in tears, and emaciated with disease and sorrow, who continued almost to drag me into a miserable hovel in the passage, where I found she was attending upon two or three unhappy children in the confluent small-pox, and in the same apartment, not above ten or twelve feet square, the wretched man whom I had convicted was sewing up little religious tracts, which had been his principal employment in his trade; and I was fully convinced that his poverty, and not his will, had led to the publication of this infamous book, as, without any kind of stipulation for money on my part, he voluntarily and eagerly engaged to find out all the copies in circulation, and to bring them to me to be destroyed.

"I was most deeply affected with what I had seen, and feeling the strongest impression that he offered a happy opportunity to the prosecutors of vindicating, and rendering universally popular, the cause in which they had succeeded, I wrote my opinion to that effect, observing, (if I well remember,) that mercy being the grand characteristic of the christian religion, which had been defamed and insulted, it might be here exercised, not only safely, but more usefully to the objects of the prosecution, than by the most severe judgment, which must be attended with the ruin of this helpless family.

"My advice was most respectfully received by the society, and I have no doubt honestly rejected, because that most excellent prelate, Bishop Porteus, and many other honourable persons, concurred in rejecting it; but I had still a duty of my own to perform, considering myself not as counsel for the society, but for the crown. If I had been engaged for all or any of the individuals composing it, prosecuting by indictment, for any personal injury punishable by indictment, and had convicted a defendant, I must have impli-

34

citly followed my instructions, however inconsistent with my own ideas of humanity or moderation; because every man who is injured has a clear right to demand the highest penalty which the law will inflict; but in the present instance, I was not retained at all, but responsible to the crown for my conduct. Such a voluntary society, however respectable or useful, having received no injury, could not erect itself into a *custos morum*, and claim a right to dictate to counsel who had consented to be employed on the part of the king for the ends of justice only."

Note 3, *Page* 15.—Dr. Arnott, in his Elements of Physics, vol. 1, p. 48, illustrates the importance of physical science to the lawyer, by giving the following amusing anecdote:—"A young and not yet skilful Jehu, having run his phæton against a heavy carriage on the road, foolishly and dishonestly excused his awkwardness, in a way which led to his father's prosecuting the old coachman for furious driving. The youth and his servant both deposed, that the shock of the carriage was so great as to throw them over their horses' heads; and thus they lost the cause by unwittingly proving that the *faulty velocity was their own*."—Mr. Chitty, in his late excellent work on General Practice, gives several instances of almost incredible ignorance in the English Judges. From this work, 2d vol. p. 321, note, I take the following passage:—"It will not be denied that in many cases, it is of the utmost importance, not only that the judge should be of general ability, but also be familiarly acquainted with the subject to be tried, for otherwise he will not be able to explain and observe upon to the jury the facts and law applicable to the case, and a just result will be endangered. Lord Mansfield was celebrated for his great knowledge of insurance and mercantile law, and consequently, whilst he presided, an admirable system of mercantile law, as regarded those subjects, was established. Whilst it is well known that another judge was so entirely ignorant of insurance causes, that after having been occupied six hours in trying an action on a policy of insurance upon goods (Russia duck,) from Russia, he, in his address to the jury, complained that no evidence had been given to show how Russia ducks (mistaking the cloth of that name for the bird,) could be damaged by sea-water, and to what extent." Two ludicrous instances of ignorance of *history*, are related upon good authority. "An Irish barrister, referring to two great events, viz. the obtaining of *Magna Charta*, and the *Bill of Rights*, confounded the sovereigns from whom they were exacted; and a celebrated English barrister, having occasion to quote a statute, and being required to mention the period at which it passed, very gravely replied, that it was 'in the reign of one of the Henrys, or one of the Edwards—but he could not exactly tell which.'" Vide Will. Stu.

and Pra. of the Law, p. 31. History and law are so kindred in their nature, and so connected in their objects, that Montesquieu does not hesitate to say, "Il faut eclaircir l'histoire par les lois, et les lois par l'histoire." Esp. de Lois, l. 21, c. 2.

Note 4, *Page* 19.—The value of competent knowledge and skill, in a counsel, and the deplorable results of a want of either, may be learnt from a fact stated by Mr. Warren, in his Law Studies, (note, p. 196.) "It is said that the late eminent conveyancer, Mr. Butler, in early life, committed a blunder, in framing a will, which deprived the party whom he was expressly and anxiously instructed to benefit, of about £14,000 a year! It was the omission of *a single word*—'Gloucester,'—that was attended with these disastrous consequences." See this case referred to in Miller vs. Travers, 8 Bing. p. 254–5. Owing to the great skill and exact learning necessary for conveyancing, and the awkward blunders which arise from the dearth of these requisites, it is very desirable, for the interests of the public, that a portion of the legal profession should give their attention to this most important branch of jurisprudence. If a body of learned lawyers in Philadelphia, were to addict themselves exclusively to *conveyancing and pleading*, as a separate and distinct branch of practice, it is believed a high benefit would be conferred upon the community. The neglect however of any part of legal science, is dangerous, as it may be attended with the most serious consequences. Witness the following examples, vouched by so respectable a writer as Mr. Chitty. (See Chitt. Gen. Pr., Vol. I. Pref. 8, note (a) 2d ed.) "Recently," says he, "a *common law* barrister, very eminent for his legal attainments, sound opinions, and great practice, advised that there was *no remedy whatever* against a married woman, who, having a considerable separate estate, had joined with her husband in a promissory note for £2500 for a debt of her husband; because he was of opinion that the contract of a married woman was absolutely void, and referred to a decision to that effect, (Marshall *v.* Rutton, 8 T. R. 545,) not knowing or forgetting, that *in equity*, under such circumstances, payment might be enforced out of the separate estate. And afterwards, a very eminent *equity* counsel, equally erroneously advised, in the same case, that the remedy was only in equity; although it appeared, upon the face of the case, as then stated, that after the death of her husband, the wife had promised to pay, in consideration of forbearance, and upon which promise, she might have been *arrested* and sued at law. If, now, the common law counsel had properly advised proceedings in equity, or if the equity counsel had advised proceedings by arrest, at law, upon the promise made after the husband's death, the whole of this large debt would have been paid. But, upon this latter opinion, a bill in

36

chancery was filed: and so much time elapsed before decree, that a great part of the property was dissipated, the wife escaped with the residue into France, and the creditor thus wholly lost his debt, which would have been recovered if the proper proceedings had been adopted, in the first or even second instance!—This is one of the *very numerous* cases almost daily occurring, illustrative of the consequences of the want of at least a general knowledge of *every* branch of law."

Note 5, *Page* 23.—It may be affirmed, that the man who is under the dominion of anger, is, for the time, deprived of reason, and that his language and acts deserve little more respect or consideration than those of the inebriate or bedlamite. Cicero says, "Semper ira procul absit, cum qua nihil recte, nihil considerate fieri potest, nec eis, qui adsunt probari." What the Roman satirist said of the maudlin Darius, may be applied to the reasoning faculty of the angry man;

"Hic est damnatus inani judicio."

Seneca, in his celebrated treatise, *De Ira*, speaks of the "irae exitus furor," and *delirium* is no unnatural offspring of ungoverned passion.

Note 6, *Page* 26.—It is not attempted to be concealed, that Coke had many faults, the greatest of which, perhaps the *cause* of his private infelicity and public downfall, was his *temper*. An estrangement arose between him and Bacon, which was never reconciled. But the characters of the two men are illustrated by the conduct of each in his intercourse with the other. Bacon, envying the reputation of Coke, did all to undermine it, that meanness, aided by a fertile genius, could suggest. Coke slighted and despised the more elegant accomplishments of his younger rival, and took no pains to suppress the exhibition of his feelings. He was, in fact, too direct and manly in his character, as well as too violent and headlong in his impulses, to exercise a control or restraint in opposition to his sentiments. Roscoe gives the following anecdote: "Bacon presented to him (Coke,) a copy of his *Novum Organum*, with the title *Instauratio Magna*, and containing a device of a ship sailing. Upon the title-page Coke has written,—

'*Edw. C. ex dono auctoris.*
Auctori consilium.
'*Instaurare paras veterum documenta sophorum,*
Instaura leges justitiamque prius.'

And over the device,—

'*It deserveth not to be read in schools,*
But to be freighted in the ship of fools,'

The volume still remains at Holkham."

CHAPTER VI

THE

LAWYER,

HIS CHARACTER AND RULE OF HOLY LIFE:

AFTER THE MANNER OF

GEORGE HERBERT'S

COUNTRY PARSON.

BY EDWARD O'BRIEN,

BARRISTER AT LAW.

PHILADELPHIA:

CAREY AND HART.

1843.

O'Brien, Edward. *The Lawyer, His Character and Rule of Holy Life: After the Manner of George Herbert's Country Parson.* Philadelphia: Carey and Hart, 1843.

T. K. & P. G. COLLINS, Printers,
No. 1 Lodge Alley.

CONTENTS.

INTRODUCTION.

"So natural is the union of Religion with Justice, that we may boldly deem there is neither where both are not. For how should they be unfeignedly just, whom religion doth not cause to be such; or they religious, which are not found such by the proof of their just actions? If they which employ their labour and travail about the public administration of justice, follow it only as a trade, with an unquenchable and unconscionable thirst of gain; being not in heart persuaded that justice is God's own work, and themselves his agents in this business; the sentence of right God's own verdict, and themselves his priests to deliver it; formalities of justice do but serve to smother right, and that which was necessarily ordained for the common good, is, through shameful abuse, made the cause of common misery."—*Hooker's Ecclesiastical Polity*, book v. c. 1.

THE Author of the following work was the late Edward O'Brien, third son of the late Sir Edward O'Brien, of Dromoland. He was born in the year 1808. After taking his degree at Trinity College, Cambridge, he became a member of the Irish bar. He died in 1840 of a fever caught in consequence of his exertions on behalf of some religious and charitable societies established in Dublin; exertions which, when added to his professional pursuits, were more than his strength was equal to.

In the composition of this book the author had no thoughts of fame, or what is called literary success. His impulse was simply the love of justice: his only motive was the desire to assist others in the performance of their duty.

I can truly affirm of this treatise that it is a sincere book. It came from the heart of its author, and embodies his most solemn convictions. A book so written is as the very soul of a man conversing with his fellow men: recording for their benefit the best thoughts of his best hours: presenting them in a brief space, with principles, the sifted and select result of all his studies, meditations, and experience: counselling them, exhorting them: witnessing for what he has known of truth; and putting it forth, with his prayers; that it may serve to the need of his brethren. Such a work, if read at all, should be read with attention and respect: unless we approach it in an ingenuous spirit, willing to understand before we criticise, deeming it possible that the objections which present themselves to our minds so readily, may have occurred to the author also, and been for good reasons put aside; desiring to stand, at least for the time, on the spot which he occupied, and contemplate the subject from his point of view; if we do not possess this small measure of self-command and philosophical docility, then there does not exist between our mind and that of the writer such a degree of moral conformity as is necessary for the appreciation of his work. We shall in such a case do ourselves least injury, and our monitor least injustice, by leaving his book unread.

I have offered this caution because at the present day books are often put forth in a trifling or mercenary spirit; and are therefore as petulantly condemned as they were corruptly written. The present work is particularly obnoxious to rash judgments, because it assails popular prejudices: and it can no longer be defended by him whose vigorous intellect might at a later time have further supported his present argument; whose consistent and upright conduct as a Lawyer would have proved the best vindication of his principles. It deserves, however, a candid consideration. It is the gift, alas! the legacy of one who did not write a single line without deep reflection and a worthy intention.

From his earliest years my lamented friend was remarkable for a scrupulous regard to justice. I have never known another person so entirely conscientious. On all occasions his first desire was to know what ought to be done, and do it. The great and invisible things which belong to truth, justice, and mercy, seemed with him ever present. On the other hand, the ordinary objects of selfish ambition appeared to him fastastic and unreal. It is not uncommon to meet men who inquire, as metaphysicians, into the first principles of right and wrong: but he followed justice into its minutest details: he believed the broken bread of justice to be the food of all social life, and reverently gathered up its very crumbs: nothing seemed to him trivial in which conscience had a part. While his faith was thus strong, he was, from natural disposition, and from habits of philosophical inquiry, unusually sceptical as to matters of the mere understanding. Those who remember his extreme caution will not be tempted to think that on so important a subject he had rushed precipitately into a system of his own.

His religious convictions were profound: he knew that moral principles have their root in divine truths, and can only be realized through aid from above. This will account for the christian tone that pervades his work: indeed, but for these convictions, I do not know whether it would ever have been written. Justice is fond rather of upbraiding than assisting. It was christian zeal and christian charity which inspired him with an unceasing desire to maintain what he believed to be the cause of truth. In particular he was anxious to assist those young men of his profession, who with views in the main honourable, and average clearness of mind, are yet unequal to contend against the favourite corruption of the time, supported as it is, not only by personal interest, but by a very large number of specious sophisms offered to their choice, as well as a considerable weight of pretended authority and modern tradition.

His religion was eminently practical in the true sense of the word. It was his habit to observe the influence of christian principles as applied to the common detail of life. He disliked religious controversy; and occult dogmas, he thought, were to be believed in faithfully, not scrutinized impertinently. He loved the reflected light of christian truth; and remembered that if we fix a direct gaze too long upon the sun, our eyes are dimmed, and we walk in the dark. He meditated often on that text, "Thy word is a lantern unto my feet," and appeared to discover a spirituality in obedience which escapes the penetration of more speculative religionists. The consequence was such as might be expected. The professions, indeed all occupations by which men live, and which are permanent elements in society, seemed to him delivered from the secular character that belongs to them naturally. He did not consider the Christian commonwealth as consisting of statesmen, lawyers, physicians, farmers, and other classes of men, who, besides their social avocations, possess religious opinions: rather he viewed it as a body of Christians who are led providentially to certain outward pursuits; who undertake them on christian conditions; who speak sincerely in naming each such pursuit a calling; ("the state of life to which it hath pleased God to call me"), and who regard it not chiefly as a means of selfish advancement, but as the sphere of those labours allotted to them by the divine command, and for the good of their neighbour. Such a doctrine must always appear to the world as visionary, because it requires us to become unworldly: nay, it carries the war into the enemy's camp: and seems to violate that silent truce by which religion, on condition of not trespassing beyond bounds, or interfering with the Babel-worship of the world, is permitted to remain herself unmolested—except by being superseded. Such, however, were the opinions which my friend maintained. Had he been a statesman or a physician, I doubt not that he would have particularly considered how the duties attaching to such callings might be fulfilled in a manner confessedly christian: and I am further of opinion that his devout inquiries would not have returned to him unsatisfied; and that, without incurring the charge of being either a fanatic or a simpleton, he would have strengthened many to walk along those tortuous paths as men not ashamed of their baptismal cross, or afraid to confess themselves in their daily walk of life the "servants and soldiers of Christ."

The opinions put forward in this book were frequently tested by the author in friendly discussions; for he was most anxious to consider whatever might be urged on the other side. As a lawyer he acted religiously on his convictions: and thus became fully assured that his principles were capable of being realized, though (as is the case with all other duties) not without self-sacrifice.

He did not think meanly of those who adopt the ordinary views of the legal profession. Believing their principles on this particular subject to be worthy of severe condemnation, he yet denied not that many who act on those principles are good, honourable, and wise men. They have inherited an error, and they propagate it. Some of the best men who lived three hundred years ago deemed it a duty to persecute with fire and sword. Three hundred years hence, men not worse than ourselves may do what we should be ashamed of doing. We are clear-sighted enough concerning that evil which is foreign to us; but we lack strength to wrestle with the error of the day. We cannot even discern its true proportions; much of it remains invisible: its outline is uncertain: it is everywhere diffused: it is consistent with the philosophy of the time, and we are all indirectly philosophers: it is associated with the remembrance of those whom we revere, and we all reason through the affections: we are probably committed to it by our past conduct; or it is congenial with the principles on which we act. Moreover, to put away a conviction long entertained is not like changing our clothes: it is a painful process more analogous to flaying off a diseased part of the skin; our principles not being adventitiously picked up, but silently exuded from within, like the bark of a tree, and gradually hardened by exposure.

The few points in my friend's character to which I have adverted will best explain the design of his book, and his motives in writing it. I have recorded them for that small but fit audience which alone he wished to gather round him. What degree of popular favour may await this work is of but little importance. The grave which has closed on its author does not more securely shield him from the arrows of fortune, and the sharp or flattering speeches of men, than did his own manly and modest nature: and those who remain will possess in this book a memorial of their friend more consoling than public applause could be. In it his portraiture remains: stamped upon it they will find not his love of justice alone, but that kindness which made him seem, if injured, to remember justice only against himself: they will observe his fearless reverence for truth, and at the same time his respect for opinions long established; his slowness to oppose them; his candour in weighing them; his charitable desire to exculpate those who hold them, and that higher charity which stimulated him to combat their error: they will be reminded of his reluctance to give pain, and his greater fear of doing wrong; his distrust of his own judgment, and his invariable faith in the moral sense and the Divine commands; his indifference to promiscuous applause, and his solicitude for the esteem of those he esteemed, the love of those he loved. They will find many light traces, for memory to fill up, of his single-heartedness, his humility, his earnestness, and his courtesy. Some passages will bring back before their eyes the very gestures and expression of countenance with which he used to enunciate such sentiments.

The style of the following pages, though different from that of the present day, is entirely unaffected. The author's reading lay principally amongst old books, and he therefore wrote naturally in their manner. Should any passages be imperfectly expressed, the friendly reader will remember that this work was the only exercise which the author had in composition, and that it remains without his final corrections. Should exceptions be made against its statements in matters of detail, we must not allow our attention to be diverted by a trifle from the broad principles of the book. As for mere casuistical objections, it is a very shallow philosophy that takes fright at them. Such difficulties must ever be met in the circle of nature and duty. They are the eddying points of meeting and converse truths. Theoretic systems are easily made consistent; but their congruity does not prove their reality. The symmetry that can be measured is but a finite symmetry. That freedom from casuistical difficulties which we often find in human schemes, proves of itself that they form no part in the providential structure of things; that they possess only an isolated, arbitrary existence, and have been worked out by a single faculty of the human understanding.

For myself, I concur most heartily in the main doctrines of this book. If justice, mercy, and truth (the common root of justice aud mercy), are to forego their obvious claims on man, in deference whether to a theory imagined or a course adopted by him, I do not know how these qualities can long continue to be venerated as the attributes of God; and as such only will they maintain their ground among men. If the law courts are necessarily so depraved that, to advance the interests of society, the barrister must violate his duty to his neighbour, then I should believe with the Quakers that Christians ought to abstain from legal proceedings. To consider the matter morally:—If the rights of the individual (when we can ascertain them with that assurance on which men act generally) are to be set at nought for the greatest good of the greatest number, then the first moral distinction is done away with, however unwittingly, that namely between persons and things; and morality itself ceases to exist.

To look at the question politically:—The legal profession is now the prominent one amongst us. It is closely connected with power, and the State. What then will be the probable consequence if lawyers are bound over by an imaginary necessity to devote the larger part of their time, thoughts, and energies to exertions in which right has not the first part? But few of the soldier's hours are spent in fighting: all the toils of the physician may be mitigated by pity and generous care: intellectual labours elevate the mind: mechanical employments leave the thoughts free. What then will be the lawyer's influence on society? What will be the consequence to the nation when those men preside over her affairs, of whom the least unfavourable account would be that they had qualified themselves for their senatorial duties, by working, during their apprenticeship, as senseless parts of a great machine? I think the consequences will at last be these. A public neglect of principle, a contempt of principle, a growing incapacity to understand or believe in principle: the deplorable spectacle of a nation reduced to a commercial establishment; denying her responsibilities, and betraying her trusts: a shifting, shuffling, state-craft of expedients: a beggarly catching at momentary devices: the observation of these corruptions by the people; the palliation, the imitation: mutual distrust: infinite covetousness: a dependance on mere mercantile credit substituted for that spirit of moral uprightness which was of old the life of England's strength, the source of her prosperity, and the cause of her great estimation among foreign nations.

Law is not the rival of justice, but an instrument for the attainment of justice. It was impossible to construct such an instrument so that it should not, if used unrighteously or even indifferently, work injustice. Thus we cannot forge a weapon to cut down an enemy, which may not also be used to murder a friend; we cannot raise an altar on which it is impossible to sacrifice to idols; we cannot discover a medicine which malignity or carelessness may not convert into a poison. In all such cases a good intention and good sense are supposed on the part of those who are to use the resources they find prepared for their hand.

There are persons who imagine that if the conventional course of things be in any respect modified, the whole civil fabric must fall to pieces. It is not improbable that every evil which has not long existed, may have been so far overruled as to be made the means of some good: but surely a much higher though a different good must result wherever a moral evil is extirpated. Drunkenness, it has been said, swells the revenue; vanity stimulates to exertion: would a nation therefore suffer loss if men became sober and modest? The common interest of all will best be promoted where each person is careful to do his own duty simply. To apply this. An advocate is of course not a judge in the technical sense of the word. In a moral sense, circumstances must often enable him, sometimes compel him, to judge on which side lies the right and on which the wrong. If in such cases lawyers invariably accounted it base to insinuate error or conceal truth; to assist in violating justice and trampling the oppressed; nay, though all who enter the legal profession were to be governed therein by the same conscientious principles which direct them in their private relations, I cannot help thinking that society would sustain no greater calamity than it could bear.

In conclusion, I commend this noble and religious book to the careful attention of those, who, like its author, desire to follow the pursuits of this life in such a manner as will favour their growth in the life interior and eternal: especially I commend it to the younger members of the Bar; and to those whose opinions are not yet made up, or who have courage and candour, and patience to reconsider them. I would also recommend it to those, who, fatigued or discouraged by the laborious littleness of the law when followed as a trade, may not be unwilling to try it as a profession, in the hope that its aspect may become somewhat less dull when contemplated in a purer light, and its yoke less burdensome when taken up in the ancient spirit, with a single eye to God's glory, and a vehement desire to do good among men.

A. DE V.

THE LAWYER.

APOLOGY FOR THE WORK.

WHEN having penned the little work which follows, I thought of making it public in the hope that I might thus call attention to the principles it embodies; before I determined upon so bold a course I put it into the hands of a valued friend, whose counsel I esteemed not less highly than his friendship. In the main he commended my design; but warned me, if I would not have my book thrown aside as soon as opened, to add a preface by way of Apology for the principles contained in it: not because in truth he deemed they needed any excuse; but because they belong to a way now everywhere spoken against, though once in this land avowed and followed ere '*the useful*' and '*the expedient*' had usurped the place of '*the right*' and '*the honest*,' and ere the divine precepts of a Leighton, a Taylor, and a Barrow, had given way to the earth-born speculations of a Locke, a Paley, or a Bentham. I have listened to his counsel, and pray the patience of the reader while I attempt to comply with it.

The object of the following pages is to portray in outline the character of a British Lawyer; to suggest the motives which should animate him and the principles which should direct him in the exercise of his calling. And here at the outset I shall be asked—What need, at this period of our nation, for that which if ever necessary should have been accomplished centuries ago?—The answer to this question involves a censure on the present age, the justice of which it can scarce be expected to acknowledge readily. In earlier times[1] no manual (so far as I know) was offered to the Professors of the Law, to direct or control their conduct; to impugn false or to suggest right principles: the chivalric spirit of the profession,[2] which regarded the fee of the lawyer as the offering of gratitude, not as wages for labour, would have turned with abhorrence from a theory which makes a lawyer the mere implement of his client, to be used at his pleasure for good or for ill: and though doubtless there were but too many who by their accursed avarice and unjust arts gave occasion to the censures of the satirist and the moralist, such censures fell harmlessly upon the profession at large, which defended itself by repudiating the principles against which those attacks were directed. Now however that principles[3] in morals generally, and particularly in regard to the professional conduct of advocates, which former ages would have shrunk from with disgust are openly avowed and commonly followed, it seemed not an idle task to set forth the portraiture of that character which once was, and, though too often ridiculed, I trust yet is the property of many; to the end that those who may never heretofore have thought seriously upon the deep responsibilities which attach to the calling of the lawyer, may look upon either picture and choose which they will for their own: whether they will consider themselves in the exercise of their calling as "under no obligation to speak the truth;"[4] as "paid for affecting warmth when they have no warmth, and for appearing to be clearly of one opinion when they are in reality of another opinion;"[5] as "men who with wigs on their heads and bands round their necks may without blame do for a guinea what without these appendages they would think it wicked and infamous to do for an empire:"[6] or whether they will not rather on the other hand consider themselves as the agents of God in the work of justice;[7] as "the counsellors, secretaries, interpreters, and servants of justice, the lady and queen of all moral virtues;"[8] as "orators bound to use the power of their tongue and wit to shame impudence, to protect innocency, to crush oppressors, to succour the afflicted, to advance justice and equity, and to help them to right that suffer wrong."[9]

But let us descend to particulars and view more closely the theories which have enabled philosophers, moralists, and divines to look unmoved, ay! admiring, upon the hideous features of the former picture: and

I. *First;* let us examine that which represents the advocate as an instrument—a conduit pipe—a mere mouth-piece; whose office it is with all his powers to advance any claim, no matter how opposed to the laws of God or man, which may be committed to him; and in the exercise of this office bound, because paid, to put forward in the way of statement, argument, or opinion whatever may be suggested or enjoined by his client, no matter how false, sophistical, or unfounded. "Every member of society (it is said by those who adopt this view), whether accusing or accused, has a natural right to speak freely and fully for himself; and if either by a legal or natural incapacity this cannot be done in person, to have a *proxy* provided or allowed by the state to do for him what he cannot or may not do for himself,"[10] and this is alleged irrespectively of the justice or injustice of the accusation or defence which it may please him to make. The lawyer is the representative, the interpreter of his client, and if he does otherwise than the client bids or wills, the client is not properly represented.

The obvious error in this theory is the assumption that any one can have a *natural right* to ask the aid of another in doing what is unjust or wrong. It cannot even be asserted that a man when acting alone has a natural right to do wrong: he has, it may be, a *power* to do so; but he can have no right: much less can he have a right to ask assistance from his fellow man. And hence it would seem to follow as a necessary consequence of the above theory—a consequence which I believe is found its practical result—that a dishonest, base, and impious client should of right be represented by a dishonest, base, and impious advocate: a trusty, upright counsellor dare not—could not—with an unblushing countenance allege that as true which he believes to be untrue, or defend that as just which he knows to be unjust: and hence the duty of doing so—if duty it be—must of necessity devolve upon him, who, skilled in the ways of falsehood and fraud, can with composure act a part which habit has rendered easy to him. That in different ages there should have been found men, in all other relations of life listening with attention to the voice of conscience and earnestly seeking to obey its dictates, who, seduced by a false estimate of duty and mistaken feelings of humanity, have persuaded themselves that in the exercise of their calling they might without blame lay aside their moral nature, and, divesting themselves of the higher character of *men*, suffer themselves to be used as mere *things*—is a fact which, while it may not be denied, must ever be deplored, and which can be accounted for only by the technical habit of thought to which the study of positive law introduces its professors. For myself, I can imagine no more melancholy picture than that which is presented by an advocate, who when a client seeks his help, instead of using all his energies to deter a fellow being from the perpetration of injustice, assists him with his talents, his knowledge, and experience, in crime against man and sin before God: nor, however in its weakness the law of the land may omit him from its catalogue of criminals, do I see how the advocate who pursues such a course can, according to the verdict of right reason or of conscience, be guiltless in the eye of Heaven, until it shall be shown that the abettor in the breach of God's laws is in his eyes less culpable, than in the eye of man is the accomplice in offences against human laws.

But it is asked—Why should it be accounted more immoral in an advocate faithfully to detail a case as stated to him by his client, without troubling himself as to the truth or falsehood of the facts contained in it, than it is in an interpreter?—The simple answer is that the advocate is not an interpreter—and the difference follows necessarily from the different parts sustained by the two characters. The interpreter is the minister of the court, and as such is bound faithfully to fulfil the part entrusted to him. The advocate, on the other hand, is the assistant, the counsellor, the friend of his client, and as such is concerned that he for whom he acts do that alone which is just and right. Were the interpreter, as he sometimes is or may easily be supposed, the minister of the client and not of the court, it would be his bounden duty to his client in the exercise of his office to convey nothing to the court which he knew or was convinced was false.

II. But again:—It is said by some more careful for the common good and less tenacious of the liberty for every man to do that which is right in his own eyes—it is said:—"The advocate is part of the machine of justice,[11] for the efficacious working of which there must be a due subordination of the different parts: each lever, chain, and wheel must perform the work allotted to it and none other; otherwise, confusion and destruction will be the result. The judge must not become advocate, nor the advocate judge; the jury may not declare the law, nor the judge decide the facts." In this view it is alleged that "it is not the duty of the advocate to make statements which he knows to be false, or to urge arguments which he believes to be of no weight. He is to his client not a passive instrument but a moral representative, limited only in this;—that he is bound to appear and act for any person who may demand his services; and so acting to put forward that alone whether of law or fact which is favourable to his client; leaving it to the opposing counsel to state all that is of weight against him, and to the judge to decide between these conflicting statements: and should the case, as must often happen, be wrongly decided, either from the ignorance of the opposing counsel or the weakness and incapacity of the judge, this must be attributed to the imperfection of all human laws, and not charged on the advocate, who in urging to the best of his power whatever was to be said on the side of his client has fulfilled his allotted part; and who, had he done more, would have been guilty of a breach of professional duty. Thus for example—that advocate would be blameless who should rely upon a will executed in the presence of the required number of witnesses, though he might be well aware that the signature affixed to it was that of an idiot or a madman; or who should quote a decided case in law, without alluding to decisions which weaken its authority."

If by this mode of stating the case it were merely intended to assert that the lawyer must often, within the sphere of action in which he is placed, be witness of evil which it is not in his power to prevent without himself doing wrong, there would be no need to quarrel with the position. The whole world thus regarded is but a vast machine of which each individual is a part, with a limited sphere of action assigned to him. But if it is thereby intended to represent the advocate as divested of moral responsibility, because acting as part of a system which tends on the whole to produce good results, and therefore *useful*, and because useful *right;* the theory is as untenable as the philosophy under which it is included is unsound and debasing. I will not here enter into an examination of that withering system of morals, which beneath the whited mask of *utility* conceals within dead men's bones and all uncleanness. This has been done too often of late years[12] to render such a course necessary. I shall merely consider it as it stands applied to the particular case we have now in hand.

"The lawyer," it is said, "is part of the machine of justice:"—Be it so:—he is still a *man;* and as man is endowed with a sense of what is *right* and *wrong*, of what is *true* and *false*, of what is *just* and *unjust;* and being so endowed is bound to the utmost of his power to advance what is right, true, and just, and to oppose what is contrary to these. Now suppose that a lawyer entrusted with a client's cause—good, bad, or indifferent as the case may be—puts forward to the court that alone which is favourable to his client, carefully suppressing all that weighs against him; and so from the ignorance of the opposing counsel or of the judge, causes that more be adjudged to his client than he knows or believes to be just: though it be alleged that, looked at in regard to *general consequences*, that is the course in the main best calculated to promote the ends of justice, however it may have failed in the particular instance; is it (I ask) the course in which the lawyer has done what is right? If a client in person be admitted to plead his own cause, conscience requires, and no law forbids that he demand that alone which he believes to be just. Why then should the lawyer standing in the client's place do otherwise? If he does so at the instance of his client, he becomes a willing accomplice in a premeditated act of injustice. If he does so against the wish of his client—what excuse has he to plead for thus making his client an involuntary instrument of evil? Not the necessity of the case, for no such necessity exists: not the obligation of the law,[13] for the law does not attempt to impose any such obligation. His only plea is *utility;* and utility can never be accepted as an excuse for doing or aiding in doing what is morally wrong. "Is it then," it is asked, "is it the bounden duty of the lawyer to state to the court every thing that can be said by either party, and to argue both sides of the case?" This by no means follows: one state of facts excludes another, and one view of law negatives that which is contrary to it. The lawyer professedly makes an *ex-parte* statement of the case and law applicable to it: but this is a very different thing from a garbled or *part* statement. For example: Titus by bond binds himself and his heirs for the payment to Timothy of a certain sum of money, with a condition (expressed in a separate instrument) that in case Titus or his heir at law be in London on the 29th day of February, 1801, the bond shall be void. Titus dies and his heir at law comes to London on the 1st day of March, 1801, but is wholly ignorant of the transaction. Whereupon Timothy sues him for the money mentioned in the bond; but makes no mention of the separate instrument whereby it was conditioned to be void. This is a part statement, and under ordinary circumstances would be wholly unjustifiable. But had Timothy sued the heir at law of Titus, alleging that he was not in London on the day required to make void the bond, this would be an *ex-parte* statement, and if maintainable would exclude the opposite statement, viz: that as there was no 29th day of February in the year 1801, the day intended must have been the 1st day of March. So again to omit in arguing a law case the mention of a statute directly referring to the matter in hand would be a *part* statement of the law: while to contend that the case, though coming within the statute, came also within some exception contained in it, would be an *ex-parte* statement, the other side contending that it did not come within such exception.

III. At this point intervene a third class of theorists, who say: "A suit at law between individuals is like a war between nations, in which artifices have always been adjudged lawful. Nations at peace may not deceive one another, but when once embarked in war they may employ stratagems to destroy their enemies. So in law a man may by himself or his advocate deceive another who is seeking to inflict a wrong upon him." As to the parallel here attempted to be drawn between the cases of war and law, it is to be remarked, that in war the same principles which give me a right to kill, give me also a right to mislead; and as on the one hand killing is no murder, so on the other deceit is no lie. But in law no such liberty of injuring another is conceded. At the bar of justice, justice alone may be sought: the evil deeds of others will not justify us in doing the like; and the rules of action must be the same which govern the intercourse of men in the common conduct of life.

"Is then," it is asked, "is no concealment, no stratagem of any kind allowable in repelling the attempts of wicked men to work injustice?"[14] This question is one of the most difficult in the whole range of casuistry, and has ever perplexed those who have sought to lay down rules for human conduct applicable to all cases. It will often happen that by silence a fact is made known to another who has no right to demand a knowledge of that fact, and who having obtained such knowledge will forthwith proceed to make an ill use of it: to rob, plunder, or murder. May I under such circumstances speak so as to mislead? and if so, why may I not directly tell a lie? tell a lie to attain a useful end? do evil that good may come? It is told of one Hooker, a puritan, in the days of Charles the First, that being pursued by some of the prelatic party, a friend in whose house he was, when interrogated by his pursuers "Whether Hooker was in his house?" replied, "What Hooker? Do you mean Hooker who once lived at Chelmsford?" The pursuers replied "Yes, that is he." "If it be he whom you look for," replied his friend, "I saw him about an hour ago at such a house in the town," which was strictly true, though said with the intent to mislead, and was all one as if he had said "He is not in my house." Are such evasions lawful under any circumstances? and if they be, does it not necessarily follow that *utility* will justify any act, no matter how wrong in itself?

The escape from this dilemma lies here:[15]—In every evil act there must be, to a greater or less extent, an evil intent—in *murder* there must be *malice;* in *theft* the injurious taking of another's goods; in a lie the intent wrongfully to mislead. To this it may be replied, "If the intent consecrates the act, those were justifiable who perpetrated the horrors of the Inquisition: they did it to make converts. Who is to judge of the intent whether it be good or bad?" The only answer is that the all-seeing eye of God alone is to judge infallibly. Man may judge to a certain extent, but his judgment is always liable to error; the only infallible judge is God. To him all must one day account, and then shall it be known whether he who has misled another has done so to his hurt or to his good; whether the advocate who has aided him in so doing, has done so for the sake of charity or of his fee. This consideration will sufficiently restrain those whose endeavour it is in all things to conform to the holy will of God, and at the same time offers a sufficient answer to the theories of those who would make the advocate a mere instrument or part of a machine; inasmuch as it supposes that no man is at liberty to do any act without a conscientious intent, or with an intent to effect good through the means of ill.

"What then," it will be asked, "are the limits within which it is lawful to mislead or to use artifice?" The only reply is, that in this as in all other departments of morals, it is impossible to lay down express rules by which to bind the conscience in every possible case. All that can be done is to suggest approximate rules, which, however they may be cavilled at by the unconscientious, will form an assistance to those striving to act conscientiously. This caution premised, the following would appear to me just limitations to be proposed as to the matter in hand.

1. As to *concealment:* If not interrogated by lawful authority, I am at liberty to conceal that which it would be unconscientious in another to take advantage of. There is in almost every title something or other wanting, yet of such a nature that it would be unconscientious for those who might by law do so, to take advantage of the defect; as for instance:—I may be in possession of property under a deed not properly stamped; which defect, originally perhaps caused by an oversight, might, if known, subject me to much trouble and inconvenience: such deficiencies the principles of morality as expounded by the best divines and casuists have always permitted the possessor of property to conceal, unless where the attempt to do so would involve him in falsehood or equivocation.

2. As to *artifice:* Where it is lawful by force to repel an attempt to take my goods or to injure my life, I may by artifice do the same. If a murderer knocks at my door and asks whether my guest is within, I may shoot him if I have a gun in my hand: if I have not, I may mislead him by telling him that he is not. Surely I have a right to mislead where I have a right to kill. Or again, if one seeking to rob me of my purse ask me if it is in my possession, I may answer "It is not," even though it is. Not so, however, where I am questioned by one who, as a judge, has a right to demand from me the fact; and to whom should I declare what was contrary to it, I should sin against truth.

IV. But *fourthly,* it is said by some: "The standard to which the advocate refers the cause of his client is not the law of reason or of God, but the law of the land. His peculiar and proper object is not to prove the side of the question which he maintains morally right, but legally right. The law offers its protection only on certain preliminary conditions: it refuses to take cognisance of injuries or to enforce redress, unless the one be proved in the specific manner, and the other claimed in the precise form which it prescribes: and consequently, whatever be the pleader's opinion of his cause, he is guilty of no breach of truth or justice in defeating the pretensions of the persons he opposes by evincing that they have not made good the terms on which alone they could be legally entitled, or on which alone they could suppose themselves entitled to success." As the notion expressed in the above quotation—that it is the duty of the advocate to concern himself solely with the law of the land—is one very generally current in the present day; before entering upon an examination of the last-mentioned theory, it may be well to premise that the above notion derives authority neither from the law of the land—for that law does not attempt to lay any such obligation upon the advocate: nor from the universal practice of the profession—for many of high name in the history of our own and of other countries can be cited who have entertained opinions and adopted practices altogether at variance with it. It remains, therefore, to inquire whether there are any grounds in the nature of the thing which, according to the dictates of right reason, compel us to embrace this now generally received notion. In determining this question it will be of use to consider for a moment the origin and the object of human laws; which done, we shall more easily perceive the error of a theory which would impose upon the advocate, as a duty, the necessity of using in every case his utmost powers to give effect to those laws in all their consequences.

God in the beginning formed man after his own image;[16] and to fit him for that state of society to which the command "Increase and multiply" had destined him, He implanted in his breast the family, the social, the political affections. What was due to every one he knew by an intuition which needed no instructor, and practised with a will which needed no corrector. Love to God which reigned in his heart, by a natural and irresistible generation, begat and nourished love to his fellow-men: and the commands of the law of love (the only law then known) were obeyed implicitly because loved intensely. But man by disobedience fell from his high estate: the characters of the inner law, which before were deep and clear, became now effaced: the' voice of conscience, which before spoke with the sound of the sweetest music, now jarred with harsh severity upon the diseased ear: all became disordered, and mutual distrust and jealousy and fear divided each man from his fellow. In this unhallowed state, where right even when known was disregarded, it became necessary that obedience, not yielded for conscience sake, should be enforced by wrath: the ungrateful precepts of the parent must be enforced by the rod of correction: the angry sword of justice must compel an outward conformity to the letter of human laws. Had the parent asked only what was kind and reasonable; had the ruler enjoined only what was just and right; the case had not been altogether desperate. But alas! the ingratitude of children was rivalled by the cruelty of parents, the rebellion of subjects by the tyranny of rulers. If in this state of moral anarchy a sage had arisen, and taught his disciples that the measure of obedience they should yield to the law of the land was that alone which wrath compelled and the letter enjoined—that aught else was weakness and folly: he would have found an excuse, if not a justification in the circumstances by which he was surrounded. Yet even here God did not so leave himself without witness[17] —did not so wholly withdraw his grace from the sons of men—but that many (even among those who were not, as the Jews, favoured with a particular revelation) bore witness to the promptings of an inner law, which to disregard they accounted impious. Were such men but visionary dreamers? Assuredly not: they lived in the twilight of that bright day, which we as Christians joy to behold: of which the promise was, that God would "put his law in their inward parts, and would write it in their hearts:" Jer. xxxi. 33, of which the privilege, the condition, and the participation now is, "that God should be loved with all the heart, and our neighbours even as ourselves."

"To what ends," it will be asked, "in this state of light and life serve the laws of man?" If all obeyed the dictates of the inner law, little need there were for anything beyond. "The law is not made for a righteous man, but for the lawless and disobedient." 1 Tim. i. 9. But because all obey not the law of God, and of those who most earnestly seek to do so, the obedience is at best but imperfect: therefore it is still necessary that to the law of God human laws be superadded, not to supersede or absolve from obedience to that higher law, but so far as may be to enforce an outward conformity to what it enjoins, and to supply rules for the converse of men one with another, which the reign of perfect love, did it exist, would have rendered needless. And here are to be kept in mind two sources of imperfection which attach to all human laws, *one* the imperfection of the lawgiver; the *other* of the law itself,[18] which can indeed reach the outward man, but cannot like the holy law of God penetrate and reach the inner man; so that he who will obey the law of man, according to the will of God, must still ever look to this higher law to give life and spirit to the letter of human laws, and to determine the measure of regard that is due to them: to some a full and heartfelt obedience, as being a pure transcript of the law of God; to others a measured and limited obedience, as made for temporary ends: to others again, an unwilling and firm disobedience, as contravening the more perfect law of God.

If what is here stated be a true account of the position in which men stand to the law of the land: if there be indeed (as is conceded even by many of those who adopt the last-mentioned view of professional duty) a higher law than the law of the land, and one which anterior to and independent of all human laws demands our most hearty obedience, on what grounds of right reason can it be contended that any man, at any time, or under any circumstances, is at liberty to act as if there were no such law? or how will that advocate be excusable who, under colour of the law of the land, assists his client in trampling under foot that higher law? In reply it is said:—"Every man to whom the law of the land gives a right, is entitled to be put into possession of that to which he has such right, without reference to the use he may make of it when in possession: and the lawyer, belonging to a profession whose business it is to help men to attain their legal rights, is bound to assist him in the assertion of that right, and is no more responsible than is the judge for the ill use which may be made of it." As to the assertion that every man has a right to be put into possession of that which the law of the land gives him, the observations above made respecting the relative positions of the law of God and the law of man, supply (if just) a sufficient answer: the law of man being merely subsidiary to the law of God, and not primary; so that wherever a contest arises between these two laws, the law of God must at once prevail. Thus if I have been paid a debt due to me, but have given no receipt, I may by the law of the land demand the money again, but I am forbidden to do so by the law of God. Who will assert that I have in any sense a right to make such a demand? That there are in practice many cases of so complicated a character that it is impossible for the individuals themselves concerned, much less for their advocates, to adjust the claims of natural equity; and consequently that the readiest remedy is to adopt that approximation to right which the law of the land gives; this I readily admit. But this is not the question: the question is, Whether the position in which the lawyer is placed be such as to make it his duty to omit all consideration of the moral and to look only to the legal character of the case. And if in any instance he is to look to the moral character, why not in all? No limits can be placed. He must, if his own conscience be alive to the distinctions of right and wrong, he must in every case take these into his consideration. How they will lead him to act; whether altogether to reject a case, or to lend it only a lukewarm and hesitating support, or to prosecute it with all his powers and energies; these are questions that can be determined only by the character of each individual case that comes before him.

But it is asked, "Why if the judge, without being guilty of an offence against God's law, may give judgment according to the law of the land, though well aware that his decision will work injustice, why may not the advocate in like manner without offence plead according to the law of the land, without regard to its moral consequences." In cases where the law of the land is directly opposed to the law of God, it is agreed on all sides that the judge is not bound to follow it. In cases where the law is in itself good, and only works injustice by reason of the imperfection of the letter, there has been much controversy whether the judge ought or not to mitigate the rigour of the law by considerations of equity. In many countries this is done by the command of the legislature, and with the general consent of the nation. In England from very early times a different practice has prevailed; and the judges of the courts of common law have felt themselves constrained by the requirements of the constitution, and in some cases by their oath of office, to judge strictly according to the letter of the law, even though contrary to the spirit; leaving it to the courts of equity, in certain cases which come within their cognisance, to modify the rights of the parties according to conscience. Is it then justifiable for the judge to accept office upon the condition that he will thus give judgment simply according to the letter of the law? or will not he who for the sake of office and emolument enters into such an engagement, be guilty of the injustice which he may afterwards be called upon to work? Though the affirmative of this question has in it something both plausible and probable, the negative must be embraced, and for this reason: the judge is the servant of the prince, and the prince is subject to the law, and even if he would, he could not delegate to the judge an absolute control over the law which he does not himself possess: and hence, if there are to be judges at all, they must judge according to the letter of the law, unless (which in our country it has not done) the law itself should invest them with power in each case to mitigate and control its rigour. Hence the case is one not of expediency or of utility, but of necessity; and the judge is in the same plight as the witness, whose evidence will not be received unless given according to the forms of law, albeit these forms may cause that the impression conveyed by it shall be other than what the witness would have. But then, being as is shown a case of necessity and not of choice, our best and most conscientious judges have ever, where opportunity offered from doubt as to the meaning of the law or from other sufficient causes, leant towards the side of equity; and where obliged in judging according to the letter of the law to work injustice, have done so with pain and grief, and with reprobation of those who have thus perverted to evil ends the good intent of the law. The case of the advocate is altogether different: he is not so much the servant of the law as of his client, who is bound in conscience to use the law only for good ends; and if he seeks to pervert it to bad ends, the advocate who knowingly assists him in doing so becomes a partaker in the crime: and just in proportion as the law of the land makes it imperative upon the judge to follow the letter of the law even where that letter works injustice, in the same proportion is it incumbent upon the client and his counsel to take care that they abuse not the strength of iniquity to overthrow the weakness of equity. That this distinction is one which has its foundation in the nature of the thing, and is not a merely arbitrary line drawn for the purpose of argument, will be evident if we for a moment imagine an advocate coming forward with language such as we constantly hear from the lips of British judges, denouncing the conduct and character of those in whose favour nevertheless they are constrained to give judgment. If the lawyer were the minister of the court and of the law, his course of duty would be clear, and he would follow the same rules as the judge. But he is not such: he is the minister of his client, though subject to the control of the court, and therefore it cannot be otherwise than immoral[19] in him to lend his aid to that which he believes in his conscience to be morally wrong. This seems a harsh conclusion, when opposed to a theory supported by the practice of men the very mention of whose names commands respect, and inclines to an uninquiring acquiescence in any course supported by their authority. Yet if the relative position of the law of the land and the law of God be what is above represented, the conclusion appears inevitable, and the theory which I have maintained, that the advocate is bound to regard the moral as well as the legal merits of his client's case, becomes the only one that can be maintained, notwithstanding all the objections[20] which have been urged against it. These objections I will now proceed to examine: but before doing so I would guard myself against an exaggerated statement which is often put into the mouths of those in whose opinion I concur, as though it were contended by them that the advocate is in every case to assume that his client is morally wrong, until he shall have proved himself morally right; and as though it were attempted to impose upon him a scrutiny into the motives and intentions of his client, such as belongs to the all-seeing eye of God alone. No such assertion as this is made: all that is maintained is, that the advocate has a right to expect what every person who calls upon another to aid him in any undertaking is bound to give, an assurance that the object he is called upon to co-operate in effecting is such as may morally and lawfully be sought. This premised, I will now proceed to consider the objections usually made to this view of the lawyer's duty. And

1. *First:* It is objected "that the dimness which clouds our discernment of right

and wrong, and which scarcely permits us to judge for ourselves how we ought to act, wholly incapacitates us from imposing upon others in their conduct, our notions of right and wrong. It is the hidden thought and intent of the heart which determines the character of any act: these in our own case we may know something of; but in the case of others who shall reveal to us all the windings and turnings, all the hollownesses and dark corners of the human heart? And without a knowledge of these, how shall we be able to form a right judgment of any case?

I freely admit the existence of the difficulty which is suggested in this objection, which must often involve the lawyer in great perplexity, and must at all times make him diffident in declining to undertake the conduct of a cause in which a client asserts the justice of his side. But great as are the difficulties which the lawyer must encounter on this ground, they are not greater than many which in the conduct of life beset us at every turn. The larger number of our actions are determined by moral probabilities, the balancing of which is often as difficult as in the case proposed. It is the duty of the physician to judge of his patient's symptoms, and accordingly to give his advice. Shall he refuse to act upon information received from the patient because that patient is liable to misrepresent and misinform? It is the duty of the minister of the gospel to warn the froward. Shall he never upbraid any until he have been proved guilty by a verdict of his countrymen? It is the duty of all men to discourage vice no less than to relieve distress. Shall we therefore never be charitable because, in the ignorance in which we must be of the character of the subjects seeking our aid, we cannot be certain what results will flow from our bounty? In these, and a thousand other cases men act on moral probabilities, according to the best judgment they are able to form after careful examination. Why shall the apothecary be commended for refusing to sell a poisonous drug to one whom on moral probabilities he believes about to make an ill use of it? or a bookseller, for declining to sell books of an immoral tendency? or a vender of arms for refusing to supply them to those whom he believes to be traitors to his king and country?—and the lawyer alone be excluded from the privilege of exercising his calling with conscience towards God and his fellow men?

In reply to this it is sometimes said—"If, indeed, the cause have an aspect so dark as to leave to the advocate no reasonable doubt of its being founded in iniquity, he is bound to decline it: but where this is not the case, his general rule should be to withdraw his eyes from all but what is technical in the case, refusing to listen to what the conscience of the client would suggest." To the good man who adopts the last-mentioned theory of professional duty this follows, I admit, as a necessary consequence. But is it, I ask, a happy consequence? Is it beneficial to the client? Is it beneficial to society? Is it right before God? It is none of these. *It is not beneficial to the client*—for it often invites him to the perpetration of wrong under the belief that if his cause were as bad as he deems it, a good man, such as he believes his counsel to be, would not stand forward to advocate it. *It is not beneficial to society*—for it perverts the general sense of right and wrong among mankind, when they see men of probity, honesty, and integrity in all other relations of life appearing at the bar of justice, the aiders, the abettors, the advocates of fraud, injustice, and wrong. *It is not right before God*—for if the advocate who might but will not search out judgment shall say, "Behold, I knew it not!" He that pondereth the heart considers it, he that keeps the soul knows it, and he shall render to every man according to his works. *Prov.* xxiv. 12.

2. But *secondly:* it is objected—"Supposing that we were able to collect before us all the materials for forming a correct judgment, different minds form very different estimates of what is right and wrong, and what one may deem unlawful another may deem lawful and right. As for example, one man may think it wrong to defeat the clear intentions of a testator though informally expressed; another may think that there is no harm in doing so: one may think that he may without scruple or violence to his conscience evade the performance of a promise not in writing, by pleading the law which requires that certain promises to be binding must be in writing; another may think otherwise: so of the statute of limitations and many other cases that might be put."

To this objection the answer is clear: My conscience and not that of my client is to determine my actions. It matters not to me that another man deems this or that lawful: if I deem it unlawful, I may not aid him in it. The experience of every day tells me that thousands will think lawful, or act as though they thought lawful, things which I cannot think so. If I am a person of a morbidly scrupulous conscience, ready to suggest captious doubts and difficulties respecting every course of conduct that can be proposed (as doubtless many such are found), I may fairly expect that clients will not come to me for counsel and advice: but if I am not so—if my judgment is generally such as straightforward, honest men would form, then, should my avowal that I will not aid others in what I deem wrong drive away clients from me, I may fairly suppose that they are such as it is well for me to be quit of.

3. But *thirdly:* it is objected—"If the advocate is to take upon himself to reject the conduct of causes which he thinks wrong, he in fact constitutes himself judge, and takes upon him an office to which he has no right:" and this objection, because often repeated and confidently urged, is accepted by many as conclusive of the point in question. But is it not, after all, a mere sophism? One of the forms of fallacy technically termed *fallaciæ æquivocationis*, an attempt to apply a proposition, true in one sense, in a sense altogether different. It is true beyond dispute that a lawyer is not to set himself up as judge: he cannot, if he would: he cannot assume the robe of justice or the ermine of office: he cannot invest himself with the sacredness of the judicial character derived from Heaven through the appointment of the prince; but he may, he must, he ought to regard the moral character of each case on which his counsel is asked, and having judged to the best of his ability what is lawful, right and just, and having advised accordingly, he should send to other more or less worthy advocates those who are unwilling to abide by his counsel. If he is not to do this—if he is indiscriminately to advocate every case which any client may put into his hands, he may knowingly be made the instrument for perpetrating the most gross injustice. He may be called upon to state as true matters which he has before him the clearest evidence to convince him are false; and to put forward as sound in law propositions which he is persuaded are altogether untenable—to rely upon an act of Parliament which he knows to have been repealed (though the judge may possibly not know it to have been so), or to quote as undoubted law a decided case which he all the while knows to have been expressly overruled. Undoubtedly a heavy responsibilty lies upon a lawyer who refuses to state a case, as believing that to be false which his client asserts to be true, or that to be not law which his client asserts to be law: but the responsibility is infinitely greater of him who at the sacred bar of justice asserts for and in the name of another what he is morally convinced is false, or who demands for another that to which he is assured the other has no moral right.

4. But *fourthly:* it is objected—"Acting as I contend the advocate should act, he judges before hearing. Many cases are of such a character that their real merits cannot be known till the facts on both sides have been fully investigated, and their various bearings duly considered. So obvious is this, that it not unfrequently occurs that judgment is given in favour of a party to whom his counsel, the very same perhaps who advocates his cause, had previously given a discouraging or even adverse opinion."

That there are many cases such as that above supposed is unquestioned; and in such the young advocate who acts upon the principles I have maintained will probably find his experience agree with that of Sir Matthew Hale, of whom it is recorded by his historian, Bishop Burnet, "that as he advanced in his practice he slackened much of his former strictness of refusing to meddle in cases upon the ill circumstances that appeared in them at first." But it will not therefore follow that he will adopt the opposite alternative of undertaking every cause, no matter what its character. He will bear in mind still that if a client's case appear not just upon his own showing, it can scarce be expected to appear so upon the showing of his adversary, and though it may sometimes, it will not often happen, that the favourable features of a case remain concealed from the view of the party whose interest it is to be acquainted with them.

5. But *fifthly:* it is objected—"If advocates be allowed to prejudge the causes of their clients, and having done so to decline the conduct of those causes which they suppose unjust, clients must often be left without counsel to represent them: contrary to the sacred rule of nature and of reason, which demands that none should be condemned until he be heard."

To this I reply: The only case in which a client can be thus unrepresented is where he seeks to obtain something which the law of God forbids; and in such cases he has no better right to demand the aid of his fellow men than has the thief, the adulterer, or the murderer. In every case, except where something at variance with God's law is sought, I admit to the fullest extent the duty of the advocate to take up the cause of every client, no matter how poor, how unfortunate, how criminal; and to the utmost of his ability to watch that no more be exacted and no less be given than the claims of justice demand. But it is said, "the lawyer may be *mistaken:* he may consider that dishonest which is in reality honest, and that contrary to the law of God which is nevertheless in strict conformity with it." I answer—If this be so—if the advocate be indeed mistaken, the client will have little difficulty in finding another to plead his cause. "True (it is replied), yet even admitting this, the consequence will often prove most disastrous to the client. As, for instance: suppose a brief put into a lawyer's hands in a cause with which he is before utterly unacquainted, just in time enough for him to prepare himself on the law of the case and state it to the jury; but not in time enough for him to return it (if he think its rejection necessary) and thus enable the attorney to hand it to another counsel, by whom, perhaps, the same process is to be gone through."

In the present cumbrous and complicated state of our legal institutions this objection has considerable weight, but not such as to give to the course of conduct I suggest that character of impracticability which it is attempted to impose upon it. For *first,* in almost every cause there is at least one counsel who has from the commencement advised respecting it, and declared it a fit one to be undertaken: and next, such a state of facts as that above suggested is generally the consequence of negligence and delay on the part of the client or his attorney, for which it is only right they should be subject to the inconvenience attending upon it: inconvenience which an upright lawyer would never wantonly cause, but which, in the extreme case above supposed of more than one counsel rejecting the same case, can scarce be supposed to have been caused wrongfully.

Let, however, the weight of this objection be considered as great as it may, it is more than counterbalanced by the benefit which would result from a thorough sifting of the case to the conscience and good fame as well of the client as of the advocate; both of which are endangered when counsel, by advice hastily given, draw before the tribunals of the country causes which, on a more full examination, reflect disgrace on their authors and their patrons.

6. But *sixthly:* it is objected—"If it be your rule that the justice or injustice of each case is to determine you whether you will or will not undertake it, the greater number of causes must be at once laid aside; for the greater number are such in which it is very doubtful upon which side justice lies, and consequently all such cases must be at once rejected, in accordance with the generally received maxim in casuistry "*in dubiis nil agendum.*"

This objection is plausible, but cannot be maintained, and for this reason: The question which the lawyer is called upon to decide is not whether he will or will not take up the case of a client; but whether he will or will not abandon the case of one who has already reposed in him a special confidence—has revealed to him his private affairs—has, in short, placed him in the position of a friend. Shall the lawyer, upon a mere surmise that his cause is unjust, turn round upon such a one and say, "I suspect you are a rogue, and will have nothing further to say to you." Assuredly not. Before he would be justified in doing this he must have strong and clear grounds for adopting such a course. *In dubiis nil agendum* must be his maxim: that is—if he be in doubt whether what his client be in quest of is honest or dishonest, having commenced his intercourse with him upon the assumption that he is seeking what is honest, he is bound to continue it till he has clear reasons for believing the contrary. Undoubtedly if a client should (as many I believe will to an advocate who deems himself bound to undertake every case) openly profess that he is indifferent to the right or wrong of the matter in hand; and that he seeks that, whether just or unjust, which the law will give him, the advocate has in such a case a full right to act upon his own estimate of the moral character of the case; and if he thinks good, to decline all further co-operation in it. But if the client (as happens in the majority of cases) declares his belief in the justice of his cause, the advocate must, generally speaking, persevere in it; and the very fact above objected—that the right or wrong of each case depends upon the inward thought and intent of the heart—will form a reason why, without clear grounds to convince him of the iniquity of a cause, he may not lay it aside. The conflict which takes place in a lawyer's mind under such circumstances may be illustrated by the case of a parent who, having discovered some act of mischief to have been done in his house, and having strong reasons to suspect one of his children of having done the act, accuses the child of it. If the child deny that it is guilty, no matter how strong the suspicions of the parent may be, he may not punish the child—he may not openly act towards it as though it were guilty: all that he can do is to lay up in his mind the grounds of his suspicion, and to wait and see whether future events may not throw light upon the matter.

7. But *seventhly:* it is said—"If the theory you maintain were consistently carried out, a lawyer would be bound to refuse his aid to a man in recovering property that justly belongs to him, if convinced that, when recovered, he would make an ill use of it—would employ it in promoting treason or rebellion, or would squander it wickedly in riot and debauchery. If the civil right which the law gives to a man is to be in any degree fettered by the moral judgment of the advocate, why may it not be altogether taken away?"

Without asserting that there is no case in which it would be the duty of the lawyer to act as is here suggested, I reply that in the great majority of instances the cases thus supposed are clearly distinguishable by the judgment of sound sense and the common understanding of mankind. The civil right to property which the law gives to a man is not separable from the moral right which he has to such property in the same manner that the right *to have* is separable from the right to use. In all cases (except those in which the law of the land is in itself wicked and contrary to the law of God) the law of the land either comes in aid of the moral right, or itself constitutes and creates it; so that in no case can a civil right be conceived to exist, independent of a moral right existing either antecedently to, or created by the civil right. Not so the right to the possession of, and the right to use property. The man who has not yet obtained possession of property may have formed no idea of the way in which he will employ it; or he may destine part of it to a good and part of it to a bad use; or he may use it well one day and ill the next. Could a case be supposed in which, at the same time that I vindicated for another a right to property, I necessarily and by the very same act secured the application of that property to what is sinful, I might justly decline to meddle in such a case. The question that here arises is of the same nature as that which occurs in respect to the levy and payment of taxes. If a ruler levy a tax generally, his subjects are bound to pay such tax without inquiring to what use it is to be applied; and they have the example of our Lord and Saviour to justify them in so doing. But if, instead of levying a tax generally, a ruler commands me to give my labour or my money directly to the maintenance of irreligion or idolatry, it becomes a question of conscience, and I am bound to disobey his commands: with the apostle of old I must say, "Whether it be right in the sight of God to hearken unto you more than unto God, judge ye?"

8. But *eighthly*, it is objected—"That to allow the advocate the liberty here sought would open the door to the greatest abuses: that avarice, indolence, and cowardice would never want excuses to decline the cause of the poor, the oppressed, the weak—that the consciences of advocates would be made the absolute measure of the consciences of all their fellow men; and a liberty would be given to them,

under the pretence of moral sensibility, to trample under foot the laws and statutes of the realm."

That the utmost caution is necessary on the part of the advocate not hastily to reject a cause because of its supposed dishonesty—that he should ever be jealous and watchful over his own heart lest indolence, love of gain, or caprice, should tempt him to decline the defence of any cause, they who know best the infirmity of human judgment and the deceitfulness of the human heart will be the most ready to acknowledge, and acknowledging the most careful to practise: and so long as generosity, integrity, and courage shall adorn but one member of the order, so long shall the poorest, the weakest, the most oppressed, seek not in vain the aid they need.

9. But *ninthly*, it is said—"The course of conduct which you prescribe for the advocate is contrary to that which in the present day has been generally considered his line of duty; and while the great majority of the profession pursue the generally received course, it is manifest that the client of those who adopt a different one will labour under undue disadvantages. He must waive a right which the law of the land gives him, where that right is contrary to equity and conscience; and yet he must acquiesce in the law of the land where it deprives him of that to which he is in conscience entitled."

That this will often be the case I do not hesitate to admit; but it is no harder lot than the Christian is constantly exposed to in regard to his temporal affairs. Were this world the ultimate scene of our existence; were there no hereafter—no resurrection—no judgment to come; were the doctrine of the Sadducee the doctrine of truth; it would be difficult to find an answer to the objection. But if the eye of faith looks with no vain confidence across the waste of this world to the fair regions of another in which we shall receive, in our bodies, according to that we have done, whether it be good or whether it be bad: if the momentary triumphs of the wicked man here below only raise him on high to make his fall the more fearful, the disciple of Christ has a ready and unanswerable reply to those who would tempt him to swerve from the precepts and example of a suffering Master.

10. If, after all, it shall be asserted "that the course proposed, however beautiful in theory, is in practice utterly visionary:" I appeal from such a statement to the experience of those nations in which the civil law has been received; in most of which an oath is required from the advocate that he will defend none but just causes, and those only by just arts: and till the whole bodies of advocates in those countries shall, by better evidence than mere surmise, be proved guilty of the crime of continued and continual perjury, I fearlessly deny the assertion in the same latitude in which it is made. That difficulties will arise in the path of the advocate who seeks to carry out the principles I propose, it is impossible to deny. But these difficulties are only the same as those which every one will meet who, professing himself the friend of others, yet assumes to himself the right of denying his assistance to a friend in any undertaking which he deems wrong. The fee which the advocate receives does not alter the nature of the case, unless, forsooth, it shall be considered "that a motive sordid in its nature can so hallow a cause of cursed iniquity as to render it fit for any man to prostitute his tongue in its behalf:" and so long as it shall be right for a man to decline to participate in the evil enterprises of one whom he has heretofore deemed his friend, so long shall it be lawful for the advocate to decline the conduct of causes which he deems unrighteous. It is true, the advocate is only in a qualified manner and for limited purposes the friend of his client: yet so far as he is, the principles which should regulate the conduct of friends one with another are applicable to him; and though it may sometimes happen that a dishonest client will apply for aid to an honest counsel, and find his expectations disappointed, the injury to the client (if injury it be) is one that will occur but rarely; inasmuch as, when the principles of an advocate are known, those whose intended conduct is such as to make them dread the contact with what is highminded and conscientious, will avoid the man who himself acts upon honest principles, and counsels others to do likewise. This view of the question will not satisfy some: that the upright client, attorney, and advocate should consort together will not content those

who embrace the levelling principles of utilitarian morality. Should this rejection of clients by advocates be permitted, "the suitor would be prejudiced in proportion to the respectability of the advocate who had shrunk from his defence, and the weight of character of the counsel would be evidence in the cause."—*Erskine's Speech.*

But is it not a law of the moral world that the character of an individual may be known from his companions? The tones of philosophers and the proverbs of the simple alike bear testimony to this law, and mark the moral judgment of mankind upon the matter: and if, as a necessary consequence, the unhappy suitor who commits his cause to a disingenuous counsellor is prejudiced by the character of its supporter, it is no more than common sense and common honesty might beforehand have informed him. But common sense and common honesty seldom lead to this association. Dishonesty naturally seeks out the dishonest—infamy the infamous: not, as true wisdom would teach, seeking by penitence and restitution to make atonement for past transgressions, but miserably adding crime to crime, and filling to the full that cup of wrath which, if they repent not, advocate and client must one day drink together to the very dregs.

If, then, the image of God in which he has been created will not suffer the lawyer to be driven like a beast or used like a tool: if the voice of conscience, never silent in the good man's breast, refuses to accept the plea of *general utility* as an excuse for doing less or more in any case than duty demands: if there be indeed an inner law, antecedent and paramount to the law of man, which demands our first and willing obedience, and to which the law of man is but subordinate and assistant; what remains for the lawyer, but that asserting for himself (though it may be in opposition to the general practice of his age, and the specious reasonings of a philosophy falsely so called) the attributes of a man, and fulfilling with conscience towards God and his fellow-men his duties as a Christian, he go forward boldly, seeking as in all other things, so also in the exercise of his calling, to imitate the infinite perfections of Him whose minister he is, in working out with truth and mercy the holy work of justice.

Thus much premised, I pray the regards of the reader to the portrait of a good man's life which I have here attempted to draw: nor will I conceal my anxious wish that the principles which, on the authority of holy men of our own and other nations, I have sought to embody in the following pages, may be embraced and acted upon by every member of that noble order whose high and holy office it is to uphold the fabric of the state—a fabric second only in importance to that loftier one of the church—which latter shall, as is our hope and trust, include within itself that former one then when "the kingdoms of this world shall have become the kingdoms of our Lord and of his Christ, and he shall reign for ever and ever."—*Rev.* xi. 15.

THE LAWYER.

THE AUTHOR TO THE READER.

BEING desirous, by the mercy of GOD (whose we are and whom we ought in all things to serve), to devote to him my labours in that calling in which it hath pleased him to place me; and considering with myself the many temptations to which the practice of the law daily exposes its professors, and the obloquy and contempt[1] to which the evil practices of some among them have at all times subjected that noble calling; I resolved to set down, as best I might, the form and character of a faithful Lawyer, noting by the way those cases which have most perplexed the consciences of good men; that so I might have a mark at which to aim, and a standard whereby to measure my own performances. Not that I deem it possible exactly to define by written rules the duties of this or of any other of the callings which Providence has allotted to man: but as the anxious mariner, traversing the trackless ocean, finds in the faint glimmerings of the distant stars enough to guide him in safety to his desired haven, so have I sought herein to find some high and bright marks whereby to steer among the shoals and quicksands of the law. The which I here present to my fellow-labourers, if haply they may meet from any of them a like regard. And that I might not, in a matter of so great moment, depend entirely upon my own judgment, I have in an appendix (which I commend to the reader as the worthier part this little book) set down the thoughts of men whose opinions may not be slighted, whatever be thought of my own comment. Of each I ask, if in anything I have judged amiss, to correct my errors and supply my deficiencies: and may He from whom all holy desires, all good counsels, and all just works do proceed, grant unto us all both that we may perceive and know what things we ought to do; and also may have grace and power faithfully to fulfil the same.

E. O'B.

CHAPTER I.

THE LAWYER.

A LAWYER is the servant of his fellow-men for the attainment of justice: [1]in which definition is expressed both the lowliness and the dignity of his calling; the lowliness—in that he is the servant of all, ever ready to assist as well the meanest as the loftiest; the dignity—in that the end whereto he serves has among things temporal no superior or equal. For justice is nothing less than the support of the world whereby each has from all others that which is his due; the poor their succour; the rich their ease; the powerful their honour. For it were governments framed, and powers ordained of God: flourishing it cheers, and languishing it dejects the minds of good men: and in its overthrow is involved the ruin and fall of commonwealths. That justice should ever be contemned or trodden under foot is a grief to God and angels: how glorious then is his calling whose work it is to prevent her fall, or to raise her fallen! Truly the lawyer, while the servant of earth, is the minister of heaven; while he labours for the good of his fellow-men he works none other than the work of God.

CHAPTER II.

THEIR DIVERSITIES.

Of those called Lawyers[1] there are in this kingdom several diversities, all having, for one common origin, the complexity and difficulty of laws. In the infancy of the earth, when laws were few and patriarchs judges, every man was his own lawyer, and needed not an attorney to write, or an advocate to plead for him; but himself demanded at the hands of the judge what of right he deemed his own. Afterwards, when kingdoms became vast, and laws many, and the forms of law complicated, and the administration of laws tedious, and labour divided; necessity was that some should be set apart to demand for others from the ministers of justice, that which want of time and knowledge and opportunity would not suffer them to ask for themselves; and hence arose advocates, barristers, proctors, attorneys, and many other attendants upon courts of law, whose several duties it needs not now to define. What I shall here offer being intended chiefly of those in our courts of common law and equity, commonly termed Barristers; to whom properly it appertains legally and in order to set before judges and juries that which the diligence of the attorney has gathered from the complaint of the client; so that the whole together—barrister, attorney, and client—make as it were one man, whom of right one spirit of truth, justice, and mercy should move and animate. But as in a clock or watch the fingers may point a wrong hour though the wheel that next moves it be exactly true, if but some notch of some inferior wheel be out of order; so, let the client be false, or the attorney deceitful, or the pleader crafty, the others shall not be able by their best care to prevent but that sometimes justice shall be perverted, innocency oppressed, and guilty men justified. Wherefore, as he shall one day give an account before the Searcher of all hearts, let not the client who is to choose an attorney be careless in whom he reposes so great a confidence: let not the attorney put in jeopardy the conscience of his client by entrusting his cause to a faithless lawyer, who, in his behalf, will do that which for worlds he would not himself do: let the lawyer look well that he lend not himself heedlessly to become a fellow-worker with others in the ways of falsehood and fraud; but let the righteous client, attorney, and lawyer, strong in the confidence of an upright cause, go forward with cheerful assurance that a threefold cord so twined together shall not by the utmost malice of evil men be easily broken.

CHAPTER III.

THE LAWYER'S CHOICE OF A CALLING.

The lawyer sometimes, though but slightly gifted with those talents which the calling of the law requires, finds himself by the will of God in the choice of parents, or in the disposal of other events over which he has himself had small control, bound thereto in such a manner, that he may not without strong reasons excusing, abandon it to follow other pursuits; but must, with what talents he has, fulfil as best he may its duties and requirements. When however it happens otherwise, and the young man at entrance upon life finds himself free to elect in what calling he will labour ([1]for some calling he must needs have, wherein at once to bear the curse and reap the blessing pronounced upon our first parents), if so be the example of holy judges fearing God and hating covetousness, or the good report of noble advocates renowned in the defence of their country's liberties or venerated in the memory of the destitute and the oppressed, stir up in him high desires to minister at the altar of justice: ere yet he presents himself a probationer before the guardians of her temple, he pauses and weighs well his fitness for so high and holy a calling.

And *first*, he asks, if he have bodily health sufficient hereto? Intense study over the midnight oil, or by the first light of morning's dawn, the disquietude of hot and crowded courts, the exhaustion of long and arduous addresses to judges and to juries, the care and anxiety attendant upon the conduct of complicated and weighty causes, demand from the lawyer a bodily frame strong, enduring, and elastic. Be it he have this;

Secondly, he asks, has he strength of mind sufficient hereto? Not alone the infinite mazes of artificial laws are to be mastered in books; not alone the ill-digested facts of complicated causes are to be seen through and disentangled, and again in lucid order detailed to the judge or the jury: but the weapons of sophistry wielded by the arm of perverted talent, and the artful devices of chicanery, falsehood, and fraud, sustained by intellectual strength and moral turpitude, are to be warded off and defeated. Be it he have strength of mind for this;

Thirdly, he asks, has he moral strength sufficient hereto? Has he patience to undergo, in diligent accumulation of legal store, the tedious discipline of unemployed and unrewarded years: has he temper to endure the irritating attacks of opposing counsel, or the harsh and unmerited reproofs of petulant judges: has he courage to persevere in a good cause against the false affirmations, the wily insinuations, the audacious practices of wicked and ungodly men?

Let him come thus equipped, though but in inferior degree, and he shall not be rejected at the portals of the sacred temple of justice.

CHAPTER IV.

THE LAWYER'S LIFE.

THE lawyer having once enlisted in the service of Justice, the queen of all virtues, upon whom all other virtues wait as handmaids, strives that he may in all things approve himself a faithful follower of so good a mistress. And as without diligence all virtues do pine and languish, the lawyer's life is one of unwearied exertion; except at those times when the usage of his calling bids him rest awhile from his labours, and yield himself to the festive joys of the Christmas, or the soberer thoughts of the Easter season; or sends him to drink in bodily health and mental energy amid summer's delights. At other seasons, when clients demand not his time, he employs so much of it as is seasonable, in increasing his stores of legal knowledge, from whence as from a treasure-house to draw out sound counsel in time of need. When in health, he is ever at his post, that he may not disappoint those who, confiding in his judgment and knowledge, are in the habit of entrusting him with the conduct of their affairs: and such principally he seeks not alone that they may with the more readiness disclose to him their whole case, but that he may with the more confidence rely on their integrity and veracity. His doors are ever open to the poor as well as to the rich; and though he knows well that labour is the lot of man and the labourer worthy of his hire, yet having proposed the holy name of Justice as the object of his labour's worship, he embraces as willingly the cause of the poor as of the rich, and strives no less earnestly for him who is unable to reward, than for him who is able and willing to reward him liberally. Yet he does not here forget the deceitfulness of the human heart, nor the eager love of gain which lies deep at its root. He knows that here an enemy lurks, and he is ever on his guard against him; striving that not only in each individual case he may forget whether it be profitable to his purse or not, but that the whole tenor of his mind may be diverted from thoughts of gain. To this end he is careful so to order his affairs that his expenditure may be confined far within his income, lest want make him careless as to the means he employ to supply it. As in the affairs of others, by his counsel and his conduct, he dissuades them from seeking more than is their due; so, in his own affairs, he is exact to avoid even the appearance of evil; as knowing that for him to defeat in his own case the ends of justice by the forms of law, would not only bring twofold condemnation on himself, but subject him to solicitations to do the same for others. As business often brings him into converse and sometimes into co-operation with men of principles widely differing from his own; while he studies to be courteous to all, he is careful that he be not led by the suggestions or example of others to countenance what he himself disapproves: and when practices are proposed to him by which justice, truth, and honour would be wounded, if youth commands from him diffidence and distrust, he dissents with modesty yet firmness; if age gives him the liberty of rebuke, he censures with warmth and energy. Surrounded from the nature of his calling by evil, and forced to be ever and anon a witness to the workings of the bad passions of our nature, he relies not on his own strength alone to bear him unscathed amid the tempest that surrounds him, but ever as returning morn summons him to his daily task, he breathes forth an especial prayer to the Giver of all good that the labours of the day may be of justice, mercy, and truth, serving to the glory of God and the good of his fellow men; and whenever in the providence of God he has been made the means of succouring the oppressed, or by prudent management of relieving those distressed as to their worldly affairs, he takes not to himself the praise, but gives glory to Him from whom all power descends, to whom all praise is due.

CHAPTER V.

THE LAWYER'S KNOWLEDGE.

THE lawyer having proposed as the object of his labour the attainment of justice, the first aim of his studies is a knowledge of those laws upon which all justice depends: for justice is well defined to be "That by which we have our own in such sort as law prescribeth."* [1]Now of laws to which mankind are subject, omitting here the mention of laws *domestic*, some regard them as members of civil communities or *states*, some as members of spiritual communities or *churches*—of the former some appertain to the converse of men one with another in particular states: some to the converse of states with one another. These last which are generally termed the laws of nations, the lawyer after a cursory study thereof remits to the care and consideration of the statesman as more properly belonging to his department of labour. Those laws which regard the converse of citizens one with another (and which are the proper and peculiar study of the lawyer) [2]he finds to be derived either immediately or mediately from God: *immediately* those written at the creation on the hearts of men, and which when sin had obscured their characters, the love of God in Christ writes anew by the power of his Spirit, and witnesses in the conscience of his reasonable creatures: *mediately* those ordained by them to whom God has committed authority confirmed and testified by his own immediate law, to act in this behalf: as are in each state those—whether princes, councils, or parliaments—to whom in the providence of God has been committed by the constitution of the country the power of framing laws.

Those laws which proceed immediately from God—and which are indifferently termed the *law of God, the natural law, the moral law*—he finds, as in their immediate origin, so also in their distinguishing characteristics the more excellent. He finds them to be—universal and perpetual, binding all persons everywhere, and always; in private as in public; the secret thought as well as the outward act; requiring to be earnestly inquired after and eagerly and actively obeyed, though loss of fortune or of life should on such obedience wait. These laws he seeks for diligently in the recesses of his own heart, and in the written records, and from the living ministers of God's holy word. To these last he is ever ready to resort in all cases of difficulty and perplexity, esteeming highly of that part of divinity which is conversant about cases of conscience. In addition to these primary sources of this

* Aristot. Rhet. I. 9. Δἰ ἣν τα ἀυτων ἑκαστοι εχουσι και ὡς ὁ νομος.

transcendent knowledge, he has studied with pains the works of those who have made the natural law their study: nor does he contemn those inferior aids which are supplied by laws dictated by the natural conscience of man. Therefore he is familiar with the principles of equity embodied in the Roman law and thence embraced by a large portion of Christendom: and thus when occasion requires he is enabled to illustrate and confirm the precepts of religion and philosophy by the usages of nations.

To those laws which proceed *mediately* from God, and which in contradistinction to those divine laws before named are termed *human* or *positive;* in unison with their inferior origin the lawyer finds these characters incident—that they may in no case ordain anything contrary to the divine law—that they continue no longer and extend no further than the authority which imposes them continues and extends—that they may be altered, suspended and abrogated—and may cease to bind by contrary reason, by conflicting enactments, by extraordinary emergencies, and intolerable inconvenience. Of positive or human laws he notes two kinds by the learned Hooker, termed the one *mixedly*—the other *merely human:* the former such as by temporal sanctions enforce an outward conformity to the immediate law of God; the latter such as in diminution of the natural liberty of men, impose restraints concerning matters before indifferent. As to the study of *natural* law, the lawyer invokes the powers of his reason and moral being; so to that of positive law, he brings the patient exercise of his intellectual faculties; and full scope he finds for them high though they may be. The general usages of the realm in which he lives, and the peculiar customs of each part of it, as approved, recorded, and handed down in the successive decisions of judges from the earliest times: the written acts of the legislature, confirming, altering, or abrogating these customs and one another; and the interpretation of these acts by the judges of the land, must be sought out with care and studied with diligence—a wide labyrinth in which without landmarks to guide and direct it can scarce be but he lose his way. To obtain these he has surveyed the positive laws of his country, as well in the order of time as of their subject matter; tracing on the one hand their gradual rise and progress in the history of his country, and again on the other marking and collecting the principles from which they have sprung and the ends towards which they tend. Moreover in the course of this study he has noted in what matters the laws of his own country accord with or deviate from the maxims of natural law and the laws of other states: and thus not only is he enabled to expound with power and clearness the characters of existing laws; but should the events of his life give him at any time a place in the legislature of his country, he is qualified with wisdom and prudence to propose new laws or to amend the old wherever they may be defective.

In this study of his country's laws, the lawyer notes, what in his practice he ever keeps in mind, the necessary imperfection of all positive laws. For though the inner law which reaches to the thoughts and intents of the heart, had been sufficient, if obeyed, to answer every need of social life; and the intent of human laws be to bring men back to this inner law: yet so infinite is the complexity of human affairs that outward laws can never by their letter provide for every case that may arise, in such manner as that the perverse ingenuity of man shall not often find occasion to set them at nought: whence it comes that he who in heart desires to be conformed to the perfect will of God must look to the spirit rather than to the letter of human laws, and seek occasion to fulfil rather than to evade their requirements.

Of those laws which pertain to the converse of men as members of spiritual communities, and which are therefore termed laws ecclesiastical, some are framed by churches for their own internal discipline and order; and these of themselves are bound upon the members of such churches by no other power than that of conscience; ministers ecclesiastical having in themselves no right to enforce their commands by the exercise of temporal power: others again are ordained by the civil power for the preservation to churches of temporal goods; or for the enforcing by temporal sanctions their rules for internal discipline. The latter kind the lawyer has need to study with the same diligence that he does other laws ordained by the temporal power, inasmuch as though pertaining to religion they are drawn within the jurisdiction of the courts in which he practises: the former kind, though he needs not, except in his own particular church, to have so perfect a knowledge of them, yet inasmuch as the other kind of ecclesiastical laws necessarily require a knowledge greater or less of these also, he may not altogether omit to study.

CHAPTER VI.

THE LAWYER'S ACCESSORY KNOWLEDGE.

THE lawyer despises no knowledge; for there is no knowledge but serves either positively as it is, or else to illustrate some other knowledge. Yet some knowledges there are more peculiarly subservient to the exercise of his calling, and these he has not neglected. By a moderate skill in the art of logic he has learned to state with clearness those arguments which bring conviction to his own mind, and to detect and expose the dark sophistries of those Belial tongues which "drop manna and can make the worse appear the better reason." Rhetoric too he has studied, that he may not by the awkwardness of his manner, the obscurity of his speech, or the ill arrangement of his subject prejudice the cause of truth and justice which he has undertaken to defend. And as these are as it were the accessory implements with which he is to work, so he has studied the material upon which his labour is to be exercised; and to this end has acquainted himself as widely as may be with the rudiments of those arts and sciences which are of most common occurrence in the affairs of life, and are of consequence often drawn before the tribunals of justice. But above and before all he has made mankind, their thoughts, passions, and actions, a principal study; and is much versed in noting the countenances and outward manners of men; by deep and constant observation of which he has penetrated to a more than ordinary knowledge of their thoughts and feelings. Nor is he content with a general study of human nature, but has carefully observed the genius and character and the peculiar manners and customs of his own countrymen. Thus armed and equipped he issues forth to the contest with falsehood and wrong, prepared with every weapon both of defence and attack.

CHAPTER VII.

THE LAWYER'S DUTIES.

THE lawyer finding (as is observed by the pious Leighton) "that particular deceits are usual in several callings, and are incorporate with them through long custom, and become a part of the mystery of those callings; and therefore men dispense with themselves in them as the inseparable sin of their calling, and have no remorse for them;" and finding moreover his own calling obnoxious to this charge, and that many consider themselves bound by the rules of their profession to act in ways which he condemns; is careful that all who employ his ministries should know what services they may expect from him. This he makes known, as well by an open profession of what he will not do, as by a patient endeavour to fulfil what he considers his duty.

1. [1]And *first* he makes it known that he will undertake the conduct of none but *just* causes; and here he esteems those causes alone to be just which natural law, or positive laws, not contradicted by natural laws, do make such. For not every cause which the forms of law may sanction is therefore just. I have paid a debt; and yet because I have not a legal discharge to show, he to whom the debt has been paid may again demand it from me. But since it is not easily to be defined what are just causes, and some persons will therefore have the lawyer to undertake every cause, and such has now become a practice very commonly allowed and followed,

the lawyer sets not up his own judgment in this matter without being able to give weighty reasons which move him thereto. And *first*, he contends that so to act is to become a partaker in other men's sins. The judge is appointed to administer the laws, according to their letter: he is bound so to do by the command of his prince and the oath of his office; and if at any time he is obliged to give judgment which he knows must work injustice he does so against his will. But the lawyer who being to counsel and assist his client, willingly, no law compelling him, counsels and assists him in that which is unjust, becomes before God a partaker in his client's evil deeds. If one reply that he is no judge but an advocate, and that till the judge have given sentence he knows not whether the cause be just or unjust: he replies by distinguishing: that some causes there are which even the sentence of the judge cannot make just, and these no law obliges him to advocate: others again are doubtful, and in these he applies to the judge for the solution of the doubt, stating to him the case as in truth he believes it to be, and fairly opening to him the difficulty thereof: others again are manifestly just, and to the defence of these he brings with zeal and diligence whatever powers God has given him. *Secondly*, he considers that the maxim *qui facit per alium facit per se* has place here; and that for him standing in the place of his client to put forward on his behalf an unjust claim would reflect upon his client the heavy judgment pronounced by the apostle: "Let no man go beyond or defraud his brother in any matter, because the Lord is the avenger of all such." Yet because from the complexity of human affairs and the ignorance in which clients sometimes are of their rights, and in which the lawyer must often remain of those thoughts of the heart upon which before God the justice or injustice of the cause depends, it is not easy to judge of the real merits of a cause: and since moreover in a doubtful case it is the right of him who is in the possession of property to retain such possession until deprived of it by judgment of law; as on the other hand it is the right of him who believes he has a lawful claim to ask his rights from the ministers of justice, the lawyer will not hastily reject a cause because on the first view of it it appears weak: in this matter he recollects that which is related of Sir Matthew Hale, "that being in the beginning of his practice very cautious not to undertake ill causes, he afterwards abated much of his scrupulosity; observing that many causes which in the beginning seemed unjust, when the cause was sifted and the evidences heard, turned out to be just."

Again, the lawyer observes that there are cases in which though somewhat is due and admitted so to be, yet more being demanded than of right ought to be—as if one should seek to take both my house and lands when he had only title to my house—it is sometimes necessary for the lawyer to aid in resisting the whole demand; and having done so, to leave to the conscience of the client willingly to give up what justice requires.

2. *Secondly*, the lawyer makes it known that he will not even in a just cause make use of unjust arts: he may not do evil that good may come, for real good he is assured can never grow out of evil, to him who works it: much less will he use unjust arts in an unjust cause. Sophistry in argument—misquoting of cases—misstating of evidences—browbeatings of simple witnesses—these and all other arts by which truth is perverted or justice defeated he regards with abhorrence, as lessons learned in the school of the father of lies. And here he denies that it is his duty, let the cause be what it may, to put forward that part of it alone which is favourable to his client, suppressing all else and leaving it to the opposing counsel and the judge to find out what they can; and so if the counsel be ignorant, or the judge simple, to snatch all he can for his client. This he thinks all one as if a man should take to himself his neighbour's lost goods, because his neighbour knows not where to look for them: and this he knows is not for him to do whose rule it is to love his neighbour as himself. If it be objected that thus acting the advocate betrays his client—his answer is ready: if the cause be such that it cannot bear the broad light of day it were better it remained in darkness. He has agreed with his client not to defend his cause whether just or unjust, but to serve him for the attainment of justice. Yet in this matter of the conduct of causes something will depend on the nature of the cause and the character of the adversary; and that which against an honest fellow

citizen would be unlawful, against a highwayman may be just, since in such cases it is reason that the exactness of natural laws be mitigated by equity. Every man is bound to restore his neighbour's goods; yet if a man call for his sword to kill his neighbour withal, the sword ought not to be surrendered. [2]So he who attempts by the formalities of law to set up an unjust claim may rightly be defeated with his own weapons, so however that truth be ever observed even to an enemy. Thus, should an heir at law attempt against conscience to defeat the clear intent of an informal will, he whom the testator intended to benefit may rightfully resist the claim. So again in those smaller matters in the conduct of causes in which by negligence or inadvertence mistakes have been made of which it were inequitable for the opposite party to avail himself; these I may rightly hide, though I may not by falsehood deny or by fraud conceal them.

What the lawyer will do for his client is seen in the diligence with which he studies his case—the assiduity with which he watches that no unfair advantage be taken—that no unnecessary expense be incurred—that he be advised of the difficulties he must encounter and the doubts which attend the issue. In one word, the lawyer regards himself as put in his client's place to do for him whatever he might do for himself (had he the lawyer's skill) consistently with truth and justice: more than this he will not do; and he desires not those for his clients who dare not trust him to act with the same prudence, integrity, and zeal, as if the cause were his own.

CHAPTER VIII.

THE LAWYER ADVISING.

When the lawyer is to advise, he considers how great a trust and confidence is reposed in him, and seeks to discharge it with becoming fidelity. And here principally he avoids the unrighteous example of those who to serve the avarice of faithless attorneys and to increase their own gains, hastily involve their clients in hopeless suits, taking for facts whatever a client may let drop in the heat of passion. He remembers that which the wise man notes *(Prov.* xviii. 17), how that "*he who is first in his own cause seemeth righteous*" though in truth he be not so—and lest according to the same wise man "*his neighbour should come and search him out,*" he himself examines and pinches the case when he fears it is foundered; and having as best he can informed himself fully of the facts, he looks at them in every point of view, not omitting to weigh well the claims of natural justice, and to observe whether he who asks his advice be careful to fulfil its obligations. If on any occasion he suspects the case to be falsely or insufficiently stated—important facts to have been omitted or latent weaknesses glossed over—he requires to be made more fully acquainted with all that belongs to it. Sometimes, if the case on which his opinion is sought be one of difficulty, he is not content to advise the institution of a suit upon written instructions alone, but will (though it consume much of his time and cause him much additional trouble) seek a conference with him whose rights are to be determined, as knowing how self-interest and passion are wont to blind the eyes of men. This done, if he finds that natural and positive justice unite in giving light to his client, he acquaints him with the strength of his case—advises (if with prudence it may be done) that it be laid open to his opponent, and that restitution be demanded; which if he refuse to make, then, and not till then, he advises an appeal to the tribunals of justice. If, on the contrary, positive law alone, according to the letter, reluctantly yield to his client an advantage which the law of God peremptorily forbids him to seize, the lawyer, though he conceal not the iniquitous strength of his case, dissuades from further prosecution of it in such manner, that either he must bring new matter to show that his is other than at first it appeared, or must seek another instrument whereby to prosecute his work of injustice. If upon a consideration of the whole matter the case appears to the lawyer to be one of doubt, he states plainly his reasons for so considering it, and recommends if the claim be small that it be abandoned, or that at all events means of amicably terminating it be first tried. He knows well, for he has oft witnessed it, with how many subtleties and arts, suits at law are managed, what danger there is of miscarriage, what anxiety for the event, what animosities intervene, how many sins are secretly insinuated into the heart and thence communicated to the actions: and knowing these he will not hastily advise a frail fellow man to place himself in the way of such strong temptations.

CHAPTER IX.

THE LAWYER DRAWING PLEADINGS.

THE lawyer is skilled in all the forms of pleading, which to the unwary and ignorant are so many traps and pitfalls wherein justice may be caught and killed. To abuse them to such purposes he regards with abhorrence: yet has he not therefore omitted the knowledge of them. For, not only are the established rules of pleading agreeable to the judge, and when honestly used adapted to the good conduct of causes; but it behoves him that he give not an unconscientious opponent the opportunity through his ignorance of wounding the cause of justice. In the matter of pleadings he endeavours—*first*, that his pleadings be as concise as the nature of the case will allow; not letting them run out to an interminable length to save himself trouble, or to please those attorneys who, loving their client's purse better than his interests, will have long profits to flow from long pleadings. *Secondly*, that they be such as shall on the trial be supported by the evidence. He is not content that the attorney instruct him—" *Counsel will please draw this or that plea.*" He requests that the state of the case be made known to him: and frames his pleadings in such manner that what he therein alleges may be established at the mouth of witnesses. *Thirdly*, he will not take trivial demurrers to gain time and to harass the opposite party and put him to expense; nor will he draw false pleas in the hope that the evidence which the other side shall bring may prove defective, or that he may abuse his opponent into a belief that his cause is stronger than it really is. He considers that pleadings however technical, are the formal allegations of the parties, to be supported by evidence according to their legal intent; and hence, to plead that which he knows to be untrue, though it be clothed in the robes of form, he considers not on that account as less unjust, but rather an aggravated falsehood. In this matter he is the more constrained to exactness by those rules of the judges which require that the signature of counsel be affixed to all pleadings; being assured that this was intended not alone as a security that pleadings should be as far as may be conformable to law, but that they should in all other respects be agreeable to the rules of right and honesty. In those pleadings which the court requires to be verified by the oath of the party he is more particularly careful that they be exactly conformable to the truth; and so far from encouraging his client to think that the oath which he takes is a matter of form merely, he impresses on him the necessity of his being convinced of the truth of that to which he sets his seal, and points attention to those matters wherein his knowledge of the case makes him think that his client might be unwarily entrapped into a misstatement of facts, remembering ever that " Lying lips are an abomination to the Lord, but they that deal truly are his delight." *Prov.* v.

CHAPTER X.

THE LAWYER ADVISING ON EVIDENCE.

THE lawyer, when he has himself advised the undertaking of a cause and drawn the pleadings in it, has little difficulty when he comes to advise on evidence. For having from the first stage of the cause carefully sifted all the facts of it, and assured himself that they are such as justify the proceedings which he has recommended, he is not forced when advising on evidence (as those too often are who hastily and without due examination counsel the undertaking of suits), to bid his client sound a retreat now after the loss of so much time, trouble, and expense; because forsooth the evidence which he can bring will not support his case: nor is he tempted to advise—as it is to be feared they too often are who counsel proceedings at law without sufficient caution, that doubtful or uncertain or it may be even false matters be put forward as evidence. Nevertheless in advising on evidence much judgment and good sense is required of the lawyer, that on the one hand he omit not to bring before the court any matter of proof which may be of weight toward the right decision of the cause; and that on the other he heap not upon his client unnecessary expense, by indiscriminately advising every witness to be called who can give evidence, no matter how trivial, concerning the matter in hand: doing like those unskilful marksmen who shoot many shafts at a venture, where a single one well directed had hit the mark.

CHAPTER XI.

THE LAWYER IN CONSULTATION.

The lawyer, when he receives a summons for consultation with those engaged together with him in the conduct of a cause, regards not the meeting as a mere form whereby to put an additional fee into his purse. When properly conducted, consultations, which for the most part are then had when the pleadings are perfected and the evidences of the cause laid open, prove often a means of terminating doubtful suits by a just compromise, or hastening just suits to a favourable issue. To this end the lawyer in consultation looks at his client's case in the most unfavourable point of view, and weighs well that which appears against him, so that he may not be taken by surprise on the hearing of the cause, or startled by a new view of the case which proper diligence would have before presented to him. And herein much is required of the young lawyer. For consultations being in part for the instruction of the leading counsel in the facts of the case, which from want of time he may not so sift and examine at this stage as may the younger counsel; it behoves him to have well weighed and studied all that belongs to the suit and with readiness to impart what he has discovered; that if weighty it may be urged on the court by the character and experience of the elder counsel, or if weak may be suppressed—forasmuch as weak arguments often injure a strong cause.

In consultation the young lawyer is sometimes perplexed. For it may be he shall hear advice given, or schemes for the conduct of the cause proposed, by those elder than himself, which he cannot but deem to deserve reprobation. Yet inasmuch as from the complexity of causes that which to him appears wrong, to another not less conscientious shall appear right, he will not, unless when he is in his own mind fully persuaded, hastily dissent from that which those older than himself advise; since thereby he might seem to censure his betters: but will calmly propose his doubt, which should it not be entertained, he considers not himself therefore bound by the judgment of his seniors (should the conduct of the cause in their absence devolve upon him) to follow that which he considers wrong, but puts forward that alone and in that way which he esteems just and righteous. Yet because thus acting upon his own opinion he may seem to censure others, and those whom he would hope fellow labourers with himself in the work of justice, this when it happens grieves him sorely and distresses his mind, lest in thus condemning others he have been himself guilty of pride and arrogance.

CHAPTER XII.

THE LAWYER PLEADING IN CIVIL CAUSES.

THE lawyer when he rises to speak is full of his subject and empty of himself. He thinks not with himself, How shall I best gain the applause of the bystanders? but, How shall I best set forth according to truth and justice the cause which I have undertaken? and this communicates an earnestness to his manner which fixes the attention of his hearers and causes the judge to lend an attentive ear to all that he advances. Not that he uses the same warmth of speech in all causes, pretending always that his side is clearly right, and the other as clearly wrong; but according to his judgment of the cause so he speaks; his heart ever going along with his tongue, and his countenance being an index to his mind. If the cause appear to him just, he omits no honest act of elocution to commend it to the judge and the jury, showing that not alone the law of the land but that natural equity and good faith are with him, and endeavouring to enlist as well their feelings as their reason on this side. If his judgment is doubtful, so is his speech: he attempts not, by garbled statements and specious arguments, to make his cause appear better than it deserves; nor will he, as artful speakers sometimes do, endeavour to make a perplexed case appear more doubtful than it really is, in the hopes that his side, though the weaker, may amid the confusion prevail. If the counsel opposed to him be young, or insufficiently informed of the facts or law of the case, and if he thinks that any matter material to the merits of the case has been inadequately stated, then (as is recorded of Sir Mat. Hale), he rather mends such defective statements than avails himself of the ignorance or imbecility of his opponent to give his own cause a better colour than it deserves. He considers that to conceal a small matter in a doubtful case, is as great a sin as to conceal a great matter in a clear case: he deems it alike wrong to take a grain or a pound from the trembling scale of justice; and this because he ever denies *expediency* to be the measure of right and wrong, and utterly abhors the Spartan law of theft, which commended him who pilfered let him only do it undetected. In a word, the lawyer keeps in mind that his powers are entrusted to him by God, to be used for his glory; and he dares not prostitute them to abuse credulity or to maintain falsehood, to justify the wicked or to condemn the just. Such things he knows to be abominations in the eyes of the Lord and master whom he serves; and such they ever are in his own.

The lawyer likes best to plead those causes which he has himself advised the undertaking of: for as it is not his fee alone which makes the labour of his calling sweet to him, but the thought that he may thereby serve the ends of justice, he has a confidence in the equity of those causes which before entering upon publicly he has sifted in private. But as from the multiplicity of courts, the complexity of affairs, and the difficulty of causes, it is often necessary that several counsel be retained to plead the same suit, and it would be an intolerable burden to the client that each of these should be consulted concerning the cause in all its stages, it sometimes happens either from the exigency of the case or the carelessness of the attorney that the lawyer shall not get his brief till the cause be on the point of being heard. When this happens the lawyer has not that liberty which he always wishes he may have, of dissuading from the further prosecution of the cause or rejecting the conduct of it, if the party asking his aid will not do what is right. For in the hasty way in which he is obliged to study the case he dares not confide in the judgment he forms concerning it. As often therefore as this happens, the lawyer walks warily in his conduct of the cause, not warranting its soundness beyond what it plainly appears to him to deserve.

While fulfilling his duty to his client, the lawyer forgets not what is due to the community; and as in all commonwealths it behooves that laws be not only just and equitable, but fixed and certain; he seeks in his practice to be consistent with himself, not one day advocating principles in law which the next he is to oppose;

but determining to the best of his judgment what is expedient, and endeavouring to co-operate with the judge in building up good laws upon sure foundations.

CHAPTER XIII.

THE LAWYER OF COUNSEL FOR THE CROWN.

THE lawyer when appointed to aid the ministers of justice in visiting on evil doers the punishment due to his country's broken laws, seeks that as far as in him lies justice may be truly and indifferently ministered to the punishment of "wickedness and vice, and to the maintenance of true religion and virtue;" ever remembering by whom was committed to the hands of his prince that sword of justice which he helps to wield. Now in the discharge of this office the lawyer is watchful that he be not led on the one hand by an undue regard for power and wealth to extenuate the guilt of the rich; nor on the other hand by a love of popular applause unrighteously to spare the poor offender, or more heavily than justice demands to lean on the rich oppressor. When crimes arising out of the zeal of conflicting parties are to be prosecuted, he is especially careful lest the bias or affection of his own mind cause him either to aggravate or palliate the fault of the accused; and when, as must at times happen, he has been led at first to think worse of a case than it deserves, and so to state it to the court; if afterwards he see reasons for changing his mind, he will not from love of mastery endeavour to support the false colour he may have given to the case, but will candidly acknowledge himself to have been mistaken. When those who have been injured in their persons or their property come to offer evidence against the offenders; if at any time he sees them inflamed by passion on account of the wrong committed, while in the discharge of his duty he proceeds with the prosecution of the offence, he warns them that they forgive the injury done to them even as themselves hope to be forgiven of God their many sins against his holy law. When justice has pronounced the sentence of condemnation, if the criminal be penitent and the nature of the case permit, in the midst of justice he forgets not mercy; but when he knows aught that may extenuate the guilt of the prisoner, he makes it known to the judge, and prays that the punishment be as light as may be: for the rest he is so kind and tender in his manner even towards the most hardened offenders (for the worse they are the more he pities them) that they who by his means have been found guilty not only willingly forgive but even love and reverence him.

CHAPTER XIV.

THE LAWYER OF COUNSEL FOR PRISONERS.

THE lawyer, when engaged in the defence of persons charged with crime, is filled with a grave sense of the duty laid upon him. If the prisoner declares himself innocent and brings proofs thereto agreeing, the lawyer is careful lest by the weakness of his advocacy he may prejudice the righteous cause of his client: and again, if the prisoner be guilty and so confesses himself, the lawyer is perplexed to know how he ought to act. [1]The law of the land obliges not but yet expects of the prisoner when asked "guilty or not guilty?" that he answer to the question: yet if he will not do so but stands mute, it allows that he be considered innocent till proof be brought to the contrary. [2]Now when the prisoner declares to his counsel that he is guilty, the lawyer reflects whether he shall advise him to keep silence or to confess his guilt. [3]Did the law imperatively demand an answer, there were no alternative but he must confess: but now that the law, though it dislike that silence be kept, yet attaches no penalty, he is in doubt whether the accused may without blame assume that liberty which the law permits even while it condemns. On the one hand he reflects, that to refuse an answer savours of contumacy and rebellion; and that the law affixes not a penalty to this contumacy, rather in mercy to him who if obliged to answer would add to his other crime, the guilt of falsehood; than to encourage him to silence, who penitent for his past fault knows and wills to do what is right. Again, if the prisoner confess not his guilt, but stand mute, and is through defect of evidence acquitted, how great temptations to sin beset him on every side! For, either he must confess to all with whom he lives, that though pronounced innocent by the voice of the judge he was in truth guilty; or he must ever after wear a mask of falsehood, pretending that the verdict by which he was acquitted was a rightful verdict, and shifting upon others the suspicion of that crime which was his own. On the other hand the lawyer reflects, that the general voice of mankind and the consent of all laws require not that the guilty, unpursued by the ministers of justice, render himself willingly into their hands, but permit him to remain unpunished, so only that he do so without adding sin to sin. Why then, he asks, may not the accused stand silent, if the law permit it; provided by so doing he injure not his neighbour nor offend against truth; especially if he have aught to plead in extenuation of his fault which yet the rigour of the law would forbid the judge to regard? On the whole, therefore, though the lawyer forbid not that the prisoner, if he have courage so to do, confess openly his guilt, and often rather encourages him thereto, than dissuades him therefrom; yet if he will stand mute he refuses not to undertake his defence, so it be not supported by witnesses suborned, or any other art of injustice; and that there be, as it were, a tacit confession of the fault.

The embarrassment of the lawyer is yet greater, when the prisoner, though knowing himself guilty, asserts that he is innocent. For as in such case the lawyer is bound to suppose that his client tells him the truth, and to examine witnesses in such manner as he would do if he were innocent, he is often thus made rather the condemner than the advocate of his client.

Another question which in criminal matters it much perplexes the lawyer to resolve, is whether he may in every case take advantage of any mistake which the prosecutor in pleading makes, thereby to effect a way of escape for the prisoner. Pleading in civil causes he is compelled by that divine law which bids us do to others as we would have others do unto us, to make no objection which does not serve the ends of justice. In criminal matters no law restrains, but he may take for his client that measure of mercy which the law permits and the judge awards. And yet if the prisoner, conscious of his guilt and penitent for it, will submit himself rather to the spirit than to the letter of the law, and deems it an insult to the majesty of justice to defeat its substance by relying upon its forms, the lawyer rather commends than blames such thoughts; and takes occasion therefrom to recommend to the mercy of the judge the criminal who has given to his country so sure a pledge that he has repented him of his crime against its laws.

CHAPTER XV.

THE LAWYER EXAMINING WITNESSES.

THE lawyer, as knowing that the temple of justice must be built on the pillars of truth, esteems highly of the examination of witnesses; in that by means of it when skilfully managed, falsehood is unmasked, truth revealed, and the cause of justice aided and vindicated. To this part of his duty the lawyer brings as well the wisdom of the serpent as the harmlessness of the dove. He is wise as the serpent; for here he has to engage with falsehood Proteus-like assuming—now, the confidence of assured certainty—now, the meekness of calm conviction—now, the ardour of enthusiastic belief—now, the hesitation of ingenuous diffidence.—He is harmless as the dove; for here he meets with certainty, mistrusting its own convictions—truth unsuspecting, entangled in the labyrinthine mazes of doubt—ingenuous diffidence, betrayed into the hesitation of fraud—ignorant simplicity, unable to explain to others what it knows itself. The knave, the fool, the daring, the diffident, the cunning, the simple, all in turn present themselves. Now the lawyer has carefully studied the different phases of truth and falsehood, and exerts his powers to reveal the one, and unmask the other: his eye is single, and his course straight; truth is his game and his heart is in the chase, and with confidence he follows her footmarks no matter whither they lead. In the examination of witnesses the lawyer derives no small aid from the religious sanction of the oath which the court administers to the witness: not harshly and carelessly in the way of astonishment and terror; but meekly, religiously, and devoutly, reminding him, how by the solemn oath he has taken he has called the Searcher of all hearts to witness to the truth of that which he alleges. Not that he dares confide to this, which should of right be an all-sufficient test of truth: his knowledge of mankind teaches him far otherwise. Hence, if he sees a witness attempt to prevaricate or conceal the truth, notwithstanding the solemn oath which he has taken to disclose it simply and wholly, he spares no weapon which the storehouse of his art affords whereby to overcome the devices of falsehood. Not that he uses these weapons indiscriminately, attempting by artifice to extort that alone which may favour his client, and to draw attention from all else. If he browbeat a witness, it is because he believes him of set purpose to conceal the truth: if he startle him by sudden transitions, it is because he believes him to be moving in the narrow circle of perjury: if he impeach his character, it is because he believes him unworthy of credit. Sometimes in utter doubt in his own mind where the truth lies, he throws his darts with random aim which misses the mark he intended and wounds where he meant not. If at any time he discovers that he has so done, he is sorry for the injury, and hastens to throw balm into the wound he has inflicted.

CHAPTER XVI.

THE LAWYER DRAWING DEEDS.

The lawyer, in the drawing of deeds, is careful to obtain all knowledge pertinent to the matter in hand, and is studious well to apply it. He considers that a deed resembles a house, which, if well constructed, lasts long and gives protection and comfort to him who inhabits it; but being ill built, lets in wind and rain; and to complete all is blown down some stormy night about the ears of its possessor. Hence, when engaged in this duty, the lawyer reflects anxiously how best he may secure ease and quiet to those and to their families who repose in him so great a trust. His principal care is, so far as he may control it, that the intention of the parties be not only prudent but righteous. And observing that in matters of property the ill passions of our nature are wont, even in the best, to be stirred up and active—that distrust in Providence and in one another—love of power and of undue gain, have often way, though he may not always be able to procure the adoption of that course which all circumstances considered is most holy and highminded, yet he constantly strives after this end by suggestions made with the diffidence which is required from one who advises in the affairs of others. And *first*, he wishes that there be not too great anxiety concerning the future—too much thought of the morrow—he wishes that something be given to trust in the providence of God as ordering the affairs of men: for he sees that they who by multiplying provisoes and conditions think to secure themselves against the ills of fortune, as they impiously term them, do most often in the end, not only miss their aim, but draw upon themselves burthens more heavy than those they have sought to avoid. [1]*Secondly*, he wills that without good cause the natural rights of men be not abridged beyond what the law of the land prescribes: as, in the frame of the marriage contract, by restraining the power of parents over their children, or of husbands over their wives. [2]He commends the maxim of the common law, which is also that of piety and religion, that a man and his wife are *one;* and he cares not that provision be made by those entering into the holy state of marriage, for a separation which the church will not contemplate; but requires that they who enter thereupon pledge to one another their faith until death do them part. *Thirdly,* he wishes that when contracts are made between persons who are equal, the contract be as simple and unfettered as may be; that each may know to what he is obliged, and that the minds of men be not burdened with thoughts of complicated obligations, or their estates at some future time encumbered with unlooked-for demands. *Fourthly,* in all matters of trust, he advises that none be named as trustees who are not willing to take upon them the duties of the trust; and that to such offices men of integrity and probity be chosen, who will not use the power committed to them for their own gain and to the injury of those whose rights they are set to protect.

The lawyer, having made it his first care that the wishes of the parties be, as far as he may control them, prudent and upright, his next care is to provide that they be given effect to in as full and ample a manner as the law will permit; and that they be not disappointed by after events, or controlled and curtailed by the absence of provisions pertinent to the nature of the interests which it is the intention of the parties to create. And seeing the infinite complexity of human affairs, and that if he rely upon his own skill alone it were an hundred to one but that some circumstance escape his notice which ought to be provided for, he is careful to follow approved precedents sanctioned by time and the approbation of learned men; not that he relies entirely upon these, for every case will have its own peculiarities; and as he would be thought but a bungling cobbler who should think to fit all men of the same age from the same last, so he would be but a sorry conveyancer who should try to make one form of deed suit all conveyances of one class.

The last though no light care of the lawyer is that his deeds be concise. Prolixity in deeds he sees to spring either from indolence or dishonesty. It was no ill saying of one who, in excuse for the length of a letter, added, "that he had not *time* to be short;" and so the lawyer finds it in the drawing of deeds. It is easier, he knows, to throw into a deed all ordinary common forms and words, taking chance that some among them will suit his purpose, than carefully to weigh the wants of the case before him, and insert only what are called for. The other cause of prolix deeds, to wit, a dishonest wish to increase his own and the attorney's gains, he shrinks from with disgust, and knows not by what words sufficiently strong to denote his abhorrence of it.

CHAPTER XVII.

THE LAWYER DRAWING WILLS.

THE lawyer, in the drawing of wills, follows for the most part the same rules which he observes in the drawing of deeds. Yet some things there are peculiar to this department of his duty which belong not to that other: for whereas deeds are for the most part made openly upon much consideration, and upon debate of the different persons affected by them; wills, on the other hand, are secret, and made upon the advice of the testator alone, who, provided he observes the limits which the law enjoins, may do arbitrarily what pleases him, be it just or unjust, pious or impious, in the disposition of his own. And because the more perverse any man is in that which he wills, the more hard it is to turn him from his purpose: the lawyer, when he would dissuade from strange dispositions of property, has need of infinite discretion, that he fail not in his design, and haply earn for himself the reputation of a busybody. Seeing, however, that his first duty, when he is about to draw a will, is to inform himself concerning the particulars of the property which the testator is about to dispose of, for this purpose he requires him to look narrowly into his affairs, that he may not, as testators often do, by too favourable an estimate of his substance, disappoint the intended objects of his bounty: seeing, moreover, that duty and right reason move him thereto, it can scarce be but that a friendly lawyer shall find occasion without offence to advise that what in a testator's intention savours of impiety or wrong be altered or omitted.

Another caution which the lawyer observes in the matter of wills is, that he be not led by the misinstructions of others or mistakes of his own to make for a testator a will far other than that which he intends, as knowing how difficult it is for one unversed in the forms and technicalities of law to express with clearness his wishes respecting the devolution of property. Hence, if at any time it chances that he receive instruction from a testator in person, he requires him to write down what dispositions he chooses to make of his substance, or else that a witness be present at this conference, who may compare the instructions given with the deed as drawn into form.

CHAPTER XVIII.

THE LAWYER A PEACEMAKER.

The lawyer, remembering him of the blessing promised to the peacemakers, neglects not the occasions which his calling affords of reconciling differences, and by much study has attained an excellent skill herein. In this matter he grounds himself mainly on that which everywhere he has observed—that each, measuring the justice of his cause by his own desire, thinks himself therefore wronged because he has not what he would. Hence, when one comes to consult him concerning some wrong done to him, the lawyer leaps not at once to the conclusion which the client wishes, but listens patiently till he has told his whole tale; noting, in the meanwhile, those parts where he observes it to be defective. When he has done, he questions him as to these, to the end that, by his own answers, he may himself discover the weaknesses of his case. Having in this manner abated somewhat of his confidence, he suggests the matters of most weight which the opposite side may have to oppose: then he dwells upon the delays which he must encounter, the expense that must be incurred, the chances of failure from defects in forms of law and other causes. Having thus further shaken his confidence, he recommends that offers of compromise be made, not niggardly, but liberal; not boasting of a confidence which he does not possess (since such boasts both partake of falsehood and inflame the pride and passions of the opposite side), but meekly urging the many hazards which lie in the paths of both, the uncertainty of the issue, and the certainty of expense. Be it, however, that the cause be never so good, that a grievous injury has been wrought, and that the law is ready at hand to vindicate his right, he suggests that the law need not, therefore, as of course, be resorted to. In many things we all offend God; we are not able to answer one of a thousand; shall we not, then, where we may, seek occasion to forgive our fellow men, even as we ourselves daily pray to be forgiven of God?

CHAPTER XIX.

THE LAWYER AN ARBITRATOR.

The lawyer, ever anxious to promote peace, [1]rejoices when, to terminate differences, parties will agree to forego the contentious forms of law; and, abating somewhat from their strict rights, will submit to his judgment the matter in dispute between them. For by arbitrations, when properly employed, a means is often found to a more perfect administration of justice than the law of the land affords. For whereas, in giving sentence, the judge is obliged to decide according to the letter of the law, be it, when applied to the case in hand, never so inequitable; the arbitrator may decide wholly according to equity; and this he always does, except where they who commit their cause to his decision will of their own accord have it otherwise. Nevertheless, in the matter of arbitrations, care is necessary that they be not perverted by the ill blood of the parties or the bad designs of attorneys, to the engendering of protracted litigation: and forasmuch as the lawyer is in no case obliged to take upon him the duty of an arbitrator until he has been first advised of the nature of the matter to be referred to him, and the terms on which the parties will conduct their proceedings; if at any time he sees probable reasons for supposing an ill issue of his labours, he prudently refuses to enter upon the office until the parties have agreed to such terms as he thinks right: which if they consent to do, reposing trust in the uprightness of his intent, he is more than ever watchful that he abuse not their confidence by a hasty judgment, but patiently listens to all that either party has to allege.

For the rest, the lawyer, when appointed arbitrator, desires to bring those qualities to his aid which a judge should possess; considering, that though appointed by the parties to decide betwixt them, the judgment is of the Lord, and to him he must account: and as he is not now clothed with that dignity which the appointment of the prince confers upon the judge, he strives, by the uprightness of his intention, the moderation of his manner, and the kindness and patience of his carriage towards all who come before him, to effect that his award be respected even by him against whom it is given.

CHAPTER XX.

THE LAWYER ON CIRCUIT.

THE lawyer is anxious that the odour of a good name may follow him whithersoever he goes: and as in the courts his truth and probity earn for him the confidence of the judges; so in the towns on his circuit he gains the respect and good will of those who are in the habit of serving upon juries. These having observed his practice of saying nothing but what he deems of weight, and of stating nothing with more weight than he deems it to possess, listen with pleasure to what he has to offer; not arming themselves, as with some they are forced to do, against being surprised into false judgments by specious artifices, but thinking of him as co-operating with themselves in the work of justice which they are sworn to promote. And as, at the time of the judge coming to the county town, the minds of all are erected towards the administration of justice; and the events of each day, whether of criminal or civil affairs, are in every one's mouth; he is careful to improve the opportunities which the hospitality of his friends affords, of commending to all with whom he converses the cause of justice, mercy, and truth: and when, as too often must happen, he chances to fall in with those who prefer ingenuity before honesty, and cajolery before truth; and who think him faint-hearted and a fool who will quietly sit down under an injury received, and forgive him who has injured him, rather than seek to be revenged therefor, he fails not to declare before God the sin of such practices, and moreover exposes the evil consequences that follow from them among men: as how injustice begets injustice, and fraud begets fraud, in an infinite generation; while a patient endurance under wrong is alone able to lay a foundation whereon may be built the superstructure of love to mankind.

When on circuit, the lawyer keeps jealous watch over himself, lest the freedom of social intercourse, or the unguarded converse of convivial hours, betray him into a participation with or approval of what is immoral or profane.

When in town, though he may not decline any duty which Providence throws in his way, he has much liberty to determine whom he will cultivate as friends and associates; but on circuit the range of his choice is much narrowed, and he is often brought into converse with men whom his own judgment would not have selected, yet whose society courtesy will not permit him to shun. Hence, while he cheerfully joins in converse with those whom he happens to meet, turning conversation where he may to the profit both of himself and others; he yet observes a prudent caution, lest by his language or looks he should at any time seem to countenance what he esteems wrong. Another temptation to which on circuit the lawyer is exposed, and which he carefully guards against, is that of neglecting the duties of the Lord's day. The frequent example of others, and the urgency of important business committed to his care, make it at all times hard to maintain faithfulness in this matter; but the lawyer, feeling that in proportion to the difficulty so is the necessity, that by his example others may be encouraged to a just observance of this holy day, takes courage in the promises of Him who is a most strong tower of defence unto all that put their trust in him, and in due time reaps, if he faint not, a reward of his obedience. And thus, like the gentle rain having descended upon the land, his country duties ended, the lawyer returns again to his home, cheerful in the hope that he has not run nor laboured in vain.

CHAPTER XXI.

THE LAWYER AT ELECTIONS.

THE lawyer, when invited to act as counsel for candidates at elections of members to serve in parliament, sees before him so foul a den in which the evil passions of our nature, like beasts of prey, are wont to ravage and devour, that he scarce dares to enter therein. Yet, in the fulfilment of duty, he may not otherwise refuse than by making known to him who seeks his aid the principles on which alone he will consent to act. And, *first*, he acquaints him that he will neither directly nor indirectly be party to the bribery of votes. The law of the land, judging rightly of the nature of a vote, and intending that he who is to exercise that high privilege should do so not for private ends, but for the public good, has by heavy penalties forbidden that which, even though no law of man had condemned, must have been held in detestation by all good men. To the righteousness of this law the lawyer gives his hearty assent, and hence deems himself unfit to be of counsel for him who, regarding neither the law of God nor of man, in this behalf thinks of the purchase of voters no otherwise than as of the purchase of a flock of sheep or other commodity which may without scandal be bought and sold. For though it may be he shall not himself be asked to aid directly in giving bribes, yet forasmuch as the confidence which should of right subsist between a candidate and his counsel makes known to him the whole conduct of affairs, and he is besides to advise concerning this very matter in making known what the law of the land enjoins respecting bribery, he will not peril himself by an approach to so dangerous a precipice.

Secondly. He will not aid in giving effect to dishonest artifices whereby to hinder voters from the exercise of their franchise, nor suggest objections merely technical to invalidate what he believes to be otherwise *boná fide* votes. Such artifices and objections he sees to flow from the intemperate zeal of party spirit or the unholy desires of self-interest and pride, which charity forbids him to countenance. If he who asks his services will nobly seek to attain the high office of representative by the unbought affections of his fellow-citizens, disdaining all corrupt and petty arts; the lawyer delights to be of counsel for such an one, and with all his might strives to defeat the unjust artifices of those who would hinder the free choice of the people.

CHAPTER XXII.

THE LAWYER'S SECRECY.

THE lawyer, ofttimes becoming acquainted with the private affairs of families, as in drawing of wills and settlements, and advising in cases of difficulty and trouble, is watchful not to divulge what he may thus learn, and considers that as counsel he lies in a manner under a promise of secrecy which it behoves him to keep sacredly. Nor is this a slight task or a trivial duty. For there is in most a desire to know the secrets of other men's houses; and if any obstacle oppose, rather than altogether miss their mark, they will pass current for truths the vaguest rumours of lying fame. Hence arises a constant temptation to the lawyer. For, let him but hint that he has some knowledge of any matter that is questioned, and he shall at once command attentive listeners, and commend himself as a person of importance. Now the lawyer having, when inexperienced, been oft taken unawares by this itch of hearing, becomes after a while wary and on his guard to avoid those occasions which might tempt him to gratify the love of detraction. The best cure for this malady, which is one of little minds, he finds to be by leading the conversation to the consideration of higher matters, which quickly puts to silence those petty traders on others' faults, and makes room for the speech of better men.

CHAPTER XXIII.

THE LAWYER DISCOMFITED.

THE lawyer claims not infallibility; he oft falls into error, but, like a wise man, seeks to profit by his errors. And this he does both in the way of humility and of prudence; learning to entertain a lowly opinion of his knowledge and powers, and in every case of difficulty asking that the aid of men wiser and more experienced be called in, though it may be that by so doing he lessens the respect of his client for his services. The subtilty, the strength, the versatility of the enemies he has to encounter terrify and dismay him. For the lawyer, when he falls into error, considers not himself at liberty to correct his mistakes by artifice or fraud; and, uncorrected, they often entail upon his client great expense and loss. When this happens, he attempts not by plausible pretences to gloss over his blunders, or to charge them upon the client as though he had misled him by erroneous instructions; but he straightway confesses his error, and advises how best he may avoid the consequences, and, if the mistake be the fruit of gross negligence or unpardonable ignorance, makes what restitution he may in returning the fees he has received. If these errors happen often, he seriously bethinks him it were better his place were filled by another, and seeks some occupation better fitted to his powers: but if he finds he only commits occasional faults, though they grieve him much, he takes courage, seeing that others around him do likewise.

Difficulty of like kind, but in an another shape, presents itself to the lawyer, when the cause that at first appeared to him just, by reason that much belonging to it had been kept back from him, as it proceeds, becomes manifestly unjust. If this happen by the wilful fraud of him whose cause he has undertaken, he forthwith deserts it, and leaves the deceiver as best he may to get out of his own trap. If, on the other hand, the client was himself deceived, the lawyer, as soon as he discovers the defects in his cause, apprizes him of them; and recommends to desist from further prosecution of it, or helps to conduct it to a termination consistent with justice.

CHAPTER XXIV.

THE LAWYER IN THE MATTER OF FEES.

THE lawyer is exceeding jealous of himself in what concerns the recompense of his labours, seeing what infinite evils they engender who, in the administration of justice, regard only their own gains. Of such the wise Hooker, not without sufficient reason, affirms, that "if they who travail about the public administration of justice, follow it only as a trade with an unquenchable and unconscionable thirst for gain, being not in heart persuaded that justice is God's own work, and themselves his agents in this business; the sentence of right God's own verdict, and themselves his priests to deliver it; formalities of justice do but serve to smother right, and that which was necessarily ordained for the common good, is, through shameful abuse, made the cause of common misery." This estimate of what should be the lawyer's motive in the exercise of his calling, caused that among the Roman advocates, and among those in time past of our own nation, the lawyer's fee was regarded,* "not in the nature of wages or pay due by contract for labour or service—since no price or rate can be set upon counsel which is invaluable—but of a gift or gratuity, which albeit the able client might not neglect to give without note of ingratitude, the worthy counsellor might not demand without doing wrong to his reputation:" which consideration, though it have not like currency now that it once had—in that the administration of justice is more complex and formal, and the duties of lawyers more fixed and certain—were well kept in mind at our day, if peradventure it might curb that too eager love of gain which makes the profession of the law a by-word in the mouths of many.

In the matter of fees, the lawyer observes that rule of his profession which forbids the taking of half fees: yet only in such manner as that he will not by so doing seek to creep into business by underbidding his brethren of the bar. Hence nothing hinders but that in a poor man's cause he return the whole or any part of the wonted fees, or cares not to look for their payment till the result of the suit be known. In such cases, however, the lawyer is careful that what he so declines turn not to the attorney's profit but to the client's relief. To this end he is mindful not to put his name to any fee which either he has not received or which for charity sake he returns, that the absence of such mark may be a check upon the careless and a memento to the careful attorney. And here the lawyer wishes that rule were more narrowly observed which forbids the officers whose duty it is to tax attorneys' bills, to allow any fees to counsel which have not such mark of receipt; inasmuch as the neglect of it causes injury to the advocate as well as to the client; to the client, in that he is sometimes charged with fees which the lawyer may have returned as not deeming them well earned, or from the poverty of the party may have declined to ask; to the lawyer, in that it enables the unworthy attorney to recover counsel's fees which he has not paid and perchance shall never pay.

Other dangers there are in the matter of fees which oblige the lawyer to walk warily, observing not only his own steps but those of his fellow-travellers also, lest haply a false step made by one of them cause him to fall.

First. He is careful to return his fee in any matter in which, from accident or other cause, he has given no labour or thought: the contrary practice in which regard, has deservedly brought much scandal upon his calling.

Secondly. He is faithful to the side which first retains him, though it may be they neglect the wonted courtesy of continuing to ask his services: considering it safer in such cases to let ingratitude, and it may be dishonesty, pass unnoticed, than himself to run the risk of being false to one to whom he has engaged his services.

Thirdly. He is watchful not to countenance the making of unnecessary motions, or the taking of superfluous proceedings, only because his own and the attorney's costs will be charged by the court to the account of the opposite party. And this the

* Sir John Davies. Preface to his Report.

rather, in that it is to be feared too many motions in courts have their origin herein, and by it robbery is daily practised unpunished in the very precincts of the temple of justice.

CHAPTER XXV.

THE LAWYER'S REGARD FOR PROFESSIONAL RULES.

THE lawyer shuns their opinion who regard the professors of the law as an order whose interests are at variance with those of society at large, and therefore to be protected by walls and bulwarks raised in self-defence. Lawyers were appointed to live for society, not society framed for them to live by. [1] Hence in those rules which they make for their conduct towards one another and towards their fellow-citizens, the lawyer regards those as of no binding force which clash with the welfare of society at large: and though to the other rules of his order he pays that deference which courtesy toward his fellow labourers in the work of justice demands, he ever remembers the good of society and the principles of equity whereby to relax their rigour. Thus though it be a rule of his profession that no lawyer confer on business with a client except at the instance of an attorney (and such rule, in the present state of the law, serves to useful purposes), yet if one be so poor that he cannot pay an attorney's costs, nor find one who will of charity undertake his cause, the lawyer willingly listens to the case of such an one, and at once gives him the advice he seeks; or, if he need assistance such as may be the best given by an attorney, commends him to some charitable practitioner who will lend his aid to the distressed. In all such matters the lawyer looks to the intent of the rule; and so the abatements he makes from the rigour of it be made in honour, with a clean conscience, without left-handed designs of self-interest or avarice, he cares not what censure he may incur from those who, considering the privileges of their order as of more value than the good of society for which alone that order exists, however wise they be in their own eyes, to others resemble the fool who arrogantly thought he played on the organ when he only blew the bellows.

CHAPTER XXVI.

THE LAWYER'S REGARD FOR PROFESSIONAL CONFIDENCE.

THE lawyer, like the divine, often comes, in the exercise of his calling, by reason of the confidence reposed in him, to the knowledge of public and private wrongs, which, had he arrived at it another way, he had been bound to reveal to the ministers of justice or to the parties injured. Now, however, that such matters have become known to him under the implied promise of secrecy, though he exhorts the person asking his counsel to do what is just, he dares not himself reveal what he has thus discovered, even though by so doing he would free the righteous cause from oppression. Thus if one should, in asking counsel, confess that he has by fraud got possession of his neighbour's goods, though the lawyer shudders at the thought that one should knowingly persist in the commission of crime, refusing to make restitution; yet he dares not make known to the injured party his just rights, esteeming that he who has thus made him privy to his evil acts has done so under the confidence that he would not make them known; which confidence, though he does what he can to cause that it should not be reposed in him, yet having been reposed, he thinks he may not without wrong betray.

Still it may be that at times a higher duty shall oblige the lawyer to declare openly what he has thus learned in secret; though here, as in all questions concerning conflicting duties, as for instance—when a subject may lawfully resist the commands of his prince, or a child those of his parent—he finds it impossible as it would be inexpedient to define beforehand what circumstances will justify a deviation from the general rule of duty.

When the Church of England by her canons would determine the duty of a clergyman respecting matters revealed to him in confession, she forbids her ministers, "under pain of irregularity, to make known any crime or offence committed to their trust and secrecy, for the unburdening of the offender's conscience, except such as by the laws of the realm their own lives would be called in question by concealing." Now though the law of the land permits to its professors and servants a privilege in regard of matters confided to them in the discharge of their professional duty which it denies to all others, giving them liberty, even when interrogated by the judge, to decline an answer to any question which would oblige them to reveal such matters, the lawyer at times finds cases arise in which right reason and conscience demand that he waive the exercise of this privilege—as if he sees one about to suffer for a crime of which another has confessed himself the perpetrator—or if treason, murder, or any other heinous crime about to be committed, could, by the disclosure of facts entrusted to him, be averted. In such cases the lawyer thinks himself at liberty to reveal so much as may be necessary, considering that the promise he has made being but implied, conditions and exceptions must be implied also.

For the rest, the lawyer regards it not as any breach of the confidence reposed in htm, when, being entrusted with the conduct of a cause, he discovers to the court all that is material to the just decision of it. Thus, if being employed to demand at the hands of the law a sum of money clearly due, he might by some concealment cause that double that sum be adjudged, he stays not in such cases to ask liberty of his client, but at once makes known to the court what he deems necessary to the ends of justice; considering that to do otherwise were to act injuriously to his client in imputing to him dishonest aims.

CHAPTER XXVII.

THE LAWYER IN VACATION.

THE lawyer in vacation is like a field lying fallow, reposing from past and preparing for future labours: there is neither ploughing, nor sowing, nor reaping—neither books, nor courts, nor fees—yet here and there a flower or plant springs up. Wherever he chances to be, the lawyer refuses not advice to the poor, neither omits any opportunity which offers of reconciling differences or preventing litigation. More than this in the business of his calling he cares not to do, not only because for the most part the health of his body and mind require these seasons of rest, but more especially because he fears lest by an unbending application to the study of the law, he make narrow his mind. [1]For, strive as he may after the larger and higher principles of natural law, much of his time, he finds, must of necessity be employed in the study of those minute distinctions which the ingenuity of lawyers, aided by the infinite variety of human events, and the imperfection of positive laws, has by little and little compelled the diffidence of judges to sanction. Now, lest this microscopic study should injure his moral and intellectual vision, the lawyer delights, during these seasons of relaxation, to climb the hills which surround the narrow valley where the scene of his daily labour lies, and to view from their tops the glories of creation set before him by the hand of Almighty love. And now he frequents the joyous halls of imagination, where the handmaid poesy waits upon his feasts, and crowns with a more sparkling wreath the cup of sober-minded pleasure; or seeks the cool groves of philosophy, where discursive thought and inventive reason supply invigorating viands to enlarge and strengthen the mind. With these, if opportunity offer, he seeks in travel to expand his knowledge, as well of nature and art as of men and manners. If he bend his steps to foreign lands, he inquires, in the states through which he passes, concerning the condition of the people, noting what of excellent or defective he observes in the institutions of each, and the sources whence derived; as whether of old standing and growing out of ancient laws, or whether the fruit of modern legislation. If, as he loves rather, he betake himself to the hospitable homes of friends in his native land, he omits no opportunity of acquainting himself with whatever of useful and charitable exists in the public or private institutions of the neighbourhood; and where he may be of service (as strangers often may), he spares no labour necessary to that end. Especially he delights to further those designs which have in view the promotion of religion, knowing that where piety advances all good things will quickly follow in her train.

CHAPTER XXVIII.

THE LAWYER'S HUMANITY.

THE lawyer, when he became a lawyer, ceased not to be a man: when he received from the guardians of his order the badges of his calling, he laid not aside any of those sympathies which should warm every brother of the human race. If the pagan could say, "*Homo sum: humani nihil a me alienum puto*," much more can he. God by his providence has appointed divers orders of men in the state, even as he has in the human body set various members, no one of which can say to another, "I have no need of thee." And as in this latter though to each belongs its proper office, yet through all circulates one common blood, one common life, and all are moved by one common spirit: so in the body politic, though to each member is allotted its respective vocation and ministry, yet from all God will one day demand an account of every talent, small or great, which he has committed to their charge: nor shall he who has neglected the duties of a father, brother, master, or friend, be in that day excused because he has laboured in his calling as a clergyman, a physician, or a husbandman. Hence the lawyer, while he is diligent in the peculiar duties of his calling, strives heartily and as unto God to fulfil every other duty to his neighbour; following in His steps who visited our earth, not alone that he might be a sacrifice for sins, but also an example unto us of godly life; and that we might approve ourselves his faithful followers and friends, not by the barren leaves of Christian profession, but by the good fruit of that vine into which he has ingrafted us.

CHAPTER XXIX.

THE LAWYER'S CHARITY.

THE lawyer, though no divine, is so far versed in the knowledge of divine things as to have learned, that outward alms alone earn not a title to the virtue of charity. Not that outward alms are therefore to be omitted. Charity is the end of the commandment, and the end of the commandment is love: love to God first, and love to our neighbours afterwards, as of necessity springing from love to God: not such love as was that of the lawyer in the gospel, who, willing to escape, sought by the difficulty of the letter to make void the spirit. The lawyer's charity is his religion, and his religion is his life; and his life is twofold—*inward* in his heart, and *outward* in his actions. For that which is inward he accounts not to man, but to God: not but that he is herein so far forth accountable to man, as that inward faith must of necessity bear outward fruit; yet forasmuch as faith is an inward germ, it binds not to a legal observance of particular outward duties in set forms. These howbeit in the general shall scarcely be found wanting.

First. His heart being on fire for the spiritual welfare of his fellow men, it cannot be but that where opportunity offers, he will speak a word in season concerning divine things to those with whom business brings him into converse: and often in so doing shall it be his chance to meet a fellow-traveller to the celestial city. Be it he but casts his bread upon the waters, yet after many days shall it return to him again. This fire in his heart makes him watchful likewise for the external welfare of Christ's church, and of those religious institutions which are formed to support its mutilated fabric. To these he willingly imparts somewhat of the store with which God has blessed him, and, so far as the duties of his calling will permit, somewhat also of his time and labour.

Secondly. In his care for the spiritual, he forgets not the temporal wants of his fellow men; for though the inferior, this is yet the second part of charity. If he can spare time, he himself visits the sick and seeks out distress: otherwise, that which, according to the apostle's injunction, he has "earned with his hands to give to him that needeth," he entrusts to faithful deacons to dispense withal; or with the widow's mite throws it into the treasury of some refuge dear to the fatherless and the widow. But principally the lawyer delights in relieving those wants of the poor which concern law and justice. This he considers his proper alms, as being the advocate of Heaven, whose peculiar care the poor are.

CHAPTER XXX.

THE LAWYER'S COURTESY.

THE lawyer's courtesy flows from his charity: and as this reaches all men, so does the other; for how should he, whose thoughts are love towards all, willingly in his outward demeanour give offence unto any?

Yet because what is never so well intended shall sometimes fail in its aim, and courtesy has limits, in that it may not pass a smile of compliance on that which inwardly we disapprove; the lawyer observes measures in his courtesy. For the exercise of this virtue he finds infinite occasions, some of which in particular, as of more frequent occurrence and weightier import, he prepares himself for beforehand; and, *First, in his demeanour before judges.* To these are due not courtesy alone, but reverence also, as to God's vicegerents. Therefore he omits no occasion of showing them due respect—as in restraining all unseasonable mirth in their presence, in rising from his seat upon their entering or leaving the court, and in other such like attentions. He thinks not that time or trouble lost which upholds respect to them to whom respect is due. Yet should the judge at any time, either from impatience refuse to hear fully his client's case, or from prejudice manifest an undue bias against it, the lawyer dares to remonstrate; yet in such a respectful manner as, if it at the moment recall not the judge to a sense of his duty, shall so weigh upon his mind that afterwards he will repair the injury.

Secondly, in his conduct to his brother barristers. To these courtesy is especially due as members of the same calling, and fellow labourers in the work of justice. Hence the lawyer is ever ready to assist them with his knowledge and counsel, not fretfully resenting all interruptions of his own business, nor carelessly giving advice no matter whether sound or not, nor being jealous because a younger than himself shall profit by his knowledge; but with a single eye considering how he may best aid others in that work of justice which he has himself at heart. Yet here he needs to be on his guard, that courtesy cause him not to sanction that in the conduct of others which he himself thinks wrong, whether it be an unworthy act or profane jest. Haply he shall hereby earn for himself ridicule and reproach; yet these he gladly bears, and more also, so he might recall such as thus offend to sober thought upon the sinfulness of such practices.

Thirdly, in his intercourse with attorneys. These, in despite of the ill name which the evil practices of too many among them have brought upon their brotherhood, he regards with esteem, and considers their duties scarce a whit inferior in dignity to his own. But as elsewhere, the corruption of the best engendereth the worst, so is it here: and while he who is true to his own conscience, and faithful to his client's interest, is as gold thrice tried in the fire; he who is false to the one, and faithless to the other, stinks in the nostrils of all good men. In his intercourse with an attorney, the lawyer's manner is according to his mind. If he have not full confidence in his integrity, he is wary that he be not betrayed, by word or look, into approval; but if, on the other hand, he meet one in whom he may confide, he freely communes with him as with a friend and fellow-worker.

For the rest, the lawyer, while he guards himself against the faults of others, is jealous that he be not unwittingly led into those faults to which his calling renders him peculiarly liable; such as are—an over-confident manner, rudely bearing down all that opposes; an irritable temper, ready to rise at every supposed offence and assume the privilege of abuse; a spirit of dispute, quick to discover matter about which to differ, and ever ready to defend that side which it has adopted by captious arguments, rhetorical artifice, or unwarranted sarcasm. Rather he conforms to those precepts which the apostle Peter (himself of an abrupt and hasty temper) enjoins, "Be ye all one mind, having compassion one of another; love as brethren, be pitiful, be *courteous*."—1 Pet.

CHAPTER XXXI.

THE LAWYER'S HOSPITALITY.

THE lawyer may not, like the country gentleman or man of wealth, give up much of his time to the entertainment of guests: yet, according to his power, he forgets not to be hospitable, bethinking him how many delights flow from the exercise of this most excellent virtue: as how, first, it serves for the comfort of our earthly pilgrimage, making known to friends the passing events in the history of each, and by this communion enhancing the joys and alleviating the sorrows of life. Then, again, he considers how grateful it is to the wearied spirits of those who have no home to be admitted among the cheerful scenes of domestic life; and how much more grateful still it is to him who, enjoying thus the luxury of doing good, learns that it is more blessed to give than to receive. Moreover by hospitality opportunities are opened up for combined efforts in the cause of charity which had not otherwise been made.

The lawyer dislikes altogether the practice of those who, when they will be hospitable, put on a mask, heaping their table with unaccustomed dainties, and surrounding it with strange faces. He thinks that a friend will not the less like his feast because it invites not to intemperance, nor will be the sooner weary of his company because they present not the excitement of novelty. Yet, when occasion offers, he delights to give the stranger a place at his board; especially he loves to entertain those whom business brings to the town, and whom the unknown multitude reminds of their solitude: and while he collects from them knowledge of how the country flourishes, how the poor fare, if the laws be respected, if religion be honoured; he in turn entertains them with all of charitable, or useful, or instructive, which the busy energy of city life, and the versatile pursuits of his own calling, have made him familiar with. If at any time he observe one anxious to seek a doubtful right at the hands of the law, he brings him to the courts, and there shows him the ordeal through which he must pass before the maimed limb of his estate be restored; so that if his appetite after law be not over keen, he may reflect on the many unforeseen difficulties which lie in his way, and rather sit down content with the loss of an uncertain advantage, than incur a certain loss of so much time, and trouble, and expense.

CHAPTER XXXII.

THE LAWYER A CITIZEN.

THE lawyer, though watchful to obey the laws of the land which it is his peculiar duty to know, deems not of himself as having then fulfilled his duties, when he has outwardly conformed to all that they command, and abstained from all that they forbid, so that he may lie down at night secure from the rods and axes of the ministers of justice. Love, not fear, is the spring of his obedience; and hence he refuses no office, however burdensome, whereby he may serve the commonwealth, nor shrinks from the discharge of any duty which his station imposes, no matter how much the performance of it may expose him to the odium of those whom it is his interest to please. Some he observes who, careless about the welfare of the commonwealth, and anxious only for their own advancement, under colour that, in a free state, men, to serve their country, should act with a party, attach themselves to a confederacy of politicians, whom they slavishly follow, in hopes at some future time to receive from them or with them an ample reward for their prostituted services. Now the lawyer reprobates not alone the practices, but the theory of such men. He holds it as a maxim of political philosophy, that principles should associate parties, and not parties control principles—being well assured that the conduct of others, how high soever their station or intellect, can never sanction a departure from what in each case is right, and deeming parties to be no further good or useful than as they are formed by the union of like minds earnestly striving after high and holy ends. Hence he in no case gives a blind assent to the acts of any set; but freely weighs and canvasses all measures of which it is his duty to judge, and if in any thing he disapproves, frankly speaks his mind; considering that the liberty of speech, which the constitution gives, not only imparts a privilege but imposes a duty. And while the lawyer values highly this freedom of speech, he is careful not to abuse it for impious ends; as by reviling rulers, or by inflaming the minds of his fellow subjects upon the occasion of every grievance which ill government may cause. If abuses exist, he chooses rather that remedy which the constitution approves, and by petition sets forth the evil, and humbly prays that it be remedied: which if those in power refuse, he cheerfully bears up under the burden, regarding what may not be removed by lawful means as a judgment sent in the wisdom of God for the punishment of national sin.

CHAPTER XXXIII.

THE LAWYER A LEGISLATOR.

The lawyer, as he shrinks from no burthen which it behoves a good citizen to bear, should he be invited by any portion of his countrymen to represent them in parliament, if higher duties permit, declines not the proffered honour; so however that he may arrive thereat without the use of those evil arts too commonly practised, and that he be not required by his constituents to sacrifice that liberty of thought and action which their interests and his own honour alike call upon him to maintain. All contracts by which the freedom either of the constituent or the representative is restrained. or their conscience fettered, he considers not only inexpedient but immoral. For as, on the one hand, he who, being entrusted by God and his country with the high privilege of declaring upon whom shall be conferred a portion of the legislative power, if for corrupt ends he name an unworthy person, stands guilty before God and his country; so he, on the other hand, who receives a heaven-descended power, and yet binds himself to exercise it according to the will of his fellow men rather than of God, insults His majesty, by whom princes rule and judges decree justice. At the same time the lawyer denies not the right of the electors to know from the candidate what are his principles, and what his present views of political measures, introduced or proposed; these he makes known without distortion or concealment: but he will not bind himself to continue ever of the same mind, and unchangeably to advocate measures which more extended knowledge or altered circumstances may prove to be injurious; or, in default of so doing, to yield up his power at the moment when duty most loudly calls upon him to exercise that power for the safety of the commonwealth.

When returned to parliament, the lawyer, as best qualified thereto by his daily studies, and being besides as it were an ambassador from the court of justice, gives himself chiefly to the amendment of his country's domestic laws. And here, having noted what is observed by Lord Bacon, that "all those who have written of laws have written either as philosophers or as lawyers, and none as statesmen; and that, as for the philosophers, they make imaginary laws for imaginary commonwealths, and their discourses are as the stars, which give little light because they are so high; and that as for the lawyers, they write according to the states where they live, what is received law, and not what ought to be law:" he is careful, on the one hand, that he be not so fettered by a reverence for existing laws as to decline making any material change therein; and on the other, that he be not led by too abstract a consideration of natural law to propose alterations merely speculative and visionary. In the matter of legislation, religion is the pole-star by which he steers; and his first care is that the laws of his country be conformable to the law of God. Hence where the intemperate and unholy zeal of statesmen, or the carelessness, infirmity, or impiety of judges, have in any case framed statutes or sanctioned maxims at variance with the law of God, he is earnest to abrogate all such. Next he seeks that the laws be made, as to their meaning, clear and certain; as to their administration, impartial and equal; as to their execution, quick and easy. For the rest, the lawyer upholds by all means the authority of the existing powers; ever, where he may with a safe conscience, supporting, rather than opposing, the ministers of the crown, and steadily resisting all feverish attempts at change, as knowing that these for the most part proceed from an irreligious spirit, which vainly looks for perfection from arrangements of what is *outward* and *formal*, neglecting that which is *inward;* a right ordering of which can alone give health to the wisest institutions.

CHAPTER XXXIV.

THE LAWYER'S CONSIDERATION CONCERNING ECCLESIASTICAL AFFAIRS.

THE lawyer, not only as being himself a member of some spiritual community, and to hold converse with members of his own and of other spiritual communities; but also as being at times to advise concerning the laws relating to the goods and discipline of such communities, is constrained, as well for conscience as for peace sake, to determine [1]what he shall think concerning the outward form of Christ's kingdom upon earth—as whether there be but one visible church upon earth, united under one visible head—or several churches all united by one common discipline, derived from apostolic times, and continued by legitimate succession—or whether again there be several churches, some it may be having forms of government differing from others, and acknowledging no one visible head, and no one external bond of union. If one form alone be of divine appointment, and all others schismatic, it may not be that the lawyer lend his aid to establish what he believes to be contrary to God's holy will and ordinance. Now since to suppose that none can be members of the kingdom of Christ, no matter how strong their faith, no matter how evident the fruits of that faith—love, joy, peace, long suffering, gentleness, goodness, meekness, temperance—that none can dwell in the unity of the Spirit, unless visibly joined together by uniformity of worship, were to imitate the error of our Lord's disciples when they would have forbid those, who, though not followers with themselves, were yet in the name of their master, and by the power of his Spirit, enabled to work miracles of mercy; and of those Jews who at the first thought that none who belonged not to the stock of Abraham could be partakers of the grace of Christ; since moreover there is in the nature of things nothing obliging to such an opinion, nor anything in the history of the church compelling thereto, the lawyer is in this matter of the advice of Lord Bacon "who in revolving the scripture could never find that there should be but one form of discipline in all churches, and that imposed by the necessity of a commandment and prescript out of the word of God; but that God had left the like liberty in the church government that he had done to the civil government, to be varied according to time and place and accidents, which, nevertheless, his high and divine Providence doth order and dispose." Yet he does not therefore deny that uniformity, if it could be had, were an excellent mean towards unity; nor that some forms of ecclesiastical government have in themselves (as is the case in civil governments) a superiority over others, God having at times for national sins (as in the case of his peculiar people the Jews) permitted inferior forms of government to take the place of better. But as all forms of civil government, be they never so imperfect, require of those subject to them allegiance to the authorities therein ordained, and confer though in differing degrees protection upon those living under them; so forms of church government, inferior in kind, albeit they confer not like privileges on those subject to them which others more perfect do, may not be deemed accursed of God. And as in the civil constitution of mankind the subjects of one state, because of the overflow of evil therein, or for other sufficient causes, may place themselves beneath the dominion of another; so in the kingdom of Christ upon earth, nothing hinders but that one born and nursed beneath one form of church government, on urgent occasions thereto moving, may subject himself to the rules and ordinances of other forms—not but that there may be, as in civil communities assemblies of mere rebels and outlaws; so in churches—confederacies of mere schismatics and separatists. But to whom particularly we will give these names, especially when lapse of time in the Providence of God shall have imparted stability to governments at the first it may be founded in schism; it behoves us carefully to consider.

The lawyer having thus considered of ecclesiastical affairs, though it may be he values beyond all others that form of church government under which he has himself been nourished, yet deems not so of other forms but that he may wish them Godspeed, and if need be give his counsel and aid for the maintenance of them, especially of such as the civil power has tolerated—so, however that in no case he will be found the advocate of those, which, though holding the name of Christian churches, deny that foundation upon which every true church must of necessity be built.

CHAPTER XXXV.

THE LAWYER UPON SUNDAYS.

THE lawyer during the week bethinks him constantly of the returning day of rest, and so arranges his business [1]that he may early upon the Saturday lay aside all professional care, and make the evening of that day a preparation for the Sunday. This he does, as having found how hard it is on that day to dismiss from his mind all thoughts of worldly affairs: how ever and again, in the midst of his public and private devotions, some matter of urgent business will obtrude itself upon him and distract his attention. Hence the lawyer, upon the Sunday, not only abstains from the labours of his calling, but carefully lays aside his briefs and papers, lest the sight of them should recall his thoughts to his weekday's business. Not that he thinks of the Sunday as a day of ceremonial observances to be slavishly pursued: on the contrary, he considers it to have been ordained by God himself in the Patriarchal and Jewish churches for the ease and solace of men in communion with their Maker: and when it behoved the Christian church to appoint a festival whereupon to celebrate the triumph of its head over the powers of sin and death, it set apart for that purpose each seventh day, thereby at once to bring to mind the labour of God's love in the creation and in the redemption of the world. The lawyer receiving thus this holy day, rejoices in the opportunity it gives him of turning his thoughts from the fleeting things of this world, to the eternal joys of that heaven of which it is a type. To this end he is a constant attendant at public worship; and that he may be found an attentive observer, as of all other laws, so of the laws of his church, if some weighty hindrance prevent not, he prefers before all other places his parish church; and to whatever place he goes to that he is constant, and this for these reasons. First—he considers that it serves to the maintenance of order, and has in it as it were the sentiment and notion of law. Next—he reflects, that of hearing many preachers there is no end; and that variety in this matter rather engenders a judgment of the preacher, than an humble seeking of truth from his lips. Moreover he frequents the temple of God mainly to pray to him, and to praise him for all his manifold mercies. If, as must at times happen, the preacher be careless or indifferent, he thinks not of public worship as thereby rendered naught, but humbly repairs his loss by more deep thought of his own infirmities, or by studying a sermon of some holy father of the church. When public worship is ended, he goes forth to meditate like Isaac of old upon divine things, or communes with a friend as he walks after the manner of the disciples journeying to Emmaus: or he seeks out the poor, or visits the sick, or assists the minister in catechising the poor children of his parish, or pursues such other work of mercy as God puts into his heart. At night he either entertains such of his relatives or immediate friends as have not a home around whose festive board to gather, or is entertained by them. There he enjoys cheerful converse seasoned with the salt of godliness: and having joined in worship round the altar of the family with whom he has kept this festival of the church, he retires to rest with an unburthened mind, refreshed for the duties of the following week; his whole soul exulting in the foretaste thus given of the joys of that kingdom for whose coming he daily prays.

CHAPTER XXXVI.

THE LAWYER BECOME JUDGE.

[1]THE lawyer, whose probity and ability have commended him to his prince's favour, refuses not at his hands the sacred office of judge, but with holy fear and many prayers enters thereon. And now he, who before was but the servant of men, according to the will of God, becomes, by the appointment of his prince, the minister of God, to dispense those laws which by God's authority committed to him for that purpose the prince with his parliament has ordained. Hence he ever keeps in remembrance the height and holiness of his office, for the due administration of which he must one day give an account before the Judge of judges; and labours earnestly to discharge its duties in all things according to the holy will of God.

His first care is, that the robe of justice which he wears be spotless. Gifts blind the eyes of the wise, and pervert the words even of the righteous. Therefore he refuses all manner of gifts, not caring to trust his own integrity. With God there is no respect of persons. Why then should there be with him his minister? Before his judgment seat the ties of blood and the bonds of friendship call in vain for favour or affection; they are as though they were not. In this matter he commends the practice of Sir Thomas More, who to his relations who prayed his favour was wont to reply, "I assure thee on my fayth, that if the parties will at my hands call for justice and equitie, then although it were my father whom I reverence dearly, that stood on one side, and the devil whom I hate extremely were on the other side, his cause being just, the devil of me should have his right."

The next care of the judge is that he may discharge his office with wisdom: to which end it behoves that he have, *First*—A knowledge of the law he is to administer; this he is studious to attain by unwearied study, as knowing the scandal which an ignorant judge brings upon the administration of law: and secondly, sound sense in the application of them to the circumstances of affairs which come before him in judgment. And here, two principal difficulties present themselves—one, when the law, which he is to dispense, is in itself unjust; the other, when the law, though good in its intent, is by the craft of wicked men perverted to work evil. Now the judge, though it grieve him to be made the means by which to work injustice, yet dares not refuse to declare what the law is. For he is sworn to administer the laws as made, not to make new laws. His duty is *jus dicere*, not *jus dare;* and so that no ill intent of his cause the law to work injustice, he considers not himself therefore culpable because the sentence he pronounces fails to dispense what is altogether just. Yet he labours that the law may be as little injurious as possible: for first if the law itself be bad, he earnestly seeks from those to whom the power belongs, that it be repealed or altered; and again, if the law be good in its intent, but by wicked men is drawn to work injustice, [2]unless plainly obliged he suffers not the law to be so perverted, but where without sophistry he may, gives effect to the spirit rather than to the letter: and where he is so constrained that he may not decide otherwise than according to the letter, he metes out only what he must, and sharply reproves him and his counsellors who have turned the law to such ill purposes.

Next to wisdom the judge brings courage to his work. The cause of the widow, the fatherless, and the oppressed, though all forsake it, he dares to uphold against the mightiest, yea, even against the very prince at whose hands he has received his office. The fear of God being ever before his eyes leaves no place for the fear of man. But chiefly in times of political trouble the courage of the judge is seen. The sullen frown of the enraged prince, and the tumultuous murmur of an angry populace, are alike unnoticed by him: and when all the pillars of the state are shaken, and the minds of men quail amid the confusion that prevails, his unshaken courage in judgment, like oil poured upon troubled waters, is able to produce a calm. Next to courage the judge brings patience. He does not hastily suffer himself to be prepossessed with either side of the case until the whole be heard; nor does he consider any case heard till he has patiently exhausted all that either party have to allege, whether of fact or of argument, as knowing how often matters of moment in the heat of debate are overlooked even by the most experienced.

And now having added to probity wisdom, and to wisdom courage, and to courage patience, he sums up all with a holy zeal and love for truth and justice, which quicken and enliven him in the work in which he is engaged, and cause that forgetful of himself he yields up his whole powers to his service who has called him to so exalted a station.

CHAPTER XXXVII.

THE LAWYER'S DEATH.

[1]IT was a bright evening in summer—the rays of the declining sun fell full upon the couch where the old man lay—round him were gathered his wife and children awaiting in sorrow, rendered peaceful by the sweet smile which played upon his lips, the moment that should summon to a better world the departing spirit of a kind and affectionate father, husband, and friend. His domestics stood in the farther part of the room scarce able to suppress their sobs.

He raised himself with an effort and spoke. "Beloved wife and children, God, who has comforted and succoured me all my days, bless, preserve, and keep you. To his heavenly guidance I commit you: despise it not: his law written on your hearts, set before you in the ensample of his dear Son, and taught you by his Holy Spirit, regard with holy fear and follow with fervent love. Let no power force you, no wealth tempt you, no earthly splendour allure you to swerve from allegiance to this holy law. I have lived long, and in a long life been often called upon to encounter the enemies of this holy law, and often alas! have I seen it trodden down and trampled under their feet: but sure I am that no peace fills their dwellings, no joy swells their breasts; but the worm that dies not gnaws their hearts, and a fearful looking for of fiery indignation haunts and disturbs them in the midst of their loftiest triumphs. Envy not then the oppressor and choose none of his ways. Listen to the law of God—the voice of heavenly wisdom—it will be a light to your feet, and a lamp to your paths; a shield against every foe, and a shelter from every blast: its ways are ways of pleasantness, and all its paths are peace. Such has it ever been to me amid all the strifes and struggles of this transitory life —and now I go, where wars and tumults shall be no more heard, where strife and struggle shall have no place, but justice, peace, and righteousness shall reign eternal. Father of heaven, grant that in that kingdom of bliss we may all meet and join in the song of praise 'unto Him that has loved us and washed us from our sins in his own blood, and hath made us kings and priests unto God and his Father: to him be glory and dominion for ever and ever.—Amen.' "

CHAPTER XXXVIII.

THE LAWYER'S PRAYER.

O LORD, our heavenly Father, who in thy providence hast appointed governors, thy ministers, to dispense thy laws among all nations: grant that we and all thy servants ministering in things pertaining to justice, may faithfully fulfil the duties of our calling, with a single eye to thy glory, and a humble dependence upon thy heavenly blessing. Mercifully, we beseech thee, turn us away from all undue love of wealth and earthly power; keep us from all pride, malice, and evil speaking; preserve us from the fear of evil men and the contagion of ill-example; strengthen in us the love of truth, justice, and mercy; and so quicken our hearts with love towards thee that we loving thee above all things may so love our fellow creatures even as thou hast loved us. Grant this, O Lord, for Jesus Christ's sake, our only Saviour and Redeemer.—Amen.

APPENDIX.

APPENDIX TO THE APOLOGY FOR THE WORK.

[1] IN *the earlier times*. Except in the short notices of the subject which occur in the writings of the casuists, I have not found any treatise upon the duties of advocates considered peculiarly in reference to morality. The subject is incidentally mentioned by several writers, especially divines; and the views almost uniformly put forward by them justify me in supposing the principles of the legal profession in the elder ages of our nation to have been in accordance with the views here maintained, however in many cases the practices of its members may have deviated from those principles.

The titles of some of the tracts touching upon the subject of the duties of lawyers, and their deviations from them, as mentioned in Watt's Bibliotheca Britannica, are amusing. Among them are the following:—

"The voyce of the laste trumpet blowen bi the seventh angel, as is mentioned in the Eleventh of the Apocalyps, callyinge al the estates of menne to the right path of their vocation; wherein are contained xii lessons to twelve several estates of menne, whych if they learne and follow al shall be well, and nothing amise. The contentes of thys booke: the Beggar's Lessone, the Servante's, the Yeoman's, the Lewde Prieste's, the Scoler's, the Learned Man's, the Phisician's, the Lawier's, the Merchante's, the Gentilman's, the Magistrate's, the Woman's. In metre. Lond. 1549, 1550. Octavo." *By Robert Crowley, Crole*, or *Croleus*, an English Printer, Divine, and Poet, born either in Gloucestershire or, according to Bayle, in Northamptonshire, and died 18th June, 1588.

The Familiar Epistles of *Sir Anthony of Guerara*, Preacher, Chronicler, and Counsellour to the Emperor Charles the Fifth. Translated out of the Spanish tongue by Edward Hellows, Groome of the Leash. Wherein are contained very notable letters, excellent discourses, curious sayings, and most natural reasons. Wherein are contained Expositions of certain figures, authorities of Holy Scripture, very good to be preached and better to be followed; Declarations of Ancient Stamps of writing upon Stones, Epitaphs of Sepulchres, Lawes and Customes of Gentiles, doctrines, examples, and counsels for Princes, for Noblemen, for Lawyers, and

Churchmen, very profitable to be followed and pleasant to be read. Lond. 1574, 4to.

Downfall of the Unjust Lawyers, and Rising of the Just. By Edmund Leach. 1652, 4to.

Sagrir, or Doomsday drawing near, with Thunder and Lightning to Lawyers. Lond. 1654, 4to. By John Rogers.

A Rod for the Lawyers. By Wm. Cole. 4to. Lond. 1659.

Essay for the Restoring of our decayed Trade, wherein is described the Smugglers', Lawyers', and Officers' Frauds. By J. Treveris. 4to. 1675.

[2] *The chivalric spirit of the profession, &c.* This was the doctrine of the civil law, and is of ours; as may be seen by consulting Sir John Davis's Preface to his Reports, and Blackstone's Commentaries, vol. iii. p. 28; though, in the present day, it is to be feared it is too much lost sight of.

[3] *Now, however, that principles, &c.* The theories of professional duty which are entertained in the present day are the natural offshoots of those low and inadequate theories of morals which make utility, expediency, self-love, the general good of mankind, and other external and experimental standards the complete measures of right and wrong; nor is it to be wondered at that the young man who at the university has imbibed the principles of Paley's Moral Philosophy, should, when he comes to the practical business of life, carry out those principles in the adoption of some one or other of those erroneous views which I have noted.

[4] *Under no obligation to speak the truth.* This is Dr. Paley's estimate of the lawyer's duty. In the chapter on "Lies," in his Moral Philosophy, he writes thus:—

"There are falsehoods which are not lies, that is, which are not criminal; as, 1. where no one is deceived, which is the case in parables, fables, novels, jests, tales to create mirth, ludicrous embellishments of a story, where the declared design of a speaker is not to inform but to divert; compliments in the subscription of a letter, a servant's denying his master, a prisoner pleading not guilty, *and an advocate asserting the justice or his belief of the justice of his client's cause.* In such instances no confidence is destroyed, because none was reposed; no promise to speak the truth is violated, because none was given or understood to be given."

[5] *As paid for affecting warmth, &c.* The shrewd biographer of Dr. Johnson has preserved to us the sentiments of that author on the morality of modern legal practice in the following colloquy. "BOSWELL: I asked him whether, as a moralist, he did not think that the practice of the law in some degree hurt the nice feeling of honesty. JOHNSON: Why no, sir, if you act properly. You are not to deceive your client with false representations of your opinion: you are not to tell lies to a judge. BOSWELL: What do you think of supporting a cause which you know to be bad? JOHNSON: Sir, you do not know it to be bad till the judge determines it. I have said that you are to state facts fairly, so that your thinking or what you call knowing a cause to be bad must be from reasoning, must be from your supposing your arguments to be weak and inconclusive. But, sir, that is not enough. An argument which does not convince yourself may convince the judge to whom you urge it; and if it does convince him, why then, sir, you are wrong and he is right. It is his business to judge, and you are not to be confident in your own opinion that a cause is bad, but to say all you can for your client and then hear the judge's opinion. BOSWELL: But, sir, does not affecting warmth when you have no warmth, and appearing to be clearly of one opinion when you are in reality of another opinion, does not such dissimulation impair one's honesty? Is there not some danger that a lawyer may put on the same mask in common life in the intercourse with his friends? JOHNSON: Why no, sir, *everybody knows you are paid for affecting warmth for your client*, and it is therefore properly no dissimulation; the moment you come from the bar you resume your usual behaviour. Sir, a man will no more carry the artifice of the bar into the common intercourse of society, than a man who is paid for tumbling upon his hands when he should walk on his feet."—*Boswell's Life of Johnson*, Croker's edit. vol. ii. p. 48.

[6] *As men who with wigs on their heads, &c.* For this eloquent description of one of the modes of thought upon the subject of legal practice we have to thank the

writer of an article in the 65th vol. of the Edinburgh Review (generally supposed to be the late Chief Indian Law Commissioner.) In examining Mr. Montagu's defence of Lord Bacon's conduct in the prosecution of the Earl of Essex, the reviewer expresses himself thus:—"Mr. Montagu conceives that none but the ignorant and unreflecting can think Bacon censurable for anything that he did as counsel for the crown, and maintains that no advocate can justifiably use any discretion as to the party for whom he appears. We will not at present inquire whether the doctrine which is held on this subject by English lawyers be or be not agreeable to reason or morality;—whether it be right that a man should, with a wig on his head, and a band round his neck, do for a guinea what without these appendages he would think it wicked and infamous to do for an empire;—whether it be right, that not merely believing, but knowing a statement to be true, he should do all that can be done by sophistry, by rhetoric, by solemn asseveration, by indignant exclamation, by gesture, by play of features, by terrifying one honest witness, by perplexing another, to cause a jury to think that statement false. It is not necessary on the present occasion to decide these questions. The professional rules, be they good or bad, are rules to which many wise and virtuous men have conformed, and are daily conforming. *If, therefore, Bacon did no more than these rules required of him, we shall readily admit that he was blameless.*"

[7] *As the agents of God in the work of justice, &c.* I quote here the words of the learned Hooker in a passage from the fifth book of his Ecclesiastical Polity, worthy to be written in letters of gold, and which I have placed as a frontispiece to this little volume.

[8] *As the counsellors, secretaries, &c.* These are the words of Sir John Davies, attorney-general for Ireland in the reign of Charles II. They are taken from the eloquent preface to his Reports, a copious extract from which will be found in a subsequent part of this volume.

[9] *Orators bound to use, &c.* These eloquent words are from an Assize Sermon of Bishop Sanderson, preached at Lincoln, 4th August, 1625.

[10] *Every member of society, &c.* This statement is from Bishop Warburton's Divine Legation, vol. i. p. 397, 3d edition, where, speaking of the character of Cicero, he says, "As an orator he was an advocate for his client, or more properly *personated him*. Here then without question he was to *feign* and *dissemble* his own opinions and to speak those of his client. And though some of those who call themselves *casuists* have held it unlawful for an advocate to defend what he thinks an ill cause, yet I apprehend it to be the natural right of every member of society, whether accusing or accused, to speak freely and fully for himself. And if, either by a legal or natural incapacity, this cannot be done in *person*, to have a *proxy* provided or allowed by the state to do for him what he cannot or may not do for himself. I apprehend that all states have done it, and that every advocate is such a proxy. Tully, therefore, feigning and dissembling his own opinions under this character, acted, I say, neither a weak nor an unfair part."

[11] *The advocate is part of the machine of justice, &c.* This is the theory in substance proposed by Mr. Basil Montague. In his little tract describing what the character of "*The Barrister*" should be, we meet the following:—"He (the barrister) exerts his power to strengthen his own case and weaken his opponent's, because he knows that taking all things into consideration, justice is best promoted by collision of intellect, and that the whole truth will be eviscerated by the opposite counsel, or that the intelligence which presides will not permit truth to be misrepresented by any partial examination." And again—"The statements by opposite advocates may not be most beneficial to the practitioner; and as the advocate may profess feelings which he does not feel, and may support a cause which he knows to be wrong: as it is a species of acting without an avowal that it is acting; it may appear at variance with some of our best feelings. It is, however, nothing but appearance. The advocate is in reality an officer assisting in the administration of justice, and acting under the impression that truth is elicited and difficulties disentangled by the opposite statements of able men. He is only troubling the waters that they may exert their virtues.

[12] *This has been done too often of late years, &c.* The first writer who appears

to have raised his voice against the specious and captivating exposition of this theory contained in "The Principles of Moral and Political Philosophy," by William Paley, D.D., was the Rev. Thomas Gisborne, the amiable author of the "Duties of Man," and of other useful works on morals. In a work entitled "The Principles of Moral Philosophy investigated and applied to the Constitution of Civil Society," that writer protests strongly against the introduction of Dr. Paley's work among the class-books of the University of Cambridge. That protest was unheeded; and the consequence may be stated in the words of Professor Whewell, "Preface to Four Sermons on the Foundations of Morals." "The general currency which Paley's Moral Philosophy has acquired (a currency due in no small degree to the adoption of the work by the University of Cambridge) has had a very large share in producing the confusion and vacillation of thought respecting the grounds of morals which is at present so generally prevalent in England even among persons of cultivated minds." Since the appearance of Mr. Gisborne's work, the errors of Dr. Paley's system have been well exposed by many writers.

[13] *Not the obligation of the law of the land, &c.* On the contrary. The following case, in which, an action having been brought by a client against his attorney for refusing to urge a plea furnished him by the client, on the ground that the plea was false, the judges held that the attorney in so acting had done his duty, affords strong ground for contending that the law of the land does not require from those who represent others in the courts that they should be made the conscious instruments of wrong. "*Attourné qui est informé de pléder matter* que il ne peut pléder par conscience, il peut pléder—quod non est veraciter informatus, &c. et hoc sufficit in breve de disceit versus son client." Note, this case is wrongly quoted both in Brooke's Abridgment, title "Attorney," plac. 76, and in Jenkin's Reports, p. 52, from the year book 20 *Edw.* 4, *fo.* 9. I have not been able to discover the correct reference.

Quite consistent with the above judgment is the oath which is taken by attorneys of the Court of Common Pleas in Ireland, of which the following is a copy:—

Oath taken by every Attorney of the Court of Common Pleas.

"You shall do no falsehood or deceit, nor consent to any to be done within this court; and if you know of any to be done you shall give notice thereof to the Lord Chief Justice, or other his brethren justices of this court, that it may be reformed. You shall delay no man for lucre or malice. You shall increase no fees, but you shall be contented with the accustomed fees. You shall plead no foreign plea, nor sue any foreign suits unlawfully to the hurt of any man, but such as shall stand with the order of the law and your own conscience. You shall seal all process that you shall sue out of this court with the seal thereof, and see the Queen's majesty and Chief Justice discharged for the same. You shall not wittingly or willingly sue, or procure to be sued any false suit, or give aid or consent to the same, on pain of being expelled the court for ever; and further you shall truly use and demean yourself in the office of an attorney within this court according to your learning and discretion. So help me God."

[14] *Is then (it is asked) is no concealment, &c.* Jer. Taylor, in the second part of his sermon on the text, "And harmless as doves," Matt. x. 16, where discussing the question whether it be lawful to tell a lie to save a good man's life or to do him a great benefit? notes, "that it was a question which St. Austin was much troubled withal, affirming it to be of the greatest difficulty, for he saw generally all the doctors before his time allowed it, and of all the fathers no man is noted to have reproved it but St. Austin alone, and he also, as his manner is, with some variety. Those which followed him are to be accounted upon his score. And it relies upon such precedents which are not lightly to be disallowed. For so Abraham and Isaac told a lie in the case of their own danger to Abimelech; so did the Israelitish midwives to Pharaoh, and Rahab concerning the spies, and David to the King of Gath, and the prophet that anointed Saul, and Elisha to Hazael, and Solomon in the sentence of the stolen child; concerning which Tremeus hath given us a *rule.* That

those whose actions the Scripture hath remarked and yet not chastised or censured, we are not without great reason and certain rule to condemn."

Though much that Jer. Taylor says in the above sermon, and also in the Ductor Dubit. book iii. ch. 2, rule 5, where he again discusses the matter, is good, yet he seems to me not to have perceived the right clue to the labyrinth, which I apprehend is that I have noted in the text.

[15] *The escape from the dilemma lies here, &c.* This appears the judgment of St. Austin. I quote from Jeremy Taylor, Ductor Dubit. book iv. ch. 2, rule 398: "Ut noverimus omnia opera nostra tunc esse munda et placere in conspectu Dei si fiant simplici corde id est intentione superna fine illo caritatis, quia et plenitudo legis caritas est. Oculum ergo hic accipere debemus ipsam intentionem quâ facimus quicquid facimus: quæ si munda fuerit et recta et illud aspiciens quod aspiciendum est omnia opera nostra quæ secundum eam operamur necesse est bona sint." By which he cannot be supposed to mean that every act which seems right in a man's own eyes is therefore good, but those acts only which are consecrated by the love of God constraining thereto.

It is remarkable that while those commandments in the two tables which forbid murder and theft do so generally—malice and ill intent being necessarily implied in the words there used; the commandment which forbids lying couples with it the notion of injury to our neighbour. Whence probably it is that Melancthon defines a lie to be, "to deceive our neighbour to his hurt." "Mendacium est petulanter aut cupiditate nocendi aliud loqui seu gestu significare et aliud sentire."

[16] *God in the beginning formed man after his own image, &c.* The following beautiful description of man's moral character in his state of innocency is from South's sermon on the text.

"The image of God was (in the state of man's innocence) no less resplendent in that which we call man's practical understanding; namely, that storehouse of the soul in which are treasured up the rules of action and the seeds of morality. Now of this sort are these maxims, 'That God is to be worshipped,' 'That parents are to be honoured,' 'That a man's word is to be kept.' It was the privilege of Adam innocent to have these notions also firm and untainted, to carry his monitor in his own bosom, his law in his heart. His own mind taught him a due dependence upon God, and chalked out to him the just proportions and measures of behaviour to his fellow creatures. Reason was his tutor, and first principles his *magna moralia*. The decalogue of Moses was but a transcript, not an original. All the laws of nations and wise decrees of state, the statutes of Solon and the twelve tables, were but a paraphrase upon this standing rectitude of nature, this fruitful principle of justice, that was ready to run out and enlarge itself into suitable determinations upon all emergent objects and occasions. Justice was then neither blind to discern nor lame to execute. It was not subject to be imposed upon by a deluded fancy, nor yet to be bribed by a glozing appetite, for an *utile* or *jucundum* to turn the balance to a false or dishonest sentence. In all its directions of the inferior faculties it conveyed its suggestions with clearness and enjoined them with power; it had the passions in perfect subjection; and though its command over them was but suasive and political, yet it had the force of co-action and despotical. It was not then as it is now, where the conscience has only power to disapprove and to protest against the exorbitancies of the passions, and rather to wish than make them otherwise. The voice of conscience now is low and weak, chastising the passions as old Eli did his lustful domineering sons: 'Not so, my sons, not so;' but the voice of conscience then was not, 'This should or this ought not to be done,' but 'This must, this shall be done.' It spoke like a legislator; the thing spoke was a law, and the manner of speaking it a new obligation."

[17] *Yet even here God did not so leave himself without witnesses, &c.* The following remarkable passage from Cicero is a striking instance of that moral enlightenment vouchsafed to pagans to which I have here alluded. "Est quidem vera lex, recta ratio, naturæ congruens diffusa in omnes, constans, sempiterna; quæ vocet ad officium jubendo, vetando a fraude deterreat; qua tamen neque probos frustra jubet aut vetat, nec improbos jubendo aut vetando movet. Huic legi, nec abrogari fas est, neque derogari ex hâc aliquid licet, neque tota abrogari potest. Nec vero per sena-

5

tum aut per populum solvi hâc lege possumus, neque èst quærendus explanator aut interpres ejus alius. Nec erit alia lex Romæ, alia Athenis—alia nunc, alia posthac; sed et omnes gentes et omni tempore una lex et sempiterna et immortalis continebit; unusque erit communis quasi magister et Imperator omnium Deus. Ille legis hujus inventor, disceptator, lator: cui qui non parebit ipse se fugiet, ac naturam hominis aspernabitur; atque hoc ipso, luet maximas pænas, etiam si cætera supplicia quæ effugerit."

[18] *The other of the law itself, &c.* This truth is well expressed by Barrow in his sermon upon Ecclesiastes iii. 17. "As for human laws, made to encourage and requite virtue, or to check and chastise vice, it is manifest that they do extend to cases in comparison very few; and that even as to particulars which they touch, they are so easily eluded or evaded, that without entrenching upon them, at least without incurring their edge or coming within the verge of their correction, men may be very bad in themselves, extremely injurious to their neighbours, and hugely troublesome to the world; so that such laws hardly can make tolerable citizens, much less thoroughly good men, even in exterior demeanour and dealing. However, no laws of men can touch internal acts of virtue or vice. They may sometimes bind our hands, or bridle our mouths, or shackle our feet; but they cannot stop our thoughts, they cannot still our passions, they cannot bend or break our inclinations: these things are beyond the reach of their cognizance, of their command, of their compulsion, or their correction; they cannot, therefore, render men truly good or hinder them from being bad.

[19] *And therefore it cannot be otherwise than immoral, &c.* Jer. Taylor, Ductor Dubit. book iv. ch. 1, thus asserts this truth and the authority by which it is supported:—

"He that gives counsel or aid to an action, good or evil, consents to it, and it is imputed to him as a product of his will and choice.

"This is expressly affirmed by all laws civil and canon, and the municipal laws of all those nations of which I have seen any records concerning this matter; and the interpreters universally consent, with this proviso—that the counsel be so much cause of the action, that without it it would not have been done."

[20] *Notwithstanding all the objections, &c.* Several of these difficulties are strongly stated in the following passages, the one from the little work of Mr. Basil Montague, called *The Barrister*, which I have before mentioned, p. 154, the other from an article in the 129th number of the Edinburgh Review, p. 16.

Mr. Basil Montague, in describing the ideal of a Barrister such as he would have him, has the following as a part of his character:—

"*In general he (the barrister) does not exercise any discretion as to the suitor for whom he is to plead.* If a barrister were permitted to exercise any discretion as to the client for whom he will plead, the course of justice would be interrupted by prejudice to the suitor, and the exclusion of integrity from the profession. The suitor would be prejudiced in proportion to the respectability of the advocate who had shrunk from his defence, and the weight of character of the counsel would be evidence in the cause. Integrity would be excluded from the profession, as the counsel would necessarily be associated with the cause of his client.

"'From the moment (says Erskine, in his defence of Thomas Paine) that any advocate can be permitted to say that he will or will not stand between the crown and the subject arraigned in the court where he daily sits to practise, from that moment the liberties of England are at an end. If the advocate refuses to defend, from what he may think of the charge or of the defence, he assumes the character of the judge; nay, he assumes it before the hour of judgment; and, in proportion to his rank and reputation, puts the heavy influence of perhaps a mistaken opinion into the scale against the accused, in whose favour the benevolent principle of English law makes all presumptions, and which commands the very judge to be his counsel.'

"Our advocate, therefore, does not exercise any discretion; to him it is a matter of indifference whether he appears for the most unfortunate or the most prosperous member of the community; for the poorest bankrupt or the noblest peer of the realm; for a traitor or for the king."

The author of the article in the Edinburgh Review thus writes: "If it depends on the opinion of an advocate whether he shall make any statement or not (that is, any statement given by his client, and the bringing which forward is admitted to be for his benefit), how long will it be before it depends upon his opinion of the whole case, whether he shall undertake the cause or not? If the lending of his assistance to the client is to depend upon the opinion he forms of the case, how long will it be before it depends upon his inclination? Can there be the least doubt that this preliminary inquiry must open the door to the grossest of all abuses, and the one most fatal both to the character of the profession and the administration of justice—the choice of clients and causes by whatever advocates are most in request? How easy will it be in each case to say, 'I don't believe your story,' or 'I don't agree with your law,' and thus to refuse being the defender of the poor and the oppressed on pretence of refusing to assist an unjust cause! In truth, the silly charge against the profession that its aid is lent to all causes indiscriminately, and that it may furnish instruments to oppression, and may help injustice to its objects, leads at once, by a very direct and short route, to a course of proceeding which makes it truly and almost in every case the means of overwhelming innocence and working injustice. For this whole charge resolves itself, whenever it is examined, into a complaint that advocates undertake either side; and as one must be wrong, it is contended that there is in each case an advocate defending injustice. True, but till the event of the trial you have no right to say which side is wrong. Therefore the charge is, that the advocate has undertaken the cause without previous examination. Consequently the remedy proposed is making this previous examination, which of course implies the right to refuse the cause; and this at once gives the rich, and the powerful, and the popular, a monopoly of legal resources, and (if it shuts not the courts to all who are desolate and oppressed) at least precludes them from the assistance of those whose ability and experience qualifies them for the safe conduct of suits. Indeed, were this preposterous but very prevalent notion once established, once firmly rooted so as to produce its legitimate fruit—the obligation in each case to institute a preliminary inquiry before undertaking it—there are times in every country when the result would be, the utter exclusion of certain parties from all professional assistance whatever. Suppose a season of great political violence, and an arbitrary power established, in the hands either of a tyrannical court, as in this country a century and a half ago, or of a ferocious multitude, as in France during the first revolution; what chance could the victim either of the despot or of the mob have of obtaining any defender at all, even among the humbler members of the profession, if the undertaking his cause was optional and not imperative? If the advocate, when applied to, was bound by such an absurd rule to institute an examination and satisfy himself, would he not be sure to employ the rule for his own protection, and refuse the defence of all whom the tyrant, be he of one head or of many, had marked out for destruction? Nay, would not this very rule be the source, and the only source, of the advocate's danger? For as long as he has no choice, but is bound by strict rule to defend every client and undertake every cause, he is necessarily free from all responsibility. Tyranny itself cannot frame a charge against him while the performance of the duty is compulsory; but make it optional, and there is some ground for questioning, and there will soon enough be found reasons for punishing, the exercise of the discretion. Under our Charleses and Jameses there was no material risk encountered by those who defended causes against which the tyrannical court was most strongly biassed. Honesty was punished in the judges when it now and then broke out; the advocates never suffered. Even during the Reign of Terror at Paris, when the execrable revolutionary tribunal had wholly yielded to the menaces of the blood-thirsty rabble, there never wanted advocates to maintain a defence, rendered unavailing by the ferocity or by the pusillanimity yet more despicable of the judges. Had advocates been clothed with the attributes of justice which those who inveigh against them are ever requiring them to display, had they been in the practice of what is daintily termed 'refusing to undertake an unjust cause,'—that is, of previously examining each case, and refusing it if they chose,—we may be well assured that instead of few decisions being pronounced against the English court, there would have been none at all, and, what is of far more importance, all the noble displays of learning and reasoning would have been lost which served to promote the flame of liberty in those dismal times, and the destruction of the tyrants which it ultimately accomplished might have been indefinitely delayed. Even in France, where much less was effected by the exertion of the bar, there can be no doubt that whatever it contributed towards the restoration of liberty, first by preparing the revolution of 1784, and then by the overthrow of the mob-tyranny of 1793–4, would have been wholly lost had the lawyers exercised any discretion in undertaking the defence of the accused; and in later times the lawyers of both countries have beyond all dispute been enabled, with comparatively little risk to themselves, to resist the oppressions of the government, chiefly by the maintenance of the rule which, depriving them of all power to refuse their assistance, secures the administration of justice in evil times, and is by *ignorant declaimers* complained of as the fountain of injustice."

I hope to show, in the appendix to this work, that in the number of these *ignorant declaimers* are to be found many of the most able lawyers of our own and other countries, and by far the larger proportion of those casuists, moralists and divines, who have handled the subject of the duties of lawyers.

[21] *I appeal from the assertion to the experience of those nations in which the civil law, &c.* By the Roman law the advocates in each case were obliged, at the commencement of it, to swear upon the Holy Evangelists that they would defend with all their force what they should judge to be true and just; and that they would abandon the defence of any cause which they should find in the beginning to be unjust, or which in the progress they should discover to be unjust. "Patroni autem causarum, qui utrique parti suum præstantes auxilium ingrediuntur, cum lis fuerit contestata, post narrationem propositam, et contradictionem objectam, in qualicunque judicio majore vel minore, vel apud arbitros sive ex compromisso sive aliter datos vel electos, sacrosanctis Evangeliis tactis, juramentum præstent quod omni quidem virtute suâ, omnique ope, quod verum et justum existimaverint clientibus suis inferre procurabunt, nihil studii relinquentes quod sibi possibile est; non autem creditâ sibi causâ cognitâ quod improba sit vel penitus desperata, et ex mendacibus allegationibus composita ipsi scientes prudentesque malâ conscientiâ liti patrocinabuntur, sed et si certamine procedente aliquid tale sibi cognitum fuerit à causa recedent ab hujusmodi communione sese penitus separantes.—*Cod. l.* 14. § 1 *de Judic.*

The ancient law of Scotland required, that "Advocates in the time of their admission, and yearly, should be sworn to execute their office of advocation diligently and truly; and that as soon as they understand their client's cause to be unjust or wrongful, that they should incontinent leave the same, and desist from all further pursuit or defence."—*Statute of the Lords*, 13th June, 1537.

The law of Spain requires an oath from advocates, "That they will conduct themselves faithfully, and will not defend unjust causes."—Institutes of the civil law of Spain, by D. Ignatius Jordan de Asso y del Reo, and D. Miguel de Manuel y Rodrignez (translated by Lewis T. C. Johnston), p. 303.

The following is the form of the advocate's oath prescribed by a law adopted by the representative council of Geneva, 20th June, 1834.

"I swear before God to be faithful to the republic and canton of Geneva; never to swerve from the respect due to the tribunals and to the authorities; not to advise or maintain any cause which does not appear to me just or equitable, unless in the defence of an accused; not to employ, knowingly, in order to maintain the causes which shall be confided to me, any means contrary to the truth; and not to attempt to deceive the judges by any artifice or by any false exposition of facts or of law; to abstain from all offensive personality, and not to advance any fact against the honour and the reputation of the parties, unless it be indispensable to the cause with which I shall be charged; not to encourage the commencement or the carrying on of any process from any motive of passion or of interest; and not to refuse, from any personal considerations, the cause of the feeble, the stranger, or the oppressed."

The only case I have been able to find which gives any intimation of what the law of England is upon this subject, is the one I have above alluded to.

APPENDIX TO PREFACE.

[1] AND *the obliquy and contempt, &c.* It would be easy to fill a volume with quotations from poets, historians, moralists, philosophers and divines, marking the scorn which the evil practices of the professors of law brought upon their calling; let the following suffice.

Swift describes lawyers as "A society of men bred up from their youth in the art of proving, by words multiplied for the purpose, that white is black, and black is white, according as they are paid."

"They were lawyers . . . . men full of subtility."—*Burke's French Revolution.*

"Lawyer! I believe there's many a cranny and leak unstopped in your conscience. If so be that one had a pump to your bosom, I believe we should discover a foul hold. They say a witch will sail in a sieve, but I believe the devil would not venture aboard your conscience."—*Congreve.*

An old proverb, to characterize that which is heartless, describes it "As cold as charity in the heart of a lawyer."

"If you go to law for a nut, the lawyers will crack it, give each of you half the shell, and chop the kernel themselves."—*Carey's Present State of England*, 4to. 1627.

"Whether it was the ever open hand of a practising lawyer always ready to grasp a fee, or the extravagant deference paid to that fee, as if a motive, sordid in its nature, could so hallow a cause of cursed iniquity as to render it fit for any man to prostitute his tongue in its behalf, and to employ what talents he has (either in argumentation, eloquence, skill in the quirks of the law, or in outfacing truth itself), to pervert justice, to impose on the minds of jurors, and influence them to an unjust verdict; or whether a strong bias, habitual disposition, and fruitful genius in too many, for turning every trust and situation in life to their own private advantage, were the reason why one of the wisest of our kings, with his council composed of great men, and parliaments themselves, thought it necessary to incapacitate practising lawyers from sitting in the House of Commons; it is certain they were the first set of men expressly excluded."—*Carte's Hist.* vol. iii. p. 480.

"I speak to the face of many here present, the lawyers, of all the people in the land, are the greatest grievance to my subjects; for when the case is good to neither party, yet it proves good and beneficial to them."—*King James I. last speech in Parliament.*

Milton, in his Treatise upon Education, speaks of men "allured to the trade of law, grounding their purposes not on the prudent and heavenly contemplation of justice and equity, which was never taught them; but on the promising and pleasing thoughts of litigious terms, fat contentions, and flowing fees."

"To deal freely with you counsellors, it is a matter that they who are strangers to your profession can scarce put any fair construction upon, that the worst cause, for a little money, should find an advocate among you! This driveth the standers by upon this harsh dilemma—to think that either your understandings or your consciences are very bad. If, indeed, you so little know a good cause from a bad, then it must needs tempt men to think you very unskilful in your profession. But when almost every cause, even the worst that comes to the bar, shall have some of you for it, and some against it; and in the palpablest causes you are some on one side, and some on the other; the strange differences of your judgments doth seem to betray their weakness. But if you know the causes to be bad which you defend, and to be good which you oppose, it more evidently betrays a deplorable conscience. I speak not of your innocent or excusable mistakes in cases of great difficulty, *nor yet of excusing a cause bad in the main from unjust aggravations:* but when money will hire you to plead for injustice against your own knowledge, and to use your will to defraud the righteous, and spoil his cause, or vex him with delays for the advantage of your unrighteous client; I would not have your conscience for all your gains, nor your account to make for all the world."—*Baxter.*

"I oft have heard him say how he admired
Men of your large profession, who could speak
To every cause, and things indeed contraries
Till they were hoarse again, yet all be law:
That with most quick agility could turn
And return, make knots and undo them,
Give forked counsel, take provoking gold
On either hand and put it up. These men
He knew would thrive with their humility:
And for his part he thought he should be blessed
To have his son of such a suffering spirit;
So wise, so grave, of so perplexed a tongue
And loud withal, that could not wag, nor scarce
Lie still without a fee."—*Ben Jonson.*

Even the meek Wordsworth cannot let the profession escape. His "Poet's Epitaph" contains the following lines—

"A lawyer art thou?—draw not nigh:
Go, carry to some fitter place
The keenness of that practised eye,
The hardness of that sallow face!"

APPENDIX TO CHAPTER I.

[1] IN *which definition, &c.* Having freely quoted from those who have looked on the dark side of the lawyer's character, I shall be excused for the length of the following extract in favour of lawyers, and of the law when rightly applied, from the Preface to the Reports of the eloquent Sir John Davies, before alluded to.

"These vulgar errors respecting the laws of England and its professions being thus reversed, so we may truly say that there is no such uncertainty in the rules of the law, no such delay in the proceedings, no such prevarication or corruption in the professors thereof, as is by some unjustly pretended; why may we not proceed further, and affirm confidently, that the profession of the law is to be preferred before all other humane professions and sciences, as being most noble for the matter and subject thereof, most necessary for the common and continual use thereof, and most meritorious for the good effects it doth produce in the commonwealth.

"For what is the matter and subject of our profession but justice, the lady and queen of all moral virtues? And what are the professors of the law but her counsellors, her secretaries, her interpreters, her servants? Again, what is the king himself but the clear fountain of justice? And what are the professors of law but conduit pipes, deriving and conveying the streams of his justice to all the subjects of his several kingdoms? So if justice be rightly resembled to the sun in the firmament, in that she spreadeth her light and virtue to all creatures, how can she but communicate part of her goodness and glory unto that science that is her handmaid, and waits upon her? And if kings be God's scholars (as Homer writeth) and that the rules of justice be their principal lesson; and if God do honour kings with his own name, *Dixi quod dii estis* (as a more divine poet than Homer singeth), especially for that they sit upon God's own seat, where they minister justice unto the people; do not kings again highly honour those persons whose subordinate ministry and service they use in performing the principal part of their kingly office? Undoubtedly: touching the advancement of such persons, Solomon the king speaketh, 'that they shall stand before kings,' and 'God will set them (saith David) with princes, even with the princes of his people.'

"Neither is this profession ennobled in regard of the dignity of her employment only, but she is to be honoured so much the more for the necessity and continual use of her service in the commonweal. For if we must honour the physician *propter necessitatem*, as the wise man prescribeth; much more must we honour (for the same cause) the professors and ministers of the law. For neither do *all men* at any time, nor any one man at *all times*, stand in need of the physician; for they that are in health (which are the greatest number of men) *non egent medico*, saith the great Physician of our souls, and our only Advocate which is in heaven. But *all men* at *all times* and in *all places* do stand in need of justice, and of law, which is the rule of justice, and of the interpreters and ministers of the law, which give life and motion unto justice.

"For do not *all persons* stand in need of justice, when, without her rule, the prince himself knows not how to rule, nor his people how to obey? When without her support the nobleman cannot uphold his honour, nor the common subject hold his liberty? When without her safeguard, the rich man cannot be free from spoil, nor the poor man from oppression? Briefly, when without her no man living, be he virtuous or vicious, can enjoy his life, nor anything that makes his life delightful. For the covetous man cannot increase his profit, nor the sensual man enjoy his pleasure, but under the shadows of her wings.

"Again, is not justice needful at *all times*, when we can neither travel safely by day, nor sleep securely by night, without her protection? When if such a law were indeed made, as was propounded by a wicked emperor, *that all laws should cease for four-and-twenty hours*, that short cessation would be sufficient to give opportunity to wicked men to make a greater combustion in the whole world, than that which happened when the chariot of the sun did want a guide but half a day, as it is lively expressed in the fable of Phaëton?

"Lastly, is not justice necessary in *all places*, when we cannot without peril make a voyage by sea, unless she waft us; nor a journey by land, unless she convey us? When we should be oppressed by force in the country, if she did not defend us; and undone by fraud in the city, if she did not relieve us? When she encloseth every man's garden and field, and makes every man's cottage his castle of defence. So as we have not such a universal and continual use either of the light of the sun, or of fire or water, as we have of the light and heat and comfort of justice: for a man may remain alive for some hours without the use of those common benefits. But a commonwealth, wherein each private man's weal consisteth, cannot stand and continue one minute of an hour, if justice, which is her soul, be departed from her.

"If, therefore, justice, and the law which is but a rule and lesson of justice, be so necessary for all persons, times, and places, as no family, no city, no commonwealth, no kingdom, can stand without the support thereof; how needful is the service of learned men in the law, without which justice itself cannot possibly stand! For *justitia periret* (saith the president Cassanæus) *si deesset qui justitiam allegaret.* For if no man did study the reason of the law, if no man kept in memory the rules of the law, if no man knew the form of pleading, or the course of proceeding in the law, what would become of public justice in a short time? Or how should the benefit of the law be derived and communicated unto the people? For as in a natural body, the reasonable soul cannot use or transmit any of her powers but by special organs of the same body, disposed of and fitted by nature for every function, as the eye to see, the ear to hear, the tongue to speak, and the like of the rest: so in the body politic of a commonwealth, the law, which is the soul thereof, produceth no effect on operation at all, but by such of her ministers, as by art and experience, are enabled and qualified for her service. For "*lex est justitia inanimata,*" saith the schoolman; "*lex est mutus magistratus,*" saith Cicero. The law of itself is dumb, and speaks not but by the tongue of a learned and eloquent lawyer: she is deaf, and heareth no complaints but by the ear of a grave and patient judge: she is blind, and seeth no enormities, but by the eye of a watchful and diligent officer.

"Again the law is nothing else but a rule which is made to measure the actions of men. But a rule is dead and measures nothing, unless the hand of the architect do apply it. It is indeed an excellent instrument to make harmony and concord in the commonwealth; but the best lute that ever was made could never make music of itself alone, without the learned hand of the lute-player.

"Therefore, though Jupiter (as Protagoras in Plato telleth us) did first invent and give the law, yet was Mercury sent with that heavenly gift to deliver it over unto mankind. So as it is manifest, that without the ministry of these Mercuries, of these interpreters of the law, namely, the learned professors thereof, there can be no use or application of the law, and consequently the law or justice itself cannot consist without them.

"But as the estimation and price of this profession is exceedingly raised by the necessary and universal use thereof, so do her great *merits* to the commonwealth deserve a far greater exaltation of honour. For, first, the commonwealth is indebted to the law for all her temporal blessings and felicities whatsoever: for all our peace, plenty, civility, and moral honesty dependeth upon the law. That we enjoy our lives, our wives, our children, our goods, our lands, our good names, or whatsoever is sweet and dear unto us, we are beholden unto the law for it. *Quid sunt regna nisi latrocinia, sine justitia?* saith St. Augustine. Without justice the land would be full of thieves, the sea full of pirates, the commons would rise against the nobility, the nobility against the crown: we should not know what were our own, what another man's: what we should have from our ancestors, what we should leave to our children. *Major hæreditas venit unicuique nostrum à Jure et legibus quam à parentibus*, saith Cicero. In a word, there would be nothing certain, nothing sure, no contracts, no commerce, no conversation among men; but all kingdoms and states would be brought to confusion, and all human society would be dissolved.

"But, on the other side, the law is a fortress for the weak to retire into, a sanctuary for the oppressed to fly into; it restraineth the boldness of the insolent, it tieth with manacles the hand of the potent, and, like Orpheus's harp, or Noah's ark, it charmeth the fierceness of the lion and tiger, so as the poor lamb may lie in safety by them.

"If, then, the law itself doth merit so highly of all mankind in general, for that it is the fountain of all these benefits; what do the professors of the law deserve which draw these benefits out of that fountain, and derive the same unto every particular person? *Namsi non habes quo haurias, et puteus altus est*, as the woman of Samaria saith of Jacob's well in the gospel, 'How canst thou refresh thyself with the water of that well?' *Si veritas sit in profundo demersa*, as Democritus was wont to say,—If human actions be so carried in clouds, as it is hard to find what is true and what is false, and when the truth of the fact is found, it is as hard many times to distinguish what is just and what unjust; if in all causes that come in question, either *quæstio facti* or *quæstio juris* must first be decided before a man can receive the benefit of the law; (for, as the wise man saith, *Deus fecit hominem rectum, sed ipse miscuit se infinitis quæstionibus:*) what a meritorious work it is to resolve these troublesome questions which arise in the civil life of man, either by laying open the truth of fact, or by clearing the doubt of the point in law, that speedy and equal justice may be done unto all, and every one may have and enjoy his own in peace. How often would the truth be concealed and suppressed, how oft would fraud lie hid and undiscovered, how many times would wrong escape and pass unpunished, but for the wisdom and diligence of the professors of the law? Doth not this profession every day comfort such as are grieved, counsel such as are perplexed, relieve such as are circumvented, prevent the ruin of the improvident, save the innocent, support the impotent, take the prey out of the mouth of the oppressor, protect the orphan, the widow, and the stranger? Is she not *oculus cæco, et pes claudo*, as Job speaketh? Doth she not withal many times stretch forth *brachium seculare* in the defence of the church and true religion? All which are works of mercy and of singular merit. Again, doth she not register and keep in memory the best *antiquities* of our nation? Doth she not preserve our ancient *customs* and *forms of government*, wherein the wisdom of our ancestors doth shine far above the policy of other kingdoms? Are not the records of her acts and proceedings so precious, as they are kept in the king's treasury, like jewels of the crown, and reputed a principal part of the royal treasure? Lastly, is not a worthy professor of the law a star in the firmament of the commonwealth? Is he not *lux in tenebris* wheresoever he dwelleth? Is not his house as it were an oracle, not only to a town or city, but to a whole country round about him? So as he may truly say of the people that seek his counsel, as Apollo Pythius spoke in Ennius of such as resorted to his temple,—

'*Suarum rerum incerti, quos ego ope meâ*
Ex incertis certos, compotesque consilii,
Dimitto, ne restemere tractent turbidos.'

Therefore one of the Roman emperors doth not without cause give this honourable testimony of the professors of the law—*Advocati, qui dirimunt ambigua facta causarum, suæque defensionis viribus tam publicis in rebus quam in privatis lapsa erigunt, fatigata reficiunt, non minus humano generi provident quam si prætiis atque vulneribus patriam parentesque salvarent: neque enim solos nostro imperio militare credimus qui glodiis clypeis et thoracibus utuntur, sed etiam Advocatos. Militant namque causarum Patroni, qui laborantium spem vitam et posteros defendunt.* For if it be a worthy deed (as doubtless it is) for a man to defend his friends or country with his right hand and his sword only; what an excellent service is it to defend them with his speech, his reason, and wisdom, wherein the excellency of man doth principally consist.

"Therefore both the schoolman and the politick do prefer justice before fortitude; and the statute of 31 Hen. VIII. cap. 10, which ranketh the great officers of the kingdom in their due places, doth place the constable and marshal beneath the chancellor in all assemblies of counsel; for *ille semel* (saith *Cicero*, speaking of the martial man) *hic semper proderit reipublicæ*, meaning the learned man of the long robe.

"And in very truth, as the commonwealth is beholden to the profession of the law, so are the professors of the law not a little beholden to the commonwealth. For if they procure and preserve her peace and plenty, doth not she requite them again with riches and with honour? Doth she not advance them to her chief benches and offices, and trust them with the livelihood and lives of all her good people? Neither do our learned men of the law grow to good estates in the commonwealth by any illiberal means (as envy sometime suggesteth), but in a most ingenious and worthy manner. For the fees or rewards which they receive are not of the nature of wages or pay, or that which we call *salary* or *hire*, which are indeed duties certain, and grow due by contract for labour or service; but that which is given to a learned counsellor is called *honorarium*, and not *merces*, being, indeed, a gift which giveth honour as well to the taker as to the giver: neither is it certain or contracted for; no price or rate can be set upon counsel, which is invaluable and inestimable, so as it is more or less according to circumstances, namely, the ability of the client, the worthiness of the counsellor, the weightiness of the cause, and the custom of the country. Briefly, it is a gift of such a nature, and given and taken upon such terms, as albeit the able client may not neglect to give it without note of ingratitude (for it is but a gratuity or token of thankfulness); yet the worthy counsellor may not demand it without wrong to his reputation, according to that moral rule, *Multa honestè accipi possunt, quæ tamen honestè peti non possunt.*

"Lastly, it is an infallible argument, that the estates of such as rise by the law are builded upon the foundation of virtue, in that God's blessing is so manifestly upon them, not only in raising but preserving their houses and posterities: whereof there are examples not a few, and those not obscure, in every *shire* of *England*, and of the *English pale* in this kingdom of *Ireland*."

The following eloquent description of justice is from the "*Holy Court*" of Father Caussin, translated by Sir F. Hawkins.

"If the world be a harp (as saith the eloquent Synesius), justice windeth up the strings, stirreth the fingers, toucheth the instrument, giveth life to the airs, and maketh all the excellent harmonies. If the world be a music-book, framed of days and nights as of white and black notes, justice directeth and composeth: if it be a ring, justice is the diamond: if it be an eye, justice is the soul: if it be a temple, justice is the altar. All yieldeth to this virtue, and as it is enchased in all laudable actions, so all laudable actions are incorporated in justice. It is an engine much more powerful in effect than was that of Archimedes in idea; for it doth that in kingdoms which this man could never so much as imagine in his mind, though ambitious enough in inventions. It maketh, I say, heaven to descend upon earth, and earth to mount up to heaven: heaven to descend, in introducing a life wholly celestial in the uncivil conversation of men: earth to mount up, in drawing it from the dregs and corruption of a covetous and bloody life, to enlighten it with rays of a prudent knowledge, to embellish it with virtues, diversify it with beauties, and settle it in the centre of repose."

APPENDIX TO CHAPTER II.

(THEIR DIVERSITIES.)

[1] OF *those called Lawyers, &c.* Those who wish to inquire into the history of advocacy will find the subject treated of in the "Histoire abrégée de l'Ordre des Avocats, par M. Boucher d'Argis," republished, together with several other interesting treatises upon the subject of the duties of Advocates, by M. Dupin, in a work entitled "Profession d'Avocat." Paris, 1838.

The necessity of the order of lawyers in advanced stages of society is so obvious as to need no comment. I would here, however, particularly call attention to the path of duty which the consideration of the origin and necessity of this profession seems clearly to point out to the advocate. For if, as is obvious, the *resulting* force (to speak mechanically) of the three persons united—the client, attorney, and advocate—ought to be the same as that of the client alone, were he endowed with the powers and knowledge necessary to plead his own cause, it follows, as a necessary consequence, that the advocate should not lend himself to produce, in concert with his client and the attorney, an effect which could not with justice be produced by the client alone when filling all the three characters in his own person. I am aware that a different conclusion is attempted to be drawn by some who assert, that inasmuch as in a simple state of society every client, no matter what his character, has the power of stating his own case in his own way, therefore in a more complicated state of society every client should possess a similar right; and that hence the duty of the advocate is not to seek what *he* thinks just in the way that *he* thinks right, but to seek that and in that manner which his client wills. I have, in the preface of this work, attempted to show the theory of advocacy which asserts this conclusion to be unsound and irreligious. At the same time I am aware, that as the data on which the arguments for and against it must be eventually grounded are determinations of the moral sense, no positive proof can be given save that which the conscience may supply.

APPENDIX TO CHAPTER III.

(THE LAWYER'S CHOICE OF A CALLING.)

[1] FOR *some calling he must needs have, &c.* On the necessity, choice, and exercise of a calling, without which, as he says, "we despise God's ordinance and smother his gifts, we expose ourselves to sinful temptations; we deprive ourselves, our families, and the poor of due maintenance; we withdraw our bounden service from the commonwealth." See Bishop Sanderson's Sermon on the text, "Brethren, let every man wherein he is called therein abide with God." 1 *Cor.* vii. 27.

"I confess it is a very sad consideration to see how much men abuse their callings, the end whereof is to serve God by serving men. He that employs his talents only to get honours, profits, and pleasures, profanes his calling, living to another end than God hath appointed him. It is true every man must labour in his calling to maintain his family, but that is not the main scope and end of our lives. The true end of life is to do service to God in serving men in our several stations. And for a recompense of this service God blesses men's honest travails, and allows them to take moderately for their labours according to the judgment of godly men. But I see it is a very hard thing to find a man that labours in his calling in love to God and his brethren's good."—*Cooke's Vindication of the Professors and Profession of the Law.*

The author of the "Broad Stone of Honour," in his review of the callings which present themselves to the notice of young men on entering upon life, thus speaks respecting the choice of the legal profession:—"The profession of the law will, of course, present itself, and the question will arise whether it be consistent with your order. Now this appears to me to be altogether a question of individual character, and not one that will admit of any general conclusion. If you are of studious habits; of a decided disposition of mind, not to be influenced by the subject of your study; and of a devotion to truth not to be perverted or overcome by sophistry; if you are firmly established in the principles of religion, and if you are one of those elevated spirits that are raised above the world, above its temptations, and its opinions—in that case you may embrace this profession, and look up to a Cicero, a Sulpicius,* a D'Aguesseau, a More, a Bacon, a Clarendon, a Hale, a Mansfield, and an Eldon, as your dignified masters. But if this be not your character; if nature has not so fashioned, and practice confirmed these habits; if a higher power has not so refined and elevated your mind; I exhort you not to undertake it.

"I confess this is the only conclusion I can come to on the subject. What authority more weighty, what judgment more sound and impartial, than that of Lord Clarendon? And yet what observation does he make upon the effects of a legal education? He says, 'It introduces men into the language and practice of business; and if it be not resisted by the great ingenuity of the person, inclines young men to more pride than any other kind of breeding, and disposes them to be pragmatical and insolent, though they have the skill to conceal it from their masters, except they find them (as they are too often) inclined to cherish it.' And with what a lively image does Lord Bacon represent the danger of an indiscriminate defence of right and wrong, though the mind may be convinced at the time, when he says that 'certain it is that words, as a Tartar's bow, do shoot back upon the understanding of the wisest, and mightily entangle and pervert the judgment;' which is not wonderful if we consider what Cicero has said: "Nihil est tam incredibile quod non dicendo fiat probabile: nihil tam horridum, tam incultum, quod non splendescat oratione et tanquam excolatur,'† which may be regarded as the judgment of Heaven by those who hold the opinion of Socrates, *οὐ γαρ που θεμις τῳ ὀρθως λεγοντι μη συγχωρειν*.‡

"It is not that I object *in toto* to the theory of the legal profession; for though Cicero perceived the grand objection to which it is exposed, and seemed to distrust his own sentence against the objection and in favour of the practice (very remarkable indeed are his words, and very slender the authority which removed his scruples);§ but that I observe and deprecate its practical tendency, its effect upon the mind, upon the judgment, and upon the heart. It is not that I would subscribe to the definition of an advocate as lately (1823) delivered and laid down before the most solemn audience that the world could produce.|| Of that portrait there certainly can be but one opinion among honest men. It has, however, I trust, no original to make it of importance, and therefore cannot be too quickly effaced from our memories; for while there are diseases of the body which it is dangerous to behold, there are also mental images from which we should turn aside to escape pollution, to both of which that verse is applicable—

> 'Dum spectant oculi læsos læduntur et ipsi.'

The arguments of Cicero are the same as those of the later writers who profess to defend the ordinary practice of the profession, although the Roman lawyer seems

* The legal character of Sev. Sulpicius was admirable: "Neque ille magis juris consultus quam justitiæ fuit: neque constituere litium actiones malebat quam controversias tollere."

† Paradox vi.

‡ Plat. Hipp. Major.

§ Quod scribere (præsertim cum de Philosophià scriberem) non auderem, nisi idem placeret gravissimo stoicorum Pametio.—Cic. De Off. 11. xiv.

|| The character here alluded to would seem to be that drawn by Lord Brougham, in his defence of Queen Caroline, before the House of Lords, in which we find the following:—"An advocate, by the sacred duty which he owes his client, knows, in the discharge of that office, but one person in the world, *that client and none other*. To save that client by all expedient means—to protect that client at all hazards and costs to all others, and among others to himself—is the highest and most unquestioned of his duties; and he must not regard the alarm, the suffering, the torment, the destruction, which he may bring upon any other. Nay, separating even the duties of a patriot from those of an advocate, and casting them, if need be, to the wind, he must go on, reckless of the consequences, if his fate it should unhappily be to involve his country in confusion for his client's protection!"

less confident of his argument than content with his authority: '*vult hoc multitudo, patitur consuetudo, fert etiam humanitas.*' It must be confessed also, that were the question one that could be determined by the conclusion from a naked abstracted theory, the writers who support it would easily overcome their opponents. But this is not the case, as I have before observed. We must pay attention to a multitude of effects, connections, and circumstances, which follow from it, and which must be taken into account when we are to decide for ourselves, or for any individuals who are estimating its advantages. The reasoning upon the one side is plausible, and perhaps unanswerable; yet from the abstracted line of the argument, without being guilty of resisting truth, the mind may remain in suspense, till the experience, the observation, and the individual feeling of the inquirer may at length confirm him in the opposite opinion, that 'the indiscriminate defence of right and wrong contracts the understanding while it corrupts the heart. Subtilty is soon mistaken for wisdom, and impunity for virtue. If there be any instance upon record, as some there are undoubtedly, of genius and morality united in a lawyer, they are distinguished by their singularity, and operate as exceptions.' In this very severe sentence the author of Junius has excluded all considerations of a religious nature, though it certainly appears to me it is from such the objection can be most forcibly urged, and it was not incumbent upon either the philosopher or the politician to exclude them from his regard. I confess, however, freely, that views and reasoning of this kind have appeared to me to determine the question. That desire of establishing a legal reputation, so essential to the candidate for future employment, while the words of Cicero are before me, 'Difficile est cum præstare omnibus concupieris, servare æquitatem quæ est justitiæ maxime propria,' that habit of regarding the side of justice (vain men, how little qualified are we to judge!) instead of mercy; that habit of looking up to authority and law as the restraining principle of human conduct, instead of relying for virtue upon the piety and principles of individuals (Montesquieu, Esprit des Loix, 3 v.); that disposition to regard the utility and practical result of measures as the criterion of their value, and that custom of office which identifies impunity with innocence; which is ready to sacrifice the end to the means, the object of the legislator to the letter of the law; these effects all and separately are death to the high and generous feelings which refine and purify the soul; they tend to destroy those grand general impressions of right and wrong which must be kept alive, and ready at the call of a moment to direct you; that habit of mercy, which must be the first feature of your character; that full confidence in the virtue of other men which must spring from the conviction of your own; that unqualified preference of principle and worth above the mere service of interest and necessity; that disdain for the bands and trammels of the letter of our rule; that utter indifference to the utility and consequences of virtue, which are all and separately essential to that elevated character which you desire and are bound to imitate. Upon the whole, then, after a consideration of the question with all its relations, and after an honest examination of your own powers, habits, and disposition, you will make that decision which disowns every base and unworthy motive; the decision of conscience and of honour, which will ensure to you your own respect, whatever may be the subsequent opinion which experience shall induce you to adopt."

APPENDIX TO CHAPTER V.

(THE LAWYER'S KNOWLEDGE.)

[1] Now *of laws, &c.* The distinction which (following Hooker) I have here drawn between the different kinds of laws to which mankind are subject, is one of great importance. But because in the present day it has been much overlooked, and its place supplied by the theories of two classes of persons, each widely differing from the other, I will first briefly allude to these latter, and will then illustrate and support, by quotations from authors of high authority, the views I have put forward in the text.

The first class of persons to whom I allude are those, who like Hobbes, Mandeville, Hume, Paley, and Bentham, denying the existence of conscience as the faculty by which we judge of right and wrong, and with it the permanent and immutable character of the laws which it discovers to us; substitute in its place, as the test of moral worth, the varying and uncertain standards of the supreme power, self-interest, utility, the general good of mankind, and other external or experimental standards. These by denying the moral nature of man, and forbidding him to look *within* for that whereby to judge of human conduct, send him to the cumbrous accumulations of a painful experience to determine, not what is *right* but what is *useful*, not what is *honest* but what is *profitable*. Even the pagan orator, unenlightened by the sun of Christianity, could discern the fallacious character of speculations such as these. Speaking of those who made power and utility the measures of right and wrong, he indignantly exclaims: " *Quod si pœna, si metus supplicii non ipsa turpetudo, deterret ab injuriosâ facinorosâque vitâ nemo est injustus, at incauti potius habendi sunt improbi. Tum autem qui non ipso honesto movemur ut viri boni simus, sed utilitate aliquâ atque fructu, callidi sumus non boni.*" Cicero de Legibus. lib. i. What is right we feel assured is even in this world useful, expedient, conducive to our own and to the public interest; but if we are to hesitate to call right *right*, until we have proved it by experience to be all these, we shall act like a man who should refuse to call white *white*, until he had analyzed the rays of light of which it was composed. And if (as is the case in morals) we have no instrument by which to effect this analysis, we must remain for ever in the same state of scepticism as to right and wrong, in which the philosopher would be as to colours, who was ignorant of, or had not at hand, an instrument by which to effect a separation of rays, or who, having separated them, should consistently call for a further analysis to convince him that each of the colours was in reality what it seemed.

The second class of persons to whom I have above alluded are those who, while they admit the existence of conscience, yet distrust altogether the intimations which it gives respecting what is right and wrong, and refer every question respecting human conduct to the decision of the Bible, looking in every case to it for a solution, direct or indirect. This form of thought, though less injurious than the other first mentioned, becomes, in the extreme to which it was carried in the days of the puritans, and is by many in our day, the source of most serious and dangerous consequences. Some of these have been most wisely noted by Bishop Sanderson in his fourth Sermon, *Ad. Clerum*, where, after asserting that for the maintenance of the doctrine " that the Holy Scriptures are the sole rule of all human actions whatsoever"—" there was never yet produced any piece of an argument, either from *reason*, or from authority of Holy Writ, or from the testimony either of the ancient fathers, or of other classical divines of later times, which may not be clearly and abundantly answered to the satisfaction of any rational man, not extremely forepossessed with prejudice;" he warns his hearers " to beware of it, and that so much the more heedfully, because of the evil consequents and effects that issue from it; to wit, a world of superstitions, uncharitable censures, bitter contentions, contempt of superiors, perplexities of conscience. First, it filleth men's heads with many *superstitious* conceits, making them to cast impurity upon sundry things, which yet are lawful to as many as use them lawfully. For the taking away of the indifferency of anything that is indifferent, is in truth *superstition:* whether either of the two ways it be done either by requiring it as necessary, or by forbidding it as unlawful. He that condemneth a thing as *utterly unlawful*, which is yet *indifferent*, and so lawful, is guilty of superstition, as well as he that enjoineth a thing as *absolutely necessary*, which yet indeed is but *indifferent* and so arbitrary. They of the church of Rome, and some in our church, as they go upon quite contrary grounds, yet both false, so they run into quite contrary errors, and both superstitious. They decline too much on the left hand, denying to the Holy Scripture that perfection which of right it ought to have, of containing all things appertaining to that supernatural doctrine of faith and holiness which God hath revealed to his church, for the attainment of everlasting salvation: whereupon they would impose upon Christian people, and that with an opinion of *necessity*, many things which the Scriptures require not; and that is *a superstition*. These wry too much on the right hand, ascribing to the Holy Scripture such a kind of perfection as it cannot have; of being the sole director of all human actions whatsoever: whereupon they forbid unto Christian people, and that under the name of sin, sundry things which the Holy Scripture condemneth not; and that is *a superstition* too."

"From which *superstition* proceedeth in the second place uncharitable censuring: as evermore they that are the most superstitious are the most supercilious. No such severe censurers of our blessed Saviour's person and actions, as the superstitious Scribes and Pharisees were. In this chapter the special fault, which the apostle blameth in the weak ones (who were somewhat superstitiously affected), was their rash and uncharitable judging of their brethren. And common, and daily experience among ourselves, showeth how freely some men spend their censures upon so many of their brethren, as without scruple, do any of those things which they, upon false grounds, have superstitiously condemned as utterly unlawful.

"And then, thirdly, as unjust censures are commonly entertained with scorn and contumely; they that so liberally condemn their brethren of profaneness, are by them again as freely flouted for their preciseness: and so while both parties please themselves in their own ways, they cease not mutually to provoke, and scandalize, and exasperate the one the other, pursuing their private spleens so far till they break out into open contentions and oppositions. Thus it stood in the Roman church when this epistle was written. They judged one another and despised one another, to the great disturbance of the church's peace: which gave occasion to our apostle's whole discourse in this chapter. And how far the like censurings and despisings have embittered the spirits, and whetted both the tongues and pens of learned men one against another in our own church, the stirs that have been long since raised, and are still upheld by the factious opposers against our ecclesiastical constitutions, government, and ceremonies, will not suffer us to be ignorant. Most of which stirs, I verily persuade myself, had been long ere this either wholly buried in silence, or at leastwise prettily well quieted, if the weakness and danger of the error whereof we now speak, had been more timely discovered, and more fully and frequently made known to the world than it hath been.

"Fourthly, let that doctrine be once admitted, and all human authority will soon be despised. The commands of parents, masters, and princes, which many times require both secrecy and expedition, shall be taken into slow deliberation; and the equity of them sifted by those that are bound to obey, though they know no cause why, so long as they know no cause to the contrary. *Delicata est obedientia quæ transit in causæ genus deliberativum.* It is a nice obedience in S. Bernard's judgment, yea rather troublesome and odious, that is over curious in discussing the commands of superiors, boggling at everything that is enjoined, requiring a *why for every wherefore*, and unwilling to stir until the lawfulness and expediency of the thing commanded shall be demonstrated by some manifest *reason* or undoubted authority from the Scriptures.

"Lastly, the admitting of this doctrine would cast such a snare upon men of weak *judgments* but tender consciences, as they should never be able to unwind themselves thereout again. Men's daily occasions for themselves or friends, and the necessities of common life, require the doing of a thousand things within the compass of a few days; for which it would puzzle the best textman that liveth readily to bethink himself of a sentence in the Bible, clear enough to satisfy a scrupulous conscience, of the *lawfulness* and *expediency* of what he is about to do; for which, by hearkening to the rules of *reason* and *discretion*, he might receive easy and speedy resolution. In which cases if he should be bound to suspend his resolution, and delay to do that which his own reason would tell him were presently needful to be done, until he could haply call to mind some precept or example of scripture for his warrant, what stops would it make in the course of his whole life, what languishings in the duties of his calling? How would it fill him with doubts and irresolutions, lead him into a maze of uncertainties, entangle him in a world of woful perplexities, and, without the great mercy of God, and better instruction, plunge him irrecoverably into the gulf of despair? Since the chief end of the publication of the Gospel is to comfort the hearts, and to revive and refresh the spirits of God's people with the glad tidings of liberty from the spirit of bondage and fear, and of gracious acceptance with their God; to anoint them with the oil of gladness, giving them beauty for ashes, and instead of sackcloth girding them with joy: we may well suspect that doctrine not to be evangelical which thus setteth the consciences of men upon the rack, tortureth them with continual fears and perplexities, and prepareth them thereby unto hellish despair."

The same subject is more fully treated of by Bishop Sanderson in the fourth chapter of his treatise *De Conscientia*, in which he proposes and answers the question *Wherein is to be found a complete rule of conscience?* After commencing with the position "That God alone exercises a complete and direct command over the consciences of men," he infers, "That the proper and complete rule of conscience is the will of God, in whatever manner made known to mankind," and then states that will to be discovered in three ways; "1st, by the light of Nature; 2ndly, by the light of Scripture; and 3dly, by the light which is conveyed by meditation and instruction exercised upon the knowledge conveyed to us by the light of Nature and the light of Scripture;" a distinction nearly corresponding to that which I have made in stating that the knowledge of natural laws is "to be sought in the recesses of the heart, and in the written records, and from the living ministers of God's holy word."

To the same effect as the passages in the writings of Bishop Sanderson, to which I have above alluded, are the remarks of the learned Hooker, in the third book of his Ecclesiastical Polity; in which, considering the assertions of those who urged "That in Scripture there must be of necessity contained a form of Church Polity, the laws whereof may in no wise be altered," he asserts, "That no sound divine in the world ever denied that the will of God, which we are to judge our actions by, was in part made manifest by light of nature, and not by Scripture alone."

I have been the more anxious to point out the errors of the two classes of theorists above mentioned, because they each in their way tend to insufficient notions of the force and obligations of laws, lowering the character of *natural* and exaggerating that of *positive* law. While they obtrude the aid of the philosopher to say what is *useful*, and of the lawyer to say what is *lawful*, they disregard the conscience which would tell what is *right*, and wholly dispense with the aid of the *Divine*, whose business it is to assist the conscience by lights drawn from the Scriptures of truth, and the opinions of pious and holy men.

I now proceed to illustrate by a few quotations the view I have adopted: And first from Hooker. In his first book of Ecclesiastical Polity, "Law Rational," he says, "which men commonly use to call the Law of Nature, meaning thereby the law which human nature knoweth itself in reason universally bound unto, which also for that cause may be termed most fitly the Law of Reason; this law, I say, comprehendeth all those things which men by the light of their natural understanding evidently know, or at leastwise may know, to be beseeming or unbeseeming, virtuous or vicious, good or evil, for them to do." And again, "All laws human, which are made for the ordering of politic societies, be either such as establish some duty whereunto all men by the law of reason did before stand bound; or else such as make that a duty now which before was none. The one sort we may for distinction's sake call *mixedly*, and the other *merely* human." In the same book, speaking of the cause why so many natural laws are set down in Scripture, he says, "The Scripture is fraught even with the laws of nature; insomuch that Gratian defining natural right, whereby is meant the right which exacteth those general duties that concern men naturally, even as they are men, termeth 'Natural Right, that which the Books of the Law and the Gospel do contain.' Neither is it vain that the Scripture aboundeth with so great store of laws in this kind: for they are either such as we of ourselves could not easily have found out, and then the benefit is not small to have them readily set down to our hands; or if they be so clear and manifest that no man endued with reason can lightly be ignorant of them, yet the Spirit as it were borrowing them from the school of nature, as serving to prove things less manifest, and to induce a persuasion of somewhat which were in itself more hard and dark, unless it should in such sort be cleared, the very applying of them unto cases particular is not without most singular use and profit many ways for men's instruction. Besides, be they plain of themselves or obscure, the evidence of God's own testimony added to the natural assent of reason concerning the certainty of them, doth not a little comfort and confirm the same."

In his sermon upon the text, "His mind swelleth and is not right in him; but the just by faith shall live," Hab. ii. 4, he makes the following forcible remarks upon that obscurity concerning justice, which is caused by the want of properly distinguishing between laws natural and immutable, and laws subject to change, otherwise called positive law. "It is," he says, "no small perplexity which this one thing hath bred in the minds of many, who, beholding the laws which God himself hath given, abrogated and disannulled by human authority, imagine that justice is hereby conculcated; that men take upon them to be wiser than God himself; that unto their devices his ordinances are constrained to give place: which popular discourses, when they are polished with such art and cunning as some men's wits are well acquainted with, it is no hard matter with such tunes to enchant most religiously affected souls. The root of which error is a misconceit that all laws are positive which men establish, and all laws which God delivereth, immutable. No—it is not the author which maketh, but the matter whereon they are made, that causeth laws to be thus distinguished. Those Roman laws, '*Hominem indemnatum ne occidito,*' '*Patronus si clienti fraudem fecerit, sacer esto,*' were laws unchangeable, though by men established. All those Jewish ordinances for civil punishment of malefactors, 'The prophet that enticeth into idolatry shall be slain,' 'A false witness shall suffer the same hurt which his testimony might have brought upon another,' 'Life for life, eye for eye, tooth for tooth;' all canons apostolical touching the form of church government, though received from God himself, yet positive laws, and therefore alterable. Herein, therefore, they differ: a positive law is that which bindeth them that receive it in such things as might before have been either done or not done without offence, but not after, during the time it standeth in force. Such were those church constitutions concerning strangled and blood. But there is no person whom, nor time wherein, a law natural doth not bind. If God had never spoken word unto men concerning the duty which children owe unto their parents, yet from the firstborn of Adam unto the last of us, 'Honour thy father and thy mother,' could not but have tied all. For this cause, to dispense with the one can never possibly be justice; nor other than injustice sometimes not to dispense with the other."

Domat, in his treatise upon Laws, prefixed to his work upon the Civil Law in its natural order, thus expresses himself:—"All the different ideas which it is possible to conceive of the several sorts of laws that are expressed by the names of divine and human laws, natural and positive, spiritual and temporal, law of nations, civil laws, and by all the other names that can be given them, may be reduced to two kinds, which comprehend all laws of what nature soever: one is, of the laws which are immutable; and the other, of the laws that are arbitrary. For there is not any one law but what has one or other of these characters. Which it is of moment to consider, not only for apprehending aright this first general distinction of laws into these two kinds, which ought to precede the other ways of distinguishing them; but because it is these two characters which are the most essential part of the nature of all laws, and therefore the knowledge of them is necessary and of great use in the study of the civil law.

"The immutable laws are so called because they are natural, and so just at all times and in all places that no authority can either change or abolish them; and the arbitrary laws are those which a lawful authority may enact, change, or abolish, as there is occasion."

The importance which Bishop Sanderson attached to a knowledge of the distinctions between different kinds of laws, is seen in his answer to one who asked him what course a young divine should take in his studies to enable him to be a good casuist. After recommending a sufficient understanding of the learned languages and of moral philosophy, "The second thing (he said) which would be a great help and advantage to a casuist, was a convenient knowledge of the nature and obligation of laws in general; to know what a law is; what a *natural* and a *positive* law; what is required to the *latio dispensatio derogatio* vel *abrogatio* legis; what promulgation is antecedently required to the obligation of any positive law; what ignorance takes off the obligation of a law, or does excuse, diminish, or aggravate the transgression: for every case of conscience being only this, *Is this lawful for me or is it not?* and the law the only rule and measure by which I must judge of the lawfulness or unlawfulness of any action, it evidently follows that he who (in these) knows not the nature and obligation of laws, never can be a good casuist, or rationally assure himself or others of the lawfulness or unlawfulness of actions in particular.—*Life of Bishop Sanderson, by Izaak Walton,* ad finem.

[2] *He finds to be derived, &c.* Jeremy Taylor, whose work entitled *Ductor Dubitantium* is well worthy the study of every lawyer, thus prefaces his observations upon the nature and character of laws:—"That the laws of God and man are the great measures of right and wrong, of good and evil, of that which is to be followed and what is to be avoided, in manners of men and the intercourses of societies—is infinitely certain and universally confessed. Since, therefore, human laws are one moiety of the rule and measure of conscience, and that we are bound to obey our lawful superiors in what they command, it is naturally consequent to this that we acknowledge the conscience bound, and that in human laws as well as divine (though according to their several proportions) the conscience ought to be instructed. And indeed there is more need of preachers in the matter of divine laws, and more need of wise and prudent guides in the matter of human laws. For the laws of God are wiser and plainer, few and lasting, general and natural, perceived by necessity, and understood by the easiest notices of things; and, therefore, men have more need to be called upon to obey than taught how; and, therefore, here the preacher's office is most necessary and most required. But human laws are sometimes intricate by weakness, sometimes by design, sometimes by an unavoidable necessity; they are contingent, and removed far from the experiences of most men; they are many and particular, difficult and transient, various in their provisions, and alterable by many parts and many ways: and yet because the conscience is all the way obliged, she hath the greater need of being conducted than in the other, where every wise man can better be a guide in the little intrigues, and every child can walk in the plain way."

APPENDIX TO CHAPTER VII.

(THE LAWYER'S DUTIES.)

[1] AND *first he makes it known, &c.* As the duty here asserted, of regarding the moral as well as legal merits of a client's case is one in the present day very generally denied among British lawyers, I shall offer no excuse for the numerous quotations which follow (and which, if need were, might easily be multiplied) from the writings of eminent Divines, Casuists, Moralists, Lawyers (both of our own and other nations), and Legislators, expressive of opinions in accordance with those which in this little work it has been my anxious wish to recommend to the attention of my brethren of the bar. If they should fail to convince, I trust they may at least cause some to suspend their judgment ere they join in characterising as "*ignorant declaimers*" those who agree in the thoughts and sentiments they contain.

I. DIVINES.

1. BISHOP SANDERSON, in an Assize Sermon, preached at Lincoln, 4th August, 1625, thus addresses the bar:—"If thou comest hither as to thine harvest, to reap some fruit of thy long and expenseful study in the laws, and to assist thy client and his cause with thy counsel, learning, and eloquence, think not because thou speakest for thy fee, that therefore thy tongue is not thine own, but thou must speak what thy client will have thee speak, be it true or false; neither think because thou hast the liberty of the court, and perhaps the favour of the judge, that therefore thy tongue is thine own, and thou mayest speak thy pleasure to the prejudice of the adversary's person or cause. Seek not preposterously to win the name of a *good lawyer* by wresting and perverting good laws, or the opinion of the *best counsellor* by giving the *worst* and *shrewdest* counsel. Count it not, as Protagoras did, the

glory of thy profession, but subtilty of wit and volubility of tongue, to make the worse cause the better; but, like a good man as well as a good orator, use the power of thy tongue and wit to shame impudence and protect innocency, to crush oppressors and succour the afflicted, to advance justice and equity, and to help them to right that suffer wrong. Let it be as a ruled case to thee in all thy pleadings, not to speak in any cause to wrest judgment."

That no doubt may remain as to the full meaning of this passage, I will quote two more passages from sermons by the same good bishop. In an Assize Sermon, preached at Lincoln, 7th March, 1624, is the following:—"I know not any extremity of wrong beyond the extremity of right: when laws intended for *fences* are made *snares*, and are calumniously wrested to oppress that innocency which they should protect. And this is most properly calumny in the prime notion of the word: —for a man upon a mere trick or quillet from the letters or syllables of the law, or other writing or evidence pressed with advantage to bring his action or lay his accusation against another man, who yet *bonâ fide* and in equity and conscience hath done nothing worthy to bring him into such trouble." And again, in the same sermon, describing the ways in which a "false report" (Exod. xxiii. 1) is raised, he says, "The third way is, when, taking advantage of the law, we prosecute the extremity thereof against our brother, who perhaps hath done something contrary to the letter of the law, but not violated the intent of the lawgiver, or offended either against common equity, which ought to be the measure of just laws, or against the common good, which is in some sort the measure of equity. In that multitude of laws, which, for the repressing of disorders, and for the maintenance of peace and tranquillity among men, must needs be in every well governed commonwealth, it cannot be avoided but that honest men, especially if they have much dealings in the world, may have sometimes just and necessary cause to do that which, in regard to the thing done, may bring them within the compass of some statute or branch of a statute; yet such as, circumstances duly considered, no wise and indifferent man but would well approve of. Now if in such cases always rigour should be used, laws intended for the benefit should by such hard construction become the bane of human society."

2. HOOKER.—It will hardly be contended that Hooker had not in his view lawyers as well as judges in the following passage:—"So natural is the union of religion with justice, that we may boldly deem there is neither, where both are not. For how should they be unfeignedly just, whom religion doth not cause to be such; or they religious, which are not found such by the proof of their just actions? If they, which employ their labour and travel about the public administration of justice, follow it only as a trade, with unquenchable and unconscionable thirst for gain, being not in heart persuaded that justice is God's own work, and themselves his agents in this business, the sentence of right God's own verdict, and themselves his priests to deliver it, *formalities* of justice *do but serve to smother right, and that which was necessarily ordained for the common good, is through shameful abuse made the cause of common misery.*" (Hooker's Eccles. Polity, book v. ch. 1.) What Hooker here means by formalities of justice, he has more fully explained in the 9th chapter of the same book. "General laws (he says) are like general rules of physic, according whereunto as no wise man will desire himself to be cured if there be joined with his disease some special accident, in regard whereof that whereby others in the same infirmity but without the like accident recover health, would be to him either hurtful, or at the least unprofitable: so we must not, under a colourable commendation of holy ordinances in the church, and of reasonable causes whereupon they have been grounded for the common good, imagine that all men's cases ought to have one measure.

"Not without singular wisdom, therefore, it hath been provided, that as the ordinary course of common affairs is disposed of by general laws, so likewise men's rarer incident necessities and utilities should be with equity considered. From hence it is, that so many privileges, immunities, exceptions, and dispensations, have been always with great equity and reason granted; not to turn the edge of justice, or to make void at certain times and in certain men, through mere voluntary grace or benevolence, that which continually and universally should be of force (as some understand it), but in very truth to practise general laws according to their right meaning.

"We see it in contracts, and other dealings which daily pass between man and man, that, to the utter undoing of some, many things by strictness of law may be done, which equity and honest meaning forbiddeth. Not that the law is unjust, but imperfect; nor equity against, but above, the law, binding men's consciences in things which the law cannot reach unto. Will any man say, that the virtue of private equity is opposite and repugnant to that law, the silence whereof it supplieth in all such private dealing? No more is public equity against the law of public affairs, albeit the one permit unto some in special considerations, that which the other agreeably with general rules of justice doth in general sort forbid. For sith all good laws are the voices of right reason, which is the instrument wherewtth God will have the world guided; and impossible it is that right should withstand right, it must follow that principles and rules of justice, be they never so generally uttered, do no less effectually intend than if they did plainly express an exception of all particulars, wherein their literal practice might in any way prejudice equity."

3. BAXTER, in his Christian Directory, part iv. ch. iv. giving directions to lawyers about their duty to God, says: "*Be not counsellors or advocates against God, that is, against justice, truth or innocency.* A bad cause would have no patrons if there were no bad or ignorant lawyers. It is a dear bought fee which is got by sinning; especially by such a wilful aggravated sin as the deliberate pleading for iniquity or opposing of the truth. Judas's gain and Ahithophel's counsel will be too hot at last for conscience, and sooner drive them to hang themselves in the review than afford them any comfort: as Saint James saith to them that he calleth to weep and howl for their approaching misery, 'Your riches are corrupted, and your garments moth-eaten; your gold and silver is cankered, and the rust of them shall be a witness against you, and shall eat your flesh as it were fire; ye have heaped treasure together for the last days.' Whatever you say or do against truth, and innocency, and justice, you do it against God himself. And is it not a sad case that among professing Christians there is no cause so bad but can find an advocate for a fee? I speak not against just counsel to a man that hath a bad cause (to tell him it is bad, and persuade him to disown it); nor do I speak against you for pleading against excessive penalties or damages; for so far your cause is good, though the main cause of your client was bad; but he that speaketh or counselleth another for the defence of sin, or the wronging of the innocent, or the defrauding another of his right, and will open his mouth to the injury of the just for a little money, or for a friend, must try whether that money or friend will save him from the vengeance of the Universal Judge (unless faith and true repentance, which will cause confession and restitution, do prevent it)."

4. BISHOP COLLYER, in his *Moral Essays*, part iv. p. 198, expresses his opinion upon this matter in the following dialogue:—

"*Philotimus.* Pray what is your opinion of those lawyers who appear in a foul cause?

"*Philalethes.* I think if they know it they misbehave themselves, and have much to answer for. What can be more unaccountable than to solicit against justice, and lend the credit of our character to an ill business?—To throw in dilatory pleas and false suggestions—to perplex the argument or entangle the witness?—To make a mercenary noise against right or reason?—To misapply precedents and statutes, and draw the laws into a conspiracy, to endeavour to surprise the judge and mislead the jury?—To employ learning, and lungs, and elocution to such purposes as these, is to disgrace the bar, and mismanage to a high degree.

"*Philot.* Must the counsel start at every dark appearance, and the client be dismissed at the first information? that is hard: a cause which has an ill face at first, clears up sometimes in the court, and brightens strangely upon the pleading. This observation prevailed with Sir Matthew Hale to discharge his scruples and practise with more freedom.

"*Philal.* I grant this reverend judge relaxed a little, and gave his conscience more room for the reason you mention. When his business lay at the bar, he made no difficulty to venture through suspicion and dislike: he thought it no fault to bring the matter to an issue, and try the strength of either party. But when he once found it work foul and shrink under the test, he would engage no further, nor ever encourage the keeping on the dispute.

"*Philot.* What then—must a man turn away his clients and baulk his profession?

"*Philal.* It is no part of a lawyer's profession to promote injustice, or help one man to that which belongs to another. The laws are made to secure property, to put an end to contests, and help those to right that suffer wrong. They were never designed to entangle matters, to perpetuate quarrels, to enrich any set of men at the damage of the community. To engage in an ill cause when I am conscious it is so, is, in plain English, to encourage a litigious humour, to countenance a knave; it is to do my best to disseize an honest man of his birthright, and wrest his money or his land from him. If the privilege of practice, if the pretence of taking a fee, will justify us in this liberty, why may not the consideration of money bear us out in other remarkable instances? Why may not we be hired for any other mischief? Why may not a physician take a fee of one man to poison another?"

5. FULLER's estimate of a lawyer's duty will sufficiently appear from the following description of *the Good Advocate*, which I have extracted entire from his Holy State, book iii. chap. 1. "He is one that will not plead that cause wherein his tongue must be confuted by his conscience. It is the praise of the Spanish soldier, that (whilst all other nations are mercenary, and for money will serve on any side) he will never fight against his own king: nor will our advocate against the sovereign truth, plainly appearing to his conscience.

"Maxim 1. *He not only hears but examines his client, and pincheth the cause where he fears it is foundered.* For many clients in telling their case rather plead than relate it, so that the advocate hears not the true state of it, till opened by the adverse party. Surely the lawyer that fills himself with instructions will travel longest in the cause without tiring. Others that are so quick in searching, seldom search to the quick; and those miraculous apprehensions who understand more than all, before the client hath told half, run without their errand, and will return without their answer.

"2. *If the matter be doubtful he will only warrant his own diligence.* Yet some keep an assurance office in their chamber, and will warrant any cause brought unto them, as knowing that if they fail they lose nothing but what long since was lost, their credit.

"3. *He makes not a Trojan siege of a suit, but seeks to bring it to a set battle in a speedy trial.* Yet sometimes suits are continued by their difficulty, the potency and stomach of the parties, without any default in the lawyer. Thus have there depended suits in Gloucestershire, betwixt the heirs of the Lord Berkely and Sir Thos. Talbot Viscount Lisle, ever since the reign of Edward the Fourth, until now lately they were finally compounded.

"4. *He is faithful to that side that first retains him.* Not like Demosthenes, who secretly wrote one oration for Phormio, and another in the same matter for Apolliodorus his adversary.

"5. *In pleading he shoots fairly at the head of the cause, and having fastened, no frowns nor favours shall make him let go his hold.* Not snatching aside here and there to no purpose, speaking little in much, as it was said of Anaximenes, *That he had a flood of words and a drop of reason.* His boldness riseth or falleth as he apprehends the goodness or badness of his cause.

"6. *He joys not to be retained in such a suit, where all the right in question is but a drop blown up with malice to be a bubble.* Wherefore in such trivial matters he persuades his client to sound a retreat, and make a composition.

"7. *When his name is up his industry is not down, thinking to plead not by his study but by his credit.* Commonly physicians like beer are best when they are old, and lawyers like bread when they are young and new. But our advocate grows not lazy; and if a leading case be out of the road of his practice, he will take pains to trace it through his books, and prick the footsteps thereof wheresoever he finds it.

"8. *He is more careful to deserve than greedy to take fees.* He accounts the very pleading of a poor widow's honest cause sufficient fees, as conceiving himself then the King of Heaven's advocate, bound *ex officio* to prosecute it. And although some may say that such a lawyer may even go live in Cornwall, where it is observed that few of that profession hitherto have grown to any livelihood, yet shall he (besides those two felicities of common lawyers, that they seldom die either without heirs or making a will) find God's blessing on his provisions and posterity.

"We will respite him awhile till he comes to be a judge, and then we will give an example of both together."

II.—CASUISTS.

1. THOMAS AQUINAS, in his book entitled *Summa Theologiæ*, 2. 2. quæst. cap. 71, art. 3, to the question, whether it is sinful in an advocate to defend an unjust cause, answers, "It is unlawful to co-operate with any one in doing what is wrong, whether it be by advising, or assisting, or in any manner consenting: for he who counsels and assists in any thing is in a manner the doer of it. And the apostle Paul (Rom. i. 23) says, that they are worthy of death 'not only who commit sin, but who have pleasure in those that do so.' . . . Now the advocate clearly counsels and assists him whose cause he undertakes; and, if he knowingly undertakes an unjust cause, is without doubt guilty of heinous sin, and is bound to make restitution to the party who by his assistance has been unjustly injured. If, however, he should undertake an unjust cause thinking it to be a just one, he has that measure of excuse which ignorance in such case offers. 'Utrum advocatus peccet si injustam causam defendat? . . . Respondeo dicendum, quod illicitum est alicui cooperari ad malum faciendum sive consulendo sive adjuvando, sive qualitercumque consentiendo: quia consilians et coadjuvans quodamodo est faciens; et Apostolus dicit, *Rom.* i. 32, quod digni sunt morte non solum qui faciunt peccatum sed etiam qui consentiunt facientibus. Unde et supra dictum est (quæst. 62, art. 7) quod omnes tales ad restitutionem tenentur. Manifestum est autem quod advocatus auxilium et consilium præstat ei cujus causæ patrocinatur. Unde si scienter injustam causam defendit, absque dubio graviter peccat et ad restitutionem tenetur ejus damni quod contra justitiam per ejus auxilium altera pars incurrit. Si autem ignorantur injustam causam defendit putans esse justam, excusatur secundum modum quo ignorantia excusari potest."

2. Dr. ARNES, in his work *De Conscientiâ*, lib. v. ch. 54, when treating of the duties of advocates, asserts that no advocate ought to undertake or prosecute a cause which he knows to be unjust. "Nullus Advocatus debet suscipere aut defendere causam quam novit esse injustam. Nam, 1. Hoc esset mentiri et contra conscientiam peccare. 2. Hoc esset fraudem facere proximo (contra Levit. xix. 13) et perversitatem exercere in judicio (ibid. v. 15). Hoc esset non tantum communicare peccatis judicis et aliorum inique facientium, sed etiam eisdem occasionem efficacem aut causam præbere. Unde etiam fit quod ars advocatoria (prout hodie a plerisque exercetur) nihil aliud sit quam sophistica perniciosa ex dolis fraudibus technis cavillationibus laqueis captiunculis insidiis tricis ambagibus et circumventionibus conflata."

3. LUDOVICUS MOLENA, in his treatise *De Justitiâ*, tract ii. disp. 81, lays it down that an advocate, when asked to plead for an heir-at-law against devisees, under a will not formally executed, is bound in conscience to ask his client whether he believes it was the intention of the testator that the will should not take effect; and that if he should say it was not, or if from circumstances the advocate be morally convinced that it was not, to decline to advocate the client's claim as being against conscience. "Denique dicendum est advocatos, qui sibi persuaserint eam fuisse legumtalorum mentem (non quidem irritas reddere minus solemnes testatorum ultimas voluntates impedire ve ne ex eis ea naturalis obligatio emanant quæ ex naturâ rei nata est oriri, neque item ex præsumptione falsitatis eas nullas pronunciare jusque concedere hæredibus ab intestato, sed duntaxat non admittere eas tanquam legitimas ad probandum eam fuisse voluntatum testatoris) teneri in conscientiæ foro interrogare clientulos, qui eorum petunt patrocinium ut ipsis tanquam hæredibus in exteriori foro adjudicentur bona defuncti in minus solemni testamento aut codicillo aliis relicta, num sibi persuadeant illam fuisse voluntatem testatoris: quod si annu-

ant, aut ipsimet advocati, illis negantibus, id sibi persuadeant, non posse illis præstare patrocinum utpote ad rem injustam, tenerique illos admonere non posse petere ea bona in foro conscientiæ si semoto omni dubio arbitrentur eam fuisse voluntatem testatoris; et in dubio teneri facere compositionem ut dictum est."

N. B. The sentiments of many other casuists to the same effect will be found collected by Vasquez, in D. Thomæ, col. 595.

III.—MORALISTS.

1. OWEN FELTHAM, in his *Resolves*, cent. ii. ch. 82, thus expresses his opinion: —"Questionless there are of this profession (the law) that are the light and wonder of the age. They have knowledge and integrity; and, by being versed in books and men, in the noble acts of justice and of prudence, they are fitter for judgment and the regiment of the world than any men else that live. And their honesty truly weighed is the gallantest engine that they can use and thrive withal. A faithful advocate can never sit without clients; nor do I believe that man could lose by it in the close that would not take a cause he knew not honest. A goldsmith may gain an estate as well as he that trades in every coarser metal. An advocate is a limb of friendship, and further than the altar he is not bound to go. And it is observed of as famous a lawyer as I think was then in the world, the Roman Cicero, that he was slain by one he had defended when accused for the murder of his father. Certainly he that defends an injury is next to him that commits it. And this is recorded not only as an example of ingratitude, but as a punishment for patronizing an ill cause. In all pleadings, foul language, malice, impertinence, and recriminations are ever to be avoided. The cause, more than the man, is to be convinced. Overpowering oratory is not ever to be practised. Torrents of words do often bear down even trophies of truth, which does so fret and anger the party overborne, that the resort is no more to paper and pleadings, but to powder and steel.

2. GROTIUS, speaking *De Officio Advocati*, says,

"Qui sancta sumis arma civilis togæ
Cui se reorum capita, fortunæ, decus
Intenda credunt, nomini præsta fidem
Juris sacerdos: ipse die causam tibi
Litemque durus arbiter præjudica
Voto clientum jura metiri time,
Nec quod colorem patitur, id justum puta.
Peccet necesse est sæpe, qui nunquam negat."

3. COLERIDGE, by the editor of his *Table Talk*, is made to lay down the limits of the advocate's duty as follows:—"There is undoubtedly a limit to the exertions of an advocate for his clients. He has a right, it is his bounden duty, to do every thing which his client might honestly do, and to do it with all the effect which any exercise of skill, talent, or knowledge of his own, may be able to produce. But the advocate has no right, nor is it his duty, to do that for his client which his client *in foro conscientiæ* has no right to do for himself; as, for a gross example, to put in evidence a forged deed or will, knowing it to be so forged."

4. JONATHAN DYMOND, a late American writer, whose *Essays on the Principles of Morality* have been republished in this country, thus speaks (Essay ii. ch. 5):— "We affirm that a lawyer cannot morally enforce the application of legal rules, without regard to the claims of equity in the particular case. If it has been seen, in the preceding chapters, that morality is paramount to law; if it has been seen that there are many instances in which private persons are morally obliged to forego their legal pretensions; then it is equally clear that a lawyer is obliged to hold morality as paramount to law in his own practice. If one man may not urge an unjust legal pretension, another may not assist him in urging it."

IV.—LAWYERS.

1. CHRISTOPHER ST. GERMAINS, the supposed author of the celebrated work entitled *Doctor and Student*, has given us very clear means of ascertaining his general

opinion on the question of what causes an advocate may rightly undertake, by the solution he gives in that work of several particular questions there proposed and answered. Take, for example, the following dialogue respecting cases in which the advocate may plead the statute of limitations.

"*Student.* Whether may a man with conscience be of counsel with the plaintiff in action at the common law, knowing that the defendant hath sufficient matter in conscience whereby he may be discharged by a *subpœna* in the Chancery, which he cannot plead at the common law, or not?

"*Doctor.* I pray thee put a case thereof in certain, for else the question is very general.

"*Student.* I will put the same case that thou puttest in our first dialogue in Latin, the twelfth chapter, that is to say: If a man bound in an obligation pay the money and taketh no acquittance, so that, by the common law, he shall be compelled to pay the money again, for such consideration as appeareth in the fifteenth chapter of the said dialogue, where it is showed evidently how the law in that case is made, upon a good and reasonable ground, much necessary for all the people, howbeit that a man may sometime, through his own default, take hurt thereby: herein, I pray thee, show me thine opinion.

"*Doctor.* This case seemeth to be like to the case that thou hast next before this, and that he that knoweth the payment to be made doth not as he would be done to, if he gave counsel that an action should be taken to have it paid again.

"*Student.* If he be sworn to give counsel according to the law, as serjeants at the law be, it seemeth he is bound to give counsel according to the law, for else he should not perform his oath.

"*Doctor.* In these words, *according to law*, is understood the law of God and the law of reason; as well as the laws and customs of the realm: for, as thou hast said thyself, in our dialogue in Latin, that the law of God and the law of reason be two special grounds of the laws of England, wherefore (as methinks) he may give no counsel (saving his oath) neither against the law of God nor the law of reason; and certain it is that this article, that is to say, that a man should do as he would be done to, is grounded upon both the said laws. And, first, that it is grounded upon the law of reason, it is evident of itself. And in the sixth chapter of St. Luke it is said, '*Et prout vultis ut faciant vobis homines et vos facitis illis similiter;*' that is to say, that 'All that other men should do to you do you to them,' and so it is grounded upon the law of God. Wherefore if he should give counsel against the defendant, in that case he should do against both the said laws.

"*Student.* If the defendant had no other remedy but the common law, I would agree well it were as thou sayest; but in this case he may have good remedy by a *subpœna:* and this is the way that shall induce him directly to his *subpœna,* that is to say, when it appeareth that the plaintiff shall recover by law.

"*Doctor.* Though the defendant may be discharged by *subpœna,* yet the bringing in of his proofs there will be to the charge of the defendant, and also the proofs may die ere they come in. Also there is a ground in the law of reason, *Quod nihil possimus contra veritatem,* that is, we may do nothing against the truth. And since he knoweth it is truth that the money is paid, he may do nothing against the truth; and if he should be of counsel with the plaintiff, he must suppose and aver that it is the very due debt of the plaintiff, and that the defendant withholdeth it from him unlawfully, which he knoweth himself to be untrue; wherefore he may not with conscience in this case be of counsel with the plaintiff, knowing that the plaintiff is paid already. Wherefore if thou be contented with this answer, I pray thee proceed to some other question.

"*Student.* I will with good will."

2. JOHN COOKE, who was solicitor-general of the Commonwealth at the trial of Charles I., in his *vindication of the professors and profession of the law,* published 1646, thus expresses his own opinion and practice, in which he expresses his belief that many of the great practisers of his day agreed. "The client (he says) I look upon as a sick man, distempered, passionate, wilful, and extremely in love with his own cause whatever it be; and many times the best advice to a resolute client is but as a good lesson set to a lute out of tune—for affections pre-engaged draw away

the judgment. Now the counsellor in the least measure ought not to feed the corrupt and peccant humour; for that is not to act the honest lawyer, but the flattering courtier, who steers his advice by the star of his prince's inclination, as our adversary Satan works upon our fancies, and the wind makes the waters rage. Nor is it enough to tell the client faintly that he doubts his cause but will do the best he can: but to deal freely with him—'Sir, thus I would do if it were my own case; if you will not follow my advice, go to another; you are in a fever, and must not eat and drink after your own appetite.' I assure you there is great difference between one counsellor and another; therefore the precious ought to be distinguished from others. The shepherd and the butcher look upon the sheep with a different eye, the one to do him good, the other to eat him. The client retains two counsel; the one cares not for the cause further than that he may gain by it; however it succeeds, he deserves little in conscience: the other desires his client may have his right, and what is given him freely he accepts contentedly. But to speak truth, many times the clients deserve the blame and not we, for they conceal the worst of their cause, and so for want of a true confession, as the priest says, the absolution is worth nothing; for proof being the chariot which carries the judge to give sentence, how can the counsel tell what the success of a difference will be; which answers a common cavil that lawyers will be of any side, and there is but one side true. The truth is many times in such a deep well, that every lawyer hath not a bucket to draw. Titles of law are very difficult perplexed knotty cases, which will hardly be made plain; the judge hath one ear for the plaintiff, another for the defendant; but the counsel hath both ears for his client, yet so as if he can discover the injustice of his client's cause (and many times light may be seen at a little hole), I am persuaded many of our great practisers will not maintain him in it. For truly to speak well in a bad cause is but to go to hell with a little better grace without repentance: it is but a kind of juggling by an over curious flourish to make a shadow seem a substance. If any of my profession think they may for their fee maintain a side which they think is dishonest........I would fain but ask them some such questions, Whether the least evil may be done to procure the greatest good? And whether every particular calling must not yield to the general of Christianity? And whether a Christian may do anything against the truth, or must do everything for the truth? And whether to be willingly instrumental to condemn the innocent, and to justify the wicked, be not both an abomination to the Lord? And whether he can answer it at the bar of Heaven that many a poor man should be undone and want food and raiment, because he found out some formality of law or defect in the proceedings, yet persuaded in his conscience that the poor man had right to the thing in question. If any man practise upon such principles, I had rather be tongue-tied nor not know how to write my name—rather be the hall sweeper, and should die with more comfort. But enough: I doubt not, but good men will hear reason from their inferiors, now the client must be admonished who will bring himself into a labyrinth do we what we can."

N. B. I quote with diffidence the last named author, as I can neither admire the character in which he appeared on the trial of Charles, nor the mode in which he sustained that character; but on the contrary think them both worthy of the severest condemnation. There is, however, so much sound sense in his remarks that I have given them as I found them.

3. SIR MATTHEW HALE. A question has been raised, as we have seen in the quotation above made from Bishop Collyer, p. 75, as to the principles and practice of this great man when at the bar, in respect to the undertaking of causes. The view of Bishop Collyer will be confirmed by the following extracts from the life of Sir M. Hale, by Bishop Burnet, and from his own contemplations. "If he found the cause doubtful or weak in point of law, he always advised his clients to agree their business; yet afterwards he abated much of the scrupulosity he had about causes that appeared at first view unjust. Upon this occasion there were two causes brought to him, which by the ignorance of the party or their attorney were so ill represented to him that they seemed to be very bad, but he, inquiring more narrowly into them, found they were really very good and just; so after this he slackened much of his

former strictness of refusing to meddle in cases upon the ill circumstances that appeared in them at first.

"In his pleading he abhorred those too common faults of misreciting evidences, quoting precedents or book falsely, or asserting things confidently; by which ignorant juries or weak judges are too often wrought on. He pleaded with the same sincerity that he used in other parts of his life, and used to say 'it was as great a dishonour as a man was capable of that for a little money he was to be hired to say or do otherwise than as he thought.' All this he ascribed to the unmeasurable desire of heaping up wealth, which corrupted the souls of some that seemed otherwise born and made for great things." When we take this coupled with Sir M. Hale's own declaration in his "*Contemplations*," little doubt will remain as to the opinion of this great man. In his "*Great Audit*" we find him giving the following account of his use of the *gift of elocution.*

"1. I have ever used that gift with *humility;* not thereby seeking applause to myself, or owning it; because pride and ostentation in this gift would be secret idolatry to myself, and sacrilege to Thee, robbing Thee of Thy glory, and therefore signally vindicated in the example of Herod. (Acts xii.)

"2. With *truth.* I never used the advantage of my elocution, either to maintain a falsehood or to abuse credulity into a foolish opinion or persuasion.

"3. With *integrity.* I never used the advantage of elocution or rhetoric to deceive people or to cozen them into a thing. My heart always went along with my tongue, and if I used intention of speech upon any occasion, it was upon an intention of conviction in myself of the truth, necessity, usefulness, and fitness of what I was persuaded; if my judgment was doubtful or uncertain, so was my speech. I never used elocution or specious arguments to invite any to that, which in my own judgment I doubted, or doubted whether it were fit or seasonable, all circumstances considered. I never used my elocution to give credit to an ill cause, to justify that which deserved blame, to justify the wicked or to condemn the righteous, to make anything appear more specious or enormous than it deserved. I never thought my profession should either necessitate a man to use his eloquence by extenuations or aggravations to make anything worse or better than it deserves, or could justify a man in it; to prostitute my elocution or rhetoric in such a way, I ever held to be most basely mercenary, and that it was below the worth of a man, much more of a Christian to do so. When the case was good and fully so appeared to me, I thought then was that season that the use of that ability was my duty, and that it was given me for such a time as that, and I spared not the best of my ability in such a season; and indeed elocution or rhetoric is a dead and insipid piece unless it come from and with a heart full of the sense and conviction of what the tongue expresseth, and then, and not till then, elocution hath its life and energy. I esteemed these cases best deserving my elocution, and in these I was warm and earnest: the setting forth of Thy glory; the asserting of Thy truth; the detection and conviction of errors; the clearing of the innocent; the aggravating sins, oppressions, and deceits: and though I was careful that I did not exceed the bounds of truth or of moderation, yet I ever thought that these were the seasons for which that talent was given me, and accordingly I employed it."

4. SIR JOHN DAVIES, in the passage from his preface already quoted, says: "Good lawyers have not with us that liberty which good physicians have; for a good physician may lawfully undertake the cure of a foul and desperate disease, but a good lawyer cannot honestly undertake the defence of a foul and desperate cause. But if he fortune to be engaged in a cause which, seeming honest in the beginning, doth in the proceeding appear to be unjust, he followeth the good counsel of the schoolman (Thos. Aquinas, 2. 2. Quæst. 71, art. 3.): *Advocatus si in principio credidit causam justam esse quæ postea in processe apparet esse injusta, non debet eam prodere, ut scilicet alteram partem juvet revelando causæ suæ secreta; potest tamen et debet, causam deserere, vel eum cujus causam agit inducere ad cedendum, sive ad componendum, sine adversarii damno.*"

5. DOMAT in his *Civil Law*, book ii. tit. 6, s. 2, thus speaks respecting the duties of advocates: "It may be remarked here on all that has been said concerning the duties of advocates, that there are three sorts of causes in which they are employed;

one sort is, of those that are *notoriously unjust;* others are *manifestly just;* and there is a third sort that are *doubtful.*

"As for the causes which are *notoriously unjust,* whether they be contrary to the law of nature, or against the positive law, it is never lawful to defend them, in the same manner as it is never lawful to steal, nor to defend an unjust act. And if the parties themselves cannot carry on these sorts of causes without abandoning the rules of their conscience and committing a most enormous crime which is odious in the eye of man, and still more abominable before God, because they use his authority to make it serve as an instrument of their injustice; the advocates who maintain and defend those causes are so much the more guilty and criminal, in that they make themselves accomplices in the malice of their clients, and prevaricate in the exercise of their function, and in the most essential duty belonging to it, which is that of dissuading their clients from prosecuting causes that are unjust. But those who undertake the defence of such causes against poor and indigent persons make themselves accessories to a crime the enormity of which can hardly be well expressed. The Holy Scripture compares the offering of him who offers to God the goods of the poor as an alms or sacrifice, to the oblation which one would make to a father by sacrificing his son before his eyes (Eccles. xxxiv. 20). By what words therefore could it describe the action of those who present themselves before the tribunal not of the mercy, but of the justice of God; not to offer to him the goods of other people and to divest themselves of them, but to wrest them out of the possession of the right owners, and to appropriate them to themselves; and who have the boldness to invocate the judges to be executors of this injustice?

"As for causes that are *just* and equitable, the only rule is to defend them by no other ways than what are just, without lying and without trick; for if actions that are just of themselves become unjust when they are not performed with the circumstances of justice, according to the saying of the wise man, (Wisd. of Sol. vi. 10,) much more ought the actions of justice itself to be accompanied with truth and with justice; and if all men owe to one another in all their actions truth and godly sincerity, according to the expression of St. Paul, they owe it infinitely more to God himself, and in his tribunal which is the seat of justice. (2 Cor. i. 12.)

"As for causes that are *doubtful,* the chief rule whereby advocates are to govern themselves therein, is not to take those causes for doubtful which may be rendered such by covering injustice with the appearance of justice; but to take sincerely all those for doubtful whose decisions are uncertain, whether it be on account of the circumstances of the facts or by reason of the obscurity of the law, or because of other considerations which makes justice doubtful in such sorts of causes, and advocates ought to determine themselves therein according to their own knowledge and conscience; and they ought neither to engage in them, nor to defend them in any other manner, nor by any other means, than such as are lawful in the defence of causes that are just.

"All these rules of the duties of advocates may be reduced to two maxims: one, never to defend a cause that is so unjust; and the other, not to defend just causes but by the ways of justice and truth; and these two maxims are so essential to the duties of advocates, and so indispensably necessary, that although they seem to be rather maxims of religion, they are, however, in proper terms expressed in the laws of the Code and Digest."

6. CAMUS, a French advocate of considerable eminence, in his little treatise entitled *Etudes nécessaires à l'Exercice de la Profession d'Avocat,* thus speaks of the duty of an advocate:—"Toutes les personnes qui s'addressent à lui sont écoutées indistinctement; mais il ne défend pas les causes de tous sans distinction. Son cabinet est un tribunal prive; il y juge les causes avant de se charger de les défendre. Ce serait faire un usage criminel de ses talens, que de les employer à pallier l'injustice; en manquant à son devoir on s'exposerait à perdre sa réputation."

The same sentiment as is here expressed runs through the several French works collected by M. Dupin in his book entitled Profession d'Avocat.

7. DAVID HOFFMAN, an American advocate and author now living, in a work entitled, *A Course of legal Study addressed to Students and the Profession generally,*

among the rules which he has proposed for the professional deportment of lawyers, has the following:

"X. Should any client be disposed to insist on captious requisitions, or frivolous and vexatious defences, they shall be neither enforced nor countenanced by me. And if still adhered to by him from the hope of pressing the other party into an unjust compromise, or with any other motive, he shall have the option to select other counsel.

"XI. If after duly examining a case, I am persuaded that my client's claim or defence (as the case may be) cannot, or rather ought not, to be sustained, I will promptly advise him to abandon it. To press it farther in such a case, with the hope of gleaning some advantage by an extorted compromise, would be lending myself to a dishonourable use of legal means, in order to gain a *portion* of that, the whole of which I have reason to believe would be denied to him both by law and justice.

"XII. I will never plead the statute of limitation when based on the *mere efflux of time;* for if my client is conscious he owes the debt, and has no other defence than the *legal bar*, he shall never make me a partner in his knavery.

"XIII. I will never plead or otherwise avail myself of the bar of *infancy* against an honest demand. If my client possesses the ability to pay, and has no other legal or moral defence than that it was contracted by him when under the age of twenty-one years, he must seek for other counsel to sustain him in such a defence. And although in this, as well as in that of limitation, the *law* has given the defence, and contemplates in the one case to induce claimants to a timely prosecution of their rights, and in the other designs to protect a class of persons who by rea n of tender age are peculiarly liable to be imposed on, yet in both cases *I shall claim to be sole judge* (the pleas not being compulsory) of the occasions proper for their use.

"XIV. My client's conscience and my own are distinct entities: and though my vocation may sometimes justify my maintaining as facts or principles in doubtful cases, what may be neither one nor the other, I shall ever claim the privilege of solely judging to what extent to go. In *civil* cases, if I am satisfied from the evidence that the *fact* is against my client, he must excuse me if I do not see as he does, and do not press it; and should the *principle* also be wholly at variance with sound law, it would be dishonourable folly in me to endeavour to incorporate it into the jurisprudence of the country, where, if successful, it would be a gangrene that might bring death to my cause of the succeeding day.

"XV. When employed to defend those charged with crimes of the deepest dye, and the evidence against them whether legal or moral be such as to leave no just doubt of their guilt, I shall not hold myself privileged, much less obliged, to use my endeavours to arrest or to impede the course of justice by special resorts to ingenuity—to the artifices of eloquence—to appeals to the morbid and fleeting sympathies of weak juries, or of temporizing courts—to my own personal weight of character—nor finally, to any of the overweening influences I may possess, from popular manners, eminent talents, exalted learning, &c. Persons of atrocious character who have violated the laws of God and man, are entitled to no such special exertions from any member of our pure and honourable profession; and indeed to no intervention beyond securing to them a fair and dispassionate investigation of the *facts* of their cause, and the due application of the law; all that goes beyond this, either in manner or substance, is unprofessional, and proceeds either from a mistaken view of the relation of client and counsel, or from some unworthy and selfish motive, which sets a higher value on professional display and success, than on truth and justice and the substantial interests of the community. Such an inordinate ambition I shall ever regard as a most dangerous perversion of talents, and a shameful abuse of an exalted station. The parricide, the gratuitous murderer, or other perpetrators of like revolting crimes, has surely no such claim on the commanding talents of a profession whose object and pride should be the suppression of all vice by the vindication and enforcement of the laws. Those, therefore, who wrest their proud knowledge from its legitimate purposes, to pollute the streams of justice, and to screen such foul offenders from merited penalties, should be regarded by all (and certainly shall by me) as ministers at a holy altar full of high pretension, and apparent sanctity, but inwardly base, unworthy, and hypocritical; dangerous in the precise ratio of their commanding talents and exalted learning."

8. LORD LANGDALE. It is cheering in these days, in which our judges too often regard with apathy the arts of legal cunning, to hear language such as the following, which I quote from the observations of the present Master of the Rolls, in the case of Hutchinson *v.* Stephens, reported 1 Keen's Reports, 669. "With respect to the task which I may be considered to have imposed upon counsel, I wish to observe that it arises from the confidence which long experience induces me to repose in them, and from a sense which I entertain of the truly honourable and important services which they constantly perform as ministers of justice, acting in aid of the judge before whom they practise. No counsel supposes himself to be the mere advocate or agent of his client, to gain a victory if he can on a particular occasion. The zeal and the arguments of every counsel, knowing what is due to himself and his honourable profession, are qualified not only by considerations affecting the general interests of justice. It is to these considerations that I apply myself; and I am far from thinking that any counsel who attends here will knowingly violate, or silently permit to be violated, any established rule of the court, to promote the purposes of any client, or refuse to afford me the assistance which I ask in these cases."

LEGISLATORS.

I have already, in the Appendix to the Preface, p. 61–62, noted the opinion of legislators as shown in the laws of different states, where the civil law has been adopted. I have also alluded to the only decided case in our own country which I have been able to find bearing upon the subject, from which, if any inference may be drawn it is that the decision of our own law, if called for, would be in conformity with the opinion of the civil law.

[a] *So, he who attempts by the formalities of law, &c.* The limitation here proposed in our dealings with unscrupulous opponents to that perfect openness and candour which in all dealings with honest men ought to characterize our conduct, whether in private or in public, are sanctioned by most writers upon casuistry. *Jeremy Taylor* in his *Ductor Dubitantium,* book iii. chap. 2, rule 5, has the following observations pertinent to this matter: "This (viz. that it is not lawful to tell a lie) is also to be extended to the case of advocates, who in a good cause must not use evil arts. For we must not tell a lie for God, and therefore not for the interest of any moral virtue, nor for the defence of righteousness; for a cavil or an injurious lie is out of the way of justice, and she must not be directly wronged that she may be indirectly righted. In the civil law it is permitted, that to avoid abuses and the injurious craft of the opposite party, the advocate of the right may use all arts that are not lies and falsity. *Nec videtur dolo fecisse qui fraudem excluserit,* says the law (L. Compat. Sect. Titio, ff. de Legat. Secundo). He may be overthrown by art, so he be not by that which is false. *Sic ars deluditur arte.* But in the case which the lawyers out of Baldus put, the question is evident. Agricola borrows of Sempronius five hundred pounds and pays him at the day, but without witness. Sempronius sues him for the money: Agricola owes him none, but cannot prove the payment; but yet may not, when he is particularly interrogated, to save himself from injury deny that he received any. He must confess the truth, though he pay the money again. Covaruvius affirms, that he may in this case lawfully deny that ever he received any; because he is not indebted, he received none that remains in his hand: and to other purposes the judge cannot question him; and if he does, he is unjust, and therefore Agricola is not tied to answer rightly. But this is not well said nor well considered. For the judge being competent may require him to answer; and the intention of the question is not to know whether Agricola had paid the money, yea or no; but whether he borrowed it: for if he did, the judge is afterward to inquire concerning the payment: and as Sempronius was tied to prove that, so is Agricola tied to prove this; and a lie is not to be confuted by a lie, nor the error of Agricola in not taking witnesses or an acquittance to be supplied by a direct denial of a truth. But if Sempronius had lent

Agricola five hundred pounds, whereof he hath received two hundred pounds, if the judge ask whether he owes him that sum which Sempronius demands, he may indefinitely without more punctuality deny the debt, that is of five hundred pounds, saying he owes it not; and if the law be such that the confession of one part entitles him to the whole, he may deny the whole to be due, in case he hath paid a part. But with these two cautions, 1st. That if he be asked concerning a part, he answers to that as justly as he answers to the whole; 2d. That he do not make use of this subterfuge to defraud Sempronius of what is due debt, but only to defend himself from the undue demand. These cautions being observed, he hath liberty so to defend his cause, because, *majori summæ negative prolatæ minorem nec naturaliter nec civiliter inesse*, say the lawyers. A man by denying the whole does not deny part, though he that affirms the whole affirms the part; and therefore his defence is just because it is true. But now if in a just cause the advocate or party may not tell a lie, I conclude that much less may he do it in an unjust cause, and for the defence of wrong. But much less signifies nothing, for it may not all be done in either, and in pure negatives there can be no degrees. But in artifices and crafty intercourses there is some difference. These may be used to defend a just cause that can no other way be defended; but they may not be used to promote an evil cause, because they of themselves, though they be indifferent, yet not serving a good end but an evil, do therefore become evil. And therefore the Greek that denied the *depositum* of his friend, and offered to swear at the altar that he had restored it already, did not preserve his conscience and his oath by desiring his friend to hold the staff in which he had secretly conveyed the money. It is true he delivered it into his hand, desiring that he would hold it until he had sworn; but that artifice was a plain cozenage, and it was prettily discovered, for the injured person, in indignation at the perjury, smote the staff upon the ground and broke it, and espied the money. But that made all right indeed, though against the intention of the perjury. Such like arts as these must not be used to do a mischief; if they do charity and justice, though they have not something to legitimate them, they have very much to excuse them."

APPENDIX TO CHAPTER XIV.

(THE LAWYER OF COUNSEL FOR PRISONERS.)

[1]THE *law of the land obliges not, &c.* By the common law upon an indictment of high treason, petit larceny, or misdemeanour, standing mute was always equivalent to conviction. Upon appeals or indictments for other felonies or for petit-treason, the prisoner who stood mute subjected himself to the terrible sentence of *peine forte et dure* (the nature of which is described by Blackstone vol. iv. p. 326), until by the 12 Geo. III. c. 20, standing mute was in these cases also made equivalent to a conviction. The questionable mercy of the present day towards criminals has effected the change noticed in the text, and now by the 7 and 8 Geo. IV. c. 28, s. 2, it is enacted, "That if any person being arraigned upon or charged with any indictment or information for treason, felony, piracy, or misdemeanour, shall stand mute of malice, or will not answer directly to the indictment or information, in every such case it shall be lawful for the court, if it shall so think fit, to order the proper officer to enter a plea of 'not guilty,' on behalf of such persons; and the plea so entered shall have the same force and effect as if such person had actually pleaded the same."

[2]*Now when the prisoner declares to his counsel, &c.* The question here mooted is surrounded with great difficulty, and I do not feel sure that the conclusion at which I have arrived is the correct one. I have been mainly induced to adopt it by the consideration that the general voice of mankind permits a person who has offended against the laws of his country to conceal such offence, except in instances when doing so could entail injury upon others.

[3]*Did the law imperatively &c.* This is the conclusion of most of the casuists and divines.

Thomas Aquinas, 2a. 2æ. quæst. lxix. lays it down, "that a criminal is bound to answer truly to what the judge may ask lawfully, but is not bound further to criminate himself."

DR. AMES, in his treatise *de Conscientiâ*, lib. v. c. 54, s. 45, is of the same mind. "Q. Quid juris sit de reo vel accusato? R. Si reus legitimè interrogatur, tenetur suum crimen fateri. Ratio 1. Quia neque negare potest veritatem notam, sine mendacio; neque tacere, respondendi officium detrectare, quando interrogatur a superiore qui jus habet interrogandi, sine inobedientiæ peccato. 2. Quia crimen divinâ providentiâ manifestatum (prout debet manifestari ut reus de illo legitimè et juridice interrogetur) vel mendacio vel artificio abscondere est aliquo modo contra gloriam Dei. (John vii. 19.) 3. Quia publicum illud bonum quod a judice in interrogatione legitimâ debet spectari non debet a reo impediri. 4. Quia reus denegando crimen legitimè objectum, indirectè et per consequentiam, dicit eum qui objectat per calumniam esse mentitum cum gravi injuriâ ipsius."

So also REVITUS in his *Prælection* in the twentieth chapter of Exod. ver. 14. "Reus tenetur judice ordine juris interrogante. 1. Dare gloriam Deo, et veritatem aperire, quamvis sciat se ex eâ confessione damnandum fore. 2. Non se debet per calumniam defendere etiam si innocens sit, sed licitis uti mediis."

JEREMY TAYLOR, in his *Ductor Dubitantium*, book iii. c. 2. rule v. discussing the rule which he there lays down, viz. "That it is not lawful for a guilty person to defend himself by calumny or a lie from the penalty of the law, though it be the sentence of death," after contending that it may be sometimes allowable to tell a lie for the purpose of preserving another from imminent danger, proceeds: "But then from these premises the truth in the instance of the rule is established; for it is not lawful for a guilty prisoner to say 'not guilty,' when he is justly interrogated. *Christianum non mentiri, etiamsi moriatur ex tormentis*, said Clemens Alexandrinus: A Christian will not lie, though to escape death with torments: for the law says, 'Thou shalt not kill,' and the law says, 'Thou shalt not lie;' but the law itself does sometimes kill, but the law does never lie. For although it be said that no man is bound to accuse himself, and indeed the laws of man do not tie him to do it; yet this hinders not the conclusion in this case; for in the present case the man is accused already, and he is not called to be his own accuser, but to confess the fact, if he be justly accused by the law. For why does the judge ask, but to be answered truly? For there being three ways in law of proceeding to definitive sentence, 1, The notoriety of the fact; 2, the conviction of witnesses; and 3, the confession of the party; in the destitution of the first, to prevent the trouble of the second, the law interrogates concerning the third: and it is as in the case of Joshua and Achan, 'My son, give glory unto the Lord, and confess thy fault.' It is true it is a favourable case; and when a man's life is at stake, he hath brought himself into an evil necessity; but there is no excusing of a false denial, but it is certainly criminal, and nothing can excuse it, unless the law should give leave to such persons to say what they would, which cannot be supposed in any good government: for then trials of criminal causes between the judge and the thief would be like a match at fencing; and it is infinitely confuted by those laws which use to examine by scourgings or torture: which, whether it be lawful or unlawful, I do not here determine; but I affirm it to be a great testimony that laws do not love to be played withal, and when they ask soberly, intend to be answered truly.

On the other hand, Puffendorf, *On the Law of Nations*, book 4, ch. i. s. 20, 21, having stated it to be a question of difficulty, *Whether a criminal or an offender arraigned on any account may deny the fact with which he is charged, or endeavour to elude the accusation by feigned arguments, and yet not incur the guilt of lying*, sets out the arguments used on both sides, and embraces the opinion that he may, and consequently that the advocate may aid him in such defences.

BISHOP HALL, also, in his *Resolutions and Decisions of divers Practical Cases of Conscience*, after noting the differences of the casuists upon the subject, contends that "It is lawful for the prisoner, though convicted in his conscience of the fact, yet to plead *not guilty* to the indictment at the bar: for as much as he doth therein, according to the sense both of the judge and jury, only hide and keep back that truth, the finding out and eviction whereof lies upon their further search and proof; so as he doth in pleading *not guilty* in effect as good as say, Whatever I find in myself, I have no reason to confess my guiltiness. I stand upon my lawful defence, and cast myself upon my just trial, yielding myself only so far guilty as your evidence and proofs can make me: let justice pass upon me; I have no reason to draw on my own condemnation. The plea thus construed is lawful and just, wherein not the shuffling equivocation of the offender, but the upright verdict of a legal jury, must carry the cause: to which purpose, that which sounds as a denial in the accused, is nothing else but a professed referring himself to a judicial trial of that fact; which he is not bound to confess.

" But when the hand of God hath once found out the man in his sin, and he finds himself legally convinced of his crime, it greatly behoves him (as Joshua charged Achan after the lot had discovered his sin) to give glory to God in a free and full confession of his wretchedness, and to be more open and ingenuous in his acknowledgement than he was close and reserved in his plea;.wherein as he shall discharge his conscience to that great and holy God whom he hath offended, so he shall thus tender some kind of poor satisfaction to that society of men whom he hath scandalized by his crime. In which regard I cannot but marvel at the strange determination of learned *Axpelaceta*, the oracle of confessaries, who teaches that the prisoner, who being rightly interrogated by the judges, stood stiffly in denial of the fact, and is upon his condemnation carried to his execution, is not bound at his death to confess the crime to the world, if he have before secretly whispered it in the ear of his ghostly father, and by him received absolution: a sentence that allows the smothering of truths, and the strangling of just satisfaction to those who are concerned as parties in the offence, and lastly, highly injurious to public justice, whose righteous sentence is by this means left questionable and obnoxious to unjust censure. How much more requisite were it that a public confession should in this case save the labour of a private, whereby certainly the soul of the offender would be more sensibly unloaded, justice better vindicated, more glory would accrue to God, and to men more satisfaction.

" But however it be lawful for the accused to stand upon these points of legality in the proceeding against him; yet, for my own part, should I be so far given over as to have my hand in blood, and thereupon be arraigned at the bar of public justice, I should out of just remorse be the first man that should rise up against myself and (which in other men's cases were utterly unlawful) be my own accuser, witness, and judge: and this disposition I should rather commend in those whose conscience hath inwardly convicted them for heinously criminous, that since they had not the grace to resist so flagitious a wickedness, yet they may endeavour to expiate it before men by an ingenuous confession, as before God with a deep and serious repentance."

APPENDIX TO CHAPTER XVI.

(THE LAWYER DRAWING DEEDS.)

[1] SECONDLY, *he wills that, &c.* The following just observations on the prevailing form of settlements are from a note in Hayes, *On Conveyancing*, 3 edit. p. 371:—" The policy of such settlements is extremely questionable: it is difficult to refer them in the absence of the motives already indicated (the desire to support hereditary rank or to found a family) to any rational principle. The present possessor has the absolute dominion; his character is known, his right unquestionable. He is asked to reduce himself to a mere tenant for life in favour of an unborn son, of whose character nothing can be predicated, and who, if he can be said to have any right, cannot possibly have a preferable right. At no very distant period the absolute dominion must be confided to somebody, and why should confidence be reposed in an unborn child rather than in the living parent? Such a settlement has no tendency to protect or benefit the father whose advantage and comfort ought first to be consulted. It does not shield him from the consequences of his own imprudence. On the contrary, if his expenditure should in any instance exceed his income, he, as a mere tenant for life, is in danger of being obliged to borrow upon annuity, a process which, once begun, proceeds generally, and indeed, almost

necessarily, to the complete exhaustion of his life income. But it may be urged, that the settlement preserves the inheritance for the son, or his committee or creditors. The son may be an idiot or a spendthrift. He may be tempted to raise money by *post obit*, to levy a fine, and by that means acquire a bare fee in his father's lifetime. If to these not improbable results we add all the family feuds generated between the tenant for life and remainder-man, in regard to the enjoyment and management by the former of that estate which was once his own, particularly with reference to the cutting of timber, the disadvantages of thus fettering the dominion will appear greatly to preponderate. At best, such a settlement is a speculation; at worst, it is the occasion of distress, profligacy, and domestic discord, ending not unfrequently, as the Chancery Reports bear witness, in obstinate litigation ruinous alike to the peace and to the property of the family. Sometimes the father effects an arrangement with the eldest son on his coming of age; the son stipulating for an immediate provision in the shape of an annuity, the father for a gross sum to satisfy his creditors, or to portion his younger children, and for a resettlement of the estate. This arrangement, perhaps, is brought about by means, or imposes terms which, in the eye of equity, render it a fraud upon the son; and here we have another source of litigation. If, however, a strict settlement is deemed expedient, the objections here urged may be in some degree obviated by reserving to the settler a power of appointing to any of the sons or issue male of the marriage for any estate or interest, and he should also be invested with ample powers and discretion in regard to leasing, as well for husbandry as for mining purposes, and in regard to timber, buildings, alterations," &c.

[2] *He commends the maxim, &c.* Previous to the interference of our courts of equity in the matter, the whole law relating to husband and wife was controlled by the maxim, "That a husband and wife are one person." It is not easy to trace in the Reports, the rise of that branch of equity which gives to a woman rights in property separate from her husband. So late as the year 1710, (Harvey *v.* Harvey, 1 P. W. 125), the *power* of courts of equity to decree such rights seems to have been questioned. The *policy* of their doing so may still be doubted.

APPENDIX TO CHAPTER XIX.

(THE LAWYER AN ARBITRATOR.)

[1] REJOICES *when to terminate differences, &c.* The policy of referring disputes to arbitration has been questioned on the ground that arbitrations so often end in protracted litigation. The experience of those societies, whose members are in the habit of settling their differences by arbitration, shows that this consequence is incident rather to the frame of the submission, and the mode of proceeding under it, and more than all, to the interference of lawyers imbued with technical habits of thought, than to the nature of arbitrations generally. In the Society of Friends, all differences among the members of which are terminated by arbitration, we do not hear that such consequences ensue, but the contrary.

[2] *The arbitrator may decide wholly according to equity, &c.* It has been attempted, at different times, to make it imperative upon arbitrators, acting under the control of our courts of law and equity, to decide according to the strict rules of law and technical equity, and to restrain them from deciding according to conscience. These attempts have fortunately failed, and the law would now seem to be as stated by Lord Eldon in Younge *v.* Walter, 9 *Vesey*, 365. "If there is a question of law, and the parties choose to refer that to the decision of an arbitrator, instead of the court, why may not he take all moral considerations into his judgment? If they refer to a person to decide all matters in difference, according to law, and he *means to decide according to law*, and mistakes, the court will set that right. But if a distinct question of law and nothing else is referred, and the parties choose to say they will not take the decision of the court, but will take whatever an arbitrator shall say is the law between them, why may they not so agree?"—See *Watson on Arbitrations*, p. 228.

APPENDIX TO CHAPTER XXV.

(THE LAWYER'S REGARD FOR PROFESSIONAL RULES.)

[1] HENCE *in those rules, &c.* The manner in which professional rules may clash with conscience and good feeling is often illustrated in the matter of *retainers*. Some instances of this are given by a writer in the *Law Magazine*, vol. iv. p. 417, in an article on Retainers. "It is well known (says the writer) to every practitioner, that the papers in a cause are frequently laid before some barrister in its earliest stage; that he even recommends the bringing or defending of the action in the first instance; that he draws all the pleadings of one party, and advises on the evidence; in short, that he brings the case down to the point of hearing or trial, and is, in some degree, answerable for its success or failure. Yet after all this, unless the form of an express retainer has been gone through, some sharp practitioner may, at any moment before the brief for trial or argument is actually delivered, thrust into his hand a retainer for the adverse party. Now what a situation is this for a man who has any feeling or conscience? for we plead guilty to the credulity of supposing that such a monster may exist as a lawyer with a conscience. To be compelled to maintain that all that he has done and advised is wrong; to unravel the web that he has himself spun, or else be wanting in duty to his newly acquired client; to be a deserter to the enemy's camp, and treacherously to discover the weak points of his *quondam* friends: or to be conscious of possessing such a secret, and doubtful whether he ought to avail himself of the knowledge or not; in short, to be driven to the alternative of sacrificing the interests either of his new client or of his old one. Is it right, we ask, to place any man in such a dilemma? Nor let it be thought that the case is imaginary; we have ourselves known instances of its actual occurrence. A person, deservedly eminent at the Chancery bar, had recommended a suit, advised upon the answer, and drawn exceptions which stood for argument, but he had not been formally retained for the plaintiff. The attorney, for the defendant, in the mean time, offered him a retainer to argue against his own exceptions. which he thought himself bound, however of course reluctant, to accept. Another learned gentleman, celebrated for his practice in bankruptcy, had resisted, no doubt, with his accustomed zeal and ability, the claim of a creditor upon a bankrupt estate, in behalf of which he had frequently appeared, on other occasions, also as the advocate. Well, he succeeded after several meetings before the commissioners in procuring the rejection of the disputed claim; whereupon the creditor petitioned, and lo! who should appear in support of the petition, labouring with equal zeal and ability to establish that the proof ought to have been received, but the same learned gentleman who had so successfully advocated its rejection. To be sure he had not been *retained* upon the *petition*, and was, therefore, *compelled* to accept the retainer of the creditor, which arrived before the brief of the assignees. Are these instances enough? If not, we can multiply them *ad nauseam*."

APPENDIX TO CHAPTER XXVII.

(THE LAWYER IN VACATION.)

[1] FOR *strive as he may, &c.* This sentiment is put into the mouth of Coleridge, by the editor of his *Table Talk*, vol. ii. p. 7. He is made to say, "I think that, upon the whole, the advocate is placed in a position unfavourable to his moral being and indeed to his intellect also in its higher powers. Therefore, I would recommend an advocate to devote a part of his leisure time to some study of the metaphysics of the mind, or metaphysics of theology: something, I mean, which shall call forth all his powers, and centre his wishes in the investigation of truth alone, without reference to a side to be supported. No studies give such a power of distinguishing as metaphysical, and in their natural and unperverted tendency they are ennobling and exalting. Some such studies are wanted to counteract the operation of legal

studies and practice, which sharpen indeed, but, like a grinding stone, narrow whilst they sharpen."

APPENDIX TO CHAPTER XXXIV.

(THE LAWYER'S CONSIDERATION CONCERNING ECCLESIASTICAL AFFAIRS.)

WHAT *he shall think in respect of the outward form, &c.* I have here intended to allude to the three principal forms of opinion upon the subject of the visible church which now divide Christians.

I. The *first* is that of the Roman Catholics, thus expressed at length by Domat in his *Civil Law*, tom. ii. book 1, text x. "There is this in common to the clergy and to the laity in every Catholic country, that they compose all of them together two different bodies, of which every one is a member; the body spiritual of the church, and the body politic of the state: for all the laymen of a state are, as well as the clergy, members of the church; and all the clergy, as well as the laity, are members of the body politic, and subjects of the prince. But there is this difference between these two bodies, that the spiritual body which is made up of the clergy and laity in a kingdom, makes a part of the body of the universal church which reaches to the whole universe, and which being only one, comprehends all the catholics of all countries, whether clergymen or laymen: whereas the politic body of a state has its limits within its own territories, under the government of its prince, and independent of all others in matters temporal: so that the clergy and laity who are under the government of one prince, are members of no other body politic: but all the clergymen and laymen of all the kingdoms and churches are united and linked together as to spirituals in such a manner as that they compose all of them together only one church, the unity of which consists in this, that all the nations have been called to one and the same faith, to one and the same law of one only God in one only religion, which he has established and taught unto men by his only Son, which is preached in all places, and is perpetuated throughout all ages by the bare mission of his apostles and their successors, under one sole head of the said church, successor of St. Peter, upon whom Jesus Christ hath founded it, and which he has always governed and will govern to after ages, by the channel of the said mission, which nothing can ever interrupt, and to which nothing strange or foreign can be united."

II. *The second* is that held by some early divines of the Church of England, and latterly put forward by the writers in the *Tracts for the Times.* That I have not misstated the views of these writers, the following quotations from their Works will show:—"The doctrine (of apostolical succession) in dispute is this: that Christ founded a visible church as an ordinance for ever, and endowed it once for all with spiritual privileges, and set his apostles over it, as the first in a line of ministers and rulers like themselves, except in their miraculous gifts, and to be continued from them by successive ordination; in consequence, that to adhere to this church thus distinguished, is among the ordinary duties of a Christian, and is the means of his appropriating the gospel blessings with an evidence of his doing so not attainable elsewhere."—*Tracts for the Times*, vol. iii. no. 74.

"Herein is the difference between the ministry of such persons as have received this commission from the bishop, and of those who have not received it: that to the former, Christ has promised that his presence shall remain, 'Lo, I am with you always, even to the end of the world:' and that when they minister the word and sacraments (which are the keys of the kingdom of Heaven), what they do upon earth in His name, according to His will, shall be ratified and made good in Heaven. 'Whatsoever thou shalt bind on earth shall be bound in Heaven; and whatsoever thou shalt loose on earth shall be loosed in Heaven.' But to those *who have not received this commission*, our Lord has given no such promise. A person not commissioned from the bishop may use the words of baptism, and sprinkle or bathe with the water *on earth*, but there is no promise from Christ that such a man shall admit souls to the kingdom of Heaven. A person not commissioned may break bread and pour out wine, and pretend to give the Lord's supper, but it can afford no comfort to any to receive it at his hands, because there is no warrant from Christ to lead communicants to suppose that while he does so here *on earth*, they will be partakers in the Saviour's heavenly body and blood. And as for the person himself who takes upon himself without warrant to minister in holy things, he is all the while treading in the footsteps of Korah, Dathan, and Abiram, whose awful punishment you read of in the book of Numbers. (Compare Numbers xvi. with Jude ii.)"—*Tracts for the Times*, vol. i. no. 35, and afterwards in the same Tract.

"Remember, then, that whether your pastors be rich or poor, honoured or despised by the world, it is only the having received this commission that makes us 'bold in our God to speak unto you the gospel of God' (1 Thess. ii. 2): and it is only this that can give you any security that the ministration of the word and sacraments shall be effectual to the saving of your souls. Learn, then, to cherish the blessing which God has vouchsafed to you, in having given you pastors who have received this commission. *The dissenting teachers have it not.* They lay no claim to regular succession from the apostles: and though the Roman Catholic clergy have indeed been ordained by the hands of bishops, they are mere intruders in this country, have no right to come here, and besides, have so corrupted the truth of God's word, that they are not to be listened to for a moment."—*Tracts for the Times*, vol. i. no. 35.

In the 33rd of the *Plain Sermons by Contributors to the Tracts for the Times*, headed *The Apostolic Church*, and upon the text, "And they continued steadfastly in the apostles' doctrine and fellowship, and in breaking of bread and prayers. And fear came upon every soul;" we find this passage, to the same effect as the one last quoted: "And as we have by God's blessing the apostles' doctrine, so also the apostles' fellowship. Our bishops derive all their spiritual authority by succession from the apostles downwards, we, the inferior clergy, all ours from the bishops. If this be denied us, we are nothing better than usurpers, self-appointed ministers, useful, perhaps, for the peace and order of society, but spiritually powerless."

"Surely there is a close analogy between the state of the Jews after the captivity and our own; and if so, a close understanding and acknowledgment of it will tend to teach us our own place, and suggest to us our prospects.

"It is scarcely necessary to notice the general correspondence between the fortunes of the two churches. Both Jews and Christians 'left their first love,' mixed with the world, were brought under the power of their enemies, went into captivity, and at length, through God's mercy, were brought back again from Babylon. Ezra and Nehemiah are the forerunners of our Hookers and Lauds, Sanballat and Gesham of the disturbers of our Israel. Samaria has set up its rival temple among us." —*Tracts for the Times*, vol. i. no. 31.

III. *The third* view above stated is that which satisfied the comprehensive mind of Bacon, as is seen in the quotation made in the text: and (whatever may be urged to the contrary) is that embraced by Hooker, who in the *forms* of ecclesiastical governments could see nothing that was not *positive*, and consequently liable to change. This is the drift of the whole of the third book of his *Ecclesiastical Polity*, in which he defends Episcopacy from the attacks of the Presbyterians of those days, who asserted "That in Scripture there must be of necessity contained a form of church polity, the laws whereof may in no wise be altered," and that Presbyterianism was that form. In that book, alluding to the conviction in his own mind that Episcopacy was the form of church government (as he elsewhere in the same book expresses himself) "which best agreeth with the srcred Scriptures," he says: "If we did seek to maintain that which most advantageth our own cause, the very best way for us, and the strongest against them, were to hold even as they do, that in Scripture there must needs be found some particular form of church polity which God hath instituted, and which for that very cause belongeth to all churches, all times. But with any such partial eye to respect ourselves, and by cunning to make those things seem the truest which are the fittest to serve our purpose, is a thing which we neither like nor mean to follow. Wherefore that which we take to be generally true concerning the mutability of laws, the same we have plainly delivered, as being persuaded of nothing more than we are of this, that whether it be in matter of speculation or of practice, no untruth can possibly avail the patron and defender long, and that things most truly are likewise most behovefully spoken." Book iii. c. x. s. 8.

[2] *Nor that some forms, &c.* This sentiment is thus expressed by Hooker, *Eccles. Pol.* book iii. ch. xi. 14. "In which respect (viz. that much which the Scripture hath taught concerning church polity may become unrequisite, sometime because we need not use it, sometime also because we cannot) for mine own part, although I see that certain reformed churches, the Scottish especially, and French, have not that which best agreeth with the sacred Scripture, I mean the government that is by bishops, inasmuch as both those churches are fallen under a different kind of regiment; which to remedy it is for the one altogether too late, and too soon for the other during their present affliction and trouble; this their defect and imperfection I had rather lament in such case than exagitate, considering that men oftentimes without any fault of their own may be driven to want that kind of polity or regiment which is best, and to content themselves with that which either the irremediable error of former times, or the necessity of the present, hath cast upon them."

APPENDIX TO CHAPTER XXXV.

(THE LAWYER UPON SUNDAYS.)

[1] THAT *he may early upon the Saturday, &c.* This suggestion is taken from Sir Matthew Hale. In his advice to his children he says, "I would not have you meddle with any recreations, pastimes, or ordinary work of your calling, from Saturday night at eight of the clock till Monday morning. For though I am not apt to think that Saturday night is part of the Christian Sabbath, yet it is fit then to prepare the heart for it."

APPENDIX TO CHAPTER XXXVI.

(THE LAWYER BECOME JUDGE.)

[1] THE *lawyer whose probity, &c.* Having before (p. 76-77) given Fuller's beautiful description of the *Good Advocate,* I here give his description, equally beautiful, of the *Good Judge.*

"The Good Advocate, whom I have formerly described, is since, by his prince's favour and his own deserts, advanced to be a Judge: which his place he freely obtained with Sir Augustine Nicholls, whom King James used to call *the Judge that would give no money.* Otherwise they that buy justice by wholesale, to make themselves savers must sell it by retail.

"Maxim 1. *He is patient and attentive in hearing the pleadings on both sides, and hearkens to the witnesses though tedious.* He may give a waking testimony who hath but a dreaming utterance; and many country people must be impertinent, before they can be pertinent, and cannot give evidence about a hen, but first they must begin with it in the egg. All which our judge is contented to hearken to.

"2 *He meets not a testimony half-way, but stays till it come at him.* He that proceeds on half evidence, will not do quarter justice. Our Judge will not go till he is led. If any shall browbeat a pregnant witness, or purpose to make his proof miscarry, he checketh them and helps the witness that labours in his delivery. On the other side he nips those lawyers, who under pretence of kindness to lend a witness some words, give him new matter, yea, clean contrary to what he intended.

"*Having heard with patience, he gives sentence with uprightness.* For when he put on his robes he put off his relations to any; and like Melchisedec, becomes without pedigree. His private affections are swallowed up in the common cause, as rivers lose their names in the ocean. He therefore allows no noted favourites, which cannot but cause multiplication of fees, and suspicion of by-ways.

"4. *He silences that lawyer who seeks to set the neck of a bad cause once broken with a definite sentence;* and causeth that contentious suits be spued out as the surfeits of courts.

"5. *He so hates bribes, that he is jealous to receive any kindness above the ordinary proportion of friendship;* lest like the sermons of wandering preachers they should end in begging. And surely integrity is the proper portion of a judge. Men have a touchstone whereby to try gold, but gold is the touchstone whereby to try men. It was a shrewd gird which Catulus gave the Roman judges for acquitting Clodius, a great malefactor, when he met them going home well attended with officers: '*You do well* (quoth he) *to be well guarded for your safety, lest the money be taken away from you, you took for bribes.*' Our judge also detesteth the trick of mendicant friars, who will touch no money themselves, but have a boy with a bag to receive it for them.

"6. *When he sits upon life in judgment, he remembereth mercy.* Then (they say) a butcher may not be of the jury, much less let him be the judge. Oh let him take heed how he strikes that hath a dead hand. It was the charge Queen Mary gave to Judge Morgan, Chief Justice of the Common Pleas, that notwithstanding the old error among judges did not admit any witness to speak, or any other matter to be heard in favour of the adversary, her Majesty being party; yet her Highness' pleasure was that whatsoever could be brought in the favour of the subject should be admitted and heard.

"7. *If the cause be difficult, his diligence is the greater to sift it out.* For though there be mention (Psalm xxxvii. 6) of righteousness as clear as the noonday, yet God forbid that that innocency which is no clearer than twilight should be condemned. And seeing one's oath commands another's life, he searcheth whether malice did not command that oath: yet when all is done, the judge may be deceived by false evidence. But blame not the hand of the dial if it points at a false hour, when the fault is in the wheels of the clock which direct it and are out of frame.

"8. *The sentence of condemnation he pronounceth with all gravity.* It is best when steeped in the judge's tears. He avoideth all jesting on men in misery: easily may he put them out of countenance whom he hath power to put out of life.

"9. *Such as are unworthy of life, and yet unfitted to die, he provides shall be instructed.* By God's mercy and good teaching, the reprieve of their bodies may get the pardon of their souls, and one day's longer life for them here may procure a blessed eternity for them hereafter, as may appear by this memorable example. It happened about the year 1556, in the town of Weipenstein, in Germany, that a Jew, for theft he had committed, was in this cruel manner to be executed: he was hanged by the feet, with his head downwards, betwixt two dogs, which constantly snatched and bit at him. The strangeness of the torment moved Jacobus Andreas (a grave, moderate, and learned divine as any in that age) to go to behold it. Coming thither, he found the poor wretch, as he hung, repeating verses out of the Hebrew Psalms, wherein he called to God for mercy. Andreas hereupon took occasion to counsel him to trust in Jesus Christ, the true Saviour of mankind. The Jew, embracing the Christian faith, requested but this one thing, that he might be taken down and be baptized, though presently after he were hanged again (but by the neck, as Christian malefactors suffered), which was accordingly granted him.

"10. *He is exact to do justice in civil suits betwixt sovereign and subject.* This will most ingratiate him with his prince at last. Kings neither are, can, nor should be lawyers themselves, by reason of higher state employments; but herein they see with the eyes of their judges, and at last will break those false spectacles which (in point of law) shall be found to have deceived them.

"11. *He counts the rules of state and the laws of the realm mutually support each other.* Those who made the laws to be not only desperate, but even opposite terms to maxims of government, were true friends neither to laws nor government. Indeed, *salus reipublicæ* is *charta maxima:* extremity makes the next best remedy: yet though hot waters be good to one in a swoon, they will burn his heart out who drinks them constantly when in health. Extraordinary courses are not ordinarily to be used when not enforced by absolute necessity.

"And thus we leave our good judge to receive a just reward of his integrity from the Judge or judges at the great assize of the world."

The following are noted by Sir Matthew Hale as "*things necessary to be continually had in remembrance*," written when he was a judge.

"1. That, in the administration of justice, I am entrusted for God, the king, and country; and, therefore,

"2. That it be done (1) uprightly; (2) deliberately; (3) resolutely.

"3. That I rest not upon my own understanding and strength, but implore and rest upon the direction and strength of God.

"4. That, in the execution of justice, I carefully lay aside my own passions, and not give way to them however provoked.

"5. That I be wholly intent upon the business I am about, remitting all other cares and thoughts as unseasonable and interruptions.

"6. That I suffer not myself to be prepossessed with any judgment at all, till the whole business and both parties be heard.

"7. That I never engage myself in the beginning of any cause, but reserve myself unprejudiced till the whole be heard.

"8. That in business capital, though my nature prompt me to pity, yet to consider there is also a pity due to the country.

"9. That I be not too rigid in matters purely conscientious, where all the harm is diversity of judgment.

"10. That I be not biassed with compassion to the poor, or favour to the rich, in point of justice.

"11. That popular or court applause or distaste have no influence in any thing I do in point of distribution of justice.

"12. Not to be solicitous what men will say or think, so long as I keep myself exactly according to the rule of justice.

"13 If in criminals it be a measuring cast, to incline to mercy and acquittal.

"14. In criminals that consist merely in words, where no more harm ensues, moderation is no injustice.

"15. In criminals of blood, if the fact be evident, severity is justice.

"16. To abhor all private solicitations, of what kind soever, and by whomsoever, in matters depending.

"17. To charge my servants (1) not to interpose in any matter whatsoever; (2) not to take more than their known fees; (3) not to give any undue precedence to causes; (4) not to recommend counsel.

"18. To be short and sparing at meals, that I may be fitter for business."

[2] *Unless plainly obliged, &c.* Lord Kenyon, in the cause of Webb *v.* Russel, 3 Term Rep. p. 403, concludes his judgment with these words:—"It seems to me, with all the inclination which we have to support the action (and we have hitherto delayed giving judgment in the hopes of being able to find some ground on which the plaintiff's demand might be sustained) that it cannot be supported. The defence which is made is of a most unrighteous and unconscientious nature, but, unfortunately for the plaintiff, the mode which she has taken to enforce her demand cannot be supported."

APPENDIX TO CHAPTER XXXVII.

(THE LAWYER'S DEATH.)

[1] IT *was a bright evening, &c.* I cannot better conclude this little volume than by the following beautiful extract from Bishop Burnet's *History of his own Times*, written June 1708, when he thought himself near his end. "I will conclude this whole address to posterity with that which is the most important of all things, and which alone will carry every thing else along with it; which is to recommend in the most solemn and serious manner the study and practice of religion to all sorts of men, as that which is *the light of the world and the salt of the earth.* Nothing does so open our faculties, and compose and direct the whole man, as an inward sense of God, of his authority over us, of the laws he has set us, of his eye ever upon us, of his hearing our prayers, assisting our endeavours, watching over our

concerns, and of his being to judge and to reward or punish us in another state according to what we do in this. Nothing will give a man such a detestation of sin, and such a sense of the goodness of God, and of our obligations to holiness, as a right understanding and a firm belief of the Christian religion; nothing can give a man so calm a peace within, and such a firm security against all fears and dangers without, as the belief of a kind and wise providence, and of a future state. An integrity of heart gives a man a courage and a confidence that cannot be shaken. A man is sure that, by living according to the rules of religion, he becomes the wisest, the best, and happiest creature that he is capable of being. Honest industry, the employing of his time well, and a constant sobriety, and undefiled purity and chastity, with a quiet serenity, are the best preservers of life and health: so that take a man as a single individual, religion is his guard, his perfection, his beauty, and his glory. This will make him the *light of the world*, shining brightly, and enlightening many around him.

"Then take a man as a piece of mankind, as a citizen of the world or of any particular state. Religion is indeed then the *salt of the earth;* for it makes every man to be to all the rest of the world whatsoever any one can with reason wish or desire him to be. He is true, just, honest, and faithful in the whole commerce of life, doing to all others that which he would have all others do to him. He is a lover of mankind and of his country. He may and ought to love some more than others; but he has an extent of love to all, of pity and compassion not only to the poorest but to the worst; for the worse any are they are the more to be pitied. He has a complacency and delight in all that are truly though but defectively good, and a respect and veneration for all that are eminently so. He mourns for the sins and rejoices in the virtues of all that are round about him: in every relation of life religion makes him answer all his obligations. It will make princes just and good, faithful to their promises, and lovers of their people. It will inspire subjects with respect, submission, obedience, and zeal for their princes. It will sanctify wedlock to be a state of Christian friendship and mutual assistance. It will give parents the truest love to their children with a proper care of their education. It will commend the returns of gratitude and obedience from children. It will teach masters to be gentle and careful of their servants, and servants to be faithful, zealous, and diligent in their master's concerns. It will make friends tender and true to one another: it will make them generous, faithful, and disinterested. It will make them live in their neighbourhood, as members of one common body, promoting first a general good of the whole, and then the good of every particular as far as a man's sphere can go. It will make judges and magistrates just and patient, hating covetousness and maintaining peace and order without respect of persons. It will make people live in so inoffensive a manner that it will be easy to maintain justice whilst men are not disposed to give disturbance to those about them. This will make bishops and pastors faithful to their trust, tender to their people and watchful over them; and it will beget in the people an esteem for their persons and their functions. Thus religion, if truly received and sincerely adhered to, would prove the greatest of all blessings to a nation. But by religion I understand somewhat more than the receiving some doctrines, though ever so true, or the professing them and engaging to support them not without zeal and eagerness. What signify the best doctrines if men do not live suitable to them; if they have not a due influence upon their thoughts, their principles, and their lives? Men of bad lives with sound opinions are self-condemned, and lie under a highly aggravated guilt; nor will the heat of party arising out of interest, and managed with fury and violence, compensate for the ill lives of such false pretenders to zeal, while they are a disgrace to that which they profess and seem so hot for. By religion I do not mean an outward compliance with forms and customs; in going to church, to prayers, to sermons, and to sacraments with an external show of devotion, or which is more, with some inward forced good thoughts, in which many may satisfy themselves, while this has no visible effect on their lives, nor any inward force to subdue and rectify their appetites, passions, and secret designs. These customary performances, how good and useful soever when well understood and rightly directed, are of little value when men rest on them, and think that because they do them they have therefore acquitted themselves of their dnty, though they continue still proud, covetous, deceitful, full of envy and malice. Even secret prayer, the most effectual of all other means, is designed for a higher end, which is to possess our minds with such a constant and present state of divine truths as may make these live in us and govern us; and may draw down such assistances as may exalt and sanctify our natures.

"So that by religion I mean such a sense of divine truth as enters into a man and becomes a spring of a new nature within him; reforming his thoughts and designs, purifying his heart and sanctifying him, and governing his whole deportment, his words as well as his actions; convincing him that it is not enough not to be scandalously vicious, or to be innocent in his conversation, but that he must be entirely, uniformly, and constantly pure and virtuous; animating him with a zeal to be still better and better, more eminently good and exemplary; using prayer and all outward devotions, as solemn acts testifying what he is inwardly and at heart, and as methods instituted by God, to be still advancing in the use of them further and further into a more refined and spiritual sense of divine matters. This is true religion which is the perfection of human nature, and the joy and delight of every one that feels it active and strong within him. It is true this is not arrived at all at once; and it will have an unhappy allay hanging long even about a good man; but as those ill mixtures are the perpetual grief of his soul, so it is his chief care to watch over and to mortify them; he will be in a continual progress, still gaining ground upon himself, and as he attains to a good degree of purity, he will find a noble flame of life and joy growing upon him. Of this I write with the more concern and emotion, because I have felt this the true and indeed the only joy which runs through a man's heart and life; it is that which has been for many years my greatest support. I rejoice daily in it; I feel from it the earnest of that supreme joy which I pant and long for; I am sure there is nothing else can afford any true or complete happiness. I have, considering my sphere, seen a great deal of all that is most shining and tempting in this world; the pleasures of sense I did soon nauseate; intrigues of state and the conduct of affairs have something in them that is more specious: and I was for some years deeply immersed in these, but still with hopes of reforming the world, and of making mankind wiser and better. But I have found *That which is crooked cannot be made straight.* I acquainted myself with knowledge and learning, and that in a great variety and with more compass than depth; but though *wisdom excelleth folly as much as light does darkness*, yet as it is a *sore travail*, so it is so very defective that what is *wanting* to complete it *cannot be numbered.* I have seen *that two were better than one*, and that a *threefold cord is not easily loosed;* and have therefore cultivated friendship with much zeal and a disinterested tenderness; but I have found this was also vanity and vexation of spirit, though it be of the best and noblest sort. So that upon long and great experience I could enlarge on the preacher's text, *Vanity of vanities and all is vanity;* but I must also conclude with him, *Fear God and keep his commandments, for this is the All of man*, the whole both of his duty and of his happiness. I do therefore end all in the words of David, of the truth of which upon great experience and a long observation I am so fully assured, that I leave them as my last words to posterity. '*Come, ye children, hearken unto me; I will teach you the fear of the Lord; what man is he that desireth life and liveth many days, that he may see good: Keep thy tongue from evil and thy lips that they speak no guile; depart from evil and do good; seek peace and pursue it. The eyes of the Lord are upon the righteous, and his ears are open to their cry, but the face of the Lord is against them that do evil, to cut off the remembrance of them from the earth. The righteous cry and the Lord heareth and delivereth them out of all their troubles. The Lord is nigh unto them that are of a broken heart, and saveth such as be of a contrite spirit.*"

THE END.

Chapter VII

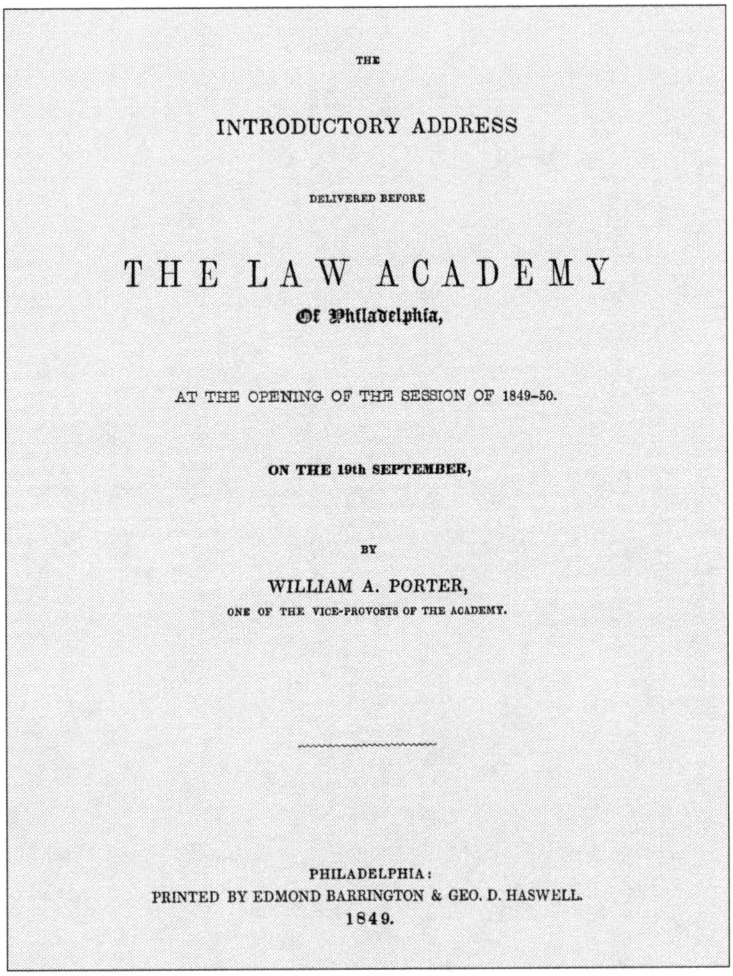

THE

INTRODUCTORY ADDRESS

DELIVERED BEFORE

THE LAW ACADEMY

Of Philadelphia,

AT THE OPENING OF THE SESSION OF 1849–50.

ON THE 19th SEPTEMBER,

BY

WILLIAM A. PORTER,

ONE OF THE VICE-PROVOSTS OF THE ACADEMY.

PHILADELPHIA:
PRINTED BY EDMOND BARRINGTON & GEO. D. HASWELL.
1849.

Porter, William A. *The Introductory Address Delivered Before The Law Academy of Philadelphia, at the Opening of the Session of 1849-50.* Philadelphia: Printed by Edmund Barrington & Geo. D. Haswell, 1849.

PHILADA., OCT. 1, 1849.

GENTLEMEN:

In placing at your disposal a copy of the Address delivered before the Academy, I am not without apprehension that you will find it, on closer inspection, entirely unworthy of the terms in which you have been pleased to speak of it.

Very truly yours,

WM. A. PORTER.

MESSRS. TRIMNEL,
FISH, and
HARDING, } *Committee.*

GENTLEMEN OF THE LAW ACADEMY :—

IT is reasonable that we should feel some attachment to our profession. An object of anxiety and toil, if it possess any merit, easily engages the affections. The commonest rewards of success are fitted to stimulate the growth of such a sentiment. Professional labour, rightly pursued, supplies the wants of many, enlarges the usefulness of others, and promotes the happiness of all. In his books, the professional man finds friends who do not repel him with coldness, do not betray his confidence, do not weary of importunity; who cheer him in his labors, who instruct him in his duty, and strew about him the treasures of knowledge with liberal hand. His clients necessarily supply him with a variety and accuracy of information pertaining to their respective pursuits, which another will find it impracticable to obtain; and thus provide the means of illustration for public argument, and of instruction for those to whom nature has made him the chief dispenser of knowledge. To his opponents, he stands indebted for that quickness of apprehension and promptness of action which constitute his chief efficiency, and not less, for their readiness to bear testimony to whatever is elevated in purpose, or brilliant in achievement.

But the reasonableness of the sentiment must

depend on the dignity of its object. I propose, on this occasion, to consider some of the views popularly entertained of the profession of the law, and to exhibit, incidentally, some portion of its title to public confidence. My aim is practical. I know nothing better fitted to chill the ardor of a generous mind, first entering on the practice of the profession, than a suspicion that, in order to achieve entire success, something may be required, which a sound reason, or a pure morality, must disapprove. My aim is still more practical. Success itself is dependent, to a large extent, on an elevated estimate of the profession. Preparation for practice, labor in conducting it, and patience in discomfiture, are large draughts on human nature. That they can be met under a consciousness, that when the highest result shall be attained, it must necessarily fall below that of other pursuits, cannot be reasonably expected.

I will suppose a man of sound understanding, desirous to acquire information on the subject which has been proposed. I will suppose him elevated above the superstition which would cause learning to be feared, and the prejudice which would cause it to be despised. I will suppose him competent to appreciate the difference in value between intellectual and purely physical labor. I will suppose him to have informed himself, how long our present system of law has prevailed, without material change, except to expand itself to the increasing wants of civilization, and the progress of kindred sciences.

If such a man were to require a lawyer to declare to him the objects which the law professes to accomplish, he would probably be told: It secures you in the possession of your house; it enables you to hold the acquisitions of your industry; it prevents your neighbour, not only from seizing your property, but from using his own in such a manner as to injure yours; it assists you to buy, to sell, and to get gain, by providing that the smallest appreciable fraud shall, under all circumstances, infect with fatal taint, whatever it may touch; if, in the transaction of your affairs, you employ a clerk or an agent, it binds him to the utmost use of his skill and integrity; if any one fraudulently misrepresent the character of a purchaser it places the former in the position of the latter; if any one injure your business by misrepresentation, or character, by the imputation of crime, it furnishes the only means of redress and prevention. — He would, probably, go further, and declare, that it affords a remedy, for every injury that may be inflicted; that not a duty in domestic life, whether necessary for existence, as maintenance, or fitted to embellish, as intellectual culture, but receives its care; that no human condition exists too exalted for its power, or too degraded for its protection; that it alike binds down the king and the commonwealth, and protects the meanest of its own assailants from punishment, except by its own hands; that, in innumerable instances, it consummates over the victims of vice and disease, those stupendous plans to which the hand of charity finds itself unequal; that it adapts its especial solicitude to the protection of the persons and property of those, who by age, natural incapacity, or the want of other protection, present the strongest claim on its care; that, when accident or negligence has rendered it necessary, it directs the transmission of property after the death of the possessor, oftentimes, with a more exact propriety than he would have displayed. A bolder tone might be employed :—The speaker might challenge his interrogator to mention a settled law of nature which the municipal law contravenes; a social duty which it does not aim to enforce; a wrong to society, down to gaming, borrowing money to game, or intemperance, which it does not aim to repress. If he doubted, let him attempt enforcing the performance of a contract which has the violation of a moral duty for its support. The challenge might be extended to the production of a principle, binding to the utterance of truth, nay, forbidding the suppression of truth, which it does not practically adopt. If he doubted, let his ship be insured, and an important fact suppressed, or his horse sold, and a false warranty given, and he would be in the highroad to discovery. In fine, an offer might be reiterated, in the spirit of that memorable eulogy, which has never been found overwrought,—a good lawyer can show to be law what any other man can prove to be right.

We can anticipate the rejoinder. If it embodied the popular idea, it would probably be conveyed thus: "Your profession has failed to accomplish its proper object. Judges and lawyers, yielding to the natural tendency of intellectual pursuits to subtlety, have been carried into unnecessary refinement. The result is, that justice is sacrificed to form, and to the policy of sustaining pre-established rules."

Before discussing the question thus presented, the truth of the following propositions must be assumed: 1. The profession is necessary. So long as the law is the only barrier against force, it will be necessary that a class of men should be exclusively devoted to the study of its principles. This is as much required as the division of labour in any department of science or art—as much, as that one set of artizans should be employed in making the hull, a second the engine, and a third the rigging, and not the same set in constructing an entire steamship. 2. It is the interest of those chiefly instrumental in perpetuating the profession of the law to perfect it. To debase it, is to destroy it. The point of its highest elevation, is that at which it yields the largest reward of honor and emolument. Conduct on the part of its practitioners, fitted to depress it below this point, pre-supposes a spirit of self-sacrifice, to which natural diffidence, or some other cause, has heretofore prevented them from making claim. In other words, to suppose a body of men, whose highest profit it is to elevate their occupation, capable of degrading it, when it is conceded they have the ability to perceive their true interest, is contrary to our experience of human nature. 3. So extensive a science as the law, and the mode of its reduction to practice, cannot be accurately estimated in a moment. A criticism on the most inconsiderable work of art would possess little value in the eyes of men of taste, if the author were candid enough to avow that he had examined it but infrequently, at short intervals, and at a great distance from the object. The testimony of the humblest artisan, who had left upon it the evidence of his labour, would, to a discriminating mind, carry superior force. 4. That which is difficult of comprehension, should not be branded as subtle and useless. Many of our most familiar ideas are those which, in their acquisition, caused most perplexity and confusion. It would be easy, by going back but a short distance, to refer, in illustration, to many a well-remembered mathematical problem,—but I have no right to excite such unpleasant emotions. The recollections of that, and the results of more general experience, should render men cautious in condemning that which they have failed to possess, the inclination or opportunity of thoroughly understanding.

It is necessary to ascertain the scope of the view which I have supposed to be expressed. I do not understand it a ground of objection, that the truth and utility of legal principles are not, in every instance, obvious even to a clear mind. That would embrace a wide circle, both of the principles of science, and the works of art,—the productions of reason and imagination. It would blot out a large part of metaphysical philosophy. It would pass censure on most of the liberal arts. It would lose us the best passages in poetry.—I do not even understand it objected, that many of the legal rules, pursued and insisted on, are purely arbitrary in their character, and commended over others, by no sound reason, except, in some instances, a supposition, perhaps a mistaken one, of their convenience,—such as the distinct forms of action required for slightly different injuries. These are quite as reasonable as the rules which regulate the quantity of verse, or the number of acts in a play. A volume before me, shall suggest illustrations of what is meant. Suit is instituted for a sum of money due more than six years; the defendant admits he contracted the debt; does not allege its payment; has the means to pay it; but the law does not compel him. In filing the copy of a promissory note, an unimportant word is omitted; the supposed copy is held a nullity; judgment cannot be rendered for the plaintiff; a less meritorious creditor steps in, and the former loses the debt. An action is brought for the amount of a tradesman's bill; the plaintiff's receipt in full is offered in evidence; he knows the instrument to be genuine; his name has been written but seldom; no mode of proving it exists, and the law assists him to recover money which has once been paid. The deposition of a witness now dead is offered in evidence; no doubt exists as to the truth or pertinency of the statement; but it appears that the oath was not administered, until after a portion of the testimony had been committed to writing; the deposition is excluded, and no other proof of the fact can be obtained. Counsel are satisfied that a witness has testified falsely; on the subject matter of the suit, he commits no blunder; ask him a question collateral to that, and he falls into wilful error; offer to prove the falsity of his last answer, and thence to infer that of his entire testimony, and you are overruled; the witness is believed, and the cause is lost. You have bought a house, and obtained possession; an erasure is detected in a material part of the deed, of which no note was made before execution; the instrument, without other proof, passes for nothing. Suit arises in relation to the performance of an article of agreement; an offer is made to show that, when the paper was signed, a verbal agreement on a particular point was entered into by the parties; the court say, we do not find it in the instrument; and the wrong once more triumphs. To go further, would be to cite a volume of reports. Do you call this the administration of justice? Is this what you mean by enforcing the principles of morality? Is this all your profession has been able to do, after some centuries of effort, to provide for the honest settlement of human controversy?

Let us not be precipitate. A competent Judge, before pronouncing a decision, would desire to "hear from the other side." A bill of merchandize is bought and paid for; after the death of the parties acquainted with the transaction, suit for the price is brought against the buyer's executors; the receipt, if taken, has been mislayed; what injustice in allowing the seller a long term of years for the assertion of his claim, or what reason in granting him more than the lifetime of every party then living, in which to make it? In filing a copy of a promissory note, what justice, what advantage to my credit, or what encouragement to general accuracy, to allow a plaintiff to write *one month*, for *one year*, or *one thousand,* for *one hundred,* dollars? What security to my property, if the man who desired to effect it by my signature, were relieved, in any instance, from the necessity of proving it? What advantage in clothing a Justice of the Peace with power to determine in what part of a deposition a witness shall testify under oath, and in what without it? If the answer to a collateral question might be contradicted by other testimony, how stop short of determining the affairs of a neighbourhood, in the same cause, and without the knowledge of those most affected by it; or how probable that a just opinion would be formed by the jury of the facts they were called to try? If a party were permitted to sustain his cause by an instrument in which an erasure appeared, what safety to any one in executing a written paper? If a written agreement deliberately entered into shall not control the subject, what utility in committing it to writing, or what refuge from the ignorance, caprice, or dishonesty of casual bystanders?

The principle is obvious. If I submit to the law, and assume my proportion of the burden of maintaining it, in consideration of its protection, so long as I perform the stipulation on my part, I have a right to its absolute protection,—how much soever others may suffer from ignorance or disregard of the forms which are essential to my safety. And the principle is equally sound in reason and morals. If I enter into the simplest contract with any one, he is bound, without regard to the convenience of others, to protect me from the injury which would result from his failure of performance.

16

But, are not the objections which presume unnecessary strictness of form, generally overstated, in point of fact? Take, for example, the most abused of all subjects in this respect, Special Pleading. What are its leading rules? That the plea contain pertinent matter; that an immaterial point be not denied; that it be free from duplicity of idea and phraseology; that when time, place, quality, quantity, and value are introduced, they should be specified with convenient certainty; that it should not contain one statement repugnant to another; that unnecessary averments should be avoided, &c. If we leave out the idea of ornament, what are these but tolerable guides for writing English? Could an essay in the Spectator, have been written in disregard of them?—Nor ought the idea of ornament to be allowed too much dominion. However the speeches of Burke, or the sermons of Robert Hall, might lead us to regard it as necessary, Butler and Edwards, not to mention our most distinguished legal writers, have shown it by no means essential, even to agreeable writing.

Take the subject of Evidence, in which fraud must be allowed most practicable, and the inducement to prevent it strongest. Is there unnecessary rigor here? That a witness shall state fact and not inference; that he shall state that only which is relevant to the issue; that he shall speak from his own knowledge, and not from the knowledge of others; that he shall not be so interrogated as to indicate the desired answer; that the best evidence which appears to exist shall be first offered, and no other, until the production of the former shall be proved impossible; that the burden of proof shall rest on the party who makes the allegation; the superiority of written over oral testimony; the value set on the admissions of a party, and their exclusion, when procured by the presentation of wrong motives; the judicial notice taken, without the necessity of proof, of that wide range of facts, in which the danger of fraud is small; the various modifications of the principle, that a man's own act or declaration shall not be received in evidence in his own favour; what are these, and other rules of evidence, but dictates of the soundest common sense? Let it first be shown, that an honest man shall not suffer by their relaxation, before it be concluded, that science has been pushed too far in their construction.

If we consider the distinctions drawn between the law and the fact, and the distribution of powers made between the court and jury, we shall discover as little for the disapprobation of reason. Strong advocates of a change of the present system have usually been found (and perhaps will continue to be) among counsel for plaintiffs, when verdicts have gone for defendants, and contrariwise. That the action of the jury is too frequently the result of ignorance or caprice must be conceded; but the system comes to us commended by too high an antiquity, constitutes too vital a part of Anglo-Saxon liberty, and possesses too many advantages, to admit the possibility of essential change. Its chief excellence is easily discernible,—it presents no mark for popular violence. Judges may shield themselves behind the doings of their predecessors, but a permanent body for the determination of facts, would poorly withstand the discontent which it would provoke. The instant of the rendition of a verdict is that of the dispersion of the tribunal,—never again to be convoked. Twelve separate riots, in as many different portions of the county, would afford ample time to the most cautious and deliberate Sheriff for contriving a mode of prevention.

It is time that we consider the conduct of the cause in court,—which will bring up for examination questions of a different character. By what rules shall the advocate regulate his conduct? Do your professional ethics approve such principles as the following: "that an advocate, by the sacred duty which he owes his client, knows, in the discharge of that office, but one person in the world: that client, and none other. To save that client by all expedient means,—to protect that client at all hazards and costs to all others, and among others to himself,—is the highest and most unquestioned of his duties; and he must not regard the alarm—the suffering—the torment—the destruction, which he may bring upon any other."* Are these the approved maxims of your craft? When such a course may benefit the client, shall he not spare a witness who has no reply to his attack? Shall he not know his professional brother, who has a reputation to preserve? Has the opposite party no rights to be regarded? Is no respect due to the court,—no fairness to the jury,—

* Lord Brougham's Speech in the Queen's case.

nothing to his own personal character,—nothing to his profession,—nothing to public virtue? Such doctrines, it may well be supposed, would require more than the authority of a great name to secure their adoption. A common result to the cause, the advocate and the profession would expose, if not their fallacy, at least their impracticability. It is a more just sentiment, that he who possesses power of any kind, holds it as a trustee for others,—and the office of the advocate furnishes no exception to the rule.

A question of some interest presents itself at this point. Can a lawyer, in every case, act honestly and conscientiously? Must not one side be right and the other wrong, and are not the chances abundantly in favour of his knowing when he is in the wrong? The late Judge Hopkinson, in the place I now occupy, more than twenty years ago, presented an answer to this question. The conclusion at which he arrived may be reached by a somewhat different process. The nature of the cases litigated in courts of justice is not generally apprehended. I do not speak of those instances, in which time for the payment of money is desired by a defendant, where judgment is taken by default, and the legal proceedings are matter of form; nor of those which result from inexperience or error,—commonly atoned for in so ample a manner, as to prevent their recurrence with the same practitioner. I refer to cases usually tried in court,—in the vast majority of which the soundest understanding might be challenged to pronounce a judgment satisfactory even to itself. To illustrate this by practical examples, would be to cite an entire trial-list. To those familiar with the proceedings of courts, the remark will commend itself. With all the evidence before him, it is sufficiently hard for any man—as those who have served as jurymen could attest—to ascertain the truth. How shall he, when he cannot, by any art, know more than that which bears on one side?—When the advocate comes to the trial of the cause, what is he to do? To state his client's position with clearness; to marshal the facts which support it, in the most effective order; to elicit the truth from an opposing witness, or to disconcert an unfair one; to ascertain the relative weight of conflicting statements; to present the proper inferences from the entire testimony; and to apply to the solution of the facts, the established principles of law. Were that not a most fastidious morality which should proscribe such an employment?

Is this a sketch from real life, or the product of imagination? Do you tell us, that such ideas find any realization in the actual practice of the profession? Are the duties which the position of an advocate imposes ever thus discharged, or the rights which it confers ever thus exercised? What is this but a stale reflection on human nature? What duties are ever perfectly discharged, or rights properly exercised? Are not all our tastes and appetites abused? Is not every privilege, personal, social, and political, at one time or other, abused? Is not every faculty, physical, moral, and intellectual, with which nature has endowed us, at one time or other, misemployed? In the case of the lawyer, observe how vastly superior to that of most others is his opportunity to do wrong,—yet how many breaches of faith are heard of? Observe, also, how generally his worst errors are on the side of duty. What is personal friendship, or political connection, or the social position of a witness, when he shows himself prejudiced or unwilling? Doubtless, disaster is thus frequently brought on the cause; but what other principal has reason to complain of his agent doing too much?

The ground on which an opposite view of the legal character rests is unsolid. The true question is, whether an eminently successful lawyer may be a purely just man? If this be established, I am not aware that what any other man may choose to do, and in order to relieve himself lay to the charge of his profession, would affect the logical accuracy of the statement. Is it so, or is it not? Where shall we look for the proof of it? Unhappily, gentlemen, the seal of death hath, within a few days, been set to a fact, which, more than all the power of words, attests the truth of the proposition. I do not desire to trench on the prerogative of his contemporaries, nor to anticipate the voice of the religious teacher, but it would be unseemly, at such a time, on such a subject, and in the midst of many who enjoyed his friendship and instruction, to omit to declare how large a debt the profession of the law owes to CHAUNCEY and his associates, for the character for integrity with which they impressed it. He assisted to bind together the ideas "lawyer" and "honest man," in a union which, we may hope, shall long remain unbroken. His life while it convinced the understanding, like the result of the clearest problem, did more than that,—it shot the truth into the heart both of lawyer and layman, that the highest professional elevation, so far from requiring the sacrifice of moral principle, may repose on it with additional dignity. He did more; he practically showed, that the same man may discharge the severest professional duties with the most scrupulous exactness, and at the same time do much in diffusing about him the charities of life, in consoling misfortune, alleviating distress, and reducing the sum of human misery. To secure so large a business,—to attract the merchant, the shipper, the owner of real estate, the mechanic, the day-labourer, the trustee and the executor, and to convince them by experience that they could obtain no more valuable services elsewhere, required distinguished ability; natural evenness of temper and cordiality of manner, were useful in facilitating business intercourse; but what proportion would remain of that vast structure which he has reared for our contemplation, if we were obliged to make deductions for infidelity to engagements, inconstancy in friendship, or the general absence of virtue? I indulge in no unnecessary encomium; I merely adduce a witness. The fame of Chauncey is safe where it now rests: in the results of his active benevolence, in the principles he assisted to establish, in the memory of the friends whom he counselled, in the hands of those numerous students of the law, who received from him their first instruction in the science, and have since attained important positions in society.

The youthful artist will seldom study without profit the great picture which his life presents.*

I return to the general subject; and proceed to consider the decision of the cause by the Court. By what process shall the law of the case be settled? Shall it be decided in conformity to a principle established in some preceding action, and because the principle has been so established? Is this not to perpetuate error? Why not pursue the course adopted in all other inquiries after truth, and allow the Judge to decide the cause on those grounds which commend themselves to his own mind? Why lay his own reason at the feet of another? What were moral, political, or any other science, if its investigations were controlled, to any extent, by such a rule? The answer is obvious. The law experiences no terror so great as that of her own minister. The great effort has been to bind him down by bonds from which he could not escape. This appears to be right, if he be unjust, for then he might upturn the system by destroying public confidence in it; and more so, if just, for then he should not be required to bear so great a burden, as would be otherwise imposed on him; and not much less so,

* When the present address was prepared, it seemed probable that some public occasion would be taken to commemorate the virtues of the deceased. This has since been done in a sermon delivered by the Rev. Dr. Boardman of the Presbyterian Church, which, I am informed, is in the course of publication. I am conferring an obligation on the professional reader, while I indulge a feeling of private friendship, by pointing his attention to that discourse, as among the highest efforts which the pulpit has made to elevate the character of the bar.

if it were possible for him to be neither, for the consequences of caprice would be scarcely less fatal than those of wrong intention. This explains and smoothes down what philosophy might otherwise stumble at; namely, that courts are frequently found conceding the unreasonableness and even absurdity of a principle, and yet determining an important controversy by re-affirming it. It is better for society, where no moral wrong is done, thus to preserve, as far as possible, the dominion of the law over the Judge, unbroken, than to relieve cases of individual hardship, however acute. If we reflect that contracts have been formed, rights acquired, and responsibilities incurred, on the faith of the past decision, we shall perceive more clearly the correctness of the course.

A subject of louder complaint has been found in the reversal of adjudged cases. Mr. Greenleaf's labors have shown that the profession has less to complain of on this score than it supposes. Conceding the number larger, how does the science of the law compare, in this respect, with other sciences, which depend either on moral or demonstrative reasoning? What would the reputation of a medical adviser be worth, who should treat disease on the principles recognized thirty years since? Who quotes in political economy at this day the writers of the last, or the beginning of the present century? In what school of morals would the doctrines of Paley, once so undisputed in their sway, be taught without qualification? In intellectual philosophy, which bounds the law on another side, and is so interwoven with it as to render the line of boundary indistinct, the main business of each writer seems to have been, to write down whatever his immediate predecessor had advanced. Why grieve over an incident of all learning? Why make it cause of complaint, that a bench educated in a different manner from their predecessors, should not always be able to coincide in the reasoning of the latter, or that they should not themselves always entertain the same views on a subject, on which, it may be, time and experience are diffusing a valuable light?

There are immediate inducements to the study of the law which I ought not to conclude without presenting.

A common obstacle to the prosecution of intellectual pursuits is their remote bearing on the practical affairs of life. I do not advert to its effect on the general diffusion of knowledge, but on the mind of the student himself. The question is constantly recurring,—what good? Who the better of all this? How, when, where, and to what, apply this knowledge? In the study of the law, these inquiries have no place. Every principle which the student is required to comprehend has sprung from a case which has actually occurred, and which has been contested and decided. That it has occurred is sufficient reason that it may occur again. When the case does arise, it effects not an abstract question, about which men may differ in opinion, whether or not it possess any practical value, but palpable and absolute interests, which all men acknowledge,—personal security, property, and reputation. In the acquisition of such principles, time and labor are not misspent.

The tendency of our professional pursuits to invigorate the mind is on all sides confessed. It is difficult to conceive of an educated person, without ability to furnish a plausible answer to an argument susceptible of answer, if the time and circumstances are committed to his own choice. To state at a moment's warning and with self-possession nice distinctions, on which large amounts of property depend,—to present objections which shall bear the scrutiny of a court, and a year afterwards, of an appellate tribunal, and to state all the objections,—to answer ingenious argument in a fiftieth of the time which it has taken to construct it and to answer it correctly, demand a training which it may be safely affirmed, no other profession is capable of imparting. Its effects have been witnessed in other professions, which legal talent has gone to adorn. The splendor it has diffused in deliberative assemblies has commanded general admiration. How inferior that toil which, while it brings the largest immediate fruits, imparts no necessary increase of power and no capacity for higher effort!

The study of the law opens to the student a vast expanse of literature, almost untraversed by others. Some degree of proficiency in intellectual philosophy is justly considered a part of a finished education. We are conducted to the investigation of moral and theological sciences, by the imperative personal claims which they have upon us. The excellence of our legal literature is known only to the student of law. Any well-read lawyer might confidently challenge the production, from any other department of literature, of performances which should excel in all the qualities of a vigorous, perspicuous, and elegant expression of thought, those which the records of our judicial proceedings contain. Why should not the man perform it well who writes or speaks to be read through all time and wherever law shall be administered; to furnish the guide for important contracts; to defy elaborate critical review before his own eyes, and before a court, whose right it is to differ from him; to lay the foundation of future decision; to illumine the page of philosophic disquisition? What would the scholar have? Would he have forcible argument? There are all the labours of English and American judges. Would he have profound learning and subtlety? There are Coke and Eldon. The highest accomplishments, decorating the extreme of professional skill? There are Eskine and Romilly. Clear, polished, and attractive exposition? There are Blackstone and Kent.—The chief glory of a country is its literature. The highest intellectual attainment is made in the pursuits of literature. The most effective and permanent power is the power of the pen. Where are now the contemporaries of Coke, who assisted to bring that great intellect to its perfection? Yet doth his genius blaze, through the gloom of centuries, with undiminished lustre.—

28

The highest boast of the law is its literature. Let us study it, gentlemen. It is a large repository of human wisdom. It is a profound commentary on human nature. It is a true history of human progress. To ourselves it opens the only road to usefulness; to our clients it gives the only assurance of safety; to our profession it supplies the only hope of elevation.

Chapter VIII

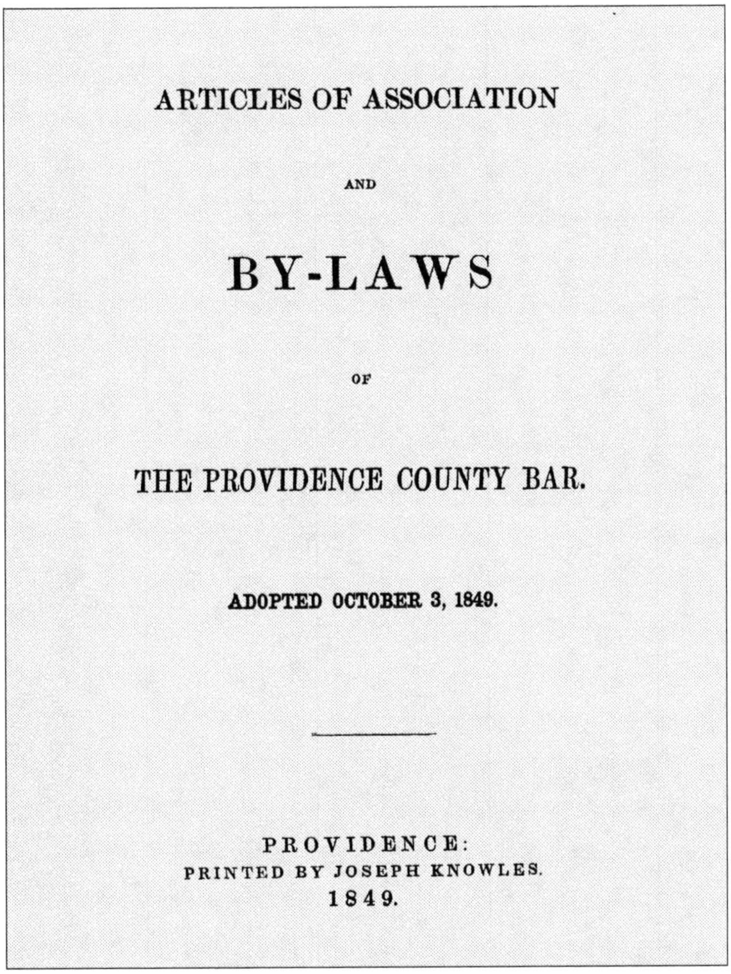

ARTICLES OF ASSOCIATION

AND

BY-LAWS

OF

THE PROVIDENCE COUNTY BAR.

ADOPTED OCTOBER 3, 1849.

PROVIDENCE:
PRINTED BY JOSEPH KNOWLES.
1849.

[Providence County Bar]. *Articles of Association and By-Laws of the Providence County Bar. Adopted October 3, 1849*. Providence: Joseph Knowles, 1849.

ARTICLES OF ASSOCIATION.

I. AN annual meeting of the Association shall be holden on the first day of every December Term of the Court of Common Pleas in and for the County of Providence, and special meetings may be holden at any time on the written request of five members, addressed to the Secretary. Seven members shall constitute a quorum for any business other than the suspension, alteration, abolition or enactment of a By-Law, or the censuring or expelling of a member; for either of which purposes the presence of at least fifteen members shall be required.

II. At the annual meeting, or in case of a vacancy, at any special meeting, officers shall be elected to hold their offices for one year, or until others are elected, as follows:—a President, who shall preside at all meetings at which he shall be present; a Secretary, whose duty it shall be to keep a record of the proceedings of the Association, to give notice of meetings, regular and special, and to receive and record the names of persons who may from time to time become students in the offices of members of the Association; an Examining Committee of three mem-

4

bers, who shall examine all applicants for admission to the Bar, and report upon their proficiency in legal studies; and a Standing Committee of three (the senior member of which shall, in the absence of the President, preside at the meetings and discharge his functions) whose duty it shall be to receive and investigate all complaints against members for violations of the By-Laws, and if they so elect, bring such complaints to the notice of the Association for its action.

III. Any member of the Bar of this State may become a member of this Association, on application to the Secretary, purchasing of him a copy of the By-Laws, and subscribing these articles, by subscribing which he shall be deemed to have assumed the obligation following, to wit:—*The undersigned, members of the Providence County Bar Association, hereby severally express their approbation of the By-Laws thereof, and agree to conform to them in their practice.*

BY-LAWS.

1. Every member shall be notified of a meeting, and so far as may be, of the business to be transacted, either by personal notice from the Secretary, or by printed or written notice left at his place of business or his residence, or forwarded by mail, at least twenty-four hours previous to the hour appointed.

2. Every member who shall receive into his office any person as a student of Law, shall within thirty days after so receiving him give notice in writing to the Secretary of the Association of the fact, stating the name and prior residence of the student, and if he be a graduate from any College, the name of that College, and the date of his graduation; and shall charge such student for his tuition (if he charge him anything) at the rate of one hundred dollars per annum.

3. No person (not a member of the Bar of another state) shall be recommended for admission to the Bar, unless he be of good moral character, and at least twenty-one years of age, and be recommended as a suitable candidate by some member, and shall (without pursuing any other employment and without engaging in the practice of law) have studied as required by the rule of the Court, or at some Law School in the country, and at least six months in the office of

some Attorney in this State, and shall, as a further evidence of his qualifications, have sustained a satisfactory examination by the Examining Committee ; nor shall a member of the Bar of another State, who has not been in practice at least three years, be recommended for admission, except upon proof that he has studied the term of time required by the rule of the Court, and has for six months at least been a student of some Attorney in this State, and is recommended by some member as aforesaid ; nor shall any of either class here named be recommended for admission, until it is shown that his instructor's claims for tuition, if any he have, have been satisfactorily adjusted.

4. The notice of a meeting at which the qualifications of candidates are to be considered, shall set forth the name of the candidate, and state by whom he is recommended ; and to this end it shall be the duty of a member proposing a candidate, to give all necessary information to the Secretary previous to the issuing of such notice.

5. No member of this Association shall permit any student of his, on pain of expulsion from his office, to practice in any Court.

6. All mistakes of an Attorney, his clerk or student, shall be amended, and all disputes and differences between members, originating from professional intercourse and dealings, shall be adjusted, on such terms as any three of the Bar, to be selected for that purpose by the President, may think reasonable.

7. No member of this Association, where he is

interested as Attorney or Counsel, shall become bail for the defendant in any proceeding civil or criminal, nor surety for the complainant in any criminal proceeding, or for the plaintiff in any bond in a replevin suit, or for costs in any suit in which a surety is ordered by the Court.

8. No member of this Association shall be concerned or associated in any professional business with any member of the Bar who shall have been expelled from the Association, or who shall refuse or knowingly omit in his practice in this county to conform to the By-Laws of the Association ; nor shall he engage for a party who to his knowledge shall have made application to any other member for counsel or assistance in the same cause, unless such other member shall have engaged or refused to engage in the cause, or been reasonably compensated for all his advice and services therein and dismissed by his client.

9. Any member of this Association who shall make a practice of soliciting employment, or of offering any special inducement to officers or others to procure business for him, shall be deemed guilty of mal-practice, and liable to the censure of the Association.

10. No member of the Association shall perform professional services of the character below described, for a lower rate of compensation than the following—which fees and compensation shall not be reduced or compromised.

Advice upon any matter of Law, -	$1 00
Drawing a Deed, Bill of Sale, Power of Attorney, or other instrument (in the city of Providence,) - -	1 00

8

Drawing a Mortgage Deed of real or personal property, - - -	1 25
Drawing such Mortgage with power of sale, - - - -	1 50
Drawing a Deed of Trust, -	2 00

[The magistrate's fees for acknowledgement not included.]

A Letter demanding payment of a claim, settled or withdrawn before suit,	
for a sum under $20, - -	25
over $20 and under $100, -	1 00
over $100, - - -	2 00
Drawing a Bill, Petition or Answer in Equity, when the amount in controversy is over $500, - -	10 00
Term fee in such cause, - -	8 00
When the amount in controversy is under $500, drawing a Bill, Petition or Answer, and for Term fee, -	5 00
Writ in suit not entered in Court,	
From a United States' Court, -	10 00
From Supreme Court or Court of Common Pleas, on a claim under $200,	3 00
over $200, - - -	4 00
Declaration, (chargeable after last day of service) - - -	1 00
Writ of Replevin and Bond, -	5 00
Special Court Writ and Declaration, (suit not entered,) - -	4 00
Prosecuting Special Court Suit (not answered) - - -	3 00

[For advice relative to suits thus commenced, a further charge if circumstances warrant it.]

9

Term fee in an answered or continued case, and on an Appeal or Petition, at every term at which it shall not be tried—		
in U. S. Courts, - - -	10	00
in Supreme Court or Assembly,	5	00
in Court of Common Pleas,	4	00
Answering fee—in U. S. Court, -	10	00
in Supreme Court,	5	00
in Court of Com. Pleas,	4	00
Arguing fee—in U. S. Courts, -	20	00
in Supreme Court or Assembly, -	15	00
in Court of Common Pleas,		
in an original action, -	10	00
on an appeal, - -	5	00
Filing reasons of appeal, complaint for confirmation of judgment, bill of exceptions, or motion in arrest of judgment or for a new trial,		
in the Supreme Court, -	5	00
in Court of Common Pleas,	4	00
Petition for Divorce or benefit of the Insolvent Act, or preparing Writ of Habeas Corpus, and services in trial of same, - - -	10	00
Petition for Naturalization, -	5	00
Opposing Petition for Divorce or benefit of Insolvent Act, - -	10	00
Filing Petition under the Lien Law (settled before Court) besides taxed costs, - - -	5	00
Drawing Petition to General Assembly,	2	00

[For Services in an answered case in which no trial is had, a reasonable compensation in addition to the Term fee.]

10

Attending a hearing before Referees, Auditors, Masters in Chancery, and on a Rule Day of the Supreme Court, - - - -	1 00
Arguing fee at such hearing, the same as for argument in the Court where the suit is pending.	
Services in attending the taking of a Deposition, - - -	1 00
Writ returnable to the Court of Magistrates, if settled before Court, -	50
Prosecuting a claim for $5 or upwards to judgment in the Court of Magistrates, the suit not having been answered, - - -	1 00
Writ of Replevin and Bond returnable to the Court of Magistrates or a single justice, if not returned to Court, - - - -	2 00
Preparing same, if returned to Court, (whether answered or not,) -	1 00
Answering or defending a case, civil or criminal, in the Court of Magistrates or a Justice's Court, -	3 00
Prosecuting a complaint or an answered suit in such Court, - -	3 00
Opposing or advocating an application for the poor debtor's oath, at jail or elsewhere, - - -	3 00

The Attorney shall be entitled to the taxable costs, except in cases where judgment is rendered against his client.

In all retainers, general or special, a reasonable fee shall be charged.

11

Commissions for collecting moneys
for persons out of the State,
on sums not exceeding $100, - 5 per cent.
over $100 and not exceeding
$200, - - - - 4 " "
over $200, - - 3 " "
For persons living within the State—
on sums not exceeding $100, 2½ " "
over $100 and not exceeding
$200, - - - 2 " "
over $200, - - - 1½ " "

and these commissions shall be chargeable on all sums secured or paid on demands left for collection, whether before suit or after, to the Attorney or to the client; and shall also be chargeable on moneys paid in discharge of mortgages upon which suits for possession are instituted or ordered to be instituted.

11. It shall be the duty of every member of the Association to acquaint the Standing Committee, by a written communication, with every violation of the By-Laws, and every instance of disreputable, oppressive or illegal practice which may come to his knowledge; and every member who shall after an investigation before the Association, on complaint of the Committee, be found guilty of the offence charged, shall be liable, for a first offence, to the censure of the Association, expressed by vote or resolution, (to be published in one or more of the public newspapers if the Association so direct,) and for the second offence shall be liable to expulsion from the Association, the vote of expulsion also to be published, if the Association so direct; provided, however, that a vote of censure, a vote of expul-

sion, or a vote to give publicity as aforesaid to such votes, shall be approved by at least two-thirds of the members present, the question in every case to be taken by ayes and nays, and the names entered on the record.

12. No member of the Association shall be required to adopt the foregoing Tariff of Fees in his charges for business already in litigation.

13. The foregoing By-Laws, so far as they relate to the examination of students, shall not be deemed to apply to any student who shall be admitted to the Bar before the rising of the Supreme Court at the next September Term thereof (1850) in this county; nor shall any of the foregoing Articles or By-Laws take effect until forty practising members of the Bar shall have subscribed the said Articles.

CHAPTER IX

THE

UNITED STATES

MONTHLY

LAW MAGAZINE.

VOL. I. No. I.

EDITED BY JOHN LIVINGSTON,

OF THE NEW-YORK BAR.

JANUARY, 1850.

NEW-YORK:

PUBLISHER'S OFFICE, No. 54 WALL STREET

$5 00 PER ANNUM, (in advance.)

NESBITT, PRINTER, COR. WALL AND WATER STS., N. Y.

[Anonymous]. "The Morality of the Bar: The Principles of Advocacy as Developed in the Lawyer's Practice." From Livingston, John, ed., *The United States Monthly Law Magazine*. Vol. I. No. I. New York: January 1850.

THE MORALITY OF THE BAR: THE PRINCIPLES OF ADVOCACY AS DEVELOPED IN THE LAWYER'S PRACTICE.

THE prejudice which has for a long time existed among a portion of the public against Lawyers, and the attacks on the profession of the Bar, which have for years past appeared in some of our journals, induce us to consider the principles by which it is governed, and the course of practice which it sanctions. The morality of the Bar is precisely the same as it was before it incurred the displeasure which has animated the invectives which have denounced it; and it is far more important to inquire whether these are just, than to assail the motives or impugn the conduct of those who have urged them. A profession which, far more than any other, holds its course before the public eye, affecting vast interests, and conducing to important issues—whose daily efforts are watched by the just vigilance of the Press, and whose severest struggles have a place in national history, cannot suffer from the reiteration of the bitterest invective unless there is something essentially base *in itself,* which deserves the hatred or contempt of the world before whom it lives. If, therefore, the attacks on the Bar had been confined to general vituperation, illustrated by the few examples of the alleged abuse of its powers, which have alone been adduced as evidence against it, we should have been contented to leave its character to the great Arbitrament of Time. But when the principle of advocacy itself is assailed as immoral, and its habitual practice as that of falsehood, by writers of just reputation and extensive influence, we think it right to meet the general accusation directly by a calm investigation of its merits; to inquire whether, in truth, our advocacy involves "an inherent baseness;" to distinguish its honorable exercise from its incidental abuses; to estimate as well the benefits it confers as the temptations by which it is beset; and to trace its influences, both on the moral character of those who practise it, and on the society with whose interests and passions it is intimately blended.

The principle of advocacy consists in the substitution of persons professing skill and learning in litigated matters for the actual litigants, to do on their behalf and in their stead, all which they might, if gifted with sufficient knowledge and ability, do for themselves, with fairness to their opponents. To the operation of that principle it is a necessary condition that the advocate shall receive such reward for his exertions as may compensate him for the preparatory study and active labor which occupy the prime of life; and it is a condition scarcely less necessary that he should be willing, as a general rule of conduct, to render his professional services without previously deciding on the merits of the cause for which he is retained. We shall have occasion as we proceed to illustrate this latter condition, and to consider its just exceptions; at present we state it broadly, as a concession to the opponents of the Bar on which they found their principal accusations.

If advocacy, thus explained, shall be proved to be a pursuit of dishonor, the conviction will, at least, be attended with disastrous consequences; for that its existence is indispensable to the administration of justice in this country can scarcely be denied. In the rudest condition of society unless the power to expose wrong were invariably associated with its endurance, and innocence when accused were always gifted with eloquence to defeat its foe, the party complaining or accused must often plead through the medium of other organs than his own, and find other affections to represent his feelings and his wishes. But in a society like ours, interveined by the ramifications of artificial law, where the tenure of real estate, the operations of commerce, the transmission of property from one generation to another, induce a complicated system,—to require that all men, women and children who may be involved in litigation, shall plead their own causes or present them only through the medium of unpaid and unskilled friendship, would amount to a practical repeal of all laws, and a resolution of the society into its elements. Even in cases which, involving no doubtful matter of law, require only aptitude, presence of mind and discretion, and in which parties endowed with capacity and courage have appeared as their own advocates, how rare are the instances in which they have not exemplified the old proverb at a ruinous expense of the time which is the property of the public! Experience has shown that, even in these peculiar cases, the duration of the proceedings has been often increased tenfold without the least practical benefit to the suitor, so as to prove that, if such examples became universal, the result would be, not merely inconvenience to a few devoted judges and juries, but the necessary multiplication of judges to an enormous cost, and an intolerable addition to the duties of juries. To be consistent, therefore, the writers who would uproot the profession of advocacy must seek the destruction of the Law itself—not its simplification merely, for that would not avail—not only the destruction of our system of English Law, but the abolition of all Law by which definite rules are applied to the complicated relations and passions and usages of mankind. To the integrity of the Bar the most important interests are daily intrusted; and, we fearlessly assert that, with rare and odious exceptions, the trust is faithfully performed. Rules, for example, are every day in term granted by the courts on the *ex parte* statements of counsel, which have direct influences on fortunes of individuals; which, for example, may suspend proceedings till bankruptcy or insolvency intervenes, or an assignment or flight defeats a creditor. In the hurry of *Nisi Prius*, occasions frequently occur when the misstating or garbling a document, the disingenuous concealment of part of a correspondence so as to give a false effect to the portion produced, a thousand modes of trickery open to an unscrupulous advocate, may work irreparable ruin. And in the advice given out of court, the power to excite or discourage litigation, or regulate its course if inevitable, counsel possess large capacities which must exist for good or for evil.

If, however, the practice of advocacy can be proved to be inconsistent with personal truth and honor, we grant that the necessity for its continuance should not rescue it from disgrace. Still, the necessity for the continuance of an order, whose influences intermingle with an infinite variety of social relations, is a strong presumption that the necessary modes of its action are not wicked; that Providence, which "shapes our ends, rough-hew them how we may," has rarely, if ever, permitted anything to be inextricably interlaced with the fibres of our social existence which is essentially evil. A yet stronger presumption in favor of the Bar arises from the conceded fact that its members, when not practising their profession, are among the most truthful and honorable of men. A writer of distempered romance may find scope in depicting the moral anomaly of a man stained by some one dark crime, who atones for his secret guilt by exercising the most generous virtues; but he would scarcely venture to represent even a single human being, the business of whose life is one lie; who shall exult in the perversion of justice, not merely to the impunity of guilt, but the punishment of innocence, and who shall yet, in social and domestic relations, in the hours of relaxation, repose, sickness and death, be good and just and kind. Still less would he venture to multiply the prodigy by hundreds—to image a race of men not devoting to falsehood merely their intellects but their tastes and affections,—ever passionate to do injustice—and yet themselves remaining all the while steady to truth and justice!

Let us, then, follow into detail the application of advocacy to the various classes of opportunity in which it is exerted, and inquire, in relation to the requisitions of each, whether its exercise involves the conscious support of falsehood against truth, of injustice against right. The vituperations bestowed on the Bar seem generally founded on the assumption not only that all litigated questions involve a direct opposition of truth and falsehood, and with it of justice and oppression, but that the advocate engages in the support of the worse cause with full knowledge of its hollowness, and does a violence to his own convictions for the sake of gain, similar in baseness to that of a philosopher, who should impugn some important truth revealed to his consciousness with mathematical certainty, or of a politician who should accept the pay of those whom he believes to be the enemies of his country and of mankind, to aid them with the blandishments of his sophistry. A glance at the intellectual and moral position of the advocate in cases dependent on legal argument where the facts are undisputed; in cases where the result depends more or less on the truth or falsehood of allegations of fact; in others, where the result depends not on the truth or falsehood of alleged facts, but on the inferences to be drawn from them; in questions of unliquidated damages, where the result altogether depends on considerations of morality and feeling; and in the conduct and defence of criminal prosecutions, which, though involving considerations like those which govern civil litigation, present some points of duty and of danger to the advocate which do not arise in civil proceedings—will better enable us to test the justice of those charges than any general reasonings.

First, then, let us consider the position of an advocate retained to support in argument a legal proposition which his client desires to maintain, with a view to decide whether there is any thing in the duty he undertakes, if fairly performed, akin to falsehood or partaking of baseness. In principle, this class of cases would seem most favorable to the objector, because no partial statement of facts, colored by the passions and the wishes of the litigant, disturbs and sways the judgment of his counsel. Nor, with those frequent exceptions in which he is required to support an opinion formed previously and communicated by himself, (and in which his office is surely beyond all impeachment,) can he enter on his work with an assurance that the proposition he is engaged to maintain ought to prevail. To require such previous mental assent from the advocate would be to invest him, not only with powers of a judge—or of any number of judges—but of the highest tribunal in the last resort, before which the question may finally be argued, without the benefit of suggestions from other minds to dispel the errors of a first impression; and would condemn the suitor to take the chance of successive experiments before he could find an advocate with a judgment happily attuned to his purpose. Cases may, indeed, be presented to a lawyer, which his discrimination may at once perceive to be "too clear for argument;" and in such case his duty is equally clear—to refuse to debase himself, and waste the public time by a vain attempt to distinguish an authority unquestionably in point, or to unsettle a principle of clear application. He will use caution, indeed, before he decides on this course—recollecting, that sometimes objections, thought too manifestly groundless by learned judges even to be reserved for consideration, have been found valid. The great majority of cases, however, present no such difficulty in their apparent clearness; the position in which they stand for solemn argument alone implies, that, to ordinary legal apprehensions at least, they are doubtful; and the question is, whether they shall be decided by the judges without argument, or—if necessarily to be argued—whether the parties to whom each side of the question is assigned, act wicked and base parts in endeavoring to support the position of their respective clients by authority and reasoning. Surely no one who desires that justice should prevail, would deprive the judges of the aids which they derive from the research and the reasoning of laborious and acute lawyers, presenting in turn each aspect of the case; investigating the principles which should govern it; collecting and explaining the authorities which bear upon it; and suggesting the distinctions and the analogies which must be regarded in each decision, if it should not introduce that inconsistency into the system, which is the worst of tyrannies. So needful to the due administration of justice in difficult questions is this sifting of their elements by legal minds, sharpened by professional zeal, that in cases of peculiar difficulty and importance—like that to which we have just alluded—the judges desire for their assistance a second argument, conceiving that even the associated experience of all the judges may be aided by such a process. The counsel, then, though *selected* by their respective clients, are really ministers of justice—contributing to the attainment of justice in the particular case by the lights they cast on it, and to the general harmony of the law of which it will become an example. Up to the height of this position they are bound to act—zealously for their clients, but fairly by the court; and, therefore, the counsel, who, in argument, should attempt to suppress or pervert the materials of judgment, as if he should quote a statute as subsisting which he knew to be repealed, or suppress an adverse authority in the hope that it might be overlooked, or wilfully stop short in reading a passage when the residue would weaken his inferences—would betray his higher duty to the court and to justice, and incur the just censure of the Bar and of the judges. But is there anything disgraceful in the office of avowedly bringing before the judicial mind all that can be fairly urged on one side of a doubtful question of law? Is any deception practised or endured? Is the mental operation of the reasoner debasing? It is not, indeed, so noble an exercise of the human faculties to explore the labyrinth of any science with the purpose of finding materials for the support of a previously adopted theory, as with the pure and passionless aspiration for abstract truth;—but of the great benefactors of mankind, how many have been partisans of theory, how few single-minded seekers after wisdom? Human nature is essentially partisan. Our minds select their favorites on lighter grounds than the confidence in a lawyer's talent implied by a retainer;—nay, on mere caprice, like that which Wordsworth exemplifies in one of his noblest sonnets, by the adoption of a single ship from a fleet under sail for the peculiar sympathy of the observer:—

"This ship was naught to me, nor I to her,
Yet I pursued her with a lover's look.
This ship to all the rest did I prefer;
When will she turn, and whither?"

Let us follow, then, the retained advocate into the studies which prepare him for the delivery of learned argument on some question arising on the law of real estate. He penetrates the maze of precedents and authorities to search after the leading principle of his subject, and traces its application in the succession of decisions with strenuous care. Dry, hard, and uninteresting as the labor seems, it soon generates its own fervor, and becomes its own reward. The faculties which would else be relaxed and dissipated among various exciting pursuits are braced and strengthened by the silent toil; the very remoteness of the subjects of inquiry from the ordinary aspects of business imparts a certain elevation and refinement to the study which masters them; while the habit of continuous exertion, frequently piercing through the accumulated illustrations and distinctions of ages to the same ancient principles of law, though in different directions, invests life itself with the consistency which belongs to singleness of purpose and aim. His progress is not uncheered by reliefs the more welcome as they are laboriously earned; a sidelong glimpse into history and ancient manners; a quaint jest of some judicial reporter in which the stout-hearted writer seems still to live and to enjoy; some classical allusion redolent of the days of youth, whereby Coke or Hale refreshed themselves as they wrote; some antique pleasantry which breathes a sort of wall-flower perfume from the solid mass which centuries have darkened but have not shaken. Nor let it be thought that the lawyer, whose toils are akin to that of the student of an abstract science, pursues them without the infusion of some warmth of partisanship which, if he begin his researches without bias, or with a distrust of the side on which they are engaged, will soon render him the convert of his own industry, and induce him to hail with satisfaction the conquest of every difficulty and the achievement of every fresh illustration. In this respect, his mental operation resembles that of some high casuist, who has undertaken to establish a favorite theory of history or literature; who surveys everything by its light, and devotes all the spoils of time to its service; as when old Jacob Bryant assails the material existence of Troy, or Wolfe or Heyne attacks the personal identity of Homer; and the process leads to a conviction, strong as that of the knights who surveyed the shield from opposite sides and fought to the death for the aspect each beheld. Such studies and such reasonings, so far from corrupting or debasing the minds of lawyers who have chiefly pursued them, often preserve a guileless simplicity of character, maintained by few who mingle largely in the feverish business and pleasures of life.

Let us next observe the moral position of the advocate in cases of disputed fact, of which it is impossible for him to ascertain the truth before he accepts the retainer, unless, indeed, he could summon all the witnesses, sift their evidence, and anticipate every aspect the case may assume when tried before a jury. He may possibly find grounds to believe that his client has no cause of action or ground of defence, and, if so, he will, if he acts rightly, take the earliest opportunity of expressing his opinion, and, if expenses can be yet saved, of urging a withdrawal or a compromise; and if neither can be obtained, he will, if for the plaintiff, make a fair statement of the case in the true aspect in which he has discerned it, and let it meet its doom as speedily as it can; or, if for a defendant, will content himself with watching and scrutinizing the plaintiff's proofs precisely as the judge himself does when no counsel appears for the defence. But the unprofessional reader may be assured that, of cases seriously litigated, those which call for this exercise of duty are comparatively rare. In many cases the client himself is only acquainted with the circumstances of his own case through the medium of other minds, of servants or other agents at a distance, all more or less disturbed by interest or colored by prejudice; and, in more, his own perceptions are moulded by his resentments or his wishes.

It is matter of curious observation, how any event, which is shared, or witnessed merely, in a state of hurry or excitement, presents different and even opposite aspects to the memory, and how a bias, from some almost or wholly imperceptible cause, converts spectators, who are without interest and above suspicion, into partisan witnesses. Such is almost every case of litigated collision by land or water; in which it is usual to find both bystanders and passengers differing, not only on the looser points of sobriety and speed, but on such matters of direct opposition, as on which side of the road or river each carriage or vessel was proceeding, and even on which side of a carriage or vessel a blow was struck. If such differences arise in the recollection of impartial persons, surely it cannot be surprising that each party is confident that he is injured, and communicates his case, in that confidence, to his counsel. The result is, that, with the exception of cases admitted to be without defence, and committed to counsel merely to watch the proofs of the adversary, and cases in which no struggle is anticipated on the facts, but their legal application alone is disputed, or technical objections are suggested, the statement presented to counsel is almost always such as to induce a strong belief in the justice of the cause, and to enlist his feelings powerfully in its success. To one thus prepossessed, who can wonder that in the animation of the contest the first impression is deepened; and as the little chapter of life, with all its living interest, opens around him, his client's case becomes part of his own being; that his belief in its justice insensibly but inseparably blends with his natural desire to succeed; and that he hears all the arguments and regards all the testimony against it with the surprise, dislike, and incredulity of inveterate opinion sharpened by zeal. The irregularities which counsel sometimes commit, when betrayed into conversational attacks on each other, and the petulance with which they occasionally treat opposing witnesses,—faults often to be severely censured, and always to be deplored,—generally arise from the excess of this conviction, and the irritation consequent on an attempt to defeat it. No counsel who regards the interests of his client, or his own duty to justice, will ever cross-examine with deliberate severity a witness whom he does not believe, for the time at least, to be swearing falsely; still less will he condescend to the more insiduous art of inducing the witness to answer with one meaning, and assume his reply to bear another, and thus lead him to give evidence which, intended to be true, shall have the effect of falsehood—a species of criminal trickery nearly allied to guilt of the deepest dye. In commenting on the testimony of witnesses he will never indulge in attacks which he does not believe to be deserved, and which he does not also deem essential to the just result of the cause; remembering that witnesses do not, like the parties, come voluntarily before the court, and are not, like them, represented by counsel; but if the evidence has important bearing upon the result, and he believes it untrue, he is bound to deal with it as false, though the imputation of perjury may thus be cast on one who has no present means of repelling it. Unless the cross-examination which may (though we believe very rarely) succeed in developing premeditated falsehood, and the remarks which, supplied by surrounding circumstances, may lead to its disbelief, were not fearlessly administered by counsel, trial by jury would be divested of its most valuable characteristics, which surely consist less in the enforced unanimity of twelve men, than in the public investigation of evidence, conducted by the vigilant scrutiny of conflicting minds. To avoid all harsh remark as far as possible, to reconcile opposing testimony by any theory rather than that of wilful falsehood, and never to impute it unless in the full belief that it has been committed, is the wisdom no less than the duty of the advocate. As the vehemence of counsel is justified by the strong belief they imbibe that the cause they maintain is just, so they are bound to conduct it as befits an honest cause, leaving the consequence of its falsehood to fall on the client who has deceived them. Although not bound to state or prove the case of an adversary, they are bound, if they anticipate it, to do so fairly; to state the entire material effect of an instrument; to produce no document with the hope of raising an impression they believe to be untrue by the ambiguity of its language; to garble nothing; to conceal nothing; to misrepresent nothing; but to present every argument and illustration which the zeal of the most earnest friendship could urge, and which are rarely urged with powerful effect unless in the conviction that they are urged for justice. As the zeal of an honorable advocate during the progress of a cause is in proportion to the confidence he feels in its merits, so we believe that the continuance of that confidence or its overthrow determines the feeling with which he regards the issue. He often remains unconvinced though conquered; but we venture to assert that the only regret, beyond the disappointment of an excited moment, which he feels, arises from an impatience of a failure of justice, mingled often with vain regrets for the insufficiency of his own exertions; and that the only permanent feeling of pleasure he cherishes in success is nurtured by the consciousness that right has been done by his victory. That there are instances in which the pride of intellect, in its unhallowed vivacity, may at the Bar, as in other spheres of action, exult in the triumph of evil, or in a heartless indifference to evil and good, we do not deny; but that a disposition to glory in the success of wrong is a general characteristic of the Bar, we do solemnly deny; and we esteem the charge so utterly groundless that, freely acquitting those who have urged it of intentional falsehood, we can only regard it as a proof of the force of bias in disturbing the aspects of truth, which not only influences lawyers, but all men who reason through the medium of the prejudices or the affections.

If we have afforded a glimpse of the manner in which counsel may be honestly engaged in each side of a cause dependent on disputed facts, where there *is* a direct opposition of truth and falsehood, and the result lies in their development, we may approach with confidence those far more numerous cases in which no such antagonism prevails. Of this character cases of circumstantial evidence partially partake, where the circumstances are admitted to be true, and the question involves only the inference which the jury should derive from them. If, in reference to these cases, we consider what a strong tendency there is in every mind, however disinterested, to weave for itself a theory out of the minute incidents which surround a transaction, itself shrouded in mystery, and to bend everything to its purpose—a disposition requiring to be checked by the strongest vigilance of juries in trying charges of secret crime—we shall not wonder that counsel, having been assured of the fact itself by his client as he desires to establish it, should find in everything a tendency to prove it true. In such cases, however, there *is* an ultimate question of truth and falsehood, though depending not on the verity of evidence, but on the strength of inferences; but there are many others which are questions of judgment, of science, of skill—questions of degree, not of opposition—which engage all the accomplishments which the advocate may happen to possess in literature, science, or art. Such are questions of copyright and patent, when the contest is whether the work for which protection is sought has such originality as to deserve it; whether an alleged imitator has sought to monopolize a principle, or only a new mode of application; how far similarities are indicative of piracies; what steps and gradations of improvement can be withheld from public endeavor for private recompense; which are not questions involving truth or falsehood, but matters of skill, on which an ingenious mind, having once received its cue, will proceed with increasing ardor, and bring to unskilled judges and juries the most important aid. Thus when rights alleged to have been acquired by prescription or user are questioned, and acts of enjoyment are proved on the one side, met by proofs of interruption on the other, the mind has only to estimate a question of degree, and will decide on a mere balance of admitted facts according to its own tendency. Thus, in the most interesting of all questions which engage the powers and affections of an advocate—questions of mental competency to perform important acts—which involve the highest moral considerations—which border on the most affecting solemnities of life and death, and render "metaphysical aid" far more needful than skill in analyzing evidence, not the ordinary prepossessions merely are enlisted in the cause by the first view presented; but the highest faculties, the noblest prejudices, the finest trains of speculative thought, all find delighted exercise in the vivid operations of the mind, thus awakened from its languor and impelled along the course of profound and subtle inquiry. In these contests, particular facts may be disputed; the wish of a witness will sometimes be "father to the thought," and circumstances will be confused by the affections; but the result will rather depend on philosophical inference applied to the affairs of life than on the veracity of witnesses. The celebrated cause, "Doe on the demise of Tatham v. Wright," in which the title of the estate of Hornby Castle in Lancashire depended on the validity of the will of Mr. Marsden, which was after two successive verdicts in its favor ultimately set aside, supplies a signal example of this position. In support of the will, which was elaborately prepared by a solicitor of high character, it was proved that the testator had lived to the verge of old age, apparently at the head of a liberal establishment, entertaining guests with courtesy—that he had bought, sold, exchanged, and mortgaged largely—that he had executed a great number of deeds, attested by witnesses of unblemished honor—and that he had corresponded with numerous persons in different periods of his life by letters, which, if the genuine products of his own mind, could leave no doubt of his competency; and had partaken of the holiest rites of religious worship. On the other hand, it was alleged that being a person of feeble understanding, never developed beyond the state of ordinary childhood, he had been all his lifetime in bondage—the puppet and the slave of his steward, whose family, engaged with their father in a conspiracy for years to acquire dominion over his estate, had contrived to present him to casual acquaintances and guests in favorable aspects—to engage him in various matters of business, and really to guide him in all,—nay, to write for him the letters he was to copy, and which were, in due season, to be adduced as evidence in support of final dispositions made under their control. This case also was sustained by a great body of proof, consisting of instances of great debility of intellect, and of base subjection to his inferiors, extending over many years, and strong grounds were suggested, as apparent in his letters, to indicate that they were not the unaided productions of his mind. The facts of both cases were probably true in the main, notwithstanding some natural mistakes and exaggerations—the truth probably lying between both theories, and the real question resolving itself into that which the law must leave as much to the feelings as the reason of juries—what degree of intellect and will should suffice to give validity to a solemn act, disposing of property which the owner can no longer enjoy? In questions of character again, involving the import and effect of words spoken or written, and sometimes contrasting the inevitable mischief accruing to individual reputation with the supposed duty of the utterer,—questions in which the noble office of law in protecting as substantial property the impressions wrought on men's minds by individual conduct—the breathing fragrance of life—is regarded with reference to the exigencies of society which may require an individual sacrifice—the office of the advocate on either side is surely neither deceptive nor ignoble. In questions of the amount of unliquidated damages, the counsel who pictures the wrong to be compensated, and he who suggests the grounds of mitigation, may not only both be honest, but both right—each taking his own share in presenting the truth, so far as it can be elicited, to the minds of the jury,—the extent of wrong on the one side, the just allowances for human frailty on the other.

At the trial, it is his province to represent the true interests, not the aimless passions of his clients; to soften, not to exasperate hatreds; and to substitute, for the naked struggle of conflicting interests, the dazzling fence of graceful reasoning, and encourage the gentler play of the affections. Thus practised, advocacy is the application to an immense variety of human affairs of cultivated and honorable minds; substituting on the arena of inevitable litigation, wiser and calmer proxies for the actual combatants; securing an approximation to equality between those who, by talent, education, fortune, sex or age, are unequal, and the preservation of order aud decorum in the discussion of matters most productive of excitement; and assuaging disappointment by the recollection of the ability and zeal which have been employed to avert it.

The exercise of the advocate's profession is unquestionably attended with peculiar temptations and dangers, not without counterbalance of influences for good. Its soul is SYMPATHY. The chief excellence of the advocate is in proportion to the facility with which he can become a party in the most momentous concerns of strangers—admitted by their choice into a little world of anxious hopes and fears, affections and resentments—and identifying his own existence, for the time, with the sharp and giddy crisis of alien fortunes. As thus he lives in the lives of others, the vicissitudes of interest, while it involves no indifference to personal hypocrisy or falsehood, may tend to relax the sterner fibres of the mind, and render it less capable of discerning and appreciating abstract truth. A pliancy of character may thus be fostered unfavorable to the maintenance of political consistency,—a weakness which the advocate shares with the poet, who, accustomed to "accommodate the shews of things to his desires," is open to the seductions of sentiment when he would scorn those of lucre. Such, however, is not the invariable effect of the practice of advocacy—in some minds the very habit of rapidly passing from one range of sympathies to another begets an earnest aspiration after conditions which are stable and enduring, and fixes the roots of individual principles deeper; and therefore, the Bar has at all times boasted examples of political consistency, maintained against the most flattering temptations. The more immediate danger of advocacy arises from the heat and activity of its struggles—the suddenness with which its resources are called into action—the surprises which occur in the disclosure of an adverse case, or the unexpected failure of its own,—which are too apt to produce those flaws of temper of which witnesses complain, and may sometimes, though we believe rarely, lead to expedients which deliberation would not sanction, and which are afterwards deplored in vain. Against this temptation—we believe the most perilous of all to which a Lawyer at *Nisi Prius* is exposed—it behoves him to exert his utmost vigilance, as we believe the charges which have been preferred against the practice of the Bar have received more support from such hurried lapses from candor, than from any habitual or deliberate baseness, even in the few who have deserved them. On the other hand, the rapid intercourse with numerous forms of many-colored life, which the practice of the Bar involves, tends to destroy all intolerance, religous, political, or moral—to nurture the affections—to quicken and enlarge the sympathies—to induce allowance for human frailty; and these influences are, we believe, deeply interfused in the personal character of lawyers. The very practice of representing the feelings of others is, at least, one remove from self-love, and though very far from approaching the comprehensiveness of true humanity, breaks the crust of selfishness, which courses of worldly success in other occupations too often engender. Whatever of passion or of weakness may be mingled with the practice of the Bar—and we do not deny the frequent intrusion of each—we fearlessly assert that they scarcely ever betray its members into the expression of opinions calculated to relax the moral sense; to impair love and veneration for the good and pure; but that counsel frequently obtain and use opportunities of enforcing high duties by generous expression; of exposing and denouncing baseness, which would else remain undetected and unpunished; and if, from the failure of human institutions, they cannot always prevent the success of the wrong-doer, of associating it, not with triumph, but with infamy.

Chapter X

The Rewards of the Profession of the Law.

A SERMON,

PREACHED

IN TRINITY CHURCH, N. Y., MAY 10, 1868,

BEFORE

THE GRADUATING CLASS

OF THE

Law School of Columbia College,

BY THE

REV. PHILANDER K. CADY, S. T. D.,

Rector of Christ Church, Poughkeepsie, N. Y.

NEW YORK:
PUBLISHED BY THE TRUSTEES.
1868.

Cady, Rev. Philander K. *The Rewards of the Profession of the Law. A Sermon, Preached in Trinity Church, N.Y., May 10, 1868. Before the Graduating Class of the Law School of Columbia College.* New York: Published by the Trustees, 1868.

SERMON.

MATTHEW vi. 5.

"Verily, I say unto you, They have their reward."

I PROPOSE to consider, in this discourse, the spirit and expectation in which a liberal profession, and, in particular, the profession of the Law, should be entered upon and prosecuted. My remarks will take their shape and complexion from the principle contained in the sentence which I just announced to be my text: which principle, therefore, I am first called upon to develop and illustrate.

4

Our Lord is speaking of the hypocrites of His day, or those who did good works, not to the glory of God, but for the sight and praise of men. When they gave alms, they sounded a trumpet before them; when they prayed, they stood conspicuously in the synagogues or at the corners of the streets; when they fasted, they assumed a sad and disfigured countenance. And our unerring Master asserts that they had their reward. They did what they did to be seen of men, and they *were* seen of men. They attracted attention, and gained notoriety, and a wide reputation for extraordinary sanctity.

The same result, I pass on to remark, will invariably follow the use of the same or similar arts and methods, it matters not where or by whom practised. The Hindoo Fakir, who sits cross-legged for twenty years and more, or who reclines constantly, day and night, upon a bed of

5

sharp iron spikes, or who permits himself to be swung high in the air, his body fastened to the swing by hooks of steel run through his living flesh, will gather a throng of spectators around him, and will fill them with admiration and awe. The Stylite, who in ancient times took up his abode upon the summit of a lofty pillar, burned by an eastern sun through the day, chilled at night by dews and frosts, living on the chance offerings which pilgrims, drawn by the odor of his sanctity, brought to him, fasting sometimes, it is affirmed, throughout the forty days of Lent, won for himself a name and fame renowned throughout the land of Egypt or of Syria, and perhaps secured himself a place in the calendar of the Saints. The busy, fussy religionist of this day, conspicuous on the platforms of religious anniversaries, prominent and loud in the petty discussions which distract his sect, accustomed to interlard his speech at all times and before all persons, with the pious commonplace phrases and truisms current in his little ecclesiastical sphere, is regarded by his admirers as a pillar of the Church and a bulwark of Zion. The way to success is direct and easy to any one who wishes to be talked about and lauded for his zeal, or strictness, or liberality, or orthodoxy. Let him do his good deeds openly, ostentatiously, obtrusively, and he will not fail.

But this proposition of our divine Lord, I go on to say, is capable of a far wider application than to the case of the Pharisees, or of those who in any age or country reflect the spirit and repeat the artifices of those Jewish devotees and partisans. It asserts a fact, to which, when certain conditions, so obvious and palpable that they needed not explicit statement, are borne in mind, there is scarcely any exception. Men can make themselves, what they choose to make themselves. They can get, what they set their hearts and minds upon. Take those who succeed in life, as the phrase goes, and it will be found, that nine achieve success to one who has success thrust upon him; for what the ignorant and thoughtless ascribe to luck and fate, to good fortune and a favorite star, in the immense majority of instances, is due to sagacity, and application, and energy, and indomitable perseverance. We can sometimes get behind the screens, and discover, at their painful labors of preparation and elaboration, those who have made a name which men will not willingly let die. We may read of the incredible toil and time which the greatest of orators spent in remedying his natural defects of speech and manner, and in acquiring the skill and power which enabled him to move and sway his Athenian audience as though they were puppets in his hand. In the papers of some eminent poets there have been found the first drafts of the poems which immortality tenaciously preserves, and we are surprised to find, in the mass of changes, erasures, additions, corrections and re-corrections which they exhibit, what a world of labor and thought, the matchless simplicity, grace, ease, and beauty in the finished work, have cost. Men have never ceased admiring the fertility of Raphael's invention and his facility of execution; but in his letters to his friends, he is found making the most minute inquiries in history, geography, popular manners and customs, and whatever may bear upon the truth and effectiveness of the pictures he is meditating; and in the museums of European capitals there are reverently preserved the first sketches and studies of many of his unapproachable paintings, and in them he is shown experimenting, with the greatest pains and patience, upon the positions and attitudes of his figures, the expression of their countenances, the folds of their draperies, and all those details, which, in his completed works, the world unites in

9

proclaiming to be the marks and proofs of his supreme, unrivalled genius. And how, let me ask you to recollect, are great fortunes, for the most part, accumulated? I believe that any man, with a sound mind and a sound body, can become a rich man, if he wishes and resolves to become one. Let him set his whole heart upon wealth; let him make it his one thought by day and his incessant dream by night; let him get every dollar that he can, and spend no cent that he can possibly save; and if he lives to be three-score years and ten, and continues through life as indefatigable in acquisition and as parsimonious in expenditure as he began it, his name will figure in the newspapers among those of the largest payers of income-tax in the land. "Verily, I say unto you, They have their reward." I do not care what may be the goal and prize men set before themselves, fame, or place, or power, or pleasure, or wealth; let them love it, pursue it, work for it, with all their heart, mind, soul and strength, and they will reach it.

But you must not fail to observe, my friends, that it is *what* they seek supremely and pertinaciously that men obtain; the same thing, and not another. If you wish a sound physical constitution you may have one, if you will live tranquilly and temperately, exercise habitually, sleep sufficiently, avoid exposure, and follow the other recognized rules of hygiene. You will have your reward. But then you cannot also be a great scholar and thinker. To be these, you must consume your patrimony in books, and chain yourself to a table, and wear out your eyes with poring over print and manuscript, and grow pale and thin and bent, and abuse your digestion, and cramp your respiration. You cannot have *both* rewards by working for one of them alone. Make your choice in advance, then, whether you will be as strong as an athlete or as learned as a pundit; you may be either the one or the other, but not the two. You. cannot be a brilliant *littérateur* and a first-rate man of business; you cannot be the most accomplished artist and the most powerful statesman of your day; you cannot be the best soldier and the ablest jurist in the land. The principle we are considering is rigorous and exacting. *You* have *your* reward. Choose your ideal and day-dream, O young man; make it the supreme, engrossing object of your pursuit; toil after it with an unresting perseverance and an invincible enthusiasm, and at last it will succumb and surrender itself to your passionate, irresistible approaches and efforts. But you must not be disappointed, and fancy yourself ill-used, nor complain of fate or Providence, because you find only one prize in your hand, and not several. *That,* which at the start you deliberately selected, which you pursued with an application and ardor that would not be denied, *that* at length you seized and retained. It would be the height of silliness and stupidity to be surprised, or chagrined, or angry, because, in addition to the reward which you chose, struggled for, and secured, you find, in the event, that there are other rewards, which you never sought, and which are now hopelessly beyond your reach.

To come to my immediate theme, young gentlemen of the Law School, I remark that the profession for which you have been in preparation and training, may be chosen and pursued in more than one spirit, and for several distinct and quite different ends. One man may choose the Bar simply as a means and instrument of making money; another, because he deems it the quickest and surest avenue to political place and influence; a third, because he is enamored of its subtle distinctions and the intricate,

13

enigmatic questions it continually presents for solution; and a fourth, because the Bench appears to him the highest, most august and most powerful seat of authority which the State has instituted.

Now what I am aiming to impress upon you, my young friends, is, that whatever kind of success in the Law men make choice of, and earnestly, inflexibly pursue, *that* certain form of success, *exceptis excipiendis,* they will obtain. Is it riches, for example, that the youthful lawyer sets his heart upon? in that case, he shall become rich. He can use his legal knowledge and experience, as the merchant uses his stock in trade or the banker his capital, simply with a view to material profit and accumulation. He can take advantage of the secret information which the nature of his pursuit constantly furnishes him with, and can often buy from those who are compelled to sell at ruinous sacrifices, and sell at enormous profits to those who have confidentially entrusted to him the management of their estates. He can resort to every art of ingenuity to swell the items and the amounts in his bills of costs; and in time, what with his industry, prudence, sagacity, and insatiable avarice, he will gain his end, and acquire his tens and hundreds of thousands of dollars.

Or, is it the fame of a successful advocate in desperate or infamous causes, he has resolved to win and hold? for, strange to say, this is the high ambition of some! the method is stereotyped and familiar. It is to accept any case, however unclean, villainous, or monstrous it may be; to blacken all testimony that may be antagonistic, and to gild all that may be favorable; to insult, abuse, and, if possible, put to the torture, the witnesses and counsel on the other side; to resort to every trick, artifice, evasion, falsehood, or piece of charlatanism that can give any advantage to the one party, or do any injury to the other; to coax, or flatter, or hoodwink, or frighten a jury; to maintain, with all the earnestness and emphasis of simulated sincerity and conviction, that black is white, and white is black, that sweet is bitter, and bitter is sweet, and that guilt is innocence, and innocence is guilt; to crush out of existence all instincts and feelings of delicacy, courtesy, honor, purity, and integrity: this is the unfailing way to become famous—or shall I say infamous?—for a certain sort of success at the Bar.

Then, again, there are some who prosecute the study and profession of the Law chiefly for its own sake. They have been called to it by a summons they could not choose but obey, just as the true artist or poet has his calling and work assigned to him by angelic mysterious whispers from the skies. They work not for pay, no more than did Milton, who sold his manuscript of The Paradise Lost for the sum of five pounds, or the architects of those magnificent European cathedrals, another of which will never be built, who were so absorbed in their art, and so intent upon the glory of God, that it never came into their minds to inscribe their names upon the imperishable buildings they were creating, or to put their own statues in the humblest niche around the sacred fane, while there were so many glorious saints deserving and awaiting honor. They find a pleasure and a satisfaction in their musty studies, as some would call them, and their dry, prosaic investigations, such as poets and painters know.

Then, once more,—or am I foolish in the thought?—there are some who have devoted themselves to the Law from a higher, more unselfish motive than even this last one that I just pointed out to you. They consider the discovery of Truth to be one of the noblest and most ennobling pursuits to which any one can consecrate his time and abilities. There is to them something awful, sacred, god-like in the dispensation of Justice; something chivalrous and knightly, yes, even angelic, in the work of defending the innocent, protecting the weak and feeble, and redressing the wrongs of the persecuted and oppressed. To paint falsehood so that it shall wear the features and countenance of truth; to connive at fraud, false-witness, or perjury; to pervert the principles of the pure and lofty science of Jurisprudence; to assist, in the most remote and casual way, in an act of deception, or treachery, or crime: this would be to them a piece of sacrilege, the very thought of which is distress and horror. To others, their feelings and views may appear ridiculous, romantic, quixotic: to themselves, they are incorporate, ineradicable parts of their souls, I was going to say, and of their religion.

Now, my young friends, to whom I am specially speaking, I call upon you to remember that each of these various classes of students and practitioners in the Law has its own line and kind of success. There are numerous prizes in your profession. As I have pointed out, there is wealth, and there is notoriety, and there is honor, and there is political position, and there is the judicial chair, and there is the enjoyment and satisfaction which good and true work, done for its own sake, invariably yields, and there is the high and proud consciousness of being a "minister of GOD" for the punishment of the guilty, the rescue of the innocent, and the deliverance of the wronged. Which will you have? For, speaking as the mouth-piece of observation and experience, I can promise you, if you are determined not to be drones and idlers in your chosen profession, but earnest, hearty, resolute, indomitable workers in it, that you shall obtain the reward which you select. What is it then? Money, or office, or the reputation for audacity, recklessness, and triumphant unscrupulousness, or profound respect and veneration for thorough, exhaustive knowledge in the science of the Law, for illustrious, incorruptible integrity, for ardent, quenchless love of truth and right, or for serene, impartial, sacred administration of justice? Whatever it may be, you shall have your reward. You shall succeed, some of you more eminently than others, as abilities and opportunities may variously affect your exertions; but, to a greater or less degree, you shall be successful.

But, mark this, I beseech you, which I next press upon your consideration. You must be content with the special reward which you had in your mind when you chose the legal profession, and for which you toiled in constant labors until you obtained it. When at length you shall have clutched the long-coveted, long-fought-for prize, you must not affect surprise, or sorrow, or indignation, that it is only one. You shall have what you chose: take your own, and go in peace. Did you love the law for its own sake? Did you pursue it, as does the enthusiastic student of natural science, chemistry, or geology, or astronomy, out of pure disinterested affection for knowledge, and desire for its discovery and dissemination? Well, you will have your reward. You will have found an unspeakable satisfaction and pleasure in your favorite study, a perennial delight in the solution of involved and knotty legal problems, which money could not have purchased for you, nor can words describe. You will have made yourself a profound, accomplished, erudite jurist. But you must not begin to complain that you have not made a fortune in the Law, or that your reputation is restricted to the few and the fit, and is not the theme of all babbling tongues. Let me again remind you, that you yourself made deliberate final choice of one particular reward, and that it will be very foolish, after you shall have secured it, to fret and murmur, because, in addition to it, you will not have won other rewards, which you never selected nor sought. That successful lawyer, whom, for the moment, I will suppose, you may be envying, in the beginning of his career chose money, or a cheap and vulgar fame, for his portion; he labored for the one or the other, and he acquired it. He despised your choice, and has none of your reward. You declined the prize that allured him, and consequently you do not share its possession with him. Each shall have what he originally preferred, and neither ought to complain of the respective final results. He has heaps of riches, and you are comparatively poor. Well, he set his heart on money; he sacrificed himself on the altar of Mammon; he starved all pure, all tender, all elevating tastes and affections out of his mind and heart; he has come to mock at poetry and sentiment, at disinterestedness and generosity; he measures men and principles by the standard of gold. Look at his keen, hard eye; remark that eager, covetous expression; take notice that accumulation has become the breath of his life, and the only food and aliment with which he feeds his immortal part. Do you desire to become such as he? Do you shrink in horror from the thought? Or, let us suppose, that your companion in the Law School has achieved a wide and remunerative popularity as a criminal lawyer. He is retained in almost every celebrated cause. His speeches are reproduced in the daily journals. By his art and adroitness; by his matchless skill in eliciting from witnesses just such evidence as he wants, and in frightening into confusion and contradiction the witnesses whose evidence he fears; by his facility in scattering at his will, now sweetest flattery, and now foulest billingsgate, he has often compelled victory when victory seemed hopeless, and has made himself a power and a terror that few are daring enough to defy. But, remember, he had to pay the price for the position in popular estimation he holds. It cost him all the honor, all the courtesy all the high principle, all the manliness, all the conscience, he ever had. Are you willing to pay what he did for the reward he has obtained?

Let me suppose, gentlemen of the Graduating Class, and let me hope and believe too, that you will be hard, diligent, conscientious students; that you will never soil your hands with filthy practices; that you will always hold a high and proud estimate of your profession; that you will ever delight to recall and celebrate the illustrious names that have adorned it, and to point to the science you have chosen as one of the greatest and noblest trophies and monuments of the human intellect; that you will always hasten to rescue the distressed, and to wreak punishment upon the oppressor, the robber of the widow, the fatherless, the helpless, as some Bayard of the middle ages, without fear and reproach, leaped to the enterprise of delivering some forlorn orphan out of a dungeon, and slaying the brutal baron who had defrauded, imprisoned, and cruelly treated the child; that you will do whatever work may be entrusted to you, honestly, thoroughly, to the best of your skill and strength; and that, after years have gone by, you can look into the past, and will not be ashamed of yourselves nor of your labors. If such be the case, without pretending to any skill in soothsaying, but only pronouncing upon the future from the experience of the past, I can safely predict and describe your reward. In hard cash, in noisy popular estimation, it may not be as great as that which others have won. But you will have earned a competence, if not more, and, together with this pecuniary recompense, whatever be its amount, you will have self-respect, and honor unsullied by a speck and integrity priceless beyond any sum of money, and a conscience void of offence toward GOD and toward man, to lose which is the greatest of all earthly losses; and, besides all these, you will have had exceeding delight and abiding satisfaction in your chosen pursuit, and the consciousness that you have done your share toward preserving in the high and honorable esteem of men your eminent profession. In addition to being a cultivated, well-furnished, experienced, skilful lawyer, you will be a gentleman, an ornament to the order of which you are a member, the object of regard and reverence by all those in the community whose good opinion is worth having, and last, though chiefest of all, your secular work will have been a help, and not an insuperable hindrance, in that work, which may not be neglected without infinite peril by any one, young or old,—the work of conforming every thought, word, and deed of the whole life to the holy, just, and supreme LAW of GOD.

CHAPTER XI

THE

DUTIES AND RIGHTS

OF

COUNSEL.

Field, David Dudley and Samuel Bowles. *The Duties and Rights of Counsel. Correspondence between Samuel Bowles of the Springfield Republican and David Dudley Field.* [n.p.] 1871.

The following correspondence explains itself, except in respect to the last letter of the Appendix. This was intended to serve as the reply to a letter to my brother from an English friend, inclosing an article of the New York *Times*, which had been copied into the money article of the London *Times*.

This pamphlet is not published generally. Whether it will be so published must depend on circumstances. For the present it is distributed confidentially among a few persons for their own perusal.

D. D. F.

New York, January 20, 1871.

CORRESPONDENCE

BETWEEN

SAMUEL BOWLES

Of the Springfield *Republican*,

AND

DAVID DUDLEY FIELD.

NEW YORK, *Dec.* 27, 1870.

DEAR SIR: I address you thus, taking it for granted that the scurrilous attack upon me, in the form of a letter published in a late number of the Springfield *Republican*, was inserted without your consent or knowledge.

Allow me to call your attention to this attack, and to ask you for a public disavowal of it.

I did not see it till this morning, when a friend showed it to me in yesterday's New York *Times*. The *Times* I do not mind, for it is the weak and wicked "sound and fury, signifying nothing," of three or four renegade Englishmen, but the Springfield *Republican* I do mind. Your relations with me make me believe that you would not willingly lend its types to abuse me, and your relations with others make me also believe that you would not knowingly consent to its degradation.

Yours very truly,
DAVID DUDLEY FIELD.

SAMUEL BOWLES, ESQ.,
Springfield Republican, &c.

2

THE REPUBLICAN,
Springfield, Mass., Dec. 29, 1870.

MY DEAR SIR: I did not see the letter about the New York lawyers, in which occurred the paragraph offensive to yourself, until after it was published in the *Republican*; nor did I read it, indeed, until since the receipt of your letter. I regret very much that it did not do fuller justice to the qualities that have won for you the position, which the letter assigned, of the leader of the active members of the New York bar. And I am especially mortified and indignant that the line concerning your personal qualities, or rather the supposed opinion, of your brother lawyers in regard to them, should have appeared in a paper under my control. Whether any or all of your associates think you "avaricious" or "mean," is a matter I know nothing about; but their judgment to that effect would not, knowingly by me, have found expression in the *Republican*. But as to the general judgment concerning your professional association with notorious parties, with generally conceded corrupt schemes, and the effect of them upon your professional standing, I should not have changed the character of the letter, though the wording of it is not exactly to my taste. Whether right or wrong, I think there is but one feeling among your old friends in Western Massachusetts on this subject, and that is one of mingled sorrow and indignation at your professional association with Fisk and Gould and their desperate schemes. I enclose an editorial paragraph in the *Republican*, a few days since, expressive, I think, of this common feeling. The judgment would have been rendered earlier, and, I think, made more condemnatory, but for the long-time pleasant personal relations between myself and your family. I shall be quite willing, if you desire it, to express the *Republican's* regret at

3

the appearance in its columns of the peculiarly personal portion of the letter in question; but I could not conscientiously do it without repeating anew, in the most positive form, its condemnation of those professional associations which are made the subject of criticism in the same paragraph. I enclose to you also a full copy of the letter in which the offensive paragraph occurred. It is one of a series of letters from a young man, in whose integrity and intelligence I have every reason to confide, and who, I am sure, had no personal motive to especially misrepresent you. It would evidently seem, however, that he had gathered his information and formed his judgment from those who are inimical to you.

I am, Sir,

Yours very truly,

SAMUEL BOWLES.

DAVID DUDLEY FIELD, Esq.,
New York City.

NEW YORK, *Dec.* 30, 1870.

DEAR SIR: Your letter of the 29th, in answer to mine of the 27th, was received this morning. The disavowal of any knowledge of the offensive letter, till after its publication, and the expression of your regret for its omissions, and of your mortification and indignation for some of its expressions, are very well; and if you had stopped there, I should have had nothing more to say. But when you add, that "as to the general judgmant concerning" my "professional association with notorious parties, with generally conceded corrupt schemes, and the effect of them upon" my "professional standing," you "should not have changed the character of the letter," and send me, be-

4

sides, a most offensive editorial paragraph previously published, saying of it that "the judgment would have been rendered earlier," and, you think, "made more condemnatory but for the long-time pleasant personal relations" between yourself and my family—when you add these expressions to your disclaimer—I am amazed and indignant.

Do you not mistake your own position as well as mine? What gives you, sitting in private and writing anonymously, authority to render "judgment" upon me? I am not disputing your right, as a collector of news, to publish any *facts* concerning anybody; but you have, certainly, no greater right to publish your *opinions* respecting the character or conduct of a private person, than you would have to publish them to his face in a private company; and you must know, that you would not have ventured to say what is contained in that paragraph to my face, in any company whatever. It seems to be imagined in some quarters, that as soon as one can get the control of types and write anonymously, he may publish whatever he pleases about whomsoever he will. For many of the conductors of the public press I have great respect, as for intelligent, cultivated, large-hearted men; but there are others, as you must know, who are "hostes humani generis," and who evidently fancy, that as soon as they can fill the columns of a newspaper, they may put off the character of gentlemen and take on that of ruffians. Such, I hope, is not your opinion; it certainly is not mine.

So much for your position; now for my own. You assail me for what you call my "professional association with notorious parties, with generally conceded corrupt schemes." Your meaning is cloudy, and I am not sure whether it be that I have a professional association with notorious parties who have "generally

5

conceded corrupt schemes," or a professional association with notorious parties and also "with generally conceded corrupt schemes." You may take whichever meaning you please. If the latter, I must ask you to state what "generally conceded corrupt schemes" I have a professional association with. If the former, then the complaint is of my "professional association with notorious parties," having "generally conceded corrupt schemes," by which I suppose you mean that I have a "professional association" with Messrs. Gould & Fisk, and that they have "generally conceded corrupt schemes." Now, I will not stop to argue with you whether they have "conceded" that they have corrupt schemes in view, or whether, without any concession on their part, it is true in point of fact that they have them. My place to discuss that question is in court, and not before you. But assuming, for the sake of the argument, that they have, I must ask you what you mean by "professional association." Is it giving them legal opinions and arguing cases for them in court? Or, is it something else? If it be something else, I must ask you what that something is, as I do not know. If it be only giving them legal opinions and arguing cases for them, all that I need say is, that I have done not only what I had a right, but what I was bound, to do. If, in giving an opinion, I have perverted or misunderstood the law, point out the instance, and I will admit myself wrong. If, in arguing a cause, I have suppressed evidence or misled the court, point out an instance of that also, and I will again admit myself wrong. I deny that I have done any one of these things, in any one instance. If you say I have, mention the instance, or admit yourself a false accuser.

You must remember that a lawyer, who is denied the shelter of his professional character, is necessarily put to great disadvantage. His communications with his clients are confidential. He cannot, in most cases, say what advice he has given, because he cannot disclose the information which his client has given him. In that respect his lips are sealed. But if I cannot tell you now what advice I have given, I am, I suppose, at liberty to tell you what I have not been consulted about; and, availing myself of this liberty, I say to you, that I have never been consulted beforehand about the management of the Erie Railway Company, or the issue of any of its stock or bonds, or the payment of any dividend to any stockholder or class of stockholders, or about what is known as the Erie Classification Bill, or about the gold operations of 1869, or any of the private transactions of Messrs. Gould & Fisk, or either of them, or about any transaction whatever of this company, or these gentlemen, to which, so far as I now recollect, any exception has been taken. If you think there is any defect in the comprehensiveness of this statement, you may question me to your heart's content. My son has shown me the copy of a letter which he wrote you after mine was sent, and which I should think would satisfy the most prejudiced person. But you must judge for yourself. I have no favor to ask, and can afford to wait.

The article in the Westminster *Review*, to which you refer, is, so far as I am concerned, a tissue of misrepresentations. It was written, doubtless, by an American, and, I think I could show, for sinister purposes. You should know that lawsuits of great magnitude are depending, which that article is well suited, and probably was designed, to affect. If these suits were pending in England, the publication of the article would, for that reason, be punishable as a contempt of court. Here, if a public opinion can be created which shall influence juries or judges to decide in favor of

7

those who write, or pay for, or inspire, this and the like articles, a great deal of money may be made. Do you understand this?

The storm of abuse that is poured upon me is really, however designed, an attack upon the independence of the Bar. Such abuse of an advocate is not a new thing in the world. They who hate a client fancy, in their folly, that, if they can frighten his advocate, they may destroy the client, not reflecting that they would thus weaken their own security. When Erskine, defending Thomas Paine, rose to address the jury, he said: "Every man within hearing at this moment, nay, the whole people of England, have been witnesses to the calumnious clamor that, by every art, has been raised against me. In every place where business or pleasure collects the public together, day after day, my name and character have been the topics of injurious reflection." "And for what," he asked; and thereupon replied, that it was due to the fact that he had not shrunk from the discharge of a duty, "which no personal advantages recommended, and which a thousand difficulties repelled." Then he boldly vindicated himself, saying, "I will forever, at all hazards, assert the dignity, independence, and integrity of the English Bar, without which impartial justice, the most valuable part of the English constitution, can have no existence." Do not mistake me by supposing that I am likening myself to Erskine, or my clients to Paine. I am stating a principle in better terms than I can state it myself. I am not insensible to the respect of my fellow-men, and, especially, of my fellow-members of the bar, who are in the main a noble but much calumniated body of men; but I value still more my own self-respect, and, if I were to be driven by clamor, or by any means whatver short of absolute force, to abandon my clients, I should lose my self-respect. That I will not do, be the consequences what they may. I am resolved that, so far as I am able to effect it, my clients shall be judged according to the law of the land. I shall, whenever I speak for them in the courts of the country, stand between them and popular clamor, just as I would stand between them and power, if they were menaced by power of any kind, monarchical or republican.

I have never cared for popularity. I have met many a scowl in my day ;—as when I defended the fugitive slave, or when I inveighed against arrests without legal warrant, under color of the war power, or when I denied the legality of test oaths, or argued against the constitutionality of the military governments in the South.

Do not imagine that, in fulfilling my duties as advocate, I mean in any manner to abet or justify what I think wrong. You, of all men in the world, ought not to think so. You know, or should know, that after your arrest, which, however provoked, I did not approve, I set myself to prevent a similar act in the future ; that I drew an amendment of the Code of Procedure to effect that object, and urged it upon the Legislature, and that, after having failed in my effort the first year, I renewed it the next, and finally got it as it now stands, in these words, appended to section 186 : "The defendant may give bail, whenever arrested, at any hour of the day or night, and shall have reasonable opportunity to procure it before being committed to prison."

After what has passed, you must judge for yourself whether you will publish any and what disclaimers. You may publish this correspondence if you please. I should think you would consider it fair to do so. If you do not, I shall think myself at liberty to publish

9

it, unless you object. And if, hereafter, you publish, in your own name or anonymously, anything else concerning me, I have to ask that you will send me a copy, and that you will give equal publicity to any reply I may make.

Very truly yours,

DAVID DUDLEY FIELD.

SAMUEL BOWLES, Esq.,

Editor of the Springfield Republican.

THE REPUBLICAN,

Springfield, Mass., January 3, 1871.

DEAR SIR: Of course I could not expect that my explanatory note of the 29th would satisfy you. Had it been possible, to my own sense of truth and justice, to have stopped short at the point that you say would have satisfied you, the imperious tone of your first note would have forbidden it. But I did not suppose that you would be surprised at my opinions. I have found them so common among gentlemen of all professions, and especially among gentlemen of the Bar in this State; they have been so often expressed in the independent press of the country, that I had supposed you were familiar with their popularity, and had ceased to be surprised, if not annoyed, by their utterance.

Of course I cannot accept the limitations which you put upon journalism. The gathering and publication of *facts* is but one part of its vocation. To express *opinions* is a higher and larger share of its duties. The conduct of public men, before the public, is the legitimate subject for their discussion. The lawyer before the court, as the minister in his pulpit, the executive in his chair of state, and the legislator in his hall of assembly—all these are alike public men, and their conduct in their public vocations, the proper theme of both journalistic report and discussion. Nor is such arraignment the province of the press alone. Without invading the sanctities of private character, or the courtesies of personal life, reason and the habits of civilization give to every man the right to arraign and discuss the public or professional conduct of his fellow-men. The politician on the stump discusses his fellow politicians. The minister in his pulpit summons his fellows for inconsistency, or unreason, or infidelity. So the lawyer arraigns his fellow lawyers in court, or in public gathering. And each, too, crosses the line of his own profession, and disputes the conduct of men of the other professions. There is no court more thoroughly established than this of public opinion, and no right more finally settled, or more largely improved, than this of the free discussion of the public and professional conduct of all our fellow-men; and I am surprised to find you disputing it. Thus, however mortifying and trying it may have been to yourself, there certainly was no invasion of the proprieties of private life, no outrage upon the decencies of the occasion, when, at a public gathering and entertainment of the Bar of your own native County of Berkshire, last week, a distinguished citizen of the county, now in public life, alluded to your professional conduct in the same spirit, if not in like terms, to those which in the *Republican* have aroused your "amazement" and provoked your "indignation."

You are more fortunate, I trust, in the statement of your own position. That, certainly, is entitled to every possible respect; and I have neither the disposition nor the power to criticise it in detail. I have "walked backward with averted eyes" through much of the history of your professional association with those no-

11

torious clients that have dragged down your professional fame. And I cannot measure the precise extent or character of the services you have rendered them. I can only say, my judgment has been formed from the general observation of your name in connection with their most desperate causes, and with some of the more extraordinary proceedings which have been had in their behalf in the New York Courts, as well as from the testimony of some of the local public journals and of prominent members of your local Bar, as, likewise, further, from gentlemen of your profession in this State, all of whom would, naturally, watch the details with greater closeness and discrimination than either my ability or inclination allowed. I am glad that you are able to satisfy yourself of the propriety of your conduct. I hope you may be able to satisfy your friends, your profession, and the public. But I must tell you frankly, that if you are right, they are widely and deeply wrong, and you are one of the most misunderstood and best abused men in the country.

It certainly will be a satisfaction to your personal friends to know that you were not associated, in advance, with those most notorious and audacious proceedings of your distinguished clients which you have catalogued. But may it not be said, that, while those proceedings were initiated and advanced to more or less of achievement without your knowledge, they had more or less of your ability, and of your services, in maintaining and defending them and their results, when disputed in the courts. Is there not such an offence, known to the laws as that of being accessory after the fact? And does it not often rise to a degree of responsibility and guilt, nearly or quite equal to that of the origination and execution?

The province of professional duty to causes and clients, is, I believe, an open question among lawyers themselves. Even the principles of it have never been stated to general acceptance, but it is much easier to agree upon a principle than to decide upon practice under it. Perhaps none would dispute the statement of Erskine. Certainly, posterity honors him for the defence of a man, who was arraigned for opinions on abstract questions. But your clients, for whom you have incurred deep responsibilities and dared professional dishonor, are no martyrs to opinions, and are not arraigned for a bold adherence to, and publication of, unpopular principles. Their offences are against the peace and integrity of business. They have achieved and hold possession of a railroad, by means little short of robbery itself. They have sought, for mere purposes of personal aggrandizement, to corrupt the very head of the nation. And they have, with like purposes in view, brought temporary disorder into the financial condition of the country, and spread ruin, with a wanton hand, among its people. It is in assisting or defending these men in such plans, and in such operations, in borrowing the forms and technicalities of law to sustain them in their position, or to screen them from justice ; it is in lending your great ability and your legal knowledge either to the concoction or the defence of gross schemes of stock speculation, or railroad and business aggrandizement, at the expense of innocent parties and the public ; it is in interposing yourself and your professional services between men whom the nation supposes rightly or wrongly, aye, *believes*, with a faith that cannot be readily shaken, are men of public corruption, and men of business dishonor ; between such men and their dispossession of their ill-gotton gains and powers, and the relief of the business of the country from their paralyzing control and corrupting example ; it is for acts and influences like these that you have been

13

arraigned before the public, and that not only professional, but popular, opinion sits in judgment upon you.

I beg you, as one who has long honored your family, who takes pride in its association with his own part of Massachusetts, and in the distinguished services of its members to education and religion, to commerce and to civilization in every form; as one who has had a pride in your own professional attainments, and your own wide reputation, to make haste and do what is still possible to retrieve your character from these suspicions and these judgments. If they are all false, it is quite time that the public mind was disabused. If there is any degree of truth in them, let it be reduced to the lowest possible element.

I did not dream, in writing my first letter, that there would ever be any call or motive for the publication of our correspondence, or, indeed, for its continuance beyond that. But I am quite willing, if you desire it, that any or all of my letters shall be published in connection with your own. I do not care to appear before the public as the personal champion of a cause which I am so inadequate to represent; and I would, therefore, prefer to leave with you the responsibility of any publication. At the same time, in view of your demand, I may conclude it is my duty, as I retain the right on my own responsibility, to publish the entire correspondence.

I am, sir, yours, very truly,

SAM'L BOWLES.

DAVID DUDLEY FIELD, Esq., New York.

NEW YORK, *January* 5, 1871.

DEAR SIR: Your letter of the 3d inst., received this

14

morning, seems to have been written for publication, and is filled with as much general disparagement as could well be got into so many pages, without stating a single fact, from which lawyer or moralist could form an opinion, except the fact that the clients to whom you refer are, as you say, bad men. To give this as a reason for not defending them is equivalent to saying that the saints must have a monopoly of lawsuits. If a saint sues a sinner, the sinner shall not be defended. If it should happen that a saint wrongs a sinner, the sinner cannot sue the saint. This is putting your case in a more palpable form than has occurred to you, perhaps, but I think it is essentially your position. Were you, however, to change it, and say that you make no question of *parties*, but of *causes*, and that a lawyer should never engage on the wrong side of a cause, I must ask you what is to be taken beforehand as the test of wrong. If the lawyer were omniscient and the judge infallible, if all the facts on both sides and all the law could be known from the beginning, then, indeed, the lawyer would be justified in saying to a client, I will not assist you. But in the present condition of humanity, facts are often misunderstood, the law often mistaken, and one Court frequently pronounces right what another Court has pronounced wrong. In this state of things, I know no better general rule than this: that the lawyer, being intrusted by Government with the exclusive function of representing litigants before the Courts, is bound to represent any person who has any *rights* to be asserted or defended. If a person has no rights, the lawyer is not bound to assist. If he has any rights, the lawyer is bound to see them respected if he can. Let me apply this rule to your case and that of my clients. You were guilty of a gross libel on one of them, for which you should have been severely punished. Was it un-

15

lawful for a lawyer to defend you? Suppose them, on the other hand, to be guilty of all the wrongs you charge them with, have they still no rights? If a ruffian beats one of them in the streets, may he be sued for it? If he utter a falsehood concerning them, may he be prosecuted? Or suppose one who has a spite against them to buy a share or two of stock in the Erie Railway Company, for the purpose of harassing them with a lawsuit, is it lawful to defend them against such a suit? Or suppose a speculator, who has sold stock on time, to bring a suit, for the purpose of affecting the price, may such a suit be resisted? Or suppose an enemy, unwilling to take the responsibility himself, puts forward a third person, to bring suits against them, and keep them in continued litigation, for the gratification of revenge, are these suits to go on without resistance? Or suppose them to have enough of the stock of a corporation to give them the majority at an election, and the managers to manufacture secretly new stock to overcome their majority, using the property of the Company to pay for it, and making away with the books to complete the secrecy, must the wrong be acquiesced in, and redress by the Courts given up? Or suppose still further, that actions are brought against them for damages on alleged sales of gold, which they say they never bought, is it unprofessional to put in their answers and try the causes for them? These are not imaginary cases. They are mostly real cases, for engaging in which I am assailed. And you, smarting under a sense of personal grievance, look on with distorted vision, and applaud the assault.

Let us look at the question from another point of view. It is lawful to advocate what it is lawful to do. Would you have a judge decide against these men, because he thinks them of bad repute, or of bad lives, or of evil example? What would you think of him if, in pronouncing judgment, he were to say, I do not think the proof sustains the charges of this complaint, but the defendants are outraging decency and corrupting justice, and I shall decide against them? Nay, suppose you were a juror, trying one of the suits for damages on alleged gold contracts, would you violate your oath and find a verdict against them, contrary to the evidence, because they "have sought, for mere purposes of personal aggrandizement, to corrupt the very head of the nation," or because "they have, with like purposes in view, brought temporary disorder into the financial condition of the country, and spread ruin, with a wanton hand, among its people"? Of course, you answer that you are not a knave, or a dog, that you should do this thing. But how, in the name of all that is reasonable, are you to be informed of the real case before you, if nobody may explain it to you? How is the evidence to be forthcoming, if they cannot have the aid of the law in obtaining it? How are they to get the facts fairly before you, if they are denied the privilege of counsel?

You should not answer me like a sentimental school girl, by talking about walking "backward with averted eyes," or by uttering the politician's slang about my being "one of the most misunderstood and best abused men in the country," as if that had anything to do with the question between us; but you should have given me facts and reasons. Instead of doing so, you have dealt me a volume of vituperation. Let me tell you, that you had better at once confess yourself wrong, and accept the theory, that the lawyer is responsible, not for his clients, nor for their causes, but for the manner in which he conducts their causes. Here I admit the fullest responsibility. I do not assent to the theory of Brougham, that the lawyer should know nobody but his client. I insist that he should defend his client *per fas* and not *per nefas*. By this rule I am willing to be judged. That was the point of my letter to which you have given no answer, but the general one, just mentioned. You can not escape in this way. You have ventured to arraign my professional conduct. I repel your charge, and challenge you to specify an instance. You fail to specify any; but say, public opinion is against me. That may be so or it may not be so. I will not stop to discuss the question with you. You do not advance a step by declaring, never so confidently, that you think so or say so, because somebody else, or all men else if you please, think so or say so. That will not do; you must go farther or submit to be branded as a libeller.

I need scarcely say more. My views of your rights and duties as the conductor of a newspaper have been already set forth, and I need not reiterate them. The Berkshire entertainment I never heard of before, and shall say nothing about till I can learn what was said and who said it. I will not stop to comment upon your inconsistency. You applaud Erskine. Yet he defended a man who was believed by nearly the whole people of England to be undermining the foundations of all religion and all morality, aiming to subvert the throne, and blot out the name of God. All that Messrs. Gould & Fisk are charged with is as nothing, in quality or in consequence, compared with what he was charged with. His advocate was denounced, hunted, dismissed from office, for defending him. Now you say "posterity honors him for the defence."

The prevalence or unanimity even of public opinion is quite foreign to our controversy. I should hope that you are mistaken; but whether reproached or not, I am confident that I have not deserved reproach.

18

Perhaps my knowledge of professional opinion is as good as yours. I have certainly one test of it that you have not, and that is the experience of the Erie office. In answer to my inquiries made to-day, I am informed that within the last three years the present managers of the Company have employed many lawyers of the highest repute in New York, New Jersey, Pennsylvania, Ohio, Illinois, Missouri, and even Massachusetts, and that not in a single instance has a retainer been refused. I do not believe there is a lawyer in the United States who would to-day refuse it. In nearly every litigation in which I have been concerned for them, I have been associated with the most respectable and eminent counsel. Indeed, in almost the only *bona fide* suit ever brought against the present managers, for most of the rest have been what I should call fillibustering expeditions, the defence is conducted with the counsel and co-operation of the foremost lawyer, not only of Massachusetts, but of all New England.

In conclusion, I have to say that I have discussed these questions on your own assumption, that my clients are all that you charge them to be. It should seem scarcely necessary to add, that the assumption is taken only for the sake of the argument. If they are justly chargeable with what is alleged against them, that will be made known when the cases are tried, and then, as at all times, I shall hope to act, as I think I have hitherto acted, according to the best lights I have, the part of an upright lawyer and honest citizen.

Your ob't serv't,

DAVID DUDLEY FIELD.

SAMUEL BOWLES, Esq.

19

THE REPUBLICAN,
Springfield, Mass., Jan. 10, 1871.

MY DEAR SIR: I have read with profound attention yours of the 5th, received yesterday, in the hope to find some reason for the modification of my judgment in the matter between us, even if not "to confess myself wrong." But I am utterly unable to do so. I am only impressed with the fact that you believe yourself right, and that you are acting sincerely, if not intelligently. But the grounds of your action, as of your defence, seem to me purely technical and altogether narrow. They do not reach the question, as it lies in my mind, and as it presents itself to the mind of the great public. It is not a question of law, nor even of abstract individual right, but of broad public morality. You have sinned against no statute; I will not undertake to say, even, that you have violated any prescript of the Code professional. Within those lines, you are wiser than I, and I shall not follow you. But that you have offended the moral sense of the public, that is what I insist upon; that is what, in my duty as a journalist, I have proclaimed to the public. If I am wrong, it is simply in reading wrongly the public judgment, in transcribing incorrectly its verdict. Time, and the developments of public testimony, will judge between us here.

Thus I dismiss the most of your argument, as purely technical, and not pertinent to my view of the subject. Still, let me say that your assumption that your clients are not to suffer for their bad character, is neither good law nor good sense. Hardly a cause is tried, where the character of the parties for good or bad is not an element in the argument of the Counsel, in the opinion of the Judge, and in the conclusion of the Jury. It should, if it does not, go back to the assumption of the case by the Counsel. A man *should* suffer for his bad character, as he should gain for his good character; and nothing more convinces me of the perverted views which you take of your conduct and of the province of your professional duty, than your more than ignoring this consideration, your denial of it.

You traverse, almost insultingly, let me say, the grounds you assume for yourself and your clients, when you charge me with a "gross libel" upon one of them, as when, also, you accuse me of being actuated by a "personal grievance" in the judgment I have rendered upon them and yourself, as in both suggestions, you illustrate anew that perversion of the moral sense, that seems to me, more than anything else, to have led you into your present unfortunate position. I was quite willing, certainly, to leave even to a New York Court the question whether I had grossly libelled your client. And as certainly, if either he or you has ever inflicted "a personal grievance" upon me, I am not aware of it. He essayed one, indeed, but did not get beyond a temporary personal annoyance. If anybody is "smarting" under that transaction, it certainly is not myself.

The only "personal grievance" that I can admit in the matter is, that which I share with the great body of the community, a grievance which every citizen *should* feel, and which most citizens *do* feel, at the success of the attacks of your clients upon the moral order of society and of business. It is under this grievance that I have written and published. It is a grievance with which you must be coupled, because of the aid you have rendered them in their conspiracies,—because of the success with which you have been able to crown them,—because of the higher character which you have dragged down, in your undiscriminating, though zealous, labors in their behalf.

21

Do not deceive yourself, my dear sir; history may be relied upon to defend freedom of opinion and to avenge its martyrs, but it will never put James Fisk, Jun., by the side of Thomas Paine, nor, for daring and losing for his cause, will it put David Dudley Field on a page parallel to that belonging to Erskine.

If I seemed to write as if for publication, in my last letter, it was because you set me the example, and openly challenged me to the types. But I await still your final desire as to the publication of this correspondence; and also your wish as to such publication, including the letters that have passed between your son and myself.

I know very well it is impossible to disassociate personal feeling wholly from such discussion of public or professional conduct, as you and I have engaged in; but I wish you to try to believe, at least, that this judgment of mine in the Republican, and in this correspondence, is, as far as possible, removed from all personal unfriendliness to yourself, and to your family, and is not inspired by any personal provocation, but is born strictly of my deepest convictions of duty as a journalist and a citizen.

I am yours, very truly,

SAMUEL BOWLES.

DAVID DUDLEY FIELD, ESQ.,
New York.

NEW YORK January 12, 1871.

DEAR SIR: Your letter of the 10th, just received, makes no progress whatever towards the support of your previous positions. In one respect it recedes from them, in so far as it admits that I am "acting sincerely if not intelligently." When you have got so far, I should think it would not be difficult for you to get further. Indeed I am quite confident, that if instead of attacking me publicly, you had written me a line, or, what would have been better, had sat down with me for an hour, I could have satisfied you that I was acting "intelligently."

This, however, is of no importance now. I am quite willing to leave to time the formation of a just public opinion. When that time comes, it will be known, that, whatever may be the faults of the clients, their Counsel, or that one of them for whom I speak with knowledge, has been governed by nothing but a sense of duty. You may well suppose, that the litigation has not been in any respect to my taste. Besides, I have been for five years, as you may chance to know, seeking to retire from active practice. Nothing but a profound conviction, that I could not with honor retire from these suits, has kept me in them. Being in them, I shall do my whole duty to my clients. I have not knowingly defended them in a single wrongful act. I am assured by them, in the most solemn manner (thus much I am permitted to say), that they have never appropriated to their own use one dollar's worth of the Erie Company's property.

Our correspondence, up to your last letter and this reply, I have had put into type and sent to a few friends, under injunction not at present to make any public use of it. A copy is sent you by to-day's post. I will add these two letters, and the correspondence between you and my son to the same pamphlet. This I will distribute among my friends, and I will send you fifty copies for yours; but I will not publish it in the newspapers, without giving you due notice.

Yours truly,

DAVID DUDLEY FIELD.

Samuel Bowles, Esq.

APPENDIX.

---

4 PINE ST., NEW YORK, *Dec. 27th*, 1870.

SIR: I am not personally acquainted with you, but I once put myself to serious inconvenience to do you a favor. When you were arrested here, and lodged in Ludlow-street jail, you wrote to my father, Mr. David Dudley Field, begging him to use his influence to get you released. We had nothing whatever to do with the suit against you, and did not know anything of it, but, at my father's request, I set off to see Mr. Fisk and intercede for your discharge. He was out, and I took a carriage and drove from place to place where I thought I might find him, continuing for hours, until I finally found him at one o'clock at night. I then insisted upon his consenting to your immediate release, telling him that I would myself become your bondsman, and that if he would give me a written assent and the address of the lawyer who brought the suit, I would go myself, late as it was, and get you out of jail. Mr. Fisk had been a client of mine for years, and I resented his refusal to take my advice in this instance. He was very indignant at your having published a statement about his father's lunacy, and was much displeased at my undertaking to interfere at all. The next morning early, I went with my uncle, Mr. Cyrus W. Field, to the Sheriff's office, and he became one of your bondsmen. Neither my father nor I ever receive

24

a word of thanks from you, and we do not want any. On the contrary, having done you one favor at your solicitation, I propose to do you another unsolicited, viz.: to give you an opportunity to make reparation for an attack upon my father in your newspaper.

Somebody connected with the New York *Times* has a spite against our firm, and almost every day some malicious and lying article appears about some of us. When this began, some years ago, we attempted to answer, but they altered our reply, and each lie refuted enabled them to answer with a new one; so we have since paid no attention to them.

Not satisfied with attacking us in their editorial columns, they take a malicious pleasure in digging out anything against us in other papers. Yesterday I was surprised to find in its columns what purports to be an extract from the correspondence of the Springfield *Republican*, as follows:

" *Correspondence of the Springfield Republican.*

" David Dudley Field, though hardly old enough to be called a veteran, is one of the ablest lawyers in New York, and has by far the largest practice. His receipts as counsel for the Erie Railway Company alone are understood to have exceeded $200,000 in a single year, and his regular income is enormous. His connection with Fisk and Gould secures him the favor of Barnard and other Ring Judges, though it has destroyed his reputation as a high-toned lawyer with the public; while the Bar always disliked him for his avarice and his meanness. David Dudley Field is a strong free-trade advocate, and often presides at the meetings of the Reform Club. He is an authority on international law, and was also the chief codifier of the present Code of Procedure of the State of New York. His reputation as a lawyer is based upon his knowledge of legal technicality, and once during a legal controversy with the late James T. Brady, the latter dubbed him 'the king of the pettifoggers,' which title has stuck to Field ever since."

Now the firm of Field & Shearman consists of three persons, myself, T. G. Shearman, and John W. Sterling, my father being counsel connected with us. He

25

has had a large practice for many years, and since I have been with him, which is 18 years, we have probably had as much legal business as any other office in New York, and we have been fairly remunerated for it. The Erie Railway Company has much litigation and many different lawyers. Some—a small proportion—of their suits are sent to us, and we are paid by it as by other clients. Neither my father nor the firm ever had $200,000 from the Erie Railway Company in one year, nor any sum in any manner approaching it.

We are not bound to tell you or the public the exact sum that we receive, but we endeavor to get fees proportionate to the labor in each case, and if our clients do not complain, I do not perceive who else can. However, if, when you are in New York, you will call at our office, I will give you a list of the services performed and the fees received by ourselves and other lawyers who have been employed from time to time by Mr. Fisk, Mr. Gould, or the Erie Railway, and leave you to judge of the adequacy of the compensation of each.

As to my father's regular income, it is derived from professional services to many clients, from mortgages, rents and the investments of a life-time. Last year and year before his sworn returns to the Internal Revenue Assessor were about $75,000.

So much for the first statement.

The second is that my father's connection "with Fisk and Gould secures him the favor of Barnard and other ring judges" He has no "connection" with Fisk and Gould beyond being retained by them in lawsuits. Within the past three years, at various times, the following New York lawyers, among others, have also been retained by the same persons, or by the Erie Railway Company: William M. Evarts, Edwin W. Stoughton, James T. Brady, Samuel J. Tilden, Aaron J. Vanderpoel, Dorman B. Eaton.

26

William Fullerton, John E. Burrill, John K. Porter, Hamilton W. Robinson, Joseph S. Bosworth, F. J. Fithian, and Clarence A. Seward, and any one of them has as much influence with any and every Judge as we have. I defy any body to point to a single instance where we have exercised any influence upon, or received any favor or any order from any Judge which we had not a right to consider justified by the law and the facts.

The communication further states that "the bar always disliked" my father "for his avarice and meanness." Now, my father is the principal author of the New York Code, which was for a long time very unpopular with the bar. He has been prominent as a lawyer, free-soiler, and free-trader, and public speaker for many years, and, naturally, has many enemies, but if there is a single member of our bar who has given away as much in public and private charity, during his life, he is unknown to me. As but one example of this, I may take an institution near you, and well known to you, Williams College, to which he has given above $30,000. I could cite many other instances, and could bring many a poor family as witnesses to the truth of my assertion, but my object is not to eulogize my father, but to defend him from aspersions.

Your article winds up with stating that "James T. Brady dubbed him the king of pettifoggers, which title has stuck to Field ever since." Mr. Brady was a personal friend of mine, and, during the latter part of his life, a friend also of my father. They, at one time, were engaged in a great legal contest, where both combatants used warm language, but Mr. Brady never gave him any such title in my hearing, and I am sure I was present during the entire controversy.

I have exposed four untruths in an article of 23 lines,

27

the whole of which is evidently dictated by malice. You can best judge whether one who knows personally of what he is talking, or a newspaper correspondence, who gives no authority and can have no personal knowledge on the subject, is most worthy of credence. The attacks in the *Times* are curiosities in their way. One article asserts that our excuse for taking a retainer from Mr. Fisk is, that we are legally bound to take *all* retainers. The Indianapolis *Journal*, an extract from which is published in the *Times* just above the extract from your paper, refutes this supposed proposition of ours with great force and fury. The truth is, that we never did make any such proposition, or defend ourselves at all. The *Journal* says in effect: Mr. Field says black is white—black is not white—therefore Mr. Field is a liar; a beautiful syllogism, and quite true, supposing Mr. Field *did* say black was white. But suppose he did *not* say so, who is the liar then? The *Times* has another article, in which it says the case would have been quite different if Mr. Fisk had been a client of Mr. Field before he became so widely known, but that he retained Mr. Field after he became notorious, &c., &c. On this text it preaches a sermon of a column. The truth is that Mr. Fisk became a client of mine years ago, when my father was in Europe, and has since continued to send more or less suits to our office. The Indianapolis *Journal* aforesaid says, 1st, we "have accepted a general retainer from James Fisk." We have not. 2d, we, "in other words, have agreed in advance for a stipulated sum to advocate all of his schemes, and defend all his villainies," &c. This is also untrue. In fact, if we were to copy all the false accusations, all inspired by the *Times*, or taken from its pages, and refute them one by one, we should have to make that our sole business. So I will go no further.

28

But I am addressing a respectable man, a man who knows, or ought to know, what the standing and position of both my father and myself is—a man who, even if he is indifferent to what wounds he inflicts upon people in general, is certainly under an obligation to me, and I want to ask you if you consider a respectable paper justified in inserting, without inquiry as to its truth, such an article as this in your correspondence, and whether you always publish any charge, no matter how vile and malevolent, from anybody against anybody. Many of the newspapers are getting to be public nuisances, and I should be sorry to have that tendency spread to old Massachusetts, which prides herself on her respectability.

I remain, sir,

Your ob't serv't,

DUDLEY FIELD.

SAMUEL BOWLES, Esq.,
Springfield, Mass.

THE REPUBLICAN,
Springfield, Mass., Dec. 29, 1870.

DEAR SIR : My letter to your father, in reply to a note from him, answers, in large part, your own letter, and I beg to refer you to it. But there are other points in your letter that seem to call for some explanation or comment. I never was aware, until a few weeks ago, from an incidental conversation with your relative, and my friend, Mr. Ashburner, of your prompt, but unavailing, efforts to relieve me from Ludlow street, for the sake of my wife ; and I then determined to take the first opportunity to express to you my grateful sense of your kindness. Let me now render to you my thanks, and say that I fully appreciate your kind

29

ness, and shall not be likely to forget it. I never for one moment believed that any "Field" had aught to do with with the trick of putting me in jail. I applied to your father, as to Mr. Seward, for relief, solely for my wife's sake—so stating it in my notes, which, by the way, your distinguished client had made it impossible, so far as he could, that I should send out that night. For myself, since the disagreeable notoriety of the arrest and imprisonment were unavoidable, I cared nothing. My sense of humor, and my love of experience, amply sustained me through the prospect of the night in jail. But my wife was in a peculiarly delicate condition of health, and very nervous ; and for her sake I did wish to be relieved. I never had any reply to the note to your father, and did not know what was done in response to it, until, as I have said, Mr. Ashburner told me. Mr. Cyrus W. Field sent me word, after I returned home, that your father was ignorant of the suit, and did what he could, after my note was received, to relieve me, but what this was, was not stated. When the suit first appeared in Court, after the jail experience, on an incidental preliminary motion, my friend and attorney, Mr. Bliss, was met by your father as the representative of the plaintiff ; and the suit, I believe, though not originating in your office, was transferred at once to your care. Soon after this, I had a note from Mr. Henry M. Field, in which; alluding to his brother Cyrus's indignation at my treatment, and saying that it was fired, in part, by the fear that his brother might, at least, have known something of it in advance, if he did not participate in it, he renewed the assurance that I had previously had verbally, of the innocence of your father in the premises ; adding, I believe, that he shared the feeling of the family on the subject. I replied to this, that I had never for a moment doubted your father's ignorance of

30

the imprisonment transaction ; and never held him, or his office, in any way accountable for it ; but I felt bound to add that, considering the incipient circumstances of the suit, I was surprised that he had afterwards consented to associate himself with it ; and that I had only one wish in regard to the whole matter, which was, that it should be either left to the blackguards who began it, or been managed by gentlemen from the beginning. All this is not exactly pertinent, perhaps, but after your generous share in efforts to release me, I think it is due to you and I that I should make this full explanation. The history of the transaction certainly never left with me anything but the kindest personal feeling towards all the Field family. I never had any other relations with them, and I never dreamed of having, or wished to have.

On the professional point, however, involved in the conspicuous relations of your father with Fisk and Gould and their desperate measures, I believe the feeling expressed by the New York "*Times*," and finding utterance in the "*Republican*," is almost a universal one; at any rate, I share it very decidedly, and the *Republican* would long ago have given most decided and sharp expression to it, but for my personal relations with your family, and the thought that its judgment might be associated in the public mind with some supposed grievances connected with the Fisk suit. The right or wrong of this feeling need not be discussed between you and I. It is a very large question, and I well understand that there is something to be said on the other side, but the *Republican* had long ago maintained, and applied to cases in Massachusetts, the doctrine that a lawyer was responsible, in a decided degree, for the character of his clients and the character of the suits which he undertook in their behalf. I believe no professional conduct is more open to criticism, in this respect, than that of your father's. If he is no more guilty than other prominent gentlemen of the New York Bar, so much the worse for the New York Bar. But, whether correctly or not, the public identify your father especially with the more desperate and notorious causes of your distinguished Erie clients, and are disposed, it would seem, to concentrate upon him a responsibility which perhaps should be shared, in some degree, by others. I say all this with obvious frankness, yet with the kindest feelings towards yourself and your father, and with no disposition to be drawn either into a public or private controversy in regard to the question involved. I could hardly say less, indeed, and make a proper answer to your letter.

The closing judgment of your letter concerning the tendency of newspapers to be public nuisances, and the contagion of the disease in this quarter, I can but think carelessly uttered. It, certainly, was unnecessary, and I forbear to enter upon the responses which it naturally provokes. I beg you to believe, sir, that I remain, yours, very truly and very gratefully,

SAMUEL BOWLES.

DUDLEY FIELD, Esq.,
No. 4 Pine street, New York.

P. S.—Pardon me, if I yield unfairly to the temptation to say that I don't think I ever thought a harsher judgment in all this matter than the one reported to me as from your lips, the very evening of the memorable Ludlow street, to wit: that you told your father that "it was a disgrace to the family to have such a client as Fisk."

4 PINE STREET, NEW YORK,
January 9th, 1871.

DEAR SIR: I am in receipt of your letter dated the

32

29th, in answer to mine of the 27th ult., and have been prevented by illness from sending an earlier reply. I think, with all respect, that if you had written such a letter as mine to those gentlemen whom you term my "distinguished clients," and they had returned such an answer as yours, the "*Republican*' would have pronounced the answer evasive, to say the least.

I took the pains to explain to you our relations with certain clients, and to point out four distinct mistatements in twenty-three lines of your paper. Your main answer is, that you refer me to a letter to my father, written by you to him on the same subject; and on reference to that I find that you "*regret*" certain matters that were stated in that article, but insist on your opinions in regard to his professional conduct in the Erie suits. You do not draw my attention (nor his, in yonr letter to him,) to any disavowal in the columns of the *Republican*, of what you do not deny to be false assertions, nor to any public expression of that "regret" that you seem privately to feel, but intimate that you are willing to correct a part of your misstatements, provided you couple with your correction further abuse. Is that quite fair and manly?

The rest of your letter amounts to this:

First. That you acknowledge my efforts to obtain your release from jail. We will pass that over, since you are unwilling to accord simple justice to those who exerted themselves in your behalf.

Second. That we afterwards acted in the libel suit brought by Mr. Fisk against you. I believe yon are mistaken in this, but I assure you I should most cheerfully have taken charge of that suit, and have carried in on to the extremity of the law. As the facts appeared, your paper had been guilty of a most gross attack on Mr. Fisk's family. Had you confined yourself to abuse of Mr. Fisk, you might shield yourself under the pretence of a high professional duty ; but you went further, and stated that his father was a lunatic. There was no excuse whatever for this. It was deliberately intended to wound and annoy him, and the author of the statement, whether it be true or false, deserves the censure of all honorable men. When I interceded for your release, Mr. Fisk asked me what remedy he had. I answered, "The only remedy known to the law is an action for libel. Your suit is well enough ; all that I object to is the time and manner of the arrest. I only want this man released till to-morrow morning, to enable him to give bail." Now, I considered, and still consider, Mr. Fisk's *suit* against you as not alone proper, but meritorious. Under the old English system, libels were so severely punished as to amount to a censorship of the Press, and, in fact, a suppression of free opinion. In our eagerness to correct this evil, we have fallen into the opposite extreme, and as our laws are now administered, actions for libels are but a farce. Still, such an action is the only *legal* redress that can be obtained. In certain parts of this country an editor was formerly constantly liable to be cowhided, shot in the street, or called out to fight a duel ; and there are States where public opinion even now sanctions that mode of punishing a libel. But here, where we at least pretend to enforce the laws, I consider a lawyer justified in advising a suit, to the exclusion of the more barbarous though more efficacious remedy.

Third. That you heard "I told my father that it was a disgrace to the family to have such a client as Fisk." I have never said or intimated anything of the kind to him or any one else.

Fourth. That (in your own words) "In the professional point, however, involved in the conspicuous relations of your father with Fisk and Gould, &c., I be-

34

lieve the feeling expressed by the New York *Times*, and finding utterance in the *Republican*, is almost a universal one, and at any rate I share it very decidedly, and the *Republican* would long ago have given much decided and sharp expression to it, but for my personal relations with your family, and the thought that its judgment might be associated in the public mind with some supposed grievance connected with the Fisk suit."

You do not state what my father's "conspicuous relations with Messrs. Fisk & Gould" are. I have explained to you that those relations are the same as exist between any lawyer and his client. If you knew of any other, I should like to have heard what they were; but you evade this, and talk of the "conspicuous relations," and of "universal feelings." You forget that I did not invite you to a discussion of universal feelings, but gave you an opportunity to correct an outrageous attack in your paper, which you still leave uncorrected. It will not do to shield yourself behind the *Times*; you should have before you *facts* that will justify the statements in *your* paper. You claim credit for not having attacked my father more sharply, owing to your personal relations. Are not those positions a little inconsistent? If, indeed, you are so far above other men as to have a right, and, in fact, to have imposed on you the duty of criticising and proclaiming to the public their private character, should you allow personal feelings toward another to stand in the way of that high duty, and should you allow fear of what the public might think of *you*, to deter you? No, the only possible defence for such criticisims is that they are prompted by the highest motives; and if they are, the critic should not allow personal feelings, much less fear of criticism on *himself*, to deter him.

35

Fifth. That "the right or wrong of the feeling need not be discussed between you and *I.*" That is to say: "I, Samuel Bowles, the responsible editor of a paper, have accused F. of certain things. I am told they are gross and malicious falsehoods, and am furnished with the evidence to that effect, and am asked to withdraw them. My answer is that *I do not care to discuss the matter.* I think the public believe them." The criminal in the dock would much prefer not to discuss the matter of the watch that he stole, but we do not expect a gentleman accused of misstatement to take refuge in this way.

Sixth. That the *Republican* has long ago maintained and applied to cases in Massachusetts, the doctrine that a lawyer was responsible in a decided degree for the character of his clients, and the character of the suits which he undertook in their behalf.

My letter was not to the *Republican*, but to you, and as you are its editor, I am justified in assuming your meaning to be that you maintain that doctrine. Put in that light, it has at least the merit of frankness, except as to the words "decided degree." These words are ambiguous, and as what is the extent of a degree, and especially of a "decided degree," can hardly be determined, it is no more than fair to state the proposition thus: "A lawyer is responsible for the character of his clients." Shades of Webster, Choate, and the numberless great Massachusetts advocates, that have passed away, defend us! Most of those men whom Massachusetts delighted to honor, defended and prosecuted at divers times divers men accused of crime. When they represented the accused, and he was found guilty did they share his guilt? When they represented the prosecution and the accused was acquitted, did they share in the guilt of a wrongful prosecution?

In almost all criminal prosecutions, there is a right

36

and a wrong. In a large proportion of civil suits, there is also an absolute moral right and wrong. Where the right rests is determined by a jury, and upon your doctrine their verdict determines the moral character of the counsel for the defeated party.

Now, as in almost all cases, there are two lawyers, and as in all cases where the jury does not disagree, there is a verdict one way or the other; and as every lawyer of any considerable practice loses and wins a number of cases each year, it follows that all lawyers must necessarily be wicked men. We have a traditional joke in our profession of a client who instantly discharged his lawyer, because he saw him conversing with the lawyer on the other side. He hated his adversary, of course. He hated his adversary's lawyer, because he was (in his mind) identified with his adversary, and the idea of friendly intercourse between *his* lawyer and *that* lawyer was too much for him to bear. I did not think to see the joke ever actually adopted as truth. It is true that there is a class of people who consider all lawyers thieves. These same people generally call physicians murderers, and clergymen imposters, and probably nine-tenths of them believe all that they read in the newspapers. I supposed few educated persons like yourself belonged to this class. Upon this monstrous doctrine, a surgeon should refuse to set a broken limb till he got a certificate of the good moral character of his patient; a clergyman should refuse to preachor minister to the low and debased, and a newspaper editor should restrict the sale of his paper to the most respectable families; if a lawyer on A's behalf brings an action against B on a promissory note, and A has been guilty of bigamy, the lawyer should go to the State prison; or, to put it in the most favorable terms for your theory, if on the trial B proves that the note was procured by fraud, and

37

defeats A, the lawyer is as guilty as A, because "he is responsible for the character of his client, and for the character of the suits he undertakes on his behalf!"

Seventh.—You end by excepting to my observation that the tendency of newspapers is to become public nuisances, and suggest that it may provoke "*responses.*" I did not say so. I said that *many* of the newspapers are tending in that direction; and whenever an editor of a newspaper (being shown that he has inadvertently or otherwise allowed his columns to be the medium of undeserved abuse) does not hasten publicly to rectify his error, but contents himself with evasive letters expressing private regret, I think *that* man's newspaper *is* a public and private nuisance. As to "provoking responses" to this part of my letter, I may excite your surprise when I say that the threat does not alarm me at all. I concede beforehand, if you will, that in assailing others with your pen, you can surpass any man not a professional newspaper writer. Now that you have not done what I supposed you would do, I am indifferent to any course you may choose to take The only "response" that I intended to "provoke" was either an immediate public statement that you had erred, with an expression of regret, or an equally public reiteration of your charges, coupled with the *facts* (not derived from hearsay or from other papers, but) from named reliable sources, with place, date and circumstance. That is what most gentlemen would do, if called to account for some statement about another made privately by them. Why should an editor of a newspaper conduct his sheet on a different principle from that adopted by himself or any respectable man managing his social relations with other men? Why is there this extraordinary dread on the part of editors of making in public an apology, which in private would be considered

38

manly and honorable? I shall not assume to "sit in judgment," as you term it, on newspaper editors. I will only say that I deny their right to allow their papers to abuse anybody at the instance of anybody.

Your obedient servant,

DUDLEY FIELD.

SAMUEL BOWLES, Esq.,
Springfield Republican,
Springfield, *Mass.*

New York, *January* 12, 1871.

MY DEAR BROTHER: Lord Borthwick's letter, which you sent me last evening, is perhaps sufficiently answered by the correspondence I have already had with Mr. Samuel Bowles, and of which I beg you will send him a copy. But I will add a few observations:

I. The New York *Times*, under its present management, is a paper of no authority. It is, in fact, a worthless and insignificant newspaper. When Mr. Raymond had charge of it, there was force in its columns. After his death, Mr. Bigelow took charge for a while, but he seems to have left it in disgust. And now it is trying to save its declining fortunes by sensational personal abuse. It is daily filled with attacks upon the best men we have; denouncing Mr. Astor, Mr. Taylor, Mr. Roberts, and others, in the coarsest language. These gentlemen take no notice of the articles, and nobody thinks any the worse of them for anything that is published. When I was first attacked, I asked two gentlemen in the front rank of our journalists, whether I should take any notice of the *Times*, and they answered no. Every friend who has been spoken with on the subject has given me the same advice. English gentlemen do not understand the difference

39

between journalism here and in England, owing to the fact that, practically, we have no adequate means of punishing libels. The law is powerless to repress or punish the audacious assaults upon private character, which a portion of our press indulges in. The consequence is, that persons assailed repose upon their characters, and let the libellers keep on. This is certainly deplorable, for two reasons; one, that the right of reputation is unprotected, and the other that what should be the wholesome restraint of the press upon bad men, is lost, because there is so little discrimination between the bad and the good. All are assailed alike, by anonymous and irresponsible accusers.

II. I wish there had been some specifications under the general expression, about "the scandal and offence against all public and private morality, in the manner in which the robbery has been carried through, by aid of the law Courts." By the "robbery" is meant, I suppose, one of three things: either;

1. The taking and holding of the offices of Directors of the Erie Railway Company; or,

2. The taking and holding by the Directors of the property of the Company; or,

3. The failure of the Directors to render an account of their transactions, beyond the annual Reports, required by law. If anything else is meant, I hope it will be specified.

I will refer to these three in their order:

1. The taking and holding of their offices by the Directors I have as little concern with as you or Lord Borthwick himself. I never attended an election. I never gave my assistance to the procuring of votes or proxies, and was never consulted on the subject. At the time of the election, in October, 1867, I was in Europe; that election which brought Messrs. Eldridge, Gould, and Fisk into the Board. Neither that elec-

40

tion, nor any subsequent one, has been disputed, so far as I know. And, therefore, I cannot see with what propriety it can be said, that the present Directors hold their offices "by aid of the law Courts," or by any aid or act of mine.

The act passed by our Legislature in 1869, providing for the classification of Directors in the four great railway corporations—the New York Central, the Hudson River, the Harlem, and the Erie—I did not suggest, advise, advocate, or by any means assist in procuring. Of its policy I have nothing to say, except that the principle of classification is taken from English precedent. But I go further, and profess myself in favor of, and ready to urge upon the Legislature, the passage of an act which shall apply the principle of proportional representation to all corporate bodies. My opinions to that effect were freely expressed during the last session, and will be so expressed during the present. Thus, if the stock of a corporation were divided into 150,000 shares, and there were 15 Directors to be chosen, I would give one Director to every 10,000 shares.

2. The present Directors of the Company, having an undisputed certificate of election, and being in possession of the offices, hold the property of the Company of course. None but the Directors can hold it, unless a Receiver be appointed, and no application for such appointment is now pending, or has been made since 1869.

3. As to the failure of the Diretors, to render an account. Four litigations have been set on foot against them; two in 1868, one in 1869, and one in 1870. The last is the only one brought in good faith, as I understand the facts and the law of the cases. The first two were disposed of two years ago. Abundant reasons, founded on English precedent, appeared against

41

their being sustained. The third, that of Ramsey, deserves only to be turned out of Court, by any Judge before whom it comes. This man, by his own avowal, bought ten shares of preferred stock, three shares of common stock, two sterling bonds, and four other bonds, for the purpose of bringing the suit. He certainly has no claim to consideration any where. The fourth suit, that of the English shareholders, was brought in the Circuit Court of the United States, in April of last year. Of all "law courts," any where in the world, that Court is entitled to the fullest confidence. It will swerve neither to the right nor to the left. It will yield nothing to clamor, nothing to chicane. No amount of newspaper writing will move it an inch. The suit is now going on regularly. A demmurer, for what we think sufficient reasons, has been filed by the three counsel of the Company, Mr. B. R. Curtis, Mr. E. W. Stoughton and myself. We are ready for the argument, and hope it may be reached during the present month.

Let me now ask Lord Bosthwick, if in all this there be anything on my part worthy of censure. I go further, and invite all reasonable discussion of my acts and motives. So far as I can do so, without disclosing my client's case, I shall be happy to answer any inquires which he or any other candid person may choose to make. I shall gladly seek every opportunity to justify myself to my English friends, whose good opinion I value much.

Perhaps I should add, that I am not the standing counsel of the Erie Railway Company, or of any of its managers. Whenever I act for them, it is upon a special retainer. And I should also, perhaps, take some notice of the article in the Westminister for October. But it is enough for me to say here, that I had no more to do with the "Gold Conspiracy" than the Gov-

42

ernor of the Bank of England; and that all I did afterwards in respect to the controversies growing out of it, was to give my opinion, that the Gold and Stock Exchanges had not authority to alter the terms of contracts, and that an attempt on their part to enforce their will by means of arbitration and expulsion, might rightfully be restrained by injunction, an opinion which I still hold and am ready to justify, as I have already done by argument in the Courts. But I forget that you are charged in the same libellous article, with having sat, as one of the conspirators, at supper beside the President! To such length will hate and falsehood bear an unscrupulous wretch, willing to falsify and loving to defame.

Ever affectionately, your brother,

DAVID DUDLEY FIELD.

CYRUS W. FIELD, Esq.

CHAPTER XII

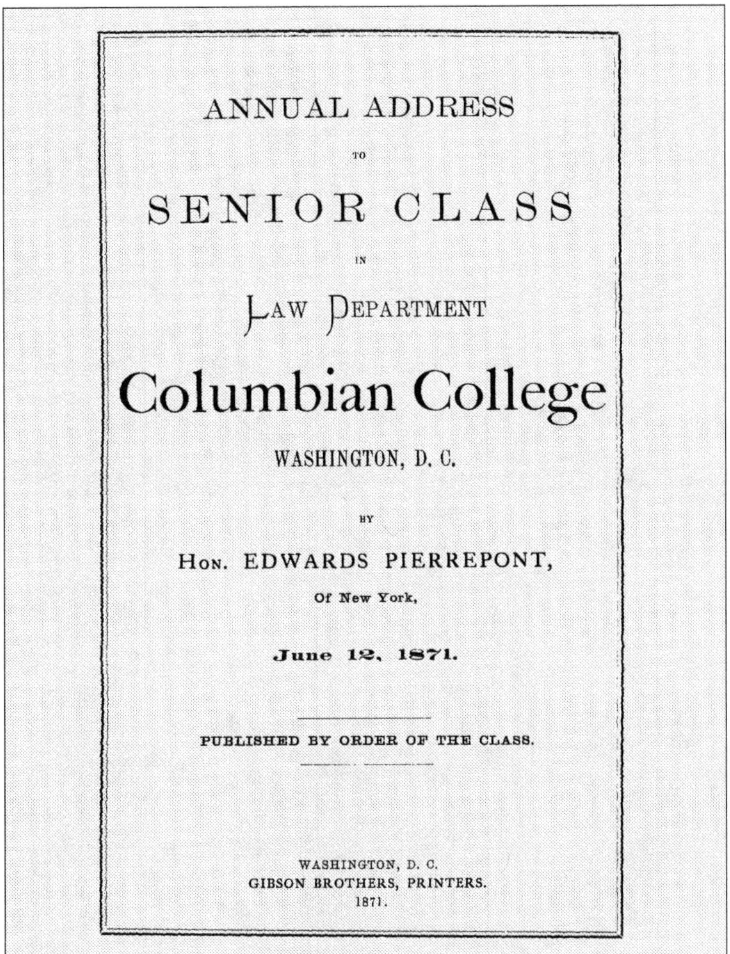
ANNUAL ADDRESS

TO

SENIOR CLASS

IN

LAW DEPARTMENT

Columbian College

WASHINGTON, D. C.

BY

HON. EDWARDS PIERREPONT,

Of New York,

June 12, 1871.

PUBLISHED BY ORDER OF THE CLASS.

WASHINGTON, D. C.
GIBSON BROTHERS, PRINTERS.
1871.

Pierrepont, Edward. *Annual Address to Senior Class in Law Department Columbian College Washington D.C. June 12, 1871.* Washington, D.C.: Gibson Brothers, 1871.

ADDRESS.

Mr. President and Gentlemen of the Graduating Class of the Columbian Law School: When your invitation to address you reached me I did not see how, in the midst of professional engagements, I could accept it, and I resolved to send you my reasons for declining. But the next morning there crowded upon me thick memories of my early professional life; and I reflected how grateful I should have been to any one who had gone before, who knew the weary road, who had been through its toils, its trials, its temptations, and who would honestly have told me what they were, and how to meet them; how eagerly I would have listened; how much weariness and anxiety and wasted labor I might have saved; and I felt that I had no right to allow professional exactions to interfere; and the pen which was dipped to frame an excuse wrote the acceptance which brings me here.

I have not come to charm the hour with pleasant words of classic lore, nor to make an ornate speech in praising great names of departed times. I have come to talk to you of the living things of our own days; of the real present; of the sturdy future; of the earnest life which you to-day begin; and if in after years these simple words of mine shall have aided one of you in lifting his heavy burdens, in overcoming his many difficulties, in manfully resisting the natural buffetings of the world, and in smoothing the steep declivities in that rugged road to professional success, then I shall have had my exceeding great reward, and though I may never hear of the result, I shall never doubt it; such is my faith in truth honestly told.

A band of young men starting at the morning dawn to begin the battle of life is most interesting. To you the past is nothing; you have no power, no fame, no riches, save in your bounding hopes and bright and airy spirits; your future is all untried; you cannot read a single page of your destiny; and if you could it would unfit you for the duties of life, diminish your happiness, and destroy the possibility of real success.

2

Start with a firm determination to perform each day's duty as it comes, having full faith that Divine Providence will then dispose your lot, and give you just that measure of prosperity which is for your greatest good.

If I mistake in assuming that you are without fortune and find that you have much of this world's goods, then I would say you may as well abandon the profession at once, for in our day it is harder for a rich young man to enter into the inner temple of the law than it was in earlier days for a rich man to enter into the kingdom of heaven. The allurements of riches are sure to seduce the young from the drudgery, the self-denial, and the enduring toil which are essential to professional success. The law tolerates no indulgent idlers among its able men, and by an inexorable rule excludes the rich from its aspiring ranks, and demands that eminence shall precede riches, and that riches shall never precede eminence at the Bar.

Neither inherited wealth nor hereditary name will give you position in the law ; you must rely upon your own individual merits. The young man who wraps himself complacently in the mantle of his sire, whether of cloth, of gold, or of laurel leaf, had better choose some other path to honor than the legal road.

The lawyer deals with this world and its every day affairs ; in things which touch men immediately and closely ; things which are understood ; about which there is little room for mistake, and no chance for blind trust. We take the medicines of the physician and the doctrines of the priest on faith, but whether the doctrines are sound or the drugs healthful we can never certainly know until we have reached a place where censure of the mistake cannot be of much avail ; but if your client loses his liberty or his estate through your negligence or blunders, neither he nor you will have to wait for the next world to find it out.

You have chosen a profession in which you may be sure that your abilities, your fidelity, your industry, your character and integrity will be fully appreciated, and so will the lack of these qualities.

You will gain all that you deserve ; settle this at the outset. It is an unerring law ; it is a law of God. Go onward in full faith from this day forth, and never doubt this primal truth, so essential to success. The world's estimate of you will, in the long run, be just, and to youth it will be generous. Never murmur that you are not appreciated.

3

You will be fairly valued, and rest assured that "the fault is not in our *stars*, but in *ourselves*, if we are underlings."

I once heard a clergyman state from the pulpit, that he left the bar, and turned to the church, because he found the temptations to dishonesty so great in the profession of the law. I dare say he did; a few years later he was disciplined for yielding to certain gentle temptations in his church. To the upright mind there is no calling which offers fewer temptations to wrong than the profession of the law. Its very business is to aid in justice, to prevent wrong, to defend the right.

No man without an upright mind, and no man who has not preserved his integrity, has ever died leaving the reputation of a great lawyer. No man can habitually espouse the side which his mind and his conscience advises him to be wrong, without final ruin to the power of his intellect.

Few seem aware of the strength which comes of the continued use of the mind on the side of right; and few seem aware of the certain weakness to the intellectual force which comes of habitual efforts to make the wrong appear right, and the right wrong; the one is the worship of God, and grows in power; the other is the worship of the devil, and tends to ruin.

This explains why you will often see a man whose natural endowments are moderate, but who never does violence to the integrity of his mind, grow stronger each year; while his more gifted rival, from pursuing the opposite course, grows weaker with time. You can train the appetite to prefer poisons to healthful food, but you will thereby weaken the body; you can train the mind until it may see the evil as good and the good as evil, but its strength and its power will have departed.

Laymen are apt to suppose that one side or the other of every cause is clearly right and the other wrong, and that the lawyer knows or ought to know which is the right. No idea is more erroneous. A man makes a will, and gives his entire estate to one child, cutting off his other children entirely. If the testator was of sound mind, and under no undue influence, and made his will strictly according to law, then it is right that the will should stand. But if he was of unsound mind, and did not execute his will as the law requires, or was unduly influenced, then the will ought to be set aside, and the children be left to share their father's estate alike.

4

A merchant, in the full belief that he is rich, devises to his wife the mansion-house and $20,000 a year for the maintenance of the widow and children. After his death it is claimed that the testator was a shareholder in a company, which by the fraud of its officers has become insolvent, thus rendering the entire estate liable to the creditors of the company. Whether the widow and children shall be beggared, or whether the creditors of the bankrupt corporation shall fail to get their pay, is a question of law, dependant upon many complicated facts, impossible to be ascertained without the fullest investigation, and until that is had neither side is more right or more wrong than the other, so far as human sagacity can tell.

It is quite common in business affairs that one of two innocent men must lose his property, and it becomes a matter of the nicest consideration to determine which of them shall suffer.

A broker of good credit goes to a merchant in New York and buys ten thousand barrels of flour to be delivered on board a Liverpool steamer; the terms of sale are cash on delivery; the merchant delivers the flour, and receives the ship's receipts; the buyer calls at the seller's counting-house, takes the ship's receipts, and obtains a bill of lading, which he endorses over to a banker, who, on the faith of it, advances $90,000 to the broker, who takes the money and absconds. The seller has been deprived of his flour, and the banker has parted with his money; a fraudulent absconder has got it, and which of the two innocent men shall lose it? Can any of you tell me? Can you say which is the wrong and which is the right side of this case? Certainly no one can tell; it requires more elements than I have given, a careful ascertainment of very many questions, both of law and of doubtful and extremely delicate facts, before we can know at all the right or the wrong of the case.

I have given you a few of the common examples of actual life; they fairly illustrate the great mass of contested cases, and prove how mistaken is the idea that law-suits have each a clearly defined side of right or of wrong.

But you will ask what is the duty of a lawyer who is called to defend one accused of murder, or of other great crime? If on examination he finds the accused to be innocent, his duty is plain. But suppose he is satisfied of his client's guilt; then what? It is right that he should see that the trial is fair; that it is conducted according to the

5

strictest rules of law; that no illegal evidence be admitted. But after much reflection upon this subject, and after reading all that I have found upon it, from Dr. Johnson to Lord Brougham, and from Lord Brougham downward, I cannot believe that it is ever right for counsel to persuade either court or jury that anything is true which he knows to be false.

In the haste which a young man feels to get on in his profession, he is sometimes tempted to espouse a cause which it were better to let alone. But let him remember that reputation, like wealth, is slow in the beginning. No sudden wealth or sudden fame was ever yet enduring. The foundation must be solidified by time and by patient toil to make the structure lasting. Begin with this fixed purpose—to deserve the confidence of the community in which you live. Deserve it by your industry, your integrity, your fidelity to every duty; and as sure as day follows night, so sure will you gain your just reward. Think only of deserving, and never doubt the good results of your good deservings.

Starting as you now do upon your professional career, you see no reason why people should select you to manage their business, and in the slow beginning you will sometimes feel discouraged. Take heart when depression comes; remember that others no older and no worthier than you have succeeded. Remember that each man who is willing to perform his part in life has his own fit place, from which *no one can crowd him.*

Be attentive to the business entrusted to you, however unimportant it may seem; be faithful and be prompt, and if you collect money, even of the smallest amount, remit it at the earliest day; let your promises be held sacred, and your lightest pecuniary obligation be discharged; and when you do not know how to manage the business entrusted to you, ask aid of some older lawyer, who will gladly advise you; and step by step, and day by day, you will gain confidence in yourselves, and gain the confidence of your fellow-men.

All your efforts will be noticed, however humble, and in after years you will find that men employ you because of the energy and ability which impressed them long before, and of which you were not in the least aware.

The respect of your fellow-men, and the trust which follows, is not a matter of accident, nor does it depend upon human will. It follows a law which keeps society together, and without which society could not exist. Ability and good conduct command respect, and men cannot help yielding it.

When a man's estate is imperiled, or his liberty is at stake, he will seek the man who can aid him. The boon companion of the night, or the popular friend of gay pleasure, will not be sought in the day of trial. The selfishness of human nature is an enduring force—always reliable.

In comparing two lawyers, you will frequently hear it said that the more successful one is of inferior ability ; and when you ask how this is, you are told that the abler one is indolent, has bad habits, or is careless of his obligations. This is simply saying that the man would be great if he had the essential requisites for greatness ; which he has not.

Never rely much upon your relations, nor too much upon your personal friends, for success in the law. Rely upon your brave purpose, your faithful work, your good common sense. Waste no time in courting the patronage of the great ; they will never bestow it until they need you more than you need them. When they find your assistance useful and your opposition dangerous, then they will employ you, and not till then.

The difficulties of professional success make the success so valuable. If the road were easy it would be overcrowded. Great success in every department of life is the result of great labor, self-denial, time, patience, and force of character.

Money is not the fair measure of a lawyer's success. In this honorable profession, honor is part of the reward. In England, from the early days of her civil liberty, the eminent barrister has held high place in the affairs of the Government, and very many of her noble families were founded by lawyers. In America, from the beginning of our Government, lawyers have held the most conspicuous place in the administration of the State. There is no better training for affairs than the severe discipline of the Bar, and no calling which wins the public confidence more than an honorable career in the profession of your choice.

It offers the highest inducements to the aspiring man, who is willing to work, to wait, to endure.

But excellent as is the training of the law for public affairs, yet so jealous is its demand upon your time that you cannot hope to succeed as a lawyer if you enter early into

7

political life. The mind and the time, the heart and the soul, must for many years be devoted exclusively to the law, if you expect success. The honors of political power must be postponed, and come to you in later life, or not at all. This is more eminently true as the country advances. Division of labor and specialties in pursuit always follow accumulated wealth and crowded populations.

In the young life of Marshall, of Clay, and of Webster, the rising lawyer could be a member of the legislature or of Congress without much detriment to his professional career. This is no longer true; and in all our great cities the young lawyer who enters the political field will be sure to fail in his professional life, not because the men of our day are inferior in varied capacity to those who have preceded us, but because in great communities concentration of all the faculties upon fewer things becomes an absolute necessity; and hence you now find the eminent lawyers in the Senate of the United States proportionately few, and from the great cities of the older States—not one.

You can read in Horace, in Juvenal, and in Cicero, who lived in the great days of Rome, how the past generation was praised as superior; you will find in Montaigue the same record touching the past generations of France. In the time of Chatham, of Fox, and of the younger Pitt, you will read lamentations over the decay of statesmanship, mingled with eulogiums over those who were dead. And now you will hear any amount of depreciation of the men of our time, with laud plaudits of the "giants" of the past, as though the lawyers, the judges, the statesmen, and all the eminent men of to-day were greatly inferior to our buried sires.

Dreams from the distant past forever deceive the dreamy men of each living age. How vanish these shadows in the light of truth! In England, now the foremost of civilized nations, the length of human life is many years longer, every comfort vastly superior, the laws much wiser, the people better governed, justice far more certain, and every kind of prosperity immensely greater than in the time of Walpole. And you have lately had within your midst English statesmen superior to any who ruled Great Britain a century ago.

In America, the great lawyers of to-day perform more intellectual labor and conduct more heavy causes in a single year than did the lawyers of Chief Justice Marshall's day in thrice that time.

8

The bench of the Supreme Court, with Chief Justice Chase at its head, is an abler bench than it was when Chief Justice Marshall was at its head.

The Cabinet of Mr. Lincoln was, in the aggregate, an abler Cabinet than had ever before advised a President.

The financial achievements of that Administration cast into shade any that had gone before. The colossal work of our armies, the conduct of the war, the management of our foreign affairs, and the vast and difficult labors which our statesmen performed, were never equalled in the history of mankind.

You can always tell the progress of a nation by a comparison of its laws.

The banker-poet, Rogers, who died in London a few years ago, leaves this record in his diary:

> "When I was a lad, I recollect seeing a whole cartful of young girls, in dresses of various colors, on their way to be executed at Tyburn. They had all been condemned on one indictment, for having been concerned in (that is, perhaps, for having been spectators of) the burning of some houses during Lord George Gordon's riots. It was quite horrible. Greville was present at one of the trials consequent upon these riots, and heard several boys sentenced, to their own excessive amusement, to be hanged. 'Never,' said Greville, with great *naiveté*, 'did I see boys CRY so.'"

Do you think that under the laws of England or of America to-day you could find judges who would consider it constructive crime, punishable with ignominious death, for like boys and girls to run to see a house on fire which the mob had kindled?

Compare the laws of New England and of Virginia, when Chief Justice Marshall was a lad, with the laws of these States to-day, and you will not again talk of the superior wisdom, justice, and humanity of by-gone times. This sickly praise of the past and depreciation of the present is the birth of narrow minds, which cannot comprehend the robust advance which the great world is making.

> "Say not thou, what is the cause that the former days were better than these? for thou dost not inquire *wisely* concerning this."

Much as the profession of the law has done for civil liberty, it has been slow at reform, clinging to musty precedent, and it still respects much antiquated nonsense. It is within the memory of the youngest here when courts of justice, whose sole business was to arrive at truth, scrupulously excluded the chiefest means, and in many cases the only means, of ascertaining the truth. The parties to the controversy could not say a word, however great their knowledge or credibility. The manager of an incorporated company, having the entire knowledge of its affairs, could give no evidence if he held a share of stock. Yet the defrauder, whose oath could be purchased for a trifle, might swear away the property of the just man who sat silent by, though his word would have been believed and his testimony would have secured a just judgment. Anywhere but in a judicial tribunal the way to truth was different. The common sense of mankind had settled it that the testimony of all parties who knew of the facts should be taken.

A judge, who would have shuddered in his seat at the idea of allowing a man to testify about a matter to which he was a party, when his two sons quarrelled in the field, where no other person was present, called them before him to ascertain the cause of the quarrel. He asked the eldest son to give a true account of the matter ; the youngest son objected, and urged that it would shock justice to allow a person to testify in his own case. The judge replied that the rule was a good one, and ought never be departed from in any court of justice ; but that his object was to find out which of his sons was to blame, and that he wanted to know the truth.

Solomon has always been commended for his wise judgment in the case of the two women who claimed the live child ; but *he* admitted the testimony of the claimants.

We shall never return to the good old times, when lawyers were so much abler, when judges were so much wiser, when the only way to obtain truth for judicial use was to exclude the chiefest witnesses who could know anything about it ; when little girls were hanged for running to see a fire which rioters had lighted ; and when also, to add contempt to the wrong, the witness, excluded on the ground of interest, could step from the stand, sign a paper which his lawyer had drawn in presence of the court, transferring his interest to some friend, who would reassign it the next hour, return to his place all purified and white for the most credible testimony, which a moment before was black disgrace to the elucidation of judicial truth.

This age has made great advance in wise administration of the law, but much is left to be done. We still imprison in unhealthy jails innocent men, upon whose humble labor sad wives and helpless children sometimes depend ! Are they innocent ? you ask. Yes, innocent ! Are they not accused of crime? Not at all. The only suspicion against them is that they are honest men who will tell the truth, and we want them as witnesses against wicked men who have committed crimes, and who are at large on bail, living in Paris, Montreal, or elsewhere, and who can go free by forfeit of their bail! But, you ask, do you keep poor, innocent men in jail who are charged with no crime, merely as witnesses against criminals who are out on bail? Yes, we do; all summer long! they are too poor to give bail, and we think them too honest to spare their testimony.

A writer of rather advanced ideas has lately said that the time is near when laws against *killing* a man will be as needless as laws against *eating* a man. The practice which I have just cited does not look that way.

Under an old rule of law which had its origin in ignorant times, we undertook to impannel a jury the other day in New York to try a murderer. Eleven hundred and fifty jurors were summoned and many days were wasted before we could find twelve men who were competent. Intelligence and reflection had disqualified most of our citizens for the solemn duty. And here let me pay a deserved tribute to a learned and eminent judge of your own city.

In the celebrated Surratt trial, Judge Wiley, who presided at the empanneling of the jury, relaxed the senseless rule, and excluded none who were ready to give their verdict according to the law and the evidence, as the same might appear on the trial, without regard to preconceived opinions founded upon uncertain reports, and which opinions the jurors were willing to change as the testimony might warrant. The more liberal rule adopted by Judge Wiley will finally prevail.

Let me warn you against an error which young lawyers often commit. The error lies in supposing that the people who have never studied law know nothing about it. You will find that they know much about it, and they will be quick to discover whether you know much about it or not.

If you ask every client who consults you, and who thinks he has right on his side, to give the reason for his belief, you will often find that he gives a better legal reason than, perhaps, had occurred to you—the legal phrase may be wanting, but the substance will be there—and if you are diligent, you will be pretty sure to find the law confirming the client's reason. And when the verdict of a jury disappoints you, ask some of the more intelligent the ground

11

of their conclusion, and in most cases you will find the ground solid, and the reason just. In these ways you may grow wiser, and you will then find that the learning of the books alone will not make a great lawyer, but that you need the added knowledge which comes of frequent intercourse with your fellow-men.

Causes are not gained by eloquent speeches delivered in the court-room. They are gained by careful preparation, and by skillful and judicious management in the conduct of the trial. In the handling of witnesses, it requires as much judgment to know what *not* to ask as what to ask, and it is often wise to let an opposing witness go without a word. For this, no rule can be given ; each case depends upon its own peculiar features and the inspiration of the hour, and your own awakened perceptions must be your guide. But never cross-examine a witness save for some specific end ; never, that you may *appear to do something.*

Prepare for the trial with unremitting care ; overmuch will do no harm ; too little may lose your cause. And when you come to the evidence which is to sustain your case, never neglect the little things ; they often determine the most important of human affairs, often they are of a kind which cannot be made up, and which, in their very nature, are controlling in their influence.

When the King of Ithica, driven by adverse fate, had been a wanderer for twenty years, he returned to his palace, filled with suitors for the hand of his wife and for the spoils of his kingdom. His wife, the faithful, did not recognize him, and his trusty servants denied his identity. But a poor old dog, dying of age, and starving from neglect, crawled fawning to the feet of the stranger, and died of joy, licking the hand of his restored master. This little bit of evidence to identity was stronger than oaths, and nothing more was needed to prove that this was indeed Ulysses, the veritable king.

Public opinion is the highest tribunal known to this country. From it, once settled, there is no appeal.

You hear the ill-considered statement that the people, after all, have nothing to do with this Government ; that a few wire-pulling politicians rule it ; that they arrange the nominations, perhaps for pay, and that the ignorant people have to vote the ticket which is not their choice.

It will be found, in this intelligent country, that the people's will *does get expressed.* The aggregate culture,

12

morals, manners, and political desires of the people tell in average resultant, and produce first that effect which, on the whole, the people wish.

All will concede that General Washington was the true representative man of his time; he was not a scholar; he was not a man of science; he had but small literary attainments; but he was the greatest man of his age. He represented the resultant force of the nation's aggregate will. He was borne to his high place by the power of public opinion, not by any political manœuver. He was the natural chief ruler of America at the time. But he was not a whit more the representative man of his day than was Mr. Lincoln or General Grant the representative man of *his* day. Each reached his place because the average judgment of the people so determined; and in precisely the same way a President will be selected next year, *whoever he may be.*

Quite the most influential, unofficial person in public affairs, whom this country has produced, told me that he never had succeeded in making any man senator, governor, or cabinet minister, by any efforts of his; that his reputation for giving men high place was due solely to the fact that he watched the drift of public sentiment, and noted the progress of men toward public favor; that every attempt of his to place men in power whom the public sentiment had not indicated was a failure; that his only merit consisted in having earlier perceptions of the public will than most men. He summed it up by saying, "I cannot *make* any man; he must make himself; and many hate me because I have told them this, which they do not believe."

The generation of lawyers to which you belong will have an important share in shaping the future of our country.

Never indulge in the shallow cant that a regal government is better than our own. If you could have the wisest and best for king, and if he would always remain the wisest and best, the evil would be less. But all history proves that long-continued power corrupts the best of men, and that after a while access to the throne is through the favor of the courtier, the harlot, and the worst of men. You have a fresh example of the effect of absolute power. A great heroic nation, whose soldiers, under the inspiration of liberal ideas, could march over the world less than twenty years ago, surrendered its liberty to the will of one man. Great prosperity followed; and the material wealth of France increased beyond that of any other period; and Americans who vis-

13

ited Paris were charmed with the smooth working of Imperial rule. Life, property, and freedom of motion were safe. Refinements, luxuries, pleasures were protected. It was a personal government of the prince, in which the people had no share, and for which they felt no responsibility.

The soldier was pampered and pleased with his indulgent life; he liked "the Empire, which was peace," and ease and sensual pleasure. He was willing to march to war to fight the adversary with fine array, but when he was called upon to fight and to die, he ran; and why not? What had he to die for? France held up no prize of glory for him. It was a personal government. The *Emperor* was the State! Why should he die for Louis Napoleon? He preferred to live; and he *ran* for life. His cannon, his chassepôt-rifle, his equipments, all were far superior to those of his enemy. He was the same Frenchman, save in the hope and spirit of liberty, which the Great Napoleon had led tattered and bare-footed to glorious victory. He was better clad, better fed, better armed than the soldier of the Army of Italy, but the spirit of individual liberty and individual responsibility was dead. He met in the field pale-faced Prussian boys fresh from the universities, with spectacles over their eyes, but with educated minds, and with purposes above the indulgence of the appetites; young men who felt their personal responsibility, who dared to die, but did not dare disgrace.

The sons of Bismarck fought as common soldiers in the common ranks, and one of them was carried severely wounded from the field. And not a single battle could the Frenchman win! This came of the eighteen years of Imperial rule. The soul of France died with her liberties. Her fate no man can tell.

In his "Spirit of Laws" Montesquieu says:

> "When Sylla wanted to restore *Rome* to its liberty, this unhappy city was incapable of receiving it. She had only some feeble remains of virtue; and as this was every day diminishing, instead of being roused out of lethargy by Cæsar, Tiberius, Caius, Claudius, Nero, Domitian, she riveted every day her chains: the blows she struck were levelled against the tyrants, but not at the tyranny."

It is often said that the agitations incident to our frequent elections of a President are expensive, and injurious to our prosperity, and many advocate a longer term for the Presidential office. Frequent elections are expensive; but liberty never was a cheap luxury. Give a President ten years of rule, and the people would never elect another President.

14

Nothing but the frequent call of the people to exercise their rights can preserve our freedom.

Never consent to increase the term of office for a single hour; never grudge the cost and turmoil of an election every four years. Never listen with patience to those who advocate an increase of the term of power. All valued things are costly, and liberty is the costliest of all. Preserve it at any price.

England grows more republican, and England grows more strong. Her Government is more stable, because more liberal. The suffrage of England to-day is about as free as the suffrage of Massachusetts; and the public opinion of England is quite as powerful upon the action of her Government.

In obedience to this opinion, she sent her nobles to Washington to treat with us; and her envoys were wise enough to know that a treaty must be made. Able statesmen from England met with discreet statesmen of America, and the two great English-speaking nations have ceased to talk of war. The weightiest fact of modern times is the treaty of Washington.

The Prussian Crown-Prince had married the daughter of England's Queen, and by this recent convention the three foremost nations of the world are united friends. We had heard somewhat boastful prophecy about the unity of the Latinrace; causes, silent, but resistless as the course of nature in her work, moved the strong Teuton to the field, sent the Anglo-statesman to New York, and the nations are not yet awake to the fact that the three great Protestant powers of the earth are in firm accord, and that the Latin race must keep the peace!

A few words more and I have done. To those who can receive them, they are more important than all that I have said or can say. They will tell you the best way through the perplexing affairs of this life, give a calmness to the judgment, a cheerfulness to the spirit, and an even temper; a courage serenely lifted above all passions, and which nothing can daunt. They will help to lighten every disappointment, render duty pleasant, and make you satisfied with your lot; and year by year you may grow stronger, wiser, and more happy. This may come. This *will* come to him who, with an earnest wish, seeks only the right, and in every trouble, in every joy, in every important undertaking in life, and every day, with honest heart and willing mind, asks enlightment and guidance from the *Great Lawgiver, our Father in Heaven.*

Chapter XIII

ADDRESS

DELIVERED BY THE

HON. EDWIN GODWIN READE, LL. D.,

BEFORE THE

CONVENTION

OF THE

LEGAL PROFESSION

OF

NORTH CAROLINA,

AT

ASHEVILLE, N. C., JULY 9TH, 1884.

RALEIGH:

EDWARDS, BROUGHTON & CO., STEAM PRINTERS AND BINDERS.

1884.

Reade, Hon. Edwin Godwin. *Address Delivered by the Hon. Edwin Godwin Reade, LL.D., before the Convention of the Legal Profession of North Carolina at Asheville, N.C., July 24th, 1884*. Raleigh: Edwards, Broughton & Co., 1884.

ADDRESS

DELIVERED BY THE

Hon. Edwin Godwin Reade, LL. D.,

BEFORE THE

CONVENTION OF THE LEGAL PROFESSION OF NORTH CAROLINA, AT ASHEVILLE, N. C., JULY 9TH, 1884.

Some fifty years ago, at Granville court, there was an important suit on trial. ROBERT B. GILLIAM, afterwards the distinguished Judge GILLIAM, and WILLIAM H. BATTLE, afterwards the distinguished Judge BATTLE, both rising to fame, appeared for the plaintiff. And GEORGE E. BADGER, always distinguished, and FREDERICK NASH, afterwards the the distinguished Chief-Justice NASH, appeared for the defendant.

After the testimony had been closed, Mr. BATTLE arose to open for the plaintiff. And, although a little tremor of the hand and voice was apparent, yet, he stated his points clearly. And then, in order to have the points on both sides before the jury at the beginning, he said: "But, gentlemen of the jury, it will be contended by the distinguished gentlemen on the other side." And then he hesitated, and his face flushed. Collecting himself, he began again: "But, gentlemen of the jury, it will be contended by the distinguished gentlemen on the other side." And then he hesitated again, and his face flushed, and he dropped back in his seat, and put his face in his hands and could not utter another word.

If, when confronting only two "distinguished gentlemen on the other side," that gifted and learned advocate failed, how shall I stand before a Convention of the whole Bar of North Carolina!

4

On an occasion when I had to pass a severe ordeal, some friends who felt anxious for my success, enquired of an acquaintance, whether he thought me equal to the task? After a complimentary answer, he added: "But if you want to hear him at his best, you must make him mad or scare him."

I have neither of these inspirations to day. After practicing with my brethren for a half century, and receiving from them all the kindness and honors which they could bestow, none of which was more esteemed than this, I am *delighted* to meet them to day; and I have a heart for them as large as these great mountains. I am not "*mad*" to-day.

Nor am I "*scared*" to-day. I always feel safe in the presence of ladies; for the first case I had at the Bar, was in favor of a merchant against a stingy husband, who refused to pay for his wife's silk dress on the ground that it was not "a necessary." It was a fine theme for the sarcasm of a young lawyer; and I indulged in it freely; and barely escaped a whipping for it. But I gained the case.

And when the first and only woman that obtained license to practice law in North Carolina, applied for her license, it fell to my lot to conduct the examination; and I did it so gently and sympathetically, that my associate justices said enviously, that I did not ask her a single question that would have bothered a child. Well, whether it would have bothered a child or not, it did not bother her; for she answered promptly and correctly and got her license.

And whereas, formerly a woman was allowed nothing except "a wheel and cards and a feather bed," I asked, why allow these, without a shelter from the rain and storm? And, therefore, I claimed for her a home, a home that she could beautify and adorn, a home that she could call her own "from turret to foundation stone."

Having, therefore, spent a long professional life in maintaining, that every woman is entitled to a silk dress, an occupation for a living, and a "home," I shall never be "scared" in their presence, although I be confronted by an army of "distinguished gentlemen on the other side!"

5

What then shall be my inspiration to-day? It shall be

THE LEGAL PROFESSION OF NORTH CAROLINA—WHAT IT IS, AND WHAT IT OUGHT TO BE.

Law is defined to be "a rule of action." And it embraces everything on the earth, in the sea, and in the heavens. The laws of many of these subjects are of great importance to be studied and known, and many of them are studied as specialties. The usefulness of the seas would be very much circumscribed if the laws of navigation were unknown. So would it be of the productions of the earth, and the influences of the heavens. The laws of others of these subjects are of little importance, and are studied for pleasure, or ornament in leisure hours, or by eccentric men. One of these eccentric characters asked me in company, "How many legs has a spider?" Now, I did not know how many legs has a spider; but, not to let him "show off" at my expense, I answered promptly, "six." Wrong, said he, "eight." No, said I, the two front ones which you take for legs are *feelers*. "Is that so?" said he. "You have been looking into it, have you?" No, said I, but any body ought to know that a spider has feelers; else, how could he make his webb in the dark? "I believe you are right," said he. Now, whether he or I, or neither was right, is of but little importance. Curious, but not useful. It is, therefore, the *subject* that gives importance to the study and knowledge of the law or rule of action that governs it.

The subject which engrosses the study of the legal profession, is the rule of *human* action. Embracing every relation of life, every right of person, property and character, the liberty of the individual, the principles and powers of the government and of all governments.

And these subjects of human action are so nearly related to, and so intermixed with, all other subjects, that the intelligent lawyer, who is studying his specialty of human action, is learning something of the laws of all other subjects. While he has hold of one, he can lay his hand on the other.

6

Hence it is common to say of an intelligent lawyer, "Why, he knows everything!" And the wonder is that he knows so much. But the wonder is greater than need be when we remember the close relation of one thing to another. The intelligent lawyer, who has well learned the law of parent and child, has almost learned the laws of all the other domestic relations, husband and wife, master and servant, teacher and pupil. So when he has learned the law of principal and agent, he easily learns all the fiduciary relations. So when he learns the law as to one species of property, it is analogous to the laws of all other property. So while he is learning what is right, he is learning what is wrong. So when he is learning the duties of citizenship, he is learning the constitution and principles of the government. And when he has learned the principles of his own government, he has learned, or can easily learn, the principles of all governments.

So much, therefore, does an intelligent lawyer know, or can readily know, that with a little license of speech, we may say, "He knows everything."

He never saw a steam ship, it may be, but he takes a case to-day involving its proper construction, and on the trial he will know more about it than the man that built it; he never studied medicine, but he tries a case involving the question of the disease of body or mind; and he confounds the physician and the expert. He tries a controversy in the church, involving property or doctrine, and he knows more of church government and doctrine than the preachers. Nations quarrel, and his diplomacy settles it: failing in which he cuts it with the sword; he settles the disputes of his neighbors, not always for a fee, but gratuitously (the best fee I ever received was a piggin of butter from a poor woman, in thankfulness for gratuitous services); he makes the laws in the Legislature, construes them on the Bench and executes them from the Executive chair.

Just as the whole religious and moral law is embraced in two commandments, "Thou shall love the Lord thy God with all thy heart, soul and mind, and thy neighbor as thy-

7

self," so the law of human action is embraced in the precept, "As ye would that men should do to you, do ye even so to them." This embraces everything. It leaves out nothing. These are the texts from which all the sermons in the world are preached, and from which all the relations of human beings are formed, and on which all rights of person and property are founded, and all civilized governments based.

The severe logic of the intelligent lawyer analyzes these fundamental principles, and draws from them all that is useful—just as he takes his a, b, cs, and forms them into words and sentences, and into every book that is written, and every argument that is made.

My familiarity with the profession for a half century, would enable me to illustrate this variety and versatility by many instances: one will suffice.

I believe the first time that I ever heard Mr. BADGER was at Granville court in the prosecution of TURNER in a murder case. He was convicted. The next morning Mr. F. NASH and Mr. W. H. HAYWOOD, who defended the prisoner, moved for a new trial on the ground that the declarations of the deceased, made some days before his death, but after he knew that he must die soon, were admitted in evidence as "dying declarations." During the arguments of Mr. NASH and Mr. HAYWOOD, which were very able, Mr. BADGER sat like a statue; so wholly absorbed in his own thoughts that he did not notice the close of the arguments on the other side, until the Judge called him. And then he arose, and with a solemnity of voice, and elegance of manner, and beauty of language, he discussed the solemnity of an oath, and the superior solemnity of the near and certain approach of death, and the appearance of the soul before God with a power that I never heard excelled or equalled. It was so exciting, that a distinguished minister of the gospel slapped me severely on the shoulder and said, "I will give a hundred dollars for that man to come and preach for us once a month." I heard him again at Hillsboro court when a New York merchant had an important suit against one of his customers. Mr. BADGER made an eloquent speech in a captivating manner. And the merchant, who thought that all excellence centered in a good salesman, said in ecstacy, "Now would not he make a splendid hand behind the counter!" I believe it was at the same court that there was a dinner party at Gov. GRAHAM'S, at which there were a number of young lawyers. I do not know whether it was by accident or design, that the subjects of the existence of God, and the truth of the christian religion were introduced by Mr. BADGER; and they were presented by a force of logic, a beauty and simplicity of language, and a reverence and impressiveness of manner that amazed me, and that I have never heard equaled in the pulpit or out of it. He seemed deeply to feel the importance of impressing these great truths on the minds of the young brethren before him; and grandly and nobly did he bear himself. I was proud of him as an elder brother, a splendid genius, and a simple christian. He was always ready on any subject, and always great, and always a child when not at work.

With so many noble North Carolinians scarcely inferior, it seems invidious to mention only him. But I must pass on.

These are the subjects of study of the legal profession, and as they are the noblest and most useful subjects, so they make the noblest and most useful profession.

In view of the usefulness and high calling of the legal profession, what manner of man should a lawyer be?

Justice BLACKSTONE says, that the study of the law is not merely a matter of amusement, and that the student will be disappointed if he expects entertainment without attention, and that such knowledge as is necessary for a Judge, can hardly be acquired by twenty years' lucubrations; but that if he has a good mind and industry he need not despair. And then he says, that to the qualities of the head which he enumerated, he must add those of the heart. A zeal for liberty and the constitution, a sense of real honor, and well grounded principles of religion, are neccessary to form a really valuable lawyer.

It is barely possible that a man may be a *learned* lawyer without a good moral character; but it is impossible for him to be a *valuable* or a *successful* lawyer without a good moral character, and I think I ought to add, with JUSTICE BLACKSTONE, without a religious character.

In view of the large influence which the legal profession exercises, and the privileges which they enjoy, a lawyer with a *bad* moral character is a nuisance. And I think this is the opinion of the public; not of the cultivated public only, but of the masses also; and especially of the immoral classes. A lawyer must hold himself up and respect himself, else he will not only not be respected, but he will be despised by the classes to whom he condescends, and to whom he thinks it necessary to condescend in order to be popular. They know that he has advantages superior to theirs, and that he claims to be above them, and they look on his condescension as meanness; as indeed it is, and they despise him.

By this is not meant that he must be proud, haughty, or exclusive: quite the reverse. He must be urbane, dignified and approachable. He must lift up every one that approaches him, and inspire confidence in all who know him; so that every one may lean on him, and trust him.

A distinguished example of such a lawyer, lately passed from among us, known to all of us. No man ever enjoyed more respect than Hon. WILLIAM A. GRAHAM. A playful incident will tend to illustrate this: At Hillsboro court a young member of the bar was amusing himself by caricaturing his older brethren. I remember his caricature of Hon. A. W. VENABLE, who was one of the best talkers I ever heard, and was very fond of talking:

> "Venable talks little, what a pity!
> What he does say is so witty,
> One hates to lose a single whisper,
> Of this slow-talking tongue-tied lisper."

And I remember his caricature of the mild demeanor of another member:

> "Reade's a queer one, let him alone!
> He ain't much more than skin and bone,
> But if you rouse him, now take care!
> He growls and bristles like a bear."

I could probably recall scraps of his other caricatures.

10

When, however, we asked to see what he said of Mr. GRAHAM, he said that he had such respect and veneration for Gov. GRAHAM, that he could not venture a caricature.

Another instance: There was in the county in which I lived a representative bad man. All the vices were his. He made money by usury and oppression, but still his leisure and shrewdness gave him influence. He was the severest critic I ever knew on men like himself, and had the highest appreciation of a gentleman. If a lawyer was careless in his practice or behavior, he would say, now how would that look in Billy GRA*ham*, as he always called him, emphasizing the last sylable. Do you think you could catch Billy GRA*ham* at a thing like that? Gov. GRAHAM, who had not a single quality in common with him, was his *beau ideal* of a gentleman, and lawyer, and statesman. And this was the estimate of the character of Gov. GRAHAM with all classes; and yet no man ever saw him let himself down to court popularity.

Pardon a personal allusion: when I commenced practice, I needed a horse to ride to court, and I had no money. I gave my note for one; and I soon found the note in the hands of this hard man. I told him I had nothing to pay with except the horse; but if he could indulge me I would pay him the first fees I could get. I did so. I never took a receipt, or saw an entry. When I made the last payment and took up the note, everything was correct. I thanked him sincerely, and told him, that I was agreeably disappointed; for I had heard that he was a hard man, and that I had expected hard treatment. He looked at me quizzically and said, "If you had had me in your power, would you have taken the advantage of me?" No sir! No sir! said I. Well, said he, when I deal with a gentleman, I deal as a gentleman, but when I deal with a sharper, he may look out for himself. I knew him long afterwards and did much professional business for him. I never encouraged or countenanced his vices, and yet I think he came to esteem me as next to "Billy GRA*ham*."

It is a great mistake for a lawyer to let himself down to

II

be popular. He need not and must not be proud and haughty; but he must be a gentleman, with a sound heart, and good moral and religious principles.

Not long ago a great moral reform was attempted and failed by the popular vote. A distinguished lawyer who was active in it, said, that he supposed he must go down with it. No, said I, you will not. It will not hurt you; but it will help you. If you want to be a constable, it may hurt you; but if you want to be a Judge, or Senator, or to fill any other high and honorable position, it will help you. In less than two years that gentleman was on the Supreme Court Bench.

Eloquence at the bar is ornamental and useful, and ought to be cultivated; but it seems not to be indispensable to success. The crowd is apt to say of one who cannot talk, "He knows a heap if he could tell it;" and of one that talks glibly, "He can tell more than he knows."

Mr. GASTON and Mr. BADGER were learned, eloquent and successful. Chief Justice RUFFIN and Chief Justice PEARSON were learned and successful without eloquence. I have heard that Chief Justice RUFFIN was a vehement speaker, and would sometimes knock the floor instead of the table with his knuckles; while his cotemporary and rival, Judge Murphy, was as soft as the lute, and would steal on the jury, and tap his snuff box and offer a pinch.

Study, industry, urbanity, dignity, and sound moral and religious principles, will make a great and valuable lawyer. Any other course will be fatal.

Your success or failure in your profession depends on yourselves. No one can either help or hinder you. And in this it differs from other professions and occupations. All has been done for you that can be done. It is true that friends may give you business in the beginning, but that will amount to but little; for, if you show yourselves worthy, you will get business without this aid; and if unworthy, the assistance will only make your failure the more conspicuous.

Not only is your success or failure dependent on yourselves, but its *measure* is also yours. And it is a pleasure to me to assure you, that with fair natural abilities, which you are supposed to possess, you may fix your own standard of excellence ever so high and reach it.

But be not deceived, this comes not of indolence, not of chance, not of fortuitous circumstances, nor yet of natural parts; but of industry untiring, of will unconquerable, of nerve undaunted, and probity incorruptible. I think it was Mr. CALHOUN who said that any one who would fix his aim on the Presidency and spend all his energy in that one direction, he might attain unto it. Literally that can scarcely be true, for, fortunately, there are not presidencies enough to supply the demand. But there is a sense in which it is substantially true. If any one will fix his aim on any thing, and spend all his energy in that one direction, he may at least approximate it. Aim at the moon, and you will at least shoot high.

When I was about to start out to practice law, I asked the advice of Judge MANGUM. He named the Courts which he advised me to attend. But, Judge MANGUM, said I, the oldest lawyers in the State practice in those Courts, and have all the business. And I have neither reputation, nor friends, nor money. No matter, said he, go where there is business, do not fear competition. The examples of these great men are just what you need. If you want to find tall trees you must go among tall trees. I took his advice and proved its wisdom. I was soon in full practice; and never met those great men that I did not feel a longing to be like them—BADGER, NASH, DEVEREUX, HAYWOOD, GRAHAM, MOREHEAD, NORWOOD, SAUNDERS, MANGUM, WADDELL, GILLIAM, BRYAN, MILLER, IREDELL—an abler bar than that of the United States Supreme Court, as I have heard Mr. BADGER say.

What shall be your behavior in your profession? Your oath will oblige you, to well and truly demean yourselves. This comprehends the whole duties of a courteous gentleman and faithful agent. There must never be the slightest departure from the strictest rule of propriety, nor the shadow of a shade of professional delinquency.

Temptations, in whatever shape they may come, and whether they threaten harm or promise favor, must not only have no force or charm, but they must be severely despised.

> "For me, so low I canna bow,
> For, Lord be thankit, I can plow,
> And when I canna yoke a nag,
> Then, Lord be thankit, I can beg"—

Is the spirit in which every temptation to error should be met.

But this inquiry is intended mainly, as to your general and public bearing as lawyers, officers of the court, engaged in administering the law. The laws of this country are its majesty. The courts and their officers are the representatives of majesty. Your deportment should be as in the presence of majesty; not with arrogance, but with gentleness and dignity, towards the court, and all who have business there.

I suggest that in the investigation of any case you never look at a book until you have mastered the facts, and come to your own conclusion, after full and impartial reflection, as to how the law *ought* to be. And then, when you go to the books, you will be surprised at the ease with which you will find your views confirmed or refuted.

I suggest that you never go into the trial of a case without the fullest preparation which it is possible for you to make. Have both the facts and the law at your fingers' ends. This is due to your client, and to the court, and to yourselves. When on the Bench, I so often heard the lawyers say, "I am not as well prepared as I would like to be. I was employed only a few days ago," or "I did not get the papers until yesterday;" and then, he fumbles over the papers, misrepresents the facts, knows nothing of the law, and hems and haws as if to show how utterly useless he is. And I have sometimes found myself involuntarily sinking lower down in my chair, as if to hide with shame and mortification, at the man's lack of consciousness of the position

14

which he ought to occupy. Why did he not set up last night, not until midnight, not until almost day, but *all night*, and get the facts by heart, and examine the law, and prepare his argument; or else continue the case, or refuse to appear. Do you say this is hard measure? Undoubtedly it is; but it is indispensable. I do not offer any level or down hill road to success; those ways are for the common herd; let them walk in them; but your way is upward and hard to climb.

> "Ah, who can tell *how hard* it is to climb,
> The *steep* where fame's proud temple shines afar!"

I hope you will not consider the personal allusion indelicate when I say, that I could count the stars as easily as I could count the nights, the whole nights, which I have consumed in such preparations. It was so much a habit with me that I came to like it. And, when engaged in a trial one day, which I had to argue the next, I preferred not to sleep at all, but to dwell on the case, and get by heart the facts and the law, and even the very words of my argument. And then, when I made the argument, if it was not the best that could be made, as it was not, it was the very best that I could make. And it sometimes gave satisfaction. It is not a natural faculty. It is hard to acquire, and few will undergo the cultivation.

I do not discourage writing; you cannot write too much. It is indispensable to accuracy. It should be used with a view to accuracy. But accuracy cannot be attained by it during the confusion and variations of a trial. All the powers must then be attentive to what is transpiring. A single moment diverted to your notes may be fatal. I would advise not to take notes in a trial. I never knew a lawyer who took notes that could represent the testimony correctly to the jury. In taking down the testimony he unconsciously shades it as he would have it to be. While he is taking down one thing, the witness is saying another thing, which he does not hear, and which qualifies or contradicts what he has put down. If he stops his argument to consult his notes, it looks awkward, it breaks the chain;

it becomes patchwork; it often confuses him, and sometimes breaks him down. Mr. BADGER took no notes. I followed his advice and example.

The substitute for notes is, by strict attention to photograph the testimony on your mind as if the whole case were a picture.

I was advised by Judge MANGUM, who was one of the finest speakers I ever heard, not to fall into the common error, that it is necessary for a speaker to *let himself down* to the comprehension of hearers. He said he always found his difficulty to be, to keep himself up to the full measure of their capacity. I have found this to be true. If you will use plain, strong language, with distinct enunciation and proper emphasis, with a lucid arrangement of propositions, the most important principles, the profoundest truths, and even obstruse problems will be readily comprehended by average minds.

The best practitioner sometimes finds himself at fault; and then indulgence or favor from the opposing counsel is very grateful: some are so liberal as to grant any favor at any time, others neither grant nor ask them. There may be nothing dishonorable in either; but I advise liberality where a brother has made a slip, a slip which would injure him if taken advantage of, and when no substantial right of your client is surrendered, and when you do not put yourself in fault by seeming indifference to your client's advantages. My own practice was to allow a brother to supply defects, correct errors, and do almost anything he desired to do, in *fixing up his case before trial;* but when the trial commenced, and swords were drawn, I threw away the scabbard and fought for a funeral.

I advise not to use forms habitually; because there will be frequent occasions when you will have to act promptly without access to forms. And then, if you have habitually used and depended on them, you will be as much at a loss without them, as if you had never seen one. You ought to be able at any moment to draw out of your own head any form which you may have to use. This will give you great advantage, not only in preparing your own forms, but in detecting faults in others. I do not mean that you are not to consult and follow forms, I mean precisely the contrary—nothing is more important,—I mean that you should make them so entirely your own that you can prepare them without reference to them. The best way to accomplish this, is to prepare a form of your own, on any given subject from your own idea of what it *ought* to be, and then compare it with the established form in such case, and then you will never forget it. When I drew my first bill in equity I had never seen one, and I had no lawyer nor form-book to consult. I was ashamed to tell my client that I did not know how to draw it, and yet it could not be delayed; so I drew up *something* and sent it fifteen miles to Judge MANGUM, with the request that he would put the *thing* in proper form for me. Instead of attempting so vain a thing, he returned it with "Barton's Equity," a little book containing the forms and proceeding in a suit in equity. In comparing my *thing* with BARTON'S form, I found Mr. BARTON wide of the mark! But still out of respect for Mr. MANGUM, I adopted Mr. BARTON'S form; and, determining that the world should never be the wiser from my unappreciated production, I threw it in the fire. I am sorry I did it. I would like to see it. If I had it I would read it to you. It was such a useful lesson to me that, as a friend told me, Chief Justice RUFFIN said, that I drew the best bills that came to the Supreme Court. If there was the slightest foundation for Judge RUFFIN'S kind remark, it was all owing to that terrible scare and to the completeness with which I then and there mastered BARTON'S forms.

MY BRETHREN:

"When ranting round in pleasure's ring,
Religion may be blinded;
Or if she gie a random sting,
It may be little minded;
But when on life we're tempest driven,
A conscience but a canker,
A correspondence fixed with Heaven,
Is sure a noble anchor."

CHAPTER XIV

A TREATISE

—ON—

AMERICAN ADVOCACY

A treatise covering succinctly the entire range of advocacy, trial tactics and legal ethics, together with the publication as an appendix hereto of the American Bar Association's Canons of Professional Ethics

—BY—

ALEXANDER H. ROBBINS

Professor of Advocacy and Legal Ethics in he Saint Louis University Institute of Law.

SECOND EDITION

ST. LOUIS:
CENTRAL LAW JOURNAL COMPANY
1913

ABA Code of 1908. From Robbins, Alexander H., *A Treatise on American Advocacy, Second Edition*. St. Louis: Central Law Journal Company, 1913.

APPENDIX.

CANONS OF PROFESSIONAL ETHICS*

I

PREAMBLE

In America, where the stability of Courts and of all departments of government rests upon the approval of the people, it is peculiarly essential that the system for establishing and dispensing Justice be developed to a high point of efficiency and so maintained that the public shall have absolute confidence in the integrity and impartiality of its administration. The future of the Republic, to a great extent, depends upon our maintenance of Justice pure and unsullied. It cannot be so maintained unless the conduct and the motives of the members of our profession are such as to merit the approval of all just men.

*[NOTE.—The following Canons of Professional Ethics were adopted by the American Bar Association at its thirty-first annual meeting at Seattle, Washington, on August 27, 1908.

The Canons were prepared by a committee composed of
Henry St. George Tucker, Virginia, Chairman.
Lucien Hugh Alexander, Pennsylvania, Secretary.
David J. Brewer, District of Columbia.
Frederick V. Brown, Minnesota.
J. M. Dickinson, Illinois.
Franklin Ferriss, Missouri.
William Wirt Howe, Louisiana.
Thomas H. Hubbard, New York.
James G. Jenkins, Wisconsin.
Thomas Goode Jones, Alabama.
Alton B. Parker, New York.
George R. Peck, Illinois.
Francis Lynde Stetson, New York.
Ezra R. Thayer, Massachusetts.]

II

THE CANONS OF ETHICS

No code or set of rules can be framed, which will particularize all the duties of the lawyer in the varying phases of litigation or in all the relations of professional life. The following canons of ethics are adopted by the American Bar Association as a general guide, yet the enumeration of particular duties should not be construed as a denial of the existence of others equally imperative, though not specifically mentioned:

1. **The duty of the Lawyer to the Courts.**—It is the duty of the lawyer to maintain towards the Courts a respectful attitude, not for the sake of the temporary incumbent of the judicial office, but for the maintenance of its supreme importance. Judges, not being wholly free to defend themselves, are peculiarly entitled to receive the support of the Bar against unjust criticism and clamor. Whenever there is proper ground for serious complaint of a judicial officer, it is the right and duty of the lawyer to submit his grievances to the proper authorities. In such cases, but not otherwise, such charges should be encouraged and the person making them should be protected.

2. **The Selection of Judges.**—It is the duty of the Bar to endeavor to prevent political considerations from outweighing judicial fitness in the selection of Judges. It should protest earnestly and actively against the appointment or election of those who are unsuitable for the Bench; and it should strive to have elevated thereto only those willing to forego other employments, whether of a business, political or other character, which may embarrass their free and fair consideration of questions before them for decision. The aspiration of lawyers for judicial position should be governed by an impartial estimate of

their ability to add honor to the office and not by a desire for the distinction the position may bring to themselves.

3. Attempts to Exert Personal Influence on the Court.—Marked attention and unusual hospitality on the part of a lawyer to a Judge, uncalled for by the personal relations of the parties, subject both the Judge and the lawyer to misconstructions of motive and should be avoided. A lawyer should not communicate or argue privately with the Judge as to the merits of a pending cause, and he deserves rebuke and denunciation for any device or attempt to gain from a Judge special personal consideration or favor. A self-respecting independence in the discharge of professional duty, without denial or diminution of the courtesy and respect due the Judge's station, is the only proper foundation for cordial personal and official relations between Bench and Bar.

4. When Counsel for an Indigent Prisoner.—A lawyer assigned as counsel for an indigent prisoner ought not to ask to be excused for any trivial reason, and should always exert his best efforts in his behalf.

5. The Defense or Prosecution of Those Accused of Crime.—It is the right of the lawyer to undertake the defense of a person accused of crime, regardless of his personal opinion as to the guilt of the accused; otherwise innocent persons, victims only of suspicious circumstances, might be denied proper defense. Having undertaken such defense, the lawyer is bound by all fair and honorable means, to present every defense that the law of the land permits, to the end that no person may be deprived of life or liberty, but by due process of law.

The primary duty of a lawyer engaged in public prosecution is not to convict, but to see that justice is done The suppression of facts or the secreting ot witnesses capable of establishing the innocence of the accused is highly reprehensible.

6. Adverse Influences and Conflicting Interests.—It is the duty of a lawyer at the time of retainer to disclose to the client all the circumstances of his relations to the parties, and any interest in or connection with the controversy, which might influence the client in the selection of counsel.

It is unprofessional to represent conflicting interests, except by express consent of all concerned given after a full disclosure of the facts. Within the meaning of this canon, a lawyer represents conflicting interests when, in behalf of one client, it is his duty to contend for that which duty to another client requires him to oppose.

The obligation to represent the client with undivided fidelity and not to divulge his secrets or confidences forbids also the subsequent acceptance of retainers or employment from others in matters adversely affecting any interest of the client with respect to which confidence has been reposed.

7. Professional Colleagues and Conflicts of Opinion.— A client's proffer of assistance of additional counsel should not be regarded as evidence of want of confidence, but the matter should be left to the determination of the client. A lawyer should decline association as colleague if it is objectionable to the original counsel, but if the lawyer first retained is relieved, another may come into the case.

When lawyers jointly associated in a cause cannot agree as to any matter vital to the interest of the client, the conflict of opinion should be frankly stated to him for his final determination. His decision should be accepted unless the nature of the difference makes it impracticable for the lawyer whose judgment has been overruled to cooperate effectively. In this event it is his duty to ask the client to relieve him.

Efforts, direct or indirect, in any way to encroach upon the business of another lawyer, are unworthy of those who should be brethren at the Bar; but, nevertheless, it is the right of any lawyer, without fear or favor, to give proper advice to those seeking relief against unfaithful or neglectful counsel, generally after communication with the lawyer of whom the complaint is made.

8. Advising Upon the Merits of a Client's Cause.—A lawyer should endeavor to obtain full knowledge of his client's cause before advising thereon, and he is bound to give a candid opinion of the merits and probable result of pending or contemplated litigation. The miscarriages to which justice is subject, by reason of surprises and disappointments in evidence and witnesses, and through mistakes of juries and errors of Courts, even though only occasional, admonish lawyers to beware of bold and confident assurances to clients, especially where the employment may depend upon such assurance. Whenever the controversy will admit of fair adjustment, the client should be advised to avoid or to end the litigation.

9. Negotiations With Opposite Party.—A lawyer should not in any way communicate upon the subject of controversy with a party represented by counsel; much less should he undertake to negotiate or compromise the matter with him, but should deal only with his counsel. It is incumbent upon the lawyer most particularly to avoid everything that may tend to mislead a party not represented by counsel, and he should not undertake to advise him as to the law.

10. Acquiring Interest in Litigation.—The lawyer should not purchase any interest in the subject-matter of the litigation which he is conducting.

11. Dealing With Trust Property.—Money of the client or other trust property coming into the possession of the lawyer should be reported promptly, and except with the client's knowledge and consent, should not be commingled with his private property or be used by him.

12. Fixing the Amount of the Fee.—In fixing fees, lawyers should avoid charges which overestimate their advice and services, as well as those which undervalue them. A client's ability to pay cannot justify a charge in excess of the value of the service, though his poverty may require a less charge, or even none at all. The reasonable requests of brother lawyers, and of their widows and orphans without ample means, should receive special and kindly consideration.

In determining the amount of the fee, it is proper to consider: (1) the time and labor required, the novelty and difficulty of the questions involved and the skill requisite properly to conduct the cause; (2) whether the acceptance of employment in the particular case will preclude the lawyer's appearance for others in cases likely to arise out of the transaction, and in which there is a reasonable expectation that otherwise he would be employed, or will involve the loss of other business while employed in the particular case or antagonisms with other clients; (3) the customary charges of the Bar for similar services; (4) the amount involved in the controversy and the benefits resulting to the client from the services; (5) the contingency or the certainty of the compensation; and (6) the character of the employment, whether casual or for an established and constant client. No one of these considerations in itself is controlling. They are mere guides in ascertaining the real value of the service.

In fixing fees it should never be forgotten that the profession is a branch of the administration of justice and not a mere money-getting trade.

13. Contingent Fees.—Contingent fees, where sanctioned by law, should be under the supervision of the Court, in order that clients may be protected from unjust charges.

14. Suing a Client for a Fee.—Controversies with clients concerning compensation are to be avoided by the lawyer so far as shall be compatible with his self-respect and with his right to receive reasonable recompense for his services; and lawsuits with clients should be resorted to only to prevent injustice, imposition or fraud.

15. How Far a Lawyer May Go in Supporting a Client's Cause.—Nothing operates more certainly to create or to foster popular prejudice against lawyers as a class, and to deprive the profession of that full measure of public esteem and confidence which belongs to the proper discharge of its duties than does the false claim, often set up by the unscrupulous in defense of questionable transactions, that it is the duty of the lawyer to do whatever may enable him to succeed in winning his client's cause.

It is improper for a lawyer to assert in argument his personal belief in his client's innocence or in the justice of his cause.

The lawyer owes "entire devotion to the interest of the client, warm zeal in the maintenance and defense of his rights and the exertion of his utmost learning and ability," to the end that nothing be taken or be withheld from him, save by the rules of law, legally applied. No fear of judicial disfavor or public unpopularity should restrain him from the full discharge of his duty. In the judicial forum the client is entitled to the benefit of any and every remedy and defense that is authorized by the law of the land, and he may expect his lawyer to assert every such remedy or defense. But it is steadfastly to be borne in mind that the great trust of the lawyer is to be performed within and not without the bounds of the law. The office of attorney does not permit, much less does it demand of him for any client, violation of law or any manner of fraud or chicane. He must obey his own conscience and not that of his client.

16. Restraining Clients from Improprieties.—A lawyer should use his best efforts to restrain and to prevent his clients from doing those things which the lawyer himself ought not to do, particularly with reference to their conduct towards Courts, judicial officers, jurors, witnesses and suitors. If a client persists in such wrong-doing the lawyer should terminate their relation.

17. Ill-Feeling and Personalities Between Advocates.—Clients, not lawyers, are the litigants. Whatever may be the ill-feeling existing between clients, it should not be allowed to influence counsel in their conduct and demeanor toward each other or toward suitors in the case. All personalities between counsel should be scrupulously avoided. In the trial of a cause it is indecent to allude to the personal history or the personal peculiarities and idiosyncrasies of counsel on the other side. Personal colloquies between counsel which cause delay and promote unseemly wrangling should also be carefully avoided.

18. Treatment of Witnesses and Litigants.—A lawyer should always treat adverse witnesses and suitors with fairness and due consideration, and he should never minister to the malevolence or prejudices of a client in the trial or conduct of a cause. The client cannot be made the keeper of the lawyer's conscience in professional matters. He has no right to demand that his counsel shall abuse the opposite party or indulge in offensive personalities. Improper speech is not excusable on the ground that it is what the client would say if speaking in his own behalf.

19. Appearance of Lawyer as Witness for His Client.—When a lawyer is a witness for his client, except as to merely formal matters, such as the attestation or custody of an instrument and the like, he should leave the trial of the case to other counsel. Except when essential to the ends of justice, a lawyer should avoid testifying in Court in behalf of his client.

20. Newspaper Discussion of Pending Litigation.—Newspaper publications by a lawyer as to pending or anticipated litigation may interfere with a fair trial in the Courts and otherwise prejudice the due administration of justice. Generally they are to be condemned. If the extreme circumstances of a particular case justify a statement to the public, it is unprofessional to make it anonymously. An *ex parte* reference to the facts should not go beyond quotation from the records and papers on file in the Court; but even in extreme cases it is better to avoid any *ex parte* statement.

21. Punctuality and Expedition.—It is the duty of the lawyer not only to his client, but also to the Courts and to the public to be punctual in attendance, and to be concise and direct in the trial and disposition of causes.

22. Candor and Fairness.—The conduct of the lawyer before the Court and with other lawyers should be characterized by candor and fairness.

It is not candid or fair for the lawyer knowingly to misquote the contents of a paper, the testimony of a witness, the language or the argument of opposing counsel, or the language of a decision or a text-book; or with knowledge of its invalidity, to cite as authority a decision that has been overruled, or a statute that has been repealed; or in argument to assert as a fact that which has not been proved, or in those jurisdictions where a side has the opening and closing arguments to mislead his opponent by concealing or withholding positions in his opening argument upon which his side then intends to rely.

It is unprofessional and dishonorable to deal other than candidly with the facts in taking the statements of witnesses, in drawing affidavits and other documents, and in the presentation of causes.

A lawyer should not offer evidence, which he knows the Court should reject, in order to get the same before the jury by argument for its admissibility, nor should he address to the Judge arguments upon any point not properly calling for determination by him. Neither should he introduce into an argument, addressed to the Court, remarks or statements intended to influence the jury or bystanders.

These and all kindred practices are unprofessional and unworthy of an officer of the law charged, as is the lawyer, with the duty of aiding in the administration of justice.

23. Attitude Toward Jury.—All attempts to curry favor with juries by fawning, flattery or pretended solicitude for their personal comfort are unprofessional. Suggestions of counsel, looking to the comfort or convenience of jurors, and propositions to dispense with argument, should be made to the Court out of the jury's hearing. A lawyer must never converse privately with jurors about the case;

and both before and during the trial he should avoid communicating with them, even as to matters foreign to the cause.

24. Right of Lawyer to Control the Incidents of the Trial.—As to incidental matters pending the trial, not affecting the merits of the cause, or working substantial prejudice to the rights of the client, such as forcing the opposite lawyer to trial when he is under affliction or bereavement; forcing the trial on a particular day to the injury of the opposite lawyer when no harm will result from a trial at a different time; agreeing to an extension of time for signing a bill of exceptions, cross interrogatories and the like, the lawyer must be allowed to judge. In such matters no client has a right to demand that his counsel shall be illiberal, or that he do anything therein repugnant to his own sense of honor and propriety.

25. Taking Technical Advantage of Opposite Counsel; Agreements With Him.—A lawyer should not ignore known customs or practice of the Bar or of a particular Court, even when the law permits, without giving timely notice to the opposing counsel. As far as possible, important agreements, affecting the rights of clients, should be reduced to writing; but it is dishonorable to avoid performance of an agreement fairly made because it is not reduced to writing, as required by rules of Court.

26. Professional Advocacy Other Than Before Courts.—A lawyer openly, and in his true character may render professional services before legislative or other bodies, regarding proposed legislation and in advocacy of claims before departments of government, upon the same principles of ethics which justify his appearance before the Courts; but it is unprofessional for a lawyer so engaged to conceal his attorneyship, or to employ secret personal solicitations, or to use means other than those addressed to the reason and understanding to influence action.

27. Advertising, Direct or Indirect.—The most worthy and effective advertisement possible, even for a young lawyer, and especially with his brother lawyers, is the establishment of a well-merited reputation for professional capacity and fidelity to trust. This cannot be forced, but must be the outcome of character and conduct. The publication or circulation of ordinary simple business cards, being a matter of personal taste or local custom, and sometimes of convenience, is not *per se* improper. But solicitation of business by circulars or advertisements, or by personal communications or interviews, not warranted by personal relations, is unprofessional. It is equally unprofessional to procure business by indirection through touters of any kind, whether allied real estate firms or trust companies advertising to secure the drawing of deeds or wills or offering retainers in exchange for executorships or trusteeships to be influenced by the lawyer. Indirect advertisement for business by furnishing or inspiring newspaper comments concerning causes in which the lawyer has been or is engaged, or concerning the manner of their conduct, the magnitude of the interests involved, the importance of the lawyer's positions, and all other like self-laudation, defy the traditions and lower the tone of our high calling, and are intolerable.

28. Stirring up Litigation, Directly or Through Agents. —It is unprofessional for a lawyer to volunteer advice to bring a law-suit, except in rare cases where ties of blood, relationship or trust make it his duty to do so. Stirring up strife and litigation is not only unprofessional, but it is indictable at common law. It is disreputable to hunt up defects in titles or other causes of action and inform thereof in order to be employed to bring suit, or to breed litigation by seeking out those with claims for personal injuries or those having any other grounds of action in order to secure them as clients, or to employ agents or runners for like purposes, or to pay or reward, directly or indirectly, those who bring or influence the bringing of such cases to his office, or to remunerate policemen, court or prison officials, physicians, hospital *attachés* or other who may succeed, under the guise of giving disinterested friendly advice, in influencing the criminal, the sick and the injured, the ignorant or others, to seek his professional services. A duty to the public and to the profession devolves upon every member of the Bar, having knowledge of such practices upon the part of any practitioner, immediately to inform thereof to the end that the offender may be disbarred.

29. Upholding the Honor of the Profession.—Lawyers should expose without fear or favor before the proper tribunals corrupt or dishonest conduct in the profession, and should accept without hesitation employment against a member of the Bar who has wronged his client. The counsel upon the trial of a cause in which perjury has been committed, owe it to the profession and to the public to bring the matter to the knowledge of the prosecuting authorities. The lawyer should aid in guarding the Bar against the admission to the profession of candidates unfit or unqualified because deficient in either moral character or education. He should strive at all times to uphold the honor and to maintain the dignity of the profession and to improve not only the law, but the administration of justice.

30. Justifiable and Unjustifiable Litigation.—The lawyer must decline to conduct a civil cause or to make a defense when convinced that it is intended merely to harrass or to injure the opposite party or to work oppression or wrong. But otherwise it is his right, and, having accepted retainer, it becomes his duty to insist upon the judgment of the Court as to the legal merits of his client's claim. His appearance in Court should be deemed equivalent to an assertion on his honor that in his opinion his client's case is one proper for judicial determination.

31. Responsibility for Litigation.—No lawyer is obliged to act either as adviser or advocate for every person who may wish to become his client. He has the right to decline employment. Every lawyer upon his own responsibility must decide what business he will accept as counsel, what causes he will bring into Court for plaintiffs, what cases he will contest in Court for defendants. The responsibility for advising questionable transactions, for bringing questionable suits, for urging questionable defenses, is the lawyer's responsibility. He cannot escape it by urging as an excuse that he is only following his client's instructions.

32. The Lawyer's Duty in Its Last Analysis.—No client, corporate or individual, however powerful, nor any cause, civil or political, however important, is entitled to receive, nor should any lawyer render, any service or advice involving disloyalty to the law whose ministers we are, or disrespect of the judicial office, which we are bound to uphold, or corruption of any person or persons exercising a public office or private trust, or deception or betrayal of the public. When rendering any such improper service or advice, the lawyer invites and merits stern and just condemnation. Correspondingly, he advances the honor of his profession and the best interests of his client when he renders service or gives advice tending to impress upon the client and his undertaking exact compliance with the strictest principles of moral law. He must also observe and advise his client to observe the statute law, though until a statute shall have been construed and interpreted by competent adjudication, he is free and is entitled to advise as to its validity and as to what he conscientiously believes to be its just meaning and extent. But, above all, a lawyer will find his highest honor in a deserved reputation for fidelity to private trust and to public duty, as an honest man and as a patriotic and loyal citizen.

III

OATH OF ADMISSION

The general principles which should ever control the lawyer in the practice of his profession are clearly set forth in the following Oath of Admission to the Bar, formulated upon that in use in the State of Washington, and which conforms in its main outlines to the "duties" of lawyers as defined by statutory enactments in that and many other States of the Union*—duties which they are sworn on admission to obey and for the wilful violation of which disbarment is provided:

I DO SOLEMNLY SWEAR:

I will support the Constitution of the United States and the Constitution of the State of...

I will maintain the respect due to Courts of Justice and judicial officers;

I will not counsel or maintain any suit or proceeding which shall appear to me to be unjust, nor any defense except such as I believe to be honestly debatable under the law of the land;

I will employ for the purpose of maintaining the causes confided to me such means only as are consistent with truth and honor, and will never seek to mislead the Judge or jury by any artifice or false statement of fact or law;

I will maintain the confidence and preserve inviolate the secrets of my client, and will accept no compensation in connection with his business except from him or with his knowledge and approval;

I will abstain from all offensive personality, and advance no fact prejudicial to the honor or reputation of a party or

*Alabama, California, Georgia, Idaho, Indiana, Iowa, Minnesota, Mississippi, Nebraska, North Dakota, Oklahoma, Oregon, South Dakota, Utah, Washington and Wisconsin. The oaths administered on admission to the Bar in all the other States require the observance of the highest moral principle in the practice of the profession, but the duties of the lawyer are not as specifically defined by law as in the States named.

witness, unless required by the justice of the cause with which I am charged;

I will never reject, from any consideration personal to myself, the cause of the defenseless or oppressed, or delay any man's cause for lucre or malice. SO HELP ME GOD.

We commend this form of oath for adoption by the proper authorities in all States and Territories.

CHAPTER XV

LAWYERS AND MORALS

BY NEWMAN LEVY

OF THE NEW YORK BAR

Levy, Newman. "Lawyers and Morals." A reprint from the February, 1927 issue of *Harper's Magazine*, made with consent of the authors and publishers, for distribution to members of the California State Bar Association in attendance upon the Eighteenth Annual Convention at Coronado, California, September 15-17, 1927.

LAWYERS AND MORALS

BY NEWMAN LEVY

THE practice of law has for generations had the curious, paradoxical reputation of being the most learned, the most dignified, and the most distrusted of professions. In every age the bar has enjoyed the cynically contemptuous admiration of its contemporaries and has been the faithful recipient of the secrets and confidences of a people that did not trust it.

This popular lack of faith in the honesty and the integrity of the legal profession exists today. There has never been a time when the lawyer has been so active a participant in the business affairs of his community; there has, perhaps, never been a time when his advice, his trained judgment, and his technical knowledge have been so essential an element in every business enterprise. The lawyer is an indispensable adjunct to almost every branch of human activity. Yet the very individuals who employ him and rely so heavily upon him form that large collective body called The Public, and it is this Public that holds the legal profession in such low esteem.

The reason for this is fairly obvious. In most other fields of endeavor the prevailing standards of conduct are conditioned by a frank and cheerfully cynical utilitarianism. The merchant does not assume a moral superiority that he does not possess, nor does he wear his virtue on his sleeve. The popular aphorism "business is business" indicates the current commercial attitude toward ethics. But the bar imposes upon itself a higher standard of behavior. The practice of law, it has repeatedly been said, is not a trade or business but a profession of great antiquity and dignity. It involves social obligations and duties that are of vital importance to the preservation of our institutions. At the same time there are the specific obligations of loyalty and service which the lawyer owes to his client.

The ambition of every lawyer is to be a successful lawyer. There are, however, varying definitions of success; there is the definition contained in the lofty idealistic utterances found in the year-book obituaries of bar associations and in the philosophic literature of the profession; there is also the more widely accepted definition exemplified by the careers of the outstanding figures of the profession, the so-called leaders of the bar, the models according to which the young practitioner seeks to shape his career. Stripped of all euphemistic verbiage, the successful lawyer, according to the popular conception, is one who has the most respectable and most remunerative clients, and who best serves the interest of those clients.

We have, therefore, a large, intelligent, and influential body devoting its energies and its genius almost exclusively to the selfish interests of individuals. If these interests conflict with the welfare of society, so much the worse for society.

We hear much talk, for instance, about justice. Lawyers frequently describe themselves as ministers of justice. In the abstract it is a beautiful and desirable concept. But justice *per se* plays a small part in the daily activities of the busy practitioner. A few illustrations will suffice: A client brings a contract to his attorney and asks to have it broken. Will the lawyer consider the possible unfairness to the other contracting party who entered into the agreement in good faith, or will he examine the document for flaws and technical defects

---

A reprint from the February, 1927, issue of Harper's Magazine, made with consent of the author and the publishers, for distribution to members of the California State Bar Association in attendance upon the Eighteenth Annual Convention at Coronado, California, September 15-17, 1927; through the courtesy of a retired lawyer, formerly a member of the Los Angeles Bar—and no doubt the victim of an enlarged perspective.

and endeavor to find some legal means to invalidate it? A lawyer in the trial of a case realizes that, although the law is on his side, his client is in the wrong, and that if he wins a grave injustice will be done. What does he do about it?

There is no doubt as to the answers to these questions, nor is there any question as to the clear, unmistakable professional duty of the lawyer. These cases are not cited in a spirit of criticism. They are mentioned to illustrate the fundamental fact that a difference exists between the profession of law and the practice. The evil, if there be an evil, lies in the refusal of the bar to face the fact squarely. The faculty of rationalization and self-deception, which is an almost universal trait of mankind, is found conspicuously in members of the legal profession. Until the bar is prepared to assume a more realistic attitude toward its functions and its activities, this clash between professional aspirations and professional conduct will continue to exist. And so long as it exists, the popular distrust of anything that savors of sham and hypocrisy will exist with it. The practice of of the law needs to be debunked.

II

This debunking process will not be easy. The bar, apart from its function as the coadjutor of private interests, is the inheritor of an ancient tradition of gentility. For centuries the practice of law was one of the few professions open to a gentleman. A ceremonial dignity, a medieval ritualism invested it and marked it as something apart from the baser pursuits of trade and labor. It thus acquired certain aristocratic attributes that survive in a vestigial form today. Among these survivals is the tradition of a higher standard of conduct than that which is customarily expected from those who engage in less exalted pursuits.

This tradition is embodied in what are called codes of ethics adopted by various bar associations, but what, actually, are refined codes of professional etiquette. The Canons of Professional Ethics Adopted by the American Bar Association, for instance, are largely a manual of polite behavior for lawyers. They deal with such matters as the respectful attitude a lawyer should adopt toward the judge, the duty of a lawyer not to overcharge a client, not to browbeat a witness, and not to insult his adversary.

It is not claimed that these canons embody the whole duty of a lawyer; there are others which are less ritualistic in their purpose. Nevertheless, the emphasis is on manners rather than morals. The questions and answers of the Committee on Professional Ethics of the New York County Lawyers' Association illustrate the same tendency. For fourteen years this committee, composed of eminent members of the New York bar, has answered questions on professional ethics propounded to it by practicing lawyers. More than half the questions deal with matters of professional good form and have nothing to do with ethics. Forty-three questions, for example, out of two hundred and twenty-nine deal with the propriety of advertising by lawyers. A great many others have to do with solicitation of business.

These matters are not unimportant. It is desirable, undoubtedly, that certain formalism and dignity surround the administration of law. A respect for institutions is gained by the preservation of ceremonial trappings and incidents, and a certain amount of stagecraft is useful even in a democracy. The ministers of justice should be trained in the ritual of their profession. It is equally desirable, however, that those trained in the ritual of their profession should be ministers of justice.

The important question which a lawyer has to decide at the outset of every professional undertaking is how far he may properly go in representing his client. Canon 5 of the Canons of Ethics of the American Bar Association attempts to define his duty in criminal cases:

> It is the right of the lawyer to undertake the defense of a person accused of crime, regardless of his personal opinion as to the guilt of the accused; otherwise innocent persons, victims only of suspicious circumstances, might be denied proper defense. Having undertaken such de-

fense, the lawyer is bound by all fair and honorable means to present every defense that the law of the land permits, to the end that no person may be deprived of life or liberty, but by due process of law.

The primary duty of a lawyer engaged in public prosecution is not to convict, but to see that justice is done. The suppression of facts or the secreting of witnesses capable of establishing the innocence of the accused is highly reprehensible.

Canon 15 defines his duty generally:

Nothing operates more certainly to create or to foster popular prejudice against lawyers as a class, and to deprive the profession of that full measure of public esteem and confidence which belongs to the proper discharge of its duties, than does the false claim, often set up by the unscrupulous in defense of questionable transactions, that it is the duty of the lawyer to do whatever may enable him to succeed in winning his client's cause.

It is improper for a lawyer to assert in argument his personal belief in his client's innocence or in the justice of his cause.

The lawyer owes "entire devotion to the interest of the client, warm zeal in the maintenance and defense of his rights and the exertion of his utmost learning and ability," to the end that nothing be taken or be withheld from him, save by the rules of law, legally applied. No fear of judicial disfavor or public unpopularity should restrain him from the full discharge of his duty. In the judicial forum the client is entitled to the benefit of any and every remedy and defense that is authorized by the law of the land, and he may expect his lawyer to assert every such remedy or defense. But it is steadfastly to be borne in mind that the great trust of the lawyer is to be performed within and not without the bounds of the law. The office of attorney does not permit, much less does it demand of him for any client, violation of law or any manner of fraud or chicane. He must obey his own conscience and not that of his client.

It will be seen that while the prosecutor in a criminal case is charged with the duty of seeing that justice is done, no such obligation is placed upon the counsel for the defense. It is his duty to present "every defense that the law of the land permits," even at the sacrifice, inferentially, of justice and the public good. In civil, as well as criminal cases, he owes "entire devotion to the interests of his client." Short of "violation of the law or any manner of fraud or chicane," he may go the limit.

The subtle ingenuity of the legal mind is capable of finding justifications and excuses even for fraud and chicane. An interesting illustration of this is found in the matter of Palmieri (176 App. Div. 58, reversed in 221 N. Y. 611). This was a disbarment proceeding brought against an attorney on the ground of professional misconduct. This lawyer was defending a man charged with a rather serious crime. One of the state's principal witnesses, a young woman, had disappeared shortly before the trial, and it was believed that she had been induced by the defendant to leave the jurisdiction.

On the afternoon of the second day of the trial the young woman appeared in court, carrying a suit-case. She was called to the stand by the defendant's lawyer. It was quite important for him to show that she had appeared in court voluntarily, and had not been in touch with the defendant. Otherwise her interest in the case would have been apparent, and her testimony would have been discredited.

"Where do you come from, Miss A——?" the lawyer asked.

"Why, I just came from Mayfield, New York."

"Where is Mayfield, New York?"

"It is up the state; just how far I couldn't tell you."

"How did you get from Mayfield to New York?"

"Why, I came down on the train *last night*; I came down here because I read in the paper that Mr. D——'s case—"

The witness produced a newspaper clipping from which, she said, she had learned that the case was about to be tried. The suit-case she carried was offered in evidence to emphasize the fact that she had just come from the train.

The defendant's lawyer, summing up for the jury, referred to her testimony thus:

"We have got her here, and, thank God, gentlemen of the jury, that Divine Providence has brought that woman here. If it was the *Evening Journal*, I thank the *Evening Journal*. If it was anybody else—she said it was the *Evening Journal* that she read it in, and by the way she produced a clipping to the judge—thank God, I say to the press."

The disbarment proceedings against the lawyer disclosed these facts: that the woman came to New York from Mayfield because the defendant had called her up on the long-distance telephone and had asked her to come, not because she had read about the case in a newspaper; that the witness had gone to the lawyer's house on the day on which the trial was to commence, and had had an interview with him there; that she again visited the lawyer's house at seven-thirty o'clock in the morning on the second day of the trial; and, consequently, when she appeared in court that afternoon with her suit-case in her hand the lawyer knew that she had been in New York nearly two days, and that her testimony was false. And, despite his eloquent remarks to the jury, he knew that neither Divine Providence nor the *Evening Journal* had anything to do with her arrival.

Nevertheless, the highest court in the State of New York, by a vote of five to two, found that the evidence did not "warrant the conclusion that there was intentional misconduct" on the part of the lawyer, and the disbarment proceedings were dismissed. This case is now a precedent—at least in the State of New York—and any young attorney who may have any doubts as to the proper course to pursue in a similar case need only read the record and govern his conduct accordingly.

Illustrations might be multiplied. There was the *cause célèbre* of a year or so ago, a sensational matrimonial action, in which the plaintiff's mother, an elderly lady, was called to the stand as a witness for her daughter. This woman, who had lived an irreproachable life for a generation or more, had been guilty in her youth of an unfortunate lapse from virtue.

The distinguished counsel for the defendant subjected her to what is called in contemporary journalism "a grilling cross-examination" in which he went into the details of her ancient departure from rectitude. The entire performance was cruel and unnecessary. The examination, which had nothing to do with the issues involved, was permitted presumably as tending to impeach her as a witness, on the theory that a witness who has once slipped is somewhat less credible than one who has lived a life of unmitigated impeccability. The actual purpose, of course, was to besmirch, indirectly, the plaintiff, and to create atmosphere.

The chief significance of this case lies in the fact that the attorney happened to be one of the most eminent members of the bar; a man whose professional career entitled him to the respect and emulation of his brother attorneys. The Committee on Professional Ethics of the New York County Lawyers' Association, in reply to a question in a similar case, had this to say on the subject:

"The Committee considers that wanton, unnecessary or unreasonable inquiry or comment respecting the discreditable past history of a witness or party, is unethical and improper professional conduct; it cannot, however, assume to say that such inquiry or comment, whether admissible or not under the law of evidence, was, in the case suggested, wanton, unnecessary or unreasonable."

This practice is, nevertheless, a frequent occurrence in our country. Usually the lawyer is some obscure practitioner whose transgression is relatively unimportant. When, however, the offender is a man of prominence and conceded virtue and respectability his conduct assumes the importance of a precedent of professional behavior.

Another pillar of the bar recently, in the trial of an important case, denounced a witness as "a scoundrel and unfit to practice law" although, according to the New York *World*, "there was not one jot of evidence to support the attack." The lawyer subsequently, *after the trial,* wrote a letter of apology concerning which the *World* commented editorially as follows:

"In his letter, Mr.——begins by saying, 'My attention has been called by Judge —— to the fact that comments concerning you which I made . . . were unwarranted by the record.' This is a tacit admission that the apology did not come on his own motion but was crowbarred out of him by the court. He then goes on to explain that he had 'never read a word of the testimony given at the trial and relied entirely on my recollection thereof' and that 'I was led by my false impression of the testimony to make statements concerning you, which, of course, I would not have made but for my false belief.' This, if it were true, would be one of the most amazing confessions ever made by a lawyer; it would indicate a degree of irresponsibility incompatible with the trust he discharged; it would prove Mr. ——, if not exactly a 'scoundrel,' then at least a lawyer who will stoop to character assassination just in order to win his case."

Here again we have an example of professional impropriety in which the offending lawyer happens to be an outstanding embodiment of professional success. The belated apology and somewhat specious explanation cannot obscure the fact that litigation is a form of warfare in which loyalty to the client is the lawyer's primary duty, and that a successful result usually is a justification for lapses from strict ethical conduct.

The famous utterance of Lord Brougham in the defense of Queen Caroline has long been accepted in practice if not in theory by a large part of the profession as the classic statement of a lawyer's duty to his client:

"I once before took leave to remind your Lordships—which was unnecessary, but there are many whom it may be needful to remind—that an advocate, by the sacred duty which he owes his client, knows, in the discharge of that office, but one person in the world, that client and none other. To save that client by all expedient means—to protect that client at all hazards and costs to others, and among others to himself—is the highest and most unquestioned of his duties; and he must not regard the alarm, the suffering, the torment, the destruction which he may bring upon any other. Nay, separating even the duties of a patriot from those of an advocate, and casting them, if need be, to the wind, he must go on reckless of the consequences, if his fate it should unhappily be, to involve his country in confusion for his client's protection."

This unswerving devotion to the client's interests is the rock upon which the practice of law is builded. It has resulted, by the operation of a sort of ethical Gresham's law, in the supplanting of the idealistic lawyer morality by the more utilitarian client morality. This might be quite all right were the legal profession to recognize it and admit it. But the bar continues to adhere to the tradition of an obsolescent gentility and an ethical fundamentalism in the face of the obvious fact of professional evolution.

III

The truth is that the old order has passed—if, indeed, it ever existed. The great democratic experiment with its unrestricted opportunities for education and the selection of a career has completely demolished the professional caste system. With it has gone, unfortunately, the accompanying aristocratic concept of ethical obligation. Today, almost any one can become a lawyer; in fact, almost any one does.

The bar is making a praiseworthy effort to raise the tone of the profession by demanding higher educational qualifications from candidates for admission. This commendable attempt loses sight of the regrettable fact that morals and education do not necessarily go hand in hand. The most flagrantly anti-social practitioners are not exclusively among the semi-educated hangers-on of the police courts; they are quite as frequently found among those paragons of professional propriety who adorn the bar associations and who prepare codes of ethics for their less affluent brothers. There is little difference in the essential morality of the police-court lawyer who seeks to delay the machinery of law on behalf of his poor pickpocket client, and the eminent barrister who does precisely the same thing for his oil magnate or ex-cabinet official client. In the one instance the dilatory tactics may delay the case for six months or a year, and the fee is fifty dollars; in the other, the delay will be for years, if not forever, and the fee amounts to hundreds of thousands. In the one case the profession proceeds solemnly to view with alarm and passes virtuous and patronizing resolutions to purge the bar of shysters; in the other case it bestows its unqualified admiration upon the resourcefulness and skill of the lawyer who can succeed indefinitely in keeping a wealthy malefactor away from a jury.

The guardians of the aristocratic traditions of the profession are the teachers of law who are sheltered from the conflicts and temptations of active practice, the members of the judiciary who have emerged from them, and those distinguished, high-priced, successful practitioners generally referred to as the leaders of the bar. Ultimate responsibility for the standards of conduct of the legal profession rests upon this last group. By virtue of their preeminence, their professional behavior should afford criteria by which the young lawyer might properly gauge his professional conduct.

No lawyer ever finds difficulty in giving whole-hearted endorsement to those excellent platitudes and moral precepts that constitute the window-dressing of his profession. He believes courageously in Honesty, Purity, and the other collateral virtues and he is not afraid to say so. It is only when the fundamental moralities collide with some specific problem of his practice and threaten to hamper his activities that he brings into play all the ingenuity of the professional sophist, and attempts, according to the custom of the bar, to reconcile or distinguish. In such a case a large retainer is usually an excellent solvent for ethical embarrassments.

Thus we have the not infrequent spectacle of a distinguished attorney pleading for special tax legislation or special tariff legislation on behalf of some powerful corporation regardless of the economic consequences to society at large. Thus we see another eminent lawyer, who has been a strong conservationist all his life, arguing in Washington that there is no present need for certain governmental steps in connection with the conservation of oil. Thus, too, we see, occasionally, prominent ex-judges appearing before their former associates selling their prestige and their friendship and putting their names to briefs they have scarcely read.

IV

The bar has the popular esteem that it deserves. It cannot nourish its prestige upon an antiquated mysticism, it cannot achieve virtue by talking about it. With perhaps one exception, there is no other profession that is so loud in voicing its own respectability. There is no other profession quite so smug and self-satisfied, and at the same time quite so lacking in a sense of social obligation. An occasional rare soul, a Clarence Darrow, may dedicate his energies to the defense of unpopular causes and earn the supercilious disapproval of his more orthodox brethren. Here and there in the lower courts may be found some obscure lawyer battling for the poor, the needy, and the oppressed without regard for the pecuniary rewards that spell professional success. But these are the freaks of the profession; they are, to use that most devastating epithet, the radicals. Most lawyers prefer to seek the more comfortable and reputable rewards of pecuniary success.

One of the incidental consequences of this commercialization of the practice of law is the low repute in which the practice of criminal law is held. Compared with the emoluments of a high-class civil practice, as it is called, the practice of criminal law is notoriously unremunerative. There are certain breaches of the penal statutes which, because of the vast sums of money involved and the social eminence of the offenders, are surrounded by an aura of respectability. But on the whole the criminal lawyer is professionally *déclassé*. The average successful lawyer will say, "I never take criminal cases," in pretty much the same tone of voice as he would say, "I never pick pockets." The young lawyer, just admitted, is cautioned by his more experienced elders not to take criminal cases.

Professor Roscoe Pound once wrote: "Three stages may be perceived in the development of the American bar. The first stage is marked by the leadership of the trial lawyer. The great achievements of the bar were in the forum, *and the most conspicuous success was success before juries in the trial of criminal cases* . . . In the second stage leadership passed to the railroad lawyer. The proof of professional success was to represent a railroad company . . . Criminal law became the almost exclusive field of the lower stratum of the bar . . . Want of education, want of organization, want of discipline of those who are habitually most active in defending accused persons in our large cities, are conspicuous and significant facts."

Just at present the subject of crime and reform of criminal law is very much in the air. Learned discussions are being held, and ingenious suggestions are being made, principally by lawyers who have never seen the inside of a criminal court. Eminent barristers, skilled in the intricacies of corporation law, but who would not know an indictment from a blackjack, discuss with great solemnity whether or not there is justification for Mr. Justice Taft's much quoted dictum that "the administration of criminal law in the United States is a disgrace to civilization."

The criminal court is a laboratory in which problems of the most vital social significance are daily being solved. Eminent members of the medical profession habitually give their services in free clinics, and feel that they are adequately rewarded by the opportunities presented for service and experimentation. The standards of pecuniary success that prevail in the legal profession make similar clinical activities in the criminal courts impossible for the attorney who would retain the respect of his clients and his brother attorneys. The result is that a branch of professional activity of the utmost sociological importance is left in the hands of those who belong to what Professor Pound calls "the lower stratum of the bar."

It may be that the time has come for a revaluation of values, for a new statement of professional aims and purposes. It may be that the standards of contemporary materialism need to be accepted and recognized as existing and essential facts in the practice of law. But it is more hopeful to believe that the legal profession still contains within itself the essence of a higher morality and an enduring sense of public obligation. The abstract ethical beliefs of a community may approach the splendid ideals imposed by the churches and the schools; its ethical conduct can never rise above that of its lawyers.

Part Two

Chapter I

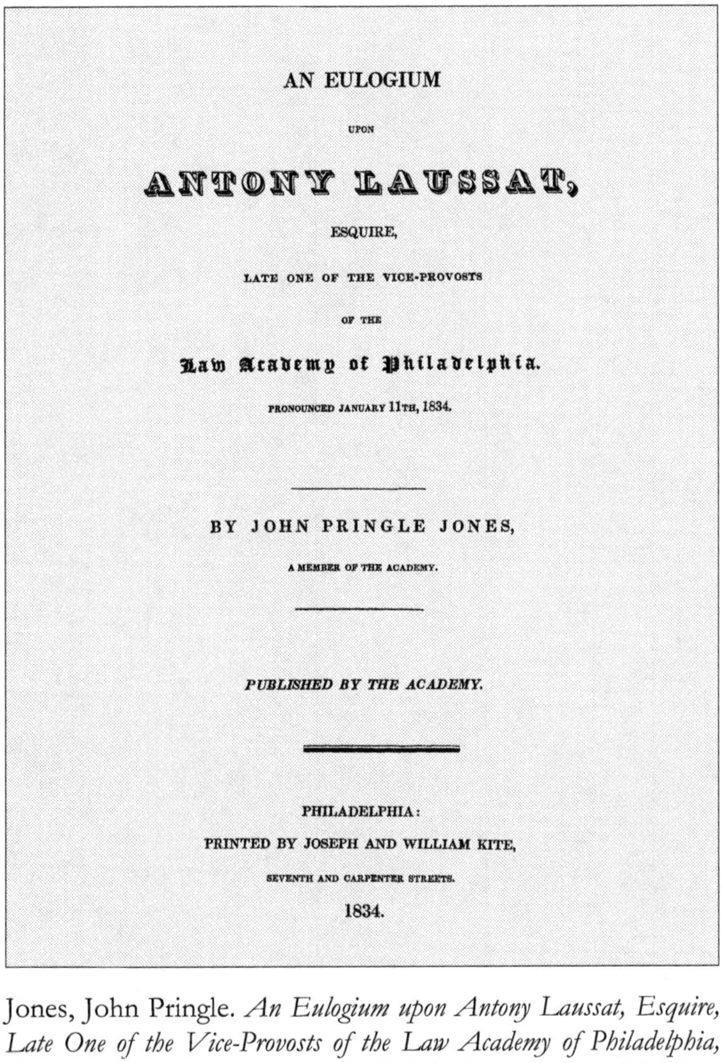

AN EULOGIUM

UPON

ANTONY LAUSSAT,

ESQUIRE,

LATE ONE OF THE VICE-PROVOSTS

OF THE

Law Academy of Philadelphia.

PRONOUNCED JANUARY 11TH, 1834.

BY JOHN PRINGLE JONES,

A MEMBER OF THE ACADEMY.

PUBLISHED BY THE ACADEMY.

PHILADELPHIA:

PRINTED BY JOSEPH AND WILLIAM KITE,

SEVENTH AND CARPENTER STREETS.

1834.

Jones, John Pringle. *An Eulogium upon Antony Laussat, Esquire, Late One of the Vice-Provosts of the Law Academy of Philadelphia, Pronounced January 11th, 1834*. Philadelphia: Joseph and William Kite, 1834.

EULOGIUM.

WE have not assembled, Gentlemen of the Law Academy, for the purpose of gratifying an illusive vanity under the specious pretext of honouring the dead, but for the honest purpose of paying a debt of private gratitude to the memory of a man, who was most active in bringing this institution into existence, in sustaining it during the feebleness of its infancy, and in conferring upon it honour and reputation by the exertion of his brilliant talents. We have followed him to that grave, in whose dreary depths are forever buried the bright and rational hopes, which his country, his profession and his friends, had built upon his youthful promise. And *now*, when the bitterness of grief is somewhat passed away—when the mind is no longer influenced by the heavy pressure of recent affliction—we have met together to indulge those melancholy feelings, which such a loss is calculated to inspire. The feeble voice, which you have designated to give utterance to your sorrows, will not elevate itself, in this time of mourning, into a strain of extravagant panegyric, outraging alike the sanctity of the tomb and the feelings of its hearers, but will endeavour to present an account of the life and character of the lamented *Laussat*, simple and unostentatious as was the man himself. It is believed that such an eulogium—if that the disembodied spirit hovers around the once-loved scenes of pleasure—would be to the invisible auditor the most fragrant incense praise could offer; and that to you, Gentlemen, nothing could be acceptable that is not strictly true. Another inducement to the design prescribed, arises from the consideration that the indi-

4

vidual, whose memory we cherish, was not much advanced beyond ourselves in the number of his years, and that therefore the faithful portraiture of his labours, may serve to guide some kindred spirit in the pathway of distinction, or rouse into active exertion some energies, which, though not less vigorous than *Laussat's*, have hitherto lain buried in obscuring inactivity. The brief career of an ambitious professional student, devoted to the pursuit of fame, cannot be expected to yield his eulogist much of that agreeable variety in which the memorials of all other classes of the *honoured* dead are so prolific; the deep seclusion in which such a man is ordinarily involved, covers his life with a veil impenetrable to the gaze of curiosity; he lives apart from the great mass, devoting his strength of mind and body to the gratification of his immortal passion, and leaves us nothing whereby to judge of him, except the production of his unseen, but untiring labours.

To review minutely the life of a man of this stamp, to search after the first development of his genius, to lay bare his efforts to surmount the rugged steep, from whose top he might "be known to all posterity," would be a delightful and instructive task; but it is one, from entering upon which I am precluded by an almost utter ignorance of the early and private history of the man. However, the meagre details, which an unceasing application has been enabled to procure, shall not be withheld; and, though vague and unsatisfactory, they cannot prove altogether devoid of interest, connected as they are with one, who inspired so much of that absorbing feeling.

The father of *Antony Laussat* was one of those unhappy fugitives, whom the unfavourable termination of the servile wars in St. Domingo drove forth from that lovely island to seek new fortunes in other climes. The ruined planter came to this city, bringing with him no resources, save the indestructible capital of honour, talents and industry, sustained by which, he rose superior to two subsequent prostrations of his self-acquired fortunes, and was enabled, in the decline of life, to retire to the enjoyment of ease and happiness upon a fine estate, far removed from the scenes of commercial perplexity. It may well be imagined that a man, who had experienced so severely the vicissitudes to which material wealth is subjected, would feel most sensibly the importance of giving to his children a possession, over which external causes can but rarely exercise an influence. Impressed thus with expanded views of the necessity and value of education, he proceeded upon the most liberal principles, in extending the means of its attainment to the objects of his nearest solicitude; and before the good old man was gathered to his fathers, he had lived long enough to rejoice over the wisdom of the course he had pursued, made manifest in its fruits, and to feel a sweet assurance that he himself had opened to an aspiring mind, the portals through which it was pressing onward to immortality. I must solicit your indulgence for thus attracting your attention to an individual so connected with the object of our meeting; but the reputation of one's offspring is so often no more than a reflection from the mirror of the parental virtues, that upon principles of general morality, it belongs to the source from whence it is derived; and we cannot too highly appreciate the worthy man, (however unknown to fame,) who gives to the republic a distinguished citizen, whose character is formed upon an imitation of the domestic model.

It was observed as a peculiar feature in the dawning intellect of our friend, that he displayed no decided preference for either of the great initiatory branches of learning, but was equally and eminently successful in his cultivation of those abstract sciences, which give to the reasoning faculty force and strength; and of those ancient languages which offer imperishable instruction, whereby to form the heart or elevate the taste. Proficient, far beyond his years, in these, the prerequisite studies, he entered the University of Pennsylvania, and before he had attained the age of sixteen, was admitted by that venerable and excellent institution to the first degree in the arts. That he did not graduate with the highest distinction, in the largest class that ever left the halls of the university, is to be ascribed, rather to his extreme youth, than to any cause unfavourable to his application or moral standing, for both of which the professors gave an unequivocal proof of their estimation, in assigning him a public exercise on the day of Commencement. The subject which he selected for his discourse, shows, that even then, his mind had turned in upon itself for the task of self-examination, and the discourse itself, (on the Various Sources of Mental Improvement,) exhibited a vigour of thought and an elegance of style, quite unusual on such occasions.

We now approach a period of his life, which, in the case of every individual, involves considerations of the deepest moment; intimately connected as it is with the realization of his fondest hopes of usefulness, happiness or renown. The process of his collegiate education, enabling him to form an impartial opinion of his talents, had prepared him to meet without prejudice and without distrust in himself, the great question, upon whose resolution so much depends; and calm, deliberate conviction of the propriety of the choice, led him to adopt the profession of the law. In this bold step, (for as such we must look upon the action of a boy not yet sixteen, abandoning the flowery fields of literature and the delights of science, to enter upon what are called the laborious and painful mysteries of legal learning,) we may easily recognize the promptness of purpose and clearness of judgment, for which our friend was afterwards so much distinguished. Conscious that no profession, that no business of life, however humble, opened an avenue to its highest appropriate reward, unless pursued with a concentration of all the powers to the one object, and prepared for the utmost devotion that might be required, he looked forward, not in idle vanity of heart, but with a certain prospect of attainment to the most dazzling distinctions of his chosen avocation. He fixed on the sun of honour an eagle-gaze, that

7

could not be averted. With such views of the importance of persevering application and industry, with an inflexible determination of spirit, that would not quail under difficulties, however weighty, he obtained admission into the office of a member of the Philadelphia bar, eminent for every qualification that can adorn the lawyer or dignify the man.*

For a few moments let us pursue our friend through the course of his professional life, and see how well he sustained the practice of those rigid principles, which he had marked out for the government of his conduct, the early formation of which is of inexpressible importance.

We sometimes behold a mind, gifted with transcendent powers, breaking through the ordinary restraints which an Infinite Wisdom has imposed, and soaring on the wings of its heaven-born energies, to command at once the wonder and delight of man. In contemplating such a character, that of a Patrick Henry for instance, how many, how very many unthinking men have formed to themselves the idea of emulating the seductive example; and in idle anticipation of a propitious hour, when, meteor-like, they should burst upon the astonished world,

——— have vanished from the earth,
Leaving no vestige of memorial there.

It is not by following these delusive phantoms, that in any profession we can rationally hope to realize success; but in *that* in which our lot is cast, more than in any other, he who turns him from the clear light of the torch of science, and pursues the glaring splendour of some gay deception, will find it "darken to despair," and when repentance comes at last, *too late*, will find the glorious vision all dissolved in disappointment. There are other dangers, scarcely inferior to that of relying upon some subsequent development of eloquence or genius, which assail the student in a thousand shapes, and require him to be constantly panoplied in the armour of resolution, to resist their insidious temptations, or to repel their more

* Charles Jared Ingersoll, Esquire.

active, and more open assaults. The refined enjoyments of society, the allurements of Protean pleasure, are alike, though in different degrees, and by different means, calculated to withdraw him from deep and intense application.

How few are they, who have not listened to the bland and soothing whisperings of a vanity, that would penetrate the gloom of coming years, and make flattering promises, never, never to be fulfilled. How few are they, who have not mingled in, and felt the difficulty of withdrawing from the intoxicating delights of society? How very few are they who have dashed untasted from their lips, the chalice, whose potent draught is mixed by death, presented by deceit.

Through all the unreal and shadowy forms, in which these temptations hung around his path, our friend, erect in reason's majesty, passed on unharmed. To *him* the syren sung her song in vain. His mind of burning thought, his nature of deep feeling, his soul of lofty aspirations, were all averse to an inglorious use of life. The intellect of this kind can never stagnate into useless, miserable indolence; its faculties reach forth, and grasp at what is mighty; its course is like the living waters, invigorating all it touches; its sojourn on earth we measure not by time—"actions are its epochs." Original, powerful, and capacious, it moves not in the common sphere, but driven into motion, is governed by its own peculiar laws. Such is the character of mind, which can mould itself into any form of greatness; the impression of any passion, once stamped upon it, can never be effaced. The choice of a profession was in *Laussat* the 'impression of a passion,' and the untiring cultivation of it was necessarily the moving principle, the spring of every action. To attain the "vantage ground" of the science, his clear conception at once struck out the unerring road; and in patient investigation, severe, though made without the appearance of much effort, he laboured onward with a natural ardour that could not be resisted. Doubts and difficulties vanished before a perseverance, which was rather animated than depressed by their presence; before a resolution which gathered strength from their opposition. In these conflicts, from which common men retire disheartened, he gained lasting advantages; his mind was disciplined into habits of reflection; he learned to think for himself; and giving, as he did, to every subject, the most unwearying attention, his opinions were remarkable for the force of argument and ingenuity with which they were sustained, and for the extensive research with which they were illustrated.

Bearing constantly in memory the observation of the author of Eunomus, "that knowledge is not so much increased by a "continued accession of new ideas, as by accurately comparing "the relations of those ideas, which we have already received," he did not launch out into vague and various reading, but confined himself to a well-directed course. On this he brought every energy of his intellect into operation, and chaining down imagination and the restless love of change, which might otherwise expose abstracted reason to their infinite intrusions, he pursued each principle, as it arose, up to its very source. The man who thus investigates our science, whose object is to penetrate the very sanctuary of its truth, can never degenerate into the mere "*acutus præco actionum, cantor formularum,*" he must one day take a stand among the sages, whose philosophic minds have dignified and illuminated the subjects of their inquiry; among those, who, in departing hence, carry not with them, *all*, wherewith they have adorned the world.

To us, Gentlemen of the Law Academy, it might be a source of profitable gratification, taking into view our destination in the same profession, to examine minutely the system of elementary instruction which was adopted in the legal education of *Laussat,* and which was so felicitous in its results, but circumstances sufficiently obvious, forbid our entering upon this fruitful and inviting theme.

There is, however, another subject connected with this period of *Laussat's* life, to which, in inviting your attention, I may be allowed to indulge those feelings of honest pride, that it must ever inspire in the members of our Academy. His Essay on Equity in Pennsylvania was an academic exercise—a performance produced in the discharge of an academic duty, written without the expectation of its being known or heard of beyond the walls of the institution, and presented with an entire unconsciousness of the value of its contents. If the Law Academy had no other claim to notice than what is conferred by having stimulated the production of this essay, by having given forth this able vindication of our judicial polity, it is humbly conceived that such a claim should entitle her to no small share of public estimation. But apart from this, she can point to a living son whose Treatise on the Penal System* has greatly enhanced the force of that claim; and to the many luminous addresses and opinions, which from time to time she has elicited from the distinguished gentlemen who constitute the faculty.

Permit me, now that we are met together to lament over the premature fate, which has forever deprived us of *Laussat,* to present to you an account of this essay; to some of you its history is well known; to many, nothing is known beyond the fact of its existence.

In the April of 1825, the Provosts appointed "for the subject of dissertation during the approaching recess," Equity in Pennsylvania. The outline, which they sketched for the government of the writers who might be selected, embraced the much vexed question, whether, in this state, a separate Court of Chancery is indispensably necessary; and if a writer maintained the negative, he was farther required to point out the manner in which that court may be supplied. In the language of *Bolingbroke,* "To discover the reason of laws—to "trace the laws of particular states, especially of his own, "from the first rough sketches to the more perfect draughts—"from the first cause or occasion that produced them, through "all the effects, good or bad, that they produced," was an em-

* J. R. Tyson, Esquire, now one of the Vice-Provosts.

11

ployment particularly congenial to the taste and habits of *Laussat,* and one, for the effective prosecution of which, the attention he had bestowed upon his previous studies was a certain pledge; with all the enthusiasm of nineteen, for he had then but very recently attained that age, he entered upon the labours of the appointment, and, incredible though it may appear, I am sustained by the very best authority in asserting, that in less than four months the work was finished. It is not by reference to the size of a book, that we can estimate the difficulty which attended its production. This is wholly independent of such a consideration, and, in the case before us, was, undoubtedly, much increased by unusual causes. The negative of the question proposed never had been a favourite with the profession; in fact, an almost unanimous voice condemned it; great caution, therefore, was requisite, in conducting its defence; in addition to this, it involved grave inquiries into civil policy, and deep antiquarian research; and as it was also to be treated in a legal point of view, the collection and arrangement of apposite authorities formed a difficulty, which no one can so well appreciate as the unpractised student. Submitted to the inspection of the Provosts, the essay drew from them the most flattering encomiums, and they urged upon the academy the propriety of publishing it, as a measure well calculated "to give a favourable opinion of the institution abroad." It was not without extreme reluctance that the youthful author assented to the proposition. His modesty was disinclined from appearing before the tribunal of public opinion; he shrunk from even the appearance of presumption; what were his feelings upon this point, we may gather from his own words in the short preface, that he affixed to the printed work;—"as the publication of this essay is to "be ascribed exclusively to those who are at the head of our "institution, the writer trusts that he will be acquitted from "the imputation of a desire to obtrude himself upon an en- "lightened profession, from whom he has yet much to learn, "and whom he certainly will not presume to instruct." To canvass the intrinsic merits of this essay is not within my present duty; the question it discusses is one, which is, perhaps, definitively put to rest; and it only remains for us to hope that time will produce a perfection in our judicial constitution, from which it now is confessedly far removed. There have been, however, opinions upon the merits of this essay, which cannot be suppressed—that justice to the dead requires me to exhibit.

Chief Justice Marshall writes to our venerable Provost,* that "if any thing could move his prejudices in favour of the "separation of the Courts of Common Law and Equity, it "would be the argument of this essay." An American lawyer could wish no higher commendation, than such a testimonial from that great father of the profession. Chancellor Kent declares, that before reading it, he had never been able to imagine how we administered justice in Pennsylvania, and congratulates, not merely the bar of Philadelphia, but every bar where the English Common Law is the basis of legal science, upon what might be anticipated from the future exertions of so vigorous a mind. Nor was this applause imited to our own country. Several British periodicals noticed the work in a tone not usual, in commenting upon things American; and the late Mr. Park, Professor of Law in King's College, London, himself a well-known writer, entered into a correspondence with *Laussat,* which terminated only with his life.

Upon a man of less solid understanding, this accumulation of delightful praise would have fallen with an overwhelming force, and contenting him with what he had achieved, would have been fatal to all further effort; upon the well-regulated mind of our friend, it acted only as a strong incentive to urge him forward, and relaxed not in the slightest degree that severe and arduous toil, for which he had thus far been so worthily rewarded. About one year after the publication of the Essay on Equity in Pennsylvania, its author's legal noviciate was

* Peter S. Du Ponceau, L. L. D.

13

brought to a close by his admission to practice. Before leaving this portion of his life, I cannot forbear a remark upon the fidelity with which the duties of instruction were performed by his eminent preceptor; and I am the rather inclined so to do, from an apprehension that it would be beneficial to students, if all, who open offices for their reception, would pay equal regard to their interests; he, to whom the charge of *Laussat's* instruction was confided, did not thrust out the feeble bark, freighted with all the young aspirant's hopes, into the vast cloud-covered ocean, to struggle through its dangers, to sink or swim, as *chance* might dictate; but with great care, great skill, he piloted it himself through the voyage, in whose success so much was staked. Left to himself, an ardent youth *may* sometimes " steer aright;" but for the many

> O'er them and o'er their names the billows close;
> Tomorrow knows not they were ever born.

Issuing from the hands of one, who had taken so much pains to form his professional character, it cannot be matter of astonishment that *Laussat* at once assumed a prominent rank among the junior members of the bar. It was not by eloquence that he expected to rise; " an accurate judgment" (it is said,) " is seldom friendly to copious declamation," and luxuriant fancy and wild imagination were not his. If, with him, an appeal, clear and forcible, fluently expressed, carried not conviction directly to the reason, he sought not to mislead by calling to its aid the passions. There was nothing cold or dull, however, in his speaking; on the contrary, it was impetuous, and gleamed with all the fire and ardour of his soul.

In his intercourse with the court and jury, he was uniformly regulated by rules of strictest truth and honour; from these plain, yet noble guides of conduct, no temporary advantage to be gained could tempt him to depart. The wretched sophism,which throws the gloss of virtue over the deviations from her precepts, which stifles the accusing voice of conscience with a paltering subterfuge, a mental lie, found

14

no favour in his sight; whatever conscience could not reconcile with perfect purity of heart, *that* was rejected; for he wisely deemed no gain a recompense for loss of self-esteem. Bold and independent, he feared no frown, he courted no protection, he could not compromise his stern, unbending dignity, for any earthly favour. In his attention to business, no man was ever more prompt or more devoted; the client left his office with the full assurance that his advocate would take the liveliest interest in his cause, and that no measure to ensure its success would be neglected, which human foresight or sagacious prudence could suggest. The preparation, which he made to appear in court was elaborate and thorough, and in conducting a suit through trial, his ability has been frequently felt and freely acknowledged. Amid the care and anxiety ever attendant upon an extensive practice, our friend still found time to prepare an edition of Fonblanque's Treatise on Equity, which, from its numerous notes and references to American decisions, is regarded as a valuable addition to the stock of legal learning, and is cited with approbation throughout the union. He occasionally contributed to the American Quarterly Review, in which his *critiques* exhibited abundant proof, that his taste in polite literature was as elegant and refined, as his learning in law was various and profound.

We have now completed the survey of a professional character, that perhaps approached as near perfection, so far as it was developed, as any which it has been our fortune to behold; that its future would have been one of surpassing brilliance, had fate permitted, is a conjecture which irresistibly forces itself upon our minds, and we therefore lament over the early death of *Laussat,* not so much from a consideration of what he *really* was, as from an anticipation of what he must, at no distant period, have been.

Exclusive of ambition and talents, the other elements of his success are within the reach of every one; without *them,* talents will lead to infamy, and ambition be of no avail. Industry and integrity were those other elements. He who possesses them, let him guard them well; they are the most current coin of time, they may be of eternity; he who has them not, let him look to it; he is a moral bankrupt; he stands upon the brink of everlasting ruin. In our profession, Gentlemen, the man, who lacks these unpretending qualities, *may* sometimes rise, but his elevation only serves to make his fall more signal, more impressive. Industrious cunning, and the miserable arts of mean chicane, pandering to crime and prostituting justice, *may give one* practice, they can never give one honour. We have been told that the lawyer should "spurn at "baseness, abhor fraud, advocate pure morality, uphold truth, "and illustrate virtue." How can he meet these duties, if he lack integrity?

The same constitution of mind and morals, which insures honourable success to the lawyer, opens likewise a similar prospect to the politician. In that character, the example of *Laussat* is equally worthy of our regard and imitation. It is a generally received opinion, that the politician of this country must sacrifice every principle of manly independence, and shutting up his motives in the most secret chambers of his soul, must, by intrigue, dissimulation and servility, creep into notice. This crooked, dangerous course, thronged by the worthless and depraved, had no charms for one, whose honest spirit could not brook the contact of deception, who could not "make debasing signs to catch the public eye." Not actuated by that mean selfishness of motive, which directs the office-hunting politician, *Laussat* connected himself with the party which has been dominant in Pennsylvania for many years, and in 1830 was elected to represent this city in the State Legislature. Attending closely to his duties in that body, he laboured for the interests of his party, but with a wider range of feeling, he also laboured for the public good. His speeches were numerous, and always commanded "a most breathing silence." All measures of obvious utility found in him an able advocate, and al-

16

though nearly the youngest member of the house, he was among the most respected. That the manner in which he discharged his duties was acceptable to his constituents, is proved by the fact, that he was again invited to present himself before the people, a candidate for their suffrages, an honour which he was obliged to decline. Leaving the halls of legislation, and returning into the ranks of private life, he still actively co-operated with the leaders of the Democratic party, and constantly enjoyed their fullest confidence and regard.

The severe mental exertions, which were required to meet his professional and political engagements, acting upon a delicate constitution, subject already to the ravages of a disease, that baffles every effort of the healing art, at length prostrated the enfeebled frame. His sufferings were not protracted ; they rapidly advanced to their fatal termination; and in the last, dread hour,

> A peace above all earthly dignities,
> A still and quiet conscience,

sustained the courage of the sinking heart, and composed and calmed the wandering mind, to meet the awful change, unawed, unmoved. O'er the wreck of all the visions of beguiling hope, o'er premature decay, he murmured not, but sunk into the embrace of death, as best became a philosophic man.

If the contemplation of some faultless model is pregnant with instruction to the thinking mind, there stands not, in all the niches of ambition's temple, one more worthy of our reverence and imitation, than that which bodies forth the memory of our departed friend.

CHAPTER II

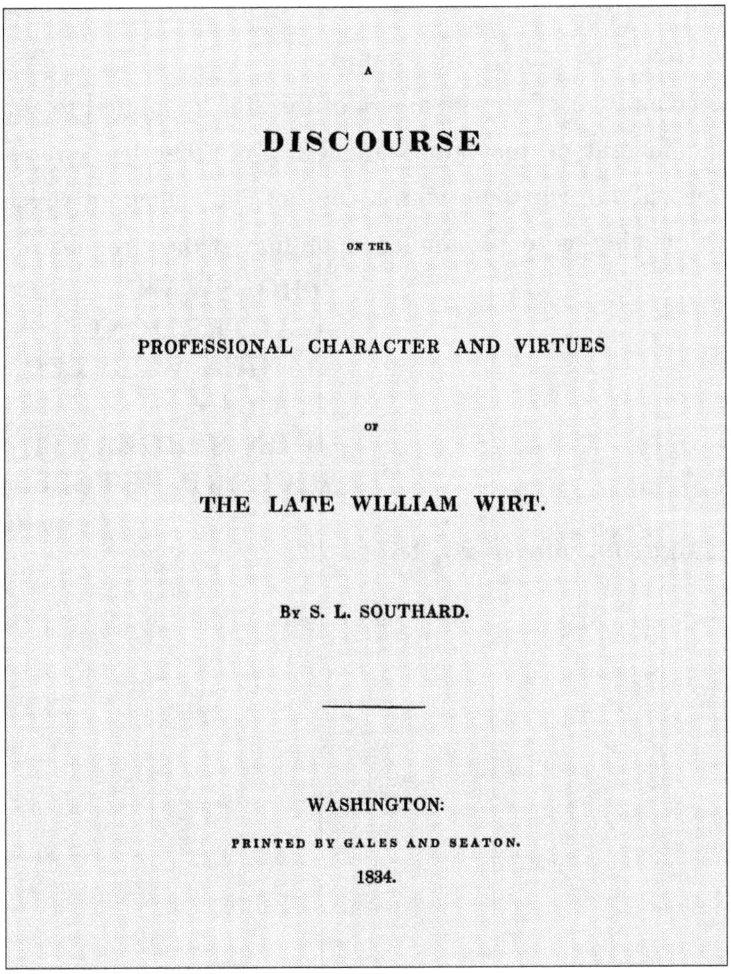

A

DISCOURSE

ON THE

PROFESSIONAL CHARACTER AND VIRTUES

OF

THE LATE WILLIAM WIRT.

BY S. L. SOUTHARD.

WASHINGTON:

PRINTED BY GALES AND SEATON.

1834.

Southard, S. L. A *Discourse on the Professional Character and Virtues of the Late William Wirt*. Washington: Gale and Seaton, 1834.

To the Hon. SAMUEL L. SOUTHARD:

The committee of the members of the Bar appointed to superintend the funeral of the late WILLIAM WIRT, beg leave to request that you will furnish them with a copy of the eulogium which you were so obliging as to pronounce upon him at their request.

THO. SWANN,
WALTER JONES,
DANIEL WEBSTER,
H. CLAY,
JOHN SERGEANT,
RICHARD PETERS,
Committee.

WASHINGTON, *March* 20, 1834.

DISCOURSE.

Is death, then, an eternal sleep? Do genius, and learning, and virtue, slumber forever in the grave; or perish like things of earth? leave no monument of good behind them? and offer, in the anticipations of the future, nothing of immortality and glory? It is the atheist's creed. It is the Christian's abhorrence.

He, whom, without affectation of grief, we mourn, has refuted the odious doctrine. *He* had the capacity to affect the conduct and character of many of his contemporaries. *He* has left memorials which will be regarded with profit by posterity; and, by a meritorious life and pious death, has furnished a persuasive argument for that religious faith which guides us here, and points to an eternity of happiness beyond the tomb. The power of virtue and talent is not unfelt at the moment of their exertion. They *do* produce salutary effects on the conduct of mankind, and often act, with increasing energy, as time rolls on. Centuries have not paralysed the examples of the patriots and scholars of

4

Greece, and Rome, and England. He who can, by a life of energetic virtue, excite the approbation of compeers, and enkindle the emulation of the young, must, in equal degree, operate on the prosperity of his fellow men; and he knows not when or where the influence of his life shall terminate. Examples for evil or for good, which reach our contemporaries, act, through them, on our children, and our children's children.

The partial triumph of virtue, then, is *here* and *now;* but it perishes not with the close of life. It acts upon the years which are yet to come; and its ultimate reward is the Christian's destiny.

They who survive departed worth and greatness have a legacy in the actions and sentiments of the deceased, rich in the possession, and which they are bound to secure to those who have right to the inheritance. They have a duty to discharge, to the dead and to the past; but more—to the living and to the future. It becomes them to cherish the memory of the wise and the good; to exhibit them for imitation, and to make their renown a nation's property—a nation's wealth.

In this duty, it is the privilege of afflicted friendship to partake; to aid in proclaiming the worth which it admired and loved; and thus to repay a portion of the debt which has been cast upon it.

You, brethren of the bar, have not been insensible to these truths; and our surrounding fellow-citizens testify, that you are not alone in your sensibility. A whole nation feels, with you, that HE has

5

departed, who was one of the strongest among her strong; one of the learned among her scholars; one of the most eloquent among her advocates; one of the most elevated among her dignified; one of the most virtuous among her wise; one of the most admired among her beloved. And while we are here, to commune together, and recount the story of his life and merits, we are permitted to rejoice that he has left behind him nothing to impair the ardor of our admiration—nothing to weaken the warmth of our attachment—nothing to diminish unanimous applause. His bold and manly independence of thought, expression, and action—his unbending perseverance in the pursuit of duty—forty years of steady, and often triumphant intellectual competition and conflict, were so controlled and regulated by purity and kindness of heart and purpose, that he created, even with inferiority, no envy; with generous rivalry, no embittered feelings, no smart. "We loved him, for we knew him; and who that knew him, loved him not?" His loss will not, speedily, be repaired to our profession, to our tribunals of justice, nor to our country; and, to ourselves—never.

"The professional character and virtues" of William Wirt are inseparably combined with the incidents of his life, and cannot properly be estimated without a brief allusion to them. But these must be repeated, with rigid simplicity, and unadorned narrative of the facts, as they have been, in various ways, stated by himself to others, or communicated to the speaker in that uncovered friendship which

6

laid bare the illustrations of character and the feelings of the heart. Such narrative and statement alone would have satisfied his own judgment, in his own case, and been required by him as the only fit tribute from his associates and brothers. I cannot but regard the selection of your organ on this occasion, as indicating your will, that equal simplicity and absence of ornament should mark the attempted portrait of his character and virtues. The task is essayed, with feelings, in which intimate, and now agonized friendship, bears a painful part; and it shall be discharged, with honesty in the detail, even at the expense of dulness in the speaker, and fatigue in the hearer. But I shall draw, from his own words and writings, and descriptions of qualities and manners, much that I have to say in relation to himself. In portraying the virtues of others; in describing the properties, at which a high, but chastened ambition ought to aim, both for the benefit of the individual and the public, he often, unconsciously, sat before the mirror; and has thus enabled me, as to several of the traits of his mind and heart, to use his own language in speaking his eulogy, and his own pencil in drawing his portrait.

The parents of William Wirt were a Swiss and a German, who resided, at the time of his birth, on the 8th of November, 1772, at Bladensburg, near this city. He was the youngest of six children. His father died when he was an infant; and his mother, when he had reached his eighth year. Being in very moderate circumstances as to property, they left him barely sufficient means to support him at school, until he was fifteen years old. Neither distinguished ancestry, a father's fame, nor abundant wealth, aided his acquirements, excited his ambition, nor guided in the formation of his character. To him, they were not necessary. To his eminence they might have been auxiliaries, but not essentials. Resting upon his own native powers; favored by the institutions and habits of his country; and urged on by the rugged and enterprising spirit of liberty, which pervaded others and possessed himself, he formed and executed those generous and lofty purposes, which made him what he was—*suæ fortunæ faber*.

His preparatory education was received in Georgetown, in Charles county, and at the school of the Rev. Mr. Hunt, in Montgomery. In the two former, he commenced the study of the Latin; but in the latter, where he remained from his 12th to his 15th year, he received the most valuable part of his instruction.

On the closing of Mr Hunt's school, he earnestly desired to be transferred to the college at Princeton, of which his teacher had been a graduate; and at the time felt deep regret that the *res angustæ domi* had prevented the gratification of his wishes.

For two years after he left the school, he lived in the family of Mr. Benjamin Edwards, in Montgomery county; gave instruction to his children and to others, and pursued his own studies with diligence and profit. Some of those whom he instructed were of greater age than himself, and had been his schoolmates, with equal advantages. But he was eminently successful in their instruction, and derived essential benefit to himself, by impressing more indelibly upon his own memory the studies of which he was obliged to be master enough to teach them. At the age of 17 he commenced the study of the law, with a son of Mr. Hunt, at the court-house of the county; and he subsequently continued it, at Leesburg in Virginia, in the office of Thomas Swann, one of our present associates; who, I feel assured, partakes with no ordinary feelings in the mournful tribute which we attempt to pay to his worth; a tribute rendered more dear to him than to others, by his recollections of the budding blossoms which preceded the rich and ripened fruit, and by more than forty years of unalloyed, congenial friendship.

Many incidents in this early period might be exhibited for the gratification of our feelings, and excite to emulation; but they are appropriate to his biography, and would inaptly protract my discourse.

Of that part of his life to which I have adverted, he always retained an evergreen remembrance. His native home; the family circle; the surrounding scenery; the youth; the manhood; the age; the neighborhood; the companions of his play and of his studies; his teachers; the incidents of labor and of sport, were always present in their minutest details, whenever he chose to recall them; and of each and all, though long separated from them, he was capable of giving the most amusing and graphic descriptions. This was, indeed, one of the striking features of his intellect and his affections. No scenery; no person; no peculiarity of conduct, or even of dress; no development of principles of action, escaped his observation. No favor, or kindness, or act of benevolence passed unheeded. He seized and stored them all, in the treasury of his memory and his heart, from which they did not escape; nor were they lost in the lapse of years. His sensibility to the beauties of nature and conduct; the retention of his memory, with his power of description, appeared in his private conversations, and in his public exercises; and furnished anecdote and illustration even in the midst of his closest argument.

When he entered upon his profession, and sought a residence beyond his native State, with the exception, perhaps, of an offended usher whom his wit and waggery had chastised, but who in after years loved and was proud of him, he left behind him nothing but affectionate regards, united with warm aspirations for his prosperity. Although an unprotected orphan, he had found in every house, a home; in every companion, a friend; and in every teacher, a parent.

He obtained his license in 1792, a few days before he was 20 years old; and, with the difficulties which surrounded him, it is not probable that his preparation was enlarged and full. His first reading, independent of classical studies, was not calculated to invigorate his mind, or hasten a reputation for learning. Works, like Guy Earl of Warwick, and Peregrine Pickle, are said to have first fed his literary appetite, and increased his desire for more and stronger aliment. In the libraries of his preceptor, Mr. Hunt, and his friend, Mr. Edwards, he found a few others better calculated to assist, and polish, and strengthen his mind; and he devoured them as whim, or fancy, or accident, directed. Pope, Addison, and Hume, with some of the historians of past ages, completed the circle of his general reading.

He probably carried into the study of the law less accurate knowledge in other branches of learning than in the Greek and Latin languages. Those who were familiar with him as a companion and speaker, must have observed the promptness and the aptness of his quotations from both the ancient and modern classics. This had its origin in the exercises of the grammar schools, such as capping verses and reciting passages from memory, which were similar to those in the schools of England, and which he remarked "give to the speakers in St. Stephen's chapel quite as much facility and reputation, on this point, as their own warm poetic sensibility;" and was perfected by the labor of instruction. He retained, through all his professional life, great fondness for Horace, Virgil, Cicero, Seneca, and the other Latin classics; one of them, usually Horace, was an inmate of his valise in all his rides to the county courts; and the candle often flickered in its socket, before he bade good-night to the satirist.

He, very early, attempted the art of writing; but nothing is to be found of his schoolboy efforts, which can justify an estimate of his success in the imitation of Pope and others, whose precocious authorship inspired his emulation. We only learn that he wrote a satire on the usher, for some real or imagined injustice towards himself, which amused the principal, and inflamed the resentments of the usher, and induced him to withdraw from the school. And also, that having attended a few times at the court of the county, and heard some causes tried, he drafted a constitution and body of laws for a court to be composed of his playmates, accompanied by a letter of apology for the deficiencies of his work. Whether the letter was in imitation or ridicule of the example of his seniors, we are not told. What was the real merit of these performances, it is too late to decide ; but they and other efforts occasioned an augury of future reputation, and secured useful favors to him. The latter, especially, attracted the notice of Mr. Edwards, of whose kindness he always spoke with grateful sensibility. Mr. Edwards, though a man of limited education, had strong and original conceptions—benignity and sportiveness of disposition—a clear and even polished mode of speaking—ardent love of the principles of liberty—and deep veneration for those, in every age, who had been its advocates and defenders. He saw the embarrassments which his young friend had to encounter; and labored, as a parent labors, to urge him on to their overthrow. One of these was a painful timidity, amounting to absolute bashfulness—so oppressive, that it produced confusion, impediment, and fluttering of speech, even in common conversation. In addition to this, his enunciation was bad. Although he did, on one occasion, bear off the palm of eloquence in the school, yet he attributed it rather to the vanity of the teacher, who had written his speech, than to his own oratory. They who have since been familiar with the clearness, music, and flexibility of his voice in conversation, and his distinct, emphatic, and unembarrassed pronunciation in public speaking, may find it not easy to credit that then, and even after he entered on the practice of his profession, his utterance was thick—his tongue clumsy, and apparently too large—his pronunciation of words clipping—and, when excited by feeling, his voice unmanageable; sometimes bursting out in loud, harsh, indistinct, and imperfect articulation. But history tells us of the pebbles of Demosthenes; and it is over such adversaries that labor and genius obtain their triumphs. He did not sink into despondency under them, as thousands would have done. He knew that to conquer nature must be his own work—and his success was complete.

After he obtained his license, he went into the counties of Culpeper, Orange, and Albemarle, in the State of Virginia, to select a place for his professional action, and subsequently pursued the practice there. On this trip, he first met *one*, before whom he has so often since discussed the interests of his clients, abstruse legal questions, and the principles of the constitution—who has so long held the scales of law and justice, in a hand that never trembled—

and whose name may not now be repeated, although it is so deeply lodged in our affections, and so often bursts, with almost involuntary emotion, from our lips.* On his return, he drew, for his friend Swann, the portrait of that individual, present and prophetic; and never after desired to change its colors or its features.

He was, probably, moved to the selection of his residence by the belief that he should find a wider sphere for exertion, more sure prospects of wealth, stronger competition, and loftier distinctions in the then palmy state of that ancient commonwealth. The result proved the wisdom of his choice. Wide as was the sphere, he was found capable of filling it; strong as was the competition, he did not sink under it; lofty as were the distinctions which she bestowed on learning and eloquence, they, more than once, courted his acceptance; rich and abundant as were her jewels, her adopted son became one of the most precious.

His first appearance was in a cause, in the county court of Culpeper, which had fallen into the hands of a young acquaintance. It was their joint and only stock, with which their adventure was to be made; and deserves remark, only, as the first effort of the mind of William Wirt in a profession, which, for more than forty-one years, he pursued, dignified and adorned. There had been a joint judgment against *three* for assault and battery; two had been released subsequent to judgment; the third taken in

* Chief Justice Marshall was present at the delivery of the discourse.

14

execution and imprisoned. Our tyroes did not resort to the old remedy by *audita querela*, but asked relief by the more summary mode of motion, according to the indulgence of courts in more modern times. The motion was presented and argued by his associate. Some of the members of the bar, dissatisfied with the mode of proceeding, and the principles advanced in relation to the release, interposed their advice, as *amici curiæ*—a practice at that time, and perhaps yet, quite common in that class of tribunals ; arising, probably, from their composition, and the courtesy existing between the court and the bar. They possessed both common law and chancery jurisdiction, and were, in former times, composed of intelligent gentlemen of the counties, who, without fee, rendered to their fellow-citizens the service of deciding their controversies, and were anxious to have the lights which could be afforded by learned practitioners. I know not whether they have degenerated ; but at that, and a period more recent, the principles of justice, law, and equity were administered by them, with a correctness which would have done credit to less unpretending tribunals. The pride, the ambition, and perhaps some portion of the resentments of Mr. Wirt, were roused by the interference with his motion, and the manner in which it was treated; and his reply was animated and ardent, yet firm, collected, and successful. It extorted the approbation of the court and audience, and introduced him to more than one individual who predicted his future reputation, and followed him with firm and constant friendship through life.

His practice increased with some rapidity, and was pursued in those counties for nearly seven years, four of which he passed in the family of Dr. G. Gilmer, to whose daughter he was married in 1795. The bar in those counties, as elsewhere in Virginia, was candid, urbane, and respectable for talent and acquirement. His associations among them were pleasant, and he speedily acquired an uncommon share of reputation, both as a lawyer and an advocate. It is not to be believed that his legal learning then merited very high applause. Stores of this kind of knowledge are not laid up in a brief space, or with few advantages of books and study. He probably owed his reputation more to his labor in his preparation for each case, to his prompt and skilful use of what he possessed, and to the force of his own talents, than to any extensive or accurate acquirements. His extra-professional reading had also been generally desultory, and often light—rather calculated to furnish amusement and the gratification of his taste and fancy, than solid instruction. His difficulty in speaking was, however, wearing away under the self-discipline which he imposed, aided by his fine ear for music, and a correct sense of what is requisite, in the voice and manner, for success in oratory. His reputation for eloquence was high. Stronger and more cultivated minds were pleased with the vigor of his conceptions and the cogency of his arguments; while inferior ones were delighted with his exuberant fancy, and almost wild imagination. Among the former were men whose history belongs, not to a county, but to a nation; and they gave evidence of their respect and regard for him; and the most amusing anecdotes are recollected of the impressions which he made upon the great mass, who esteemed him as a master spirit in the art.

This period was also a time of imminent peril to his future hopes. He had then a vigorous constitution—fine mould of person—open, frank, and prepossessing countenance—graceful carriage and manners, though sometimes quick and impetuous. He was social in his disposition—fond of music to excess—performed skilfully on some instruments, and sung with uncommon ease and melody. He was full of animation—fond of anecdote, and told them with remarkable point and brilliancy. His powers of conversation were of a polished and classical kind; so that he was, literally, a fascinating companion. These are dangerous possessions to a young man, especially to one who has been early bereft of the shield and the refuge which the family altar and domestic fireside afford. It was natural that he should be sought by the young, the gay, and the ardent, and urged to partake in all the sprightly and dissipating amusements of the day. The trial was severe—his temper was social and yielding—his resistance too feeble for his own profit—too unsteady for the avoidance of some of the natural consequences. He lost firmness, and time and progress, in the road to distinct eminence. He was in jeopardy of shipwreck; and with less of native vigor, less of high and generous ambition, less of virtuous principle, he would, like thousands of others, have been borne on those waves beyond the sight of beacon, shore, or harbor, and lost forever. But there was a redeeming spirit in his nature—a light which penetrated the darkness; and, let me add, a saving hand in that Providence which cast succeeding events in his pathway.

His residence in the family of Dr. Gilmer, until the death of his wife, in 1799, was useful to him. Dr. Gilmer had a high professional and classical reputation, pure wit, and warm benevolence. The society around him exhibited a fine specimen of Virginia intelligence, elegance, and hospitality. Such a mind as Mr. Wirt's could not fail to profit of these circumstances. He mingled much in society, and formed an acquaintance with Monroe, Madison, Jefferson, and others, whose affectionate attachment remained unabated and ardent in his subsequent career, and was manifested by them all on every suitable opportunity. But he did not satisfy himself by social intercourse and professional pursuits. It was a period of immense importance to his future fame. He read and wrote diligently, and devoted an earnest attention to composition and to the formation of a correct style, which he had previously too much neglected. He also stored his mind by the earnest study of Bacon, and Boyle, and Locke, and Hooper, and other fathers of English literature; and the effects upon his intellectual powers were apparent and permanent. Although the exuberance of his prolific fancy was not yet subdued to the tone of his latter years, yet its wanderings were, in some degree, better corrected and controlled.

After the death of his wife, in 1799, he was elected clerk of the House of Delegates of Virginia—an office of larger profits and higher grade of respectability than in some of the other States. Here he became conversant with a large proportion of the gentlemen of talents in that part of the country, and with the deep agitations of political controversy. It was a time of great excitement; and the proceedings of the Assembly in that year have been the subject of more discussion, and produced a stronger effect on the formation and fate of parties, and the construction of the constitution, than those of any which has assembled in that or any other State. They have been text books for succeeding politicians; although, I believe, *their precise meaning* is, even yet, subject of debate. Of their merits, the occasion does not require me to speak. The constitutional opinions of the clerk, at that period of his life, may be inferred from the fact, that he concurred in their general principles. The impression which he made upon the members of the Legislature, by the manner in which he discharged his office, and by his intercourse with them, was exhibited in his selection, two years afterwards, for a high and weighty office.

His first appearance in Richmond, as a speaker, was upon the 4th of July, 1800, and in the defence of Callender. This oration is in print, and worthy of perusal. It exhibits a fine contrast with the more chastened productions of later years; showing the effect of labor and study upon a mind capable of great effort and steady advancement. It is fervid, rapid, imaginative, descriptive—full of imagery, fine feeling, and principle—not destitute of sober thought, but not carefully and diligently arranged or pruned. The trial of Callender brought him into notice, as well from his performance, as from the treatment of the court. It will be recollected that the conduct of Judge Chase gave rise to one of the charges on his impeachment. His interruption of Mr. Wirt, and commanding him to sit down, were considered by many as harsh and intolerant. But the recollections of the parties justify a favorable inference as to both. The advocate retained no resentments, and did not appear as a witness against the accused. The judge afterwards spoke of the talents and manner of the advocate with kindness, and felt an interest in his prosperity.

Previous to 1802, but one Court of Chancery existed, having jurisdiction throughout the State, and held by the learned and profound Chancellor Wythe. In that year three courts were created. The court of the Lower District was directed to be held at Williamsburg; and the Legislature, most unexpectedly, without solicitation, with great unanimity, and greatly to his own surprise, appointed Mr. Wirt Chancellor of that District. The idea of this appointment was suggested to him on the evening preceding its occurrence; but he supposed it to be, and treated it, rather as the light and free suggestions of some intimates, than the fixed purpose of the members; and he took his seat at the clerk's table as usual. When the nomination was to be made, he was privately requested to retire, but, still under the same impression, refused; and the person nominating him had risen to speak, and was embarrassed by the awkwardness of his position, which the Speaker perceiving, leaned forward and requested Mr. Wirt to leave his seat for a few minutes. He did so; the nomination was made, and seconded by two of the most respectable of the members, and carried without opposition—a most gratifying and uncommon evidence of attachment and confidence in the learning, talents, and virtues of a man, not a native of the State; not then quite thirty years of age; without a particle of extraneous influence, which his own character had not produced; and in a community abounding with men eminently qualified for the station. He did not seize with avidity upon the offer. He felt the weight of the trust, and apprehension of the unfitness of his age and qualifications. He hesitated painfully; and consulted his friends, and, among others, Mr. Monroe, then Governor of the State, on whose wisdom he always felt great reliance. He did, however, accept the office; and, during the short period in which he discharged its duties, added to his reputation by a patience, industry, and learning, suited to its important functions.

21

In the autumn of that year he married Miss Gamble—for thirty-three years the *wife*, and now the *widow*. Of her, I shall not attempt here even the outlines of a picture ; but it is due to both to say, that seldom, in this world, have there been more congeniality and happiness. And he has left the declaration, that, to her purity and intelligence, wisdom and piety, he owed a large amount, not of his enjoyments and happiness alone, but of his intellectual, moral, practical, and religious worth and usefulness. That sacred relationship produced, in these cases, its appropriate and beneficent effects. One of the joys of the garden, it alone, of all the relations of man, survived the ruins of the fall, to scatter light, love, and blessings amid its desolations.

This marriage, the incompetency of his salary to meet the wants of a family, and, perhaps, the unextinguished ardor for that kind of distinction which results from professional celebrity, induced him to resign the office of Chancellor, with an intention to seek for fame and fortune in the great and growing West. From this intention he was diverted by the advice and solicitation of his friends, and especially of the Governor elect of Virginia, who tendered to him a participation in the extensive practice which his commanding talents had secured at the bar, in Norfolk—an offer made in a generous spirit, and as generously declined. He, however, went to Norfolk ; and after a residence there of about three years, returned to Richmond, where he continued until his removal to this place, in 1817.

22

During the period of about thirteen years in Norfolk and Richmond, he was engaged in every variety of cause, civil and criminal, and under all the jurisdictions known to our State and Federal institutions. It is a period replete with incidents of importance to those who seek a knowledge of his professional character, of the qualities of his mind, and of the force and depth of his virtues. But it would be improper in me to fatigue your attention by any thing more than a hasty allusion to a few of them.

His practice was, principally, but not exclusively, confined to the courts in those cities. He was sometimes called to other and to distant places, where his powers, both in civil and criminal causes, were understood and valued. He had to contend with the master spirits of the Virginia bar—the Tazewells, Taylors, Wickhams, Randolphs, and other *clara nomina.* To have been able, at his age, and with the obstacles which had impeded him, to sustain the conflict without discomfiture and disgrace, gives proof of no ordinary mind. But he emerged from it with the generous applause of his competitors, and the augmented regard of his fellow-citizens. The competition was useful to him. It required that every hour should be devoted to literary and professional exertions; and every hour new and merited confidence and respect followed those exertions. It is only in the conflict of mind with mind, that the highest intellectual powers can be developed and invigorated. He who would triumph greatly, must not seek inferiority with which to contend. The struggle must be with the strong, and the preparation for that struggle incessant. The Olympic wreath must be won by unceasing discipline, and by straining every nerve and muscle in the game. It was so with him. He entered the lists, not only there, but here, with bold and vigorous champions. The conflict kept his armor always bright, and proved the good temper of the steel. His bow he permitted to be only so far unstrung as to retain its elasticity and strength ; his quiver he furnished with arrows of the purest and finest point ; and he sped them with Apollonian skill and grace.

One of the first causes which engaged his attention, after his return to Richmond, was the trial of Aaron Burr, in 1807. He was employed in it, to aid the District Attorney, by the direction of Mr. Jefferson, then President of the United States. It were useless to comment at large on that trial. It agitated both patriotic feeling and party passion. It rendered the names of those concerned in it familiar at every fire-side in the nation. To Mr. Wirt it gave his full share of celebrity ; but, I believe, at the same time, did real injustice to his reputation, by the general circulation of an extract from his principal speech, which described the character and situation of Blennerhasset and his wife. That extract was regarded as the work of fancy only, while its most glowing colors were justified by the evidence in the cause. But it led to the impression that law and reasoning were neglected by him, for the play of imagination. They, however, who have read with attention the whole of his arguments on that occasion, will not hesitate to apply, as well to him as the other counsel, the commendation of the court, that "a degree of eloquence, seldom displayed on any occasion, embellished solidity of argument and depth of research." It was, also, probably true with him then, and at other times, as it is often with earnest, brilliant, and impassioned speakers. More injustice is done to them, in the reports of their speeches, than to more cool and deliberate, though inferior men. The reporter, whether skilled in the art of stenography or not, cannot follow them. His feelings become interested; his pen is not rapid enough for the flight of mingled thought and fancy; he loses self-possession and composure, and necessarily presents an enfeebled and disjointed picture of the argument, perhaps even more than of the illustration. The loss is irreparable. The address carried along the hearer with irresistible power; but it cannot be recovered, even by the speaker himself, after the excitement has passed by. The victory has been won, but the weapons are scattered, and the order of their combination and use cannot be restored. Is it not, in great part, owing to this fact, that we have now to rely on contemporary fame, and the effects which he produced, for our estimate of that great orator of nature, Patrick Henry; and that not even a single perfect specimen can be found of the most commanding efforts of Pinkney's mind?

In 1808 Mr. Wirt was elected by the people of Richmond a member of the House of Delegates, without the canvass which is usual in that State—an unsolicited tribute by his fellow-citizens, and the only occasion, through life, on which he permitted himself to be a candidate for the popular vote, except at the last presidential election. While in the Assembly, as a member of a special committee on the foreign relations of the country, and the measures of the general administration, he wrote a report defensive of those measures. It was strong, impartial, indignant at the injuries inflicted by France and England, and in all respects worthy of the times, the occasion, and the man.

In July of that year he prepared an address to the people of that State, on behalf of the Manufacturing Association of Virginia, which reviewed the acts of the belligerents, exhibited their operation on our commerce and other interests; urged the propriety of fostering domestic manufactures; and insisted that the country was prepared, by its capital and enterprise, to accomplish it successfully. He also addressed three letters, signed "One of the People," to those members of Congress who had protested against the nomination of Mr. Madison for the presidency. They were written with a polish and force of style seldom found in the newspaper essays of this country; and they bear an emphatic testimony to the services and merits of Mr. Madison. They were generally published through the nation, and are said to have produced great effect, not only on those to whom they were addressed, but on popular opinion. Of the political opinions contained in all these papers, it is not my purpose to speak. They are mentioned as evidences of his style of composition; of the interest which he took in the concerns of the country; and of that industry which was not confined to professional occupation alone.

But there is other and stronger evidence on these points. In 1803 he wrote the letters of the British Spy; in 1812 those of the Old Bachelor; and in September, 1817, published the Life of Patrick Henry. The two former were newspaper essays, which have been collected into volumes, and have been sufficiently popular to pass, the one through three, the other through ten editions. The severity of criticism ought not to be applied to the style or matter of these works, without recollecting the circumstances under which they were produced. They were essays intended to appear in the ephemeral journals of the day, and expected to perish with them. They were the results of a few leisure hours stolen from the laborious pursuits of his profession. They were not subjected to the *limæ labor et mora.* When these facts are considered, they may defy the severity of criticism, and claim equality with any which have been produced under similar circumstances. They add a wreath to his fame, which any jurist might desire to have bound around his own brow.

He commenced one of them, it is said, to repel the rude insolence of foreign travellers and critics upon our country. But he had a higher aim—to turn those very strictures to our own profit; to prune away our faults, and thus wipe off the reproaches which had been cast upon us; to increase the love of literature; to benefit the manners and morals of society, and to hold out to the young fit objects of pursuit. He designed to draw a picture of living manners, and he has given one, new, original, and entertaining. He went into what, in his own language, "was a vast field covered with a heavy harvest, which no sickle had entered," and which, some other has remarked, no reaper of equal skill has since entered. All his sketches, whether of persons or manners, bear evidence of close observation. He endeavored to bring his lectures home to the bosoms of his readers; but not in the mode of Aristophanes, who hoisted his philosopher to the clouds in a basket, thence to lecture his pupils below; nor like Villiers, who exhibited the living general and the admired poet in farce; or, like Foote, who entertained the public with the natural defects of the impassioned minister of the gospel, and assumed the dress and mimicked the manners of those he satirized and burlesqued; but, like Addison, he presented a delightful, moral, literary work, drawn from living manners, with the interest of fiction, and the illustration and force of moral truth.

At this period of his life, and up to the time when he received the appointment of Attorney General, I believe the prevalent impression, out of the circle of his practice, was, that he possessed rather showy than solid talent and acquirement—more of belles

28

lettres and classical, than abstruse legal learning. Such was my own impression; but when I expressed it to a most competent judge, intimately acquainted with him, and the witness of many of his arguments, he replied, " Your estimate is wrong. His true character is that of a laborious, profound lawyer, more conversant with the *black letter* than even with works of taste, poetry, and fiction." He lived long enough to correct the false opinion which the public had formed of his intellect and acquirements. Their error had resulted from some of his lighter productions having been generally read, while there was comparatively an entire ignorance of the vigor and learning which he brought to the discussion of his causes. They had seen his 4th of July oration ; a sketch of his speech in the singular case of Shannon ; the letters of the British Spy and Old Bachelor ; and parts of one of his speeches in the trial of Burr, and some other fugitive pieces ; and they inaccurately inferred that the mind which produced *them*, in the midst of a professional career, must have tendencies and occupations which would prevent it from being stored with the more dry, and, to most men, tedious doctrines of the law books ; and that his excelled in the ornamental, rather than the severe and cogent properties of oratory. The inference was, in part, correct. The bias was strong; but imagination, taste, and fancy, were not the ruling powers of his mind. They held, even then, but a divided empire ; and, as he advanced in life, it became more and more apparent that masculine judgment, and close, logical, and lucid argument, were his decisive characteristics.

When Mr. Jefferson retired from the presidency in 1809, he felt a very natural and earnest solicitude for the future course of the Government, and the success of those who were to succeed him; and he desired to strengthen the hands of those to whom the destinies of the country were, for the time, to be committed. With these feelings, he urged Mr. Wirt to enter on a career of political distinction, and held up before him confident calculations of success. Mr. Wirt did not perceive that duty to the country required it. He was not dazzled by the prospect, and would not be withdrawn from literary and professional pursuits; and he had his reward in a calmer life, a less assaulted reputation, and higher renown for intellectual vigor. The example deserves at least the sober thought of the young men of the country. They who have, from choice, or the apparent necessities of their situation, ventured on another voyage, may tell them of dangers, and storms, and losses, and shipwrecks, to which that voyage is liable, and that it is wise to repress the propensity to venture upon it for the gratification of selfish ambition alone. When their country calls, they have, and ought to seek no alternative. She claims the homage of their hearts. Their services are her due. On her altar private comfort, personal interests, even fame and life, are to be laid, as offerings, not of *constraint*, but of *devotion*.

30

In 1816 an opportunity occurred for Mr. Madison to give to Mr. Wirt an expression of his regard, in the sphere which he had chosen for himself; and he was appointed District Attorney of the United States for Virginia.

In the following year, at the age of forty-five, he received from Mr. Monroe, one of his earliest friends, the appointment of Attorney General of the United States ; and with the kind of preparation which has been detailed, and the reputation which I have endeavored fairly to estimate, he accepted the appointment, and moved to this city—to the vicinity of his native home, from which he had been so long separated. The change which had been effected in himself and the surrounding country must, to a mind and memory like his, have been full of sensibility, even to overflowing. He left a family circle ; he found a closed home and scattered relatives. He left his little village in the animation of prosperity ; he found it palsied and sunken. But, in contrast of these, he went a pennyless orphan, with no human hand to protect and guide him ; he returned himself the guardian of others, and the dispenser of opinions which were to affect the rights and interests of thousands. He went unknown and with a name untold ; he returned with that name upon the lips of millions. He left the hills and valleys which surround us, and over which his boyhood had sported, occupied by few inhabitants, and sprinkled here and there with the results of human labor and industry ; he found them covered with a population of ten thousand souls, and on their heights the magnificent edifices where a nation's power and sovereignty were represented, and a nation's agents assembled to guard her interests. He left his native State a feeble and struggling member of an inefficient and almost powerless confederacy; he found it the thriving and prosperous equal and constituent of a Government—strong, because the emanation of a people's power, sustained by a people's love, and acting with beneficent influence on a whole people's prosperity—holding out to other nations a united sovereignty, which demanded and enforced respect and justice—designated by its flag, whose combined stripes are not pale, nor its stars dim; and bearing aloft, high enough to be seen by the scattered and oppressed millions of the human family, the beacon lights of liberty and law—"hope of the fettered slave, and glory of the free."

In such a Government he was to bear an important part. The station which he was to occupy was difficult enough to try the strongest powers and purest virtues; and, when filled with talent and learning, efficient in producing a regular and safe administration of the laws.

The office of Attorney General for the United States was created, and its duties defined, by the 36th section of the judiciary act of 1789; and had been held in succession by Randolph, Bradford, Lee, Lincoln, Smith, Breckenridge, Rodney, Pinkney, and Rush. The duties are, "to prosecute and conduct all suits in the Supreme Court, in which the United

States are concerned; and to give advice and opinion upon questions of law, when required by the President of the United States, or when requested by the heads of any of the Departments, touching any matters that may concern their Departments." He is thus constituted the legal adviser of the executive branch of the Government—the counsellor of the nation in the execution of the laws. He is, at the same time, and has so been from the commencement of the Government, a member of the confidential council or cabinet of the President; and is thus compelled, not only to discharge duties appropriately professional, but to mingle in the deliberations and express opinions upon those general questions and interests which spring out of the action of each of the Departments, and of the whole combined, which affect the internal prosperity and external relations of the nation. He must, therefore, be not only a good lawyer, but a safe statesman. There is a peculiarity in the responsibility of this officer, which requires the exercise of more than common care in his selection. He does not deal with the ordinary routine of business, which inferior intelligence and system can manage; but when doubts and difficulties intervene upon the powers conferred by law, or the rights intended to be secured, the appeal is made to him. His labors are always connected with perplexing subjects; and his opinions, as well as his arguments in court, relate to every variety of questions which can arise under our institutions, or from our connexions with the commerce and Governments of the world. *Hic labor, hoc opus.* His opinions, too, are official; not merely persuasive upon the judgments of other officers, but, *so far as the construction of the law is concerned*, regarded as binding; and, if error be committed, the responsibility is, in a great degree, taken from them, and cast upon him—a responsibility by no means light, to a sensitive and well organized mind.

The character and action of this office, and the mode of performing its duties, were essentially changed by Mr. Wirt. Before his time, those who held it, although the confidential counsellors of the President and legal advisers of the departments, did not reside constantly at the seat of Government, except his immediate predecessor, who lived here at the time of his appointment. Mr. Wirt removed with his family, and continued here throughout his whole period of eleven years and four months, more than twice the time during which the office was held by any other; and, by his residence here, the labors of his office were much more than doubled.

In one respect he contracted the action of the office, or rather, he refused to be led beyond the limits prescribed by law; and the incident not only furnishes a guide to his principles of action, but fixed a salutary boundary for the Legislature, in relation to his department. In a few instances, (I believe they were but few,) the Attorney General had been called on, either by Congress or by committees, for opinions in matters which were before Congress. His residence here was calculated to increase such calls. In the spring of 1817 the House made an order to refer to the Attorney General sundry documents in relation to the accounts of an officer during the late war. He found these papers, in his office, in the succeeding fall; and in December made a report, in which he expressed an opinion on the legal liability of the party in the supposed case, but altogether declined giving an opinion upon the merits, or even considering the facts. On the 28th of January, 1820, the House referred to him the petition of Joseph Wheaton, and accompanying documents, with the report of the Committee of Claims. Five days afterwards he returned the papers to the House, with a letter, in which he explained his views of his official duties under the law, which he recited and discussed; declared that the service required of him was extra-official; and that he should violate his sense of his oath if he was instrumental in enlarging the sphere of his official duties, among which was not that of being the legal counsellor of the House of Representatives. He adds: "It would be incal-"culably dangerous to permit an officer to act, under "color of his office, beyond the pale of the law. "The precedent is not less dangerous, on account "of the purity of the motives in which it originates. "The maxim is as old, at least, as republican Rome, "that *omnia mala exempla ex bonis orta sunt.* "It gives me more pain to be thus obliged to de-"cline, than it would give me trouble to make the "report; but, in a conflict between my wishes and "my sense of duty, there ought to be no question "which I should obey." The practice since has been in conformity with the views thus expressed; not only in relation to Congress, but other officers.

He had, previous to this time, in the year succeeding his appointment, addressed a letter to the chairman of the committee of the House, which is still, I believe, on file, calling attention to the state of the office, and requesting a remedy for certain defects, which he regarded as injurious to the public interests. The remedy was not then applied. One of his requests was, that means might be provided for furnishing a record of the proceedings of the office. This he had already commenced without aid. He had found no opinions of his predecessors, no papers, no notes, to inform him what had been done by them; or the construction put on the numerous laws which had been subject to question and debate. This he regarded as an unfit state of things, in an office whose sphere of action was so wide; whose decisions are of such extensive and unremitting practical effect; and where consistency and uniformity should prevail. He, therefore, determined to make a regular record of every official opinion and letter written by him; to file the papers and documents on which they were formed, with corresponding references, to give facility in their future examination. This record bears date on 12th of November, 1817, the day he entered on the duties of his office; and the last recorded opinion is on the 17th of January, 1829, though some of the letters are of a later date. They fill two large volumes and nearly half of a third, besides a letter book; and contain, I doubt not, more opinions and letters than were written by all his predecessors, from the establishment of the Government. They amount to more than one for every week that he held the office; and were prepared with care, elaboration, and thorough investigation of facts and law. One of them, which had been given as advice to President Monroe, was subsequently, upon a call, sent to the Senate, and fills nearly fifty pages of congressional printing. They all relate to matters of importance in the construction of the laws; many of them to the most difficult and interesting subjects of municipal and constitutional law, as well as the law of nations, which occurred during three presidential terms. They will prevent much uncertainty in that office hereafter; afford one of the best collections of materials for writing the legal and constitutional history of our country; and remain a proud monument of his industry, learning, and talents.

It is difficult to state the precise number of causes in the Supreme Court, in which the United States were concerned, because they often have an interest, though not a party on the record; but the number on the docket, for several years past, which he had to prepare, do not, I believe, average less than forty, and those argued and disposed of not less than twenty-five at each term. These causes were usually of magnitude, and always brought him in conflict with minds of the highest order. That court is the very battle ground of intellect. In every cause he was thoroughly and minutely prepared ; its slightest incidents, every question of law, applicable to it, were examined upon principle and authority ; and to every cause in which he represented the Government he did entire justice. The rights of the United States were most fully and amply guarded by him.

It will be recollected by all whom I address, that, in the year 1826, the fourth of July was, in the dispensations of Providence, consecrated anew by the death of Mr. Jefferson and Mr. Adams ; an event which has since been rendered more memorable and impressive by the death of Mr. Monroe, on the same great anniversary. The citizens of Washington, desiring to give appropriate expression to their feelings on that occasion, selected Mr. Wirt to deliver an address. It was delivered in this hall, to an immense multitude of hearers ; and the public judgment has assigned to it a place among the most masterly efforts which the literature and eloquence of our country have produced.

In the winter of 1822, when the court was in session, his vigorous constitution received a sudden and violent shock, which had the appearance, and some symptoms, of an apoplectic kind ; and he did not, during the remainder of his official term, nor, indeed, during his life, entirely recover from its effects. It was, probably, the result of a labor too intense and unremitted for the human body to bear ; and would have induced any other man, with whom I have been acquainted, to relax ; but it did not produce this effect on him. To the last moment of his life, disease and impaired health seemed neither to weaken the vigor of his intellect, to repress the ardor of his feelings, nor to enfeeble his exertions. He lived in one perpetual struggle, and died almost in the very act of conflict. On the 3d March, 1829, he resigned his situation as Attorney General, under circumstances known to all. It was during the sitting of the Supreme Court; and there were several causes on the docket in which the United States were interested, and which his successor might not be prepared to discuss, so as to protect their rights. He, therefore, in the most courteous and generous spirit, tendered to him any aid in his power, either of advice or argument. The offer was not, I believe, accepted.

Mr. Wirt carried out of that office a reputation augmented, wide spread, most splendid. His course in it had been fearless and patriotic; governed always by the candor, honor, truth, and justice which become an Attorney General for the United States. He pressed the claims of the Government with befitting earnestness; but never, knowingly, passed the line which law and truth designated. He felt that the just Government of a free country can have no interest in the wrongs of its citizens; no profit from injustice; no glory from oppression.

Retirement from office did not diminish the respect of his country, or his professional reputation. He removed to the capital of his native State, and continued a practice both extensive and lucrative. His aid was sought by individuals; by corporations, in every part of the Union ; by States ; and even by the Government itself, in causes of large importance. On one or more occasions he was called to Philadelphia, New York, and Boston. It was natural that his reputation should *there* be put to a severe trial. He would necessarily be met by the strongest, and they sustained in their efforts by the countenance of admiring friends. Report may well be credited when she declares that those trials were giant struggles of giant intellects. They attracted the taste, the fashion, the learning, and the wisdom of those cities ; and the award, while it sustained the merited distinction of his antagonists, gave assurance that his own fame was *just.*

It would be a vain and hopeless effort in me to attempt the designation of those cases, in which his learning as a jurist, and his eloquence as an advocate, were best displayed. Each successive effort, where the cause demanded it, seemed to surpass its predecessor ; but, among them, we may refer to the steamboat cause, to the Cherokee case, and to the impeachment of Judge Peck, as furnishing specimens of all the properties which adorn the jurist and advocate—inferior to none which have ever been exhibited at the American or British bar.

In July, 1830, at the request of one of the literary societies, he delivered an address to the students of Rutgers' College, New Jersey ; and in October of that year, another to the people of Baltimore, at the celebration occasioned by the recent revolution in France. These addresses afford examples of his mature style of composition, sentiments, and feelings.

In 1832 he was nominated and supported as a candidate for the Presidency. We are too near the time of that event, and it was too closely connected with the excitements of the day, for me, here, to comment on that nomination and its acceptance. He has taken care to record, for future use, every thing which occurred on that occasion; and it will be the duty of his biographer to give it to the world. It is my part only to say, that the selection, under the circumstances, is an evidence of his imposing character in the country; and that it was justified by all the high properties which can give honor and dignity to that elevated station.

I have thus, brethren of the bar, attempted a sketch of the life of our departed brother. It has been hastily drawn, and, I fear, tedious in the repetition. My object has been, in the incidents of his life, to discover and exhibit the traits of his professional character and virtues. Will you bear with me while I further allude to a few of the characteristics of his mind and heart, and his qualities as a man and orator, as drawn from this history and from observation? They influenced his professional character, and formed a part of it. I mean to attempt no general portrait or full-length likeness. A different pencil would be required to combine the features, and give the living expression.

His manly, graceful, and elegant person; his powerful, clear, musical voice, are well remembered by you all. His countenance exhibited a happy combination of intellect and sensibility; broad and open, yet delicate, cheerful, and benignant; giving, perhaps, at first view, more the impression of his generous and benevolent heart, than of his strong mind and lofty genius. The first impulse was to love; the second, to admire; the third, to revere and venerate its possessor.

His manners were a singular union of artless simplicity, and polished elegance and dignity. In the private and social circle his conversation always breathed a pure and gentle spirit, while it was animated, judicious, and instructive; not wasted in idle professions, but shedding the active influence of his own learning and wisdom on those around him. There his genius often showed itself, not merely unfettered, but luxuriant in its sports and movements—abundant in stores of classical and general reading. His benevolence never permitted his keen and Attic wit to give pain; his fancy played in innocent gambols, with amusing and animated variety; or shot its flight with rapid and exalted wing, dropping the balm of peace as well as joy; so cheerful and gay, that it "lent a new spring to the pulse of the heart." In intercourse with the world, his manners had a large share of dignity and firmness; never offensive, never sycophantic; a just medium, and equally opposed both to that confident self-esteem which justly gives offence, and that cringing suppleness which as justly loses respect. They were the united result of native ease and grace; pure and refined sentiment; self-respect, and tender regard for the feelings of others. They were also, without doubt, in some degree, affected by his just estimate of female character and virtues, and enjoyment of female society. He has declared that "the genuine virtue and refinement of any man might be safely estimated by the delicacy with which he regards the purer and softer sex; and, that irreverence to them was evidence that the brain was obscured by the meanest pride, or the heart corrupted by the grossest vice." No one felt more deeply the sympathy, respect, and protection which a generous and ennobled nature is always ready to extend to the gentleness and sensibility of virtuous woman; to the disinterested generosity and enthusiastic love, which makes her forget her own ease in the promotion of ours; and, in spite of constitutional feebleness and delicacy, enables her to defy climate and toil, while she believes that she can advance the convenience and happiness of the lord of her affections. He, at least, did not make a poor and base return. His pen loved to portray her virtues, and his heart delighted in elevating her character and cultivating her intellect. In his home, his manners assumed their most exquisite form—combining all the fondness and affection of the father, all the tenderness and assiduity of the husband, with all the cheerfulness and warmth of the beloved companion.

He had one peculiarity, in his intercourse with the young, of more marked excellence than I have ever seen in any other man. He loved them with ardor, and joined in their conversations and amusements with infantile ease and simplicity, until they forgot his age, and opened their feelings before him, as if he were their playmate. Yet they never lost their veneration, and respect, and love for him ; and, without their perceiving it, he so guided their amusements and remarks, as to leave some strong sentiment, some useful truth, fastened in the right place in their hearts. I never knew him leave a child, even after a short conversation, without having produced in the child affection for himself, some elevation of feeling, some well directed thought and purpose. You can all estimate his family circle from this statement, better than I can describe it. No parent ever felt there a purer rapture or a prouder triumph. Had he, like the Teacher of Crotona, preferred to his profession the instruction of youth, and the formation of the future patriots, and orators, and statesmen of his country, he would, like that Teacher, have conferred lasting blessings, and won immortality.

In his instance, the controlling qualities of the mind—memory, imagination, and judgment—were strong. He had a keen and intuitive perception of fact, character, and the beauties of nature ; and his memory, quick and tenacious, retained his observations with the freshness of the moment when they were made. It gave him no trouble to recall them, whenever they were needed, in conversation or public debate. His imagination was luxuriant but not extravagant ; perhaps too rich in resources, and too active, in early life, for the staid and sober concatenation of precise argument; but study and labor brought it to the just position which it ought to occupy, as the handmaid of reason. His judgment was quick, clear, and accurate; his power of reasoning comprehensive, yet close; embracing, without confusion, all those matters which justly affect the decision, and arranging them in their relative order of weight and force. These properties combined, gave unusual energy and power to the argument which he presented, whether in public or private discourse.

His reading was extensive. He visited every haunt of genius, and travelled over every region where science had shot its rays. Over its whole empire he had ranged with irrepressible ardor; examined its almost boundless extent; and penetrated the mystery and obscurity in which many parts of it lie covered and involved to less penetrating eyes.

He read much upon the philosophy of the mind, as he did upon the philosophy of the law. The Bridgewater Treatises and corresponding topics were among his last studies. Astronomy, with the phenomena of nature connected with it, which are so apt to excite the curiosity and speculation of mankind, were with him a favorite theme, both of study and conversation.

With poetry and other departments of taste he was familiar; and his memory retained, with accuracy, the finest passages in works both ancient and modern. Shakspeare and Cicero were, with him,

45

not amusement alone, but study; and all their illustrations were the commonplaces of his mind.

His labor was without limit. I know of but one individual (Pinkney) who in this respect equaled him. They both improved steadily and rapidly, to the last moment, as advocates, counsellors, and scholars; exhibiting to the young aspirant after fame the true and only road to eminence; and proving, to demonstration, the error of the common opinion, that the mind attains its usefulness, and vigor, and abundance, before the age of forty or forty-five; and that the struggle afterwards is to maintain its strength and acquirements, and to use them for the individual and public benefit. Their progress in intellectual wealth, and its active use, was at no period more rapid than the last fifteen years of their lives.

On few points were Mr. Wirt's habits of labor more useful to him than in the correction of his style of writing and speaking. He has been accused of being too florid in style, too ornamented in diction, and approaching that which Cicero calls *Asiatic*, and condemns. The criticism was just, to some extent, when applied to his earlier productions; but if his professional arguments, and the later efforts of his pen—those, for example, to which I have referred—be examined, it will be found that he was able to correct his error, and that his neatly condensed and chastely ornate style may be added as another proof of his steady advancement—another merit worthy of imitation.

His principles of conduct were those of punctilious honor, refined and guarded by moral and religious sentiment. He did not give, and was not willing to receive offence. Sensitive himself to the slightest impeachment, he avoided, upon principle, all imputation upon others, which was not justified by the clearest evidence. He was open to the approaches of civility and the courtesies of social intercourse, and willing to receive advances from all; a shrewd observer of character, with an almost intuitive perception of the appropriate feelings, thoughts, and language of every situation. Yet, it sometimes happened that he had to recall confidence and the praises bestowed in advance. This arose, not from an inability to inspect and judge deeply, nor from want of knowledge of human nature, or the motives, springs, and purposes of human action; but from the generosity of his whole temperament, which abstained from condemnation in advance, and made him yield to appearances, in the hope that subsequent experience would justify the adventure. But he never made intimate friends incautiously. Those whom he chose, through his whole life, were among the sober, the sedate, and the diligent. The gay and the dissipated were, at some periods, his companions, but never his friends. His standard was too high for such. He regarded friendship as necessary to our happiness and our virtues. His heart was open to its brightening countenance and its inspiring salute. He insisted that we all require its offices, not only to console us in adversity, and rejoice with us in prosperity, but to chastise our immoralities, and correct them in their source; to watch over our manners with benignant solicitude, and admonish us without reserve. These offices he received kindly, and ministered freely.

He possessed strict and scrupulous integrity, enthusiastic warmth and bravery of spirit, and that *moral and civic courage* which is the most uncommon, most difficult of attainment, and most valuable and commanding of all the qualities which dignify and adorn the man and the citizen ; without which the public agent is a public curse.

With such personal advantages, manners, learning, powers of intellect, principles of conduct, and severe labor, it could not be that Mr. Wirt should have fallen short of the highest elevation in the profession of the law. They are the component parts, the necessary constituents of real greatness, in that profession—a profession which ought not to corrupt the heart, or narrow the understanding, because superiority in it is the first distinction in a free State. When strongly united and combined, these properties form the very *beau ideal* of a great American constitutional lawyer.

His eminence did not create hatred, or envy, or jealousy. His rivals regarded him as a competitor worthy of their powers, and of the field on which they contended; one who never intentionally wounded their feelings ; never, if successful, manifested the self-complacency of triumph ; never, when defeated, detracted from their merits. They had no disposition to be at enmity with him. If they had, they would have found themselves in the predicament which Dr. Johnson described, when he said of Sir Joshua Reynolds that he was one of those men with whom, if a person desired to quarrel, he would have been most at a loss how to abuse.

His inferiors and juniors loved and respected him, for he was always ready to treat them as equals; always prompt, without the appearance of condescension, to afford them counsel, advice, and assistance.

The Judges also regarded him with attachment and respect; and have given feeling testimony to his worth and ability.

His manner in forensic argument was earnest, and often impassioned. With a voice clear, full, sonorous, articulate, and flexible; modified as feeling or argument required, regulated so that it did not escape his control, into monotony or harshness; with an expression of countenance sincere and animated; gestures, natural, easy, and forcible; an attitude, graceful and dignified; he was always ardent and zealous. It was the combination of these particulars which Demosthenes denominated action; and they constituted the action of Mr. Wirt. He understood a truth, not always felt to be a truth, that arguments addressed to the understanding require an impassioned manner, as well as appeals to the passions. It is necessary to produce a conviction that the speaker feels that he is right; to command confidence in his argument and in his feelings; to make a lodgement in the affections, and drive home to the judgments and hearts of hearers the warm appeal, the cogent reasoning, the strong conclusions, and the deep convictions of the orator. The earnestness of Wirt appeared in his brow, his voice, his gestures ; and yet his unwavering lip, clear and firm enunciation, distinct strokes of thought, connected movement of the mind, proved that, though ardent, he was collected ; though vehement, profound ; though in the excitement of feeling, temperate, even to smoothness.

His earnestness, at no time, made him overlook the respect due to the court, and to the feelings and rights of his adversary. There is here a narrow and almost imperceptible line, which is to be trodden by the practitioner. It lies between the vigilant attention and ardent prosecution of the client's rights on the one side ; and proper respect for, and submission to the court, and regard for the feelings of the opponent, on the other. It is a point, in our practice, less successfully reached than any other. It can only be attained by him who possesses a clear, unclouded judgment, decisive control over his own feelings and movements, and perfect sensibility to the rights and feelings of others. It is not unjust to my professional brethren to say, that Mr. Wirt reached that point more successfully, and walked upon this narrow line with more unerring certainty, than any man with whose professional course I am intimately acquainted.

His arguments usually embraced all of the law which was requisite for a decision. I do not assert that he presented clearer views of the law, nor seized and exhibited the strong points of a cause with

50

greater force than some others. It was not so; he had his equals, if not his masters, in that respect. But while few could equal his potency in this, his peculiar merit lay in a lucid order—in that power of combination and arrangement, which collected, as he progressed, every topic of fact, of argument, of illustration; arranged them without the slightest confusion, and brought their combined weight to bear upon the conclusion at which he aimed; and, like the mountain torrent which had gathered up the rivulets in its course, he swept the feelings and judgment along with mighty power. His mind embraced the *whole* of every controversy in which he was engaged, and suggested every consideration which ought to bear on its decision, even to the remotest consequences; and his comprehensive thought found illustrations and analogies in universal reason and abstract truth, as well as in the moral sublime of nature and feeling. Many others reason clearly and cogently; many declaim splendidly and pathetically; but few are great in both departments. In him, rhetoric and logic were combined in high perfection. He reasoned with such Herculean force, as rendered resistance always difficult; he declaimed in such manner, that the overwhelmed hearer was often carried unresistingly to his conclusions. And he had the immense advantage of moral weight of character to aid him. The hearer felt that no sordid sycophant, no vicious intriguer, no guilty mind, addressed him; but that the great orator was also the good man.

I mean, on this topic, to draw no comparisons with the past or the present; but I protest against the promulgation of the opinion, that modern times, and especially this land of light and liberty, must be humbled in comparison with other nations and other times. Give to American orators (and Wirt was among them) "the same themes, the same surrounding circumstances, and they will stir the blood as freely; agitate the heart as deeply; control the will and lead the judgment as triumphantly; rival Tully, in unveiling a conspiracy; and the speaker of Athens, in drawing a circle round his beloved city, and hold ing a victorious tyrant at bay."

The theatre on which Wirt appeared, in the latter part of his life, was one cause of his splendid reputation. The tribunal which he addressed demanded the best efforts of the human mind, in argument. It was the concentrated judicial power of a mighty Union of free States. It stands the pride and the boast of legal science. Its learning, integrity, and firmness, have been equal to its magnificent jurisdiction. It is the Areopagus of a great nation; the Amphyctionic assembly of confederated powers; the Aulic council of a combined empire; and on its decisions, past and future, hang more of the destinies of free institutions and the liberties of the world, than upon any other tribunal upon earth.

My brethren, if I have rightly exhibited the character and virtues of Mr. Wirt, may I not declare, that, as he inscribed the life of Patrick Henry to the young men of Virginia, to increase their virtues and public spirit, so his own life should be dedicated to the young men of the nation; to those who are rising, the hopes of our profession; to all the young, who are to form the nation; who have before them a destiny of glorious and increasing brightness, but on whom will rest a fearful responsibility—fearful, from the felicity and honor which Providence has bestowed, and which they must sustain, protect, and defend; fearful in its account to God and the world of man.

But, brethren of the bar, I should be untrue to his memory, unfaithful to you and to my own feelings, if I closed this notice of his character and virtues without a distinct testimony, in relation to another and nobler trait of character—his attribute in health, his consolation in death. William Wirt was a *devout Christian.*

In his infant years he received instruction, which produced a favorable bias towards religious truth, from his aunt, under whose care he was after the death of his mother. She was a woman of great firmness, yet of equal sensibility; and often read, with devotional voice and feeling, several pious books, and especially the old family bible; the appearance of which, even to the clasps and binding, was held in remembrance by him. At about eight years old, an incident occurred, simple in its facts, yet sublime in the moral meaning and tendency; and which he related as producing an abiding effect upon his feelings. A storm arose, in which the mingled wind and rain, and thunder and lightning, were terrific to the stoutest—giving awful evidence of the power of Him who wields and controls them. In the midst of its violence, the lightning struck and rent a large tree before the door, and sent one of its branches into the house. The inmates were stupified, and trembled, and sought impotent refuge in the darkest part of the room. His aunt calmly took down her bible, and, placing it upon the table, read, in an audible and composed voice, some of its sublime passages; thus deriving courage and support from the words of Him who was speaking in the tempest. This simple act of piety, and the confidence which it exhibited, produced a deep impression on the observant boy; and was recurred to as evidence of the power and dignity of faith in the humblest Christian.

As he advanced further in life, there was a period when he had strong convictions upon the subject; but they were not permanent. He was thrown into society where infidel works were often read, and in which it was not unfashionable at that day to give utterance to that scepticism which had been imported from the region where the Goddess of Reason was worshipped, and where the unnatural alliance between infidelity and liberty had been consummated. Misled, for a time, the mind of William Wirt doubted the authenticity of the sacred volume. But he was not of a temper, on this or any other subject, to rely long upon the opinion of others, nor to rest satisfied with doubts which his own efforts could confirm or remove; and this was especially true in regard to a point of infinite magnitude, affecting all his relations and duties, present and future. He determined, therefore, to bring his mind to the investigation; and, after full examination, to adopt the conclusions to which it should lead him.

Without neglecting his professional engagements, he discharged this office; and the result may be regarded as a triumph to Christians every where; for where is the mind more competent to the task; possessing larger views of all the relations of man to man; better knowledge of the aids which science and learning afford; stronger powers of investigation; better acquaintance with the principles by which error is to be detected, and truth established; or governed by more candor and sincerity? Tell me in whom of all those that have disputed the Christian doctrine? I have neither known nor read of any such.

Mr. Wirt examined, with care, the evidences of Christianity, both internal and external. He read, with close attention, Butler, Addison, Watson, Home, Keith, Campbell, Faber, and others. He examined also every doubt suggested by the sceptic; every argument and dogma which the infidel had uttered, and which fell under his notice. He pushed the inquiry until he found the doubt dissipated, and the argument answered. He literally studied Hobbes, Voltaire, Hume, Paine, Bolingbroke, and the whole host who have been marshaled against the Christian cause; and the result was, deep conviction, unhesitating, assured reliance on its authenticity and truth.

But he did not stop at the assent of the understanding. He openly professed his belief, and was enabled to lay all his talents and learning, with deep humility, before the cross of Calvary. He was not ashamed of the gospel of Christ.

Before the sceptic shall sneer, or the infidel rail, at the annunciation of this fact, let him bring to the investigation of the same great and leading truths the same labor, skill, talent, learning, knowledge of the rules and principles of evidence, the same candor and integrity of purpose.

These opinions and feelings of Mr. Wirt could not fail to influence his professional character and virtues; and the effect upon them must be, to the members of the bar and to others, a subject of interest and solicitude. An opinion has prevailed, that deep sensibility to religious truths, and an open profession, were calculated to weaken the power and efficiency of the practitioner. It was not so with him. In proportion to his investigations, he acquired additional elevation of purpose, renewed efforts, bolder and stronger views of duty; and, by his active virtue, preached, sublimely, the doctrines which he professed. It is not too much to allege that his growth in power and reputation was in proportion to the clearness and enlargement of his views, in regard to the great questions which act upon all the personal and relative duties of man, and give authority and sanction to all the laws and obligations of society. At no period of his life was he more faithful to the interests of his clients, more patient in the investigations of his causes, more forcible in argument and illustration, or more zealous in all the duties of his calling. He did not become an ascetic nor a fanatic. And why should it be otherwise? He has said that the true office of religion is to exalt our reason, enlarge and sublimate our affections; and, in a letter written in 1833, he contests the notion to which I have referred with earnestness and demonstration.

It is an interesting fact, that his last effort at composition, which bears date on the 6th January last, immediately before he left home to attend the Supreme Court, was upon a religious subject. The work of Mr. Rennell's Christian Advocate, in the University of Cambridge, on the sceptical opinions propounded by some eminent physiologists of France, and adopted and echoed by those of England, was about to be republished in this country; and he was requested to prepare a preface. The attempt, in his hands, swelled to a long essay. In it, the doctrine of Bichat, that "*organization of itself constitutes the whole of life;*" and that of Lawrence, that "*medullary matter thinks,*" are contested with wit, ridicule, and argument, as but a new form for the old notions of the materialists of the last century—leading to the unavoidable conclusion that we are a mere mass of organized matter; that there is no necessity for a vital principle to impel and sustain our organization; no moral responsibility in man for any act to which his passions may urge him; no necessity for an intelligent spirit, and no function for it to perform. And he insists upon the conclusion, that, "if the Christian opinion be superstition, it is one which ennobles and exalts us, by disposing us to aspire to the imitation of angelic natures, and giving us the hope of immortality; theirs is a superstition which levels them, in life and in death, with the beasts that perish. Our belief is one which tends to the order and peace of society; to the promotion of decency, purity, benevolence, and all the kind charities and affections of life; theirs is the one which transformed, for a time, the most refined and courteous people of Europe into a nation of unchained, ferocious bedlamites; their moral sense extinguished, and all the profligate passions of their nature let loose, with a phrensy, ungovernable, irresistible, and terrific."

If his biography shall be written, and his writings collected, this short but able work will merit publication and notice.

The last acts of Mr. Wirt, on the day when he was seized with his fatal illness, were those of private and public devotion. It was the Sabbath. He was bowed down by no fears of approaching dissolution, to excite the anxious expression of his feelings. Within the twenty-four hours preceding, he declared to me, that he felt all the firmness of re-assured health, and the anticipation of days which did not yet seem to be numbered. In this assurance, in private, with humble penitence and holy ardor, he commended himself, and those he loved, to the keeping of covenanted Grace and Mercy ; and asked, fervently, for the extension of the Redeemer's kingdom. And in public, in this hall, surrounded by the evidences of human power, and the allurements of human ambition, his tears testified his sensibility, while the preacher, with apostolic eloquence, illustrated the declaration: "We preach Christ crucified ; unto the Jews a stumbling-block, and to the Greeks foolishness ; but unto them which are called, Christ, the power of God, and the wisdom of God."

He died as a Christian ought to die. After a torpor, which lasted several days, and rendered him almost insensible to surrounding objects, he was enabled to revive, and to recognise his beloved family, and give them hopes and consolations, infinitely more precious than those which Tacitus has suggested for the weeping relatives of Agricola—such as the world could not give, and cannot take away. His death, in the anticipations which lay before him, was peaceful and triumphant ; not the triumph of the scholar, who had conquered the difficulties of science, and acquired applause by the extent, and accuracy, and abundance of his learning ; not of the patriot, who had given his all to his country and his fellow-men, which they had a right to ask at his hands ; not of the profound jurist and eloquent advocate, who had reached the summit of his profession, and received the award of equal rank with the proudest and the strongest ; no, nor even of the father and the husband, who had discharged all his duties with a beauty and fidelity which left nothing to regret; but it was the triumph of faith in the redemption purchased by atoning blood.

Death is not, to ***him***, an eternal sleep. The bonds which have been sundered shall be reunited. He has left memorials of good to his contemporaries, and those who shall succeed them. He had a hope of immortality and glory beyond the tomb.

THE END

Chapter III

THE

IMPORTANCE OF RELIGION

TO THE

LEGAL PROFESSION:

WITH SOME REMARKS ON THE CHARACTER

OF THE LATE

CHARLES CHAUNCEY, Esq.

A DISCOURSE DELIVERED ON SUNDAY EVENING, SEPTEMBER 30TH, AND REPEATED ON SUNDAY EVENING, OCTOBER 14TH, 1849, IN THE TENTH PRESBYTERIAN CHURCH, PHILADELPHIA.

By HENRY A. BOARDMAN, D. D.

PHILADELPHIA:
PUBLISHED BY WM. S. MARTIEN,
No. 142 Chestnut Street.
1849.

Boardman, Henry A. *The Importance of Religion to the Legal Profession: With Some Remarks on the Character of the Late Charles Chauncey, Esq. A Discourse Delivered on Sunday Evening, September 30th, and Repeated on Sunday Evening, October 14th, 1849, in the Tenth Presbyterian Church, Philadelphia.* Philadelphia: Wm. S. Martien, 1849.

PHILADELPHIA, October 15, 1849.

Rev. and Dear Sir:

In pursuance of the intimation contained in our note of the first instant, the undersigned, members of your congregation, now ask the favour of a copy of the discourse repeated by you at our request and that of other gentlemen of the profession, on the fourteenth instant, for publication.

The name of CHARLES CHAUNCEY, so happily introduced by you in illustration of the great leading object of your discourse, belongs to the whole community, as well as to the legal profession. His great virtues and rare endowments—his talents, learning, and practical benevolence—guided withal by "that wisdom which cometh from above," cannot be too often, nor too widely commemorated.

With a strong desire to cultivate the sentiments of your excellent discourse,

We subscribe ourselves, your friends and servants,

R. C. GRIER.	CHAS. B. PENROSE.
JOHN K. FINDLAY.	JAMES ROSS SNOWDEN.
W. H. DILLINGHAM.	CHARLES GILPIN.
JOHN R. VOGDES.	WM. A. PORTER.
SAMUEL HOOD.	E. SPENCER MILLER.
W. B. HIESKELL.	EDW. ARMSTRONG.

To the Rev. Dr. Henry A. Boardman.

PHILADELPHIA, October 15th, 1849.

Rev. and Dear Sir:

The undersigned, several of whom united with the Gentlemen of the Bar of your own congregation in the expression of a wish that you should repeat your able and eloquent discourse upon the importance of religion to the legal profession, now, with equal pleasure, join them in asking for its publication. We listened with great satisfaction to your graphic description of the character of the late CHARLES CHAUNCEY, Esq., universally and justly regarded as one of the brightest ornaments of the profession. The whole discourse might well be characterized as one of the happiest efforts of clerical eloquence. We regard it as calculated to do great good, and shall be happy to see it widely disseminated.

We are, very respectfully and faithfully, yours,

ED. E. LAW.	J. R. INGERSOLL.
JOEL JONES.	H. J. WILLIAMS.
JAMES DUNDAS.	WM. E. WHITMAN.
FERDINAND W. HUBBELL.	GEO. EMLEN.
B. GERHARD.	CH. GIBBONS.
SAMUEL H. PERKINS.	GARRICK MALLERY.
EDWARD HOPPER.	DAVID PAUL BROWN.

To the Rev. Dr. Boardman.

PHILADELPHIA, October 19th, 1849.

Gentlemen:

I am quite sensible that the interest excited by the discourse which you have done me the honour to request for publication, must be ascribed mainly to the subject and the occasion. The discourse was prepared from a conviction, that the death of that eminent and excellent man whom an all-wise Providence has lately taken from us, afforded a suitable opportunity for inculcating, especially upon the Legal Profession, the virtues which were so happily illustrated in his life. That this humble attempt to improve a bereavement which affects our "whole community," should have met with the approval of a body of gentlemen so honourably representing both the Bench and the Bar, is extremely gratifying to my feelings. I cannot refuse a request emanating from such a source, and herewith submit the manuscript to your disposal.

I am, Gentlemen, with great regard, your friend,

H. A. BOARDMAN.

To the Hon. R. C. Grier, Hon. John K. Findlay, Hon. Joel Jones, and Edw. E. Law, Joseph R. Ingersoll, H. J. Williams, James Dundas, Ferdinand W. Hubbell, B. Gerhard, Samuel H. Perkins, Wm. E. Whitman, George Emlen, Ch. Gibbons, Garrick Mallery, Edward Hopper, David Paul Brown, Wm. H. Dillingham, John R. Vogdes, Charles B. Penrose, James Ross Snowden, Charles Gilpin, Wm. A. Porter, Samuel Hood, E. Spencer Miller, William B. Hieskell, Edward Armstrong, Esquires.

DISCOURSE.

MARK THE PERFECT MAN, AND BEHOLD THE UPRIGHT: FOR THE END OF THAT MAN IS PEACE.—*Psalm* xxxvii. 37.

WE read in the Gospel of Luke, that, on a certain occasion, a lawyer stood up and "tempted" our Saviour, saying, "Master, what shall I do to inherit eternal life?" It was a good question, though prompted by a bad motive—a question every way to be commended, whether we regard the subject to which it relates, the Being to whom it was addressed, or the individual who propounded it. It were a waste of words to undertake to prove that it must be to every individual the most momentous of all questions. And just in proportion to the gravity of the question, is it of importance that we should look well to whom we apply for an answer. For the answers it has received, and is daily receiving, are extremely various and contradictory; and if we happen to be misled, the consequences must be disastrous, and may be irretrievable. This lawyer set us a wholesome example, not, indeed, in respect to the spirit which suggested his inquiry, but in respect to the source at which he sought information. He alone who has salvation to bestow, can teach us how it is to be obtained. If we rely upon a teacher of philosophy, or a teacher of religion, however learned and exemplary, we may fall into error; if we follow implicitly the utterances of this or that sect, or venture to lean upon what we believe to be "the Church," as an infallible guide, we may possibly rest our hopes for eternity upon a foundation as truly foreign from the real foundation, as Platonism or Buddhism is from Christianity. Life and immortality have been brought to light in the gospel: and the gospel is the only chart which can conduct us to heaven. He who takes up with any other teacher than Christ, may expect to come short of eternal life.

It is not to be overlooked that the person who put this question to the Saviour was a lawyer. We know nothing of his character beyond what is revealed in the brief account of this transaction; and he is exhibited to us here in no very prepossessing aspect. Arguing from this interview, we do him no injustice in supposing that he was a man too much immersed in the cares and conflicts of the world, to have given much attention to the claims of spiritual religion. A Pharisee he might have been, and a zealous devotee in his way, but he was manifestly a stranger to genuine piety. It had been well for him, befitting both himself and his calling, had he asked in sober earnest, as he asked in subtlety, "Master, what shall I do to inherit eternal life?"

Nor let it be deemed invidious if the remark is made, that this duty is no less incumbent upon every lawyer. I say this, not to disparage but to honour the profession. There are cogent reasons, aside from those of a private or personal nature common to the members of the legal pro-

7

fession with all other persons, why they should be men of Christian integrity and purity—WHY THE PROFESSION, AS A BODY, SHOULD BE PERVADED WITH A SOUND RELIGIOUS SENTIMENT. The moral character of the Bar, no less than its character for learning and ability, is a matter of deep and universal concern. It is not a matter, Gentlemen of the Bar, which pertains merely to your reputation as individuals, nor to the relations between yourselves and your clients. Even if it were, it might be pertinent to ask, Who are your clients? For the purposes of this argument, the whole community are your clients. There is no citizen, however humble or however exalted, who may not at any time become your client. There is not one among our honourable and opulent merchants, among the ministers of religion, among the able and upright jurists who preside over your own courts—nay, not one among these refined and gentle females, our mothers, wives, and daughters, who make our homes the purest and the happiest homes on earth, who may not, on any day, be compelled to invoke your protection. You are the conservators of our property, of our liberty, our lives, our characters; the guardians of our firesides, the defenders of our altars. Have we no stake, then, in your character? Have we no right to insist that a profession which is the depository of our most sacred earthly interests, shall omit nothing that may help to qualify them for their high trust? that they shall not only make themselves masters of their noble science in its principles and its technicalities, but cultivate those elevated moral sentiments which alone can assure us that our confidence will not be misplaced?

8

Let us look at the profession in another aspect. The Bar must always, in a country like ours, be the chief avenue to civil distinction—the main road to posts of emolument and power. As such, it will embrace a large proportion of the educated and able men of the Union; and the influence of such a body must necessarily be very great, irrespective of their strictly professional functions. How much, then, must this influence be augmented, when it is considered that they exert an immediate and powerful agency in moulding the popular will. They are usually the leaders in the collisions of parties, and the chief speakers even in the primary assemblies of the people. They fill the principal offices. They direct our legislation, and make the laws which it devolves upon them to administer. They shape our policy, domestic and foreign. They control our intercourse with other countries; and do more than any other class among us, to decide the relative position we are to occupy among the nations of the earth. Not to expatiate on these topics, the bare hint of them must suffice to show, that every citizen is implicated in the character of the Bar; and that a profession clothed with so lofty a mission, needs, both for its own sake and for the sake of the country, to be pervaded with a wholesome religious sentiment. Piety alone will not, it is true, fit men to become jurists, diplomatists, or legislators. But piety is the basis of good morals. It makes men conscientious. It stimulates them to acquire the qualifications demanded by the stations Providence may assign them, and puts them upon using their abilities for the best ends. If evangelical Christianity were enthroned, not in our halls of justice merely, but in the hearts of all who serve at her altars, their great influence would tell, if the expression may be pardoned, far more auspiciously than it does now, upon the leading interests of the country. It would moderate the spirit of faction—the bane of all republics. It might repress the idolatry of mammon, and curb the lust of conquest—two of the brood of baser passions which have acquired an Herculean growth in our soil. It would check the prevailing tendency to rash and hasty legislation, and teach visionary reformers that they "should approach to the faults of the State as to the wounds of a father, with pious awe and trembling solicitude."* It would be felt through all the frame-work of society, in extinguishing vice, alleviating misery, fostering education, and consolidating the institutions of Christianity.

Even if the members of the Bar, then, could dispense with religion as a personal concern, the just claims of the country upon the profession, would forbid them to slight its obligations.

But they cannot well dispense with it as a personal concern. Christianity challenges their homage, not only as revealing to them the way of salvation, but as supplying the most valuable aids in the practice of their profession. Let us dwell for a few moments on this topic.

A very little consideration will suffice to show that an intelligent, scriptural faith, must be of great assistance in forming a just estimate of the nature and objects of the legal profession. How grossly these are misconceived, not only by many of the populace, but by no inconsiderable number of those who write themselves "Attorney and

* Burke on the French Revolution.

Counsellor," must be but too well known to every respectable member of the profession. In the judgment of these persons, the law is not a science, but a trade—not a trade even, but a system of trickery. They come to the Bar as a gambler to his club, to be honest where it is politic to be honest, and to practice fraud and chicanery where chicanery and fraud promise larger gains. They see nothing in a law-suit but a private dispute or quarrel, a sort of pugilistic encounter, in which it is all one to the community who beats and who is beaten. Their grovelling minds cannot expand sufficiently to take in the idea that the processes going on before their eyes in the courts, are processes in which we, who seldom or never enter a court-room, have an interest second only, and in some instances not second, to that of the parties litigant; that a claim for the worth of a lamb, or a case of assault and battery between two inebriates, may fairly "bristle with points of law—law that is involved in a large proportion of the common transactions of life;" that the dollars and cents involved in any suit, though amounting to millions of money, are of as little relative value when compared with the principles at issue, as was the tea thrown overboard in Boston harbour, when weighed against the emancipation of a great nation. To all this, the reckless pettifoggers of the profession are blind. But there can be no occasion to remind *you*—and if there were, it would not be decorous in the speaker to become your mentor—that "the science of Jurisprudence, the pride of the human intellect, with all its defects, redundancies and errors, is the collected reason of ages, combining the principles of original justice with the infinite variety of human concerns."* You have not to learn that next to the influence of the gospel, it is the presence and pervading power of LAW which distinguishes free from despotic governments, Christian from Pagan nations—that to annihilate law, is to extinguish all incentive to industry, and all motive to honourable ambition—that where there is no law, science will languish and the arts decay; factories will be closed, commerce will dismantle her ships, capital will hide itself, credit, and all that is built upon it, will die, confidence between man and man will be destroyed; and in place of thrift and comfort, there will be universal suspicion and distrust, violence and misery.

These views are familiar to you. In so far as they go, they are right views. And while they may undoubtedly be entertained and acted upon by individuals who are not under the control of religious principle, it is no less obvious that they are the views which a Christian lawyer *must* take of his profession. It is the uniform and necessary tendency of Christianity to expand and liberalize the mind, while it informs the conscience. It is the essential habit of men who live under its influence, to connect all themes, all interests, all pursuits, with the great First Cause. And such men, when called to the Bar, must belie every principle of their new nature, if, instead of framing a comprehensive and dignified estimate of the profession, they dwarf it down into a system of legerdemain, or an arena for gladiatorial shows.

It would not be easy to exaggerate the value of personal religion in the actual practice of your profession. Whether

* Mr. Burke.

regard be had to its temptations, its trials, or its duties, to the dangers to be shunned or the difficulties to be met; in every view, religion must be considered as of the last importance. It will not, it is true, supply the absence of the requisite intellectual furniture; it will neither confer learning, nor genius, nor eloquence. But it will do much to correct the evil tempers, and shield from the temptations, which are so often fatal to the youthful aspirant at the Bar; and to foster those moral qualities and habits on which respectability and success largely depend. Among these qualities are self-control, benevolence, candour, kindness of heart, and a love of truth and justice. That the characters of individuals who make no pretensions to personal religion are sometimes graced with these attributes, is readily conceded; but it is a circumstance too certain and too serious to be overlooked, that a large part of the virtue current in the world, is the virtue rather of education, of habit, of interest, of listless conformity to the prevailing usages of society, than the virtue of principle. Mr. Coleridge has expressed this thought with his customary felicity, in language which, with very little alteration, would be quite as applicable to our country as to England. "It would furnish grounds both for humility towards Providence, and for increased attachment to our country, if each individual could but see and feel how large a part of his innocence he owes to his birth, breeding, and residence in Great Britain. The administration of the laws; the almost continual preaching of moral prudence; the number and respectability of our sects; the pressure of our ranks on each other, with the consequent reserve and watchfulness of demeanor in the superior ranks and the emulation in the subordinate; the vast depth, expansion, and systematic movements of our trade; and the consequent inter-dependence, the arterial, or nerve-like *net-work* of property, which make every deviation from outward integrity a calculable loss to the individual himself from its mere effects, as obstruction and irregularity; and, lastly, the naturalness of doing as others do: these, and the like influences, peculiar, some in the kind, and all in the degree, to this privileged Island, are the buttresses on which our foundationless well-doing is upheld, even as a house of cards, the architecture of our infancy, in which each is upheld by all."*

It is in no censorious spirit that the opinion is expressed, that much of the "well-doing" among ourselves rests upon no firmer "buttresses" than these. Better indeed is it for society, far better, that it should be leavened with this dilute and fickle morality, than given up to the sway of rampant wickedness. But few will venture to deny, that the exigencies of our probationary state can be adequately met only by a morality which reposes on the impregnable basis of religion. The vicissitudes of life are too painful, its conflicts too violent, and its seductions too captivating, for unassisted humanity: man must be endowed with a celestial virtue, and sustained by an Almighty arm, if he would "keep himself unspotted from the world," and live as a rational and immortal being should live. And the duties of an advocate especially involve so constant and so severe a trial of character, that even on the ground of personal reputation and peace of mind, no lawyer should be willing

* Lay Sermon.

to dispense with the invaluable aid which Christianity offers him.

With other men, controversy is an incidental and occasional thing; with you, it is the business of life. Controversy is your vocation; and it is no ordinary degree of watchfulness that can preserve you from forming a petulant or imperious temper, the common vice of controversialists. No less open is the profession to the incursions of jealousy and "lean-faced envy." These twin-vipers haunt every Bar. They insinuate their venom not unfrequently into the most powerful minds; and where they have once secured a domicil, they can be driven out, like other demons, only by prayer and fasting. Is it necessary to observe, that the only effectual antidote to these vagrant tempers is to be found in the Gospel of Christ; and that the shortest and best way to acquire the mastery of one's own spirit—that most rare and difficult achievement—is, to have every power and thought brought into subjection to the will of God?

There is perhaps no sphere in which *integrity* is of greater value, and none where it is more rigorously tested, than at the Bar. The temptations to swerve from it are of daily recurrence, and are sometimes clothed with a most specious garb. The profession has to do chiefly with two classes of persons—the wronged and wrong-doers. And to deal with either, as their confidential adviser, in a perfectly frank, straight-forward, and kind manner, demands a stern and lofty virtue. We know how difficult this is even in private life; and the difficulty must be greatly increased where the parties bear to each other the relation of client and counsel. Among men who live by the law, who look to it for a support and for fame, the inducements must be very strong to encourage litigation. It has always been the opprobrium of the profession, that it was infested by individuals who were ready on all occasions to pander to the basest passions, and to become the instruments of the avaricious, the revengeful, and the hard-hearted in oppressing their victims. Such men, unhappily, rarely want for clients. For the race described by Addison is not yet extinct—a race of whom he observes, "the law of the land is their gospel, and all their cases of conscience are determined by their attorney." He adds, in that tone of quiet sarcasm, so peculiar to himself, "As for such as are insensible of the concerns of others, but merely as they affect themselves, these men are to be valued only for their mortality, and as we hope better things from their heirs."* And this is just the principle which controls the sort of lawyers in question. It is neither the love of justice nor any real regard for their clients, which makes them the ready abettors of litigation. Their employers, in many instances, become their victims, and discover too late the secret of their pretended zeal for their wounded honour or damaged fortunes.

What we require in the legal profession, is, men of principle—men whose rule of conduct shall be, not the conventional code of morals which may happen to have been adopted by their *caste*, but the law of God. The circumstances in which individuals ordinarily come to you, make it a matter of the highest moment, that they should be able

* Spectator, No. 456.

to repose entire confidence in your integrity, your discretion, and I may add, your delicacy of feeling. For what *are* these circumstances? They come to you smarting under real or imaginary wrongs, and burning with resentment—or affrighted at the thought of a prosecution they have incurred by their misconduct. They come to solicit your assistance in despoiling others of their property, or in repelling aggressions upon their own—to ask you, to exhaust the penalties of the law in wringing the "pound of flesh" from an unfortunate debtor—to protect their defenceless and terrified families from the tyranny of the great—to shield them from the tongue of the defamer—to help them in defrauding their creditors, or in garnishing their rent and blasted characters. These, and such as these, are the errands on which men invoke your aid. They come when they are in trouble—in doubt—in danger—when they are doing wrong or suffering wrong—consumed with remorse or on fire with revenge—when they are anxious and excited, and, not seldom, incapable of acting for themselves. What are you to do? Are you to inflame still further their excited feelings by expatiating on their alleged injuries? Are you to pry open the innermost chambers of their agitated bosoms, that you may afterwards use what you have seen there to bend them to your sordid purposes? Are you to join hands with them in their schemes of detraction and dishonesty? Are you with eager haste to assure them that the case admits of no compromise—that the law will award them full redress, and they should be satisfied with nothing less? Are you to bring the cause into court, and employ all the arts of chicanery, such as brow-beating the witnesses, misquoting authorities, perverting the testimony, and appealing to the baser passions or the political prejudices of the jury—to conceal the merits of the question and secure a favourable verdict? This surely is not the treatment your clients have a right to expect from you. The law has made you our advisers. We have no alternative when we are in trouble but to come to you; and if we would perpetrate a wrong under colour of law, we can do it only through your agency. You are bound then—bound not merely by your relations to us, but by your paramount obligations to society—to deal honestly and kindly by us. If you think we are in error in proposing to institute a suit, it is incumbent on you to tell us so. If you believe an equitable compromise can be effected, you should suggest it. If you perceive that we have made no estimate of the contingent consequences of the litigation we demand, you should point them out. Instead of inflaming, you should endeavour to mollify our resentments. Instead of advising us as we may wish to be advised, you should advise us according to the truth and equity of the case. When we repair to you in the first instance, it is as counsellors, not as advocates. And it is none the less your duty to give us faithful counsel, though it may not chime in with our hopes or purposes. If a surgeon orders an amputation where his patient expected a cataplasm, he discharges his conscience whether the patient acquiesces or not. And when we come to you with a question of property, liberty, or life, we have a right to look for the same candour, however we may treat your counsel.

Should you take up the cause, whether on your own conviction or from our solicitation, it is no less due to us and to society, that you should conduct it throughout in a fair and honourable manner. It is not meant by this that a lawyer is to assume the functions of a judge, and take both parties under his protection. He stands before the court as the representative of one of the parties, and he is bound to omit no legitimate means which may promise to benefit his client. He may suggest arguments which are not conclusive to his own mind: the court will allow them their due weight. He may seize upon technical informalities in the proceedings of the other side. He may avail himself of all the advantages which the law will allow him for vindicating his client and baffling his opponent. But he may not bring into the conduct of his cause a malicious or vindictive spirit. He may not needlessly blacken the character of the opposing party. He must not impugn the veracity of witnesses, whose only fault has been their modesty or their timidity. He must not seek to carry his cause by misrepresenting the facts, or by poisoning the minds of the court and jury against the antagonist client on personal or party grounds, aside from the merits of the issue on trial. These, and all similar expedients, are incompatible with that integrity which is at once the ornament of the Bar and the safeguard of our rights. And they will disappear just in proportion as our courts become transfused with the purity and benignity which accompany a cordial reception of the gospel.

Occasions not unfrequently arise in the practice of the law, which call for a high degree of *moral courage.* The most ill-assorted parties appear before the tribunals. The advocate may be called upon to espouse the cause of some obscure woman against the exactions of an opulent landlord. He may be required to enforce the law against an intractable tenant who has sought to elude the payment of his rent by raising the Agrarian cry, and getting others to raise it, of "oppression" and "persecution." It may become his duty to arraign some individual of eminent station, who has depredated upon the public purse, or employed a corporate institution for swindling purposes on a gigantic scale, with the expectation that wealth and family influence would shield him from the legal penalties of his crimes. He may be obliged to undertake the defence of a person who has made himself obnoxious both to the government and the people. The press may with one voice demand his condemnation. The populace, unwilling to await the slow process of a judicial investigation, may be panting to wreak their vengeance upon him. The Bench itself may bend before the whirlwind, and reveal by no ambiguous auguries, its purpose to abandon the victim to his fate. But the law is with him; and the blow which smites him to the earth, will shatter the pillars of the constitution. Shall his counsel desert him? He cannot desert him. His own professional prospects, the very bread which is to keep his family from starvation, may be imperilled with his client; but he cannot give him up. To his eye he is the very impersonation of the law. The office Providence has laid upon him, is not so much the vindication of the prisoner at the bar, as the protection of the State. He stands there, the sponsor of that helpless man, to guard the rights of thousands of citizens who sit quietly by their firesides, anxious only to hear that the jury have convicted him—nay, to defend the liberties of the infuriated multitude who throng the avenues of the court-room, and show by their looks and gestures how bitterly they resent this effort to deprive them of their prey. Whatever may be the consequences to himself, he will not betray his client; and if he could stoop to that meanness, he would still have too much patriotism not to shield him, if possible, from a poignard's thrust, which could not reach him without piercing the vitals of his country.

It would be claiming too much for religion to affirm that this high moral courage can exist only in connexion with personal piety. Examples to the contrary would instantly occur to the minds of my legal auditors. Among these, the name of Lord Erskine would certainly be conspicuous. Every lawyer must be familiar with the maiden speech of this great orator; that speech which brought thirty briefs into his hands before he left Westminster Hall, and which his noble biographer characterizes as "the most wonderful forensic effort" of which there is any account in the British annals. "It was the *début* (he adds) of a barrister just called and wholly unpractised in public speaking—before a court crowded with the men of the greatest distinction, belonging to all parties in the State. He came after four eminent counsel, who might be supposed to have exhausted the subject. He was called to order by a venerable judge, whose word had been law in that Hall above a quarter of a century. His exclamation [when Lord Mansfield told him that Lord Sandwich, whose name he had introduced, 'was not before the court,'] 'I will bring him before the Court,' and the crushing denunciation of Lord Sandwich, in which he was enabled to persevere, from the sympathy of the by-standers, and even of the judges, who in strictness ought again to have checked his irregularity—are as soul-stirring as any thing in this species of eloquence presented to us by ancient or modern times." *

In so far as strictly forensic efforts are concerned, this last remark may be allowed to pass; but Lord Campbell might find examples of still greater intrepidity in a volume with which he must be very conversant. One of these, is the case of the three Jews at the court of Nebuchadnezzar. The king summoned them before him and commanded them to worship the image he had set up, or be cast into a burning fiery furnace. This was a question of life or death; and they must decide it without hope of fame or fortune—without the support derived from the sympathy of a crowded court-room, or the ill-concealed admiration of the Bench itself—from the plaudits of a powerful press or the prospect of professional honours—in a word, without any of those collateral but invaluable aids which sustained Erskine in his sublime effort. And what was their decision? It ran thus, in words of quiet strength and majesty which even at this distance of time cannot be read by any one who is susceptible of admiration, without deep emotion. "O Nebuchadnezzar, we are not careful to answer thee in this matter. If it be so, our God whom we serve is able to deliver us from the burning fiery furnace, and he will deliver us out of thine hand, O king. But if not, be it

* Lord Campbell's Lives of the Lord Chancellors.

known unto thee, O king, that we will not serve thy gods, nor worship the golden image which thou hast set up." (Dan. iii. 16–18.) This was the courage inspired by *faith*. To comment on it, would be but a poor compliment to my hearers.

There is a kindred example in the New Testament—a forensic example—on a theatre no less august in Judea, than the Court of King's Bench is in England. I refer to the speech of the Apostle Peter before the great Sanhedrim, that memorable scene in which the parties exchanged places, and the prisoner, arraigning his judges, brought home to them, in a few words of eloquent and withering rebuke, the most flagrant of all crimes, the murder of their Messiah. (Acts iv. 5–12.) This again was the intrepidity inspired by true religion. For no longer before than the evening prior to the crucifixion, this same Peter, who now stood up before the high priest and rulers of the Jews, and charged them with this atrocious wickedness, had himself denied his Master with cursing and oaths. So mighty was the transformation which the baptism of the Spirit had wrought in this ardent and affectionate but hitherto timid disciple. And a similar change is gradually effected in the characters of all who experience the renewing power of the Holy Spirit. Religion may not at once convert every lion into a lamb, nor every lamb into a lion; but it is the true nurse as well of courage as of meekness. The fear of God is the best antidote to the fear of man. And in proportion as the legal profession becomes pervaded with this principle, will it be adorned with exhibitions of genuine heroism, like those we have been contemplating.

23

Some allusion has been made to the *temptations* which beset the path of the advocate. The annals of almost every Bar will bear melancholy attestation to the dangers to which the profession is exposed from this source. It would be quite pertinent to the present discussion, to show that religion offers the only effectual shield against these dangers; that a firm faith is the best of all equipments to protect the members of the profession from those enticements to dissipation, and the more subtle enticements to dishonesty, which have proved fatal to so many of their brethren. But I have already trespassed too long upon your patience, and must waive this topic, with several others no less worthy of attention.

My object has been to show the great value of personal religion, its professional value, so to speak, in the practice of the law. It is not denied that examples may be found at the Bar, of eminent moral worth and distinguished success, dissociated from real piety. But it is contended that even in cases of this sort, religion would impart an additional lustre to the character; while its influence, if diffused throughout the body, would be most advantageously felt in removing the prevalent vices and defects of the profession, and augmenting all those virtues which make it one of the chief supports and ornaments of a refined civilization. What the profession would be if it were consecrated by the pervading power of a vital Christianity, may be inferred from the instances occasionally presented, of men who combine the noblest intellectual gifts, the most accurate and profound knowledge of jurisprudence, rhetorical abilities of a high order, the purest affections, and the greatest amenity of manners, with an enlightened and unostentatious piety.

Such an example of the theme on which we have been meditating, has been before the eyes of the Philadelphia Bar for the last half century. Amidst the tears of the profession and the regrets of this whole community, death has lately set his irreversible seal upon it. The incorruptible virtue, the radiant example, the untarnished fame, of CHARLES CHAUNCEY, have become part of the moral treasure of his country. It is not for me to pronounce his eulogy: that can be done only by one of his peers. But where providence and grace conspire to form a character of so much excellence, it is due no less to the munificent Being who made him what he was, than to the profession he adorned, that some of his moral qualities should be held up, even though in a transient and imperfect way, to the study and imitation of his junior brethren. More than this I shall not attempt to do. I leave it for others to sketch his intellectual attributes and his legal acquirements: my office is to speak of him, and that briefly, as a *Christian*.

The prime quality in Mr. Chauncey's character, was his integrity. This is as much associated with his name, wherever he was known, as justice is with that of Aristides. It is impossible to speak of him without thinking of it; as it was impossible to converse with him without feeling that you had to do with a man of inflexible probity. If there are men who are honest from policy or interest—who are honest in great matters but lax in small matters—whose perceptions of right and wrong are quick and accurate on questions affecting other people's affairs, but misty and obtuse where self is concerned—he was not one of them. He was upright on principle, and from preference. The love of truth and right was part of his being. He could not have been divested of it without destroying his identity. He carried it, therefore, into every relation and circumstance of life. It controlled his most trivial pecuniary transactions; it presided over every scene of social enjoyment, even those in which he gave full play to his refined and ardent affections; it breathed through every sentence he uttered at the bar, whether in one of those luminous and eloquent arguments with which he often captivated the court and jury, or in those incidental passages between opposing counsel—the by-play of a trial—in which truthful men sometimes exceed the limits of sober verity. His clients knew that the advice he gave them, was given in all sincerity and was designed for their good, however counter it might be to their wishes. The bench and the jury knew that they were listening to a man who was a stranger to deception and finesse—a man who, though liable, like all other men, to err, could not act a part—who, when he spoke, uttered his real convictions, and believed what he was trying to make them believe. There have been lawyers whose professional has been as distinct from their personal character, as the wig and gown of an English barrister from the barrister himself; and courts and juries have instinctively, when they rose to speak, recognized their two-fold nature. But they never mistook Mr. Chauncey for one of this hybrid race. In him the union between the advocate and the man was not, as in the other case, a mere mechanical conjunction, like that which held together the different parts of Nebuchadnezzar's image, but a chemical combination—an intermixture of the elements of the one with the elements of the other. His speeches, therefore, carried with them all the weight of personal conviction—and that, in the case of a man so eminent as well for his ability and his wisdom as for his integrity, was often more than half the battle.

It were well for the younger men in the profession, to consider the great value of such a reputation for integrity, simply as a means of success. They may gain an occasional triumph by deviating from the line of strict rectitude; and the prospect of winning an important cause, may seduce them into the use of unfair weapons. But a few victories achieved in this way will ruin, or at least seriously injure, them. To a young lawyer, CHARACTER is every thing. It is character, not learning, not astuteness, not eloquence, which is the basis of confidence: and "confidence," especially the confidence of clients and judges and juries, is "a plant of slow growth." It is a sensitive plant too: its leaves will begin to curl and wither with the first rude breath of deceit and equivocation. The youthful advocate, flushed with an ill-gotten triumph, little divines what an impression he has made on that stern jurist on the bench, and even upon these emulous associates who throng around him with their congratulations. They may well congratulate a rival whose ovation, like those the Venetians used to accord to their heroes, is the pledge of his early downfall. Let those who stand on the threshold of this noble profession, learn from the example of that eminent man whose loss we now deplore, that virtue is the highest wisdom—that virtue, especially, which has God for its author and end, the word of God for its rule of duty, and the love of God for its animating principle. In this divine endowment, they may see one of the chief implements of his success. He has vindicated the profession from the vulgar cavil, that no strictly honest man can be a lawyer; and shown that the Bar forms no exception to the rule, that the path of virtue is the path to honour. In some pregnant crisis of your history, when temptation proffers you its golden fruit,

> "Fair to the eye, inviting to the taste,"

and you are just saying to yourselves,

> ———" What hinders then
> " To reach, and feed at once both body and mind?"

it may recover you from your perilous position, to recall the name of one who maintained an unspotted reputation amidst the conflicts and enticements of the Bar for upwards of fifty years, and whose pure fame is unsullied by a single mean or dishonourable action.

Mr. Chauncey was no less distinguished for his benevolence than his integrity. I do not allude in this remark merely to the charity which goes out in alms-giving, or in contributions to ecclesiastical and religious objects. This, when prompted by right motives, is a charity of high esteem in the sight of God: indeed, our Saviour teaches us that if we are destitute of it, we may scarcely presume to think we are Christians. But the benevolence of Mr. Chauncey included a great deal more than this. He was essentially an unselfish man. He had a heart as well as a head. And his heart was large enough to take in some others besides his own family and immediate friends. He was always ready to employ his great powers for the relief of the poor, the injured, the helpless; to extend to them "the charity of time, labour, and attention; the protection of those whose resources are feeble, and the information of those whose knowledge is small." This was so well understood, that there was probably no man in this community who was so much resorted to for counsel. He was so wise, so candid, so kind, and entered so readily into the circumstances and feelings of his clients, that people of all descriptions sought his advice on all sorts of subjects. Who that has entered his ante-room during his office-hours, has not been struck with the variety of characters assembled there to solicit his aid. Distinguished counsellors, young lawyers, and possibly grave judges, with their vexed questions, capitalists seeking investments, embarrassed merchants, guardians perplexed to know what to do with their wards, parents to consult him about their children, widows anxious to secure their little property, together with suitors of various kinds—such were the groups that not unfrequently met at his levees. And they went there because they knew they could confide to him domestic matters which they would scarcely breathe into the ear of another human being; and that when they had stated their case to him, he would give them judicious advice made doubly acceptable by the manner in which it was given. He might, without presumption, have appropriated the language of Job: "When the ear heard me, then it blessed me; and when the eye saw me, it gave witness to me. Because I delivered the poor that cried, and the fatherless, and him that had none to help him. The blessing of him that was ready to perish came upon me; and I caused the widow's heart to sing for joy. I put on righteousness, and it clothed me: my judgment was as a robe and a diadem. I was eyes to the blind, and feet was I to the lame. I was a father to the poor; and the cause which I knew not I searched out. And I brake the jaws of the wicked, and I plucked the spoil out of his teeth." Among all the monumental memorials which grace our cemeteries, there is not one which might with more propriety receive these words as its epitaph, than the tomb of Charles Chauncey.

Mr. Chauncey's manners, it has been intimated, partook of the kindness of his nature. Instead of that *hauteur* and reserve which great men sometimes assume, and which make them appear greater than they are, like objects seen through a mist, his manners presented a felicitous combination of dignity and ease, with simplicity and benevolence. In this respect, as well as in the genial warmth of his affections and his earnest sympathy with suffering humanity, he closely resembled that illustrious man, Dr. Chalmers. For so free was this great philosopher and divine from ostentation and assumption—so perfectly accessible—so prompt to enter with an unaffected interest into the topics of the passing hour—that his guest might, for the time, almost forget his greatness in his goodness. Am I wrong in the conjecture, that many a man who has hesitatingly approached Mr. Chauncey as a counsellor, has been made to feel during their first interview, that his counsellor was no less his friend? "If a man," says Lord Bacon, "be gracious and courteous to strangers, it shows he is a citizen of the world, and that his heart is no island cut off from other lands, but a continent that joins to them: if he be compassionate towards the afflictions of others, it shows that his heart is like the noble tree that is wounded itself when it gives the balm: if he easily pardons and remits offences, it shows that his mind is planted above injuries, so that he cannot be shot." These were marked traits in the character of our revered friend. And you will justify me in appropriating to him the beautiful sketch Mr. Addison has drawn of a great light* of the English law. "His life was, in every part of it, set off with that graceful modesty and reserve, which made his virtues more beautiful the more they were cast in such agreeable shades. His great humanity appeared in the minutest circumstances of his conversation. You found it in the benevolence of his aspect, the complacency of his behaviour, and the tone of his voice. His great application to the severer studies of the law had not infected his temper with anything positive or litigious; he did not know what it was to wrangle on indifferent points, to triumph in the superiority of his understanding, or to be supercilious on the side of truth. He joined the greatest delicacy of good breeding, to the greatest strength of reason. By improving the sentiments of a person with whom he conversed, in such particulars as were just, he won him over from those points in which he was mistaken; and had so agreeable a way of conveying knowledge, that whoever conferred with him grew the wiser, without perceiving that he had been instructed. His principles were

* Lord Somers.

31

founded in reason and supported by virtue, and therefore did not lie at the mercy of ambition, avarice, or resentment."

It has been intimated that no portraiture would be attempted, in the present service, of Mr. Chauncey's public or private life. I may be allowed to pause for a moment, before concluding this very imperfect notice of some of his prominent virtues, to remark on one or two features of his professional career. He abstained from taking an active part in politics; and with a single exception, that of his consenting to sit as a member of the Convention for revising the Constitution of this State, he uniformly declined public office. It would certainly be unfortunate for the country if all our ablest lawyers should adopt the same line of conduct. But the example may suggest a wholesome lesson to the junior portion of the Bar. No man can expect to become an eminent lawyer, who does not, for at least a score of years or more, confine himself rigidly to his profession. The temptation to embark in politics is very great, especially under a government like ours; and it has proved fatal to the hopes of many a young lawyer of brilliant talents. The rewards of jurisprudence, like the choicest crystals of the Alps, are too remote and too difficult of access, to be secured by any precarious and inconstant exertions. The path which leads to them is narrow and rugged, obstructed with rocks and exposed to avalanches: and he who suffers himself to be intimidated by dangers, or diverted into by-paths in quest of flowers, must make up his mind to relinquish the jewels to his competitors.—This subject is too large to be discussed here; but I could not refrain from making a brief allusion to it.

The only other topic to which I shall advert in this connection, is, Mr. Chauncey's respect for the Sabbath. To his eye, the Sabbath bore the KING's image and superscription: and he had no sympathy either with the presumption which would seize upon "the Lord's day" and appropriate it to private ends, or with the mock loyalty which glories in rendering to Cæsar the things that are Cæsar's, while it denies to God the things that are God's. Accepting in its just import that much-abused saying of our Saviour's, "the Sabbath was made for man," with his characteristic reverence for law, he studiously consecrated it to the purposes prescribed by its beneficent Donor—to the concerns of the soul, and the sublime realities of the life which awaits us beyond the grave. And to these well-spent Sabbaths we must look for many of the influences which contributed to mould as well his intellectual and social, as his elevated moral character.

The example is instructive. There is no need of assuming—it would be discourteous and unjust to assume—that the Bar stands in special need of admonition on this subject. But neither will it be claimed that the Bar is quite guiltless of that disposition to secularize the first day of the week, which has infected all other professions. The temptation to do this, constitutes, in fact, one of the chief snares to which the members of the profession are exposed. Could the truth be revealed, it might be found that no inconsiderable portion of our able and rising lawyers were more or less in the habit of appropriating a part of the Sabbath to the study and arrangement of their cases. They forget that there is a law in existence paramount to all earthly legislation: nor are they struck with the incongruity of preparing themselves to expound and enforce human statutes, by treading under foot the law of God. The pernicious consequences which flow from this practice, are manifold. It weakens the moral sense. No man can habitually or frequently set at nought a Divine ordinance, without blunting his conscience and impairing his reverence for the authority of God. He who begins by taking half the Sabbath for his professional business, will be likely in the end to take the whole. And how is it possible for an individual to treat one item of the decalogue as a nullity, without lessening his respect for all its other provisions, and indeed for the whole religious system of which the two tables are the moral code? "Whosoever shall keep the whole law, and yet offend in one point, he is guilty of all." For the law, though presented to us in distinct categories, is essentially one; and to violate any part of it, is really to violate the whole, just as he breaks a large mirror who only throws a pebble through one corner of it. The wilful breach of any single provision, involves, also, a contempt for that authority on which the entire law rests. And it moreover indicates a disposition which, under like provocation, would set at nought any other of its enactments.

The practice in question, removes a man from all the wholesome influences of the sanctuary. But not to dwell on the peril in which the neglect of the house of God puts the salvation of the soul, we can none of us afford to dispense with the collateral benefits which flow from the due observance of the Sabbath. If any confidence is to be placed in the opinion of eminent physiologists, the Sabbath law, though a positive institute, has its foundation in the nature of man. It is no arbitrary decree, but an ordinance indispensable to the proper culture and developement of his physical and mental powers, and to his social happiness. The tendency of an uninterrupted devotion to earthly pursuits, is, to debase the character and to induce premature exhaustion and decay. The Sabbath comes to us, as an angel of mercy, to withdraw us, at stated intervals, from the secularities with which we are engrossed—to recruit our wearied frames—to let in upon our souls and upon our concerns the light of eternity—to revive our fading impressions of spiritual objects—to bring us into communion with the Father of our spirits—and to remind us of what we are so prone to forget, that

" 'Tis not the whole of life to live,
Nor all of death to die."

The appeal might be safely made to gentlemen who have long stood in the very front rank at our own Bar, whether they have not derived the greatest advantages from the tranquilizing and refreshing influence of the Sabbath, in seasons when they have been well nigh overwhelmed with the pressure of their business. And all experience shows how keenly nature resents any attempt to despoil her of that periodic rest which is her inalienable birthright. There are doubtless exceptions, but it will generally be found that lawyers who devote the whole seven days to business, pay the penalty of their error, either in a loss of health or in falling a prey to vicious indulgences. The overtasked constitution gives way under a load it was never designed to bear. Their recuperative energies are paralysed. Physical debility is followed by mental depression. The nervous system acquires a morbid sensitiveness; and men of a serene and amiable temper and bland address, become irritable, harsh, and repulsive. Not unfrequently, stimulating drinks are invoked to inspire the strength demanded by urgent professional duties; and by degrees, the occasional expedient becomes a daily necessity, and the victim hastens with accelerated pace to a dishonoured grave. In other instances, the nerves become more and more disordered until reason is dethroned; and the once gifted advocate only lives to excite the pity of the Bar he adorned, or awakens their profounder sorrow by his suicidal death. You will not require illustrations. The wrecks are scattered all along the shore you are coasting: and even those who have but just cleared the port and spread their sails to the breeze, may deem themselves happy if they have not come in sight of some of them. If I should select a single example, it would be that of an English barrister, the splendour of whose forensic abilities was enhanced by his private virtues—I mean, Sir Samuel Romilly. My legal auditors are of course familiar with the history of this eminent person and with his disastrous end. It was the opinion of his illustrious contemporary and friend, Mr. Wilberforce, that the fit of insanity in which he terminated his life, though immediately owing to a sad domestic bereavement, was remotely induced by his uninterrupted devotion to business, without allowing himself even the repose of the Sabbath. In writing to a friend, he says, "I am strongly impressed by the recollection of your endeavour to prevail upon the lawyers to give up Sunday consultations, in which poor Romilly would not concur." Four years after his death, Lord Castlereagh came to the same untimely end. When Wilberforce heard of it, he exclaimed, "Poor fellow! he was certainly deranged—the effect, probably, of continued wear of mind. The strong impression on my mind is, that it is the effect of the non-observance of the Sabbath; both as to abstracting from politics and from the constant recurring of the same reflections, and as correcting the false views of worldly things, and bringing them down to their true diminutiveness." "It is curious to hear the newspapers speaking of incessant application to business; forgetting that by the weekly admission of a day of rest which our Maker has enjoined, our faculties would be preserved from the effect of this constant strain." Being again reminded by the death of Castlereagh, of Sir Samuel Romilly, he said "If he had suffered his mind to enjoy such occasional remission, it is highly probable that the strings of life would never have snapped from over-tension."

Let me dismiss this topic by quoting the testimony of one whose name has never been mentioned but with veneration, in either hemisphere—Lord Chief Justice Hale. "I have found by a strict and diligent observation, that a due observance of the duty of this day, [Sunday] hath ever had joined to it a blessing upon the rest of my time; and the week that hath been so begun, hath been blessed and prosperous to me; and, on the other side, when I have been negligent of the duties of this day, the rest of the week has been unsuccessful and unhappy to my own secular employments; so that I could easily make an estimate of my successes in my own secular employments the week following, by the manner of my passing this day: and this I do not write lightly or inconsiderately, but upon a long and sound observation and experience."

It has been implied in every line of this sketch, that Mr. Chauncey was a sincere and decided Christian. He not only received the Bible as a divine revelation, but embraced its doctrines with a cordial faith, and made its precepts the rule of his conduct. Deeply persuaded of his own participation in the common ruin of the race, and of the insufficiency of any works or sacrifices of his own to propitiate a holy God, he sought salvation through the blood of the Lamb, and made the righteousness of Christ the sole ground of his hope of pardon and eternal life.* His piety was equally removed from the spurious liberality which homologates all creeds and sects, and the bigotry which confounds the door of its own narrow pale, with the only door that leads into the fold of Christ. It pervaded every part of his character, and had much to do in forming him to that wonderful symmetry—that harmony of all the powers and susceptibilities of his nature—which made him

* Mr. Chauncey was a member of the Second Presbyterian Church in this city.

so *complete*, I had almost said, in the language of the text, so "perfect" a man. It revealed itself not so much in a specific substantive form, as by its influence upon the whole man; like a light behind a beautiful transparency which, unseen itself, illuminates every line of the artist's cunning handiwork. It might be detected in his temper, his conduct, his manners, in all that he did, and in all that he said. No trumpet nor phylactery was needed to announce its presence: his serene and venerable aspect, his suavity, his cheerfulness, his overflowing kindness, his prompt and generous interest in others' wants and sorrows, and the whole tone of his conversation, whether on public affairs or matters of personal concern—all betrayed the commerce of his soul with heaven, and awakened the feeling, "Thou also wast with Jesus of Nazareth."

This great and good man has gone to his reward. Full of years and full of honours, in the maturity of all his powers and without any exhibition of human infirmity, he has been gathered to his fathers. Life's work was done, and well done; and we cannot doubt that he has received that crown of righteousness which the Lord, the righteous Judge, will give to all them that love his appearing.

I may not invade the sanctity of the domestic circle, to speak of the void his death has caused there. The time forbids me to enlarge on the public loss we have experienced as a community. The legal profession have shown that they were not insensible to the greatness of their bereavement. They can best estimate their obligations to one who employed his varied talents through a long life, in maintaining the high character of the Philadelphia Bar;

and who, without disparagement to the living or the dead, did at least as much as any other individual, to preserve unimpaired its reputation for sound learning, superior abilities, incorruptible probity, and urbanity of manners. The trust confided to him and his contemporaries, (of some of whom who survive, delicacy forbids more to be said than that they were worthy to be his partners in such a trust,) is now, in so far as he was concerned, to be devolved on the younger members of the profession. It is an honourable distinction to be made the keepers of a deposit which has passed through the hands of such men as Ingersoll and the Tilghmans, Rawle and Chauncey. But the post of honour is always a post of responsibility. And there is but one way, Gentlemen, in which you can acquit yourselves of your high functions with dignity and success. The character of the Bar must depend on the characters of its members. Personal purity and refinement will insure professional integrity and courtesy. It is the prerogative of RELIGION to make and keep men pure, and to confer that refinement of feeling for which good breeding can only substitute a graceful address—in other words, to make men what good breeding requires them to appear to be. The morality which is divorced from godliness, however specious and captivating to the eye, is superficial and deceptive. The morality you require, "the only morality (I use the language of an eminent compeer of the venerated Chauncey, whose name and fame we instinctively associate with his own,)—the only morality that is clear in its source, pure in its precepts, and efficacious in its influences, is the morality of the Gospel. All else, at last, is but idolatry—the worship of something of man's own creation, and that thing imperfect and feeble like himself, and wholly insufficient to give him support and strength."*

BELIEVE ON THE LORD JESUS CHRIST, then—receive and rest upon HIM as your Saviour—and you will have the best preparation for the duties and trials of this life, and the only adequate preparation for the life to come.

* The Hon. John Sergeant.

THE END.

www.ingramcontent.com/pod-product-compliance
Lightning Source LLC
LaVergne TN
LVHW062242200926
848484LV00006B/1594